A GENERAL HISTORY OF EUROPE

GENERAL EDITOR: DENYS HAY

A GENERAL HISTORY OF EUROPE

For many years the volumes of Denys Hay's distinguished *General History of Europe* have been standard recommendations for university students, sixth formers and general readers. They offer broad surverys of European history, in which the detailed discussion (on a regional or continent-wide basis) of social, economic, administrative and intellectual themes is woven into a clear framework of political events. They set out to combine scholarship with accessibility in texts which are both attractively written and intellectually vigorous. Now the entire sequence is under revision by its original authors – most of the volumes for the first time since they were published – and the books are being redesigned and reset. The revised *General History of Europe,* when complete, will contain twelve volumes, three of them wholly new.

* AVAILABLE IN THE ORIGINAL EDITION
◇ NEW EDITION PUBLISHED IN THE REVISED FORMAT
□ NEW TITLE IN PREPARATION

EUROPE IN THE EIGHTEENTH CENTURY

1713–1783

THIRD EDITION

M. S. ANDERSON

LONGMAN
LONDON AND NEW YORK

Longman Group UK Limited
Longman House, Burnt Mill, Harlow
Essex CM20 2JE, England
and Associated Companies throughout the world

*Published in the United States of America
by Longman Inc., New York*

First published 1961
First paperback edition 1970
Second edition 1976
Third edition 1987
Second impression 1988

British Library Cataloguing in Publication Data
Anderson, M. S. (Matthew Smith)
    Europe in the eighteenth century 1713–1783
    — 3rd ed. — (A General history of
    Europe)
    1. Europe — History — 18th century
    I. Title   II. Series
    940.2'53   D286
ISBN 0-582-49389-7 PPR
ISBN 0-582-00115-3 CSD

Library of Congress Cataloging-in-Publication Data
Anderson, M. S. (Matthew Smith)
    Europe in the eighteenth century, 1713–1783.

    (A General history of Europe)
    Bibliography: p.
    Includes index.
    1. Europe — History — 18th century. I. Title.
II. Series.
D286.A5   1987   940.2'53   86-2878
ISBN 0-582-49389-7 (pbk.)

Set in 10/12pt Bembo Roman Linotron 202
Produced by Longman Singapore Publishers (Pte) Ltd.
Printed in Singapore.

CONTENTS

Contents

LIST OF MAPS

PREFACE

The writing of a book as wide in scope as this one is a difficult though rewarding task. In my case its burdens have been lightened and its attractions increased by the help of a number of friends and colleagues. I am grateful to Professor D. B. Horn of the University of Edinburgh, to Dr J. H. Western of the University of Manchester, and to my colleagues at the London School of Economics, Dr R. M. Hatton, Mr A. Davies, and Dr D. C. Coleman, who have all read parts of the book in typescript and made valuable suggestions for its improvement. My wife typed over half of it at a period when she had many other calls on her time, and has also given me useful advice and comments on a number of points. For the errors and other inadequacies which a work of this kind can scarcely hope to escape the responsibility is entirely mine.

M. S. ANDERSON

LONDON, *May 1961*

Preface to the second edition

The years since the first appearance of this book have seen the publication, notably in France, of a considerable number of works which make new and important contributions to our knowledge of eighteenth-century Europe. I have tried in this second edition to take account wherever necessary of these, and have also corrected a number of errors of fact and emphasis. This has involved not merely alteration but extensive rewriting. In addition to many minor changes and additions to the text a large amount of new matter has been incorporated in Chapters III–VI, XIV and XVI, while the discussion of the Enlightenment and of political and social ideas in general, which now seems to me inadequate as it stands in the first edition, has been expanded into an entirely new Chapter XV. I have three important debts to acknowledge. The first is to my publishers, who have been willing to allow such extensive changes. The second is to the secretarial staff of the International History Department of the London School of Economics, and in particular to Mrs N. J. Smith, for the help they have so cheerfully given. The third and greatest is to the British Library of Political and Economic Science, which for a quarter of a century has been an unfailing source of intellectual nourishment and support.

LONDON, *December 1975*   M. S. ANDERSON

Preface to the third edition

In revising this book for its third edition I have taken the opportunity to add a considerable amount of new material to many of the chapters, and also sometimes, in order to avoid increasing the length excessively, to delete material which now seems less significant and occasionally out of date. A number of footnotes have been dispensed with, partly again to keep the length within reasonable limits and partly because, in a book of this type, heavy footnoting seems ostentatious and unnecessary. Those which remain are mainly references for direct quotations. The most extensive changes have been in Chapters 3 and 4, and to a lesser extent in Chapters 5, 6, 8 and 16. Considerable attention has been given to the updating of the Bibliography, which is now grouped as a unit at the end of the book and not, as in the first and second editions, divided in the main between separate lists attached to each chapter. It is hoped that this arrangement will be more convenient for the reader, though the size of the subject and the continual outpouring of relevant work, often of high quality, make it impossible to claim with any confidence that I have listed every book and article which deserves to be mentioned. I am most grateful to the publishers for allowing me to revise the text so completely: this third edition is a small monument to a productive working relationship which has now lasted for over a quarter of a century. I am also, as in the past, deeply indebted to the British Library of Political and Economic Science. Without access to its holdings and the help of its staff my task would have been significantly more arduous.

LONDON, *December 1985*   M. S. ANDERSON

1

INTRODUCTION

The period from the early 1680s to about 1713 acts, in more than a merely chronological sense, as a bridge between the seventeenth and eighteenth centuries. It has a distinct character of its own; but if a choice must be made, it belongs rather to the former than to the latter.

In international relations it begins with the rise to its highest pitch of the influence of Louis XIV and the failure of the Turkish attack on Vienna in 1683; while its end is marked even more clearly by the Treaties of Utrecht and Rastadt in 1713–14 and by Louis's death in 1715. In this sphere it is dominated in Western Europe by the threat of French hegemony and in the East by the beginnings of the rise of Russia. Of these two factors the former bulked much the larger in the eyes of most contemporaries. France with her, by the standards of the age, huge population of over twenty million, her armies of a size no other State could match, her efficient commanders and subtle diplomats, seemed more than once during these decades to threaten all Western Europe with servitude. The aggressive and casually brutal way in which her strength was sometimes used, as in the seizure of Strasbourg in 1681 or the devastation of the Palatinate in 1688, increased the fears of her neighbours. Little seemed beyond Louis's power in the 1680s. He might secure his election, or at least that of a member of the Bourbon family, as Holy Roman Emperor. He might permanently reduce the States of West and South Germany to the position of French satellites. Above all he might secure most or all of the Spanish Empire for himself or his descendants on the death of the sickly Charles II of Spain. Such

1

a success would mean not merely a union of the French and Spanish crowns but also French control of the Western Mediterranean, an increased French threat to the security of England and the United Provinces, and the transformation of Spain's enormously wealthy American possessions into a French commercial preserve.

Thus until the end of the struggle over the Spanish inheritance in 1713 there were few international questions of any importance which were not influenced, and often dominated, by France and her ruler. Throughout this period Louis's policies and intentions were the object of anxious speculation in the capitals of Europe. This fear of France was to some extent exaggerated: the poor communications and inefficient administrations of the period made it impossible for Louis to exert to the full his enormous potential superiority to his neighbours. It was nevertheless a natural and inevitable fear; and even the victories of Marlborough and the death of the *roi soleil* could not completely dissipate it.

The rise of Russia to the status of a great European power was by contrast largely unnoticed in its earlier stages. Until her victory over the Swedes at Poltava in 1709, she impressed foreign observers by her military and administrative weaknesses rather than by her potential strength. Even after the crisis of the Great Northern War had been passed it was some time before all the implications of her new status became clearly visible. The rise in her international importance, in other words, was an eighteenth-century phenomenon, though some of its foundations had been laid in previous generations. As such it is an important theme of this volume.

For the European States, with one or two important exceptions, the transitional generation which began in the 1680s was in internal politics a period of despotism. The significant point is that almost all the despotisms of this period looked back rather than forward. They were still heavily dependent on religious sanctions. Monarchy was still a divinely ordained institution. Kings still wielded their powers as the vicegerents of God. They remained, almost if not quite as much as in previous generations, remote, awe-inspiring and essentially mysterious personages to the majority of their subjects. The theories of 'enlightened despotism' which were to be so widely diffused over much of Europe in the later eighteenth century and which sometimes (though less frequently than historians have often thought) inspired the policies of rulers, were only hinted at in the age of Louis XIV. In this respect also Europe, down to the great king's death, was still living in the seventeenth century. The generation 1685–1715 was, in its political thought, more in tune with seventeenth- or even sixteenth-century apologists for divine right than with the critical and utilitarian attitudes which were to mark much eighteenth-century thinking. Already, however, Locke had laid in England many of the foundations of the eighteenth century's attitude to human psychology, and hence indirectly to questions of political right and obligation. His ideas were beginning to have some influence outside his own country even before the death of Louis XIV; we shall see them bear generous fruit in the middle and later decades of the period covered by this book.

In economic life the last generatioin of Louis's reign was essentially a period of stability in Western Europe. We can, none the less, easily detect in it the beginnings of changes which were to become more marked in the eighteenth century. The economic, or at least the commercial and financial, importance of England was now increasing. Less visibly to contemporaries, that of the United Provinces was entering on a long though slow decline. The economies of one or two West European States were beginning, at the end of the seventeenth century, to be profoundly influenced for the first time by trade with the extra-European world. Only then were the pattern and value of England's seaborne commerce radically altered by the products and markets supplied by her possessions overseas, while a corresponding transformation of French trade was still slower to show itself.

In intellectual life this generation was in some very important respects a period of change. It was the age of Newton and Locke, the last stage in that wonderful burst of scientific and philosophical activity which in the seventeenth century accumulated a capital of basic ideas upon which the modern world is still living. Old certainties, received opinions, conventional attitudes, were holding their ground with increasing difficulty against the attacks of sceptics and the still more dangerous erosion produced by geographical and anthropological discoveries. Newton and his followers did not shake the religious or political faith of their contemporaries, and never meant to do so. Throughout the eighteenth century the development of the physical sciences, though it had revolutionary implications, had no really revolutionary effects. On the other hand the description, on a scale and with

3

a detail hitherto unprecedented, of non-European peoples and civilizations, which is one of the features of the period *c.*1680–1715, had much more serious results. The discovery by the reading public of noble Iroquois, virtuous Hindus and philosophic Chinese, inevitably shook the Christendom-centred attitudes inherited from the past.

This interest in the non-European world, and the greater width of outlook and flexibility of judgement which resulted from it, grew steadily in the eighteenth century. They confront us on almost every page written by Montesquieu and on many written by Voltaire. They were coupled with an almost equally important development of historical method, seen above all in Jean Mabillon's great textbook of palaeography, *De Re Diplomatica* (1681), and consequently of historical scepticism. The difficulties of writing reliable history were now more clearly understood and more frequently stated than ever before. Moreover rationalistic criticism of religious tradition and even of the Bible itself, exemplified by the *Dictionnaire Historique et Critique* of Pierre Bayle (1697) and by the work of the great French biblical critic, Richard Simon, was beginning to shake in a still more fundamental way traditional certainties inherited from the past. It was chiefly in this growth in much intellectual life of a critical, sometimes aggressively critical, spirit, in this developing taste for change and for rejection of the past, that the dynamism of the generation before 1715 lay. To say, as one leading historian of ideas has done, that 'virtually all the intellectual views and ideas which as a whole were to culminate in the French Revolution had already taken shape even before the reign of Louis XIV had ended',[1] is perhaps an exaggeration. But it is not a very gross one.

This generation thus shows, as any comparable period must, the interaction of conflicting tendencies. Intellectually in some ways an age of radical innovations and challenges, it saw little fundamental advance in economic life over much of the continent. During it armies came into being which in efficiency, size and cost surpassed any known for many centuries. Yet they were used, in the main, in struggles for European territorial prizes which had already been many times contested – the Rhineland, northern Italy or the southern Netherlands. Political ideas and attitudes still looked largely to the past, and were still in the main rooted in religion. Yet they were already feeling the effect of new currents of thought which were eventually to transmute them, at least in their more extreme forms, into something quite unrecognizable to seventeenth-century theorists such as Filmer or Bossuet.

On this foundation, in some parts solid and relatively unchanging, in others flimsy and unstable, the history of eighteenth-century Europe was to be built.

NOTES AND REFERENCES

1   P. Hazard, *The European Mind* (London, 1953), pp. 445–6.

2

THE SOURCES

The extent to which the history of any age can be known depends
on the fullness and reliability of the records left by it. These may
take a great variety of forms. The buildings, furniture, painting
and sculpture of a period are all illustrations of its activities, illustrations of a peculiarly immediate and tangible kind. They are
sometimes the best of all guides to its spirit, ideas and assumptions. In the main, however, the historian, especially if he is
concerned with modern history, must rely upon the books and
documents left by the period which he wishes to study. The
eighteenth century has bequeathed to scholars a varied and
formidably large legacy of this kind, although it is much smaller
than that left by the century which followed, and minute by
comparison with the one we are now accumulating for the use
of posterity. The population of Europe was much less during the
period with which this book is concerned than it was to be even
a few decades later. The States between which the continent was
divided and the administrative systems which controlled them
were primitive by comparison with their successors. Europeans
were less literate, less aware of their history and its implications
and hence less self-conscious, than they were soon to become.
Thus the output in the eighteenth century of books and documents, of those traces of the past without which it can never be
adequately reconstructed, was not great by modern standards. It
was nevertheless very large by those of any comparable preceding
period.

To the majority of eighteenth-century Europeans the State was
not an entity with which they felt a very intimate relationship.

It impinged on the life of the individual as a rule in a purely negative though important way, exacting tax payments, military
service and sometimes forced labour, and usually doing little for
him in return. Nevertheless a large portion of the material which
the historian of this period has at his disposal was the product of
the States, of the courts of their rulers, of their judicial systems
and their administrative machinery. The eighteenth century saw
over the greater part of Europe a movement towards the creation
of more efficient and more centralized bureaucracies. These, as
both a condition and a result of their increasing efficiency,
produced a growing bulk of reports, memoranda, statistics, legislative projects and correspondence of all kinds. Documents of this
essentially governmental or legal kind are available in great quantities. They can provide answers to a wide variety of questions,
many of which have, at least superficially, no connexion with
administrative or legal problems. They give the scholar not only
an immense amount of information but also very valuable insights
into the economic activity, the society and even the intellectual
life of the age. Thus for example what is still perhaps the best
account of life and society in London during this period, M.
Dorothy George, *London Life in the Eighteenth Century* (London,
1925), is based to a considerable extent on the records of the Petty
Sessions held at the Guildhall and for the County of Middlesex.
On a larger scale the reports sent to Paris by officials in the provinces during the reigns of Louis XV and Louis XVI provide not
merely information important to the historian of French administrative methods but also in many ways a remarkably complete
picture of the life of the areas concerned. They have therefore
made a very important contribution to the social and economic
studies of different regions of France which have since the 1950s
been, for all thei sometimes excessive length and detail, the
greatest glory of French historical writing. These have been
notable for their efforts to quantify the developments which they
discuss, to teach historians to count as well as to describe, and for
their attempts to draw on the insights of a wide range of disci-
plines – psychology, geography, anthropology, sociology – to
present a broader and more complete picture of the areas with
which they deal.[1]

On the other hand, materials of this legal and administrative
kind have limitations. With few exceptions they were accumulated by men struggling with immediate and concrete problems.

How could an inefficient and irrational system of taxation be made to yield more revenue? How could recruits for the army be most easily obtained from a recalcitrant population to which the idea of public spirit was almost incomprehensible? How could an archaic and often brutal judicial system be best used in the maintenance of public order? These were typical preoccupations of the eighteenth-century administrator, and the documents he produced were intended to help him answer questions of this kind. They were not meant to supply information for its own sake, much less for the convenience of scholars in the future.

The questions asked by the twentieth-century historian are, however, quite different from those which faced the eighteenth-century bureaucrat. In particular many scholars are now increasingly interested in the accurate determination of aggregate quantities – the population, imports and exports, and agricultural and industrial production of a given State or geographical area. Increasingly knowledge, however incomplete, of such quantities is being used to explain economic growth (or its absence) and social and political change. Eighteenth-century administrations were not in general equipped with reliable information of this type. What mattered to them was the number of taxable individuals and households in a State or a province rather than its total population, the yield of customs duties rather than the real quantities or values of the goods imported or exported, whether hunger was so widespread as to threaten riots and revolt rather than exactly how much grain or meat was being produced. Though many of them made during this period increasingly effective efforts to collect statistical information of various kinds (see p. 116) it remained from their point of view an administrative tool and nothing more.

What attempts were made to obtain figures of the kind sought by the present-day historian, also, were often stultified by the laziness, ignorance, or venality of the officials charged with their collection. Thus the usefulness of the trade statistics which began to be collected in England in 1696 by the Inspector-General of Imports and Exports is considerably reduced by the fact that they continued throughout this period to be based on arbitrary official values for the commodities concerned. These values were realistic in 1696 but soon became quite notional, a mere bureaucratic fiction. Moreover efforts to collect quantitative information of this type were often made still more difficult by the almost universal and often justified suspicion that they were the prelude to new taxation. A clear illustration is the enumeration of peasant households over most of Russia begun on the orders of Peter I in 1718–19 to provide a basis for the new poll tax. This was carried out with considerable difficulty and in the face of much popular opposition. As a result the total number of households given by the inquiry was clearly too low. The same weaknesses continued to a lessening extent to affect the similar censuses of 'taxable souls' which were carried out later in the century. Yet the results of these inquiries, in default of anything better, remain the basis for all estimates of the population of Russia in this period.

It must also be remembered that conditions might vary very widely between different parts of the same State. Food and drink, dress, dialects, methods of land tenure, of taxation, of agriculture, might differ strikingly even in neighbouring districts of what was politically a unit. French or Prussian provinces such as Brittany or Brandenburg might have very little in common with other French or Prussian provinces such as Dauphiné or Cleves. The historian who wishes to study many aspects of the century, above all its economic and social life, on more than a local or provincial scale, must therefore cast his net as widely as possible. He must beware of taking the particular for the general, the local for the national. This warning obviously applies to a great many types of material other than administrative documents.

The extent to which sources of this kind have been printed varies very considerably between different States. In Britain the quantity of administrative and governmental documents in print relating to this period is small by comparison with that available for the sixteenth and seventeenth centuries. (The most important collections are the *Calendar of State Papers, Colonial Series, America and West Indies* (London, 1866–   ) which has as yet reached only the year 1738; the *Journal of the Commissioners for Trade and Plantations from . . . 1704 to . . . 1782* (London, 1920–38) which also deals mainly with colonial matters; and the four volumes of the *Calendar of Home Office Papers* (London, 1878–99) which contain a good deal of miscellaneous information for the years 1760–75.) In France a vast amount of work has been done on this type of material, but its results have been embodied in monographs rather than in collections of printed documents. Prussia by contrast has produced in the *Acta Borussica. Denkmaler der Preus-*

sischen Staatsverwaltung im 18 Jahrhundert, published by the Königliche Akademie der Wissenschaften from 1892 onwards, the most complete collection of printed administrative documents available to illustrate the history of any eighteenth-century State. For Russia there is much material of this type scattered throughout the 148 volumes of the *Sbornik Imperatorskogo Russkogo Istoricheskogo Obshchestva* (St Petersburg, 1867–1916) and in smaller collections of which *Zakonodatelnie Akty Petra I*, vol. I, ed. N. A. Voskresenskii (Moscow-Leningrad, 1945) is probably the most important.

In general diplomatic documents are those which the historian finds easiest to use. They are also relatively abundant and accessible for this period. They are sometimes difficult to interpret and evaluate accurately: what statesmen and monarchs said about their foreign policies in the eighteenth century is no more to be implicitly relied on than similar pronouncements today. But however complex the gradations and local variations in the economic and social life of the States of this period they had as a rule unified and reasonably coherent foreign policies which can be followed in detail from the material available. There are exceptions to this generalization; but on the whole international relations, conceived in a narrow diplomatic sense as a narrative of negotiations and agreements between States, is one of the simpler aspects of the history of the century. It is, moreover, a subject on which a relatively large amount of information is available in collections of printed documents, such as the twenty-nine volumes of the *Recueil des Instructions données aux Ambassadeurs et Ministres de France depuis les Traités de Westphalie jusqu'à la Révolution Française* (Paris, 1884–1969) and the much skimpier seven volumes of *British Diplomatic Instructions, 1689–1789* published by the Royal Historical Society in 1922–34. Most important of all, the *Sbornik Imperatorskogo Russkogo Istoricheskogo Obshchestva*, which has already been mentioned, contains a great amount of diplomatic correspondence drawn from British, French, Prussian and Saxon archives as well as Russian ones, which it prints in the original languages. Eighteenth-century compilers also produced a number of important collections of this kind, of which J. Rousset de Missy's *Recueil historique d'Actes, Négociations, Mémoires et Traitéz* covering the period 1713–48 in twenty-one volumes (The Hague–Amsterdam–Leipzig, 1728–54) is a good example.

Government was carried on, policies formulated and new

trends in economic and intellectual life originated, in the eighteenth century as at any other time, by individuals as much as institutions. This means that our knowledge of many aspects of this period must be derived largely from private papers and correspondence. Where the individual concerned was a monarch controlling personally the fate of the State he ruled, the line dividing a private letter from a public document can become a very fine one. Thus the great *Politische Correspondenz Friedrichs des Grossen* (forty-six volumes: Berlin, 1879–1939) is in form a collection of Frederick II's personal correspondence but in fact a great corpus of official documents, many of them of the highest importance. The same is true of the papers of Peter I of Russia, a collection which began to be published in 1887 and is still far from complete; of the *Correspondence of King George the Third from 1760 to December 1783*, ed. Sir J. Fortescue (London, 1927–28); and to varying extents of nearly all the letters of monarchs and statesmen during this period. It must be remembered, moreover, that it was quite normal for a minister, on leaving office, to take with him large quantities of documents which he regarded as his private correspondence but which to modern eyes seem important State papers. This practice seems to have been particularly common where foreign policy was concerned, above all in countries where monarchical and bureaucratic centralization had not developed very far. It was notably widespread in Great Britain, whose great libraries are therefore particularly rich in material of this kind, both printed and unprinted, for the eighteenth century. Many efforts were made to prevent the retention in private hands of documents of public importance. Victor Amadeus II of Savoy even went so far as to order in 1720 that the houses of high-ranking officials should be searched after their deaths to recover materials of this kind. Such precautions, however, could not prevent a steady leakage in almost all the States of Europe of public or semi-public documents into private hands.

Personal papers are therefore useful because they often supplement the material available from purely governmental and administrative sources. They can perform a still more important function, however, by showing how policies were evolved, how they emerged in some States from the conflicting attitudes of the ministers, diplomats and officials concerned, while in others they were merely the fiat of an all-powerful monarch. It is above all through material of this kind that the individual enters the historian's picture of the eighteenth-century States and their activities.

Collections of private papers of a different and more intimate type can also throw much light on the social, intellectual, artistic and economic life of the age. Thus, to take one of the best-known examples, the vast correspondence of Horace Walpole covering the period 1731–97 can be made to yield a great deal of information about many aspects of life in eighteenth-century England. (The best edition is that in course of publication at Yale of which forty-eight volumes have now appeared.) The same is true of the most famous biography of the century, indeed the most famous in the English language, James Boswell's *Life of Samuel Johnson*, of which the best edition is that by G. Birkbeck Hill and L. F. Powell (Oxford, 1934–50). The letters of some of the great authors of this period – large collections of those of Voltaire, Rousseau, Hume and Gibbon, amongst others, have been published – are also one of the best avenues of approach to its intellectual life. However materials of this kind, no matter how eminent their authors, illuminate very unevenly the various aspects of eighteenth-century Europe. This is mainly because large collections of private papers dealing with economic life are much rarer than those concerned with politics, society and the world of ideas. A number of great economic institutions of a public or semi-public kind, particularly trading companies and banks, have preserved substantial collections of papers relating to their activities in this period. Of these, in a few cases, parts have been published. But the papers of individual merchants or industrialists, the ledgers, accounts and commercial correspondence which would be of so much value to the historian, have very often been lost or destroyed. Of the material of this kind known to exist, moreover, only a small proportion has been printed. As a result discussion of the economic history of this period has until recently been based, to a degree which all historians would now agree is undesirable, mainly on series of official documents which are usually more complete and more accessible than the relevant private papers. Economic histories of the eighteenth century have therefore tended to be histories of economic policy, of what governments or their agents did or tried to do, as much as of economic activity, which was the result of a multitude of individual decisions.

During the last generation or more this position has changed markedly for the better. The papers of individual entrepreneurs and business firms (though these are inevitably more fragmentary than those of government departments and official bodies) have been used by historians with increasing effect. They have helped to paint a picture of economic life, at least in parts of Western Europe, more detailed and realistic than any available before. In one very important way in particular there has been a successful effort, notably in France, to found discussion on more certain foundations. Historical demography, the study of the growth of population in the eighteenth century, is now more securely based than ever before. The riches of the raw material available in France for work of this type has allowed the technique of 'family reconstitution' (the reconstruction of families, normally on the basis of mention of their members in parish registers and similar documents) to be used as a tool with which the historian can come to grips as never before with the demographic, and therefore to a large extent social, realities of past ages.[2] In other parts of Europe less abundant documentation makes the use of such methods more difficult; but almost everywhere they have great potentialities.

Allied to private papers and correspondence, possessing some of the same virtues but suffering in many cases from defects of their own, are the memoirs and autobiographies which the century produced in such profusion. Like private correspondence these are an important vehicle for the transmission to posterity of the thoughts and feelings of individuals. They are one of the means by which the historian can most easily 'think himself back' into the eighteenth century. Some of them, such as the *Journal et mémoires* of the Marquis d'Argenson (ed. J. B. Rathéry, Paris, 1859–67) or the more famous *Mémoires* of the Duc de Saint-Simon (ed. A. de Boislisle, Paris, 1923–28) contain important information about political matters not available elsewhere. Others such as the *Journal historique . . . du régne de Louis XV* of E. J. F. Barbier (Paris, 1847–56) illustrate many aspects of the social and intellectual life of the age. In a few cases (the most obvious is the *Autobiography* of Edward Gibbon, of which the best edition is that published in London in 1896) they are works of literary art in their own right. They are one of the types of historical material which can be most easily enjoyed by the layman. From the viewpoint of the historian, however, they often suffer from serious defects. In some cases they are quite spurious, the work of hack journalists rather than of the ostensible authors. Thus the so-called *Testament politique du Cardinal Jules Alberoni* (Lausanne, 1753) is really the work of a French publicist. When genuine they are in many cases apologies rather than impartial statements of facts and intended, consciously or unconsciously, to influence posterity in favour of the writer. Such are the *Mémoires du Duc de Choiseul* (Paris, 1904) and the *Mémoires et lettres du Cardinal de Bernis*, ed. F. Masson (Paris, 1903). More important in many ways, they are a literary form which flourished mainly in Western Europe, notably in France, and which is poorly represented in the eastern and even the central parts of the continent. Also, like collections of private correspondence, they reflect in the main the interests and outlook of a small privileged ruling class. Memoirs and autobiographies written by merchants, by professional men, even by squires and farmers, do exist. One example of the latter, the *Pameti Frantiska J. Vavaka* (ed. P. J. Skopec, Prague, 1914–16) is the most important printed source of information about peasant life in Bohemia in the later eighteenth century. In general, however, the voice of the common man finds little expression in material of this type – less than in some classes of administrative document.

The eighteenth century was a great age of travel. It was also an age in which the reading public displayed a voracious appetite for information about foreign countries. It thus saw the publication by many travellers of descriptions of their experiences. These accounts, some of them very voluminous, vary greatly in quality. As a whole, however, they provide the historian with a vast amount of information, above all about the economic and social life of Europe during this period. Often the comments of an observant but unsophisticated foreigner, shocked by the sight of habits and tastes different from those to which he is accustomed, illustrate more forcibly and convincingly than anything else the very real psychological and intellectual barriers which still existed between the various parts of Europe. Thus an English traveller complaining that in Russia 'it is the genious [*sic*] of this country to be everything or nothing: a middle state such as happy England boasts is not understood',[3] or that in Spain 'the children in this country seem neither to play nor to work; it is nearly impossible to buy either toys or books',[4] or a German visitor annoyed by his English landlady's refusal to allow him to play the flute on Sundays, can sometimes bring contrasts of this kind home to the reader more forcibly than pages of statistics or abstract description.

Descriptive accounts of this type have none the less considerable weaknesses. Side by side with substantial works of lasting value can be found vast numbers of books of a popular and quite ephemeral kind. Their authors were often interested in externals – clothing, food and drink, the cleanliness of the inns in which they slept – rather than in political, economic or social questions. For this it is unfair to blame them. After all, in a great many cases they were travelling for pleasure. Moreover, like the volume of memoirs or autobiography, the book of travels was in the eighteenth century essentially a product of Western Europe. Many were written by Englishmen and Frenchmen, an appreciable number by Germans, Italians, Dutchmen and Scandinavians, hardly any by Russians, Poles, Hungarians, Greeks or Turks (and for that matter few by Spaniards or Portuguese). The picture which they paint, therefore, is one coloured by the assumptions which dominated the relatively wealthy and educated societies of the West, one in which the viewpoint of the poorer and more backward parts of Eastern and Central Europe finds little expression. Distance, the difficulty of travel and ignorance of the languages concerned, also meant that relatively few of the authors of this type of book travelled in Eastern or even Central Europe. Their works deal above all with the cities of France and Italy, increasingly frequented by tourists, and to a lesser extent with the Netherlands, western Germany and Spain. By contrast Russia, Poland and the Habsburg territories attracted little attention, and the Balkans (with the partial exception of Greece) very little indeed.

Besides this great travel literature the eighteenth century also produced a good deal of writing on the events of its own day. Some of these semi-historical, semi-journalistic accounts are of real importance. They are often voluminous, providing the historian with substantial bodies of facts conveniently assembled (usually in a chronological sequence). Examples of this type of work, selected almost at random, are John Entick, *The General History of the Late War* (London, 1763–64), John Andrews, *The History of the War with America, France, Spain and Holland* (London, 1785–86), and on a larger scale the *État Politique de l'Europe* (The Hague, 1742–49) of J. Rousset de Missy. (The last is really a very detailed history, including many printed documents, of the years

1734–43.) More important, such books, written by authors who may have been eye-witnesses of some of the events they describe, sometimes preserve and transmit to the reader, amid many longueurs and aridities of style, the 'feel' of the period in a way which the 'scientific' historian, writing years later, cannot hope to do.

Against these advantages, however, must be placed once more considerable defects. In the first place there is often an element of plagiarism about works of this kind. In an age when the idea of copyright was still new and very hard to enforce by law it was quite common for a writer to embody in his own book considerable portions of one written by someone else, and to pass the result off as his own work. This is particularly noticeable in West European writing on distant and little-known parts of the continent such as Russia. It is seen most clearly of all in the great commercial encyclopedias which were one of the features of the age (Malachy Postlethwayt's *Universal Dictionary of Trade and Commerce* (London, 1751–53) is the best English example) and which provide the historian with vast quantities of information whose reliability is often hard to determine. More important, the eighteenth century took, by modern standards, a rather limited view of history. The characters of kings, the intrigues of ministers, the convolutions of diplomacy, the movements of armies, attracted the attention of writers and bulked large in works on contemporary or near-contemporary events. By comparison the progress of some aspects of economic life, the introduction of new administrative methods, the development of education, even the growth of new religious sects, aroused little interest. When therefore an eighteenth-century writer attempted to narrate on a large scale the events of his own day he usually confined himself to political, military and diplomatic history and consequently produced what now inevitably seems an unbalanced picture. This is true even of so well-known a work as Voltaire's *Précis du siècle de Louis XV* (Paris, 1769) one of the best and most intelligently written examples of this *genre*. The lopsidedness of so many of these books is of course in itself a fact of historical importance. 'At any time, the conception of what is remarkable or worthy of record is a function of the whole body of current ideas, and what the writer sets down represents not merely his private judgment, but that of the community of which he forms a part.'[5] Nevertheless it clearly limits their value to the historian.

Even on this semi-journalistic level, moreover, contemporary discussion of the events of the eighteenth century was influenced, usually for the worse, by prevailing ideas about the nature and functions of historical writing. It was still widely believed that accuracy and reliability in the writing of history was unattainable, that it could never be more than a fable distorted by the ignorance or prejudices of the writer. 'O! do not read history', exclaimed the British statesman Sir Robert Walpole (an excellent eighteenth-century example of a pragmatic lack of interest in the past and its lessons), 'for that I know must be false.'[6] More important was the fact that to many of the most important writers of the period history seemed a vehicle for the exposition of ideas or the teaching of morality rather than a disinterested enquiry into the facts of the past. Bolingbroke's pronouncement in 1735 that it was 'philosophy teaching by example' (an idea then already two millennia old) set the tone for much of the historiography of the century. 'To me it appears', wrote an intelligent author near its end, 'that to write history without drawing moral or political rules from it, is little better than writing a romance.'[7] Throughout this period, therefore, writers were strongly tempted to extract moral judgements from the events which they described. Sometimes they might even manipulate or suppress evidence in order to vindicate some preconceived theory or prejudice. These tendencies are perhaps most noticeable in works dealing with classical or medieval history; and there were great writers such as Hume and Gibbon who struggled to resist them. But writing on contemporary or near-contemporary events, especially if it aspired to the rank of literature rather than mere journalism, was often heavily influenced by them. Thus Voltaire's *Histoire de Charles XII* (Paris, 1731) and *Histoire de l'Empire de Russie sous Pierre le Grand* (Paris, 1759–63), both popular and influential books, were not works of history in the modern sense of the term. Voltaire took considerable pains in collecting the information on which they were based; but they were not intended to be accumulations of accurate facts established by research. They were in part conscious works of art (in this they belong to a tradition tracing back to the Renaissance) and in part edifying stories designed to illustrate the responsibilities of rulers and thus help them to improve their judgement and act correctly in moments of crisis. When a Swedish historian, Nordberg, published in 1740 another account of the reign of Charles XII, he took the opportunity to point out a number of errors in Voltaire's book. The Frenchman replied by attacking Nordberg's work as excessively preoccupied with factual accuracy, pedantic and boring. Voltaire had the better of the exchange, but his victory does not alter the fact that Nordberg's is the more useful book of the two to the modern scholar.

It is worth noting, moreover, that in the eighteenth century as still occasionally today writers of real eminence were sometimes unwilling to concern themselves with the history of their own times, regarding it as a rather second-rate subject. 'I should shrink with terror', wrote Gibbon in an autobiographical fragment of 1762, more than two years before he conceived the idea of his *Decline and Fall of the Roman Empire*, 'from the modern history of England, where every character is a problem, and every reader a friend or an enemy; where a writer is supposed to hoist a flag of party, and is devoted to damnation by the adverse faction.' At a lower level, the factual and essentially journalistic level of works such as those of Entick, Andrews and a host of other writers, eighteenth-century discussion of eighteenth-century events does not as a rule suffer severely from the desire of its authors to import morality into their subjects. As it rises in the literary scale, however, it tends to become increasingly selective and moralizing. This makes it interesting to the historian of ideas but reduces its value to the scholar in search of accurate or balanced discussion.

During this period two classes of raw material for the historian begin to be produced in unprecedented quantities. Newspapers and periodicals are the first of these. Ancestors of the modern newspaper, brief, intermittently appearing and usually short-lived news-sheets, had been published from early in the seventeenth century. As it drew to a close it was becoming clear that at least in some parts of Western Europe, above all in England and the United Provinces, a demand for serious and well-informed journalism was developing on a hitherto unknown scale. Thus Courtilz de Sandras, a very voluminous writer on contemporary politics, founded in 1686 at The Hague the *Mercure Historique et Politique*, the first political monthly. The earliest English daily paper, the *Daily Courant*, appeared in 1702. A few years later the phenomenal success and widespread imitation of the *Spectator* showed that there now also existed a considerable public demand for a non-political periodical of this kind, a journal of ideas rather than of information, and for the attractive blend of morality and entertainment which it purveyed. The development of the Press

in Europe during the middle decades of the century was relatively
slow, but its last years saw a very rapid growth of newspapers
and periodicals over much of the continent. Eighteen newspapers
were published in London in 1782; forty-two were appearing a
decade later. Against the thirty-five newspapers and periodicals
of all kinds published in Paris in 1779 must be placed the 169
available at the outbreak of the Revolution. In the 1770s and 1780s
the French publisher Panckoucke, who has been called 'the greatest
impresario of the Enlightenment', acquired control of a number
of these and created the first newspaper empire in European
history. In the Dutch Republic, which had pioneered the development of newspapers and had still in the middle and later eighteenth century great prestige as a centre of journalism, a similar
development can be seen in the emergence of important new journals such as *Le Politique Hollandais* and the *Post van der Neder Rhijn*.
(The latter, soon after its foundation in 1781, had no less than
24,000 subscribers.) Even in Spain periodicals such as the *Gaceta
de Madrid* and the *Espiritù de los mejores Diarios* played a significant
role as vehicles of 'enlightened' thought in the later eighteenth
century.

To the historian these newspapers and periodicals have inevitably certain defects. In the first place, like so many of the more
literary and consciously-created types of evidence available to him
– memoirs, books of travels, works of contemporary history –
they were a product of Western Europe and took root only slowly
in the east and even the centre of the continent. Political journalism in particular could flourish only in countries where some
degree of political and intellectual freedom existed, in other words
in Great Britain and the United Provinces. Even France had no
daily paper till 1777, when the *Journal de Paris* began to appear,
so that during most of this period the reading public there
depended for much of its information on current affairs on newspapers published in the Netherlands, or in small neighbouring
States such as Berne, Liège and Cologne. In Germany, where the
despotic governments of the numerous small States tended to
hamper the growth of the Press, it was not until the 1780s that
serious discussion by it of political questions began to be possible.
Even then this discussion was often timid compared to that in
Britain or the Netherlands. In Russia the time-lag in this respect
as compared to some parts of Western Europe was especially
noticeable. Peter I had founded in 1703 what is sometimes

described as the first Russian newspaper, the *Vedomosti*. This however was merely a government propaganda organ, appearing very irregularly, with a small circulation, and containing little but praise of the Tsar's policies and news of his victories. Though there was under Catherine II a considerable production of literary periodicals which often took the *Spectator* or *Tatler* for their model, Russia never possessed during this period a newspaper which could comment with any degree of freedom on current politics. In other words the Press, or at least the political Press, provides much more, and much more important, information for the historian interested in some parts of Western Europe than for scholars whose interests lie farther east.

Even in Great Britain or the United Provinces eighteenth-century newspapers suffer, as raw materials for the writing of history, from considerable defects. Many of them were purely advertising organs which carried no news or editorial comment at all. Even in those which were newspapers in the true sense of the word advertisements bulked larger than is normal today. This advertising matter is of considerable interest from some points of view. It is in particular an important source of information about many aspects of social life, though one which is difficult to use and which has never been thoroughly exploited. But its prominence naturally tended to reduce the amount of space which could be given to news. In particular (as was to be expected in an era when communications were still slow and difficult) few journals or magazines were well-informed about events in foreign countries.

Moreover the Press was never, in any major European State, free from government influence and official pressure during this period. In France at the outbreak of the Seven Years War the government, using the journalist J.-N. Moreau as its agent, published a newspaper which it hoped to send abroad and also distribute in Paris in order to combat the anti-French arguments being put forward by the British Press. A few years later two of the most important French statesmen of the century, the Duc de Choiseul and the Comte de Vergennes, attempted to win over the Press to support their policies (notably that of intervention in 1778 in the War of American Independence). Frederick II of Prussia went much farther in this direction. He established in Cleves, one of his Rhenish provinces, a newspaper, the *Courier du Bas-Rhin*, designed to influence European opinion in his favour; paid the

Gazette de Berne for the same purpose; and even had the editor of the hostile *Gazette de Cologne* beaten up by his agents. In Britain, where the more rapid development and greater importance of the Press made it more worthy of the government's attentions, the politicians in power consistently attempted to influence it in their favour during most of the first half of the century. Thus in 1722 the government bought, on terms which are not precisely known, the support of the *London Journal*, its most bitter critic during the preceding three or four years. In 1731 an opposition paper alleged, probably without great exaggeration, that the ministry was spending £20,000 a year on subsidies to the Press and bribes and pensions to journalists. It is true that government influence of this kind declined from the later 1730s onwards and that by the 1750s a subsidized ministerial Press had ceased to exist. Efforts to influence newspapers in support of official policy seem however to have revived somewhat at the end of this period: in 1791 nine London newspapers were receiving regular (though relatively small) payments from secret service funds.

The pressures of this kind under which newspapers and periodicals laboured are of importance to the historian because this type of source has been used by him hitherto mainly as raw material for studies of public opinion. It is clear that a public opinion of a recognizably modern kind was emerging and assuming political importance by the end of this period in some parts of Europe, above all in Great Britain. It is clear also that the Press was the most important channel through which it could find expression. But to say with certainty how far any particular newspaper or periodical was reflecting at any particular moment a real current of popular feeling, and how far it was merely responding to government or party pressure or the prejudices of its owners, is often very difficult indeed. It is true, of course, that the Press has always been, and is today, exposed to external influences of this kind. There were however a number of factors – the small circulations and financial weakness of nearly all newspapers, the feeling still prevalent everywhere that a free Press was a danger to political stability, the resulting existence in most countries of systematic censorship – which made the eighteenth-century Press peculiarly vulnerable in this respect.

With all these defects the newspapers and periodicals of the eighteenth century provide the historian with important and still incompletely exploited sources of information. The newspapers give him, as has been seen, very important material for the study of public opinion in some parts of Western Europe. They may also, on occasion, supply him with items of political information not easily accessible elsewhere. Periodicals of an unspecialized kind, such as the *Gentleman's Magazine* which began publication in 1731, provide an illuminating commentary on many aspects of the age and sometimes contain material of political importance. Journals such as C. F. Nicolai's *Briefe, die neueste Litteratur betreffend*, founded in 1759; C. F. Wieland's *Deutsche Merkur*, founded in 1773; or E. C. Fréron's *Année Littéraire*, which began publication in 1754, are of great interest for any serious study of the literature of the period.

As well as seeing the first important growth of newspapers and periodicals the eighteenth century was also the greatest age of the pamphlet. This also was predominantly a product of Western Europe, of Great Britain and the Netherlands, to a lesser extent of Germany and France. It is therefore of great potential value to the historian of some of the Western States, of relatively little to those of the eastern or even the central parts of the continent. Pamphlets, moreover, present peculiar difficulties to the scholar who seeks to use them. They were produced in great numbers (in Britain and the Dutch Republic in thousands during this period) and are frequently hard to trace in library catalogues. Apart from these purely mechanical difficulties, the historian has also to face the fact that many of them are anonymous and that, like the newspapers of the period, they were often produced to serve the purposes of some powerful individual or interest group and are far from being impartial examinations of the subjects with which they deal. The question of authorship can often be answered and is sometimes not very important. It is usually more necessary and often more difficult to find out whose arguments are in fact being expressed in any particular pamphlet. Thus for example *The Northern Crisis, or Reflections on the Policies of the Tsar* (London, 1716), one of the better-known of those published in England during this period, has sometimes been quoted as an illustration of the hostility then felt there to the Baltic ambitions of Peter I of Russia.[8] In fact, however, this pamphlet is not English at all. It was written by Count Gyllenborg, the Swedish minister in London, in an effort to mobilize opinion in Britain in favour of his country, which was then struggling for survival in a great war with Russia. It is clear from other sources that its arguments won considerable support in Britain. But in itself the pamphlet is evidence of nothing but the desire of the Swedes for British backing.

Knowledge of the true authorship and inspiration of eighteenth-century pamphlets is important to the historian because they, like the newspapers of the period, have hitherto been used largely in studies of public opinion and in efforts to show how it influenced the development of government policy on various issues. Like many newspapers, they were intended to persuade rather than to inform their readers. Almost everywhere in Europe, until near the end of this period, they were the most effective means of mobilizing opinion on the great issues of the day. Pamphlets, especially when they deal with some limited or local issue, may contain factual information not available anywhere else. Many, notably on economic questions, were the work of experts whose views must carry considerable weight. But the highly polemical character of much of this type of writing, almost irrespective of its subject, must always be allowed for.

Finally the imaginative literature of the period – its poetry, its plays, above all its novels – is in itself a part of its history. This means that it is of interest not merely to the historian of literature but also to the student of eighteenth-century society, ideas, and to a lesser extent economic and political life. Thus the importance of satire as a literary form during the first half of the century, of which the works of Pope and Voltaire are the greatest examples, may be seen as an expression of the analytical and rationalistic tendencies which were then the most dynamic elements in its intellectual life. In the same way the success of the moralizing novels of Richardson or plays of Lessing in the middle years of the century was largely a result of the emergence, in the wealthier parts of Western Europe, of a new and important middle-class novel-reading and play-going public with new and middle-class tastes. The primitivism and exoticism which affected most branches of literature so powerfully in the last years of this period also represents the influx into European life of powerful currents of new ideas. Nor was prose literature at least, during much of this period, seriously restricted by considerations of social class or 'suitable' subjects. Indeed a good deal of it shows, by comparison with that of the age which followed, a remarkable readiness to discuss without sentimentality or even emotion the lives of the poor, and of the criminals and potential criminals who were so numerous in all great European cities. A historian who wished to study poverty and crime in London or the *demi-monde* in Paris in the early decades of the eighteenth century could do worse than start by reading Defoe's *Colonel Jack* (1723) or Prévost's *Manon Lescaut* (1731).

On the other hand imaginative literature, like all the more self-conscious types of historical material generated during this period, was in the main a product of Western Europe. It throws considerable light, from a number of different angles, on the history of England and France, and to a lesser extent perhaps on that of Italy and Germany. To the historian interested in Eastern Europe, or even in Spain or Portugal, it has less to offer. Moreover it was, as perhaps any highly developed literature must be, the product and reflection of an essentially urban society. Eighteenth-century writing was the offspring of cities, of courts, of universities, of centres in which the theatre, the *salon* and the coffee-house could flourish. It might often use the countryside as a peg on which to hang its philosophizings and displays of emotion, especially in poetry. It might sometimes idealize or sentimentalize over the peasant and the labourer. It might even (as in some of Fielding's novels) occasionally draw a realistic picture of the farmer or the squire. But it was not really concerned with, and in general had not much understanding of, the rural society in which the great majority of Europeans still passed their lives. This inevitably limits its value to the historian. The studies of almanacs, chap-books and other ephemera, the reading of the poor and the semi-educated, which have in recent years been made, notably in France (see p. 396) may in time do something to fill this gap and deepen our understanding of mass psychologies and popular climates of feeling. But however much we try to compensate for it we can never escape the fact that virtually all our sources for the study of this period, and especially the more literary and self-conscious ones, heavily over-represent the urban, educated, well-to-do parts of society everywhere in Europe as against the more backward and rural ones.

The student of the eighteenth century thus has at his disposal a wide range of materials, a series of great quarries from which he may extract virtually unlimited amounts of information and even an occasional idea. Of these sources the most important is the great mass of official papers, of reports and correspondence of all kinds, which was produced in every European State of any

significance during this period. For the historian of administration, of war, of diplomacy, of colonial expansion and of many
aspects of economic life, there is no substitute for material of this
type. It can and should, however, be supplemented by private
papers of all kinds, by memoirs and diaries, by pamphlets and
newspapers. For the historian of ideas, of culture, of society, the
range of relevant material is even wider. He may acquire valuable
insights not merely from all these sources but from the imaginative literature of the age, from almanacs and chapbooks, from
accounts of travels, from ballads and folklore, from the whole
material legacy of the age in its art and architecture, and for that
matter in its furniture, clothing and cookery.

NOTES AND REFERENCES

1   The most important examples relevant to the eighteenth century
    are listed in the Bibliography, see p. 481.

2   Family reconstruction was first illustrated on a significant scale in
    E. Gautier and L. Henry, *La Population de Crulai, paroisse
    normande: étude historique* (Paris, 1958).

3   *The Russian Journals of Catherine and Maria Wilmot, 1803–08*, ed.
    H. Montgomery Hyde (London, 1934), p. 55.

4   *The Journal and Correspondence of William, Lord Auckland* (London,
    1861–62), vol. II, p. 84.

5   F. J. Teggart, *Prolegomena to History*, University of California
    Publications in History, vol. IV, No. 3 (Berkeley, 1916), p. 179.

6   W. Coxe, *Memoirs . . . of Sir Robert Walpole* (London, 1798),
    vol. I, p. 762.

7   Sir John Dalrymple, *Memoirs of Great Britain and Ireland* (London,
    1788), vol. II, p. 177.

8   Karl Marx, among others, used it for this purpose in his *Secret
    Diplomatic History of the Eighteenth Century* (London, 1899),
    pp. 25ff.

3

THE STRUCTURE OF SOCIETY

Over most of Europe during the eighteenth century society, though slowly changing, was still in many essentials what it had been for generations. There are at least three obvious illustrations of this fact.

The first is the overwhelming importance of the family rather than the individual at every social level and the fact that the family continued, at least until well into the second half of the century and even in the more advanced parts of Western Europe, to be thought of in essentially traditional terms. It was seen, in other words, through the eyes of medieval realism rather than through those of nineteenth-century sentiment. It remained a patriarchal institution in which women and children had a definitely inferior status. Over much of Europe, if a woman committed a crime in the presence of her husband he was liable to find himself charged with it, since it was assumed that he controlled, and therefore could be held responsible for, all her actions. The family was also an institution based on continuity, on the perpetuation of the family name and the ownership of family property, rather than on the rights or sensibilities of individuals. In the upper ranks of society in particular the idea of the family as a 'house', a collectivity with imperative demands of its own rather than an association of freely interacting individuals, was still enormously powerful. This meant that at all levels of society the marriage of children, particularly of daughters, was decided by their parents, above all their fathers, and governed by family interests (which in practice meant almost always family property interests). It was quite possible for a father to feel sincerely that these things were no concern of the child in question, so that a consellor of the *Parlement* of Dijon, when approached by his son about the latter's impending marriage, could reply without any sense of incongruity 'Mind your own business'.[1] Compared to family ties, any wider loyalty, any concept of the public or collective good, was for the overwhelming majority of Europeans extremely weak, indeed more often than not almost meaningless. The continuing widespread indifference to young children, at least until late in the century, was inevitable in the demographic conditions of the period. When so high a proportion died in the first years, even the first weeks or months, of life, it was impossible and undesirable to make a heavy emotional investment in each one as it was born. It was necessary to have many children in order to keep a few; the harshness of this demographic imperative was hostile to any growth of modern 'child-centred' attitudes. There is a good deal of evidence, in fact, to suggest that the greater value which began to be attached to children in some parts of Europe in the later decades of the century was the result largely of a slow improvement in health and a corresponding tendency for infant mortality to fall. Even amongst adults the continual closeness of death, far more often than now sudden and unpredictable, the result of some epidemic against which there was no defence, made it less emotionally important than it is today. Since the family, not the individual, was the fundamental building-block of society, it must, when weakened by the death of a father or mother, have its strength restored as soon as possible by remarriage. This explains the remarkable speed with which men in particular at all social levels often remarried after the loss of a wife.

These traditional attitudes were, at least in the second half of the century and in some parts of Western Europe, slowly altering. In France and England particularly, the position of women began to improve. Hitherto they had been significant in two ways above all – through their physical indispensability as mothers, and through their theological status as occasions of sin. Now as never before they began to be regarded as true persons, individuals with feelings, abilities and rights of their own. In France this change of attitude can be seen not merely in the upper strata of society but also in the almanacs and other ephemeral literature which was the only reading matter of the masses. The extent of the change, outside a small intellectual minority, should not be exaggerated. As in the past the unmarried woman was still hardly regarded as a person in her own right. 'A spinster', wrote a Spanish author at the end of the century, 'is a nullity who usually serves only to embarrass even her own family and who finds herself in a miserable position.'[2] The marriage of girls (and almost as much that of young men) continued to be subject to strict parental control and often to take place very early in life, while in Catholic countries it was still common for a daughter to be compelled, in the interest of the family as whole, to take the veil. Change of a liberating kind, however slow and partial, there none the less was.

In Britain and France at least attitudes to children also were altering. Much more clearly than ever before, childhood was now seen as a distinct phase in the development of a human being, with its own characteristics and requirements. The child was ceasing to be regarded as merely an immature and incompetent adult, a change symbolized by the new practice of dressing children (boys more than girls) in relatively informal and comfortable clothes different from those worn by their parents. The emergence for the first time in history of specialized shops selling only clothes for children is a good illustration of this development. Growing attacks on primogeniture, on the grounds that all children had an equal right to their parents' affection and support and that the firstborn son should not be favoured as against his brothers and sisters, mark an important step away from the traditional view of the family and towards the more emotionally charged nineteenth-century one. So does the increasing emphasis, in the later decades of the century, on the duty of women to breastfeed young children and not allow them to be dependent on wet-nurses. In a few parts of Europe at least parents by the end of this period saw more of their children than ever before, played with them more and took greater pains over their education. It is significant that some of the most popular children's toys and games originated in the later eighteenth century (the outstanding example is the invention of the jigsaw puzzle in England in the 1760s) and that books designed specially for children were produced in unprecedented numbers. The English publisher John Newbery was perhaps the first to produce, in his *Little Pretty Pocket-Book* (1744) a book which aimed to please children as well as instruct them.

Yet it would be quite misleading to imagine that this picture of change was typical of Europe in general. To it two enormous qualifications must be made. The more liberal and modern attitudes to the family and to women and children which have just been described were confined almost entirely to the upper, or in England the middle, ranks of society. They were also limited in the main to parts of Western Europe. The peasantry, the overwhelming numerical majority of society almost everywhere, remained untouched by such changing ideas. For most Europeans tradition and habit continued to hold sway over family life as over all other aspects of existence. The vast majority, at least until late in the century, continued to accept almost without question the traditional Christian view that children displayed in a relatively pure and undiluted form the wickedness inherent in human nature, the taint of original sin. Spontaneous display of their essential nature was therefore by no means something to be encouraged. On the contrary they had to be curbed and moulded by teaching, by example and most of all by appropriate punishment so that they became good Christians, conscious of their own fallen state and of the need for redemption, and thus good members of society. By the later decades of the century 'enlightened' Europe was slowly abandoning such ideas: in this process the *Émile* of Jean-Jacques Rousseau (1762), the first great advocacy of child-centred education and of the free expression of the child's interests and personality, played an important role. But for most of the century and for most Europeans traditional beliefs and unquestioned assumptions continued to hold sway over family life as over all other aspects of existence. In economic terms young children were important for essentially negative reasons – because they made up everywhere the overwhelming majority of the dependent population, of those who could not earn their own bread and who therefore became, in times of economic stress, a source of anxiety, even of despair, for the working population which had to feed and clothe them. Everywhere, and especially in the larger cities, the problem of foundling children abandoned by their parents or by desperate unmarried mothers was one of the blackest aspects of eighteenth-century society. No group was more helpless and for none was life briefer or more harsh.

The second great illustration of the conservatism of eighteenth-century society is the way in which it continued, as in the past, to be dominated by division into 'orders'. Social classes in the modern sense of the term, groups defined chiefly by wealth and economic status, were still unimportant over the greater part of Europe. Their place was taken by traditional 'orders', broad groupings essentially hereditary in character, each of which united people of a particular 'quality'. Wealth as a determinant of social status, though certainly growing in importance, was still far from decisive, even in the more economically advanced parts of Europe. What mattered most was the social esteem and the combination of rights and duties traditionally attributed to the different groups which made up society. Except to some extent in Great Britain and the Netherlands, Europe before the French Revolution was still a largely closed society of orders and groups. It is misleading to analyse it in the class terms which become truly applicable only after the political and economic upheavals which began in the 1780s had done their work.

This society was bolstered by the fact that over much of Europe it still corresponded reasonably well to the economic realities of a largely pre-industrial age. It was also powerfully supported by traditional Christian teaching. This stressed heavily the need for each individual to fulfil as completely as possible the duties and responsibilities of his station in life, a station which was divinely ordained. For a man to try to change it, or to blur the distinctions between different stations, was more than merely socially disruptive: it was impious. Inequality was decreed by Providence. It was thus divinely ordained and unalterable. Without it society could not exist. For a man to fulfil the obligations of the social order in which God had placed him was to perform a religious duty. 'True piety', claimed the great Catholic preacher Massillon early in the century, 'is the order of society. Religion disavows the most saintly works which one might substitute for duties; and a man is nothing before God when he is not what he is supposed to be.'[3] The same viewpoint, the same emphasis on tradition and refusal to contemplate social change, could also be expressed in more secular terms. 'A reasonable man', wrote a commentator in the middle of the century, 'is always happy if he has what is necessary for him according to his condition [i.e. his place in the social order], that is to say, if he has the protection of the laws, and can live as his father lived before him: so that one of the essential things to the good of a nation is being governed in one constant and uniform manner.'[4] A stable social order in which change was very slow and the barriers between different groups clear-cut and difficult to cross thus seemed essential to the functioning of any stable political order. Any challenge to the social order must weaken and might destroy the political one. In France

Louis XVI himself wrote in 1788, when such a challenge was imminent, of 'the hierarchy of my subjects, without which monarchy can nowhere exist'.[5]

Ideas of this kind and the whole concept of immutable social orders were being slowly but steadily undermined in the eighteenth century. The Enlightenment was by implication hostile to them (though many of its leading figures, notably Voltaire, were in practice deeply unwilling to disturb a social structure from which they personally benefited). More important, economic change was making traditional attitudes more difficult to sustain and traditional social distinctions a barrier to progress. Nevertheless their vitality was still clear. In Central Europe, an economically stagnant area, this was especially so. The most striking illustration of this is the absolute prohibition in the Prussian law code of 1794 of marriage between nobles and middle-class women unless with special governmental permission. Without this the woman concerned was, in the eyes of the law, merely a concubine, and her children illegitimate. This was social conservatism with a vengeance; for even in backward Russia such a marriage was recognized as valid and as conferring noble status on the wife. Nowhere in Europe, again, was a clinging to traditional social distinctions more marked than in the cities of western Germany. In Frankfurt-on-Main, for example, the burghers were divided into five groups. Members of each, by medieval regulations confirmed as late as 1731, were obliged (the regulation was not in fact enforced) to wear a special dress which made their social status immediately visible. Sumptuary legislation of this kind existed, at least on paper, in such intellectually advanced areas as France and the city-state of Geneva. Even in England there were proposals for its introduction; and the revival there in 1687 of the High Court of Chivalry, dormant since 1640, was a sign that the most developed of all the major European States shared many prevailing assumptions about how society should be structured. In 1732 the King's Advocate exhibited in this court a complaint against the widow of a merchant for using at his funeral 'ensigns of honour not belonging to his condition'; and a good many similar cases had been heard in previous years.[6] Though the court ceased to function in 1737, after only half a century of intermittent life, its mere existence is a reminder of the continuing strength of social conservatism in eighteenth-century Europe. Nor were regulations regarding dress and outward appearances confined in their operation to the middle and lower ranks of society; the nobility also was often affected by them. Thus in Venice in 1710 nobles who appeared in public without wearing the *vesta patrizia*, a special dress which was a sign of their status, were threatened with fines and imprisonment; while in Russia the Table of Ranks of 1722 specified the clothes and equipage appropriate to each of the many ranks of the privileged landed class, the *dvoryanstvo*. (The wearing of lace, for example, was confined to the top five ranks in the table, and those with no official rank were forbidden to wear velvet at all.)

It should be remembered, moreover, that even without any element of legal compulsion the persistence of a wide variety of traditional and regional costumes meant that different social groups were still distinguished almost everywhere by the clothes they wore with a clarity which would be inconceivable and repugnant today. Some conservatives wished these distinctions to be made even more clear. The author of a detailed description in 1768 of the town of Montpellier in southern France, for example, argued that parks and promenades in the city should be reserved for different social groups at different hours of the day, that workers in different trades should each live in their own neighbourhood and, most important of all, that servants should be forced to wear distinctive badges so that they could not be mistaken for 'gentle people'.[7] This was an extreme attitude; but it was one which, in milder forms, was almost universal. Such clear-cut external distinctions were slowly beginning to disappear. Trousers (originally worn by seamen) began during this period to be a kind of uniform of artisans and urban workers in Western Europe. Their adoption during the later decades of the century as the dress of upper- and middle-class boys in Britain and France was the first step towards the uniformity of appearance between the different parts of society which we now take for granted. But this development was limited in scope, a mere forerunner of those to come.

The third great proof of the traditional character of society is the extent to which it continued to be an amalgam of small, well-defined and closely-knit geographical and occupational groups – parishes, manors, guilds, municipalities, at the most provinces – each with an outlook, interests and traditions of its own. To the ordinary man in Western and Central Europe the continent was divided not merely into conflicting States and rival religious confessions, but into these much smaller and more intimate units, which were of far greater practical importance to him so far as his daily life was concerned. 'Civil society', proclaimed the Prussian law code of 1794, 'consists of many small societies and estates, connected to each other by nature and law, or by both together.' This type of traditionalism, this atomization of society, was strengthened by the persistence everywhere of local and regional differences of all kinds so numerous and varied as to defy adequate description. The ordinary man lived his life within narrow geographical boundaries: at any moment in the eighteenth century a high proportion of Europeans could have said with certainty in which churchyard they would be buried. The importance therefore, so far as most people were concerned, of local rivalries, local grievances and local ambitions can scarcely be overstated. Local dialects, often confined to surprisingly small areas and difficult to understand outside them, still retained an importance of which only the developments of the next century in transport and mass education were to rob them. Thus a local official at Riom, in the Auvergne, had to abandon an attempt to interrogate a young beggar from the little town of Courpière, little more than twenty-five kilometres away, because 'the speech of Courpière differs considerably from that of Riom'[8]. This intensely local nature of reality in the eighteenth century so far as most people were concerned should never be forgotten.

Even in countries where strong centralized monarchies had emerged, the new political and administrative structure was normally superimposed on the traditional form of society without modifying it in essentials. In France, for instance, the number of guilds was considerably increased by Colbert's reforms in the 1660s and 1670s: the city of Poitiers had three times as many in the eighteenth century as in the fourteenth. Not until the 1750s did Vincent de Gournay, followed by his pupil Turgot, launch a systematic attack on French corporate bodies of this kind, and then with rather moderate success. Indeed where administrative efficiency and social traditions conflicted the forces of conservatism, so deeply embedded in society, very often proved the stronger. As a rule habit and prejudice set limits to the activities of rulers and bureaucracies rather than vice versa. The political failure and personal tragedy of the last years of the Emperor Joseph II (see pp. 205–06) are only the most striking of many illustrations of this fact.

Very few eighteenth-century monarchs or statesmen, however, seriously contemplated really fundamental social changes. To a man like Frederick II of Prussia society as it stood was something given, the work of time and nature, buttressed by a vast structure of rights and privileges (the two words very often meant the same thing) and rooted in the essentially conservative idea of natural law. Its structure might occasionally be modified somewhat if the interests of the State required it. Frederick's efforts in 1763 to abolish serfdom in Pomerania, its abolition in Lorraine in 1719 and in Savoy half a century later, are obvious examples of such modifications. It could not, however, be invaded or disregarded wholesale. The conception of society as, in a sense, a work of art, something which can and should be moulded and shaped in the interests of justice, reason, or even efficiency, can of course be found in the works of a good many eighteenth-century thinkers. But this idea, and the hostility to group privileges and traditional and local peculiarities which it implied, were still confined to a small intellectual class. It had never a dominant influence on government during this period anywhere in Europe except in the Habsburg Empire under Joseph II, and perhaps on a smaller scale in the Grand Duchy of Tuscany under his brother Leopold. Provided they could maintain a minimum standard of public order and extract from their subjects enough money and recruits to maintain their courts and armed forces, monarchs as a rule showed little interest in the lack of logic and symmetry in the social organization of their subjects.

This acceptance of traditional rights and local peculiarities is shown clearly in the treatment by all European States of territories which they conquered and annexed. The idea that the newly acquired areas should be completely assimilated by the conquering State, except as the result of a long and almost unconscious process of absorption, or that their institutions should be forcibly modified in order to speed up this process of assimilation, was almost unknown. Rapid and forcible integration of conquered territory with that of its conqueror at any level, religious, economic or social, was exceptional. Certain political and fiscal obligations had of course to be accepted by the newly acquired area; but they did not as a rule involve any drastic change in its social organization. Thus, for example, the conquest by Russia during the Great Northern War (1700–21) of the Swedish provinces of Livonia and Esthonia had little influence on society in these areas.

The traditional ruling class of largely German landowners, the 'Baltic barons', suffered no loss of influence or infringement of their rights by the change. The towns such as Riga and Dorpat, again largely German, continued to be administered very much as before except that they were now garrisoned by Russian instead of Swedish troops. The peasantry continued to be one of the most miserable and depressed in Europe. Hardly anything had changed. Even in the province of Silesia, whose conquest from the Habsburgs by Prussia in 1741 changed the whole face of German politics, the implications of the change for its inhabitants were for long relatively slight: in 1806 a Prussian official claimed, though with some exaggeration, that 'Silesia is the same as it was under the Austrians'.[9]

So much did governments respect existing rights, so little did they value social change or even administrative uniformity for their own sake, that a conquered territory was often allowed to retain privileges and institutions which clearly reduced its value to the conqueror and made more difficult its eventual assimilation by him. One of the most striking examples of this is the treatment of Strasbourg after its annexation by Louis XIV in 1681. The city had to accept a French garrison and a number of French officials and to transfer the cathedral from Lutheran to Catholic control. On the other hand down to 1789 its citizens did no militia service, could be sued in the first instance only in the municipal courts, and paid taxes only to the municipal authorities, who then negotiated with the royal treasury on the payments the city should make to it. Above all Strasbourg retained unaltered its very complex traditional constitution. It had its own system of censorship and was granted a relatively high degree of religious toleration for its Lutheran inhabitants.

Parallels to these privileges existed in many of the States of Europe. The Basque provinces of Spain, to give only one instance, collected and spent public money on their own account, paying to the Spanish Crown only specified sums which they had agreed to provide. Concessions of this kind were sometimes a result of the weakness of the government concerned. It might well be convenient for it to delegate responsibilities in this way (see p. 125). Very often, however, they were also the product of a profound unwillingness to interfere with established institutions or practices unless it were essential to do so.

Such a position was obviously very hard to reconcile with the creation of modern centralized States. The unity of nearly all the countries of Europe was weakened by the survival of a vast structure of local and traditional rights and institutions; and these were now so deeply ingrained in the fabric of European life that only a cataclysm as great as the French Revolution could begin the work of dislodging them. Even the Revolution and the series of liberalizing movements which followed it – for the abolition of slavery and the slave trade, for the removal of the age-long disabilities imposed on Jews, for freedom of trade – did not completely defeat the conservative and traditionalist forces embodied in the idea of the sanctity of ancient institutions and inherited rights.

The success with which European society resisted the forces of change meant that it remained throughout this period extremely varied and heterogeneous. This lack of symmetry and regularity can be found at every social level. It is most marked in the landowning class and the peasantry, rather less so in the case of the towns. The extent, importance and ubiquity of these local variations and peculiarities in social structure can scarcely be exaggerated. The feelings of local patriotism and local selfconsciousness which they helped to breed often meant that areas politically united by allegiance to a single ruler none the less regarded each other with indifference or even hostility. Thus a Basque and a Castilian, a Catalan and an Andalusian, a Breton and a Gascon, might feel themselves to be fellow-subjects: fellow-citizens they could not be. In a State such as Prussia, which was an artificial creation and whose provinces were not united by a common history or bound together by natural frontiers, this position was still more acute. Until at least the middle of the century most of the subjects of the kings of Prussia probably drew no real distinction between the Prussian provinces other than their own and the possessions of foreign rulers. This parochialism underlies and weakens the blanket terms – French, Prussian, Spanish, peasantry, bourgeoisie, nobility – which the historian must use for convenience and for want of anything better.

Nevertheless, eighteenth-century social structure, like the eighteenth-century family, was not completely dominated by conservatism and tradition or completely immune to the forces of change. To the description of it as static and traditional important qualifications must be made. In the first place the old groupings of the parish, the guild or the manor had decreasing meaning or relevance in the great cities which now occupied an increasingly large part of the social landscape. Traditional ideals and responsibilities were hard to maintain in such an environment. Increasingly though slowly, they were also being drained of reality by the growth of large-scale industry, which brought with it social contrasts and cleavages of a new and often unmanageable type. It was possible for the old structure of society to retain much of its vitality in Frankfurt, which in the early decades of the century had a population of about 32,000, and where economic life centred around trade and banking rather than industry. It was even possible for it to do so, to a lesser extent, in Strasbourg, which had by 1789 a population of about 50,000 and which was also not an important industrial centre. But in London, Paris and Vienna, or even in Bristol, Lyons or Bordeaux, it could not hold out indefinitely against the forces of size and economic change and the new impersonality in social relations which they brought with them. In a truly new city such as Liverpool, which was not even a parish in its own right till 1699, a society of the traditional type never really existed.

Secondly, the conservative and backward-looking social structure which still dominated Western and Central Europe in the first half of the eighteenth century was becoming noticeably weaker in its later decades. On the intellectual level it was increasingly undermined by the rationalizing influence of the Enlightenment, by its contempt for survivals of the Middle Ages and its generalizing and deductive tendencies. By 1791 intellectuals almost everywhere were prepared to give an enthusiastic welcome to the Declaration of the Rights of Man, that supreme rejection of the idea of society as a mere network of communities, interests and traditions. As the century progressed the privileges of guilds, towns, provincial assemblies, manorial courts and a host of other survivals from the past seemed increasingly opposed to the interests of the community as a whole. The assaults of the Physiocrats (see p. 115) on what seemed to them obstructive and irrational relics of feudalism, which culminated in Turgot's unsuccessful attack on guild privileges in France in 1776, were merely the most obvious example of this attitude.

Finally, this traditional type of social structure never really existed in Russia, whose rise to the status of a great power is the most important political fact in the history of this period. The reasons why medieval Russia failed to develop a society based on groups, corporations and orders, as Western and most of Central Europe did, are far from clear. Whether the failure was caused by the country's lack of natural boundaries, great area and relatively scanty population (since it is hard to imagine a social organization of this type unless population has reached a certain minimum density); whether it was simply a result of the crushing by its rulers of any social institution which might act as a focus of opposition; or whether it was caused by some other factor or combination of factors, is difficult to say. The fact is, however, that in the eighteenth century the power of the central government in Russia was limited mainly by the mere physical difficulty of enforcing its commands over such a vast area. Except in a few regions such as the Baltic provinces there were hardly any institutions intermediate between the individual and the State with rights which the latter had to respect.

In Western Europe the towns clung tenaciously to their privileges. In Russia by contrast no city in the seventeenth or eighteenth centuries was able to act as an effective obstacle to the exercise of monarchical power, or to exercise rights comparable to those of France, Spain or West Germany. Indeed even if they had possessed the pride and self-confidence of many Western European towns it is doubtful whether those of Russia could have done much to modify the autocratic character of the State: as late as 1785 there were only five in the whole empire with populations of over 30,000.

Morever the only approach to a central representative institution which Russia had hitherto possessed, the *Zemskii Sobor* (Assembly of the Land), had ceased to function by the middle of the seventeenth century. Although the country was unified in much the same manner as France, by the accretion of provinces round the central nucleus of the Grand Duchy of Muscovy, it never possessed local representative bodies comparable to the French provincial estates or the *cortes* of the Spanish kingdoms. Moreover the privileged landowning class which took shape in Russia in the early eighteenth century, the *dvoryanstvo*, never acquired the self-consciousness and corporate pride which were characteristic of the nobilities of Western and Central Europe. Perhaps the clearest indication of this is the fact that, unlike their counterparts in nearly all Western countries, Russian landowners made no attempt to assert the principle of the indivisibility of their estates. The *mayorazgo* in Spain, the entail or 'strict settlement' in

England, the *Fideikommis* in the Habsburg hereditary provinces, were all means by which the lands of a nobleman could be preserved intact after his death and thus the standing of his family maintained. When, however, Peter I attempted in 1714 to prevent by legislation the customary division of landed estates in Russia amongst all the sons of the owner the innovation was furiously opposed. In 1731 it had to be abandoned. Moreover, partly because the *dvoryanstvo* had not originated as an essentially military caste, the West European idea of 'honour' was quite foreign to it. Until the promulgation by Catherine II of her Charter to the Nobility in 1785 its members continued to be subject to the corporal punishment which was so severe and so widespread throughout the country. The Charter has been interpreted as an attempt by the Empress to create what Russia had failed to produce spontaneously, a *noblesse* of the Western type. Like Peter I, she was trying, in an effort to develop and modernize the country, to establish institutions which, if they took root, might in the long run limit the autocratic power of the ruler. In Russia, in other words, social groupings were in general not native growths fortified by the prestige of generations of uninterrupted existence, as in the West, but artificial creations imposed from above with shallow roots in the national life. It is significant that there, apart from one or two really old families descended from independent or appanage princes of the Middle Ages, such as the Golitsyns or the Odoevskiis, very few Russian noblemen took their names from those of their estates or neighbourhood, as was so common in Western Europe. It is not a great exaggeration to say that in Russia society was a creation of the State, its structure a reflection of State needs and State pressures. In Western and much of Central Europe the opposite was the case. This meant that, paradoxical as it may seem, relations between rulers and ruled were in some respects more 'modern' in backward and undeveloped Russia than in the more developed countries of the West.

In almost every eighteenth-century State society was still in the main rural, and the workers on the land (who may be conveniently if not altogether accurately referred to as 'peasants') were the largest social group. The peasant's economic and social status, his standard of living and the degree of personal freedom he enjoyed, varied enormously between different areas. They depended on whether he was a free man or a serf, on the way in which he held his land, on whether that land was adequate to maintain him and his family, on the tools and technology at his disposal and on· a host of other factors. Most of peasant society, however (insofar as it can be spoken of as an entity) was traditional and pre-modern in one very fundamental way – in the fact that freedom of personal choice, and even any need for such choice and for the making of important decisions by individuals, was still very limited. A strict rule of custom which dictated how and when the peasant planted and harvested his crops, how he built his house and even how he treated his wife and children; the prevalence of arranged marriages; the small part very often played in peasant life by cash receipts or payments (since the spending of money is the essential mode of choice in the modern world) – all these fostered a deeply conservative type of society in which individual preferences and feelings counted for little and individual initiative and refusal to conform were hardly possible.

From the legal (though not necessarily the economic) point of view the critical distinction was that between the peasant who was personally free and his fellow who was a serf. This was largely a distinction between the western and eastern halves of the continent. In the British Isles, the Iberian peninsula and Italy, legal serfdom no longer existed. In France it was a serious factor only in a few eastern areas (in 1750 there were in all about 950,000 serfs in the country). In Germany the position varied from that in the south-west, where serfdom was comparatively rare and what existed was of a mild type, through that in Bavaria and Saxony, to that in Pomerania and East Prussia. In the latter large estates were dominant, the powers of the lords very extensive, and serfdom of an often highly oppressive kind the lot of the majority of the population. In Poland political chaos and the complete domination of the government by the privileged landowning class, the *szlachta*, made the status of the peasant almost comparable to that of a Negro slave in the West Indies. In Russia the unfree status which the strains of the seventeenth century and the policies of Peter I had riveted on a great part of the agrarian population was extended still more widely by Catherine II.

It was only too possible, of course, for a peasant to be legally a free man and still live in desperate poverty and great economic insecurity. The eighty per cent of the population of Andalusia who were shown by the Spanish census of 1797 to be day-labourers, often on the great estates of absentee landowners, were certainly worse off than many serfs in Russia or eastern Germany, and the same was true of many of the inhabitants of Sicily, southern Italy, Portugal and parts of Ireland. In France by 1789 about two-fifths of peasants owned no land or hardly any, whereas in Russia, where there were still vast amounts of undeveloped land and many village-communities periodically redistributed land amongst their members, a completely landless peasant was hard to find. In terms of security and living standards this was an extremely important contrast. Over much of Western Europe, moreover, even independent peasant proprietors owning or renting land found it more and more difficult to flourish, or even to survive, as the century went on. Their small-holdings were often less efficient and more tradition-bound producers than the larger estates of the nobility and the Church. More important, these holdings constantly tended to become still smaller through subdivision, since entails were too expensive and complex for the ordinary peasant to contemplate and often also ran counter to deep-seated traditional peasant feeling. Also although the small proprietor or tenant-farmer in the West might be free from the compulsory labour-services to a lord which were the essence of serfdom he was subject to one important exaction which was unimportant or unknown in most of Eastern Europe. This was the tithe which, especially on poor and unproductive land where it might amount to as much as a third of the net yield (i.e. after allowance had been made for the grain needed to provide seed for the following year's harvest), could be a heavy and deeply resented burden. The fact that tithes were very often owned and collected by laymen, sometimes even by governments, and that even when they remained in clerical hands they were more often than not in those of abbeys and wealthy prelates who lived in cities, meant that they usually contributed little to the maintenance of the parish priest, their ostensible object: in France, the country for which the subject has been most studied, only a tenth of priests received all the tithes collected in their parishes. Tithes in other words were yet another mechanism by which resources were drained from the villages for the benefit of the towns and the ruling social groups. Apart from the hunting rights over peasant land claimed by the aristocracy in many areas, probably no aspect of the old regime in the countryside aroused so much resentment as this. None of these qualifications, however, undermines the importance of the fundamental legal and moral distinction between a peasantry of serfs and one of men at least nominally free; and this contrast, broadly speaking, was one between Eastern and Western Europe.

This East-West contrast, none the less, must not be applied too mechanically. In Denmark, for example, an edict of 1702 which attempted to abolish serfdom in Seeland, Laaland and the neighbouring islands remained a dead letter. There the position of the peasantry in fact deteriorated in the eighteenth century, largely because of extensive sales of Crown lands to speculators in 1765–76. By contrast, over a great area of North Russia with its poor soil and scanty population peasant labour services to a lord were unknown. Holstein, which can hardly be regarded as part of Eastern Europe, had one of the most oppressive agrarian régimes to be found anywhere on the continent; while the subjection of the peasantry which was so notable a feature of society in Livonia was the result of German and Catholic conquest in the Middle Ages, not of Russian rule.

Serfdom in eastern and northern Germany and in Russia differed essentially from that in France and western Germany. In the latter it was a medieval institution surviving with increasing difficulty in a changing social and economic climate, of little apparent value to the State and more and more a target for the criticisms of reformers. This period saw its legal abolition in Lorraine, Savoy and Baden. East of the Elbe, on the other hand, it was a relatively new institution which had developed rapidly in the seventeenth century. In Brandenburg and Saxony its spread was accelerated by the devastation of the Thirty Years War, and by the critical shortage of labour which the war had produced. This, coupled with a growing demand for grain for export and distilling, led the landowners of these areas to extend and intensify their control over the peasant population. As well as being obliged to provide labour services, the peasant thus lost in many parts of eastern Germany the right to choose his employment, to work outside the lord's estate without the latter's consent, or even to marry without the payment to him of a small tax. His subjection was completed by a growing tendency towards the union in the hands of the lord of landownership (*Grundherrschaft*) and rights of jurisdiction (*Gerichtsherrschaft*). This meant that in the eighteenth century the landlord was usually a judicial and administrative official, and often an army officer as well. Against this concentration of authority, and still more against the power given the landowner by the dependence on him of the Prussian administration and army for their efficient functioning, the peasant was almost helpless. In both Prussia and Saxony, moreover, there had emerged after the Thirty Years War the system of *Gesindedienst* or *Gesindezwangsdienst* by which young peasants had to serve their lord, normally on his estate, for prescribed periods at fixed (and of course usually low) wages. A similar system prevailed in parts of the Habsburg Empire, where peasant boys who had reached the age of fourteen were regularly mustered for service in the lord's house or on his domain. Those required for such purposes normally served for three years, but might have to do so for as long as seven. This system of forced labour, which was consolidated in Saxony as late as 1766, was safeguarded by efforts in many States to prevent the spread of industry to the countryside, since there it would inevitably compete with agriculture for the still limited labour force available. In Saxony there were even proposals that all children, on reaching the age of fourteen, be obliged by law to work for four years on the land.

In Russia serfdom had originated in a somewhat different way. There it arose from the efforts of the government, from the second half of the sixteenth century onwards, to pin down a scanty and shifting population in a vast undeveloped country and extract from it the money and services required for State purposes. This process was completed in the reign of Peter I by the introduction of a system of military conscription from 1705 onwards, and above all by the imposition on the Russian peasantry in 1719 of the poll-tax. Peter made the landowner responsible for the collection of this tax and for the supply of recruits from his estates. By so doing he greatly increased the lord's authority over his serfs. The nature of serfdom in Russia was thus fundamentally changed. From being primarily an attachment to the soil, as it had been under the legislation of the sixteenth and seventeenth centuries, it became increasingly one to the person of the landlord, and hence approximated to slavery. This was emphasized in 1762, when Peter III gave the lords the power to transfer serfs from one estate to another, thus depriving the serf of his traditional attachment to the land he cultivated. The abolition of slavery as a recognized legal status in 1723 thus indicated a decline in the position of the serf rather than a rise in that of the slave. Russia indeed was the one European State in which the legal position of the serf changed clearly and decisively for the worse in this period. In 1760 landowners were granted the right to exile to Siberia lazy or rebellious serfs: twelve years later there were in eastern Siberia alone over 20,000 peasants who had been sent there by their masters. The attitude to serfdom of Catherine II, after her accession in 1762, was complex and ambiguous (see p. 194) and she had certainly some grasp of the extent to which it now hampered the social and economic development of Russia. But she was unable, and probably unwilling, to do anything effective to restrict its growth.

The complete absence of any attempt by the rulers of Russia to protect the serf is all the more marked by contrast with the efforts of this kind, however ineffective, which were made by the governments of Prussia and the Habsburg dominions. Thus the Austrian government made a series of attempts in 1680, 1716 and 1738 to set limits to the labour-services exacted from the peasants of Silesia, Bohemia and Moravia. These efforts culminated in the great reforms introduced by Joseph II in the early 1780s (see p. 202). In the same way in Prussia an attempt was made in 1723 to limit the control hitherto exercised by the Junkers over the marriage of peasant girls on their estates; and in 1763, as one of his agrarian reforms of that year, Frederick II attempted without much success to give the peasantry of Upper Silesia greater security of tenure and abolished serfdom in Prussian Pomerania. In no part of Europe except Poland and perhaps Hungary was the peasant quite so completely abandoned to the mercies of his master as in Russia.

Serfdom was also becoming the lot of an increasingly large proportion of the Russian people. In the far north, where the population was scanty and the soil poor, it was never of much importance. In Central Russia, on the other hand, its prevalence steadily increased, while the territorial expansion of the later decades of the century extended it to the steppe and 'black earth' regions of the south. Its establishment in the Ukraine, made final in 1783, was followed at the end of 1796, immediately after the death of Catherine II, by its extension to the Caucasus, the Crimea and the Don region. Nowhere in European Russia was now exempt from its influence. Moreover from the reign of Peter I onwards social groups hitherto free were beginning, under the pressure of taxation and conscription, to sink into serfdom. Increasingly the population of much of the country was tending to divide, apart from churchmen and a small merchant class, into a minority of landlords and a huge mass of 'bonded people' (*krepostnie lyudi*). Thus during this period rural society in Russia, though not exactly un-European, was developing along lines which had been abandoned or were being modified over most of the rest of the continent.

Areas such as the Habsburg provinces, Poland and Russia, where serfdom was onerous and the authority of the central goverment hard to enforce, were the natural breeding-ground of peasant revolts. All of them suffered during this period from disturbances of this type. In Bohemia there was a serious rising in 1775 accompanied by a march of peasant insurgents on Prague, and a particularly brutal one broke out in Transylvania in 1784. In the Polish Ukraine there was a very savage revolt, provoked by the antagonism between an Orthodox and Uniate peasantry and a mainly Catholic landowning class, in the 1730s and another exceptionally bitter one in 1768. In Russia above all agrarian discontent and disorder were endemic throughout the century, especially in its second half. Seventy-three peasant risings, most of them of purely local importance, are known to have taken place in 1762–69; and the widespread rural disorder which marked the early years of the reign of Catherine II culminated in the revolt led by the Cossack Pugachev which broke out in 1773 and was not completely suppressed till 1775. This outbreak, which swept across a huge area of south-eastern Russia and involved Cossacks, non-Russian peoples such as the Bashkirs, religious dissidents and rebellious workers in the mines and foundries of the Urals as well as peasants, was the greatest outburst of social protest anywhere in Europe during this period. Close on three million people may have taken some part in it and for a few weeks in the summer of 1774 it seemed that it might even overthrow the ruling order in Russia.[10] In the Baltic provinces there was serious rural unrest in 1778 and 1783; and in another great wave of discontent in 1796–97 in Central Russia 278 separate outbreaks were recorded.

None of these revolts, however, in Russia or elsewhere, had any real programme beyond that of removing or lightening some of the burdens which weighed so heavily on the peasant. Nearly all were inspired by specific and concrete grievances, not by any desire to alter the structure of society, an ambition beyond the grasp of the ordinary peasant. Most of them were little more than inarticulate outbursts of hatred and resentment. Occurring as nearly all of them did in areas where towns were few and small they were deprived of the urban leadership which alone might have brought them some success. Insofar as these peasant outbreaks had any ideological content it often took the form of a pathetic belief in the benevolence of their rulers and in the willingness and ability of the monarch, once he was made aware of their justified grievances, to do something effective about them. Probably the efforts of a number of rulers to improve the position of the peasant during the later decades of the century did something to strengthen this 'naive monarchism' as a Polish historian has called it: this was certainly the case so far as the Emperor Joseph II was concerned. But the most effective threat which the peasant could offer to the regime which so exploited him was not by revolt but, where this was possible, by flight, usually to some thinly populated frontier region where the hold of the State and the landowner was weaker. In Russia, where 200,000 cases of peasant flight were officially recorded in 1719–27 and there must have been many others which escaped official notice, this was a great and intractable problem, as a mass of legislation on the subject testifies.

Almost everywhere in Europe village communities played an important and sometimes surprisingly independent role in the life of the countryside. Autonomous or semi-autonomous villages reached their highest pitch of development in the poorer and more remote mountain areas of the Alps, Pyrenees and Appenines. They could be found, however, enjoying varying degrees of self-government, in most European countries. The village community had normally a number of important functions, at least in Western Europe. It safeguarded public order in its own area and provided a minimum of poor relief. It maintained the parish church and often paid a village schoolmaster. Frequently it apportioned amongst the heads of households in the village the sum demanded in taxes by the central government.

In France the majority of villages, at least until late in the century, retained a high degree of self-government – more indeed than most French towns. 'Each community amongst us', wrote the *Parlement* of Provence to Louis XV in 1774, 'is a family which governs itself, which draws up its own laws and looks after its own interests; its municipal officer is its father.'[11] Paternalism and localism, two basic ideas of the century, are tellingly combined in this claim. Village assemblies in France, meeting periodically on Sundays after Mass, continued to regulate a wide variety of local affairs. They elected their own syndics (except for a short interval in 1702–17, when the government created perpetual syndics for each parish in order to be able to sell the office and thus raise funds). They often appointed a variety of minor officials. They controlled sales, purchases and rents of common lands. Sometimes they fixed the conditions of the wine harvest, the prices of basic commodities and even rates of pay for day-labourers. As time went on their control of communal property and funds tended to be increasingly supervised by the provincial estates and by government officials such as the *intendant* and the *sub-délégué*; but the system seems to have worked reasonably well to judge by the fewness of complaints about it in the *cahiers* of 1789. It is noteworthy, moreover, that priests and *seigneurs* had to contribute in proportion to their means to communal taxation, and were often compelled to do so, if they made difficulties, by royal officials. One historian has claimed, with some exaggeration, that 'the equality of taxation which was proclaimed in 1789 had long existed with regard to communal contributions'.[12]

In north-western Germany, again, the village community (*Gemeinde*) was important and largely democratic in its structure. Like its equivalent in France it supervised communal property, safeguarded public order, and maintained the roads and bridges of its own locality. Its position was strengthened by the fact that in this area the rights of jurisdiction enjoyed by the nobility in the Middle Ages had been largely taken over by the governments of the various States.

These village communities should not be idealized, nor their defects lost sight of. They were not democratic in any present-day sense of the term. Dominance by the richer peasants, those who could eat white bread while their poorer fellows ate soups of various sorts, or in Northern Europe potatoes and in the south chestnuts, was the norm. Quite frequently the richer peasants had become rich by acting as bailiffs and collectors of tithes and feudal dues for local landowners, a fact which tended to deepen further social divisions and resentments. The village community expressed the inveterate localism, the ingrained narrowness of view, the deep-rooted distrust of all change, which dominated the lives of so high a proportion of Europeans. The tenacious and widespread peasant resistance to new crops such as potatoes or maize, or to novelties such as inoculation against smallpox, is a good illustration of this. So is the widespread practice of the fixing by the village council of an official date for the beginning of the harvest and the fining of any cultivator who disregarded it: the traditional village was deeply distrustful of individual initiative of any kind. The same attitudes emerge clearly in the hostility with which villages so often greeted well-meant attempts by reforming officials or governments to help them, or even to acquire more accurate knowledge of their problems. In the Auvergne in 1770, for example, the efforts of the *intendant* to take a census of needy families to make easier the distribution to them of official supplies of food was resisted because of fears that the families concerned were to be forcibly deported to French Guiana. In the same area surveyors making a cartographic survey were stoned by the local peasants as sorcerers likely to attract hail which would damage the crops. In a different way the same narrowness can be seen in the prevalence of inter-village feuds. Sometimes these were over an identifiable material issue, as when one Breton village refused to allow another to collect seaweed for use as a fertilizer.[13] Often, however, their origins were lost in the mists of time and they had become no more than a form of unthinking traditionalism, a collective reflex action. The village community stood, in a limited way, for freedom in an age of despotism; but it was a freedom usually marked by ignorance, prejudice and deep and irrational conservatism. It is hardly surprising that in the second half of the century several governments made efforts to break up the common lands which many village communities still controlled into individual holdings, since these seemed likely to be more productive and also to offer some solution to the growing problem of the landless peasant. It is equally unsurprising that such efforts, in Spain in 1766–68 and in France during the same decade, encountered determined opposition from the communities concerned and achieved little.

The structure, numbers and influence of the landowning class (the term 'nobility', though its use cannot always be avoided, is too narrow to be really accurate) varied enormously in different parts of Europe. Almost everywhere, except in Britain and the United Provinces, it enjoyed important legal privileges – rights of jurisdiction, immunity from certain forms of particularly severe or degrading punishment or from some types of taxation. In many States legal barriers were opposed to the acquisition by commoners of 'noble land'. In the eastern and central parts of the continent in particular the legal superiority of the landlords to other social groups was marked. Thus in Poland they retained until 1768 powers of life and death over their serfs, and in Hungary succeeded in 1731 in asserting their right to pay no taxes at all. The diets or estates, traditional representative bodies tracing from the Middle Ages which still existed in many parts of Europe though with declining effectiveness, were normally dominated by the privileged landowning class. This was the position in Sweden, in those German States where such bodies still functioned, and in most of the Habsburg provinces. In Poland and Hungary this social group was the only one represented. Side by side with these politically and economically important privileges, moreover, were others which, though in practical terms less significant, often aroused deep resentment – the exclusive right to wear a sword, to have a coat of arms, to use a special pew in church and, often most resented of all, a monopoly of most forms of hunting. In many parts of Europe there were special schools – the *Ritterakademien* in Germany, the *colegios mayores* in Spain – which were reserved exclusively for the sons of the privileged. Provocative distinctions of this kind were often underlain by claims that the nobility was in some sense a distinct race inherently superior to the unprivileged masses. This attitude was most articulate in France, where many partisans of the nobility saw it as the heirs of the conquering Franks of the fifth and sixth centuries ruling by right of conquest a population descended from the Gauls whom Clovis and his successors had subjected: but similar attitudes were also prominent in Germany.

In many countries the landowning class was tending, as the century progressed, to become more self-conscious, more jealous of its rights and more anxious to prevent commoners achieving privileged status. This is perhaps seen most clearly in Sweden, where the constitution of 1720 severely limited the ruler's right to ennoble commoners. Everywhere there was a strong feeling that an indispensable prerequisite of true noble status was an appropriate style of life. A noble must live on the yield of his estates (which included the yield of mineral deposits discovered on them). He might become rich through industry based on the raw materials which these estates produced; but he must not engage in trade, and certainly not in retail trade, in a way which compromised his social standing. To do this was to run the risk of derogation, loss of privileged status. For the smaller landowners, squires and petty nobles, it was not always easy to observe these restrictions; and in one very important case (that of Russia, where nobles were allowed to trade without loss of status) they did not apply. In many parts of Europe, however, notably in France where the idea of 'living nobly' was more ingrained than in most other areas, even very poor members of this privileged class struggled bitterly to avoid any sort of activity which might drag them down into the ranks of the unprivileged majority.

In most parts of Europe this privileged group had originated as a knightly class with important military functions. Military traditions and ambitions still counted for much in the outlook of many of its members in the eighteenth century. Its real military effectiveness, however, was now in decline. No European army in the eighteenth century could afford to base its organization entirely on a single class or to exclude commoners completely from its commissioned ranks, though there continued to be a widespread assumption that nobles, the product of a centuries-old military tradition and imbued with a high sense of military honour, made the best officers (see p. 222). This created, in many States, an implicit conflict between military efficiency and what many members of the privileged class, especially many of its poorer members, thought of as their right to monopolize commissions (see p. 222). To some extent this conflict could be resolved by the grant of privileged status to able commoners who had reached a certain level of military rank, or whose families had established some hereditary connexion with the army. This was done most notably in Russia by Peter I in the Table of Ranks which he issued in 1722. This divided the bureaucracy, as well as the commissioned ranks of the army and navy, into fourteen distinct grades. Membership of the higher grades in the case of bureaucrats, and of all in that of army and navy officers, conferred on the holder the privileges of hereditary nobility. In a rather different way something of the same sort was attempted in France. There an edict of 1750 granted nobility to commoners who had reached the rank of general (of whom there were of course very few indeed) and also to all families whose male members for three generations had served in the army in commissioned ranks lower than that of general. In this way some 125 officers were ennobled in 1766–90. Besides this about 150 others were granted nobility in the forty years before 1789, though their families had not provided the required three generations of service. These figures merely show, however, how tiny was the change brought about by such measures in the composition of the French nobility, whose numbers ran into hundreds of thousands. Not until after the Revolution was it possible to envisage the taking-over on a large scale of its military functions by other classes.

The privileged landowning class had more than military importance in the eighteenth century. It also played a large, sometimes an indispensable, part in the running of the State administrative machines. In Prussia, where the Junkers were being transformed in the later seventeenth and early eighteenth centuries into a class of hereditary State servants, the whole administration increasingly reflected their virtues and vices. A very similar position was to be found in Russia. There Peter I had succeeded, in the face of much opposition, in asserting the principle that every landowner was bound, as a condition of holding his land, to serve the State for an unlimited period in the armed forces or the civil administration. In this way alone could the officers and officials needed for the creation of powerful armed forces and a centralized bureaucracy be found, and Russia be enabled to play the role of a great power in Europe. The onerous obligations he thus imposed on them were naturally resented by the nobility, and under his weaker successors they succeeded in having them considerably reduced. In 1736 the period of compulsory service was fixed at twenty-five years, so that if a child were inscribed for service very young, as was frequently done, he might become free of further obligations by the age of about thirty. In 1762 Peter III completed this process by liberating the *dvoryanstvo* from all legal obligation to serve the State, so that from this date onward it ceased to be a service class in the strict sense of the term.

Nevertheless it continued to dominate both the army and the administrative machine, and to retain for many years much of the outlook of a class of hereditary State servants. It was only with the issue by Catherine II in 1785 of her Charter to the Nobility that it began to be something approximating to a *noblesse* of the normal West European type. This document, the last and greatest grant of privileges by any ruler of Russia to the landowning class, created permanent and official assemblies of the nobility at provincial and district level, which were to have the right to make submissions to the provincial governors and in certain circumstances even to the ruler. This was a deliberate effort to endow the Russian ruling class with greater self-consciousness and self-confidence, to foster greater initiative and independence in it and make it a more creative element in Russian society. Henceforth members of the *dvoryanstvo* were to be exempt from corporal punishment and were to be deprived of their rank, property or lives only after trial by their peers. This was a long step away from the harsh and demanding attitude of Peter I and a real if limited effort to break with the tradition of autocracy and arbitrary power which was now so deeply ingrained in Russia. The Russian nobility by the end of Catherine's reign was still a distinctively Russian phenomenon, but in terms of its legal status and rights it was now more 'westernized' than ever before. At no time during the century, however, even after the issue of the charter of 1785, was it able or willing to act as a true social estate in the West European sense of the term, with collective self-confidence and a genuine sense of its own unity. Though on several occasions (1702, 1713, 1723) Peter I tried rather unsucessfully to make the provincial nobility elect their own representatives for various purposes (notably for the collection of the poll-tax in 1723) this was merely an administrative device. These representatives were not in the least intended to defend the interests of their districts or of those who had elected them. Moreover, throughout the century the fact that so many nobles were absent from their estates for very long periods, serving in the armed forces or the bureaucracy, meant that they had little chance to develop the local roots, the knowledge of and interest in the affairs of their own localities, which were so important to most of their West and even Central European counterparts.

In France the position was very different. There, as the old military and landed nobility, the *noblesse de l'épée*, showed itself less and less able to administer a State struggling with complex social and financial problems, it was supplemented and to some extent replaced by a new administrative nobility, the *noblesse de la robe*. This class, of comparatively recent origin and led by the holders of a number of great legal offices, was now growing in wealth and influence. It provided many of the Secretaries of State who controlled during this period the workings of most of the different departments of the central administration – Chauvelin, Maurepas, Machault, the d'Argenson brothers. Equally important, it dominated the *parlements* – powerful, conservative and largely hereditary legal corporations, twelve in number, which could possess great political importance. On the other hand, since it was composed mainly of bourgeois who had purchased government offices carrying with them the privileges of nobility, or their descendants, the *noblesse de la robe* tended to be looked down on by the older noble families. Nor had it much influence at court, or within the charmed circle immediately surrounding the royal family. Its very abilities, indeed, to some extent told against it; for learning or intellectual interests seemed to many Frenchmen the qualities of a commoner, something which a true nobleman could do without. Nevertheless it was one of the most important elements in French society during this period. The passage of time and the wealth of the great *robe* families did something to lessen the condescension with which it was regarded by the older nobility, so that by the middle of the century it had largely thrown off the stigma of its middle-class origins and could see itself as part of a united *noblesse*. Able, conservative and self-interested, it had become by the years before 1789 perhaps the greatest of all obstacles to the radical overhaul of the governmental system which was now clearly needed.

In Britain also the influence of the aristocracy and squirearchy on the government and administrative system was profound. Throughout the century the House of Lords retained a political influence and popular esteem little if at all inferior to those possessed by the House of Commons. The latter in any case consisted overwhelmingly of landowners: its members were very often related to those of the upper house and owed their seats to the money and influence of some peer. From 1710 onwards every Member of Parliament had to own land of a specified annual value as a qualification for membership of the House. Moreover to the end of this period and long after the Cabinet remained a predominantly aristocratic body. The younger Pitt, when he took office as Prime Minister in 1783, was the only member of his own Cabinet who sat in the Commons; and as late as 1830 that of Lord Grey contained thirteen peers or sons of peers, a baronet, and only one untitled commoner. In English local government also the dominance of the landowning class through the Justices of the Peace (see p. 156) was the central fact of this period. In one fundamental respect, their lack of fiscal privileges, the peers and squires in Britain differed from comparable groups in almost all of the rest of Europe: but their hold on the administrative machine was at least as great as in most other parts of the continent.

A control by landlords of the life of their own localities as complete as that in England or Prussia can be seen in many other parts of Europe. In Hungary and Poland this control was absolute, unchallenged and unchallengeable. In the Two Sicilies also the local influence of the nobility, based on their jurisdictional and economic rights over the peasants and their possession of bodyguards of armed retainers, was enormous. In spite of the efforts in the 1730s and 1740s of Charles IV and his ministers to reduce these outmoded and dangerous powers (mainly by making the decisions of feudal courts subject to appeal in royal ones, and by limiting the number of armed followers a noble might possess) it remained very great throughout the century. In Sweden, again, the nobility enjoyed great political importance. Not until 1809 was government office there made legally accessible to members of all classes.

The use of the terms 'nobility' or 'landowning class' must not be taken as implying that a homogeneous social group is being discussed. There were vast differences between the 'nobilities' of different countries. The Polish and Hungarian squires exacting directly or through manorial officials labour services from their peasants had not much resemblance to the aristocrats of England or Sweden, whose lands were for the most part leased to tenant farmers over whom they had much less direct control. The service nobilities of Russia and Prussia had little in common with the increasingly functionless aristocrats of Spain and Italy. The relatively businesslike landowners of England, often improving the part of their estates which they directly controlled and occasionally reaping great wealth from the exploitation of mineral rights, contrasted with the highly unbusinesslike and ill-informed ones of Russia, who usually had no idea whatever of either their income or their expenditure. There were also important distinctions between the different sections and subdivisions of each national 'nobility'. In England, where the peerage was a very small and homogeneous body separated by a clear line of division from non-noble landowers however wealthy, the position was comparatively straightforward. In most other countries, however, the number of people who could lay claim to the privileges of nobility was very large, and the disparities between them in wealth, education and political power might be very great.

Thus in France, where the *noblesse* towards the end of this period numbered in all perhaps some 300,000–350,000 (about one per cent of the population), there were probably as few as 4,000 noble families which had any share, however small, in the life of the court, or any direct access to the monarch. That access was now being more narrowly restricted than ever before. From 1732 onwards the grant of the *honneurs de la Cour* (presentation of female members of a family to the queen and the permitting of its male members to ride in the king's coach) presupposed that convincing proofs of nobility had been given. From 1759 it required, at least in theory, that the family in question should have been noble since before the year 1400.[14] Even within the highest ranks of the nobility there was a complex pecking-order, so that a *duc et pair* ranked above a mere *duc à brevet*. Between a great noble who could obtain for himself and his protégés the appointments, honours and pensions which only court influence could secure, and the poor provincial squire, the *hobereau*, who might live and work in conditions no better than those enjoyed by many peasants, the gulf was wide indeed. Only in a purely legal sense can they be regarded as belonging to the same social class, and the envy and resentment felt by the small noble in the provinces for the great one at Versailles was often bitter. 'The court nobility', wrote an observer in Britanny late in the century, 'has at all times been the most pronounced and most dangerous enemy of the other nobles.' The width of the economic gulf which separated different groups of the French nobility can be seen in the workings of the new poll-tax, the *capitation*, introduced in 1695. This divided the entire population of France into twenty-two classes, each supposed to be made up of individuals with a more or less equal capacity to pay. But whereas members of the first class (princes of royal blood, ministers and farmers-general of taxes) paid 2,000 livres the poorest nobles, without a fief or chateau of their own, paid a mere 6 livres.[15] The distinction between rich and poor nobles, between metropolitan and provincial, was in practice much more important than that between those of the 'robe' and the 'sword'. Even the degree of influence which the French nobility could exercise over the provincial representative bodies, the estates, in the areas where these existed, varied widely in different provinces. In Brittany perhaps as many as 3,000 *gentilshommes* had the right to attend meetings of the estates; and it was normal for several hundred (many of them very poor) to put in an appearance. In Languedoc, by contrast, only twenty-three nobles, nearly all of them much wealthier than the Breton gentry, were members of the estates.

Similarly in Spain, where in the census of 1787 half a million people (about 5 per cent of the total population) claimed to be of noble status, the difference between the poor *hidalgos* who made up the vast majority of this total and the tiny group of great land-owners at the apex of the social pyramid, such as the Dukes of Infantado and Medina-Sidonia, was immense. Within these major divisions of the Spanish privileged class, moreover, there were further subdivisions: the grandees, the highest stratum of the nobility numbering little more than a hundred in all, were them-selves classified, at least in theory, in three distinct groups. There were also enormous regional differences. The entire population of one of the Basque provinces claimed noble status, whereas in Andalusia a mere one per cent made such a claim. Contrasts were equally sharp in Poland. There the privileged class, the *szlachta*, was before the partitions an enormous group of 750,000–850,000 people (10–15 per cent of the whole population) the vast majority of whom were poor and many of whom owned little or no land. Many of them, to the casual observer, were distinguishable from peasants only by their possession of the right to wear a particular type of dress and by the fact that special seats were reserved for them in church. Between 'barefoot *szlachta*' of this type and the two dozen or so great magnates who ruled the country (in so far as it was ruled at all before the partitions) there could be no real equality. A Prince Radziwill, owning lands greater in extent than many of the German States, or a member of one of the other great Polish families, the Czartoryskis, the Potockis, the Sapiehas, was a different being from the ignorant and impoverished squires who followed and depended on him. In the same way in Hungary, where the census of 1784 (a surprisingly complete one for this period) recorded 416,000 'nobles' or about 4–5 per cent of the population, the Esterhazys, Palffys, and other great families, wealthy, cultured, and influential at Vienna, moved in a different world from the semi-educated and bitterly conservative petty landlords. Similar distinctions can be seen in Russia, where in 1760 there were perhaps 500,000–600,000 'nobles' – about 2–3 per cent of the population. There as early as the 1690s Prince M. Ya. Cherkasskii, the greatest secular landholder in the country, possessed over 9,000 peasant households, while eleven other land-owners each possessed over a thousand. Even eighty years later, by contrast, in spite of a great growth of population and considerable extension of serfdom, three-fifths of all landowners in the Great Russian provinces still owned less than twenty male serfs. Even in a state as small as the Venetian Republic a profound distinction of a different kind can be found – that between the nobility of Venice itself, declining in numbers and increasingly impoverished, and the nobilities of the Venetian possessions on the mainland of Italy. When in 1775 it was agreed to accept on payment of a large sum of money forty families of the latter into the Venetian nobility (for centuries the most snobbish and exclusive in Europe) only ten such families could be found willing to accept the honour offered them. In some areas such as Sweden and Tuscany, where the nobilities were small (perhaps 0.3 per cent of the population in Tuscany) and relatively homogeneous, internal rivalries of this kind were less pronounced: but almost everywhere they were significant.

In much of eighteenth-century Europe, therefore, and notably in Russia, Spain, Poland and Hungary (which between them contained more than two-thirds of the nobles of the continent) it is the enormous disparities between different groups within this privileged social order which stand out. As the century went on, moreover, it became more and more difficult for the poor noble to maintain his position and avoid sinking into the unprivileged mass of the population. Social status was slowly but increasingly becoming associated with education, and the very poor 'noble' of Poland or the Basque provinces was less and less able to give his sons even the basic education which was now needed if they were to hold their position in the world. Governments increasingly found the pretensions of this often unruly and more and more functionless class a nuisance. After the partitions of Poland the Prussian, Austrian and Russian governments refused to recognize the privileged status of many *szlachta* in their new territories, while in Spain the government became increasingly stringent in its demands for proofs of nobility and the number of nobles officially recognized fell by over 300,000 in the years 1786–97. A process of elimination of this kind (it has been claimed that the total size of all the European nobilities combined fell by about a third in the period 1750–1815) was an essential step towards the emergence of a more modern class structure, one based on economic status and education rather than on traditional and legal privileges.

One final point of importance must be made. Very few nobilities in eighteenth-century Europe, and no large or important ones, were completely closed castes. In Russia the Table of Ranks of 1722 made even quite modest success in state service the stepping-stone to privileged status. Almost everywhere else the golden key was money. In France there was a vast and complex structure of government offices which could be bought and which conferred noble status on the holder (many of them only gradually, after they had been held for three generations in the same family). Throughout the century successful commoners were able to use this route to social advancement, while the purchase of land with associated seigneurial rights served the same purpose. In the Habsburg dominions under Joseph II (1780–90) there was in effect a fixed tariff of payment for titles of nobility – 20,000 gulden to become a count, 6,000 to become a baron, a mere 386 to become an untitled nobleman: these widely differing sums are yet another index of the cleavages within this privileged social order. From 1758 onwards it was possible to buy *hidalgo* status in Spain, while even the Venetian nobility, driven by the needs of war expenditure, admitted 127 new families in 1646–1718 in return for a very heavy entrance fee of 100,000 ducats. Of all the major states Britain, where the peerage grew only very slightly until the 1780s, was the one in which the aristocracy was most difficult for even a very rich man to enter.

The social importance of the towns also differed enormously in different parts of Europe. No contrast between Western and Eastern Europe was more fundamental and far-reaching in its effects than that provided by the greater strength of urban life, and all it implied, in the West. By the end of the century about a third of Englishmen already lived in towns, more than eight times as high a proportion as in Russia. Moreover, in the West towns were not merely more numerous and as a rule larger than in Eastern Europe, but also enjoyed a far higher degree of effective autonomy. In Russia, Prussia and Poland they were for the most part small and, more important, timid. There centuries of subjection to autocratic government or the power of great nobles had robbed them of self-confidence and desire for autonomy. In 1699 Peter I had offered the Russian towns a degree of self-government in return for the payment of higher taxes; the proposal was rejected. In 1785 Catherine II attempted to strengthen their position and make them a more autonomous element in society by a charter which gave each of them a common council, meeting weekly, which was elected by all city-dwellers. This was an important constructive step; but it could not compensate for the effects of generations of weakness and subjection. In Western Europe, by contrast, municipal self-government had been for centuries a political and social reality. There municipal privileges in regard to such things as taxation set genuine limits to the powers of central governments. Quite apart from the imperial cities of Germany, which were formally independent States, the towns of France, Spain and England enjoyed a significant degree of real independence in the conduct of their own affairs. In France this was symbolized by the fact that until late in the seventeenth century many retained fortifications and artillery of their own; Paris still possessed its own cannon in the eighteenth century and had them recast in 1732. Except in a few areas – the Dutch Republic, England, some parts of Italy – towns-folk still made up only a small fraction of the population. Even at the end of the old regime only about a sixth of all Frenchman lived in towns of over 2,000 people, while Paris itself accounted for only about two per cent of the total. Nevertheless this urban minority often had an importance out of all proportion to its size; and there was a widespread consciousness of the differences between town and countryside and often much mutual dislike and mistrust. The contrast between the large city, a centre of education and luxury consumption, and the poverty-stricken countryside which often surrounded it, could be very sharp indeed; a completely new city such as St Petersburg, the greatest achievement of town-building during this period, showed it in its most striking form. 'The country about Petersbourg', wrote a British observer in 1741, 'has full as wild and desert a look as any in all the Indies; you need not go above 200 paces out of the town to find yourself in a wild wood of firs, and such a low, marshy, boggy country that you would think God when he created the rest of the world for the use of mankind had created this for an inaccessible retreat for all sorts of wild beasts.'[16] In Western Europe also such brutal contrast were not uncommon; for example, that between the wealthy seaport of Nantes, enriched by the slave-trade and full of fine buildings, and the desperately poor countryside in which it was placed. 'What a miracle', exclaimed the English traveller Arthur Young on seeing it, 'all this splendour and wealth of the cities in France should be so unconnected with the country.'

The peasant frequently resented what he saw as exploitation by the town, and this feeling was usually justified. Organized charity, for example, was normally much more widespread and accessible in the towns, while governments often took elaborate precautions to safeguard the food supplies of their capitals. These factors, and the position of towns as markets, meant that in times of shortage they were fed while the peasant food-producer might starve. Often a high proportion of the beggars in a town were peasants from the surrounding area reduced to this by hard times on the land. Professional services of all kinds, scanty or non-existent in the countryside, were much more plentiful in the cities. One study of a large area of France shows that in the middle of the century doctors (for what their services were then worth) were about three times as numerous in proportion to the population they served in the towns as in the rural areas around them. It was easier and usually cheaper to borrow money in the towns: in Naples, for example, the normal rate of interest during much of the century was about three per cent whereas in the surrounding countryside it fluctuated around eight or nine per cent. Conscription for the army and militia often fell much more lightly on the towns. Most important of all, they almost always escaped more lightly than the countryside where direct taxation was concerned. It was claimed, to quote only one of many possible instances, that Palermo in the early decades of the century consumed about a third of the total production of the island of Sicily while paying only about a tenth of the total tax yield. 'So long as the arbitrariness of the *taille* (the main tax on land), the fear of the militia and the horrors of *corvées* (forced labour, usually on roadbuilding) continue to oppress the countryside', wrote a Frenchman in 1762, 'one must expect that the cities, where one is sheltered from these evils, will continue to grow at the expense of agriculture'.[17] The countryside fed the towns: but except in the more developed parts of Europe it did this in large part not by producing for the market but through rents, feudal dues, tithes and other legally-enforced levies on the product of the peasant's labour. The worst examples of widespread malnutrition were in the countryside: no French town was so badly off in this respect as rural areas like the Valais and the Vivarais, where there were entire villages whose inhabitants were crippled and deformed by an inadequate diet. The resentment which these unfairnesses aroused was almost certainly intensified by the considerable purchases of land by wealthy townspeople which can be seen in some parts of Europe in the later eighteenth century. The townsman for his part often felt a scarcely suppressed fear and contempt for the semi-civilized peasant majority who surrounded him. In 1789, for example, some French towns showed themselves uneasy lest the peasantry and their grievances should be too effectively represented in the States-General when it met. Probably the widespread introduction in the second half of the century, at least in Western Europe and in the larger towns, of such urban amenities as street lighting, the numbering of houses and more or less modern fire-fighting organizations, accentuated the distinctions between town and country and hence the possibility of bad feeling between them.

In a few cities of Western Europe a small social segment of merchants, bankers or financiers was now becoming very important. In the United Provinces the patriciate of Amsterdam had long been a dominant group, enjoying great political influence as well as great wealth. In England a somewhat similar development was visible before the end of the seventeenth century; during the two generations or more which followed great London bankers, financiers or merchants, such as Samson Gideon or Sir Joshua Vanneck, had on occasion very real influence on the development of government policy. In the realm of public finance, in particular, ministers normally depended heavily on the support, and were compelled to pay attention to the advice, of a small number of great capitalists. Many of these were of Jewish, Dutch or Huguenot extraction. Moreover there was a strong tendency for this group, by marriage or by purchase of land, to become closely connected with and eventually assimilated to, the greater English landowners. (Though to the end of this period there was a strong prejudice against the grant of titles, and of the position of Justice of the Peace, to men whose money had been made in trade, industry or financial dealings, and whose property was not mainly in land.) The emergence of a similar class, even smaller in numbers but in some ways equally important, can be seen almost simultaneously in France. There the last years of the seventeenth century and beginning of the eighteenth saw the rise to positions of real though often unacknowledged power of such people as the banker Samuel Bernard, the merchant and financier Antoine Crozat (who in 1712 secured a monopoly of trade with Louisiana) or the merchant Nicolas Mesnager of Rouen (who

more than once represented his country in commercial negotiations with other States). Above all the Pâris family, whose
fortune was made by a series of army contracts in the 1690s, had
in the first half of the century great and sometimes decisive influence on French financial policy.

The growth of an *haute bourgeoisie* was encouraged in France
(and elsewhere in Europe) by the system of tax-farming, which
brought vast profits to a small number of wealthy families and
individuals. However the French farmers-general constituted a
relatively open and fluid group. On the one hand it was constantly
being strengthened by new recruits from non-noble families with
interests in trade or finance; but on the other the sons of its
members tended to use their parents' wealth as a means of
entering the *noblesse de la robe* or of obtaining commissions in the
army. There were few dynasties of tax farmers. More important
in the creation of a wealthy merchant class was the immense
expansion of French trade with the West Indies and the Levant
which followed the peace of 1763 with Britain. This made the
fortunes of an increasing number of great trading families such
as the Gradis and Bonaffé of Bordeaux and the Roux of
Marseilles. Throughout Western Europe, in Britain, France or the
United Provinces, a very wealthy urban class was almost entirely
the product of trade, above all overseas trade, and of banking or
financial dealings (tax-farming or trading in government securities). Industry, by comparison, was only beginning by the 1770s
or 1780s to produce comparable fortunes; and the social status of
the successful industrialist was lower than that of the successful
merchant or financier. Even in England an Arkwright, a Boulton
or a Wilkinson lacked the standing of a great banker or merchant.
In France the century saw the emergence of only two industrial
dynasties of more than local importance; the De Wendels with
their great interests in the iron industry, and the Van Robais
textile magnates.

On a smaller scale the growth of a commercial and financial
upper middle class similar to that of Britain, France and the Netherlands can be seen in a few other areas of Europe – Tuscany,
Genoa, some West German cities. Elsewhere it was almost
entirely lacking. Overwhelmingly agrarian countries with few
towns, small merchant marines and little capital, such as Prussia,
the Habsburg territories, Poland and Russia, could produce little
of this kind. Thus although in the middle of the century the

number of towns in Russia was reckoned, for tax purposes, at just over two hundred, in 1762 only sixteen of these had municipal budgets of over 1,000 roubles per annum (about £150 at the then prevailing rate of exchange). The position was similar in Poland, where in 1772 there were only five towns with populations of over 20,000, and also in Hungary. In both the influence of the urban population was further reduced by the fact that it was largely composed of aliens – Jews or Germans in Poland, Greeks or Rumanians in Hungary. All over Eastern and much of Central Europe, moreover, the position of the towns was weakened by the fact that landowners, using the raw materials produced by their estates and the forced labour of their serfs, often set up in the countryside industrial establishments which competed with urban factories and workshops. In Bohemia and Moravia the glass and textile industries were created in this way, while in Poland members of the Radziwill, Czartoryski and Potocki families set up important industrial enterprises on their huge estates.

It would, however, be a great mistake to assume that the urban population anywhere in Europe was composed of, or even normally led by, wealthy merchants, bankers or financiers. Everywhere small traders and artisans, and even more small landowners, were numerically and often politically of far greater importance in its makeup. Moreover it should be remembered how much in some areas the middle class (it is difficult to avoid using this somewhat anachronistic term) depended on governments for employment and economic opportunities. This was especially notable in France, where there were enormous numbers of holders of minor government offices and owners of government securities (*rentes*). It was people of this kind who were the most important element in the population of many French towns during the eighteenth century and who helped to ensure that the entrepreneurial spirit, as opposed to the legalistic, office-holding and *rentier* one, was relatively unimportant in French urban life. The predominant social values, those of the privileged landowning group and the Church, looked down on trade as an inferior, in the case of the Church perhaps even a sinful, activity. The result was that money made in business was very often used to buy land or offices, not to develop the business concerned. 'In France', wrote a contemporary, 'we have not a due regard for merchants . . . from whence it comes to pass, that the son prefers the exercise of an office that ruins him, to commerce that enrich'd his father.'[18] The greatest statistician of the century, the Abbé d'Expilly, estimated in 1763 that 60,000 French families lived from *emplois de finance* (minor offices connected with the system of taxation) and 100,000 from judicial offices, royal or seigneurial. By comparison, he calculated, bankers and merchants made up only 10,0000 families. At the outbreak of the revolution about eighty per cent of all privately owned property in France was 'proprietary' wealth in the form of land, buildings, government offices and annuities. Even in such great trading centres as Bordeaux and Rouen small landowners, officials and holders of government securities considerably outnumbered merchants and manufacturers. In other provincial capitals which were more purely administrative centres the prominence of the official element was even more obtrusive. It has been calculated that in Toulouse, for example, legal functionaries alone, with their families and servants, made up about a tenth of the city's population; while in Aix-en-Provence administrators and clerics, with their dependents, accounted for twice as high a proportion.

Not only was the patrician element of great bankers and merchants confined to a few great cities in Western Europe: it was often unable to dominate even these. Thus in London the smaller merchants, traders and craftsmen, who controlled the Common Council and elected the city's four Members of Parliament, tended as a rule to be hostile to the urban magnates whose close connexions with the government and the aristocracy they distrusted and envied. This feeling made a large part of the population hostile to landlords, aristocrats and all social institutions which recalled the 'feudal' past. As a result the city tended to be sympathetic to the reforms advocated in the 1770s and 1780s by many radical writers and politicians, such as more frequent parliamentary elections and a reduction of the standing army. A still more striking example of this tension between a wealthy oligarchy and an envious or frustrated body of smaller merchants and artisans is to be found in the city-state of Geneva. Its history throughout this period was punctuated by demands that power be more widely shared amongst the citizens, demands which culminated in 1768 and 1782 in serious outbreaks of violence. Essentially the same struggle, though in a less violent form, can be seen also in several of the cities of West Germany. In Cologne during the 1780s, for example, control of the city was contested between the *Magistrat* (the ruling oligarchy) and the *Bürgerschaft* (a much wider body of all full citizens, made up of house owners, master-craftsmen and a few professional men). Discontented urban groups of this kind often came increasingly, as the century progressed, to feel themselves excluded and discriminated against by the essentially aristocratic political systems of their countries.

The position in the great cities of France was different but not totally dissimilar. France was in the later eighteenth century the one European country in which a fairly well-to-do and fairly well-educated urban bourgeoisie was both large enough to be a significant element in society and at the same time completely excluded from political power. In the United Provinces the government had long ceased to be dominated by the nobility, though the great merchant families of Amsterdam and a few other cities formed a kind of aristocracy which aroused a good deal of envy and bad feeling in those a little further down the social scale. In Britain a bourgeois, if he were wealthy enough, would eventually be accepted, or at least secure the acceptance of his children, on equal terms by the landed gentry. The great cities and the interests which dominated them could always make their voices heard in the House of Commons. In France, by contrast, society and the political structure were still overwhelmingly aristocratic in tone, and the safety-valves for bourgeois envy and resentment which existed in Britain (and were by no means completely effective there) were much less adequate. It was not unheard-of for a French merchant, banker or even industrialist to be ennobled, even without his buying a government office which conferred nobility on the holder. In 1767 the government promised that henceforth rights almost equivalent to those of nobility should be granted each year to two important merchants, provided that their fathers and grandfathers has also been merchants. This, however, was a very half-hearted attack on a difficult problem. The obstacles in the way of the urban middle class attaining nobility are illustrated by the fact that in Brittany, a province which possessed such substantial ports as Brest and l'Orient, only twenty-two businessman were ennobled in the three generations before 1789.

Too much, however, can be made of the gulf which separated noble and bourgeois in France in the last decades of the old regime. Whether, as used to be widely believed, the eighteenth century really saw a growth of self-consciousness and exclusiveness on the part of the French nobility as a whole now seems at least questionable. The claims which the *parlements* were putting forward more and more vociferously (see pp. 177–9) were after all, in form and even to some extent in substance, those of the nation and not merely of the nobility. Neither the *intendants* and other great officials nor the upper ranks of the Church seem to have been, as a group, more aristocratic in the later eighteenth century than they had been a hundred years earlier. The decree of 1781 which attempted to prevent the granting of army commissions to non-nobles allowed many exceptions and had in any case been foreshadowed by earlier legislation of this kind in 1718 and 1727. The *parlements*, undoubtedly, were becoming more socially exclusive and increasingly refusing to accept non-nobles as members (the *Parlement* of Dauphiné, for example, declared itself a closed group in 1762 and by the last years of the *Ancien Régime* the *Parlement* of Toulouse was excluding even the sons of those recently ennobled). Nevertheless in the later eighteenth century, as nobles, or at least the wealthier ones, increasingly invested in new economic enterprises, notably mining, and as the wealthy non-noble townsman increasingly bought estates and feudal rights, the distinction between the nobility and the upper bourgeoisie tended to lose some of its clarity. As a traditional society composed of 'orders' was slowly eroded by the coming of one in which status depended more and more on money it became easier to bridge social chasms which had hitherto seemed very difficult to cross. Nevertheless when all this has been said it is clear that, as the progress of the Revolution was to show very clearly, there was discontent and readiness for change at least amongst some sections of French urban society in the later eighteenth century. The fact that educational standards were rising fairly rapidly was one element in this. Another was the steadily growing importance of new professional groups, small in numbers but self-conscious, well-educated and open to new ideas and political ambitions. These groups, such as doctors and journalists, were often more ready to envisage drastic social and political changes than older and much better established ones such as lawyers.

The fact that in many West European States during this period the towns, even if not independent as the German imperial cities and the Italian city-states were, enjoyed a considerable degree of autonomy, meant that their internal organization was of real political and economic importance. That organization varied enormously, but was almost always complex, often extremely so. Municipal rights and privileges varied moreover, as might be expected, in a highly complicated and irrational way. The extraordinary variety of franchises by which members representing boroughs were elected to the House of Commons in Britain, or the distinction in Scotland between 'royal burghs', founded by charter from the king, and mere 'burghs of barony', are obvious examples of these variations. So is the legal distinction which was often drawn in France between the original city, enclosed by its medieval boundaries, and the *faubourgs* which had grown up around it.

Certain characteristics, however, were common to most European towns during this period. In the majority of them an important role in government was played by the guilds. In Strasbourg, for example, the twenty guilds each elected fifteen members of the Council of Three Hundred and, of more practical importance, one member of the Senate. In most French towns indeed the ruling body was composed mainly or entirely of representatives of the craft and merchant guilds. Though there were some important German cities (Frankfurt for instance) in whose government guild influence was slight, here too it was usually powerful and often dominant. In practice, however, most West European towns during this period, whatever their constitution, tended to be ruled by an oligarchy of wealthier citizens, and one which was usually in large part hereditary. Thus in Berne, where the hereditary element was unusually strong, there were only about 250 families which were classified as capable of ruling (*regimentsfähig*): of these about seventy really controlled the city. In Zurich at the end of the century half the seats on the Great Council were held by only thirteen families, while in Rheims a handful of families became known as the 'Nous-ferons' because they could in effect do as they liked in local politics. In many other towns the same names can be seen recurring for generation after generation in the membership of the ruling bodies – the Dietrichs and Wenckers in Strasbourg for example. In Nuremberg a list of families whose members were alone eligible to hold all the leading municipal offices had been drawn up and given legal effect as early as 1521; and in Frankfurt a patriciate of this kind successfully defended its position in a long series of constitutional struggles in 1705–32. Sometimes in ethnically mixed areas a town oligarchy might be defined by language and nationality. In Riga, for example, the Great Guild, whose members alone had full rights to trade and own property, was composed entirely of Germans and refused to admit other nationalities. In 1753 it proposed that all land in the city belonging to Latvians should be confiscated and that they should be obliged to clean its drains and collect its refuse 'so that they should not forget their origins, nor seek the privileges assured to citizens, and should remember eternally that they are slaves'.[19] It should not, however, be assumed that oligarchical rule was necessarily hostile to all progress. The greatest achievement of urban renewal and town planning during the second half of the century, the building of the New Town in Edinburgh, was the work of a city council which was an oligarchy of the narrowest kind.

The cities of eighteenth-century Europe were thus, with few exceptions, traditional in their social structure and government and backward rather than forward looking. Their populations, notably in the larger cities, grew as they had done for generations past, by immigration from the countryside rather than by natural increase. Overcrowding, grossly insanitary living conditions, polluted water supplies, all made for high urban death-rates, especially amongst children. A continual influx of peasants driven by poverty to seek work in the cities was thus needed even to maintain the numbers living in them. A good case in point is Lyons, the second-largest city in France, which received in all about 120,000 immigrants in the years 1700–90. Unemployment, particularly for the unskilled, the day-labourer with no regular master, was heavy, and merciless in its impact on individual lives. Crime, prostitution, most noticeably of all begging, were its inevitable results. No city was without its quota of beggars, some professional but many reduced to this by the sheer need to survive. In economically stagnant towns such as most of those of West Germany and Italy begging (and for women prostitution) sometimes reached epidemic proportions. In Venice between 1760 and 1787 licensed beggars made up 3–5 per cent of the population and unlicensed ones another 13–15 per cent; while in Bologna in the same years a quarter of the inhabitants seem to have lived by begging or public charity. In Mainz it was alleged that about a third of all women were beggars or prostitutes.

In the long run the remedy for unemployment and poverty was economic and in particular industrial growth, though the experience of the generations to come was to show that even this worked only slowly. Very few towns in the eighteenth century, however, were industrial in the sense in which the term could be used in the following one. The fact that many of such large-scale industrial enterprises as existed – the great ironworks in the Ural mountains of Russia are a very clear example – were geographically remote from any large town did much to ensure that urban life in general retained its traditional character. Everywhere service trades were important. Servants – maids, footmen, cooks, grooms – made up a substantial fraction of the population of every town. Paris was reckoned in 1743 to include 40,000 liveried servants in its population; and there must have been far more in humbler households who wore no livery. It was very often as servants that immigrants from the countryside, especially women, gained their first acquaintance with urban life. Urban industry was still predominantly craft industry. Most workers laboured in workshops or in their own homes, using traditional methods to produce traditional goods. They had often close personal contact with their employers; and work-discipline was often less strict than it was to become in the different environment of the large factory. None the less their life was hard and insecure; and the gap between the master-craftsman and those under him was often widening. Any systematic discussion of wages is difficult because of the scarcity of reliable information; and the fact that payments of various sorts in kind rather than in cash were still common is a further complication. It is clear, however, that many workers were paid little more than the barest minimum. Indeed it was generally agreed that to pay them more than was needed to maintain themselves and their dependents would make them lazy, rebellious and unwilling to do dirty or unpleasant jobs. A family of this kind, living normally at little more than subsistence level, was quite unable to make savings or build up reserves of any sort. It was therefore intensely vulnerable to the sickness or unemployment of a breadwinner, to the effects of old age and to any marked rise in food prices. It has been calculated, for example, that in Aix-en-Provence, in many ways a good example of a pre-industrial city, two married workers with one child to support were likely to have a family income of about 380 livres. But bare survival cost about 336 livres, leaving a margin of less than 50 to cope with every sort of extra expense. There were elements of light and shade in this picture. Almost everywhere there was a traditional hierarchy of different trades, with such groups as jewellers and goldsmiths normally at the top of the tree. At any given moment in a particular town workers in some trades would normally be better off than those in others: marriage-contracts suggest that in Lyons, for example, bakers were relatively well off while hat-makers and dyers, who usually did not even own their own tools, were very poor indeed. Perhaps most debilitating of all, however, was not poverty but the universal assumption that the poor acting independently could achieve nothing, that they were helpless without the support of some powerful established institution or group. One of the greatest achievements of the French Revolution was to begin the process of breaking down this assumption.

The still largely traditional and static society described in this chapter was doomed to rapid decay. The network of communities, orders, privileges, peculiarities and exemptions, of which it was composed, could not hope to withstand indefinitely the forces of change which were growing stronger throughout this period. From the middle of the century at latest it was being steadily though very slowly eroded by the demands of governments for larger revenues and greater administrative efficiency. It was also being undermined, more rapidly and more fundamentally, by the development of Europe's economic life. For a society based on customs and historic rights which were everywhere different was slowly being substituted one based on ideas and economic pressures which were everywhere the same. Yet it would be a great mistake to describe eighteenth-century society entirely or even mainly in terms of 'progressive' forces. Like so many other aspects of the continent's life during this period, it must be studied with an eye to the past as much as to the future.

NOTES AND REFERENCES

1   Anne Lefèbvre-Teillard, *La Population de Dôle au XVIIIe siècle* (Paris, 1969), p. 65.

2   J. Amar y Borbon, *Discurso sobre la education fisica y moral de las mujeres* (Madrid, 1790), p. 265.

3   Quoted in B. Groethuysen, *The Bourgeois: Catholicism versus capitalism in eighteenth-century France* (London, 1968), p. 229.

4   Abbé le Blanc, *Letters on the English and French Nations* (London, 1747), vol. II, pp. 404–5.

5   J. Egret, *La pre-révolution française* (Paris, 1962), p. 54, fn.2.

6   G. D. Squibb, *The High Court of Chivalry* (Oxford, 1959), p. 110.

7   R. Darnton, *The Great Cat Massacre and other episodes in French cultural history* (London, 1984), p. 136.

8   A. Poitrineau, *La Vie rurale en Basse Auvergne au XVIIIᵉ siècle (1726–1789)* (Paris, 1965), vol. I, p. 117.

9   H. C. Johnson, *Frederick the Great and his Officials* (New Haven-London, 1975), p. 148.

10 The most detailed and accessible account of this great revolt is P. Avrich, *Russian Rebels, 1660–1800* (London, 1972), pp. 180–254.

11 C. de Ribbe, *Les Familles et la société en France avant la Révolution* (4th edn; Tours, 1879), vol. I, p. 92.

12 A. Babeau, *Le Village sous l'ancien régime* (Paris, 1878), p. 95.

13 J. T. A. Le Goff, *Vannes and its Region: A Study of Town and Country in Eighteenth-Century France* (Oxford, 1981), p. 245.

14 F. Bluche, *Les Honneurs de la Cour* (Paris, 1957), vol. I, p. 3.

15 R. Mousnier, *Les Institutions de la France sous la monarchie absolue, 1598–1715* (Paris, 1974–80), vol. I, p. 136.

16 Quoted in *Oxford Slavonic Papers*, New Series, vol. 15 (1982), p. 76.

17 J. Kaplow, *The Names of Kings: The Parisian Labouring Poor in the Eighteenth Century* (New York, 1972), p. 13.

18 Abbé le Blanc, *Letters*, vol. II, p. 122.

19 R. P. Bartlett, *Human Capital: The Settlement of Foreigners in Russia, 1762–1804* (Cambridge, 1979), p. 89.

4

ECONOMIC LIFE

The eighteenth century saw a good deal of economic progress in
Europe, but progress which was uneven geographically, in its
speed at different times, and in its effect on different types of
activity. It saw a marked development of banking and public
finance in Britain, the Netherlands, and to a lesser extent in
France. It saw a great expansion of transatlantic trade, which was
again most marked in the case of Britain. Industry on the other
hand developed rather slowly until the industrial revolution began
to affect Britain and to a much less extent France in the very last
years of this period; and the methods and productivity of agriculture did not change greatly except in a few favoured areas of
Western Europe. Geographically the rapid progress of Britain and
the continued high level of achievement of the Netherlands
contrasted with the relative backwardness of much of Germany,
Central Europe, Italy and Spain. In some parts of Poland and the
Ottoman Empire there may even have been a fall, mainly because
of political upheavals, in the already very low standards of
productivity and consumption which prevailed at the beginning
of the eighteenth century. In Russia on the other hand Peter I and
his successors fostered an impressive though unbalanced development of industry and even of trade. The first decades of this
period were a time of relative economic stagnation over most of
the continent, while after the middle of the century the pace of
advance perceptibly quickened in many areas.

Underlying and partly explaining this slow and uneven advance
was a tendency for population, especially urban population, to
increase almost everywhere. This tendency operated with varying

effect in different countries; but almost every European State had a larger population at the end of this period than at its beginning. Thus England and Wales, which had 5 or 6 million inhabitants in the reign of Queen Anne, could boast nearly 9 million by the end of the century. France, where this growth was somewhat less marked, had about 18 million at the death of Louis XIV and about 26 million in 1789. In Italy the population increased from perhaps 11 million in 1700 to over 16 million in 1770, while in parts of Spain the growth may have been more rapid than in England – from 5 or 6 million in 1700 to some 11 million a century later. In European Russia, which had about 18 million inhabitants at the death of Peter I in 1725, there were nearly 27 million by 1780; but gains of territory from Sweden, Turkey and Poland account for a good deal of this increase. Europe as a whole, which had a population of perhaps 118 million in 1700, had one of about 140 million in 1750 and about 187 million in 1800.

The distribution of this increase was strikingly unequal, not merely between different States but also between different regions of the same State and between different classes of society. Some peripheral areas grew rapidly – Ireland from 2.2 million in 1725 to perhaps 4.6 million in 1791; Hungary, helped by considerable immigration, from a little over 4 million in 1720 to a little over 7 million in 1786. In areas where industry was growing a demand for labour drew a response in the form of an increasing population, mainly by encouraging earlier marriage and therefore bigger families. But regional variations were sharp. In Italy population growth came mainly in the least developed regions, the south and the islands of Sicily and Sardinia: Palermo and Naples amongst Italian cities increased their population substantially, while Rome, Florence, Venice and Genoa showed only a feeble rise. In Spain some peripheral areas like Catalonia and Valencia saw marked population growth, while Castile and other peripheral areas such as Galicia were relatively stagnant. In the German world there was strong growth in Württemberg, Pomerania and East Prussia, but much less in Schleswig-Holstein. Birth-rates could vary in different parts of Europe from 30 to 60 per thousand of total population, while life-expectancy at birth in 1750 was 35.8 years in Sweden (an impressive figure for the time) and only 24.8 years in France. There is also clear evidence that in several parts of the continent, ruling groups – the high aristocracy in France, patrician groups in Geneva and Florence – were already beginning deliberately to limit the size of their families by the first decades of the century; but it was to take several generations for this tendency to seep down to the mass of the population over most of Europe. Demographically as in so many other respects eighteenth-century Europe was a complex network of widely varying regions and localities rather than a neat arrangement of internally homogeneous States.

The reasons for this remarkable demographic change are still far from clear. It seems certain, however, that a slow improvement in food supplies which made serious dearth or absolute starvation less likely than in the past played a considerable part. Thus in 1709 France saw large-scale famine for the past time. After that terrible year very sharp rises in the price of food as the result of bad harvests became less common than they had been in the seventeenth century: the doubling or more of the price of bread within a few months, not abnormal in previous generations, now became exceptional. The crucial decade of French history in this respect was probably the 1740s and the last really intense food shortage that of 1741–42. Though similar crises were to affect the country later in the century (for example in the early 1770s and in 1788–89) their intensity was noticeably less than in the past. In some parts of Europe the introduction of new crops played an important role in this process of slowly improving nutrition. The establishment of maize as a basic cereal crop in northern Italy and south-eastern France from the 1690s onwards meant that a very important new source of nourishment was now available there; while by the end of the century the potato had become the basic food of most of Ireland and many areas in Germany. It has been very tentatively estimated that in the first years of the century the average agricultural worker in Europe (if that phrase has real meaning) produced only 20–30 per cent more food than was needed to sustain himself and his family. By the middle decades of the century this surplus may have arisen to somewhere around 50 per cent: the implications of this in reducing the risk of famine scarcely need emphasis. More adequate diet, then, mainly through its effects in increasing resistance to disease, was certainly one mainspring of population growth. Nevertheless its contribution to what still remains in many ways a mysterious process can be overstressed. In some parts of Europe a rise in population began before marked growth in agricultural output: during the century as a whole Britain's population grew by about 71 per cent and its output of cereals by only about 46 per cent. Quite often it seems, for example in France, that population increase stimulated agricultural growth rather than the other way around. Other factors, therefore, certainly played some significant role in this unprecedented rise in the number of Europeans.

Some of the great killing epidemic diseases which had ravaged the continent in the past may, though this is disputed, have become less lethal in the early decades of the century as the predominant strains of the disease-causing organisms became less virulent. The slow replacement of wooden houses by stone and brick ones, the equally slow improvement in personal cleanliness, the removal of animals from dwellings, all reduced opportunities for the breeding of vermin and hence the spreading of many diseases. Improved feeding, which increased resistance to infection, combined with these other factors to reduce markedly the hitherto often terrible effects of epidemics. In Germany, for example, the plague of 1709–11 was the last great outbreak of the disease, so devastating in previous centuries; and after the 1720s it ceased to be a significant factor in the demographic picture of Western Europe. (Though it was not eliminated in Eastern and South-Eastern Europe until the mid-nineteenth century – a good example of the differences between East and West which were now in many ways widening and which were to persist for generations to come.) Infant mortality in particular fell in many areas in the second half of the eighteenth century. This, coupled with a continuing high birth-rate produced the growth in the sheer number of Europeans during this period.

In a few areas population growth may have been accelerated by rather more sophisticated factors. In some, notably England, growing prosperity and particularly industrialization helped by stimulating the demand for labour, making children profitable and thus encouraging earlier and more prolific marriages. The proportion of English women who passed through the child-bearing years without marrying fell from perhaps 15 per cent in the 1680s to half that figure in the early nineteenth century. This marked increase in 'nuptiality', it has been recently and forcibly argued, did more than anything else to increase the country's population. But it should be emphasized that all over Europe the ordinary man was at the mercy of natural forces, in the extent to which he reproduced himself as in almost every other respect, in a way hard to grasp completely today. A bad harvest or an epidemic, natural disasters against which there was little defence, could still very quickly have drastic effects upon an entire population (though it is also true that in many parts of the continent greater resilience than in the past was being shown in rapid recovery from such disasters). Over much of Europe also, religious feeling and tradition had considerable demographic effects. They meant that in Catholic areas at least marriages in Advent and Lent were notably fewer than at other times of the Christian year, while there tended to be a seasonal peak of conceptions in May and June. Certainly the significance of medical and sanitary improvements – inoculation against smallpox, the founding of hospitals, higher standards of personal cleanliness aided by the wider use of washable cotton clothing, improved water supplies – should not be exaggerated. Great parts of Europe were in the 1780s still virtually untouched by such developments. Medicine was still a compound of empiricism and tradition; trained doctors were still few and over large areas almost non-existent; hospitals were still of little importance outside a fairly small number of large towns, and in any case probably killed more people through cross-infections than they helped to cure.

Eighteenth-century Europe therefore lived under a demographic regime which was still very far removed from that of the present day, one in which marriages were late, birth and death-rates, and particularly death-rates in infancy, very high, and expectation of life at all ages very low. In the 1970s the median age at death for women in Britain was 80: in the 1750s it was about 35. In the 1970s 16 per cent of men in Britain died between the ages of 25 and 65 (many of these through accidents rather than natural causes); in the 1750s about 65 per cent did so. The average British woman in the 1970s finished child-bearing at the age of 28 and her last grandchild was born when she was 56, with twenty-four years still to live. In the 1750s she finished child-bearing at 39 and died twelve years before her last grandchild was born.[1] In terms of these basic life-chances as of many other things this was still a world far closer to the Middle Ages than to the twentieth century.

Whatever the causes of this unprecedented increase in the number of Europeans, the economic importance of the phenomenon is beyond question. A rising population meant an increasing demand for food and raw materials. This in its turn could mean either a considerable improvement in agricultural methods, as in Great Britain, or a large extension of the area under cultivation, as in Russia, or some combination of the two. Where these safety-valves were not available the results could be serious. Land-hunger; increasing subdivision of holdings amongst a growing population; rising rents as the scramble for land became more acute: all these outcomes of rising population in slow-growing agrarian economies can be seen very clearly. In southern France, for example, the evidence suggests that the real incomes of the peasantry fell by about a fifth between the 1720s and the Revolution of 1789, while in the country generally rents rose in real terms by 50 per cent or more between the 1730s and 1789. In the Toulouse area during the century as a whole the population grew by 40–50 per cent but the number of landholdings actually fell by about 13 per cent. In Germany rents may have trebled between the 1730s and the end of the century. All this tended to mean a marked growth in the real incomes of landowners, and particularly of great landowners, at a time when life was becoming more difficult for many peasants and agricultural workers: the bitterness which this produced was to erupt spectacularly in France in 1789.

Population growth had other important results. It created both a labour supply for the new forms of industry which were beginning to emerge in a few limited areas at the end of this period and a need for increased employment, above all urban employment, if some parts of Europe were not to become over-populated rural slums (as Ireland and parts of Spain and Italy were showing signs of doing by the end of the century). In some areas, such as Scotland, Northern Ireland and Switzerland, it provided a considerable incentive to emigration; while in countries where numbers were increasing really rapidly the existence of a high proportion of young people in the population may have had important though unmeasurable psychological effects.

Except in a few restricted areas agriculture was by far the most important form of economic activity in eighteenth-century Europe. On its efficiency and productivity, and most of all in the short term on the state of the harvest, depended overwhelmingly the economic well-being of society. This was mainly because the agricultural sector was almost everywhere very much bigger than any other part of the economy. Also movements in agricultural prices were as a rule much sharper than those in the prices of manufactured goods. Agricultural fluctuations thus determined the direction and violence of economic fluctuations in general. A crop failure meant inevitably a rapid rise in grain prices. Since cereals made up, far more than today, the vast bulk of the food intake of almost all Europeans, this inflicted immediate and often savage hardship on many people, above all on the poorest. Bread in most of Western Europe, porridge or gruel further east, were of overwhelming importance in the diet of the ordinary man and often made up almost all of what he ate. Paris, for example, with a population at the end of the century of about 700,000, had 250–300 bakers in the city proper, about 300 in the surrounding suburbs and up to a thousand others who came into the city two or three times a week. A sharp rise in grain prices could threaten the very existence of great numbers of people. A bad harvest also meant a reduction in the amount of seasonal work available in reaping and threshing, and often the dismissal of workers whom the farmer or the better-off peasant could no longer afford to feed; this happened, moreover, just when more and more labour was being forced on to the market by the need to stay alive in the face of rising prices. An economic crisis of this type therefore involved a devastating mixture of falling wages, rising unemployment and rising food prices. Such a combination, apart from its purely economic results, could have dangerous social and even political ones. Some groups – rich farmers who could afford to hold stocks of food while prices rose, landlords receiving rent in the form of a share of the crop – obviously benefited; for them the time of highest prices was also that of highest return. The spectacle of a privileged minority benefiting in this way from the sufferings of the majority could stimulate acute and potentially dangerous bitterness.

The organization, methods and productivity of agriculture differed greatly in different parts of Europe. In the West there were considerable areas in which technology was relatively advanced, capital for agricultural improvement not too hard to come by, and the population dense enough to encourage the development of intensive cultivation. Much of the Netherlands, a good deal of the south-east and Midlands of England, later in the century parts of the Lowlands of Scotland and of Catalonia, were in this position. In these areas productivity was high and increasing, interest in new methods relatively easy to arouse, and the agricultural community generally prosperous. All of them were areas where urban life was well developed and where there were cities, in particular great cities such as London and Amsterdam, which provided large markets for agricultural produce.

In the Netherlands, or at least in densely populated areas such as Flanders, West Brabant, Zeeland and South Holland, many farmers were already specializing in the seventeenth century in the production of purely commercial crops (flax, madder, woad, hops and tobacco) and had abandoned the mainly subsistence agriculture which was still dominant over a great part of the continent. By the eighteenth century Friesland and Holland were producing milk and cheese on a scale and with an effectiveness unequalled anywhere else in Europe. Market-gardening and the cultivation of fruit had also been developed in the Netherlands to a degree equalled perhaps only in a few small areas of Italy, and a considerable technical literature on agricultural questions was beginning to emerge there. Complex systems of crop rotation, the widespread use of fodder crops such as clover and turnips, heavy manuring and heavy yields, all marked the agriculture of these favoured areas as the most advanced in Europe. The Dutch Republic, largely because of its heavy production of industrial crops at the expense of less profitable foodstuffs, was also the only large and consistent importer of cereals in Europe: about a seventh of the grain it consumed was imported from the Baltic. In the eighteenth century, though they were eventually challenged and perhaps equalled in this as in other respects by Great Britain, the Netherlands remained one of the most advanced agricultural areas in Europe. In them originated the Brabant plough which, first recorded early in the century, is generally regarded as the prototype of the modern plough. During the second half of this period they became one of the first parts of Europe to cultivate the potato on a large scale. As late as 1802 a German observer, after careful study, concluded that agricultural productivity in the Austrian Netherlands was still about 30 per cent higher than in England.

In the latter the period 1600–1750 saw a remarkably large output of technical works on agriculture, many of which pointed the way towards improvements which were later to become generally accepted. Thus the first English treatise on the cultivation of clover appeared in 1663, and the first on the potato in the following year. By the 1680s as advanced an idea as that of the compilation of soil-maps was beginning to be put forward, while in 1749 (a surprisingly late date) the first English work on sheep-rearing made its appearance. However the practical effectiveness of writing of this kind, in England or anywhere else, should not be exaggerated. Successful innovation was the result of changing conditions and new opportunities much more than of the work of theorists or enthusiasts. The generally upward tendency of agricultural prices from about 1740 onwards, and the opportunities of increased profit this created, did more to stimulate change than all the theoretical writing of the century. But the change was real and important. Already in the 1720s turnips and clover were being cultivated on a considerable scale in Norfolk, and stock-breeding and land drainage were being improved. Later in the century these and other improvements in agricultural techniques were carried still further by such people as Robert Bakewell, and systematically utilized by great farmers such as Thomas Coke (afterwards Earl of Leicester). Simultaneously farms were growing larger, calling for greater amounts of capital and making more efficient use of the division of labour. The smaller squires tended slowly to give way to great landowners, and small free-holders to leaseholders who cultivated on a more extensive scale.

Throughout the century moreover, and above all in its last decades, the process of 'enclosure' was going on (perhaps 5 million acres in all were enclosed in 1760–1800). The scattered holdings which had hitherto been typical of the Midlands and much of the south were now being consolidated and fenced, and common rights in meadow, waste and woodland extinguished. The social implications of these developments were complex and have stimulated much controversy. Enclosure sometimes caused real suffering, though it is doubtful whether cottagers and squatters, the lowest strata of agrarian society in England, were forcibly driven from the land in large numbers as has sometimes been claimed. Bigger farms and greater estates, the coming of an England of large tenant farmers renting from often very wealthy landowners, meant the creation of a large class of landless labourers whose plight was largely responsible for the trebling of the amount raised in poor rates in the century before 1780. It was precisely their landlessness, however, which made them a flexible and geographically mobile work-force of a kind hardly to be paralleled in most of continental Europe, while it was their poor wages which made possible the profits which financed agricultural progress. Though the cost of increased output in human terms was certainly high the increase was very real. By the end of the century an agricultural worker in England may have been producing, on average, twice as much as his great-grandfather at its beginning.

The relative modernity of agriculture in Britain and the Netherlands contrasted sharply with the backwardness of many other parts of agrarian Europe. Over much of the continent technology and yields were still terribly low. In most areas it was still thought very satisfactory if each grain planted produced a harvest of four (a yield of four to one); and in Russia, Poland, the Balkans and parts of Germany even this could hardly be achieved. Yet such low yields meant that a quarter of each harvest had to be put aside to provide seed for the next year's planting. (In England by 1800 the average yield of wheat was ten or twelve to one.) The fact that over so much of Europe the peasant's holding was subdivided into small strips of land which might be quite widely separated was a great source of inefficiency. It meant waste of time and energy in getting from one strip to another, wasteful use of land and endless possibilities of dispute between the owners of adjacent strips. Almost everywhere outside Britain and the Netherlands animal husbandry was neglected. This was inevitable where population pressure was heavy, for a given extent of land could support many more people if it were used to grow cereals than if it were merely grazed by animals. Yet the results were serious. A shortage of animals meant a shortage of fresh milk, which almost certainly had considerable effect in increasing infant mortality. It also meant a shortage of manure and more rapid exhaustion of the soil, and often a lack of animals for draft purposes and for use as a source of power. Tools and techniques improved only with depressing slowness, while the continuing effectiveness of the village community and its regulation of the activities of its members helped to bind the peasant, over great parts of Europe, to a traditional routine. Rulers and governments made intermittent efforts to stimulate progress. They might set up model farms to act as an example and inspiration to landlords, as Frederick II of Prussia did in 1767. They might offer tax exemptions to encourage the cultivation of waste land and fallows, as the Elector of Bavaria did in 1762. They might provide loans to encourage the introduction of new crops, as again Frederick II did in 1771. But neither these spasmodic and often badly thought-out efforts nor the activities of improving landlords (in most parts of Europe a very small minority) had much effect.

Agrarian conditions in purely material terms, in those of how much the peasant had to eat and how much land he had to cultivate, were not necessarily worse in Eastern Europe, the Europe of serfdom, than in the West, the Europe of at least formal peasant freedom. Thus, for example, in Sicily a dense population, a soil often poor and hard to work, primitive techniques and a social and administrative system almost unequalled in harshness, made the peasantry one of the most wretched in Europe. The fact that very many Sicilian peasants were sharecroppers, bound by one-sided agreements to hand over to the landowner (or often to some entrepreneur who had leased an estate from its owner) a high proportion of what they produced, was an important element in this depressing situation. Though the island still exported wheat it had lost the position which it had held in the sixteenth and early seventeenth centuries as the granary of all Southern Europe; in 1763–64 a famine, one of the worst of this period, and the disease which inevitably followed, killed 30,000 of its inhabitants. In Andalusia similarly a harsh geographical environment and the prevalence of great but poorly cultivated estates led to depopulation, very low productivity, and the emergence of a large class of landless labourers. In other Spanish provinces such as La Mancha and Valladolid conditions were almost as bad. From the 1760s onwards rising food prices led to increasing investment in agriculture and a growing area under cultivation in Spain; but this had much more effect in Catalonia, where great estates were unimportant and seigneurial burdens light, than in the backward south. In Poland and Livonia also the position of the peasantry was wretched. 'The Country People', reported an observer at the end of the seventeenth century, 'are poor and miserable and are masters of nothing they have, but are subject to their Lords, who treat them as tyrannically as Galley-Slaves.'[2] In Russia the peasant was increasingly oppressed and exploited in many ways (see pp. 43–4), though the area under cultivation and possibly the productivity of his labour increased during this period. Russian landowners remained perhaps the most economically inefficient, the most indifferent to possibilities of profit and improvement, in the whole of Europe.

Between these extremes of progress and stagnation, between the Netherlands on the one hand and Sicily and Andalusia on the other, lay great areas of Europe in which, although techniques were almost unchanging and the economic and legal position of the cultivator very vulnerable, absolute starvation and large-scale agrarian revolts were comparatively rare. These included France, much of western and central Germany, northern Italy and Scandinavia. In them the life of the peasant was still hard, limited and insecure to an extent difficult to imagine today. As late as 1770, 150,000 people are said to have died of hunger in Saxony and 80,000 in Bohemia (though these figures, contemporary guesses, are certainly too high). Even in France, where total agricultural production was greater than in any other European State, techniques in general were very backward. An active school of writers during the second half of the century advocated constructive change and the introduction of new crops, machinery and methods. Henri Bertin, who for a considerable period in the 1760s and 1770s acted in effect as a kind of Minister of Agriculture, encouraged improvement of many kinds. Yet the practical effect of all this was very limited. In 1788 the great scientist Lavoisier estimated that the productivity of agriculture in Britain was on average 2.7 times that in France, while of 4 million French peasants with holdings of their own during the 1780s 600,000 at most produced for the market. Often, moreover, what the peasant sold was no more than a few leftovers from his own family's consumption. The social stresses generated by an inadequate agriculture are reflected in the constant presence in Paris during the reign of Louis XV of an army of around 30,000 beggars. Many of these were ruined peasants, or landless labourers produced by the combination of a rising population and a stagnant agrarian economy. People such as these, like their predecessors for generations, flocked to the city for the succour which the countryside could not or would not provide. Britain, almost alone amongst the major States of Europe, had by the later decades of the century little fear of such developments. With an agriculture which was rapidly developing and, at least in some parts of the country, highly productive by the standards of the age; with a great merchant marine and foreign trade and hence excellent facilities for importing grain in times of shortage; with industries which were, by the end of this period, offering in a few areas employment of a new kind on a new scale, she had no fear of famine. She was thus able to go further than any other great State in abandoning, in practice if not in theory, efforts to fix the price and control the export of food.

Accurate generalization about agrarian conditions in eighteenth-century Europe is thus very difficult. The poorness of communications, different forms of land tenure, the persistence of a vast structure of local peculiarities and traditional rights and privileges, meant that they varied enormously even between different parts of the same State. Thus the *latifundia* of Andalusia contrasted sharply not only with the scientifically run and highly capitalized estates of Norfolk, but also with the independent peasant holdings of the Basque provinces, Catalonia and to a lesser extent some parts of Aragon. Normandy, where enclosures were permitted by customary law and where techniques of cultivation were relatively advanced, contrasted almost as sharply with backward Lorraine, with barren and poverty-stricken Brittany, and even with the Ile-de-France. The obligation of individual peasants to follow a traditional system of crop rotation, so onerous and hard to escape in eastern France, was generally lighter and less well enforced south of the Loire. French Flanders, on the north-eastern fringes of the country and really part of the Netherlands, had grain yields twice the average for France as a whole, while in parts of the south or of Brittany yields were half or less the national average. Marked divergences could occur within the same province or even within a much smaller area. Thus in Brittany remnants of feudalism were much more important in Basse-Bretagne than in Haute-Bretagne, while the share of total agricultural production which went to the nobility was less in the area around Rennes, the provincial capital, than in most others. A recent study has divided the Gâtinais, a small area in central France between Orleans and Fontainebleau, into no fewer than the nine sub-areas, each with its own distinct characteristics in terms of density of population, type of holding and major products. In the German States similar contrasts are visible; for example the position of the peasant was notably better in Lower Silesia than in most other parts of the Prussian monarchy.

It follows therefore that there was no such thing as a European peasantry in the eighteenth century, in the sense of a more or less homogeneous class whose rights and obligations were similar in different areas of the continent. The fundamental legal distinction, that which divided serfs from free men, has already been mentioned (see pp. 40–5). There were, however, other and more purely economic differences between the agrarian populations of the various parts of Europe. The Basque farmer cultivating his own land was a different being from the Irish tenant paying rent through a middleman to a landlord he might never have set eyes on, or the Sicilian or Provençal share-cropper. In France the *laboureur* who owned a plough-team had not, as a rule, the same interests and fears as the *manœuvrier* who had no source of livelihood but his own hands. In Germany the vine-grower of the Neckar valley, and the peasant of the Erzgebirge or Thuringerwald who had an ancillary source of income in handicrafts and domestic work, had little in common with the serf of Pomerania or Holstein. These contrasts could be multiplied indefinitely. Throughout Europe the cultivators of the land showed certain common or at least wide-spread characteristics – technical conservatism, attachment to traditional forms of religion, hostility to great landlords and their claims – but they were not a class in any genuine sense of the term. Everywhere, however, the scales were increasingly weighted against the small peasant proprietor. His decline was slow and fiercely resisted; and high prices for agricultural products from the 1740s onwards often helped him to survive and strengthened his resistance. Not until the 1880s did the decline of the peasant in France become unmistakable and irreversible, while during the eighteenth century the proportion of the land held by peasant freeholders actually increased in Sweden as a result of deliberate government policy. But traditional peasant Europe, though still very powerful and pervasive in the 1780s, was now a declining, though only slowly declining, element in the life of the continent.

In international trade, as in every other aspect of economic life, development was more rapid during this period in some western areas than in other parts of the continent. Foreign trade was still, for most countries, much less important than it was to become in the generations which followed the industrial revolution. As in the seventeenth century, the United Provinces and Norway were perhaps the only countries whose life depended on their ability to obtain essential imports of food. Nevertheless commercial questions bulked very large, indeed misleadingly large, in the abundant economic literature of the period (partly because a high proportion of the writers who produced it were themselves merchants). Trade rivalry between States remained as keen as ever before. 'Almost every corner of Europe, in our age,' wrote a British contemporary, 'strives to gain some part of the commercial advantages which they clearly observe to contribute so much to the enrichment and the exaltation of nations.'[3] Another asserted that commerce 'should be the great object of public attention in all national movements, and in every negotiation we enter into with foreign powers'.[4]

In this competition for trade Britain, at least from the 1750s onwards, was more successful than her rivals. Though it is impossible to provide really reliable figures of her exports and imports at any particular date, it is clear that both increased rapidly in the second half of the century. The growth of her overseas trade is reflected in that of her merchant fleet. From 3,300 ships with a total tonnage of 260,000 in 1702, it grew to over 8,100 with a tonnage of 590,000 in 1764, and 9,400 with a tonnage of over 695,000 in 1776. In the last years of the century its increase was even more rapid: by 1800 its carrying capacity was perhaps five or six times as great as it had been hundred years earlier. The development of a modern system of mercantile law, notably during the years (1756–88) when Lord Mansfield was Lord Chief Justice, was also a reflection of the increasing importance of trade in the country's life; while as suppliers of raw materials and markets merchants played a significant part in the early stages of the industrial revolution in Britain.

Throughout this period the visible balance of Britain's trade was in her favour, sometimes heavily so. It is true that the official figures which the historian has to take as his starting-point over-estimated the real strength of her position. Interest charges on the capital she imported from abroad (mainly from the Netherlands), the cost of maintaining armies in Europe and paying subsidies to European allies in time of war, the fact that great though unknown quantities of foreign goods were smuggled into the country and thus did not appear in the official returns at all – these and a number of less important factors meant that the balance of payments was much less in her favour than would appear at first sight. Nevertheless her commercial position throughout this period was strong; and it was becoming still stronger as the century drew to its close. Until the end of the 1740s her trade grew at only a moderate rate (a good deal more slowly than that of her great rival France, which doubled in value in the two decades 1735–55). In the second half of the century, however, the protected market provided by her colonies, the power of her navy, and the industrial and technological progress which allowed her increasingly to undersell rival producers of manufactured goods, were the foundations of a commercial growth which was not only rapid but also soundly-based. By the end of this period the growth was becoming spectacular. In 1780 exports accounted for about 8 per cent of British Gross National Product: by 1800 they made up about 18 per cent of a considerably higher total. Even in the 1780s, moreover, two-thirds of the value of British exports represented manufactured goods, as against only about two-fifths in the case of France. This growth of her trade, as contemporaries realized, immensely strengthened her international position. In particular it helped her to emerge victorious from the crucially important colonial struggles of the age. 'What has enabled England to Support this expensive War (i.e. of 1689–97 with France) so long,' asked the economist Charles Davenant as early as 1696, 'but the great Wealth which for Thirty Years has been flowing into us from Our Commerce Abroad?'[5]

About Britain's trade with America, Africa and the East something is said elsewhere in this book (see pp. 361ff). Her trade with Europe, though it grew less rapidly than that with the other continents, nevertheless expanded considerably. From the Baltic, particularly Russia, she drew great quantities of the naval stores – masts, hemp, tar and cordage – which she could not produce herself in sufficient quantities and on which her whole position as a maritime power depended. As a result Russia was one of the few countries with which her trade balance was heavily and continuously unfavourable. From both Sweden and Russia she drew great quantities of iron, which she was forced to import by the steadily rising cost of charcoal for use in smelting her own iron ore. Not until the 1780s, with the increasing use of coke for smelting and the development of the puddling process, did she begin to make herself independent of the Swedish and Russian ironmasters who had for so long profited from her weakness in this respect. With the Netherlands her trade, though its relative importance was declining, remained very extensive. With France, until the commercial treaty of 1786, it was restricted by war, by traditional hostility and distrust, and by numerous restrictions and prohibitions imposed on both sides of the Channel. (Though a large but indefinite amount of smuggling and contraband trade went on between the two countries throughout the century.) With Spain Britain drove a thriving trade in salt fish, textiles and other manufactured goods, receiving in exchange wool, wine, vegetable oils, fruit and of course bullion from South America. By the last years of the century she was playing a greater role than any other country in Spain's foreign trade. In Portugal British merchants and British goods enjoyed a position of almost complete dominance during the first half of this period. The Methuen Treaty of 1703 is usually taken as marking the definitive establishment of Britain's leading position in the Portuguese market; for the next fifty years a steady stream of British manufactured goods flowed to Lisbon and Oporto in exchange for the wine of Portugal and the gold of Brazil. One contemporary claimed that the treaty had quintupled British exports to Portugal. During the quarter of a century (1750–77) in which he dominated Portuguese life as chief minister of King Joseph I, the Marques de Pombal made strenuous efforts to reduce this, as it seemed to him, humiliating dependence on Britain. He could do little, however, to endow Portugal with the industries and the spirit of enterprise which alone could free her from foreign tutelage. With Italy also British trade, based once more largely on the export of salt fish and woolen goods and on the import of raw silk, grew in a satisfactory though far from spectacular manner during this period. Trade with the Levant alone declined during much of the eighteenth century. Relatively flourishing until the 1730s, it then fell off rapidly, mainly because of French competition, political upheavals in Persia which disrupted the supply of silk through Smyrna and Aleppo, and the lack of enterprise shown by the Levant Company. From this decline it did not begin to recover until the last years of the century.

In France this period opened with a reaction against the strict government control of foreign trade which had marked the last decades of the seventeenth century and which is associated with the name of Colbert. The *Conseil du Commerce* which was set up in 1700 and which included representatives of eleven of the main French towns showed itself anti-Colbertist in outlook; and in 1697–1713 a series of important commercial treaties were negotiated with the Netherlands, Prussia, Denmark and the Hanse towns. This movement towards a more liberal system of trade regulation was short-lived. The period of the Regency and the régime of Cardinal Fleury (1715–43) were marked by a reversion to the regimentation and protectionism of the later seventeenth century. This return to the past was challenged or criticized by many French writers on economic affairs – Saint-Pierre, Melon, d'Argenson – and also by many of the merchants whom it affected. Thus the Marseilles Chamber of Commerce argued strongly in 1723 and 1742 in favour of some freeing of French trade. Not until the 1750s, however, did the prohibitions and regulations which had for so long hampered the development of the country's commercial life begin to be dismantled; and then only very slowly. This tentative movement towards greater economic liberty was accentuated and accelerated by the development of 'Physiocratic' ideas on economic questions (see p. 115). It contributed to the remarkable development of French overseas trade, above all colonial trade, which marked the quarter-century after the end of the Seven Years War in 1763. From 120 million livres in 1716 the value of the country's exports rose to 500 million in 1789; and the greater part of this increase took place in the last decades of the period. During the same two generations or more the value of France's imports increased sixfold.

The geographical pattern of French trade with the other European States was very different from the British one. With the Baltic France never traded directly on a large scale during the eighteenth century. British and Dutch competition; the caution and conservatism of her own merchants; the political antagonisms which divided her from Russia during much of the period; the capital needed in a trade which often required heavy investment and the ability to wait some time for returns – all these limited her throughout this period as a direct factor in the commercial life of Northern Europe. Great quantities of her wine, brandy, silks and colonial produce filtered into the area, however, through Dutch or Hamburg merchants. With Spain on the other hand her trade, encouraged by geographical proximity and political alliance, was large. The accession of Philip V to the Spanish throne in 1700 was followed by the immigration of many French technicians and skilled workers. French commercial influences remained very important there throughout the century, much to the disgust of many Spaniards: by 1789 France was exporting to Spain over four times as much as she imported from her. Italy also proved a fertile field for her trade, though the establishment of a branch of the Bourbon dynasty on the throne of the Two Sicilies in 1735 never gave her quite the commercial predominance in the southern part of the peninsula for which some Frenchmen had hoped. The most striking expansion of French trade in Europe during this period was seen, however, in the Levant. The activity of the merchants of Marseilles, the encouragement given them by the French government, and perhaps the diversion to the eastern Mediterranean of energies frustrated by Britain's victories in North America and India, had made France by the later decades of the century much the greatest force in Europe's commerce with the Near East. In the years just before 1789 it seemed that she was about to extend her influence to the Black Sea, now for the first time for centuries opening to European trade. Only the great cycle of wars which broke out in 1792 prevented the whole eastern basin of the Mediterranean from falling under her commercial dominance.

The trading importance of the two greatest States of Western Europe was thus increasing during this period, and particularly during its last decades. That of the United Provinces, still in many ways the most economically advanced area in Europe, was by contrast stagnant or even declining. By 1739 it was believed in Amsterdam that twice as many ships unloaded their cargoes at London as at the great Dutch port. Some loss of the position which the United Provinces had occupied in the commercial life of seventeenth-century Europe was inevitable as the other parts of the continent developed their merchant fleets and began to trade directly with one another, thus robbing the Dutch of their old position as the centre *par excellence* of entrepôt trade. This more than any other factor explains the fall in the commercial importance of the Dutch Republic. Its decline in this respect was probably accentuated by the rigidity of its commercial policy (for example by the failure in 1738 and 1751 of proposals to make Amsterdam a free port). But a good deal of this loss of commercial leadership was caused by factors quite beyond the control of the Dutch government or Dutch merchants. The very disruptive conflicts of the first two decades of the eighteenth century, the Spanish Succession War of 1701–13 and the Great Northern War of 1700–21, inflicted permanent and irreversible damage on Dutch trade. When relative stability returned in the 1720s the commerce of Amsterdam did not recover to the level of the first years of the century, whereas that of Britain and France was now clearly growing. This relative decline was very notable in the Baltic, whose trade in the seventeenth century had threatened to become a Dutch monopoly. At Danzig, for example, the greatest grain port in Europe, three hundred Dutch vessels on average had touched each year at the beginning of the century; and these had accounted for half the trade of the city. By 1780 the figure had sunk to 91; and these took on board only about a seventh of the city's exports. Moreover (the most ominous symptom of all), Dutch ships were now playing only a small role in trade with North America and the Caribbean; and it was here that the really explosive growth of trading opportunities and profits was to be seen. By 1740 only about 4 per cent of Dutch merchant tonnage was trading with Africa and the Americas, a striking contrast with the now rapidly growing trade of France and still more Britain.

Commercial decline was certainly accelerated by the inability of the United Provinces, partly through sheer lack of physical resources, to develop industry on any really substantial scale. The quite important industries which they possessed at the beginning of the century suffered severely during this period from foreign competition. Calico-printing and sugar-refining, for example, were badly injured by competition from Hamburg, Bremen and the Austrian Netherlands. Of the eighty cloth factories in Leyden in 1735 more than half had disappeared only sixteen years later. Developments of this kind could hardly fail to have a considerable influence on Dutch seaborne trade. Finally, this decline in Dutch trade and industry was underlain by the fact that the United Provinces were one of the few parts of Europe whose population failed to increase significantly during the eighteenth century. Amsterdam grew from 190,000 inhabitants in 1700 to about 217,000 a hundred years later. But this was an almost trivial increase compared to the upsurge of London; and some important Dutch cities such as Leiden and The Hague had actually fewer inhabitants at the end of the century than at its beginning.

Elsewhere in Northern Europe there were States with appreciable merchant navies. Sweden in 1787 possessed over 1,200 merchantmen, Prussia at the same period nearly a thousand, Hamburg perhaps 150, and Bremen something over a hundred. The majority of these ships, however, were small (the average Prussian merchantman had a crew of only seven men). The part played by such States in international trade was not negligible. Hamburg in particular was one of the major commercial success stories of the century: the number of ships touching there more than doubled in the years 1750–78. But these were minor trading powers compared to Britain, France or the United Provinces.

In the Mediterranean Venice, formerly so important in the commercial life of Europe, was now sinking into irreparable decay. The city was still a trading centre of some importance and historians have often exaggerated its commercial weakness. In 1703 it was claimed that it earned 10 million ducats a year through its activity in marine insurance. In 1759 nearly 1,800 ships touched there. However its own merchant marine was small and declining; and its growth was hampered by the rapidly increasing competition of Trieste and Ancona, and by the hostility which existed for much of the century between Venice and the Barbary States of North Africa which preyed on its trade in the Mediterranean. Leghorn, in the Grand Duchy of Tuscany, was by contrast one of the greatest commercial centres of Europe during this period. The city was a free port with admirable quarantine arrangements (a factor of importance where trade with the disease-ridden Levant was concerned) and considerable colonies of the Greeks, Jews and Armenians who played so large a part in the commercial life of the eastern and even the western Mediterranean. The Tuscan merchant marine nevertheless was completely negligible; and Leghorn depended for its importance entirely on the British, French, Dutch and Genoese ships which called there. The Kingdom of the Two Sicilies, the largest of the Italian States, was also an almost completely passive factor in the trade of Europe. The salt, grain and other commodities she exported, the manufactured goods she imported, were carried in French, British, Genoese or Ragusan ships, not in her own.

Finally the Ottoman Empire, almost the largest of European States, was commercially one of the most inert. The contempt which most Turks felt for commerce and the essentially military character they had given their empire made it impossible for them to play any real part in its foreign trade. Nor were the Jews, Greeks and Armenians who controlled almost the whole of the empire's internal trade able to play quite so important a role in its commerce with Western Europe. The result was that this was dominated by Europeans, above all Frenchmen, and that at every port in the Ottoman Empire – Salonica, Constantinople, Smyrna, Aleppo – small but very important colonies of Western merchants were to be found.

Europe was thus divided, from the standpoint of international trade, into two unequal parts. A small number of States in the West, which controlled and financed by far the greater part of the continent's commerce, existed side by side with a much larger area which provided markets and commodities for export but depended on foreign ships and merchants to supply its imports and dispose of its products. The superiority of the more advanced parts of Western Europe in commercial and financial expertise can be seen in the role which British, French, or Dutch merchants and adventurers played in stimulating the economic development of the rest of the continent. Thus the Ostend Company, through which the Emperor Charles VI hoped to obtain for the Habsburg dominions a share in Europe's trade with the East, was founded in 1722 largely on the initiative of a Scottish adventurer, Ker of Kersland; and the Swedish East India Company set up some years later was founded and managed by Englishmen. The two most important merchant houses in Sweden in the last decades of the century had also been founded by Englishmen, while a Frenchman was mainly responsible for the creation in 1782 of the Bank of St Charles in Spain.

The expansion of seaborne trade between the European states was not paralleled by any comparable increase in that by land. The seas were becoming safer with the suppression of piracy and the development of marine insurance; ships were slowly increasing in size and port facilities were being improved; but the conditions under which goods had to be transported on land changed little. It was possible for areas widely separated geographically to be close commercial partners linked by the bond of seaborne trade. Comparable areas much closer together physically, if they were connected only by land communications, might live in virtual isolation from one another. A good illustration of this is the coastal parts of the French province of Brittany. Throughout the century they looked overseas, towards the British Isles, Spain, Holland and the French colonies, rather than towards the rest of France, from which they were largely cut off, even in the later years of this period, by marsh and forest. The marked concentration of the population of the province around the coast and the barrenness and depopulation of large inland areas reflect to a considerable extent this lack of balance between communication by sea and by land, an imbalance which had profound effects everywhere.

In some parts of Western Europe a good deal was done to improve land communications. This was strikingly so in France, where from the 1730s onwards the finest system of main roads to be found anywhere in the world was built (though secondary and feeder roads remained in very poor condition and travellers were sometimes struck by how little traffic these splendid main roads carried). In Britain the creation of 'turnpike trusts', private enterprises directed towards the improvement of specific stretches of road, was especially rapid during the 1750s and 1760s. In both countries there was extensive canal-building and embanking of rivers in the second half of the century. James Brindley, the most famous of the engineers associated with canal-building in England, had a vision of a 'Grand Trunk', a network of over 260 miles of canals which would link the Mersey, Severn, Thames and Trent and revolutionize the whole communications system of the country. None the less in many parts of Europe the poorness of internal communications remained the greatest of all obstacles not merely to the growth of trade but to the development of economic life in general. In Spain, for example, serious efforts to improve the road system (or rather to create a road system) began only in 1777. Until then almost the only real roads in the country were those connecting Madrid with the various royal residences. Even in 1800 only one point on the Spanish frontiers (Hendaye in the Pyrenees) was connected with the capital by a road which could be used by wheeled vehicles throughout its entire length. In Sicily the position was even worse. There the journey between the island's two main cities, Palermo and Messina, was normally made by sea; and even in the early years of the twentieth century there were still many Sicilian peasants who had never seen a wheeled cart, so bad or even non-existent were the roads. The cost of land transport, at least in England and France, tended to fall during the eighteenth century; but it was never possible anywhere to move heavy or bulky goods by land nearly so easily or cheaply as by water. At the beginning of this period Marshal Vauban, the great French soldier and writer on economic questions, asserted that by using a boat of the normal size on a navigable river six men and four horses could transport goods which required the use of two hundred men and four hundred horses on ordinary roads. This striking equation still, by and large, held good at its end. Land communications so difficult and expensive hampered economic life in several important ways. They meant that in the larger and more backward states economic unity was a mere dream and inter-regional trade very slight; Spain is again a good example of this. In particular, because it was so hard to move grain in large quantities from areas of surplus to those of shortage violent regional disparities in food prices and rapid fluctuations in them were normal and unavoidable.

Customs barriers and tolls continued to impede the flow of trade along its traditional routes, notably along the great rivers. Thus there were thirty such barriers on the Rhine between Kehl and the frontier of the United Provinces, and nine between Bruges and Coblenz. In a number of ways the political units into which Europe was divided were far from being commercial ones. Often they were subdivided by internal customs barriers and by differing systems of weights, measures and currency. This was the position in France, where tolls were very frequent on all the main arteries of trade and where, as one of the *cahiers* of 1789 complained, 'the infinite number of weights and measures passes the imagination'. In Spain there was a customs barrier between Castile and Valencia till 1717, while Andalusia retained its own customs system till 1778. The country also suffered from a bewildering variety of monetary systems: until 1718, when Castilian coins were for the first time made legal tender in the other provinces, she could scarcely be said to have a national currency at all. In the same way Russia, politically united to most of the Ukraine since the 1650s, was not economically united with it till the reign of Catherine II.

The effects of the declining relative importance of overland trade during this period are best seen in the failure of the towns of West and South Germany to recover their former leading place in the economy of Europe. Like many of the Italian cities they were the victims of fundamental changes in the geography and techniques of European commerce. Like these cities and the United Provinces they lacked the territorial and industrial resources which might otherwise have compensated them for their commercial losses. The result was that Cologne and Mainz, Nuremberg and Trier, play in eighteenth-century economic history a role of only third-rate importance. The rise of Basle and Zürich (perhaps accelerated by the welcome which they gave to religious refugees from France and the Archbishopric of Salzburg) showed that the historic German cities were not necessarily condemned to stagnation and decline. Some – Augsburg and particularly Frankfurt-am-Main – were able to establish themselves as important financial centres and thus recoup to a certain extent the loss of their former commercial position. These, however, were the exception.

This period saw no spectacular industrial advance so far as most of Europe was concerned. The one important exception to this generalization (and it was later to be a supremely important one) is the growth of industry, and of industry of a new kind, which was beginning to show itself in Great Britain in the last decades of the century. Accompanying this growth came a whole series of far-reaching economic changes: a rapid and sustained increase in population and in particular an unprecedented rise in the proportion of that population which lived in large towns; a sharp increase in the use of sometimes quite complex machines; a tendency, though one limited to one or two industries, for units of industrial production to grow larger. Perhaps the most fundamental change of all was one still in its infancy even in the 1780s – the movement in the most rapidly growing sector of British industry, cotton textiles, towards modern flow rather than traditional batch production, and thus towards a new labour discipline and organization, stricter and more rigid than any in the past. By the 1780s, as a result of this great series of interlinked changes, Britain was on the point of showing the rest of the world that self-sustaining and accelerating economic growth of a kind new in history was now within the reach of at least a few advanced areas of Western Europe. Great increases in production were often achieved as the cumulative result of many small improvements in the methods used, without any abrupt or eye-catching alterations in technology: British coal production, for instance, trebled in 1700–75 in this unspectacular but effective way. These changes were social and organizational as much as technological. Nevertheless it was the new technology now affecting one or two industries which most impressed contemporaries. By the 1780s the manufacture of cotton textiles in Britain had been revolutionized by a series of new machines – the spinning jenny, the waterframe, the mule – while the country's production of iron, stagnant for most of the century, had been vastly expanded by the large-scale use of coke for smelting. Simultaneously the power needed to drive new machines of all kinds was beginning to be provided by James Watt's steam-engine, which had far greater economic potentialities than the expensive and inefficient 'atmospheric' engines which preceded it. The full implications of this technological leap forward were hidden from contemporaries. But the new machines and techniques were signs, clearly visible, that Britain was moving into a new age of wealth and productivity.

The 'Industrial Revolution' did not take shape suddenly and

without warning in the 1760s, in the early 1780s, or at any other date. There had, many historians have argued, been earlier industrial changes which could be reasonably described as revolutionary under the Tudors and early Stuarts, perhaps even in the twelfth century. Certainly the foundations of the growth of industry which marked the last quarter of the eighteenth century in Britain had been laid earlier by improvements in agriculture; by the growing population which these made possible; by a rapid expansion of overseas trade; and by the emergence of a government more stable and a society more free than any major part of continental Europe could boast. Yet what was happening in a few areas of Britain by the 1780s was an economic change so potentially far-reaching that no word weaker than 'revolution' is adequate to describe it. By the end of the 1780s, to take only one telling instance, Britain's consumption of iron, in proportion to its population, was about four times that of France, in spite of the quite significant industrial development which the latter had seen during much of the century.

The reasons for this great change, the explanation of why it took place when it did, are complex and still debated. Some of these reasons certainly were not strictly economic ones. The advantages to Britain of her relatively free society, for example, with the opportunities it gave for able men to rise in the social scale and the relatively high social status which it offered to at least certain types of business activity, probably did a good deal to help economic growth. Yet how much and in what way are difficult to prove. As yet we simply do not know enough about the relationship between social structure and economic change in eighteenth-century Britain to do more than assume some general causal connection.

Even if intellectual and social factors are left out of the picture and attention is concentrated on purely economic ones it is hard to produce any simple and generally acceptable explanation of the origins of the Industrial Revolution. The eighteenth century saw a great expansion of Britain's colonial trade, above all with America (see p. 361), and this, it has frequently been argued, provided the indispensable foundation of industrial advance. Commercial profits, it is claimed, were the source of the capital needed for investment in new machines and processes. Growing overseas markets meant increased demand for British goods and intensified pressure towards large-scale production of them. This line of argument can easily be pushed too far. A fairly recent study of the subject suggests strongly that even in the three crucial decades 1760–90 only about 6–8 per cent of all capital formation in Britain resulted from the profits of overseas trade, and that the maximum effect of this trade during the century as a whole was to increase Britain's total productive power only by somewhere between 5 and 11 per cent.[6] Britain's large re-export trade in tropical and colonial products such as sugar, coffee and tobacco was important in helping her to pay for raw materials imported from Europe – naval stores from the Baltic, iron from Sweden, raw silk from Italy and the Levant – which she needed as her industrial growth accelerated. But successful British merchants, virtually without exception, became landowners (sometimes owners of plantations in the West Indies) or bankers, not industrialists. The cost of the buildings and machinery needed in the first stages of the Industrial Revolution was relatively small (in the 1770s perhaps less than a million pounds was being invested each year in British mines and factories) and was met by ploughing back the profits of existing industry far more than by the bringing in of new capital from any source. An increasing population, a rise in real wages and a series of good harvests after about 1730 almost certainly did more than trade with the outside world to encourage a growth of industry. Other explanations of Britain's industrial growth in purely economic terms have been offered. It has been argued, for example, that it was powerfully stimulated in periods when interest rates were low, that the enclosure of common lands, the building of canals and turnpikes, investment in new machinery, even the taking out of patents for new inventions, were all encouraged by the ability to borrow cheaply. Certainly the long-term trend of interest rates in Britain during this period was downwards. Another suggested explanation is that for much of the century the rise in industrial wages was less than that in the prices of manufactured goods. This, it is claimed, meant large windfall profits for the capitalist and hence large investment in new factories and machines. But the second of these hypotheses is now discredited (at least so far as Britain is concerned) in terms both of historical fact and economic theory; and the first is very much open to question, for there seems no reason to suppose that interest rates were more important than other costs in the making of business decisions in eighteenth-century Britain.

In other words no explanation of the origins of the Industrial

Revolution wholly or mainly in terms of a single factor can be satisfactory. The picture at present available is that of a process of balanced and relatively slow economic growth, with its roots deep in the past, which lasted until the 1760s or even the 1780s. This growth was the product of many factors, some of them not economic in any strict sense – changing social attitudes and the extension of education; widening overseas markets; accumulating capital for investment and a growing population to provide both workers and consumers; technical innovation and improving transport facilities. In the last decades of the century it accelerated and became increasingly unbalanced as some sectors of production (iron and still more cotton textiles) developed explosively. This very rapid lop-sided growth then stimulated other branches of industry and gave new strength to the pressures making for change in the economy as a whole.

It must be emphasized, however, that really rapid industrial growth, even in Britain, was only beginning at the very end of the period covered by this book. Until late in the century it was rare for any British industrial enterprise to use steam-power on a considerable scale. A well-informed observer in 1752 thought there were then not more than a hundred 'fire-engines' in the country, and even in 1800 all the Watt engines in use in England developed between them only about 5,000 horsepower. Even in the first years of the nineteenth century cotton provided only about a twentieth of Britain's national income: not until after the end of the Napoleonic Wars in 1815 did it displace the much more traditional production of woollen textiles as the most important British industry. Long after the 1780s the availability of water-power was the most important factor determining the location of most British industries. Industrial activity still depended on the weather, and could be disrupted by either drought or flood, to a degree hard to grasp today. In 1767 the Carron works in Scotland, one of the most advanced metallurgical enterprises in Europe, was brought to a complete standstill for three months by lack of water. Outside Britain, except to some extent in parts of France, Catalonia and the Austrian Netherlands, an industrial revolution had not even begun to develop by the early 1780s. (In Germany the first Watt steam-engine was installed only in 1785.) Nowhere were large factories staffed by hundreds of workmen and containing relatively elaborate machinery more than very exceptional features of the industrial landscape. Throughout the century the greatest cities of Europe – London, Paris, Constantinople, Moscow, St Petersburg, Amsterdam, Naples – were capitals or seaports, or both, not primarily industrial centres. The new technology was introduced only where there was a demand for it and when it seemed likely to pay. It was still a factor which was governed by the state of the economy in general rather than one which governed it.

This did not mean that great industrial enterprises were unknown. In France the Anzin coal-mining company, founded in the 1750s, was employing 4,000 men in the years before 1789. The Van Robais textile factory at Abbeville, one of the industrial showpieces of the age, contained within its walls during much of the century some 3,000 workers, while many hundreds more spun yarn for it in their own homes. In Britain the silk-mill set up by Thomas Lombe at Derby in 1717–21 employed over 300 people and contained machinery with 26,000 wheels; while two generations later the great ironmaster John Wilkinson provided one of the first important examples of 'vertical concentration' of an industry, owning his own iron-mines, coal-mines and foundries. Nevertheless the typical unit of production was still extremely small: an official survey of 1764 in the Austrian Netherlands, one of the most economically advanced areas of Europe, showed that there industrial enterprises with as many as forty-five workmen were exceptionally large. Industry was still almost everywhere conservative in technique, dominated by ideas and traditions derived from handicraft production. Where substantial and highly-organized productive units existed they were often confined only to the finishing processes.

Where large numbers of workers were concentrated under effective discipline and supervision in a single enterprise it was often because they were given no choice in the matter. Every European State attempted, with varying success, to conscript for forced labour in industry the sections of its population which it regarded as unproductive and socially dangerous. Criminals, vagabonds, prostitutes, orphans, foundlings and quite often soldiers were utilized in this way in work-houses, orphanages and barracks. Thus in Bohemia early in the century beggars and vagrants were systematically rounded up twice a year by the authorities, children of up to fourteen being sent to homes for foundlings and adults to forced labour. In Berlin at the same period a large lace factory was established in an orphanage, while under Frederick William I soldiers were employed in spinning wool and cotton on a considerable scale and every barracks became a kind of industrial establishment. The description of the prisons and hospitals of Europe provided by the Quaker John Howard at the end of this period shows how widespread practices of this kind still were in such institutions. Much more important were the great enterprises which it was possible to create in parts of Eastern and Central Europe by making use of serf labour. The supreme example of this, one of importance for the economy of the whole continent, was the development of the iron industry in Russia. In the same way the remarkable growth of the textile industry in Bohemia, which involved the setting-up of relatively large unified factories for the bleaching and dyeing of cloth, was made possible by the ability of the landowning nobility to mobilize large amounts of unfree labour. It is not surprising there-fore to find in both these countries (more particularly in Bohemia) the landowning and serf-owning class playing a large role in industrial development.

The most important type of publicly owned enterprise, orga-nized on a very large scale, was the arsenals and dockyards of the great powers. Establishments such as those at Chatham, Brest and Kronstadt ranked high among the biggest and most elaborately organized productive enterprises in Europe, almost as high as the famous arsenal at Venice had done in previous centuries. Armies and navies needed large quantities of standardized equipment – muskets, cannon, uniforms – and in the supply of such items there was an incentive to true mass-production stronger than where most ordinary industrial products were concerned. It was also quite common, particularly in central and eastern Europe, for industrial undertakings to be created by a combination of govern-ment and private initiative, or to alternate between government and private control. Thus an arms factory at Spandau, near Berlin, was set up in 1722 jointly by the Prussian government and a private banking firm. The mirror factory at Neuhaus in Austria originated in 1701 as a private concern with considerable State support, lost that support two years later, and was finally taken over completely by the State in 1720.

Over most of the continent the most usual method of industrial production was the 'domestic system'. The typical industrial worker, in so far as he existed, was a domestic worker. Under this system, the details of which varied widely in different parts of Europe, the workman worked up materials supplied to him by the manufacturer either directly or, more often, through an intermediary. His tools he might either own himself or hire from his employer. The goods he produced might then be finished in a factory of something like the modern type. A good illustration is the watch-making industry of Geneva (one of the industrial success stories of the century: its output grew twentyfold between the 1680s and the 1780s). Parts for the watches were made over a wide area of the Jura and Savoy while their finishing, decoration and final sale took place in Geneva itself. An organization of this kind was almost universal in the textile industries, where the spinning of yarn and to a slightly less extent the weaving of cloth were normally done by domestic workers, the finishing processes then being often carried out under the employer's own supervision. Thus the textile factory at Nova Kydne in Bohemia had 1,400 spinners and 100 weavers working for it in their own homes in the 1770s, as against a mere 297 people employed within its own walls. On a larger scale the great State-owned woollen factory at Guadalajara in Spain employed in 1784 over 2,000 people directly; but it had another 15,000, scattered over six different provinces, spinning yarn for it. Perhaps the most striking example of all is the government-owned woollen factory at Linz in Austria which at its peak in 1786 gave work to 35,000 people, more than 29,000 of them domestic spinners. Nearly 17,000 of these lived in Bohemia, hundreds of miles away, so that complex transport arrangements were needed to supply them with raw materials and bring back to Linz the yarn they produced. The domestic system flourished particularly in textile production, but it could be found in varying degrees in almost every branch of industry. In the early years of the century, for example, a German entrepreneur claimed that his needle-making works in Aachen provided a livelihood for a thousand people the great majority of whom were domestic workers.

A system of this kind, which had gained ground rapidly in the previous century at the expense of traditional forms of handicraft production, was inherently efficient. It meant that a large amount of rural labour could be used in industry at times when it was not needed on the land and then released at harvest or sowing time. Industry of this kind was, indeed, becoming almost essential to the economic existence of large parts of Europe. Without the employment and earnings which the domestic system provided, vast numbers of peasants, dependent on holdings which were too small and tending continually to become smaller, would have found themselves much worse off than in fact they were. It is significant that it was often widespread and important in areas where the soil was poor and it was difficult to make a living from the normal peasant holding, such as the mountain districts of Silesia and Bohemia, north and central Russia and much of Switzerland, or sometimes in areas where the soil was fertile but population pressure severe, as in parts of north-eastern France. The domestic system also usually demanded a higher degree of organization and larger capital investment, mainly in stocks of raw materials, than had been needed in the relatively small-scale handicraft industries which had preceded it. Its spread thus marked an important step in the development of modern capitalism.

The geographical distribution of industry changed considerably during this period. When the eighteenth century opened the most highly industrialized areas of the continent were the United Provinces, some parts of France and a few areas of Germany, notably Saxony. Several of the Italian States also retained some of their former significance in this respect. England was a very important exporter of woollen textiles, and to a lesser extent of tin and lead, but apart from these she produced little which counted for much in the economic life of the continent. By the outbreak of the French Revolution the United Provinces had lost much of their former importance. France had maintained and perhaps slightly improved her relative position; and the Italian States had declined into insignificance. Bohemia had become an important industrial area, especially from about 1770 onwards. England, equipped with new techniques and relatively plentiful supplies of capital, was preparing to acquire an industrial predominance which was essentially qualitative, based not on superior physical resources but on superior technology and organization. Equally important, new industrial powers had emerged. Scotland in particular, backward and poverty-stricken at the beginning of the century, had become by its later decades one of the most industrially advanced countries in Europe. As the possessor of an unusually well-educated population she was well placed to produce the skilled workers and managers who were now becoming more and more indispensable.

Most striking of all in some ways, Russia had established herself as one of the great industrial powers of Europe. This position she achieved primarily because of her importance as a producer of metals – copper and still more iron. At the beginning of this period she already possessed a considerable iron industry in the Tula and Olonets areas. To this she added, during the reign of Peter I, a new and greater source of production in the southern Urals. Government encouragement, vast and accessible supplies of timber for fuel, the forced labour of peasants 'ascribed' to the foundries, a growing demand for arms while the war of 1700–21 with Sweden lasted – all contributed to a rapid growth of output. From the establishment of the first Ural foundry at Nevyansk in 1699 until Peter's death in 1725 expansion was almost unbroken. This expansion made the fortunes of a number of entrepreneurs, above all of Nikita Demidov, an illiterate artisan of Tula who founded the greatest industrial dynasty of the age. (By 1762 the family owned twenty-eight ironworks of various kinds.) The Tsar's death and the end of the war with Sweden were followed by a slackening of activity in the next two decades; but the number of metal works in the Urals doubled in the period 1745–62. The reign of Catherine II, though it was marked by the great peasant revolt of 1773–75 which completely disrupted the life of the area, saw the construction of thirty-two new ones. By 1800 the Ural deposits were producing 80 per cent of all Russia's iron and copper, and the majority of what they produced was exported. The ironmasters of Sweden, hitherto by far the greatest European exporter, combined to restrict the production of their forges in order to maintain prices and conserve fuel supplies. Their attitude, backed by the Swedish government, culminated in the creation of perhaps the most successful cartel in European history and meant that from about 1730 onwards the level of exports from Sweden was remarkably stable. Russia was thus given the chance to become a great supplier of iron to the States of Western Europe, in some of which the shortage of timber as a fuel for smelting was now very serious. This chance she seized, so that Britain, where the fuel shortage had been most acute, was importing Russian iron even as late as the 1790s at an average rate of almost 26,000 metric tons a year.

Apart from the production of metals and a few other commodities such as sailcloth, industrial development in eighteenth-century Russia was disappointing. In spite of much government encouragement and the use of foreign experts, it proved extremely difficult to stimulate the production of goods such as silk, paper or glass on any substantial or permanent scale. (A similar position is seen in Sweden where in spite of subsidies and protective tariffs industry, apart from the metal industries, never employed much more than one per cent of the country's manpower.) Of the 300 most important industrial establishments of this type in Russia in 1780 only twenty-two had survived from the reign of Peter I. Foreign competition, lack of skilled labour, the limited market provided by a peasant country most of whose needs were still supplied by handicraft industries producing for a purely local market – all these factors ensured that Russia entered the nineteenth century still an exporter of raw materials and semi-finished goods and an importer of manufactures. The part she played in the economic life of Europe had, however, strikingly increased in this period.

Eighteenth-century industry was prevented from developing more rapidly not only by the slowness of technological advance and the shortage of capital but also by the conservative and restrictive influence of the guilds. This influence was now in decline; but the decline was slow and uneven. Such unity and homogeneity as the craft guilds had possessed in medieval and early modern times had been undermined long before the beginning of this period by the action of new economic pressures and opportunities. In particular the rough equality which the medieval guilds had attempted to preserve between their members had been in most cases irreparably destroyed. Increasingly they were now divided between a wealthy merchant group and a majority of small-scale producers whose products the former marketed and whom they increasingly dominated. One of the best documented examples of this process is that of the Lyons silk industry, where a distinction of this kind was well established by 1712. Moreover many of the guilds were becoming increasingly exclusive, more and more unwilling to admit journeymen to the rank of master. In many cases (though there were wide variations between different countries and different trades) they were now closed and largely hereditary groups whose main function was a jealous guardianship of their own privileges.

Their importance was reduced during this period by a tendency almost everywhere for important new industries to be set up in the countryside, where the guilds had little or no jurisdiction. Guild restrictions often played an important part in the spread of the domestic system. The guilds were also under attack from the efforts of many governments to make them docile instruments of State policy or even destroy them. Attempts of this kind, an example of the tendency of the age towards more effective political absolutism and greater concentration of power, were particularly marked in the German States, where the powers and independence of the guilds had hitherto been greater in many ways than in Britain, France or the Netherlands. Thus in 1731 an imperial decree gave the rulers of individual States the power to dissolve refractory guilds, while in Prussia in 1734–38 over seventy new codes of regulations (*Zunftordnungen*) governing their organization and conduct were laid down by the government. Their activities were regulated in the Habsburg Crown lands under Maria Theresa, and also in Baden and Württemburg. In the same way, in 1772 and 1777 the Spanish government ordered those under its rule to be more liberal in the admission of new members, and even to accept suitable foreigners provided they were Catholics, while in 1790 it ordered a general revision of all guild ordinances. In France the guilds continued to show some capacity for growth during the first decades of this period: paper-makers, for example, were formed into one in 1739. But they too were now more and more controlled by the central government. There was a growing tendency to regard guild statutes as valid only if they had been confirmed by royal letters patent; permission to form new guilds was frequently refused by the government; and the activities of those which existed were increasingly hemmed in by royal officials, the inspectors of manufactures. By the 1750s and 1760s there were unmistakable signs that the whole structure of guild privileges was under attack in France. In 1762 legal obstacles to the movement of industry from the cities to the countryside were swept away, a measure which inflicted severe damage on a good deal of town-based industry and generated much urban resentment. This movement culminated in the abolition of most guilds in Paris by Turgot, the greatest reforming Controller-General of the century, in 1776. This measure aroused bitter opposition and was soon withdrawn, largely because of the weakness of Louis XVI; but it proved impossible in many cases to re-establish effectively what had been even very temporarily suppressed.

Nevertheless the economic importance and political influence of the guilds remained very considerable to the end of this period in many parts of Europe. In France they were able to withstand at least to some extent attacks on their privileges until the Revolution. In Germany they retained real economic importance until the middle of the nineteenth century. Over most of Europe their hostility to new productive processes, the demarcation disputes in which they frequently indulged and their tenacious insistence on their traditional rights, tended to restrain economic progress. Increasingly these defects outweighed the services they still performed in safeguarding standards of quality and training skilled workers.

The development of financial techniques during this period was seen most strikingly in Britain. There the archaic and inefficient organization of the Mint and the constant export of large quantities of silver, mainly to the East, meant that the country (like many other parts of Europe) tended to be chronically short of coin, particularly of coins of small denominations. Not until after 1821 was the Mint able to supply Britain with an adequate quantity of small change. The result was that throughout the eighteenth century private individuals, particularly industrial employers, frequently manufactured token coins of their own. By the beginning of this period these inadequate supplies of coined money were being supplemented by other forms of currency – the notes issued by the Bank of England founded in 1694 (which had little circulation outside London), Exchequer bills, lottery tickets, and above all the notes of the private banks which were now beginning to multiply. Even before the end of the seventeenth century merchants, manufacturers and lawyers, both in London and the provinces, had been performing many of the functions of bankers. By the 1750s there were twenty to thirty private banks in London; and by 1800 this number had grown to seventy. In the provinces such banks, though slower to develop, were also well established by the later years of this period: from a mere dozen or so in 1750 their number had grown to over a hundred by the early 1780s. In Scotland too a national bank had been set up in 1695; and a number of joint-stock banks, more powerful and durable than most of the English private ones, came into existence there during the eighteenth century. Their assets grew sharply in the 1750s and 1760s: here again the third quarter of the century was a great age of expansion. By the middle of the century, moreover, London was the centre of a well-organized system of marine insurance.

This did much business with foreign shipowners and hence tended to strengthen the country's balance of payments and increase her importance in international trade and finance.

This period therefore saw the creation in Britain of a range of important new financial institutions. With them there grew up a new atmosphere of trust in the country's financial stability. The growth of this feeling was sometimes interrupted by severe financial crises. In particular the 'South Sea Bubble' of 1720 severely shook public confidence in the financial system as well as in the honesty of the ministers then in power. The crisis originated in an offer by the South Sea Company (a chartered company trading with South America and the Pacific) to take over the existing national debt and accept from the government a rate of interest on it lower than the current one. The acceptance of this offer was followed by a rapid rise in the value of the Company's shares (which its directors had expected) and by an unforeseen and unprecedented burst of speculation in hundreds of schemes put before the public by enterprising and sometimes dishonest promoters. The collapse of this speculative mania in September 1720 ruined thousands of people and produced a wave of bitterness and cynicism for which there are few parallels in British history. There were also severe fluctuations in the price of government securities and other stocks during the Seven Years War (1756–63). Nevertheless the dominant feeling of this period in Britain where public finance was concerned was one of growing confidence. This confidence made it possible for the government to borrow successfully both at home and abroad on a scale which impressed and sometimes horrified contemporaries. It was thus one of the foundations of the political and military victories won by the country during the eighteenth century. In the 1730s the philosopher George Berkeley described it as 'the chief advantage England has over France'; and three decades later an expert on commercial questions spoke of the strength of England's public credit as 'the permanent miracle of her policy, which has inspired both astonishment and fear in the States of Europe'.[7] These comments had much justification: of the costs of the four great wars fought by Britain in 1702–83 three-quarters were raised by borrowing. It was borrowing, moreover, at relatively low rates of interest: the ability to raise money cheaply was a major British advantage in the country's struggles with France. In December 1779, for example, the French government had to pay not far short of 7 per cent on the loan of 60 million livres which it floated in that month. At the same moment the British government, in a situation of extreme difficulty (see pp. 343ff), could still borrow at under 4 per cent. A difference of this sort, heavily favouring Britain, operated throughout the whole of this period.

The evolution of new institutions and techniques in Britain did not rob the United Provinces of the leading position they had enjoyed in Europe's financial life during the seventeenth century. In many ways indeed they tended to strengthen it. Various forms of British government stock, and the shares of the East India and South Sea Companies, created new outlets for Dutch capital which from early in the eighteenth century came to Britain in great and increasing quantities. It was estimated in 1737 that about £11 million of Dutch money was invested in Britain, while in 1776 the Prime Minister himself alleged that this sum had risen to £59 million – three-sevenths of the whole national debt. The second of these figures at least was much too high; but there is no doubt that Dutch investment of this kind was very considerable. The hostility with which many eighteenth-century English writers and statesmen regarded the growing national debt was caused in part by the heavy burden of interest payments to foreigners which it was rightly believed to involve. Elsewhere in Europe moreover – in France, Sweden, and in the later decades of the century Russia – capital exported from the Netherlands was a factor of considerable importance in economic life and the calculations of governments. By 1790 there was probably about 800 million guilders of Dutch money invested abroad in loans to foreign governments and such things as West Indian plantations – well over three times the national income of the United Provinces. Amsterdam was thus able to consolidate and even extend the position it had established in the seventeenth century as the chief centre of Europe's international finance. Challenged by London, especially as a centre of marine insurance, and to a lesser extent by Hamburg, it retained this position until the cataclysm which followed the French Revolution. 'The Bill on Amsterdam', it has been said, 'was to the eighteenth century what the Bill on London was to become to the nineteenth century.'[8] Dutch money seemed to some contemporaries a supranational force well able to exert a powerful influence on the whole life of Europe. 'If ten or twelve businessmen of Amsterdam of the first rank meet for a banking operation,' wrote a very well informed observer in 1769, 'they can in a moment send circulating throughout Europe over two hundred million florins in paper money, which is preferred to cash. There is no Sovereign who could do as much. . . . This credit is a power which the ten or twelve businessmen will be able to exert over all the States of Europe, in complete independence of any authority.'[9] But there was another side to the picture. The Dutch were able to export capital on an unprecedented scale partly at least because there seemed little really profitable employment for it at home, because their trade was, during much of the century, growing more slowly than that of their main rivals, and because their industry was stagnant or even declining. Moreover the money lent to foreign governments was used in the main to pay for war equipment (which the Dutch did not produce in great quantities) and to hire mercenary soldiers (few of whom were recruited in the United Provinces). Dutch industry and exports therefore gained little benefit, at least directly, from even the largest foreign loans.

In France financial techniques developed more slowly than in the other leading States of Western Europe. A widespread distrust of the financial stability and even honesty of the government, and the inefficient system of taxation, tended to discourage the growth of a national debt of the British type. The 'Mississippi Bubble' of 1719–20, when thousands of people suffered heavy losses in a burst of frenzied speculation provoked by currency inflation and the hope of vast profits to be made in colonial trade (a French equivalent of the 'South Sea Bubble') had psychological effects which persisted long after its collapse. In particular it strengthened the already widespread distrust in France of paper money and large financial institutions. The effect of this is seen in the slowness with which French public finance developed and in its failure to keep pace with the growth of the country's industry and trade. Thus although the Paris *Bourse* opened in 1724 it was until 1780 robbed of much of its usefulness by the prohibition of 'forward' transactions. One of the most obvious symptoms of French backwardness in this respect was the very large role played by foreigners (Swiss, Germans or Scots) in the belated growth of the country's financial system.

The years before 1789 saw, however, a distinct quickening in the tempo of financial development in France. The *Caisse d'Escompte*, a bank of issue and discount, was founded in 1776 (significantly by a Scot and a Swiss and in face of opposition, based on traditional hostility to usury, from both the Sorbonne and the *Parlement* of Paris). The *Loterie Royale* established in the same year issued from 1783 onwards interest-bearing tickets repayable in eight years – in effect a kind of treasury bond. Joint-stock companies began to develop after the middle of the century; and this movement was greatly accelerated from about 1780 onwards. In 1788 a Swiss set up the first French company to offer insurance against fire. In spite of all this, however, France approached the Revolution with a financial organization decidedly inferior to that of her rival across the Channel. Its deficiencies, combined with those of her tax-system, meant that her government was never able to mobilize and use effectively her great economic resources.

Progress in this field elsewhere in Europe was still slower, and was concentrated largely in the later decades of the century. Genoa continued to be, as in the past, a financial centre of some importance: on a much smaller scale she acted as a kind of Mediterranean Amsterdam, a source of capital and a centre of dealings in bullion imported from Latin America. In the second half of the century both France and the Habsburgs borrowed fairly heavily on the Genoese money market; and by 1785 the Genoese aristocracy had 70 per cent of its assets in the form of cash, loans and shares and a mere 18 per cent in land. Such a distribution was without parallel in any other ruling group in Europe. Hamburg, one of the most rapidly developing cities in Europe, consolidated her position as a centre of banking and international financial dealings. She also developed from the 1720s onwards a considerable business in marine insurance; and her economic growth was probably helped by the fact that her political structure, under the new constitution introduced in 1712, was less oligarchical than that of any other German city-state. The bankers of Geneva, another town whose economic importance was rapidly increasing, were already investing on a considerable scale in England, France and even the Netherlands during the War of the Spanish Succession (1702–13). Their close contacts with Cadiz gave them an important position in the European bullion market; and in the later decades of the century their influence on the financial life of France in particular became marked. On a smaller scale both Berne and Zürich lent and invested abroad. All of these were city-states, often Protestant, with favourable geographical positions and cosmopolitan outlooks.

In other parts of Europe governments with very different outlooks and ambitions, inspired by the success of Britain and the Netherlands, attempted to stimulate the development of their relatively backward territories and gain greater control of their resources by the creation of central banks. Thus the *Bank der Stadt Wien* was set up in 1706; the *Courantbank* in Copenhagen in 1736; and the *Königliche Giro- und Lehnbank* in Berlin in 1765. Berlin equipped itself with a *bourse* in 1737 and one was set up in Vienna in 1771, while the Bourbon government in Naples made efforts to unite the seven private banks there and thus form a single state one. Few of these institutions proved very stable or permanent. Lacking skilled direction, established in States where there were few liquid resources available for investment, exposed to constant manipulation by impoverished governments, most of them disappeared or were drastically modified soon after their foundation.

In Eastern Europe the position was different again. In Poland and the Ottoman Empire banking continued to be controlled by a small number of wealthy individuals, hardly any of whom were Poles or Turks, and was in general little more than old-fashioned money-lending. Neither country possessed much which could be dignified by the title of financial institutions. In Russia the real history of banking began only in 1754, when a Noble Bank and a Commercial Bank were established simultaneously. The latter had ceased to function by 1770 and was wound up in 1782; the fact that it was concerned only with trade passing through St Petersburg had in any case limited its importance. The Noble Bank, which had a longer life and greater significance, was created not to develop Russian industry and trade but simply to safeguard by loans the economic and therefore social position of the Russian landowning class. This it did with some success; by the end of the century it and its successors had lent the *dvoryanstvo* from public funds a sum greater than the entire annual government revenue. Its very success, however, meant that scarce financial resources were being diverted from constructive purposes to consumption, often of a wasteful and unnecessary kind, and to propping up the position of a class which was now in many ways an obstacle to economic progress.

Most of the economic ideas of this period are usually lumped together by historians under the general heading of 'mercantilism'. It seems increasingly doubtful whether this term is a very useful one, or even whether it has any precise meaning at all. How far mercantilism was ever a unified body of doctrine, how far it envisaged economic progress merely as a means of increasing the political and military power of the State, the exact significance in mercantilist thought of the precious metals – these and other questions remain without generally-accepted answers. Moreover the answers hitherto given have often been influenced by the nationality of the writer and his usual tendency to emphasize evidence drawn from the history of his own country. Thus German historians have tended to stress the political, 'State-building', character of mercantilism, while those of the Atlantic countries have tended to give greater weight to its more purely economic characteristics.

Nevertheless there are a number of propositions which all mercantilist writers would have accepted. They would have agreed that a State should have a large population concentrated in its metropolitan territory, and that emigration should be encouraged only when it was clearly to the advantage of the State. Few or none of them had any clear conception of the difficulties which could be created by pressure of population, or of the workings of the law of diminishing returns. They would also have agreed that the economic interests of a State were not best served by giving unlimited freedom of action to individuals, that it was often necessary to sacrifice the immediate interests of the latter to the security and greatness of the former. Hume summed up a good deal of contemporary opinion in his remark that there 'seems to be a kind of opposition betwixt the greatness of the State and the happiness of the subjects'. They would have agreed that the wealth of the world as a whole could not be increased, at least in the short run, and that international trade was thus an incessant struggle in which one State's gain could only be another's loss. (Though only a minority would have gone as far as the German writer T. L. Lau, who in 1719 argued that plague, war, famine and other disasters in a neighbouring State were to be welcomed as increasing the relative strength of one's own.) They therefore rejected totally the idea, fundamental to the economic liberalism of the nineteenth century, of a pre-established harmony of interests, both within and between States, which would be achieved by reducing government intervention in economic life to a minimum. They would also have agreed that economic wealth and political and military strength were interdependent. Large revenues and a high taxable capacity allowed a State to maintain armies and men-of-war, protect its trade and acquire colonies, while this very trade and colonial expansion, by a circular process, paid for still more powerful fighting forces. They would have united, finally, in a common tendency to stress problems of production and consumption, and particularly on the need to keep wages and thus production costs low and in this way compete effectively for the limited and inelastic markets available for all manufactured goods. Almost without exception they were indifferent to the problems of distribution which were to bulk so large in the work of the 'classical' economists of the early nineteenth century.

Mercantilism, even if it can be spoken of as a unity, was not an inquiry into the abstract principles of wealth in the sense that Adam Smith's *Wealth of Nations*, published in 1776, was. Very few mercantilist writers made any effort to provide a comprehensive discussion of the workings of an entire economic system. Those who did fell far short of Smith in width of views and depth of analysis. The vast majority of the mercantilist writings of the eighteenth century dealt with limited and concrete issues, immediate and practical problems. They were very often produced by or for men whose own material interests were involved in the questions which they discussed. Mercantilism was thus a collection of attitudes and assumptions, almost an administrative technology, rather than a science of economics. It was also a set of attitudes which grew naturally from the realities of the age. All forms of production were still labour-intensive and new machines which increased productivity were rare. Competition was thus largely a matter of producing as cheaply as possible by keeping labour costs as low as possible. It was also a period in which the great majority of people had little or no purchasing power to spare once they had paid for the necessities of life; and this made it reasonable to think in terms of markets whose size was fixed and which grew, if at all, only slowly. In such a situation it could be very plausibly argued that any State could increase its trade and wealth only at the expense of its competitors.

Strict mercantilism was not the only current of thought to influence economic ideas during this period. In England it was possible to find even before the end of the seventeenth century a number of eminent publicists – Coke, Barbon, North, Petty –

who dared to point out the advantages of high consumption and a high standard of living as against the frugality, abstinence and low wages still so desired by most of their contemporaries. This tendency was continued in the eighteenth century in the writings of Mandeville, Hume and Steuart; it was probably strengthened by observation of the futility of the sumptuary laws which had been enacted in past generations in almost every part of Europe. Simultaneously there can be seen the beginnings of a rejection of the general mercantilist belief in the desirability of reducing imports from foreign States and replacing them at almost any cost in efficiency by domestically produced substitutes. As early as 1696 Davenant, in one of the most pregnant passages in the economic literature of the age, argued that 'Wisdom is most commonly in the Wrong, when it pretends to direct Nature . . . it can never be Wise, to endeavour the introducing into a Country, either the Growth of any Commodity, or any Manufacture, for which, nor the Soil, nor the General Bent of the People, is proper . . . a trade forc'd in this Manner, brings no National Profit, but is Prejudicial to the Publick.'[10]

The group of French writers usually known as the Physiocrats struck another severe blow at the declining prestige of mercantilist attitudes. Centred around Quesnay, Turgot, the elder Mirabeau and later Dupont de Nemours, their influence was at its height from the mid-1750s to the mid-1770s, above all in France. They equalled or surpassed the mercantilists in the stress they laid on the need to increase population. However their conception of an ultimate balance between different States and different types of activity in the same State, which would be easily achieved once governments gave up their fruitless efforts to direct economic life, was totally at variance with mercantilist presuppositions. So was their view of land as in the last analysis the only source of wealth and the attitude of implicit hostility to industry and even more commerce which followed from this. Most of all, however, it was their belief in a large degree of economic freedom, embodied in the phrase *laissez-faire, laissez-passer*, their stressing of the advantages to be obtained by allowing more play to the economic forces naturally present in any society, which ran counter to the mercantilist spirit.

The practical achievements of the Physiocrats were not great. Their playing-down of the importance of trade and industry compared with agriculture was as prejudiced and unrealistic as any of the policies of the mercantilists. Their efforts to free the trade in grain, such as those made by Turgot in France in 1776 or by the Grand Duke Leopold, under Physiocratic influence, in Tuscany a few years earlier (see p. 199) aroused much opposition and had only short-lived effects. But for a generation or so they were a major intellectual influence. They ensured that Adam Smith's *Wealth of Nations* was not given to a world altogether unprepared for it. The ideas he attacked, though widespread and influential, had already been under hostile scrutiny for several decades.

Europe's economic life was marked throughout this period by the scarcity of the commodity most essential for the formulation of effective economic policies: information. Until late in the century few governments knew with any accuracy even the number of their own subjects. Efforts to improve their knowledge on this point were likely to encounter opposition as impious, or as the likely forerunner of new taxation. Thus in Britain a Bill for the taking of an annual census of population, though passed by the Commons, was rejected by the House of Lords in 1753. Nevertheless in spite of often fierce objections and the considerable administrative difficulties involved some advances were made. In Sweden, where registration of births, deaths and marriages had been compulsory from the 1680s, a census was taken in 1749 and an embryonic statistical office set up in 1756. In Denmark–Norway censuses, though not completely reliable ones, were taken in 1769 and 1789, and in Spain in 1768 and 1787. In Russia Catherine II ordered provincial governors in April 1764 to take a thorough census of the population under their jurisdiction, to have accurate maps of the provinces drawn and to collect information about trade and agriculture. Even in remote Iceland a remarkably complete and thorough census was carried out as early as 1703. France, in this as in so many other respects, acted as a model for the rest of Europe, at least in the second half of the century. Several remarkably good censuses of individual provinces were taken by energetic and reforming intendants, for example in Provence in 1765. From 1772 onwards annual reports from each province of population changes during the preceding year were sent to Paris and collated there by a *Bureau de Statistique*.

The slowly increasing importance attached by the age to knowledge of this kind is also seen in the efforts of private individuals to compile great collections of statistical information, for example in the vast mass of material assembled by the Abbé d'Expilly in his *Dictionnaire Géographique, Historique, et Politique, des Gaules et de la France* (Paris, 1762–70) or a little later the *Vollständige Topographie des Königreichs Preussen* (1785–89) of J. F. Goldbeck and the *Statistical Account of Scotland* (1791–97) organized by Sir John Sinclair. But even in the last years of the century the most intelligent and best-informed observers in the most advanced States could be startlingly ignorant of the demographic changes going on around them. Most of the Physiocrats believed, as an article of faith, that France's population was falling; while in 1780 the radical intellectual Richard Price claimed that the population of England had declined by a quarter in the preceding hundred years and Thomas Malthus, in the first (1798) edition of his famous *Essay on the Principle of Population*, gave a figure for the population of Britain which turned out to be over a third too low.

Economic information of various kinds, particularly relating to trade, was also collected by some governments on a fairly considerable scale. Thus in England the office of Inspector-General of Imports and Exports was created in 1696. Though the figures assembled by its holder soon ceased to reflect the state of British trade with any accuracy (see p. 8) the desirability of collecting statistics of this kind was now more clearly recognized than ever before in the country's history. In France a *Bureau de Commerce* with somewhat similar functions was established in 1713. Moreover the later decades of the century saw in many countries efforts to carry out extensive surveys of landownership, usually with the intention of using them to reform or extend the system of taxation. Turgot attempted a survey of this kind in the French province of the Limousin when he was intendant there in 1761–64; and in 1763 a royal decree called for a similar effort on a national scale. Each French parish or commune, it was hoped, would henceforth be able to preserve in its archives a plan showing details of this kind for the area. Similar efforts were made in Spain in the 1760s and in the Habsburg dominions from 1785 onwards. An earlier survey had been carried out in Savoy-Piedmont in 1728–38, and a very large one begun in Russia in 1750 had been extended to nearly half the country by the end of the century.

In spite of all this, however, it is clear that essential economic information of many kinds was unobtainable in the eighteenth century. It is equally clear that governments too often lacked the will as well as the ability to collect it. In Great Britain, so relatively advanced in other respects, no census was taken until 1801; and even then its results were not completely reliable. In Russia the Minister of Finance complained as late as 1808 that no effort had ever been made to calculate the country's balance of trade with any accuracy.

The still partially medieval character of eighteenth-century economic life can be illustrated in other ways. The idea of active competition between manufacturers or merchants as a normal and desirable thing was slow to develop: governments still often attempted to prevent price-cutting. Ideas which had taken root in a pre-capitalist age, such as that of the 'just price', still retained much of their former vitality. Thus Jacques Savary des Bruslons, the author of the greatest commercial handbook of the age, *Le Parfait Négociant*, was still able in the 1724 edition to argue that the price of a commodity should be determined by what it was just that the vendor should gain. This idea was repeated by a German writer as late as 1768. On a different level the same rejection of economic individualism, of the idea that it was legitimate to charge what the market would bear, can be seen in the deep-rooted popular feeling that essential foods should be sold only at customary prices and in customary ways. Windfall profits of dealers and speculators, in this scheme of values, were unfairly extorted from the consumer and could be reclaimed by him. This meant that at times of shortage and high prices millers and bakers were liable to be intimidated by mobs into charging at the normal rate, and the houses or barns of suspected hoarders, or of merchants believed to be moving stocks from one area to another in search of bigger profits, were exposed to attack. Efforts to enforce from below this 'moral economy' were the most frequent of all causes of riot and public disorder. The strict official regulation of the grain trade which was taken for granted until the last decades of the century in many parts of Europe shows these assumptions at work on the governmental level. It expressed not merely a prudent desire on the part of rulers to keep their subjects fed and therefore docile but also a genuine feeling of duty, a belief that it was immoral to leave the subsistence of the people at the mercy of mere market forces. This is seen, for example, in the fact that in France would-be dealers in grain, before being officially registered, had their moral character investigated by the police.

A similar rejection of the capitalist spirit is seen in the widespread tendency for resources to be squandered, as they had been for centuries, in conspicuous expenditure on buildings, plate, clothes and jewellery. This tendency was almost as marked in countries such as France, where opportunities for lucrative investment in trade and industry existed, as in those such as Poland where they were much more difficult to find. Over much of Europe, especially Central and Eastern Europe, it was rare to find a landowner, though land was still overwhelmingly the most important form of capital, who looked on his property as an enterprise to be run for profit. If high agricultural prices put more money in his pocket he was much more likely to spend this windfall on luxury goods, on adding a new wing to his house, or perhaps on buying more land, than to invest it in making his estate more productive. Social prestige and family reputation, not economic gain, inspired such expenditure. Sometimes a landowner would invest in local industries which processed the products of his estates such as wool, leather or timber. The textile industries of Bohemia, in which such great families as the Kaunitz, Harrach, Gallas and Haugwitz were involved, owed much to developments of this kind. Sometimes he might invest in the exploitation of mineral deposits on his land. In France even members of the royal family profited in this way and nowhere did such activity carry the social stigma of trade. Over much of the continent, however, if a wealthy landowner invested at all it was in relatively unproductive state or private loans. The former were normally designed to fight current wars or pay for past ones. The latter were sometimes, as in Piedmont for example, made to the local village community and thus a means by which the landlord consolidated his hold over it.

Conspicuous consumption of a traditional kind can be seen most strikingly of all, however, in the maintenance by wealthy men almost everywhere of huge households of servants and hangers-on, many of whom had no real function. Inequality between rich and poor in eighteenth-century Europe showed itself even more in the consumption of services (or alleged services) than in that of material goods. These inflated households (many of whose members received food and somewhere to sleep but little or no wages) were in the main the product of two factors. One was the feeling, impossible to justify in economic terms, that the great and wealthy man must show his importance in his style of life, that he must cut a public figure which fully reflected his status. The other was a belief, surviving from the Middle Ages and still strong almost everywhere, that the rich had a moral obligation to provide subsistence in this way for the poor, by offering them employment, however fictitious, and maintenance, however scanty. The result could be seen at its most extreme in the troops of serfs to be found in the country houses of great Russian landowners and in the crowds of unemployed or under-employed servants who lounged around the palaces of Spanish and Neapolitan grandees. 'The profession of 15,000 people at Naples is to run ahead of a carriage', commented a foreign observer in 1786, 'and of 15,000 others to run behind.' Nothing could be a more flagrant infringement of the spirit of economic rationality, of measurement and calculation, which from its foot-hold in some parts of Western Europe was slowly in the next century to conquer the entire continent. The same traditionalism is seen in the fact that a prejudice against life insurance, a feeling that the life of one of God's creatures should not be made the object of what was seen as a wager, was still quite widespread in the later years of the century. Even in France life insurance remained illegal until 1818 because of emotions of this kind.

The most important of all these traditional prejudices in its economic effects was the continuing strong feeling against the lending of money at interest. In Catholic countries this often took the form of an outright prohibition of 'usury' which, though increasingly difficult to enforce effectively, was still far from meaningless. In France, for example, a group of bankers at Angoulême failed in 1745 to recover by legal process money owed them since, it was held, they had themselves by charging interest on the loan broken the law. The *Caisse d'Escompte* set up in Paris in 1776 was as a special privilege allowed to charge what was in effect an interest rate limited to a maximum of 4 per cent; but this restriction meant that in times of financial difficulty it had to ration credit rather than charge more for it, which made it unpopular with businessmen and led to accusations of favour-itism. In Spain there continued to flourish a deep traditional conviction, frequently voiced by popular preachers, that not merely lending at interest but all forms of trade and finance were, by their very nature, temptations to the mortal sin of avarice. It was only with the issue of the new Austrian law code of 1787 that the formal prohibition of interest ceased in the Habsburg dominions; and even then the maximum rate was limited to 6 per cent. In Britain throughout the century, although the charging of interest on loans was permitted, the rate was similarly limited – in this case to 5 per cent. The influence of this restriction on the economic development of the country is still unclear, but it may have been considerable.

The forces making for economic change and progress in the eighteenth century must not be undervalued: in England at least the national income may have trebled between the 1680s and the 1780s. Nevertheless it is easy to exaggerate their scope and immediate effect. If we attempt to see the period as it appeared to those who lived in it, particularly to those who were not members of the educated or privileged classes, it is impossible to see it as one dominated by banks, stock exchanges, large factories or great trading companies. The horse-drawn wagons moving painfully over wretched roads, the sailing-ships sometimes delayed for weeks or months by contrary winds, the domestic workers at their bench or spinning-wheel, the unique social prestige still attached almost everywhere to the ownership of land, the overwhelming importance of a good harvest – all these show us that we are still in many respects very close to the Middle Ages.

One final point is so fundamental that it must be re-emphasized here. This is the sheer variety and lack of uniformity of eighteenth-century Europe, a variety more clearly visible in economic terms than in most others. Not merely between different States but between different, sometimes contiguous, parts of the same State there were wide differences in terms of land tenure, in per capita product and real income, in economic sophistication generally. Highly developed or rapidly developing areas might be juxtaposed with others still sunk in tradition and little touched by the forces of modernity. What is most eye-catching and important in this respect is the distinction between two Europes. One was the Europe of the great ports and their immediate hinterlands, the Europe which had easy access to the sea and all that this implied in terms of ease of movement, contact with markets and commercial stimuli, and exposure to new ideas. The other was inland, continental Europe, the Europe which was far from the sea in an age when movement of goods and even people by land was so laborious and expensive, the agrarian and peasant Europe still so firmly gripped by tradition and routine, still for the most part living close to subsistence level and with little of the complex commercial and financial life of the great ports.

This contrast was not absolute. There were great cities in the heart of the continent which were important markets on long-established trade-routes – Lyons, Frankfurt, Strasbourg, Leipzig: and the domestic system ensured that much of rural Europe was also the site of important industries. Nevertheless it was a real contrast. There were, for example, clearly two Frances – the rural France increasingly looking to Paris for leadership and the 'rim of port towns' such as Marseilles, Bordeaux, Nantes or St Malo. Even more marked was the contrast between the poor, conservative and agrarian economy of the interior of Spain (Old and New Castile, Leon, Extremadura) and that of the more developed coastal rim (the Seville-Cadiz area, a good deal of Catalonia, the Basque provinces, to some extent parts of Andalusia and Valencia). Before the railways allowed trade and ideas really to penetrate much of the interior of the continent for the first time the great maritime centres traded with each other or with Europe's colonies overseas rather than with the more distant parts of their hinterland. Bordeaux's contacts were with the French West Indian islands, on the one hand, and the Baltic on the other, much more than with the interior of France, while Hamburg's most important commercial links were with London, not with any German city. One of the greatest economic advantages which Britain possessed during this period was her moderate geographical area and the fact that nowhere in it was very far from the sea, the sea which meant challenge, stimulus and progress. The conservative, even stagnant society of agrarian Europe could hardly exist in an island so much of which was directly stimulated by a few great ports. In the following century this situation was to change as railways made possible the growth of new factory towns – Düsseldorf, St Etienne, Lodz, Chemnitz – with an ethos and significance very different from those of the maritime centres. In a very real sense the Industrial Revolution in much of continental Europe was an assertion by the interior of claims to equality, in education, living standards and general creativity, with the hitherto heavily privileged seaboard. But even at the outbreak of the French Revolution this development and its enormous implications were still far in the future.

NOTES AND REFERENCES

1 These comparisons are taken from M. Anderson, 'The Emergence of the Modern Life-Cycle in Britain,' *Social History*, Vol. 10, No. 1 (Jan, 1985), p. 70.

2 *The Ancient and Present State of Poland* (London, 1697), p. 13.

3 D. Macpherson, *Annals of Commerce* (London, 1805), vol. III, p. 292.

4 *Mercator's Letters on Portugal and its Commerce* (London, 1754), p. 5.

5 *An Essay upon the East India Trade* (London, 1696), p. 7.

6 P. Bairoch, 'Commerce international et genèse de la révolution industrielle anglaise', *Annales*, 28ᵉ année, No. 2 (March–April, 1973), pp. 541–71.

7 Quoted in F. Braudel, *Civilization and Capitalism* (London, 1981–84), vol. III, p. 378.

8 C. H. Wilson, in *The New Cambridge Modern History*, vol. VII (London, 1957) p. 44.

9 Quoted in F. Braudel, *Civilization and Capitalism*, vol. III, p. 245.

10 *An Essay upon the East India Trade*, p. 34.

11 Quoted in M. Vaussard, *Daily Life in Eighteenth-Century Italy* (London, 1962), p. 86.

5

GOVERNMENT AND
ADMINISTRATION

During the eighteenth century few European States possessed
efficient administrations. For this inefficiency there were several
reasons. The governmental machines of the period were defective
because nearly all of them were operated, to varying extents, by
men who were not professional administrators: nearly all of them
depended on the help of unofficial or semi-official bodies of
various kinds. Moreover the officials whom they employed, as
well as being often few in numbers, were as a rule inadequately
trained and often poorly and irregularly paid. Most important of
all, they were faced almost everywhere by a complex array of
traditional institutions, often with deep historic roots and able to
call on considerable reserves of popular support in their own
localities. These were almost always hostile to any concentration
of power in the hands of a centrally controlled and efficiency-
minded bureaucracy and distrustful of any move towards administrative rationality which seemed to threaten their own powers.

The amateur and semi-official character of much eighteenth-
century administration was bound up with the nature of society
as an aggregate of traditional groupings and institutions (see
pp. 32ff). It seemed reasonable, and was often economical of
money and effort, to allow groups and institutions of this kind
not merely a high degree of autonomy in the regulation of their
own internal affairs but also a large share in the execution of
government policies which particularly concerned them. Where
this was done such bodies might become for certain purposes
virtually branches of the central administration, and their officers
practically government officials.

Thus in France the University of Paris was entrusted by an *arrêt* of 1725 (which summarized much seventeenth-century legislation on the subject) with a large degree of control of the book trade. Similarly the weights and measures used by Paris shopkeepers were checked, not by government officials, but by the *corps des épiciers*, one of the most important guilds of the city. Corporate bodies, moreover, often became intermediaries between their members and the State in the allocation and collection of taxes. The University of Paris acted in this way after it was subjected to the *capitation* (a graduated poll-tax) in 1695 and the *dixième* (a tax on incomes) in 1710, deciding on its own initiative how much should be paid by different grades of teacher. In the city the collection of the *capitation* was supervised by municipal rather than royal officials. In a somewhat similar way most towns in Castile paid the government a fixed sum in respect of the *millones* (a kind of excise on meat, wine and other commodities) and collected the tax for themselves; while in 1703 Philip V of Spain ordered that all merchants and artisans in his dominions should become members of the appropriate guilds, since only through the latter could they be taxed with reasonable ease and efficiency.

In Britain there can be seen, in a rather different form, a tendency for functions of great importance to the government to be entrusted, *faute de mieux*, to amateur administrators. By 1698, for example, the Crown had lost control of the appointment of the commissioners set up a few years earlier for the collection in each borough and county of the land-tax, then by far the most important direct tax in the country. After that date the holders of these appointments were in effect nominated by the Members of Parliament for the area concerned. This undoubtedly contributed to the steadily declining efficiency with which the tax was collected in the eighteenth century and helped to impede the introduction of new forms of direct taxation.

The autonomy enjoyed by organizations of many kinds intermediate between the individual and the State could thus be of great administrative significance. It allowed the State to leave to such organizations functions which to modern eyes are essentially governmental, but which as yet they could perform with greater efficiency than the central government. All too often, however, guilds, chartered towns, universities, legal corporations, even village communes, opposed administrative progress. Too often they used their rights and privileges to place obstacles in the way of the levelling and centralizing efforts on which that progress clearly depended. The experience of Turgot in his efforts to abolish guild privileges in France in the 1770s, or of the Emperor Joseph II in his struggle with the privileged institutions of the Austrian Netherlands during the last years of his reign, were only the most important of many illustrations of this fact.

During this period a number of European States attempted with varying success to provide their bureaucrats with some systematic training and thus equip themselves with a *cadre* of competent officials. This policy was pursued most consistently in Prussia. There Frederick William I founded chairs of 'cameral studies' in two universities for the purpose; and from 1723 onwards young recruits (*Auskultatoren*) were admitted to various branches of the administration for practical training. This system was continued by his son Frederick II, who in 1770 set up a commission to examine such men at the end of their studies; while in 1792 his successor Frederick William II provided that they should also be examined before beginning their training. But neither these measures nor the repeated efforts of rulers such as Peter I, Frederick William I and Joseph II to punish lazy or corrupt subordinates could guarantee an adequate supply of good and upright officials.

Inadequate training and ineffective central control account therefore for some of the defects of eighteenth-century administration. Equally important was the fact that many officials purchased their posts, which were thus regarded by them, and by the State, as a kind of private property of which they could not be deprived without compensation. The sale of government offices was particularly widespread, and has been most intensively studied, in France. There the growth of a wealthy middle class eager for the security and social prestige which official rank could give created a large and profitable market. The last decades of the reign of Louis XIV saw the establishment on a hitherto unknown scale of the practice of creating new government posts, or even entire new classes of posts, merely for the sake of the money to be obtained by selling them. It continued to be indulged in, in spite of the damage it did to the administrative machine and in the long run to the government's financial position, until the end of this period. Sales of offices were not a universal phenomenon. The practice never took root in Russia or Great Britain, for example. But it could be found, though usually on a smaller scale than in France, in many European States. Even in Prussia under the incorruptible and efficiency-minded Frederick William I every official newly appointed or promoted to a higher rank had to make a contribution to military funds. Some offices in Prussia were also sold outright, while officials who had been dismissed might be reinstated in return for a money payment.

The selling of government offices was justified by contemporaries on various grounds. It was argued that it ensured that important (and thus expensive) appointments were held by men rich enough to be above ordinary financial temptations. The practice was also defended as a means by which the merchant class, still without real political power in most States, could play some part in the business of government. It was impossible, however, to reconcile with any system of administration which aimed primarily at efficiency, and in the last decades of this period was increasingly recognized as an abuse.

Eighteenth-century officials, in central and still more in local administration, also differed from their present-day counterparts in that many of them did not receive fixed and regular salaries. They were paid instead, in whole or in part, by fees which they levied on private individuals for the performance of specific services, and this often applied even at the highest levels of the machinery of justice. In Prussia for example the great legal reformer Samuel von Cocceji failed to persuade Frederick II to pay judges a salary from government funds. The fact that the amount of these fees often depended on the avarice or disinterestedness of the official concerned, who might himself be struggling to pay off liabilities he had contracted by buying or even accepting his office, created opportunities for oppression and over-charging which were not easy to eliminate. A good example of this is provided by the administration of the Tolbooth, the prison of Edinburgh, in the later eighteenth century. There a woman released in August 1787, after a short imprisonment for a debt of 6s 6d, had to pay fees of £1 1s 10½d before she was allowed to leave. More striking still was the case of a debtor imprisoned six months earlier who, though he spent only two days in gaol, found himself confronted on his release with a demand for £17 6s 5½d in fees. The gaoler replied to complaints by pointing out that he had no salary and that his post was burdened with the payment of annuities to former holders of it and other unavoidable expenses to the value of about £70 a year.[1]

What functions were these eighteenth-century administrative systems intended to perform? In the first place they had to maintain so far as possible public order in the territories which they controlled or claimed to control. This was often far from easy: the law was in general poorly observed by the standards of our own day. No government possessed any real equivalent of a modern police force. France was the most intensively policed of the major European States; but even there the *maréchaussée*, the most important of a number of police forces, numbered less than 3,900 men in the later decades of the century, and many of these were hardly fit for their work. Chartres, a town of 15,000 inhabitants, had only six policemen. Paris had about 1,500 full-time ones; but in London, a much bigger city, order had to be maintained by a chaotic assortment of parish constables and locally controlled forces, most of them of less than doubtful efficiency. Not until 1784 did something effective begin to be done to improve matters there by the setting-up of the City Patrol. At the other end of the continent the Vyatka province of Russia, with 830,000 inhabitants spread over an immense area, had even after the administrative reforms of 1775 (see p. 151) a police force of only 540 men. Routine policing was almost everywhere in the hands of local authorities and independent of central government control. In Spain, for example, the only effective organ of law-enforcement was the *Santa Hermandad*, an association of towns formed to catch criminals and pursue bandits which had been formed in the later fifteenth century and which lasted until 1835. When riots or serious large-scale disorder of any kind threatened it was normally necessary therefore to fall back on the army if they were not to get out of hand. This was a clumsy and inflexible method of control. Soldiers were not always easily available in sufficient numbers, and in the pre-railway age often could not be moved quickly from where they were stationed to where they were needed. On the other hand discontent and disorder could to some extent be predicted. The most common type of eighteenth-century riot was sparked off by bad harvests and high food prices, the result of unfavourable weather, which generated mob attacks on mills and warehouses and the forcible seizure of the contents to be sold at a 'fair' price. Quite often, again, disorder might be the result of popular resistance to militia service (there were serious riots of this kind in a number of English counties in 1757 and 1761), of resentment of new or increased taxation, or of efforts to arrest smugglers, who to the ordinary man often seemed to perform a useful and even essential function. The ability of governments and their officials to foresee trouble of this kind before it happened was often an important factor in preventing things getting out of hand. But in the larger cities in particular riots could be generated by many different causes. Even a spectacular execution might have this result. Thus when the celebrated forger (and Anglican clergyman) Dr Dodd was hanged at Tyburn in 1777 the likelihood of disorder was considered so high that 2,000 soldiers were held in readiness in Hyde Park to deal with any emergency. More than half a century earlier the French government did not dare to hang publicly the great smuggler Cartouche (who had committed some twenty or so murders) for fear of triggering off a serious riot; instead he was quietly strangled in his prison cell.

No eighteenth-century government found any satisfactory answer to the problem of public order: that it was an endemic and serious one can be seen merely by recalling the most important of the riots and similar outbreaks which occurred during a few years in the 1760s and early 1770s. In Madrid in 1766 popular demonstrations forced Charles III of Spain to dismiss his chief adviser, the Italian Squillace. In London there were serious riots in 1765 and 1768; those of the latter year, provoked by the political conflicts centring on John Wilkes and the refusal of the House of Commons to admit him to membership (see p. 175) were particularly dangerous. In Moscow in 1771 a devastating outbreak of plague led to widespread disorder including the brutal lynching of the archbishop (see p. 444) and forced the government to take extraordinary measures to reassert its authority. In France in 1775 serious grain riots, the *guerres des farines*, spread to Paris from the surrounding area and had to be repressed by military measures. And throughout these years, of course, normal government was breaking down over much of Britain's colonial empire in America. Nor was this decade, from the mid-1760s to the mid-1770s, abnormally lawless by comparison with the rest of the century.

With only weak and poorly organized police forces to depend on governments were driven to two main expedients to repress and control crime. One was deterrence through very severe punishments, usually publicly inflicted – floggings, mutilations, liberal use of the death penalty sometimes in such cruel forms as breaking on the wheel or, for crimes such as theft from a church which was technically sacrilege, burning alive. The other was the offer of rewards for information leading to the arrest of criminals, and the extensive use of informers. The Paris police were notorious for the extent to which they relied on informers, while in England the 'Tyburn Ticket Acts' of 1699 and 1706 promised anyone helping in the conviction of a robber not only the substantial sum of £40 but also a certificate (which could be sold) exempting the holder from all parish duties, e.g. as constable.

The second great function of any eighteenth-century administration was to raise by taxation or other means enough revenue to allow the machinery of government, and above all its armed forces, to function with reasonable efficiency. This was also difficult to achieve. In large part this was because the financial demands of governments increased rapidly, especially after 1750. A year of war cost the British government £5–6 million in 1700: by 1800 this had increased to £40 million. The greatest difficulty, however, was that taxation systems were so irrational and inflexible. In general taxation was neither equitably assessed nor efficiently collected, so that governments found their revenues inadequate and many of their subjects laboured under a strong and justified sense of grievance. Over much of Catholic Europe the Church paid less than its share, and continued to do so until the end of this period. In most countries the nobility and the landowners were favoured: in some, such as Hungary and Poland, outrageously so. In many others, for example France and Lombardy, the towns were favoured at the expense of the countryside. Moreover fiscal systems, even when good in theory, often had their effectiveness reduced by the existence of a complex structure of local rights and exemptions. The result could be marked and even brutal inequity. Thus Necker, the Controller-General of Finance, estimated at the beginning of the 1780s that a Breton paid in all forms of taxation little more than 12 livres each year as against the 64 livres which had to be found by each inhabitant of the Île de France. Even if allowance is made for the greater wealth of the latter the disparity is still considerable. Necker also calculated that Champagne, which had only a fifth more population than the privileged frontier province of Franche-Comté, paid six times as much in taxes. Half a century earlier in Lombardy an official enquiry revealed that of a sample of eighty communes some paid as much as 10 per cent of the capital value of their land in taxes each year and others as little as one per cent. Often differences of this kind can be explained in terms of difficulties of communication, especially in the larger States. There was a fairly general tendency for areas near the capital, where the government's hand lay relatively heavy, to pay considerably more than remote frontier ones where the effectiveness of the central administration was reduced by distance. Sometimes, again, areas which could plead no legal privilege might be able to avoid paying their full share of taxation if they had some political leverage at their disposal. Thus the south-western counties of England were under-assessed for land-tax during this period mainly, it seems, because they were over-represented in the House of Commons.

Strikingly unfair differences of this kind, however, operated not merely between provinces or relatively large areas but also on a very local scale. Thus the town of Compiègne, north-east of Paris, paid an average of 4.7 livres in *taille* (the main direct tax in France) for each of its households: but the small village of Conly, close by, paid one of 30 livres. It seems likely that in France, whose fiscal system has been studied in greater detail than that of any other State, these regional and local unfairnesses were more important than those which operated between different social classes. The taxation privileges of the French nobility have attracted much attention from historians; but recent research suggests strongly that their effects have often been exaggerated and that they were in many ways less significant than the privileges of the towns and of favoured provinces and localities.

The taxes themselves varied widely in different States. They might fall on land, as in the case of the main form of the *taille* in France or the land-tax in England; or on articles of general consumption, as with the Prussian and English excise duties and the French *gabelle* (a complicated and highly unfair tax on salt); or on individuals or households, as with the poll-tax in Russia and the *capitation* in France; or on imports, as with the customs duties of which every government made use. Usually indirect taxes were more important and lucrative than direct ones. Sales taxes were very important in Spain; and in many countries government monopolies were a highly productive (and deeply resented) source of revenue. The *gabelle* in France is much the best known such case but there were many others – tobacco in France and Prussia, alcoholic drinks in Sweden after 1775, at different times caviare, saltpetre, vodka and other commodities in Russia, salt in many different States. In Britain indirect taxes were particularly important. In 1750 about 57 per cent of the whole yield of taxation there came from this source, and by 1780 the proportion had risen to 70 per cent. In France, by contrast, the significance of direct taxes was much greater. Not until the coming of income tax in 1799 was any British government able to tax its subjects directly on the scale which had been normal across the Channel for the last century or more. In the broadest and crudest terms there was, it may be argued, a certain fairness in that the wealthiest States and those with the highest standards of living, Britain and the Dutch Republic, were also the most heavily taxed. The best recent calculation shows that in Britain the total weight of taxation during this period was equivalent to 17–19 per cent of the country's total physical output, and that after 1775 it was actually increasing faster than physical output. In France during the second half of the century, by contrast, taxation averaged no more than 10–11 per cent of physical output. Britain won her colonial and imperial duel with her rival because she was willing and able to pay for victory.

In methods of collection the most obvious defect was the common though by no means universal practice of tax-farming. Though it was unknown or unimportant in many of the great States of Europe – Britain, Russia or Prussia – it was practised during this period in some of the wealthiest parts of the continent, notably in France and until 1770 in Lombardy. Reduced to its essentials it meant that the State delegated to wealthy individuals or groups of individuals, in return for a lump-sum payment, the right to collect certain specified taxes. The greater the State's need of ready money, the less favourable the terms it could expect to make with the tax-farmers it employed. Not only did the practice enable a handful of wealthy men to make great profits and deprive the governments concerned of part of their revenues; it was also an implicit admission by these governments that they did not yet possess adequate administrative machines. Moreover even in States where the taxes were not farmed their collection was often in the hands of men who were not officials and who were under only a very moderate degree of control by the central government. Thus in Russia the effective raising of taxation depended entirely on the co-operation of the landowning class. Similarly in England the collection of the land-tax was in the hands of receivers-general for each county (or for groups or subdivisions of counties) who were usually country gentlemen and were paid for their services by being given a commission on the sums they collected.

Methods of this kind inevitably involved local variations in the efficiency of the machinery of collection, and thereby added a further element of unfairness to those which already afflicted most eighteenth-century fiscal systems. Nearly all such systems, moreover, suffered from two other important defects – the tendency of assessments, once made, to remain unchanged for decades, even generations; and the difficulty, often the impossibility, of collecting the arrears of payments which constantly tended to accumulate. The first of these is particularly striking to modern eyes. In Languedoc, to give only one of many possible illustrations, the distribution of the burden of taxation between the different dioceses which made up the province had been fixed in 1530 and was still essentially unchanged in 1789. Within dioceses the tax load was allocated between towns and villages on the basis of registers of landownership which were now hopelessly out of date: the diocese of Toulouse, for example, used throughout this period one compiled in 1551 and only one diocese, Narbonne, tried to modernize its arrangements in this respect during the eighteenth century. A similar kind of unwillingness to adapt to changing conditions can be seen in the frequent tendency to assume that a particular tax yielded over a long period of time an unchanging notional sum. For example the British Treasury took it for granted for decades on end that land-tax at four shillings in the pound yielded £2 million each year in revenue (in fact the yield was much less) and that the excise on malt was always worth £750,000. When all these factors are considered it is not perhaps surprising that only two major States during this period could claim to be in a really strong financial position. One of these was Prussia. There for much of the century perhaps administrative efficiency and certainly governmental economy were more marked than anywhere else in Europe, and the royal domains contributed more to State finances than anywhere else – about half of all revenue in mid-century, still about a third in the 1780s. The other was Great Britain, where taxable capacity was increasing fairly rapidly and where governmental borrowing was easier than in any other major country.

Another generally recognized function of eighteenth-century

governments was that of increasing the wealth of their subjects. 'Prosperity by compulsion', as one historian has called it, was an objective all rulers of the period wished to attain, the 'empirical despots' of the first half of the century as much as the 'enlightened despots' who succeeded them. If achieved it meant an increase in the pool of wealth on which the government might draw by taxation or borrowing, and a consequent increase in its power (which usually meant in practice its military strength). Power, not welfare, was the guiding principle of eighteenth-century politics. The domestic policies of every country were influenced, often dominated, by the need to maintain and if possible strengthen its position in a system of ruthlessly competitive States.

The idea of State-induced prosperity as a necessary stepping-stone to power was most enthusiastically accepted in the poor and backward countries of East and Central Europe. It underlay the ambitious schemes of economic development which Peter I of Russia attempted to realize (see p. 104). It can be seen in an almost equally pronounced form in the policies of the rulers of Austria and Prussia – in the grant to Trieste and Fiume of the status of free ports in 1719 and 1729; in the creation of the Ostend Company for trade with the East in 1722; in the considerable efforts made under Maria Theresa to improve the internal communications of the Habsburg territories; in the attempts of both Frederick William I and his son to develop the industries and expand the agricultural production of Prussia. In particular it was accepted by almost everyone that it was a duty of governments to increase if possible the populations of the countries they ruled; a growing population seemed the surest of all signs of a well-governed State. Thus it is not surprising to find Frederick William I and Frederick II doing their utmost to encourage the colonization by immigrants of uncultivated areas in Brandenburg and Pomerania; Catherine II of Russia striving, with some success, to attract German and Swiss settlers to the Volga basin and South Russia; Joseph II forbidding emigration from his dominions and encouraging immigration to them; and earlier in the century a Grand Duke of Tuscany bringing Greeks from the Peloponnese to populate the Maremma (a swampy coastal area of Tuscany).

This emphasis on population as the greatest single foundation of a State's wealth had other effects. It underlay the stress laid by so much eighteenth-century economic theory on the preservation and development of labour-intensive industries, which would provide plentiful employment, on preventing as far as possible the export of food (since a cheap and plentiful food supply was correctly seen as the greatest single encouragement to population growth) and on encouraging the export of goods with a high labour content. It also meant that at least in the more developed parts of Europe governments made more or less systematic efforts to help their subjects avoid starvation in times of harvest failure and food shortage. In France this type of paternalism worked with considerable effect. In Montauban, for example, there was from 1723 onwards an official *magasin du Roi* capable of storing 3,000 quintals of grain. This was intended primarily to supply seed to needy cultivators; but in times of shortage it also acted as a source of supply for the bakers of the city. When acute crisis threatened the area millers were compelled to surrender for public use stocks of imported grain held in the nearby port of Moissac; or if necessary the intendants who administered the area might import grain on government account for distribution to those in need. In 1752 considerable quantities were obtained in this way for the *généralités* of Auch and Montauban. At Lyons, again, in the very bad winter of 1788–89, the lieutenant-general of police organized the public distribution of coal to the poor. He also kept four mills on the river Rhône at work to supply flour for the city by providing men who laboured day and night to break the ice which would have otherwise made it impossible for them to function. 'It can be said,' wrote a contemporary, 'that without his vigilance we should have lacked everything or could have obtained it only at high cost.' In the same way the government of the electorate of Mainz during the severe shortage in 1771–72 bought grain in Poland and distributed it to the population of the city at moderate prices. When the Rhine burst its banks in 1784 and the Oder did the same in the following year, causing severe flooding in different parts of his territories, Frederick II provided from state resources substantial sums for the relief of distress. Even in Great Britain the government distributed £15,000 worth of food in the Scottish Highlands during the shortage of 1783. These are merely isolated and almost random illustrations of an attitude shared to some degree by every eighteenth-century government. They did not usually attempt, except in moments of real crisis like those which have just been mentioned, to take positive measures to feed their subjects. But until late in the century at least most of them tried, mainly by regulating the movement and marketing of grain, to ensure that their subjects could feed themselves. Quite apart from the fact that hunger pushed beyond normal levels inevitably meant disorder, all of them could see the advantages of ruling a wealthy and populous State.

In Great Britain and the Dutch Republic, where a high degree of government supervision and initiative in economic life was neither so necessary nor so practicable as further east, ideas of 'prosperity by compulsion' and official paternalism were less wholeheartedly applied. There the assumption that the government had a duty to increase the wealth of the State by all means in its power was as fully accepted as in the Habsburg lands or Prussia; but by the middle of the century it was beginning to be widely felt that it could do this without increasing the scale of its interference with economic life. By then the liberalizing ideas of the Physiocrats (see p. 115) were beginning to take shape in France. By the 1770s they were exerting, through important officials such as Freiherr von Gebler and Count Zinzendorf, some influence even on the economic policies of the Habsburg government. To the ordinary man, however, freedom of trade and liberal economic ideas seemed merely a betrayal of the ruler's inescapable duty to watch over the economic well-being of his subjects and in particular to see that they did not starve. To the end of this period hardly any measure of trade liberalization failed to arouse popular opposition: the resistance to the legislation of 1763–64 which attempted to free the grain trade in France from many restrictions, and its enforced withdrawal in the early 1770s, are the most important of many illustrations of this point.

Side by side with these fiscal and economic functions eighteenth-century governments had of course to maintain a judicial system, or at least a number of central law courts. The status and political importance of the judicial system varied widely in different States. In England it was independent of the administration (except that the Lord Chancellor and the other law officers of the Crown were appointed for political reasons and were normally displaced when a change of government occurred). Judges, from 1714 onwards, held office while they were of good behaviour, and could not be dismissed on political grounds. A whole series of leading cases in constitutional law during this period (the most important was that which established in 1763 the illegality of general warrants, i.e. warrants for the arrest of persons not individually named) showed that their independence was a reality. The central courts of law in England indeed to a large extent controlled the actions of the administration, not because they were part of it but because, by the use of well-established *certiorari* and *quo warranto* procedures, they could compel officials to justify in terms of the existing law their actions or omissions to act. No other country possessed a judicial system so independent and so respected; and its existence is one of the keys to the divergence in constitutional development between England and almost all the other States of Europe during this period. In France also the *parlements* (see p. 52) enjoyed increasing prestige and popularity from the 1760s onward. They also acted as a check, though a less efficient and reliable one than the English law courts, on the activities of the bureaucracy. In particular the *Parlement* of Paris, by using its right to issue 'remonstrances' against royal decrees, could hamper the execution of measures which it disliked or which were incompatible with what it chose to regard as the French constitution. The French and English judicial systems differed enormously, not least in their size. The *Parlement* of Paris had 240 judges in 1715; and most of the provincial *parlements* had about 100. These, combined with the four royal courts of appeal which were not formally *parlements* but had some independence in fact, meant that at the highest level there were about 1,200 royal judges in eighteenth-century France. In England the number presiding in the central courts of common law and chancery (not allowing for the more specialized Admiralty and Church courts) seldom exceeded fifteen. Nevertheless there were some important underlying similarities. In both States the judicial system, at least in its higher ranks, was a conservative force. In both it restricted or attempted to restrict, for good or evil, the freedom of action of the administration.

In Eastern and Central Europe the position was quite different. In the great States of the West, England, France or Spain, it was possible to claim, with varying degrees of truth, that a constitution existed. In each there was, it could be argued, a structure of rights and established procedures which would be upheld at least to a large extent by the law courts and which could not be easily overridden by an autocrat or a great official. Even in France this claim was not altogether justified; in Eastern Europe it was even more difficult to make. In Russia, to a large extent in Prussia, and in the Habsburg hereditary lands if they are considered as a whole, the administrative system was the real

137

constitution. In all these States the judiciary, at least in its higher ranks, was a department of the administration. In them it had evolved largely as part of the machinery of absolute government. It is true that the eighteenth century saw almost everywhere in Europe an increased emphasis on the idea of governments as applying and controlled by law (which was equated with reason). This idea enjoyed growing influence in Central Europe as elsewhere. It helped to popularize there the conception of the judicial system as a regulating element within the administrative machine and to stimulate attempts to give it greater independence. Thus in 1748 Frederick II forbade administrative bodies in Prussia to interfere in judicial proceedings. In the following year the judicial functions of the central government in the Habsburg hereditary provinces were for the first time clearly separated from its administrative ones when the *Directorium in publicis et cameralibus* was set up to supervise administration and finance while a quite distinct new organ, the *Oberste Justizstelle* (in effect a combined Ministry of Justice and Supreme Court), was established to oversee judicial matters. Throughout this period, however, the administration of the law in Eastern and Central Europe continued to be essentially a branch of the administration in general. The two fields, administration and justice, continued to be difficult to separate clearly. Administrative bodies tended to acquire judicial or semi-judicial functions (the Senate in Russia under Peter I is a good example: originating as an essentially administrative organ it had become by the end of this period a predominantly judicial one). In Prussia, and still more in the Habsburg territories, legal training continued to be required for appointment to the higher ranks of all branches of the administration to a degree unequalled anywhere in the West.

In all parts of Europe the law itself, as distinct from its administration, left much to be desired. Almost everywhere the need for codification, for the law to be expressed simply and comprehensively, for redundant and outdated legislation to be amended or repealed, was great and increasingly felt. This was especially the case in France. There a number of differing legal systems, based in the main on Roman law in the south and on customary or common law in the north and centre, provoked an understandable demand for a unified and simple code – a demand expressed in many of the *cahiers* of 1789. The position was even worse in Russia. There, until the end of this period, many imperial decrees (*ukazy*) were issued without being printed or published, especially if they related to purely private or local issues. Moreover many government departments issued orders which had the force of law. Commissions to codify this chaotic system were set up by Peter I in 1700, 1714 and 1720, and another by the Empress Elizabeth thirty years later. Yet another, the most famous of all, which included elected representatives of the nobility, the towns, and most other strata of Russian society, was assembled by Catherine II in 1767. None of these had any practical result; and the chaos of Russian legislation was reduced to order only in the early nineteenth century in the great work of codification inspired by M. M. Speranskii. The eighteenth century saw several more successful efforts of this kind elsewhere in Europe. In the Habsburg hereditary lands the position was as complex as anywhere, since there prevailed in them a mixture of Roman and customary law with many regional variations, a situation which impeded economic development, led to endless jurisdictional disputes between competing courts and even made it difficult to transfer officials from one province to another. Here the ministers of Maria Theresa began the codification of civil law in 1753, though the process was not complete until 1811; and in 1769 an important effort to systematise criminal law, the *Codex Theresianus*, was produced. Most impressive of all was the great Prussian code, the *Preussisches Allgemeines Landrecht*, promulgated in 1794 but the result of work extending over several decades. Over much of the continent, however, the demand that the law be made more comprehensible and accessible to the ordinary man remained unsatisfied.

Nor was its administration appreciably improved. Slow-moving, expensive and tradition-bound, the higher law courts remained almost everywhere one of the aspects of government most frequently complained of and most resistant to change. The attempts of a number of autocratic rulers to improve their procedure and speed up their work had little effect. This was largely because hardly any eighteenth-century government was willing to spend money on a considerable scale on improving the machinery of justice. The governmental reforms of the period were almost all aimed, directly or indirectly, at increasing the military and political power of the State, at developing its capacity to survive and to expand territorially. States, it was quite correctly believed, fell or were defeated because they were weak, not because they failed to achieve some ideal standard in the administration of justice. Judicial reform thus appeared something of a luxury, admirable in principle but with a less pressing claim on available resources than the improvement of the armed forces or the development of economic life.

Underlying the structure of royal and State justice which has been briefly discussed in the preceding paragraphs there existed an enormous network of seigneurial or, to use a somewhat meaningless word, 'feudal', justice. Over much of Europe landlords had the right to hold courts of their own, to compel peasants on their land to use these courts for certain purposes, and to profit from the process. In this way they made an important contribution to the administration of justice and maintenance of order in their own localities, and one which historians have often tended to neglect. Most governments simply did not have as yet the resources to provide a comprehensive and all-embracing network of state courts. Seigneurial ones were therefore often an indispensable element in the whole structure of law and order. The importance of this can be seen in Joseph II's decree of 1786, which ordered the landowners of his dominions (many of whom now thought their rights of jurisdiction more trouble than they were worth) to continue to carry out their judicial functions until at some more or less distant date the State was ready to take them over. In France, again the country in which this aspect of eighteenth-century life has been most intensively studied, such courts were very numerous and sometimes very burdensome. In Brittany (admittedly the most 'feudal' of French provinces, and hardly typical) about nine-tenths of all judicial business was still transacted in seigneurial courts, of which there were about 2,500 in existence as late as 1789 – an average of two to each parish. There were at the outbreak of the Revolution about 70–80,000 full and part-time judges in courts of this kind in France as a whole. One result of this situation was swarms of lawyers and court officials, often poorly qualified or not qualified at all, levying dues of different sorts on the peasant; and there was an increasing and dangerous tendency for seigneurial rights of jurisdiction to be bought by well-to-do merchants or professional men as a status symbol or purely as an investment. In Prussia the local judicial functions of the landowner were one of the foundations of his power, indeed of the entire structure of the Prussian State. Elsewhere in Germany the old assembly courts of the village communities (*Landgerichte*) had been largely taken over by nobles by the end of the sixteenth century; and the Thirty Years War had seen noble influence extended in many cases over the comparable courts of the towns. In Russia the land courts, the only significant judicial institutions at the village level and important instruments of social and political control, were completely controlled by the land-owning class. In Scotland the heritable jurisdictions which had hitherto allowed their owners to control and punish their tenants and humbler neighbours were abolished only in 1747, when regality courts and heritable stewartries and sheriffdoms were swept away.

The whole question of grassroots justice of this sort, traditional, class-dominated and intensely local in outlook and operation, is complex. A single jurisdiction of this kind, and the revenue in fees and fines which it produced, was often the property of a number of different landowners and might be highly subdivided between them. Seigneurial jurisdiction over one tiny village in Lorraine, for example, was split between six individuals, one of whom took 43 per cent of the income arising from it while another received a mere 0.5 per cent. There was also an important distinction between rights of 'high' justice, which in principle gave the right to sentence offenders to corporal and even capital punishment, and the lesser rights of 'low' justice, which in practice usually meant simply the enforcement of the rights of the lord and the obligations of the peasant. (Sometimes the position was further complicated by the existence of an intermediate 'middle' justice as well.) Broadly speaking, however, there was a clear gradient of increasing seigneurial rights and controls as one moved eastwards from France to the German world and on to Poland and Russia. In the latter, as has been seen (p. 44) the legal powers of the lord over his peasants reached under Catherine II a level never seen before; and owners of large estates in Russia often drew up their own detailed regulations governing the conduct of their serfs – in effect private law-codes.

It should never be forgotten, however, how many Europeans in this period had their only first-hand experience of law and legal processes in courts of this kind. Governments increasingly made efforts to ensure that minimum standards of competence and fairness were enforced in the administration of seigneurial justice. In 1680 Louis XIV, for example, demanded that judges in the seigneurial courts exercising rights of 'high' justice should have

141

received at least two years of legal training. In Prussia it was established practice by the eighteenth century that sentences passed by seigneurial courts in criminal cases had to be confirmed by a royal one. Even in Poland the right of such courts to impose the death penalty was abolished in 1768; and this merely recognized an existing fact, since most of them were already transferring capital cases for trial to the nearest royal court. But there were many parts of Europe in which the justice which impinged directly on the ordinary man in the course of his daily life was controlled only very imperfectly or not at all by the ruler and the State. Moreover the noble landowner's position as a judge or a court-owner tended to endow him also with a wide variety of police and quasi-judicial powers with regard to public health, morals, fire precautions and economic life generally in his own locality. It has to be remembered, however, that seigneurial justice, whatever its defects, was usually accessible and cheap, virtues which many royal courts conspicuously did not possess. Moreover it was still natural in many parts of Europe for peasants to look to their lord as an arbiter in disputes and to feel that it was one of his obligations to provide a means of solving them. Justice of this type was by no means always unpopular. It seems likely that the decline of seigneurial courts in France in the generation before 1789, as landowners became more conscious of the expense and trouble of maintaining them and the difficulty of making them profitable, was one element in a growing peasant resentment of what was seen as seigneurial exploitation.

A demand for more humane and enlightened judicial systems can be seen developing during this period in several countries, especially from the 1760s onwards. The publication in 1764 of Cesare Beccaria's *Dei Delitti e delle Pene* was the first systematic attack on the unscientific penal systems of the age. Both directly and through its influence on other writers, above all on the English legal theorist Jeremy Bentham, it was to have great influence in the future. Almost simultaneously two great judicial scandals in France, the Calas and Sirven affairs[2], advertised all over Europe by the interest taken in them by Voltaire, helped to shake still further public faith in traditional procedures. Nor was this demand for a more enlightened judicial system altogether ineffective. In particular the use of judicial torture was abolished or discarded in many parts of Europe. It was ended in Prussia in 1754, in Saxony in 1770, in Poland and the Habsburg dominions in 1776, in France by stages in 1780 and 1788, and even in the Kingdom of the Two Sicilies in 1789. It seems likely that a moral and emotional reaction resulting from the work of Beccaria and Voltaire had relatively little to do with this development, however. Changing ideas of what constituted acceptable proof of guilt, a decline in the traditional emphasis on obtaining by almost any means a confession from the accused and a growing willingness to accept merely circumstantial evidence, were probably much more important. Certainly the idea that public order and the protection of the citizen demanded the severest punishment of wrongdoers was still very widespread. A decade after the appearance of Beccaria's work it was still possible for a book published in England to advocate the vivisection of murderers.

Finally there must be mentioned one function of the administrative machinery of this period which is sometimes overlooked. This was the preservation and protection of the State religion. The importance attached to this in different countries and by different rulers varied greatly, from the passionate Catholicism of the kings of Spain to the indifference of Frederick II, from the intolerance of Portugal or Savoy to the relative freedom of the United Provinces. But hardly ever were governments prepared to dissociate themselves from religion, or to abandon their traditional role as the protectors of the faith of their subjects, or of the majority of them. The idea that religious belief was the most effective of all social cements, the ultimate and irreplaceable source of all morality, was still very much alive everywhere. As a result rulers and ministers themselves completely lacking in religious feeling were willing to foster religion, as Turgot admitted, not because it was true but because it was useful. Monarchs hostile to the power or envious of the wealth of their State Churches, or of particular religious groups such as the Jesuits, never allowed these feelings to lead them into opposition to religion as such. Thus Peter I, although he destroyed the political influence of the Orthodox Church in Russia (see p. 461), was a devout adherent of its doctrines. Catherine II, who secularized its lands two generations later, lost no opportunity of advertising to her subjects her personal piety. Joseph II, though he was anxious to reform, if necessary by force, the Catholic Church in his dominions, and to inculcate a greater degree of religious toleration there (see p. 459) nevertheless considered it his duty to persecute atheists and even deists.

If the essential functions of the administrative system were the same in all parts of eighteenth-century Europe the methods by which these functions were carried out varied widely in different areas.

Throughout much of the century Prussia seemed to many contemporaries the best administered of European States, the outstanding example of what good government could do to strengthen a country and increase its power and importance. The creation of an efficient bureaucracy, like that of a powerful army, was to some extent forced on her rulers by the complete lack of any geographical unity or common history to bind together the different provinces which they controlled. A group of disjointed and disparate territories strung out across the North German plain from Königsberg to Wesel could hardly have been maintained indefinitely as a political unit without a centralized and efficient governmental machine: it should be remembered that though their ruler held the title of 'King in Prussia' from 1701 and 'King of Prussia' from 1772 it was only in 1807 that 'Prussia' became the official designation of the monarchy as a whole.

The creation of the army and bureaucracy which were to provide the backbone of the new State, the centralization of authority in Berlin and the reduction of the power of the provincial estates and the nobility which were the prerequisite of real administrative improvement, had all been begun in the previous century by the Great Elector Frederick William. They were carried further by King Frederick William I, especially in the first decade of his reign. These years (1713–23) saw the creation of a number of new government departments – the General Finance Directory, the General War Commissariat, the Audit Office and others. By the 1720s they had been combined in three great institutions; the General Directory, which supervised military, police, economic and financial affairs; the *Justizstaatsrat*, which supervised the judicial system, religion, and education; and the *Kabinetsministerium*, which was concerned primarily with foreign affairs. Under the General Directory were a number of provincial boards (essentially administrative committees) with very wide but primarily financial functions. A systematic effort, which continued to the end of the reign, was made to fuse the component parts of the monarchy more completely together, notably by refusing to employ officials in the province of which they were natives. Repeated and on the whole successful attempts were also made by Frederick William to assert the principle that the members of the bureaucracy were his personal servants and owed him implicit obedience. 'One must serve the king', he wrote in 1714, 'with life and limb, with goods and chattels, with honour and conscience, and surrender everything except salvation. The latter is reserved for God. But everything else must be mine.'[3] This attitude expressed itself in royal efforts to control and supervise the day-to-day work of the whole governmental machine, notably by an order of November 1716 which regulated in great detail the work of the chanceries attached to various government departments. It can also be seen in the extension of the system of *Fiscals* (officials charged with watching the workings of the administration and denouncing inefficiency and corruption) which the king had inherited.

Frederick William's whole reign was dominated by the desire to exploit to the full every possible source of income. This was done by the creation of government monopolies of various products; by the imposition of heavy excise duties; and by the efficient administration of the royal domains. Simultaneously by the most rigid economy in civil expenditure he accumulated a large reserve of bullion for use in emergency. The diplomat and publicist Gentz, himself a Prussian official at one stage in his career, was justified three generations later in claiming that 'the first and principal part' of the Prussian administrative system was 'the amassing of treasure'[4].

Many of these trends continued under Frederick William's more famous son. Frederick II like his father supervised personally the whole governmental machine. He did this mainly by means of written instructions and comments on reports submitted to him, partly by tours of inspection in the summer of each year during which he examined officials and heard the grievances of his subjects. The *Fiscals* continued to be extensively used; and of the forty-one provincial board presidents who held office during his reign (1740–86) eleven were dismissed in a constant though largely fruitless struggle to increase their efficiency. Government income and expenditure continued to be scrutinized with a care unknown in any other major State except Great Britain. The creation of specialized ministries, which had begun in the last years of Frederick William I, was continued by the establishment of new ones for commerce, Silesia, and army affairs – though the General Directory, the main central institution of the previous generation, continued to exist until 1806. There were few radical innovations. From 1746 onwards there slowly took shape a series of important judicial reforms, though this was the work of one of Frederick's ministers, Samuel von Cocceji, rather than of the king himself. In 1766 an independent administration of the new tobacco excise was set up. But the keynote was conservation and adaptation rather than far-reaching change.

However methods well adapted to the Prussia of 1713 were ceasing to be practicable in the much larger and appreciably wealthier State which was emerging in the two decades before 1789. In particular it was becoming steadily more difficult for Frederick II, in the second half of his reign, to exercise effective personal control of the administration, while the position was made still worse by the king's touchy vanity and resentment of criticism or even suggestions from inferiors. The result was a tendency for the orders issued from Berlin to become increasingly confused and unrealistic and for Frederick's subordinates to conceal difficulties or unpleasant facts from him. Moreover as the bureaucracy grew in size (the General Directory was roughly three times as large at the end of Frederick's reign as at its beginning) the king's jealous desire to control the entire machine and to make all decisions, often hasty and badly thought-out ones, had serious results. It tended to throw real power increasingly into the hands of his ministers and still more into those of the heads of the provincial chambers, the men most responsible for the day-to-day administration of the different parts of the Prussian monarchy. Thus East Prussia, the most remote from Berlin of the major provinces, was visited by Frederick only three times (in 1740, 1750 and 1753); and though the president of the provincial chamber there reported to the king monthly and was summoned each year in June to the capital to see him personally, it is clear that Frederick was not really well informed about East Prussian affairs. All this amounted to the growth, in the later years of the reign, of a kind of unplanned, unconscious and *de facto* decentralization of effective control. The reputation of the Prussian administrative system thus reached its peak, after the Seven Years War, at a time when its real efficiency was tending to decline.

In one important respect, moreover, Frederick II broke with the traditions bequeathed him by his father. Under Frederick William I men of non-noble birth had played an exceptionally important part in the administration, indeed a more important one than at any time before 1918. It seems clear that the king actively distrusted at least the greater and more ancient Junker families. In his *Political Testament* of 1722 he flatly described those of the Altmark and the Magdeburg area – the Alvenslebens, Schulenburgs and Bismarcks, names which resound through the whole of Prussian history – as the enemies of the monarchy. Of the eighteen privy councillors in office in 1740, when he died, only three were of noble birth. Under his son the administrative importance of noblemen increased sharply. Recruitment to important posts became more dependent than in the past on family connexions; and the higher ranks of the administration came in time to approximate to a hereditary caste. (Though the lower-ranking posts, such as *Steuerrat* and *Burgomeister* were still filled mainly by middle-class appointees). From this point of view, the cultured Frederick II was really less in sympathy with the progressive tendencies of the age than his 'mad drill-sergeant' father had been.

The administrative history of eighteenth-century Russia is in some ways similar to that of Prussia, in others very different. There as in Prussia the bureaucracy and army held the country together. The vigorous personal control by the ruler to which Prussian officials were subjected was paralleled to some extent in Russia, at least under Peter I, who borrowed from his Western neighbour the system of espionage and denunciation by *Fiscals*. Like Frederick William I, moreover, Peter was willing on occasion to entrust high administrative posts to men of non-noble birth or to foreigners (P. P. Shafirov, the son of a converted Jew, who was one of the Tsar's ablest subordinates in foreign policy matters, is a good example) though it is quite clear that he always preferred whenever possible to rely on members of the old Muscovite aristocracy. It was impossible nevertheless to create in so huge and undeveloped a country as Russia a bureaucratic machine as efficient as that of Prussia. The distances involved, the weakness or indifference of many of the rulers concerned, above all the lack of educated and honest officials; all forbade it. The result was that throughout this period the central government was very dependent on the landowning class for the execution of its policies. It could never override its wishes or interests even to the limited extent to which the kings of Prussia could disregard those of the junkers.

The administrative system inherited by Peter I at the end of the seventeenth century was the product of generations of haphazard and unplanned growth. At the centre were the *Boyarskaya Duma* (a council dominated by members of the upper nobility) and over forty departments (*prikazy*) whose functions varied very widely in importance and geographical scope and whose spheres of activity overlapped and intersected in a highly irrational way. Control of local administration was largely in the hands of the provincial governors (*voevodas*). When Peter died in 1725 the picture was quite different. The *Boyarskaya Duma* had ceased to exist (its fall was one of many indications of the declining power of the older noble families) and had been replaced by a series of new institutions, notably the Senate founded in 1711. The *prikaz* system had been largely replaced, in 1718–19, by the creation of nine administrative colleges, each with a well-defined sphere of activity. These were essentially committees (with in several cases a number of foreign members) of a sort now well established in Prussia and Sweden: this type of administrative mechanism had become popular over much of Northern Europe at the end of the previous century and the Russian colleges were based on a systematic study of foreign, particularly Swedish, models. In the provinces a series of complicated changes in 1708, 1715 and 1719 made the control of the central government more effective by subjecting local officials to the Senate and later to the colleges. By the date of the great Tsar's death the country had been divided into fifty provinces, each headed by a *voevoda*, while a large number of new local officials with specialized functions (the *ober-kommandant* the *ober-kommissar*, the *landrichter*, etc.) had been created.

Peter had thus endowed his country, mainly in an effort to mobilize and develop her resources for military purposes, with an administrative system more bureaucratic and more centralized than any she had hitherto known. Under his immediate successors the machine he had created remained intact in a number of essentials and continued to function, though with declining efficiency. A series of new central institutions for the formulation of policy was set up – the Supreme Privy Council in 1726, the *Kabinet* in 1731, the *Konferentsiya* in the 1750s – but these were all in effect the same body under differing names. The Senate lost some of its power and was divided by Catherine II into six separate departments; but it continued to transact a vast amount of business. The colleges created by Peter remained in existence, though most of them became unimportant in the second half of the century. Local government as it existed at the end of his reign was drastically remodelled in 1728, however, mainly by increasing the importance of the *gubernii* (great territorial divisions each including a number of provinces) and their governors.

The reign of Catherine II is important in the administrative history of Russia above all because it witnessed a partly unconscious decision by the government to base the administration more than ever on the privileged landowning class. In a sense the government took this class into partnership, and thus tempered the autocracy of the ruler in practice if not in theory. The closeness of the *de facto* alliance which was growing up between the monarchy and the smaller and medium-sized landowners had already been seen clearly in 1730. When in that year the young Tsar Peter II died, the Supreme Privy Council chose as his successor Anna, niece of Peter I and Duchess of Courland. Her acceptance as ruler was, however, made conditional on her agreement to a series of conditions drawn up by Prince D. M. Golitsyn, a member of the Council and also of one of the most important noble families in Russia. These conditions, which were closely similar to those imposed on the Swedish monarchy in 1720 (see p. 267), provided that she should rule with the advice of the Council, and that she should not make war or peace, or military promotions to ranks above that of colonel, without its consent. Nor was she to marry or name a successor on her own initiative. If put into force, these proposals would have substituted for the autocratic rule traditional in Russia that of a noble oligarchy; and Golitsyn is known to have planned also the creation of representative bodies for the lower nobility and the towns. But such ideas were confined for the most part to a few great noble families. The lesser landowners were anxious to obtain some share in government, above all in local government. But they were quite unwilling to limit the power of the monarchy, which they saw as the defender of their interests against the encroachments of the old *boyar* families. The result was that the attempt of Golitsyn and his associates to create some limited form of constitutional government in Russia broke down almost immediately and that autocracy reasserted itself with undiminished powers. These powers it now held, in part at least, by the will of the landowning class.

The half-century which followed saw an almost unbroken series of concessions by the Crown to this class. The obligation to perform compulsory State service which Peter I had imposed on it was progressively reduced, and finally abolished in 1762 (see p. 51). In 1775 its administrative influence was greatly increased by a very important reform of provincial government. The details of this are complicated, but its effect was to transfer many of the functions of the colleges to new institutions, the provincial chambers, which were dominated by the landowners of the areas concerned. The reform also established in every province of the empire a Board of Public Welfare with responsibility for prisons, workhouses, hospitals, schools, almshouses and orphanages. Inevitably it was difficult to make this legislation effective in practice. Often it was hard to find enough qualified men to fill the new posts which were being created, especially any which called for special skill or training. None the less it showed an interest in public welfare as distinct from State power which no Russian ruler had displayed before. Ten years later the landowning class was granted a charter which conceded it a wide range of legal and economic privileges. This extended still further its control of provincial administration, a control which was intensified by the inability of the Russian towns to play an independent role of any importance. Thus by the end of this period Russia possessed an administrative system which was in form highly centralized and autocratic. In fact, however, her government was based on the predominance of a single class and involved in practice a considerable decentralization of authority in the interests of that class. It is also clear that factional struggles within this ruling class and the formation within it of clientage groups with recognized leaders among ministers and great officials greatly influenced the processes of administration. Personal connections of this sort were much more important in the Russian bureaucracy than in those of Prussia or the Habsburg territories.

Nevertheless the purely administrative achievements of Catherine II were remarkable. She went far towards creating what eighteenth-century Russia had never previously possessed – a rationalized structure of civilian bureaucracy capable of administering this gigantic and thinly peopled empire at least in a rudimentary way. An important set of Staff Regulations for officials, enacted in December 1763 only a few months after her accession, standardized salaries and, largely by the creation of new posts, almost doubled the size of the bureaucracy. This was by far the most comprehensive review of the administrative structure ever hitherto attempted in Russia. In the following year civilian officials were ordered to assume responsibility for the collection of the poll-tax which since its introduction by Peter I from 1718 onwards had been collected by the army simply because there was no civilian machinery capable of doing the job. In 1773 a special Office of State Revenues was created as a subdivision of the Senate; the result was that in 1781 it was possible to submit to the empress the first meaningful budget in the history of Imperial Russia. Since at Catherine's accession there had been about fifty distinct government agencies with the right to collect specified revenues and to spend the money thus raised (a typical pattern of medieval public finance) this must rank as an administrative triumph. In 1782, again, the government was able to issue for the first time a clear and detailed list of all taxes and official fees. Even in the very concrete and visible form of the creation of new provincial towns, built by government decree simply for administrative purposes, a vast amount was accomplished. The provincial reform of 1775 provided for the division of the empire into districts (*uezdy*) of 20,000 to 30,000 inhabitants, each of which was to have a town to act as a centre of administration. The result was the foundation in the following decade of well over 200 such new towns, an achievement which no other eighteenth-century government could approach and which was one of the most important practical legacies of the age of Catherine. The highly rationalistic character of this town-building and its marked emphasis on uniformity (the new towns were to be of a standard size of four versts (4 kilometres) in diameter and were not to spread beyond this except with official permission) give it a certain general resemblance to the rationalizing of local government in France by the revolutionaries from 1790 onwards. However the sheer lack of resources from which the Russian government still suffered in the later eighteenth century must never be underestimated. At Catherine's accession the entire empire in all its vastness had, by one calculation, about 16,500 officials at work in the machinery of central and local administration combined; and many of these were unpaid and part-time. Frederick II, who ruled about one per cent of the land area of Russia, had at the same date about 14,000 under his control. At the outbreak of the Pugachev revolt in 1773 the huge *guberniya* of Kazan, with a population of 2.5 million, was administered by eighty permanent full-time officials. Only if facts such as this are given their proper weight can the Empress's achievements be fairly judged and her reliance on the support of the landowning class be seen for the inescapable necessity it was.

The position in the Habsburg hereditary lands resembled that in Russia and Prussia in that there too the creation of a centralized and reasonably efficient administration seemed essential if the State were to develop or even survive. But in Central Europe the obstacles which impeded the growth of a strong central government and an elaborate bureaucracy were almost as great as in Russia. The Habsburg territories were very extensive, their internal communications were poor, their economic life was generally backward. Also the Habsburgs had inherited a position of power, even leadership, in Europe which was becoming increasingly difficult to maintain: during this period they were more preoccupied than most European dynasties by the need to defend their existing possessions against encroachment and if possible to acquire others. This intensified the need for efficient administration of their territories but also helped in some respects to make efficiency harder to attain.

Moreover in Prussia noble families on the greatest scale, owning vast estates and great wealth, had never existed. In Russia they had been largely stripped of political power by Peter I. In the Habsburg lands, by contrast, they remained of very great importance throughout this period. In the reign of Charles VI, when their influence was at its height, the hereditary dominions of the Habsburgs were in some ways rather an aristocratic republic, a federation of great noble families, than a genuine monarchy. It is significant that the administrative reforms of his daughter Maria Theresa and her son Joseph II were carried out by ministers drawn largely from the nobility, even the high nobility – Haugwitz, Kolowrat, Chotek, Kaunitz and others.

Most important of all, almost every major subdivision of the Habsburg dominions – Bohemia, Milan, Upper and Lower Austria, the Netherlands – retained a distinctive character, a deep-rooted and strongly marked political tradition of its own. These were embodied in local institutions whose outlook was profoundly conservative and which often wielded considerable power. Hungary in particular continued to be in many ways a foreign country so far as the rest of the Habsburg monarchy was concerned. From 1687 onwards its kingship was hereditary in the

Habsburg family and its privileged class lost the right of armed
resistance to their ruler (*jus resistendi*) which they had hitherto
possessed. This did not, however, prevent the outbreak of a
serious nationalist revolt against Habsburg rule in 1703 which was
ended by negotiation (Peace of Szatmár) only in 1711.
Throughout the eighteenth century the country retained its own
system of administration, dominated by the gentry and based on
their county assemblies (*komitats*). Equally important, this class
retained, in spite of the efforts of the government in Vienna,
enormous privileges in respect of taxation. Moreover the middle-
class groups which in many other parts of Europe were the most
powerful supporter of the idea of centralized absolutism were in
many of the Habsburg territories, above all in Hungary, exceptionally weak. All these factors combined to make impossible
centralization of authority on the scale achieved in Prussia or even
in Russia.

Administrative improvement was inevitable none the less. The
obsolete semi-feudal system of government which had been inadequate even in the reign of Charles VI was drastically modified,
though never completely swept away, as a result of the struggles
of 1740–63 with Prussia (see pp. 288ff). Improved administration,
and above all greater administrative unity and uniformity, was
clearly a prerequisite of the recovery of Silesia, perhaps even of
the continued existence of the Habsburg monarchy. Prussia had
shown what could be done to strengthen, by efficient administration, a state otherwise apparently doomed to poverty and
weakness; and for the next half-century her example was to
inspire in Vienna efforts at change in the administrative almost
as much as in the military sphere. Thus a series of reforms in the
1740s began to break down the privileges which the nobility and
Church had hitherto enjoyed with regard to taxation. Simultaneously new agencies of the central government (*Repräsentationen*
and *Kammern*) were created in many of the provinces. The financial reforms carried through by Count von Haugwitz, one of the
greatest reforming bureaucrats of the century, in 1748 provided
for a large increase in government revenue. Moreover now taxes
were to be collected by officials of the central government, not
as hitherto by agents of the provincial estates – a crucial step in
strengthening control from Vienna. New central institutions were
developed – a State Chancery for Foreign Affairs in 1742, the
Directorium in Publicis et Cameralibus (a union of the hitherto

separate chanceries of Bohemia and Austria under the presidency of Haugwitz) in 1749, and the Council of State in 1760. In 1749 a new high court of appeal, the *Oberste Justizstelle*, asserted more clearly than ever before the principle that the higher judiciary at least was independent of the administration in general. These reforms, which at first encountered bitter opposition from the estates and nobility in all the hereditary provinces, meant that by the 1760s the Habsburg hereditary lands enjoyed a bureaucratic system more efficient and more modern than anything which Prussia herself could boast. The decline in the power of the provincial estates continued after 1763, while the social dominance and hence political influence of the nobility began to be undermined, though slowly, by legislation limiting in various ways their hitherto almost absolute control of their serfs.

The effect of these changes was geographically uneven. In particular Hungary, entrenched behind her peculiar and remote relationship with the rest of the monarchy and the self-interest of her ruling class, was little affected by them. Even in 1764, when the Hungarian Diet rejected Maria Theresa's demands for higher taxation, the other Habsburg provinces, excluding Milan and the Netherlands, paid over four times as much towards the military expenses of the State as she did. Nevertheless the foundations of many of the radical and centralizing policies of Joseph II (see pp. 201ff) had been laid long before his assumption of sole power in 1780, or even his promotion to co-ruler with his mother in 1765.

To the great States of Eastern and Central Europe reasonably efficient administration (which in practice meant centralized administration) was a necessity, almost a condition of existence. The position in Britain was completely different. To the exposed land frontiers and vulnerability to foreign attack characteristic of all States east of the Rhine, she opposed a geographical position which gave her, while she controlled the seas, complete physical security. To their general poverty she opposed a wealth whose growth was making her the envy of the rest of the continent. To the emphasis upon military needs which marked their administrative systems she opposed a distrust of and contempt for the army which made her almost unique in Europe. To the centralization which increasingly characterized their bureaucracies she opposed a system of government still in many ways highly decentralized. To an extent unparalleled elsewhere in Europe she was a State dominated by legislation, or by traditions having in effect the force of law. Her constitution was real, an amalgam of law and habit, not the system of bureaucratic practice which did duty for one in many continental States. Her government controlled its agents by legislation or, as has already been pointed out, by various legal procedures, as much as by purely administrative means. Administration in eighteenth-century Britain was the application and execution of common or statute law, and often little more.

Her central government was controlled and its policies formulated by a number of ministers and great officials: the councils and committees still so prominent in many continental States were in Britain of little importance. The Lord Chancellor, the First Lord of the Admiralty, the First Lord of the Treasury (an office which gave its holder control of many subordinate appointments and from the 1720s onwards was often held by the chief or Prime Minister) and the two Secretaries of State for the Northern and Southern Departments were amongst the more important of these ministers. Others – the Lord Privy Seal and the Lord President of the Council – had less executive power. All of these were normally members of the Cabinet, as that rather amorphous institution gradually evolved (see pp. 172–3). Most of them owed their position, at least until late in this period, largely to royal favour, and regarded the king as a master to whom they owed a personal loyalty. With few exceptions, however, they also owed something to their possession of electoral or parliamentary influence (since the government had to be able to retain the support of a majority in the House of Commons) and the importance of this factor tended to increase as political parties of a very loosely organized type slowly developed (see pp. 173ff). The king's choice of ministers was thus not completely unfettered. To the end of this period it was rare for a minister to be forced by parliamentary or popular pressure on a ruler unwilling to accept him. (The clearest examples of this occurred in 1744, when George II was compelled to give office to Henry Pelham and his elder brother, the Duke of Newcastle; and in 1757, when he had to accept the elder William Pitt as Secretary of State.) Nevertheless the men who made up the government of Great Britain were usually more than the courtiers and favourites who bulked so large in the governments of some continental States.

The departments over which these ministers presided varied

greatly in size and structure. Many of them were inefficient by the best continental standards. In spite of the relatively advanced methods of public finance which had now been evolved in Great Britain, hardly any Treasury officials were paid regular salaries until after 1782. Even then they were not paid out of public funds, but from 'a domestic fund nourished by fees'. Military administration in particular remained for nearly a century after the end of this period an administrative jungle of divided responsibilities, overlapping jurisdictions and competing vested interests. Here the Secretary at War, the Master-General of the Ordnance, the Secretaries of State and the Commander-in-Chief (when he existed; the office was in abeyance during much of the century) all had fingers in the pie. Even more striking than this inefficiency to modern eyes is the narrowness of outlook of the central administration in Britain during this period. Its utter indifference to education could be paralleled in other parts of Europe; but the extent to which it was willing to leave the development of the country's system of communications or the relief of distress to purely local initiative was unusual even in an age in which the effective powers of central governments were in general so limited.

The decentralized and amateur character of so much British administration is seen clearly in the very large part played in it by the Justices of the Peace. For the most part landowners or Anglican clergyman (the two categories to a large extent overlapped) they bore a very wide range of responsibilities and carried out, often in virtual independence of the central government, a great variety of functions. In Quarter Sessions they acted as a court of law for their localities and decided large numbers of serious and important cases. They bore the main responsibility for the maintenance of public order in the areas under their jurisdiction, helped in the recruiting of men for the armed forces, controlled the administration of the poor law and vagrancy law, and acted in many other ways as the virtual rulers of their own districts. The best-known example of their independence of central control is the introduction, by a group of Berkshire justices in 1795, of the 'Speenhamland System' of outdoor relief for heads of families who had appealed to the poor law authorities for support. The system, which was widely imitated in other parts of England, was not in fact a complete novelty. Nevertheless this episode was a striking illustration of the way in which a group of private individuals could in Britain create policy on its own initiative on a matter of great national importance, acting almost as though it enjoyed legislative power.

The French administrative system occupied a position midway between the centralization seen in Prussia under Frederick William I and Frederick II and the decentralized parliamentary system of Britain. In theory and to a large extent in practice it was highly centralized, at least in its upper ranks. At this level the power of the ruler was exercised in part through a number of councils. The most important of these were the *Conseil d'Etat*, in theory the main policy-making body, the *Conseil des Dépêches*, the *Conseil des Finances*, and the *Conseil Privé*, a kind of supreme legal tribunal. These had been very important during much of the seventeenth century but were now mere shadows of their former selves. Much more significant was a small group of ministers – the Chancellor, the *Garde des Sceaux*, the four Secretaries of State (for Foreign Affairs, War, the Navy, and the *Maison du Roi*) and the very powerful Controller-General of Finances who also supervised communications and many aspects of the nation's economic life. These were the king's ministers: their power depended on their personal relationship to the monarch and the degree of attention he paid to their advice. By far the most important royal agents outside Paris were the intendants who had evolved in the seventeenth century as a means of extending the monarchy's control of the provinces and of whom there were now thirty-four. Under the ministers and intendants functioned a great bureaucracy, both central and local. This included many men of ability and produced an immense volume of correspondence, reports and memoranda. It was also, however, complex and hierarchical and correspondingly slow-moving. The needs and wishes of provincial communities could easily be lost sight of in a morass of paper-work and official procedure. The intendants, it has been said, were 'committed to a perpetual drudgery in administrative bad habits, to a wearisome tidying of endless lumber'.[5] The administrative centralization which was so marked a feature of the revolutionary régime after 1789, and which was bequeathed with little fundamental alteration to the France of the nineteenth and twentieth centuries, was in many ways merely a streamlined and rationalized version of the bureaucracy of the *ancien régime*.

This bureaucracy, like those of Prussia and the Habsburg provinces, was essentially legal, even legalistic, in its outlook. It was an instrument of despotism, and designed as such, but of a despotism which could not in practice be unlimited or grossly irresponsible. More important, the degree of effective central control which could be achieved in pre-revolutionary France was limited by conditions and institutions inherited from the past. The fact that the country lacked any unified system of law, or even of weights and measures, and that its fiscal system was riddled with anomalies, hampered the efforts of the bureaucracy to increase the power of the central government. Above all institutions such as the *parlements*, the provincial estates, the guilds and the Church, still possessed powers which could not be easily overridden. The ability of the *parlements* to oppose and stultify the policies of the king and his ministers (see p. 178) was merely the clearest of many illustrations of this fact. In France bodies of this kind retained an importance which they had lost during the reigns of the Great Elector and Frederick William I in Prussia: in Russia most of them had never even existed. By acting as a buffer between the central government and the ordinary man they helped to ensure that France, which during this period produced more great administrators than any other European State, remained in many ways a badly administered country.

French government under Louis XV and Louis XVI therefore consisted essentially of two distinct elements. The first of these was a rationally organized and in large part recently created structure of central authority, the ministers and intendants. But this was superimposed on and struggling to control a second element, a jungle of widely varying traditional local and provincial authorities as well as a vast array of minor venal offices whose holders often regarded them simply as sources of status and income. There is much to be said for the traditional view that it was the failure of the reforming impulses represented by a number of enlightened ministers and officials to win the day against the forces of tradition and sectional and personal selfishness which more than anything else doomed the old regime in France.[6] In the middle of the century a would-be reformer of France's government, the Marquis d'Argenson, had called for 'a genius who will reduce things from the compound to the simple'; but that genius was never found.

NOTES AND REFERENCES

1   J. Howard, *An Account of the Principal Lazarettos in Europe* (Warrington, 1789), p. 76n.

2   Calas, a Protestant whose son had died violently in mysterious circumstances, was executed in March, 1762, on a charge of having murdered him to prevent his conversion to Catholicism. Sirven, another Protestant, was accused of the murder of his daughter, who had been taken from him and sent to a convent to be brought up as a Catholic. In January, 1764, he escaped death by flight.

3   R. A. Dorwart, *The Administrative Reforms of Frederick William I of Prussia* (Cambridge, Mass., 1953), p. 36.

4   F. von Gentz, *On the State of Europe before and after the French Revolution* (London, 1802), p. 33.

5   D. Dakin, *Turgot and the Ancien Régime in France* (London, 1939), p. 27.

6   But for a conflicting view by a leading authority see Olwen Hufton, *Europe: Privilege and Protest, 1730–1789* (London, 1980), Ch. XI *passim*.

6

MONARCHS AND DESPOTS: TENSIONS WITHIN THE STATE

Make argument stronger by incorporating ch.

Every St...............e, with a few relatively
unimport.............. monarchy. Almost everywhere the
monarch was, and was expected to be, the moving force behind
the machinery of government. At their highest level the internal
politics of the European States were the politics of monarchy.
Political conflicts normally took the form of struggles between
parties or individuals for influence over the ruler, struggles in
which the victor secured the all-important privilege of easy access
to him and in which the vanquished were dismissed, disgraced
or exiled. The fate of a fallen minister or favourite might be even
harder if he had aroused real fear and hatred in his opponents –
the executions (or rather judicial murders) in 1719 of Baron
Goertz, the adviser of the dead Charles XII of Sweden, and in
1772 of Count Struensee, the progressive-minded but tactless
favourite who had for several years dominated the court of
Denmark, are good illustrations of this. On the other hand
anyone who could establish a real ascendancy over a monarch
might himself become almost a surrogate ruler: the extraordinary
position achieved by Prince G. A. Potemkin in Russia through
his personal hold on Catherine II for some years before his death
in 1791 is an outstanding case in point. Perhaps the most
convincing illustration of the power of the monarchical idea and
the extent to which it was still unchallenged is the way in which
almost everywhere opposition to rulers, insofar as it was formed
or organized at all, tended to centre around the heir to the throne
or at least some member of the royal family and to use him as
a figurehead. From the 1690s, for instance, discontent with the

policies of Louis XIV gathered around his grandson, the Duke of Burgundy, and hoped for a change of course with his accession to the throne; while in the last two decades of the reign of Catherine II her son, the Grand Duke Paul, acted as the focus of potential opposition. Even in Britain it seemed almost a law of politics under George II and George III that the Prince of Wales should act as a rallying-point for all those who hoped to benefit from a change of ruler.

Few people seriously questioned the practical advantages and moral justification of hereditary monarchy as a system of government, particularly in the larger and more powerful States. Its superiority to its rivals seemed proved not merely by argument but by experience. In Italy a few famous and ancient republics – Venice, Genoa, Lucca – continued to exist; and in some of them republican government, even in the highly oligarchical form which had prevailed in these small States for centuries, continued to arouse genuine loyalty. The successful revolt of 1746, for example, which expelled an Austrian garrison from Genoa, expressed a powerful urban patriotism which drew strength from the city's long republican tradition. But none of these was strong enough to make much difference to the general picture of eighteenth-century Europe as overwhelmingly monarchical. In some other States elective monarchy provided opportunities of limiting the powers of each ruler at his election. Each of the ecclesiastical electors in Germany (those of Mainz, Cologne and Trier), on being chosen as ruler by the cathedral chapter concerned, had to sign an agreement (*Wahlkapitulation*) in which he confirmed and promised to respect its ancient privileges. The *Pacta Conventa* which the nobility imposed on each newly elected king of Poland performed, on a much more important scale, a similar function. Each Holy Roman Emperor, the supreme example of an elected monarch, had to accept the same kind of limitations when he was chosen by the imperial electors. But even this does not seriously modify the picture. Every successful large State in eighteenth-century Europe, every one which made significant territorial gains or played a great independent role in international affairs, was ruled by a powerful hereditary monarchy. Those which lacked this essential source of strength were either impotent small ones on the fringes of the great political developments of the age, such as the Italian republics, or, in the case of some more important States, were notably less well governed and less effectively led than their neighbours and competitors. Of the latter group both the United Provinces throughout the century and Sweden during the period of weak and limited monarchy from 1718 to 1772 were examples; while the destruction of Poland was the supreme warning of the fate in store for any State whose rulers were too weak to repress internal dissension or ward off the attacks of external enemies.

The United Provinces, a cumbersome federation of seven units each with estates and administrative machinery of its own, was an uneasy compromise between the monarchical and republican forms of government. Each province had its own Stadtholder (the formal head of its administration, chosen by its estates). It was possible, however, for a member of the House of Orange (the descendants of William the Silent, the leader of the struggle for independence against Spain in the later sixteenth century) to be elected Stadtholder of all or most of the provinces and thus attain the position of General Stadtholder of the federation. He thus became in a sense a monarch, though one whose powers were strictly limited and often jealously scrutinized by the provincial estates. The monarchical tendencies typified by the Orange family were stoutly opposed by the republican forces which were strong in Holland, by far the most powerful province of the federation, and notably among the great merchants of Amsterdam. The result throughout this period was a continuous struggle between republican and Orangist groups and an uneasy oscillation of power between them. The death in 1702 of the Stadtholder William III (King William III of England) who left no son to succeed him, was followed by over forty years of republican rule. His heir, John-William Friso, was Stadtholder only of the province of Friesland, while the government of the United Provinces fell under the dominance of Anthony Heinsius, Grand Pensionary of Holland, who remained until his death in 1720 one of the leading figures in European politics. The power of the republicans suffered a serious setback in 1747, at a moment of crisis when French invasion seemed imminent, by the victory of the Orangists and the accession to power of William IV, the posthumous son of John-William Friso. In that year he received the title of Captain and Admiral-General and became Stadtholder of all the provinces. When he died in 1751 he was succeeded by his son William V, then a child of three. The republicanism of Holland, however, was far from dead. Encouraged by the long minority of the new

Stadtholder it helped to influence Dutch policy in a pro-French and anti-British direction during the Seven Years War (the Orange family, now closely associated by marriage with that of Hanover, was generally pro-British in outlook). It did much to bring about the Anglo–Dutch conflict of 1780. In 1787 it led the country to the verge of civil war and provoked the intervention of the Prussian army in defence of William V and his wife, a Prussian princess.

What one British envoy called the 'crazy constitution' of the United Provinces thus appeared to contemporaries a poor advertisement for any form of government which attempted to escape from the conventional pattern of monarchy. This impression may have been strengthened by the slow decline in the country's commercial importance (see pp. 90–1), though this would have taken place whatever its political structure. Even the judicial system in the Dutch republic, in so many ways still among the most advanced parts of Europe, suffered from the lack of a powerful monarchy able to press effectively for the sort of reform which rulers in many less developed areas were now forcing upon their subjects. It is significant that judicial torture was abolished in the province of Holland only as late as 1798, while in the generally more backward Austrian Netherlands the Emperor Joseph II had ended it, at least in principle, fourteen years earlier. Moreover the United Provinces showed themselves throughout the later decades of the century notably less welcoming than their southern neighbours to ideas of penal reform of the kind now being put forward by Beccaria and others.

In the same way the constitution of 1720, which drastically limited the powers of the Swedish monarchy, hitherto one of the most absolute in Europe, seemed to condemn the country to perpetual divisions and faction-fights and therefore to impotence in international affairs. It was for precisely this reason that Russia, which had far more than any other State to fear from strong government and an active foreign policy in Sweden, did everything in its power to uphold that constitution (see p. 266). Sweden continued to be in some ways deeply divided even after the *coup d'état* by which Gustavus III reasserted in 1772 the power of the monarchy. Moreover the constitution which the Swedish Diet was forced to accept in that year (the first in the world to be embodied in a single comprehensive organized document) was in some ways relatively moderate. It left both the Senate and the

Riksdag with considerable powers. Nevertheless the king had restored to government and policy-making an element of continuity and decision which had been lacking for many years.

Most of all the fate of Poland illustrated the necessity of strong monarchy and the fatal disunity which usually followed when it was lacking. At the end of the sixteenth century the 'crowned republic' of Poland had been in some ways one of the great powers of Europe. Her decline to the position she now occupied, that of a helpless victim-State, was the product of many factors – economic and social backwardness, long frontiers unprotected by natural obstacles to invasion, religious divisions and the aggression of her neighbours. But underlying all these was the fact that the power of the Polish monarchy had evaporated since its elective character (which had existed in theory since the 1430s) had become finally established in practice from the 1570s onwards. Henceforth each successive royal election provoked party conflicts and personal intrigues which often led to civil war, as well as pressure and even forcible intervention from abroad on behalf of competing candidates. The kings of Poland, often foreigners, their hands tied by promises made to the greater nobility at their accession, had to submit to continuous scrutiny and control by the same nobles. Any effort to increase their powers, most of all any suggestion that the Crown might once more become hereditary, at once aroused the most violent opposition. At their disposal were a ludicrously inadequate army and an administrative machine so primitive that one observer in the early eighteenth century alleged that the tiny Italian city-state of Lucca possessed a larger civil service than they. Their ministers (if such a term can be used of the great officials such as the treasurers and hetmans of Poland and Lithuania) were irremovable; and the principle of the *liberum veto* meant that any of the two hundred or so members of the Diet (*Seym*) could nullify the work of an entire session by recording a single dissenting vote.

A strong monarchy could have developed a powerful army and an effective bureaucracy. It could have defended the frontiers, repressed religious intolerance and done something to accelerate economic and intellectual progress. The rulers of Russia, Prussia, and the Habsburg territories succeeded in varying degrees in achieving all these aims. Without such a monarchy progress in Poland, though not impossible, was very difficult. Only from the 1760s and 1770s onwards were there signs that it might be achieved. By then it was too late: the destruction of the country's independence was already under way. Only political units which were small and remote from the international conflicts which agitated the greater powers, as were the Swiss cantons and some of the city-states of Germany and Italy, could hope to dispense permanently with some more or less effective form of kingship.

To the greater States, on the other hand, strong monarchy was essential. It alone could safeguard them against disintegration and the disruptive effects of faction and provincial particularism. The monarch, it was argued, unable to escape from his burdens by resignation, as a mere minister could, and anxious to pass on undiminished to his heirs what he had inherited from his ancestors, was the safest and most effective possible guardian of the public welfare. 'An absolute king,' wrote Voltaire, 'unless he is a monster, can wish only the greatness and prosperity of his State, because it is his own greatness and prosperity, because every father wishes the good of his own household. He may be mistaken in his choice of means, but it is against nature that he should wish harm to his kingdom' A unified and consistent policy, it was often contended, could be carried on only by a monarch, not by a group of ministers each of whom had his own axe to grind (this was a favourite argument of Frederick II in particular). And the greater the State the more inescapable was monarchy and the more powerful it must be. The argument was well put by the ruler of the biggest of them all. 'The Russian Empire', wrote Catherine II in 1764, 'is so large that apart from the Autocratic Sovereign every other form of government is harmful to it, because all others are slower in their execution and contain a great multitude of various horrors, which lead to the disintegration of power and strength more than that of one Sovereign, who possesses all the means for the eradication of all harm and looks on the general good as his own.'[1]

Monarchy in eighteenth-century Europe was thus buttressed by powerful utilitarian arguments. It was also strengthened by the assumption, inherited from the Middle Ages and still very widely accepted, that the relationship between a ruler and his subjects was analogous to that of father and children. 'The true image of a free people, governed by a patriot king,' wrote Lord Bolingbroke, one of the most sophisticated intellects of the century, in 1738, 'is that of a patriarchal family.' Even some of the articles of the great *Encyclopédie,* the supreme general expression of a radically enlightened view of the world and society, as its successive volumes appeared in the 1750s and 1760s (see p. 410), contained distinct traces of the same pervasive traditional assumption. In small States it was often possible for the ruler to express very effectively by his own actions this paternalist view and to have some more or less personal contact with an appreciable fraction of his subjects. Thus John V of Portugal (1706–50) gave public audiences regularly twice a week at which he personally received petitions for the redress of grievances. At the same time he gave alms with his own hand to the poor from a basket of coins placed by his side. In Mainz an ordinance of 1788 announced that the elector would give general audiences every Monday at precisely 4 o'clock in the afternoon: at these every inhabitant of the electorate was entitled to attend and present in person any grievance he might have. In the larger States contacts of this direct and relatively informal kind between ruler and ruled were obviously impossible on a large scale. Even in them, however, the assumption that the monarch was in some sense a father of his people and that he should therefore be freely accessible to them died hard. In the 1760s Catherine II of Russia had in self-defence to issue decrees ordering her subjects to petition her only through the appropriate officials and not by the direct personal presentation to her of their grievances and requests. The extent of the childlike and almost filial loyalty felt by the ordinary man everywhere towards his ruler, the great fund of emotion of this sort upon which a monarch could still draw, are clearly seen in France in the crisis of 1789. Many of the *cahiers* (the statements of grievances and proposals for their rectification drawn up for the guidance of the States-General when it met in May 1789) proposed the building of public monuments to Louis XVI in recognition of his action in calling the States-General and thus restoring the 'liberties' of his people. Some also suggested that a national holiday be established in his honour or that he be given some honorific title – *le Bienfaisant* or (significantly) *Le Père du Peuple.*

Paternalist assumptions were an aspect of the deeply entrenched feeling, which time and education were only slowly eroding, that legitimate rulers were in some sense the agents of God. From this it followed that kingship, like fatherhood, was a divine institution to which resistance was not merely impolitic but sinful. Ideas of Divine Right were, it is true, becoming increasingly difficult to justify in intellectual terms. In the later decades of this period particularly, they could seldom be openly asserted with the conviction which had been possible in the sixteenth century and much of the seventeenth. Indeed the years immediately before 1789 saw in some of the greatest European monarchies (most notably in Prussia) a growing demand for the drawing up of fundamental laws which would prevent the ruler from behaving in an arbitrary manner, particularly by increasing the importance of legal institutions. Among ordinary people almost everywhere, however, the idea of monarchy had still great emotive power. The ruler continued to enjoy, unless he were unusually vicious or unlucky, a respect which sometimes verged on worship. One of the Russian admirers of Peter I actually hung the Tsar's picture among the holy ikons in his house and burnt candles before it. Few things in the history of the eighteenth century, indeed, are more significant than the unquestioning support which the Russian monarchy continued to receive from its subjects in spite of the wild vicissitudes of intrigue and revolution through which it passed.[2] Even the wars and internal reforms of Peter I, bitterly unpopular as they were with great masses of his people, could not eradicate the feeling that the Tsar was, in some ultimate sense, the father and protector of the ordinary Russian.

The institution of monarchy thus dominated the political horizon, whether it was thought of in terms of Divine Right or merely as a secular institution guaranteeing civil peace and security. Republican theories were never a serious factor in the politics of any major European State during this period. The 'republicanism' of the great merchants of Amsterdam or the nobles and gentry of Poland was in no sense a system of ideas. It was rather a façade behind which classes and individuals with a vested interest in weak and decentralized government could entrench themselves, and also a mere mechanical adherence to established practices and institutions. The ideology of republicanism aroused some interest; but it was thought of in terms of ancient history rather than contemporary politics, in terms of the world of Lycurgus, Solon and Pericles rather than that of Louis XV, Frederick II or Catherine II. Genuine republican feeling, in so far as it existed at all in the major States, was a nostalgia or very occasionally an aspiration, never a programme.

The great monarchies of eighteenth-century Europe, like its administrative systems, can be roughly classified into groups. Russia and to a lesser extent Prussia are at one extreme, Great

Britain at the other. France, Spain and the Habsburg dominions occupy intermediate positions. Of Russia and Prussia little need be said, for there, as has been seen (see p. 138) the administrative system was the real constitution. In autocratic States such as these limits to the authority of the monarch were imposed by the efficiency of the bureaucracy and the strength of the army rather than by political institutions capable of opposing him. But without political institutions enjoying some real power it is difficult to have political conflict or political life in any but a very narrow sense of the term. In Russia such institutions did not exist. In Prussia provincial estates continued; but even before the accession of Frederick William I in 1713 most of their functions had been lost to the permanent officials of the centralized royal government. It can thus be argued that Russia and Prussia have in the eighteenth century a very important and interesting administrative history but little real political, still less constitutional, history. In Russia there were not even formal rules regulating the succession to the throne until 1796, while Peter I, in an exercise of uncontrolled personal power unparalleled in any other monarch of the period, had in 1722 assumed the right to bequeath the throne to a successor of his own choice. In both Russia and Prussia, though much more in the former, can be seen struggles between competing ministers for royal favour and support. In both a change of ruler or minister often had drastic repercussions, particularly on the conduct of foreign policy. Thus the death of Catherine I of Russia in 1727 and the changes it produced in Russian policy in the Baltic brought about a reconciliation with Britain after a long period of antagonism; the death in 1762 of the Empress Elizabeth meant Russia's immediate withdrawal from the Seven Years War; and the accession to the throne of Frederick II was an essential preliminary to the Prussian attack on Silesia in 1740. In both Russia and Prussia the dependence of the government on a single class, a landowning service nobility, was complete. In both public opinion of a modern kind scarcely existed during this period. In both therefore it is difficult to speak of political life or political problems except in a limited and rudimentary sense.

At the other extreme stood Great Britain. Here too the monarchy was central to the political life of the country; but it was a monarchy to which the rest of Europe offered no parallel. Its powers were wide. The government was still the king's government: the monarch retained great influence over the administration and to the end of the century expected to have a say, even a dominant say, in the making of policy. In particular the degree of negative control he could exert over the actions of the government, his ability to obstruct change, remained important until well after the end of this period. In 1801 and 1807 ministries fell from power because of the obstinate resistance of George III to the grant of equal political rights to Catholics. Moreover there were certain branches of the governmental machine and certain aspects of policy on which the king was considered to have a special right to make his views heard. Such were the army, in which both George I and George II took a strong personal interest, and foreign policy, about which as a rule few ministers knew or cared very much. The king also retained a considerable range of prerogative powers, those inherent in the office of king and not conferred on him by legislation or the common law. Of these some, such as those of creating peers and making promotions in the armed forces, could have very real political importance. Parliament, moreover, was open to considerable royal influence, since a large proportion of its members, both in the House of Lords and the House of Commons, held offices, pensions or contracts awarded by the Crown. An effort to exclude office-holders of this type from the House of Commons was made, with no great success, by the Act of Settlement of 1701. A more thoroughgoing attempt to reduce the parliamentary influence of the Crown by the 'Economical Reform' legislation of 1782 was little more effective. Also throughout this period some members of the House of Commons, though their numbers steadily decreased, owed their election to the influence which the Treasury and Admiralty were able to exert over certain constituencies. The exercise of electoral influence of this kind, by individuals as well as by the government, was made possible by the fact that most of the members representing boroughs, who made up over four-fifths of the House of Commons, were elected by very small numbers of voters. The county members and those who sat for the few boroughs in which the franchise was reasonably wide were normally the most independent of eighteenth-century MPs; but they were in a minority. The extent to which the Crown could control the composition of Parliament was, however, habitually exaggerated by contemporaries, at least from the 1760s onwards.

The House of Commons was far from being a genuinely representative body, but it was not the mere tool of the king. It was rather a kind of oligarchy, with a strong hereditary element in its composition. It is important also to remember that a post or pension given to a member could be a reward for past services as well as a means of securing future ones.

The Hanoverian monarchy could also draw on a more profound and lasting source of strength than any of these. This was the very widespread feeling (at least in Parliament: public opinion normally tended to be suspicious of ministerial projects) that the king and his ministers had a right to the support of all loyal and patriotic subjects. In particular it was almost universally agreed, at least until near the end of this period, that it was wrong for any group of politicians to unite to offer systematic and continuous opposition to the government. A 'formed opposition' of this kind was frowned on even by professional politicians; and this feeling explains the efforts of the opposition to group themselves round some discontented member of the royal family and thus acquire a kind of respectability. Thus the death in 1751 of the Prince of Wales, who had long been on bad terms with his father, led to a virtual collapse for the time being of all political opposition. In other words monarchy was, in Britain as almost everywhere else in Europe, a genuinely popular institution. It retained its popularity even though none of the Hanoverian kings was an inspiring personality and none, with the possible exception of George I, a man of much intelligence. In any political conflict the king always tended, so far as the ordinary man was concerned, to be given the benefit of the doubt. No government which was known to enjoy the support of the Crown was defeated in a general election until well into the nineteenth century.

Nevertheless the real power of the monarchy in Great Britain declined during the three generations which followed the revolution of 1688–89. In the first place its prerogatives were considerably reduced by legislation. The Declaration of Right of 1689 abolished the power claimed by James II to suspend the operation of any law, and to some extent the power which he had also claimed to exempt individuals or groups from the operation of certain laws. Five years later the Triennial Act imposed a limit of three years on the life of any Parliament (it was raised to seven years by the Septennial Act of 1716). It thus became impossible for any king in future to prolong indefinitely the life of a complaisant House of Commons, as Charles II had done with the 'Cavalier Parliament' of 1661–79. More fundamentally, the Act of Settlement of 1701, by asserting the right of Parliament to decide the succession to the throne, struck a decisive blow at the mystique of absolute hereditary monarchy still so widely accepted in many parts of the continent.

Moreover under William III, who was a foreigner, and Anne, who was a woman and a stupid one, the influence of Parliament over foreign policy grew rapidly. The long struggle with France in 1689–1713 meant an unprecedented raising of money for government purposes by methods such as the levying of a land-tax and the creation of a funded debt. This could be achieved only through Parliament. As a result, from the end of the seventeenth century onwards both Houses increasingly demanded to be informed about the negotiations with foreign States which made necessary the taxation and borrowing to which they were being asked to agree. The position in this respect remained more or less the same in the eighteenth century. To speak of Parliamentary control of foreign policy would be quite misleading. Nevertheless the influence of Parliament in this respect could be considerable and the need to give it at least a certain amount of information about foreign affairs could hardly be avoided.

Thus the generation 1690–1720 saw a considerable transference of real power from the King to Parliament, partly as a result of specific acts of legislation and partly because of the enormous changes in the country's fiscal system and relationship to Europe which occurred in these years.

The next four decades saw a slow but fairly steady erosion of royal power. This was produced not so much by Parliamentary aggression as by the personal characters of George I and George II. The former, a middle-aged German prince at his accession, was always more interested in Hanover, and more at home there, than in England. George II was essentially a weak and second-rate man. The result was a slow leakage of power, to individual ministers and the new and still half-formed institution of the Cabinet rather than to Parliament itself. Under George III there was, in a sense, an effort to restore and increase the authority of the Crown. The king did not attempt to achieve this by over-throwing or even modifying the constitution, for which he had a sincere and perhaps exaggerated respect. Rather he asserted and tried to use effectively in the 1760s and 1770s powers which he undoubtedly possessed in theory but which under his predecessors had begun to be whittled away in practice. In particular he demanded the right to choose his own ministers, who were to be responsible to him alone, and to exercise an effective supervision over the workings of the machinery of government. During the long ministry of Lord North (1770–82) he seemed for a time to have achieved this objective. But his efforts to regain the ground which the monarchy had lost were stultified by Britain's defeat in the War of American Independence. They also aroused much antagonism; and the last years of the war saw a determined effort by the king's opponents to reduce his influence over Parliament and the political life of the country. Public discontent at the defeats Britain had suffered, coupled with resentment of the unrepresentative character of the House of Commons, helped to produce in 1779–80 a movement of an almost revolutionary kind. The County Associations which were then formed to demand a widening of the suffrage and a redistribution of Parliamentary seats, and the General Association, a substitute Parliament, or anti-Parliament, in which some of them proposed to combine, seemed for a time to threaten drastic and violent constitutional changes. In the event the movement collapsed quite quickly in the summer of 1780, largely because there was no sustained demand for such changes in the country as a whole. Nevertheless the monarchy did not escape the crisis unscathed. The 'Economical Reform' programme of 1782 was the most determined attack on the power of the Crown since 1641. Its practical effect was not very great; but it began an attack on what radicals later came to call the 'old corruption', the network of sinecures and jobbery which still played a large role in British political life.

Englishmen thought of the internal politics of their country in the eighteenth century largely in what had now become the traditional terms of a dialogue, usually though not always amicable, between king and Parliament. Almost imperceptibly, however, the dialogue was now being transformed into a general conversation by the emergence of new and immensely important institutions – the Cabinet and the political parties.

The development of the Cabinet is one of the most obscure and difficult aspects of British history in this period. By about 1740 and probably earlier a definite distinction had emerged between the 'formal Cabinet', a relatively large body which included a number of holders of great court and ceremonial offices, and the 'effective Cabinet', a much smaller and more compact group of ministers. The former met rarely and for purely formal purposes. The latter, an active body including the heads of all the great departments of State, was in fact the 'government'. However even the 'effective Cabinet' was not during this period a real political organism. Some of its members were experienced professional administrators. Others were leaders or representatives of the small and competing groups into which Parliament was normally divided. Their allegiance was thus to the king, who had appointed them and was the source of their power, and to their followers, for whom they sought offices, titles and pensions, rather than to their colleagues or to any leader amongst them. Cabinets were therefore often divided by personal rivalries – the schisms in those led by Sir Robert Walpole (First Lord of the Treasury and Chancellor of the Exchequer, 1721–42) are a good example – and this lack of unity tended to increase the influence the king could exert over individual ministers and the Cabinet as a whole. In particular the whole idea of a Prime Minister was looked on with the gravest suspicion. Walpole, who has been traditionally and perhaps wrongly regarded as the first British Prime Minister, always took pains to deny that he occupied such a position. As late as the 1760s the ideal government, in the eyes not merely of George III but of the great majority of his subjects, was one consisting of a number of heads of departments, each performing his task efficiently and responsible only to the king and Parliament. Both the unity of the Cabinet and its independence of the king began to be unmistakably and effectively asserted only after the end of this period, during the long premiership of the younger William Pitt (1783–1801).

In the long run the most fundamental check to the power of the British monarchy was that imposed by the growth of increasingly organized and coherent political parties. It was these which, by limiting the king's freedom of manœuvre, in the end destroyed his ability to play a great role in politics. At the end of this period matters had by no means gone as far as this, for the growth of political parties in eighteenth-century England was curiously erratic. Under Queen Anne parties of a modern kind did not exist; but it is possible to speak without gross inaccuracy of Parliament and the politically active part of the nation as being divided for the most part into Whigs and Tories. Between these two groups, each including within itself many sub-groups, there was on most of the great issues of the day a fairly clear division. The Whigs favoured the accession to the throne, on the queen's death, of the Elector of Hanover, the later George I. They demanded that England should give effective support on the continent to the Dutch and the Emperor against Louis XIV during the War of the Spanish Succession (1702–13). They were in general tolerant in their attitude to the Protestant Dissenters. Some of the more extreme Tories, by contrast, flirted with the idea of restoring the son of James II, the Catholic Stuart king deposed in 1688, while most of them demanded that the British war effort be concentrated on a mainly naval and colonial struggle against France. Above all they were much more aggressively Anglican than the Whigs.

Peace with France in 1713, the accession of George I in the following year, and the easy suppression of a revolt in Scotland of the Jacobites (the partisans of the exiled Stuarts) in 1715, changed this position completely. Excluded from power by the new king who understandably distrusted them, discredited by their connexion with the defeated Jacobites, the Tories as a significant Parliamentary group soon ceased to exist. In the middle decades of the century every leading figure in British politics would, if pressed, have described himself as a Whig. Parliament by then had become atomized, divided into small and continually fluctuating groups or 'connexions', which were usually formed around some leader or based on family or regional relationships. This lack of real parties during the period of Whig supremacy in 1714–60 was made possible by the lack during these years of real issues of principle around which opinion could crystallize and in terms of which politicians could arrange themselves. With the Hanoverians secure on the throne (especially after the defeat of a second and more serious Jacobite revolt in Scotland in 1745–46), with the grant of a considerable degree of *de facto* toleration to the Dissenters, the questions which had dominated internal politics in the reign of Anne appeared to have been settled. Nothing now remained to contend for but the possession of office: politics were reduced to a struggle between 'ins' and 'outs'.

In the 1760s the position began to change again. Once more genuine issues of principle arose. The career of the demagogue John Wilkes aroused political passions fiercer than any seen for half a century, passions which were often rooted in real political idealism. It was his publication in 1763 of what the courts decided to be a seditious libel on George III which led to the judicial decision that general warrants were illegal (see p. 136). His election on three separate occasions as MP for Middlesex in 1768–69, and the repeated refusals of the House of Commons to admit him as a member, did much to stimulate in London the current of political radicalism which was later to run so strongly there. Simultaneously the far more important question of relations with the American colonies, and of the moral justification of the demands which the mother-country was now making on them, roused intense feeling and stimulated widespread political discussion, much of it at a relatively high intellectual level. This injection of principles and ideas into British politics ended the easygoing cynicism which had been marked in the generation before 1760. Political groupings now began to emerge which more closely resembled modern parties than anything hitherto known. The Whig group led by the Marquis of Rockingham provided, in the 1760s and 1770s, the first example of this; while many of the ideas for which it stood inspired the somewhat similar group led by Charles James Fox in the 1780s and 1790s. More important, the younger Pitt, during his long tenure of office, laid the foundations of the nineteenth-century Tory party. By the end of this period the political groupings which were to carry out the great changes of the next century in Britain, though very far from having assumed their late-Victorian form, were slowly evolving.

It is easy with the advantages of hindsight to think of the political structure of eighteenth-century England, with all its defects, as the best in Europe. It is necessary, therefore, to remember that for most of the century this admiration was not felt by most foreigners. Not until the 1760s did Britain begin to live down her reputation (based on the violence of the period 1640–1714) as an inveterately turbulent and factious country where almost anything could happen. 'The people are really richer here than anywhere else,' wrote a French observer in 1747, 'and they partly at least owe this advantage to the wisdom of their laws. But amidst all this abundance, the nation is so disunited and rent by continual factions, that it seems at every moment to be threatened with the horrors of civil wars. . . . A man tortured by a continual fever with exacerbations, to me appears the image of the English government, constantly disturbed by parties, and

frequently altered by revolutions.'[3] It was the victories won
during the Seven Years War of 1756–63 much more than any
intrinsic merits of the British constitution which forced a revision
of disparaging estimates of this kind.

The French monarchy, like the French administrative system,
occupied during this period a position intermediate between the
extremes to be found in Russia and Prussia on the one hand and
in Great Britain on the other. The kings of France possessed in
theory great personal power. They were the supreme embodi-
ment of sovereignty; the army owed obedience to them personally; the debts of the State were their personal debts; they could
override or anticipate the decisions of any court of law. Louis XV
was stating what had, at least until very recently, been a
commonplace, when he claimed in 1766 that 'in my person alone
resides sovereign power . . . I alone possess complete and untram-
melled legislative authority.' Even the most extreme partisans of
absolute monarchy were prepared to admit that there were
theoretical limits to the power of the king. He could not change
the monarchical nature of the government or the hereditary nature
of the monarchy. Nor could he disregard the Salic Law which
forbade the accession to the throne of a woman. It was agreed,
moreover, that he must obey divine law by doing justice and
showing mercy and that, at least beyond a certain point, he had
no right to infringe his subjects' property rights or their personal
liberty. These restrictions, however, were vague and impossible
to define accurately; and the plenitude of royal power was thus
little affected by them. Most important of all there was no individual or institution in France with any right to override or
control the actions of the king.

Such was the position in theory. In practice it was strikingly
different. At certain points in the machine of government the
power of the king was still great. His ministers depended on his
favour for their continuance in office. They were thus subject to
effective control if the king chose to exercise it. The sudden fall
of an able and apparently powerful minister such as the Duc de
Choiseul in 1770 showed that even in the last years of the lethargic
and indifferent Louis XV this control was real. But it was a negative control. 'Each (minister) is absolute master in his department', wrote the Emperor Joseph II to his mother after a visit to
Paris in 1777, 'but fears to be, not controlled, but displaced, by
the sovereign. . . . The king is absolute only in his power to pass

from one slavery to another. He can change his ministers; but unless he is a transcendent genius he can never be master of the conduct of affairs.'[4] Lower down the administrative hierarchy royal influence was much less effective. In particular the fact that so many officials had bought their offices and thus made them their personal property (see p. 126) made it very hard to dismiss them, since the government could seldom afford to refund the purchase price. The lower and even the middle ranks of the bureaucracy were to a considerable extent decentralized and independent of royal power. As time went on their responsiveness to local pressures and needs, as opposed to those of the central government, tended if anything to increase. Even the intendants, who had been under Colbert and his successors the greatest of all agencies of administrative centralization, showed tendencies of this kind in the last decades of the period. 'For long [before the revolution of 1789]', wrote a contemporary, 'the intendants, directed by public opinion, sought rather to distinguish themselves by their care for the people and by works of public utility, than by their obedience to ministerial wishes.'[5] Some, such as Turgot in the *généralité* of Limoges and Orceau de Fontette in that of Caen, were much in advance of the central government in their attitude to the areas they administered. An able and strongminded intendent could enjoy during the last decade of the *ancien régime* a remarkable degree of autonomy and independent initiative.

Moreover the French monarchy found itself, in the generation before 1789, faced by increasing opposition from the *parlements* and to a lesser extent from the estates, normally dominated by the nobility, which still existed in one or two provinces. In September 1715, immediately after the death of Louis XIV, the *Parlement* of Paris had restored to it by the Regent, the Duc d'Orléans, the right of remonstrance which allowed it to impede royal legislation. This it at once began to use to hamper the government's efforts to cope with the desperate financial situation. Proposals to suppress unnecessary offices, to fund part of the state debt and to debase the currency, all had to face stubborn resistance. This increasingly impossible situation was brought to a head when the *Parlement* was temporarily exiled to Pontoise in 1720 and threatened with the creation of new judicial institutions which would take over much of its work. Such measures brought it to heel for the time being; but this was to be the last occasion before the end of the old monarchy when the government won a real victory over this increasingly dangerous opponent. On a number of later occasions – in 1749, 1753, 1771–74 and 1788 – the device of exiling the *Parlement* to a provincial town was resorted to; but every one of these struggles was ended by concessions made solely or mainly by the king and his ministers. From the moment its powers were revived in 1715 the *Parlement* was a strong supporter of the Jansenist minority in the French Church (see pp. 451–3). From the 1730s onwards, therefore, it was involved in intermittent but sometimes very bitter disputes with the government, which was notably more orthodox in its attitude to religious matters and often overbearing and insensitive in its efforts to have the papal bull *Unigenitus* (see p. 453) registered by the *Parlement*. In 1749–51, with the support of the Church and much of the nobility, the *Parlement* was able to defeat a series of efforts by Machault d'Arnouville, the Controller-General of Finance, to impose a tax of one-twentieth on all incomes. This victory of the privileged was one of the decisive events of the century in France. The struggle over Machault's proposals was fought with a bitterness which for several years partially paralysed the workings of government and led to widespread speculations of imminent revolution. The defeat of the government in this conflict condemned it, irretrievably as events were to show, to growing financial weakness and vulnerability. This, made worse by the war of 1756–63 and catastrophic by that of 1778–83, was to destroy it in 1787–89.

Moreover by the 1750s the provincial *parlements*, hitherto relatively inactive, were increasingly following the lead of that of Paris. The *Parlement* of Bordeaux, for example, gave forcible expression in a remonstrance of May 1757 to the idea that it was the guardian of the 'ancient and fundamental laws' of France and could and should not register any legislation which infringed these. In 1763 that of Toulouse placed the Governor of Languedoc under arrest merely because he had done his duty by attempting to collect new taxation ordered by the government; while for several years in the 1760s Brittany was convulsed by a violent conflict between its Governor, the Duc d'Aiguillon, and the *Parlement* of Rennes, over the same issue. In 1783–84 the *Parlement* of Bordeaux was able, after a struggle, to force the removal from office of an intendant who had tried to reform the system of *corvées* (forced labour, mainly on road-building) in the area of its jurisdiction. All this to modern eyes looks like, and indeed very often was, mere selfish defence of local and sectional interests. Yet it is important to realise that in the last decades of the old régime in France the *parlements* were often expressing more or less accurately what public opinion there was on the issues at stake, and that they had frequently widespread popular support for their attitudes. They were, after all, the only secular institutions which could claim some formal independence of the Crown and the nearest approach to a constitutional opposition which France could muster. This meant that in spite of their class selfishness and legalistic pedantry they were widely regarded as the defenders of liberty and established rights (the two were still largely synonymous) against royal autocracy and 'ministerial despotism'. This function they performed only in a limited and highly conservative way; but there was hardly any other institution in France which could perform it at all. They could therefore claim a good deal of genuine popular backing; and their power, or at least their powers of obstruction, survived almost as long as the monarchy itself. In 1771 the Chancellor, Maupeou, exiled the *Parlement* of Paris once more and abolished the offices held by its members. He thus, in the face of furious opposition, cleared the ground for the drastic overhaul of the fiscal system which was now more essential than ever. Three years later, however, he was dismissed on the accession of Louis XVI and the powers of the *parlements* restored. For the next thirteen years they offered no really serious opposition to government policies: but their refusal in 1787 to accept proposals for important new taxes and tax reforms was a crucial step in the destruction of the old regime in France.

The generation before the Revolution saw not only the opposition to royal power offered by the *parlements* and their allies but a growth in criticism of the monarchical régime of a more fundamental and ultimately more dangerous kind. Demands were now being made that the people, or at least the educated and property-owning classes, be given more effective means of making their wishes felt. Suggestions that some representative element be added to the government, an idea which very few people would have taken seriously before the 1750s, were now being put forward. In 1763 the *Cours des Aides*, one of the chief legal and financial institutions of the monarchy, asked for the convocation of the States-General (a national representative body, organized by social orders, which had originated in the later

Middle Ages and had not met since 1614). In 1775 the Physiocrat Dupont de Nemours drew up an elaborate scheme for a hierarchy of local and provincial representative assemblies with a national one as its culminating point. Three years later the Controller-General Necker created such an assembly, one-third of whose members were to be nominated by the king and the rest elected, for the province of Berry. A similar one was set up in 1779 in Haute Guienne; and in 1787, in the last desperate efforts to save the old régime in its death agony, no fewer than nineteen were established in *géneralités* throughout the country.

Underlying and largely explaining the increasingly difficult position of the French monarchy during this period were the personal characters of the monarchs concerned. Louis XV became King of France in 1715 as a child of five. His reign thus began at a moment when, as a result of defeat and financial stress, the difficulties which now faced the monarchy were beginning to be all too visible. The Regency period (1713–23), during which the government was controlled by the able if dissolute Duc d'Orléans, saw a violent reaction against the rigidity and authoritarianism of the régime of Louis XIV. The most striking political expression of this reaction was the establishment of the system known as *polysynodie* (government through councils or committees in place of Secretaries of State) in 1716–18. The experiment was short-lived and a failure; but it suggested that the young king might not be able to reckon as a matter of course on wielding all the powers of his great predecessor. It was, however, his own personality at least as much as the difficulties of the position he had inherited which prevented his following in the footsteps of Louis XIV. Served by a chief minister of some ability, Cardinal Fleury (1726–43), and a more able Controller-General, Orry (1730–45), he remained personally popular until the middle of the century; but the limitations of his character had already begun to show themselves. The sexual irregularities of which biographers have made so much were not in themselves important or unusual for a ruler of that age. The charge which the historian must bring against him is not that he was vicious but that he was timid, selfish and worst of all lazy. Apart from the system of secret diplomacy under his personal control which he developed after 1745 and which served merely to complicate and frustrate the foreign policies carried on by his ministers through regular channels, he took little interest in the machinery of government. He exercised no effective supervision of the great departments of State. His unwillingness to face serious opposition, his tendency to seek an easy solution for every difficulty at the expense of the real interests of the monarchy, are well illustrated by his abandonment of Machault's taxation proposals of 1749. In the last years of his reign, embittered by external defeat and domestic unpopularity, he sank into a kind of sullen apathy. 'His lamentable reputation in history,' it has been said, 'derives less from what he did than from what he never tried to do. For him all evils were incurable.'[6] His last years saw in Maupeou's attack on the *parlements* a real effort to give the monarchy more freedom of action, and in the radical fiscal expedients of the Abbé Terray (Controller-General, 1770–74) a partially successful attempt to ease its financial position. Nevertheless as his reign drew to a close Louis was perhaps more hated and certainly more despised than any king of France for generations. He was, wrote a contemporary critic, 'A king whose death was . . . the triumph of the nation'.[7]

His grandson and successor Louis XVI was not the man to regain either the power or the popularity of the monarchy. Well-meaning and pious, he was of mediocre intelligence and inherited the timidity which had been one of Louis XV's greatest weaknesses. His recall of the *Parlement* of Paris within a few months of his accession, his failure to support his radically reforming Controller-General Turgot (1774–76), showed that he was no more able than his grandfather to withstand the opposition of the privileged groups. More serious still, during his reign the lack of contact and sympathy between ruler and people, already growing during the last two decades of the life of Louis XV, became more marked. Apart from a visit to Cherbourg in the 1780s to see the new harbour works there his movements were confined entirely to a group of royal châteaux in the neighbourhood of Paris. To the day of his death on the guillotine in January 1793 France remained to him an unknown land.

Like France, Spain and the Habsburg territories can be regarded as occupying an intermediate position in the spectrum of European monarchy in the eighteenth century. In each rulers were faced, in their efforts to create an efficient administrative machine, by stubborn opposition from privileged groups and institutions. In each they struggled with considerable success to overcome that opposition. In the explicit limits to their power which they had to accept in some of the areas they ruled (especially in Hungary and the Basque provinces) the Habsburgs and the Spanish Bourbons had something in common with the Hanoverians. On the other hand in the fact that they were not limited by any central representative institutions, and that they based their power largely on their armies and bureaucracies, they were in the main stream of continental absolutism.

It is above all in the general success of their rulers in improving the position of the monarchy that the history of Spain and the Habsburg lands differs, at least until the 1780s, from that of France. In both the challenge offered to royal authority by provincial particularism was far greater than in France. The importance of this factor in the Habsburg territories has already been mentioned (see p. 152). In Spain the struggle over the succession in 1702–13 had seen a prolonged effort by Catalonia and much of Aragon to throw off Castilian rule, an effort which drove them to support the Habsburg Archduke Charles against the eventually victorious Bourbon claimant to the throne, Philip V, grandson of Louis XIV. Throughout the century, moreover, the Basque provinces retained a remarkable degree of autonomy (notably the right not to be taxed without their consent) while the *cortes* (provincial estates) of Castile and Navarre continued to meet, though infrequently and ineffectively.

There were thus substantial obstacles in Spain and the Habsburg lands to the creation of an effective centralized absolutism, obstacles greater than those which existed in France. Yet the Habsburgs and Spanish Bourbons attacked and partially overcame them. They did not surrender to them as Louis XV and Louis XVI did to the opponents of monarchical power. It was only in October 1714 that Barcelona at last surrendered to Philip V after a long siege. Not until the following year, when Majorca was forced to submit, did armed resistance to him in Spain come to an end. As late as 1719 there was a plot to hand over the island of Ibiza in the Balearics to the British; but by then Catalan resentment of rule from Madrid, though still a factor of importance, was ceasing to be an immediate danger to national unity. The Basque provinces, though they could not be taxed at will, were persuaded by Philip and his successors to provide the monarchy with considerable sums in the form of free gifts (*servicios*). If the *cortes* of Navarre and Castile prolonged a phantom existence that of Aragon vanished for ever. Moreover a new drive towards *desertion*

adm   ganization by 1714
of tł   French model. This
invo   ral of Finance and a
nun   some system of councils   relied so heavily in the
pre   se, the Council of Castile
aloi   system of intendants on the
Fre   hea,   nough it did not survive for
lon   1749 with marked success. The new
ma   considerable defects, proved more effi-
cie   xible than the old.

I   tories also, as has been seen, a series of
able ministers backed by Maria Theresa, the greatest ruler of the
dynasty, created from the 1740s onwards a whole range of
important new organs of administration (see pp. 153–4). They
broke down to some extent, particularly in Bohemia, the former
administrative separatism of the provinces, and provided the
monarchy with an income far greater and an army far stronger
than it had ever possessed before.

Thus in Spain and the Habsburg provinces progress was made
in the creation of powerful monarchies and centralized administrations. In France this process was halted and even reversed. The
contrast cannot be explained entirely in terms of personalities;
nevertheless the characters of the rulers concerned were of great
importance in this connexion. In Spain the feebleness of the
melancholic Philip V was partially redeemed by the energy of his
masterful second wife, Elizabeth Farnese. Charles III was hard-
working, patriotic and conscientious, though intellectually unre-
markable. In the Habsburg States Maria Theresa displayed a
courage and tenacity equalled by very few eighteenth-century
rulers, while her son Joseph II, whatever his faults, did not lack
energy and public spirit. The strength of their personalities
partially explains the fact that Charles III was able to exert more
effective authority than any ruler of Spain for generations, and
that the powers of Maria Theresa were greater than those wielded
by any of her predecessors. The French monarchy under Louis
XVI was by contrast in many ways a shadow of what it had been
under Louis XIV. In an age of monarchy there was no substitute
for an able and energetic ruler.

It is often claimed that the government of many European

States in the generation or more before the French Revolution is distinguished from earlier practice by the existence of something called 'Enlightened Despotism'. How far is this claim justified? Clearly some rulers and ministers were being affected in the second half of the century by the complex and often conflicting currents which made up the great intellectual movement of the Enlightenment (see Chap. XV *passim*). In the 1760s the Physiocrats in France laid much of the ideological foundation for a new form of monarchy by popularizing ideas of a natural social order which could be easily discovered by the use of the human intelligence and which all unbiased men of goodwill must support. This natural harmony of interests, it seemed, could be most easily given political expression by an enlightened government, which must be the work of an enlightened monarch. In 1767 one of these thinkers, Lemercier de la Rivière, in his *L'Ordre naturel et essentiel des sociétés politiques* (1767), presented such a ruler as not legislating in any positive sense but merely declaring and applying fundamental laws which were immanent in the nature of things, in the structure of the world as it is and must be. In this capacity he was entitled to obedience from the subjects whose welfare he served. This concept of 'legal despotism' had for a time considerable importance, at least in intellectual circles. The belief, universal in the political thinking of the Enlightenment, that the best form of government is one in which the individual is subject to known and clearly expressed laws, ruled out the arbitrary and uncontrolled 'oriental despotism' which every thinker of the age agreed in rejecting. But it did not at all rule out the possibility of these laws being enunciated by an enlightened monarch. Such attitudes were an expression of the tendency of the age to produce simple, general answers to what in modern eyes seem highly complex and intractable problems. Underlying them was a widespread assumption that the principles of good government were clear, absolute and unchanging, that they could therefore be applied anywhere with relatively little modification. Even a Tatar Khan in the Crimea in the years before the Russian annexation of 1783–84 is said to have wished to rule in terms of 'enlightened' ideas.

The ideology of Enlightened Despotism, however, as it existed in the three or four decades before the French Revolution, was not the expression merely of intellectual forces. Underlying it was also a vein of genuine practicality. Despotism seemed, to the French writers who were much the most important source of this

type of thinking, to promise more rapid progress than was possible under balanced and 'mixed' régimes in which power was
widely distributed, such as that in Britain. What mattered, after
all, was the use made of power, rather than its formal institutional
aspects. The enlightened ruler must first of all laicize monarchy.
He must free himself from the control of any established church
and its priests and instead subordinate them to the State. As his
ministers he must take men of true enlightenment; great nobles
with an interest in maintaining a feudal past and its practices
should be kept at arms length. A monarch who behaved in this
way could rely on the support of many of the leading intellectuals
of the age, however despotic his power.

There were important figures of the Enlightenment who
distrusted and disliked any form of despotic rule. Side by side
with Voltaire and Kant, with their admiration of constructive and
public-spirited autocrats, were others such as Helvétius, Holbach,
Diderot and Rousseau, who refused to believe that this form of
rule, however 'enlightened', could do anything for the liberation
of the individual subject. Yet often such writers, while
denouncing despotic or absolute rule in principle, were willing to
take advantage of the practical benefits it might bring. Turgot,
for example, though he denounced any form of despotism, was
himself very authoritarian in his methods during his brief term
as Controller-General of Finances in 1774–76; and even Rousseau
was opposed only to the despotism of individuals, not of groups
or collectivities. Sometimes, as with Kant, a period of more or
less authoritarian government under an enlightened prince was
seen as a necessary preliminary to the introduction of a more
liberal and representative form of rule. The intellectuals of the
Enlightenment showed, in general, remarkably little interest in
the structure of government provided it was pursuing what they
saw as the correct policies, those directed towards greater tolerance and efficiency and the happiness and welfare of mankind as
a whole. It is important to remember, moreover, that most
eighteenth-century reformers saw freedom in largely negative
terms. To them it meant primarily the sweeping away of restrictions and prohibitions, on particular forms of trade, on the free
choice of a profession or occupation, on the practice of minority
forms of religion. For this essentially destructive task, this
necessary clearing of the ground so that greater liberty for the
individual could be obtained naturally and more or less spon-

taneously, an absolute ruler seemed well suited. The most impressive contemporary tribute to the idea of enlightened despotism,
therefore, is the number of idealists who accepted that only
through this form of government had their ideals any chance of
realization. 'It is a humiliating thought, but true,' wrote one of
them, the educational reformer J. H. Pestalozzi, 'that any advance
in the good leadership of people must proceed from the cabinets
of monarchs'; and he himself acted on this thought by offering
his services to the Habsburg emperors Joseph II and Leopold II.

The difficulty is to relate this body of theory to what rulers,
ministers and officials in fact did in specific situations. Clearly it
was possible to have great administrative, fiscal and even social
progress under a ruler who was not personally at all in sympathy
with the Enlightenment. The Empress Maria Theresa presided
over a transformation of the Habsburg hereditary territories
which was the greatest achievement of its kind anywhere in
Europe during this period. Without her work the power of the
Habsburgs could hardly have survived in the predatory State
system of eighteenth-century Europe. Yet in intellectual and to
some extent in practical terms her attitudes were overwhelmingly
conservative. She was opposed to toleration of Protestants and
Jews in her dominions. She wished for good relations with the
Papacy, which was the target for the scorn and hostility of almost
every leading figure of the Enlightenment from Voltaire downwards. She regretted the dissolution in 1773 of the Society of
Jesus. She wished so far as possible to respect in her dominions
the rights of the provincial estates, the greatest bastions of resistance to change. Yet the permanent achievements of her reign were
not surpassed by any other ruler of the age. In many States, moreover, efforts at more or less enlightened reform were inspired by
history and tradition rather than by abstract ideas. They were
rooted in the necessities of the countries concerned and in earlier
efforts to meet these necessities, not in the mere words of intellectuals, however plausible. Thus in Spain the reforming work of
Charles III and his ministers was a reflection of well-marked
national traditions. The idea of radical change in terms of a few
basic ideas runs through many of the proposals for reform of
Spanish government and society made in the seventeenth and
early eighteenth centuries as well as those produced by the age
of the Enlightenment. In particular the regalism, the desire to
assert royal rights over the Church and Church property, which

was a notable feature of this movement of reform, had deep roots in the earlier history of Spain. It is note-worthy that of all Charles's ministers the one who most forcibly asserted rights of this kind, Pedro Rodriquez Campomanes, was also the one least influenced by 'enlightened' ideas, which in Spain were very much a foreign, overwhelmingly French, import. For all his regalist attitudes Campomanes showed the sincerity of his Catholicism by dying a member of the third order of the Franciscans.

Moreover, even of the rulers who were more strongly and self-consciously influenced than Maria Theresa and Charles III by the attitudes and assumptions of the Enlightenment none, with the exception of Catherine II, regarded himself as absolute in any complete sense. None wished or attempted to destroy all the institutions which acted as possible centres of opposition to their reforming efforts. None, with the possible exception of the Grand Duke Leopold in Tuscany, dreamed of challenging the principle of social and political inequality on which all European society rested.

None of this means that the element of intellectual conviction was negligible in the policies of many of the rulers of Europe in the generation before the French Revolution. It is clear that the greatest of them had beliefs about their relationship to and responsibility for their subjects different from those of their seventeenth- or early eighteenth-century predecessors. The welfare of those they ruled and still more the greatness of the State (now clearly separated from the ruler and the ruling dynasty) dominated their calculations as never before; indeed an ideal of State service was the one thing which they had in common. This ideal was some-times expressed by partisans of Enlightened Despotism with almost religious fervour. 'The State', wrote one, 'is a lifeless mass, to which the monarch first gives life; a machine without motion, which the monarch first sets moving and to whose mechanism he gives reality . . . the monarch lives for the State and the State lives through him.'[8] Attitudes of this kind meant that purely dynastic considerations played strikingly little part in the thinking of most of these rulers. Family feelings and any sense of monarchs as a divinely blessed group had in general little hold on them. In Prussia Frederick II was often on bad terms with his younger brothers, whom he treated with great severity; and he disliked and neglected his nephew and heir. His lack of family feeling and unquestioning assumption that it must always be sacrificed to

187

necessities of State emerge clearly from his political testaments of 1752 and 1768, the most revealing of all statements of his basic ideas. In Russia Catherine II, after conniving at the overthrow and murder of her husband in 1762, was on continuously bad terms with her son and heir, Paul, who feared and hated her and whom in the last two decades of her reign she scarcely ever saw. In the Habsburg territories Joseph II treated other members of the ruling family with a studied rudeness which shocked contemporaries: in the 1780s he deeply antagonized his younger brother and successor Leopold, Grand Duke of Tuscany, by pressing for the merging of the Grand Duchy with the hereditary lands of the monarchy. The history of every European dynasty is full of rivalries and antagonisms; such things could flourish very well without ideas of enlightened government to give impetus to them. Nevertheless there is little doubt that in the cases of Frederick and Joseph at least a feeling that an enlightened ruler ought to be above merely personal and family considerations, that it was his duty to sacrifice them ruthlessly on the altar of the State, was a factor in their behaviour to their own blood relations. The contrast with the dynasticism of the age of Louis XIV is a striking and significant one.

No ruler of a large State, however, could afford the luxury of uncritical adherence to an ideology, even one so loosely defined as that of enlightened government. All of them, to only slightly varying extents, were inevitably the prisoners of history. For all of them limits to possible action were set by economic, social, political or military necessities which were in the main the legacy of the past. Completely 'enlightened' government was a goal which, even had they wished to attain it, the internal complexities of their own countries and the external pressure of others placed beyond their reach. Only small States, freed from the burden of playing a leading role in international affairs and often more homogeneous economically and socially than their more powerful neighbours, could afford to apply the political panaceas of the Enlightenment with some approach to thoroughness. Thus the only European ruler to introduce, even on a restricted scale, the *impôt unique* (a single tax on land) which was perhaps the most important practical innovation advocated by the Physiocrats, was the Margrave Charles Frederick of Baden. (The experiment was a failure.) With the great exception of Joseph II the rulers of the major States in the later eighteenth century were not prepared to face the problems involved in pushing through really radical changes of this kind.

Frederick II of Prussia is of all the major rulers of the century the one about whose stature historians have disagreed most violently. There is no doubt that to his contemporaries he seemed, for much of his reign, the outstanding example of a modern and enlightened ruler. By raising Prussia from the position of a second-rate State to that of at least a kind of great power, and by achieving this with very limited physical resources, he provided the supreme illustration of what might be accomplished by an intelligent and dedicated ruler inspired by enlightened ideas. The decade after 1745, when the successful struggle for Silesia, which had transformed Prussia's international standing, was followed by internal consolidation and some limited domestic reform, saw his reputation at its height. In these years Frederick gave Europe its first real example of enlightened despotism in action. Moreover throughout his life he continued to stress very heavily in his voluminous writings the moral obligation of the ruler to use his powers selflessly, unsparing of his own peace and comfort, for the good of the State. From his *Anti-Machiavel* (1741) to his *Essai sur les formes de gouvernement* (1781) he expressed a view of monarchy which was utilitarian, secular, antidynastic and untraditional. The people, by a tacit and irrevocable act of delegation, had handed over their powers to the monarch. This surrender was legitimized only if the monarch devoted himself unsparingly to the good of the state and his subjects. Indeed he alone could see clearly what that good was; for in virtue of his position he was impartial and disinterested as no mere section of society, no corporate body or representative assembly, ever could be.

This austere doctrine meant for Frederick a lifetime of toil and effort: no monarch in the history of Europe has worked so hard over so long a period to meet obligations which were essentially self-imposed. It was also a view of monarchy quite compatible with a deep contempt for the subjects whom the ruler served from above and whose interests he safeguarded with such jealous care, often against their own misguided inclinations. Frederick himself showed this contempt, in writing and conversation, with an often brutal lack of restraint, especially as he became soured by decades of effort and struggle. The humanitarian side of the Enlightenment, the emphasis it laid on making the ordinary man happier through religious toleration, economic progress and education, always made a genuine appeal to him. But the necessities of the State, its imperative demands for physical security and therefore for military strength and administrative efficiency, took precedence over everything else. To these the happiness of individuals (not least of Frederick himself) was always sacrificed without hesitation. The idea of the humane, creatively enlightened State, which cared for ordinary men and their development, was in his thinking always overshadowed by that of the power-State, Spartan, demanding and careless of the feelings or immediate interests of the individual. Duty and service, not freedom or happiness, are the notes which reverberate through the history of eighteenth-century Prussia. Yet it must be stressed that in the eyes of Frederick and most of his contemporaries his rule was never a crude despotism. On the contrary, the Prussian State was seen as having been turned consciously, by a great act of will on the part of its ruler, on to paths which were constructive and enlightened. Justice, religious toleration and codification of the laws; economic progress through internal colonization and a great variety of government measures; intellectual life, above all through Frederick's own example as a writer and the symbol of the Enlightenment enthroned – all these seemed to be served by his rule.

Yet when we turn to Frederick in action, to the administration of Prussia during his forty-six years on its throne, the ambiguity of his position becomes fully clear. Throughout his reign he trod, where day-to-day rule was concerned, in paths already marked out for him by his father, to whom the Enlightenment had meant nothing. In spite of the profound dissimilarities between father and son, and the bitter personal conflicts between them, Frederick II remained always the executor of Frederick William I. 'Only his care,' he wrote of his father, 'his untiring work, his scrupulously just policies, his great and admirable thriftiness and the strict discipline he introduced into the army which he himself had created, made possible the achievements I have so far accomplished.'[9] Frederick was fully conscious, as perhaps his father had never been, of the State as an entity completely distinct from the person of the ruler, its greatest servant. Nevertheless he made few fundamental changes in the system of government he had inherited, and in one important respect, his active and explicit preference for aristocratic ministers and officials as against commoners, his reign sees a definite regression from what had preceded it (see above pp. 146–7). In economic life, in spite of a long series of efforts, little was achieved. Monopolistic trading companies, a state bank, efforts to stimulate industrial development; none of these had much success. The silk industry in which two million thalers were sunk (heavy investment for a poor country) produced goods of such poor quality that they were very difficult to sell. The porcelain industry, in which again much government money was sunk, was also a failure. Prussia remained, in spite of all Frederick could do, what the most severe of his modern critics has quite fairly called 'a backward, retarded, autocratic and sergeant-like (*feldwebelhaft*) economy'.[10] In cultural terms, again, it is easy to overrate what Frederick achieved. His flute-playing, the vast quantity of bad French poetry he wrote, his friendship with Voltaire (carefully advertised but when put to the test no more than skin deep) impressed many contemporaries and have impressed some historians. Yet they count for little when balanced against his blindness to the cultural ferment which was agitating educated Germany by the later decades of his reign and his ignorant contempt for most of the greatest German writers and scholars of the age. It is no accident that so many of the latter – Wieland, Winckelmann, Lessing, Gottsched – disliked both him and Prussia.

Frederick thus presents the paradox of a ruler who was sincerely attracted by many of the ideas of the Enlightenment, who voiced these ideas and advertised his adherence to them throughout his life, and yet whose policies in practice were hardly affected at all by the new intellectual currents of the age. He was, to be fair, in a position which left him little real freedom of action. Prussia, even after the territorial gains of his reign, was a relatively small and weak state surrounded by more powerful neighbours. Mere self-defence meant the fullest possible mobilization of all available resources. The king had, therefore, to command and manipulate his subjects with much of the harshness of a Prussian sergeant drilling new recruits. A more liberal regime, a greater degree of economic freedom, serious political experiment of any kind, even had Frederick ever desired such things, were luxuries too dangerous to be indulged in under these conditions. Moreover under his rule the extent to which Prussia was committed to Eastern Europe and had her centre of gravity east of the Elbe was markedly accentuated. The alliance of 1764 with Russia was a politic, even necessary, move after the frightening demonstration of her military power during the Seven Years War (see p. 300). Yet coupled with the seizure of Polish territory in 1772 it helped to emphasize Prussia's affinities with her eastern rather than her western neighbours. The deep ambiguities of the Prussian State as it existed in the nineteenth century, intellectually a part of Western Europe yet with a social and military structure much of which continually tended to align it with Russia, trace largely from Frederick's reign. He himself did not much value the small detached territories – Cleves, Mark, Ravensberg – which he ruled in the Rhineland. He discriminated against them in his tariff policies and would have been happy to exchange them for land in Pomerania, Saxony or Mecklenburg. In terms of his own situation and interests this attitude is perfectly understandable. Yet it illustrates once more how throughout his reign, in spite of his personal adherence to so many of the attitudes and ideas of the Enlightenment, he was turning Prussia's energies and attention to the East, with all that this implied for the future.

Catherine II of Russia is almost as controversial a figure as Frederick. Throughout most of her reign, and particularly in its early years, she made strenuous efforts to show herself an adherent of advanced theories of government and of the ideas of the French Enlightenment in general. On a superficial level this can be seen in her long and mutually admiring correspondence with Voltaire, and in her financial help to Diderot and the unsuccessful visit to Russia which he paid at her invitation. On a more serious one the same efforts underlay the calling in 1767 of the Legislative Commission, the most ambitious effort made in eighteenth-century Russia to provide the country with a rationalized and workable legal code. The Instruction (*Nakaz*) which Catherine personally drew up for the guidance of the deputies who made up this Commission was a conflation of ideas drawn, with little alteration, from West European writers, particularly Montesquieu and Beccaria. Though it was completely lacking in originality its publication in Western Europe drew the admiration of many of the leading figures of the Enlightenment. The Legislative Commission produced no results. The outbreak of war with the Ottoman Empire in October 1768 led to the suspension of its work; and the explosion of the great peasant and Cossack revolt led by Pugachev in June 1773 ensured that it was not reconvened. But though Catherine was clearly disappointed by its failure to produce a new code of laws as quickly and easily as she had hoped, and perhaps not very reluctant to end its activities, there is no doubt of the sincerity of her motives in calling it. Nor is there any question of the reality of the belief in the principles of enlightened government which underlay the *Nakaz*. Moreover, as has been seen (pp. 150–1), the 1760s witnessed in Russia the beginnings of a remarkable process of administrative reform which culminated in the great overhaul of provincial government in 1775.

All this gives Catherine II apparently formidable claims to be regarded as a genuinely enlightened ruler. Yet many historians would argue that these claims were fraudulent, or at least greatly exaggerated. Criticism of the empress has developed along at least three different lines. In the first place it is argued that the real motive which underlay her ostentatious partisanship of enlightenment, especially in the 1760s, was not a concern for the well-being of her subjects or even a deep belief in ideas of enlightened government, but mere vanity. She was inspired, it is argued, by nothing higher than a desire for self-advertisement and for the applause of Voltaire and his fellow-writers in Western Europe. Doubts of the sincerity of her much-advertised desire for reform were already being voiced in the early years of her reign. A British commentator, for example, writing in 1768 when her reputation as an enlightened ruler was at its height, thought that 'there is a sort of whim or affectation of singularity, in the manner of conferring her favours, that looks as if the desire of being spoken of, fully as much as the desire of doing good, was the fountain from which they flow'.[11] Certainly there is no doubt of the strength of Catherine's desire for a good press in Western Europe and of her sensitivity to criticism of any kind: vanity and *amour propre* played a greater role in her policies than in those of any other ruler of the period.

A second and more serious line of criticism is that the empress's claims to real enlightenment and concern for the welfare of her subjects are shown to be a hollow pretence by the intensification and geographical extension of serfdom in Russia during her reign. The marked deterioration in the position of the Russian peasant under Catherine's rule has allowed historians to point the contrast between the enlightened ideals which she proclaimed and the oppressive despotism which she allegedly practised. In particular the decree of May 1783, which in effect established serfdom definitively in the Ukraine, has attracted much criticism. Yet the question is not a simple one. The most recent work on the subject stresses the complexity and ambiguity of much of the legislation of this period regarding the serf population of Russia: it also suggests that after 1775 repression of peasant disorder may have been less arbitrary than before and that it was sometimes accompanied by efforts by provincial governors to persuade land-owners to treat their peasants with greater humanity. It has also been argued that the halting of peasant movement in the Ukraine and the extension to it in 1783 of the poll-tax, which doomed the Ukrainian peasant to serf status, were inspired by a desire to end the privileged position enjoyed by many border areas of the empire, and to some extent by the need to increase revenue, rather than by the extension of serfdom as a matter of policy. (The poll-tax was in fact extended in the same year to Esthonia and Livonia for these reasons.) Moreover it is true that in one or two specific minor ways the express tried positively to limit serfdom – by ordering in 1781 that war prisoners were in future to become free men if they were converted to Orthodoxy; and by reducing the possibilities which had hitherto existed of enserfment by marriage. But none of this alters the fact that when she died there were more serfs in Russia than ever before and that they were worse treated than under any of her predecessors.

Finally Catherine's claims to be a genuine enlightened despot can be impugned, like those of Frederick II, on the grounds that she was merely carrying on policies inherited from her prede-cessors. In many essentials this charge is undeniable. The reform of provincial government in 1775 had been anticipated by proposals made in the 1750s under the Empress Elizabeth. So had the great survey of landownership in Russia which Catherine set in motion in 1765 and even the Legislative Commission of two years later. The secularization of Church lands in 1764 was the completion of a process begun early in the century by Peter I. The system of government which Catherine perfected, an autocracy based on the support of the landowning class, was entirely Russian. Only in a few cosmetic details did it owe anything to French or other West European influences. Like every other ruler of a great State, the empress was the captive of the historical situ-ation in which she found herself, and in her case this forbade any radical change in the social structure of Russia or any far-reaching amelioration from above of the position of the peasant. It is unfair to see her, as Soviet historians have done, as the mere representative of the Russian nobility, trampling underfoot the interests of the great mass of the population to serve those of a small ruling class. It is significant that the huge grants of land and serfs to noble favourites and officials, for which she has been so much blamed, followed the first partition of Poland in 1772. After the original grants to her supporters in the *coup d'état* of 1762 which placed her on the throne, Catherine made very few presents of this kind during the decade 1762–72, when her dependence on noble support is usually supposed to have been at its height. Nevertheless as a woman, a foreigner and a usurper, Catherine was never in a position to dispense with the backing of the landowning class in Russia even had she ever dreamed of doing so. Throughout her reign, and particularly in its first decade or so, noble factions and the struggles between them did much to restrict her freedom of action: in 1772–73 the conflict at court between the rival Panin and Orlov parties for a time deprived her almost completely of any such freedom. This situation, coupled with the insuperable physical difficulties of governing a huge, thinly populated empire, set inescapable limits to what she could hope to achieve. As a French observer at the end of her reign pointed out, 'it was solely by suffering her power to be abused that she succeeded in preserving it'.[12]

It would be wrong to end this discussion of Catherine's work on a merely negative note. Apart from the very real administrative achievements of her reign she had some grasp of the advantages of giving the nobility, the townsfolk and even the state peasants an improved status as efficient and creative autonomous groups within Russian society (see pp. 51–2). During her reign the proportion of government revenue spent on civilian and 'welfare' objectives as opposed to military ones rose substantially. Moreover her rule saw in Russia an unprecedented growth of intellectual life and a flow and expression of ideas more free than ever before in the country's history. The members of the Legislative Commission of 1767 received from the areas which elected them both instructions and statements of grievances: digests of these were studied by the empress and had considerable influence on her later activities, notably on the reform of provincial administration in 1775. This upward flow of information and suggestions for change was something new in Russian history. A different expression of a roughly similar tendency can be seen in the fact that the total production of books in Russia during the years 1762–1800 was about three and a half times that in the entire period from the introduction of printing down to 1761. An ambitious Statute of National Education was promulgated in 1786, though lack of money and trained teachers meant that when the empress died in 1796 there were still only 62,000 pupils in all the state schools in Russia – a very small number in terms of a population of thirty million. Catherine is best seen, in the last analysis, in essentially the same terms as Frederick II. She was, in other words, a genuine believer in the ideals of enlightened government (perhaps a more sincere one than the king of Prussia); but her application of these ideals was limited to some extent by her personal weaknesses and far more by the demands and pressures of the situation in which history had placed her.

There were none the less in the later eighteenth century a number of rulers and ministers in Europe who were prepared to break radically with the past, to override vested interests and disregard deep-rooted traditions in the interests of the States they ruled. Yet in almost every case of this kind the difficulty of relating theory to practice, of showing that radically reforming policies were inspired or even strongly influenced by theories of enlightened government, is marked. Most of them are to be found in southern and Mediterranean Europe, an area in terms of its society and institutions closer to France than to Prussia or Russia. In many of the States concerned, Portugal or the Kingdom of the Two Sicilies for example, the machinery of administration was poor, very much poorer than in Prussia. Few of the rulers or ministers who attempted far-reaching reform in these areas were much influenced by the Enlightenment and none advertised his adherence to its ideas as Frederick II and Catherine II did. (This explains the small amount of attention given them by contemporary theorists of enlightenment in contrast to the adulation lavished on the Prussian and Russian rulers.)

In the kingdom of Savoy-Piedmont, whose ruler was one of the most absolute to be found anywhere in Europe, a series of remarkable reforms throughout the century went far, at least in theory, towards creating a modern State and society. A unified legal code was established there in 1725–29. The completion of a great survey of landownership in 1725–38 paved the way for a high degree of equality in respect of taxation; the nobility and clergy retained tax privileges only in respect of properties which they could prove they had held before 1584. In January 1762 King

Charles-Emmanuel III freed all serfs on the royal estates and encouraged those of the nobility to negotiate their own freedom. Another decree of December 1771 began the abolition of feudal rights, which were to be redeemed by money payments to their owners. In Savoy as elsewhere, it was one thing to issue a decree and another to make it effective. Not all this legislation was quickly or completely put into force. The poverty of the peasants and the village communes meant that in 1792, when the situation was transformed by the irruption of the armies of revolutionary France, less than half the redemptions of feudal rights envisaged two decades earlier had been completed. Nevertheless in theory and to some extent in practice a programme of very far-reaching change was carried out; and this was achieved in one of the most intellectually backward and undeveloped areas in Western Europe. Charles Emmanuel III was certainly influenced by the humanitarian ideals of the Enlightenment. Nevertheless it seems likely that change was forced on him, as earlier on such 'empirical' despots as Peter I in Russia and Frederick William I in Prussia, by the need for greater practical efficiency, and to some extent perhaps by an instinctive feeling for rationality, not by theories propounded in Paris.

The same is true of the Marques de Pombal, who for over a quarter of a century (1750–77) was virtual ruler of Portugal as all-powerful chief minister of King Joseph I. His efforts to revive the country's economic life and challenge the dominance which British merchants had for decades wielded over its foreign trade, his ferocious repression of noble opposition, his brutal expulsion of the Jesuits in 1767 (see p. 454), show a far more truly radical attitude to tradition and established interests than Frederick II displayed. In 1759 some of the greatest Portuguese nobles whom Pombal regarded as threats to his position, the Duke of Aveiro, the Marquis of Tavora, the Marquis of Alorna, were accused of conspiring against the king, tortured and in some cases broken on the wheel. Nowhere else in Europe outside Russia can one find a willingness to treat men of this social standing with such brutality. Yet however radical some of Pombal's attitudes, he has little claim to be considered an 'enlightened' minister. His policies were empirical, dictated by what he saw as the necessities of the immediate situation. Though he destroyed the power of the Jesuits he left untouched the politically less threatening one of the Inquisition (largely because he was able in 1760 to make his brother Grand Inquisitor of Portugal). Though he had served as a diplomat in both London and Vienna he owed little to the ideas of the Enlightenment: his favourite author was Molière, not any eighteenth-century writer, and under him the works of Voltaire and Montesquieu, as well as Hobbes, Locke and Spinoza, were banned. His efforts to stimulate industry in Portugal, largely by the setting-up in the 1760s of a number of privileged and mainly foreign-owned enterprises, owed more to the Colbertian attitudes of late-seventeenth century France than to any economic theories of his own day.

Rather similar arguments apply to Bernardo Tanucci, the greatest reforming minister in the Kingdom of the Two Sicilies. Tanucci was an innovator only to a very limited extent. An edict of 1738 against abuses of the judicial system, for the promulgation of which he was responsible, led to no real change. A commission for legislative reform set up in 1742 produced a decade later not a legal code but a mere collection of edicts and regulations, neither amended nor unified. In one area Tanucci did aim at far-reaching change. He was bitterly hostile to the enormous powers and privileges of the church in southern Italy, and thus abolished the Inquisition in the Two Sicilies and attacked the right of mortmain which had over generations accumulated vast amounts of property in clerical hands. In 1762 he even secured a royal edict which compelled the clergy to contribute a fifth of their income to charitable purposes, though this soon had to be withdrawn. Yet in spite of this he remained a convinced Catholic, regarding Voltaire and the *Encyclopédie* as profoundly dangerous.

Pombal and Tanucci were therefore severely practical and utilitarian in their attitude to the problems of government. To them enlightened rule, in so far as they thought in terms of it at all, meant simply effective solutions to immediate problems. Of the Enlightenment as Kant or Voltaire saw it (see pp. 411ff below), as the human mind liberating itself from the self-imposed tutelage of centuries, a new birth of intellectual adventure, they had no inkling. The same is true of Charles III of Spain (1759–88) and his most important reforming ministers, Campomanes and Jovellanos. It is important to remember that the Enlightenment as a set of economic or administrative reforms could be conscientiously and effectively applied by men indifferent or hostile to it in its higher sense as a movement transforming the human consciousness.

The Grand Duke Leopold of Tuscany (1766–90) presents a more difficult problem. He was the most remarkable and most interesting of all the 'enlightened despots'. Tuscany at the beginning of his reign was still what it had been since the formation of the Grand Duchy in the sixteenth century, a personal union of a number of medieval city-states of which the most important were Florence and Siena. These for generations had remained distinct in their administration, their laws and their economic institutions. From this unpromising inheritance Leopold had created by the end of his reign, at least on paper, one of the best-governed states in Europe. Aided by some of the ablest ministers possessed by any eighteenth-century ruler (Pompeo Neri until his death in 1776; Francesco-Maria Gianni after that date) he changed every aspect of the life of his dominions. Here as elsewhere in Catholic Europe reform meant a reduction in the stifling power of the Church. The right of mortmain was limited in 1769, the Inquisition abolished in the Grand Duchy in 1782 and in 1785 the powers of religious tribunals limited to spiritual affairs. Reform in Tuscany also had important economic aspects. In 1767 the import and movement of grain was freed from restrictions; while the craft guilds were suppressed in 1770 and a great survey of landownership begun in 1781. Municipal government throughout the Grand Duchy was overhauled in the 1770s. Most striking of all was the constitution which Leopold presented to his subjects in September 1782. This provided for the election by all landowners over the age of twenty-five of representatives to local and provincial assemblies. These in turn were to be represented in a central assembly for the entire State. Without the consent of the latter neither the succession to the throne nor the territorial limits of the Grand Duchy were to be changed; nor was war to be declared or existing legislation altered. The ruler could not on his own initiative build fortresses, hire troops or alter the judicial system. These proposals remained only a paper scheme; but they were the most remarkable constitutional document to take shape in any European State during the generation before the French Revolution. If we interpret Europe as excluding Great Britain there is a good deal of force in the claim of one historian that Leopold was 'the first constitutionally-minded monarch known to European history'.

There is no doubt, moreover, of the sincerity of the Grand Duke's belief that he was merely a trustee acting on behalf of his subjects, whose interests must always be paramount. In one of the most striking of his letters to his brother, the Emperor Joseph II, he stresses the need for a ruler always to be willing to give his subjects a complete account of the finances of the state and of their administration; such action, he writes, is 'glorious, useful and just'. The State finances are 'entirely a public matter' and the ruler merely their administrator. He is entitled to spend money only 'in accordance with the intentions of his principal' (i.e. the people), for the advantage of the State and the individuals who compose it.[13] In 1790, writing to one of his sisters, he put the case even more strongly. 'I believe,' he wrote, 'that the sovereign, even when he rules by hereditary right, is only a delegate and representative of the people, for whom he exists and to whom he must devote all his care and labour . . . . I believe that the sovereign must rule through the law and that the people are his constituents.'[14] Such attitudes are a striking reflection of the idealistic and libertarian aspects of the Enlightenment. Since Leopold ruled a small State and had neither fears nor ambitions so far as territorial changes were concerned (he wished to establish the perpetual neutrality of the Grand Duchy as a tradition of European diplomacy, to give it more or less the status which Switzerland was to enjoy in the following century) he was able to accept radical ideas and even try to realize them in practice in a way quite impossible to Frederick II or Catherine II. There is no doubt moreover that, unlike Pombal, Tanucci or Charles III, he was in close touch with the most progressive thought of the age on political and social problems. His tutor, Anton von Martini, was one of the foremost representatives of the Enlightenment in the Habsburg territories. He read extensively many leading political writers of the age, notably Turgot. He was deeply interested in the progress of the American Revolution, and owned and studied in detail a copy of the constitution of Pennsylvania. Yet not even Leopold was merely the Enlightenment enthroned. Another force underlying his policies, one which helps to explain his ready acceptance of ideas of limited monarchy and some degree of representative government, was aristocratic conservative influences, derived particularly from the Habsburg province of Carinthia and the traditions of its estates, which were strongly represented in his entourage. Unlike his brother he genuinely respected the constitutional structures of Hungary and the Austrian Netherlands: he was attracted by the possibility that the local autonomy which they so strongly represented might make government cheaper by reducing the number of centrally appointed officials needed to run it.

The only great late-eighteenth-century example of the ruler-ideologue, the monarch who attempted as an act of faith to impose enlightened rule upon his subjects, was the Emperor Joseph II, the elder brother of the Grand Duke Leopold. In outlook and temperament the brothers differed sharply. Where Leopold was uninterested in territorial gains Joseph spent much of his life in often fruitless efforts to add to the Habsburg power in Germany, Italy, Poland or the Balkans. It was his strongly expressed desire to annex the Grand Duchy of Tuscany to the hereditary provinces of the monarchy which at least in part prevented the putting into force there of the constitution of 1782. Where Leopold was cautious and realistic, Joseph was rash, obstinate and inflexible. Where the younger brother was moderate and willing to compromise, aware of the rights and claims of his subjects and of the impossibility of ruling despotically, the elder was conscious of no such limitation and, with the highest intentions, was deeply intolerant of all opposition. The contrast is well illustrated by some of the entries in Leopold's diary during a visit to Vienna in 1778–79. In these he criticizes severely his brother's régime as 'arbitrary despotism' and accuses Joseph of wishing to 'dispose despotically and capriciously of the lands, persons and goods of his subjects'.[15]

Joseph's view of kingship had no particular originality. It was essentially the same as that of Frederick II, whom he greatly admired and took in many respects as a model. He thought of his authority as delegated to him by his subjects and thus contractual in origin. He was the mandatory of his people, the trustee of the general good. The power delegated to him must never be misused for merely personal or even dynastic ends. It was, however, absolute. The people, having once surrendered it, could not revoke their delegation; and no subordinate authority in his dominions, whether of a guild, a religious order or the estates of a province, could be valid unless it emanated from or was confirmed by him. He thought always much too easily, in highly unrealistic terms, of the peoples he ruled as a mere aggregate of individuals face to face with an absolute State. The importance in many parts of his dominions of institutions intermediate between ruler and subject he underestimated grossly almost to the end of his reign.

His objectives were no more original than his political ideas. As with Frederick and Catherine, his overriding consideration was the power and well-being of the State. It was his ability to achieve that power and well-being which alone justified his despotism. In practical terms this meant curbing the powers and reducing the property rights of the Catholic Church; hence the 'Josephinism' which was one of his most important legacies to his successors (see pp. 458–60 below). It also meant centralized and rationalized administration; hence efforts were made to extend to Hungary, so jealous of its autonomy, the administrative system of the hereditary provinces. Joseph's attempts to end the dominance of the Hungarian county assemblies by the local gentry, and to substitute German for Latin as the language of administration, provoked deep and passionate national resentment. State power and the public good also demanded efforts to improve the position of the peasant: free peasants would be more productive than unfree ones. Hence the very important legislation of 1781, which abolished personal servitude, though not labour services, in Bohemia, Moravia and Silesia (it was later extended to the other hereditary provinces and in 1785 to Hungary). Hence the *Strafpatent* of the same year, which limited the lord's right to punish his peasants, and the *Unterthanspatent*, also of 1781, which allowed a peasant to lodge a complaint against his lord with officials of the central government. Hence also the introduction in 1789 of a very ambitious though shortlived scheme of tax reform which provided that in future the peasant should pay to State and lord combined only 30 per cent of his gross income. This did not in practice apply to landless labourers or peasants with very little land, a large and growing element in the rural population; but if it had been put into effect it would none the less have been the most sweeping social legislation seen anywhere in old regime Europe. Some limited degree of universal education was another obvious step towards the strengthening of the State and the fostering of general well-being. Basic literacy, which was all that was aimed at, would allow the people to grasp more easily the intentions of the ruler and thus ensure their more effective co-operation in his policies. Hence the creation in the Austrian provinces and Bohemia, beginning with the *Allgemeine Schulordnung* of 1774 (though this was the work of an official, J. I. Felbiger, not of Joseph himself) of the first truly universal system of education in European history.

None of these policies was really new. The greatest period of administrative reform in the history of the Habsburg territories had come in the two decades after 1749 (see pp. 153–4); here Joseph achieved much less than his mother. Official efforts to protect the cultivator against an oppressive lord went back at least as far as legislation by the Emperor Leopold I in 1680; and in many ways Maria Theresa showed a truer concern for her peasant subjects than her son was ever to do. In Hungary she had attempted by the *Urbarium* of 1767, against bitter opposition from the Diet, to protect the peasants against excessive exploitation. From 1771 onwards a series of codes for different provinces, beginning with Silesia, had set for the first time clear official limits to what the lords could demand of their peasants, especially in terms of labour-services. In the 1770s she had envisaged the abolition of serfdom in Bohemia, Joseph merely its amelioration: his attitude probably contributed to the outbreak in the province of the peasant revolt of 1775. 'Josephinism' in religious matters, again, it is now clear, had behind it a long tradition extending back to the first years of the century. In one significant way, it is true, the reign of Joseph marked a distinct break with the past. It saw, especially in its early years, a great advance in freedom of expression on political and other questions in the Austrian provinces and the emergence of an embryonic public opinion there. The relaxation of the censorship which was one of his first actions after the death of his mother meant that in 1780–81 an extraordinary flood of pamphlets (many of them admittedly on very trivial subjects) engulfed Vienna. In March 1782 the British ambassador there spoke of a freedom of political debate 'almost as extensive as in England'. But for the great bulk of Joseph's subjects this was a meaningless luxury; and in any case the later years of the reign, as opposition mounted, saw the government's control of publication and the press partially reasserted. In the main, Joseph's work was a logical continuation of that of his mother and her ministers.

What was novel about his reforms was not so much their content as the spirit in which they were carried out. A dogmatic intolerance which refused to recognize that he might sometimes be mistaken, a haste which incessantly demanded immediate and clearly identifiable results, undermined policies always well meant and sometimes even well conceived. About many of the emperor's actions there hangs an atmosphere of niggling dogmatism, of intolerant high-mindedness, which makes him, for all his good intentions, personally one of the least attractive of eighteenth-century rulers. Thus Joseph realized one of the objectives of radical idealists throughout Europe by virtually abolishing the death penalty in the Austrian provinces: only one execution took place there during the whole of his reign. But the hard labour for criminals which replaced judicial execution was so appalling that it was in effect a living death. The judicial reforms which he introduced in 1781 revived a number of harsh punishments which his mother's law-code of 1769 had abolished, such as the branding of life-prisoners on the forehead and the chaining of some prisoners to the walls of their cells. It is significant of Joseph's attitude that his legal code of 1787 declared that henceforth all offences were against the State and must therefore be prosecuted even if there were no individual victim willing to begin legal proceedings.

The genuine and constructive concern for elementary education which the emperor showed was combined with a marked dislike of scholars, whom he regarded as useless parasites. The result was that though his reign saw a growth in popular literacy, the setting up of Jewish and Protestant schools and the supply by the government of free textbooks for elementary teaching, it also witnessed a serious attack on secondary education and the universities. When he died there were only about half as many pupils in secondary schools as at his accession to the throne. Moreover the number of universities in Joseph's dominions had by 1790 been reduced to a mere three (Vienna, Louvain and Pest) and these had been forced to concentrate on such useful subjects as medicine and law and virtually to end the teaching of luxury ones such as foreign languages. The fostering of economic growth was a constructive objective, at bottom perhaps the most important of all. But it was not helped by such petty interferences with ordinary life as a decree of 1781 which forbade young men under the age of twenty-eight to travel abroad, or another of 1789 which forbade the granting of a marriage licence to peasant couples unless they could prove that they had already enriched the state by planting a number of fruit trees. The mental atmosphere of Joseph's reforms – idealism, effort and self-sacrifice combined with dogmatism, intolerance and a humourless lack of any sense of proportion – is very reminiscent of many aspects of the French Revolution. The emperor himself, indeed, was well aware of this similarity. Shortly before his death he complained with much justification that his Belgian subjects were refusing to receive from him as a gift benefits which the French were at the same moment extorting from Louis XVI by a great upheaval. It is suggestive that during his reign military uniform became for the first time permissible dress at the Habsburg court.

A man of this stamp, ruling what was still in essentials, in spite of the reforms of Maria Theresa, a mere group of separate provinces, was certain to encounter opposition. Of the great established interests in his dominions – Church, nobility, provincial estates, privileged towns – none was on his side. Active support Joseph could expect only from a small number of officials. Moreover his domestic position was seriously weakened by his obvious lack of success as a diplomat and a military commander. His failure to gain much of Bavaria in 1778–79, to exchange the whole electorate for the Austrian Netherlands some years later (see pp. 303–5 below), or to achieve real military success against the Turks in the war of 1788–90, undoubtedly did a good deal to increase the difficulties he faced within his own dominions. To these difficulties he himself added immensely by his insistence on extending his reforms to Hungary and the Austrian Netherlands. Had he confined his attentions to the Austrian provinces and Bohemia the story might have been very different; but the nationalism of the Hungarians (or at least their ruling class) and the ingrained particularist conservatism of the Netherlands provinces, above all Brabant, proved too much for him. Yet far from leading him to abandon or modify his policies, opposition incited him to more drastic methods. If his subjects were unwilling to accept the progress and enlightenment he offered, so much the worse for them. If they could not be enlightened by persuasion it must be done by force. We are thus faced in his later years by the paradox of a ruler who had spent his life in efforts to make his subjects prosperous and happy compelled to create a system of secret police and to hold down considerable parts of his territories by armed force. From the early 1780s onwards an increasingly elaborate network of agents and informers kept foreigners and even many important figures in the government under surveillance, and from 1782 there was provision for dangerous political prisoners to be held in complete isolation in special underground cells. Events were to show that the persuasive power of force was not lasting and that some parts of the Habsburg lands were still able to defend their privileges effectively. The emperor's reforming policies in the Austrian Netherlands, in particular his efforts to reduce the power of the Catholic Church there and to override provincial traditions and institutions, meant that from 1787 onwards much of the area was in open opposition to him. His drastic remodelling of the archaic and irrational administrative system, replacing it by a system of intendants on something like the French model, his abrogation in June 1789 of the *Joyeuse Entrée* of Brabant, the most important of the constitutional documents which limited his powers in the Netherlands, his collection of taxes which had not been approved by the provincial estates, all aroused furious opposition. Coupled with the almost equally difficult situation in Hungary this resistance disrupted the fragile unity of the Habsburg dominions. Even before his death in February 1790 Joseph, ill and discouraged, had been driven to revoke some of his most unpopular measures. His brother, who succeeded him as the Emperor Leopold II, was able to restore peace in the disturbed areas only by a skilful mixture of force and concessions.

Enlightened Despotism is not a mere figment of the historian's imagination. It had a real existence, in the sense that a number of rulers in the period 1750–90 attempted, to differing extents and in differing ways, to shape their policies in terms of a body of current theories about the duties of monarchs and the nature of good government. They were more influenced than their predecessors by consciously held and relatively sophisticated beliefs and less by unthinking traditional assumptions. Yet if we look at what they in fact did, it is striking how little practical difference these beliefs really made. In almost every case (Leopold in Tuscany is perhaps the one real exception) the new façade of fashionable ideology clothed policies which followed naturally from what had already been attempted by relatively unenlightened predecessors. No ruler of the later eighteenth century except Joseph II was willing to press home 'enlightened' policies in the face of really formidable opposition; and his fate showed the near-impossibility of doing this successfully. All eighteenth-century governments existed, in the last analysis, by the consent or at least the acquiescence of the governed. No ruler, therefore, could force his more powerful subjects to accept innovations which they really disliked. In every State the mass of the uneducated and a large fraction of the educated were deeply hostile to change, quite untouched by the intellectual currents of the Enlightenment and intensely suspicious of any government-inspired innovation. During the Hungarian revolt of 1790 against the innovations of Joseph II the new registers of land titles (an essential tool of modern government which had taken years of labour to complete) were ceremonially burnt to the accompaniment of music, drinking, feasting and general rejoicing. Members of the estates then took a public oath that no trace of these hated documents should be preserved. Everywhere measures to free the grain trade aroused the deepest suspicion and hostility. France is the best-known example of this but there are plenty of others; the riots in Tuscany in 1790 provoked by measures of this kind are a good example.

In particular any tampering with traditional religious institutions or observances, of the kind so common among enlightened rulers and ministers, was likely to generate deep resentment. In Bohemia under Joseph II opposition to the burial of Protestants in cemeteries hitherto reserved for Catholics was so great that it required the presence of a considerable force of cavalry to ensure that one such burial took place; while the disastrous flooding of 1785, when the Danube broke its banks, was widely regarded as a divine punishment for the emperor's impious attacks on the Church. Attempts to interfere with the liturgy; the abolition, for economic reasons, of some of the very numerous religious holidays; the dissolution of the Jesuits, still deeply respected over much of Catholic Europe – all these manifestations of enlightenment could easily arouse widespread and sincere opposition. The experience of the Electorate of Mainz, hardly one of the most backward parts of Europe, is illuminating in this respect. When the Jesuits were expelled from the city in September 1773 public resentment was so real that the entire garrison had to occupy key points and patrol the streets to maintain order. When in 1787 a new hymn book in German was introduced by a reforming elector this aroused bitter popular hostility. The peasants tore up and burned the copies they received; and often it was simply ignored and the singing of hymns in Latin continued. It is important to remember that however misguided, selfish or shortsighted this opposition to change may seem, it was none the less sincere. Almost always it was underlain by a passionate feeling that genuine rights were being trodden underfoot, that the structure of custom and tradition by which all but a small minority of Europeans lived was being wantonly shaken, that any increase in government activity must threaten the subject. What the ordinary man most wanted of the State was that it should so far as possible leave him alone. The more enlightened and reforming a government the more obviously it must flout feelings of this kind; and sometimes the price to be paid for flouting them was high.

However limited its immediate effects, the ideology of Enlightened Despotism was important in the long term. A heavier emphasis than ever before was being laid in the later eighteenth century, notably by monarchs themselves, on a ruler's duties to his subjects. These duties were now increasingly defined in terms of progress towards a better, or even an ideal, form of society and government. The frequent acceptance of ideas of this kind by monarchs helps to explain the lack of hostility, sometimes even enthusiasm, with which the French Revolution in its early stages was received by many of them. In St Petersburg in 1789 the French ambassador was publicly congratulated by the Grand Duke Alexander (later Alexander I) on the fall of the Bastille, while Alexander's younger brother the Grand Duke Constantine, who was later to become an extreme reactionary, was also at first an enthusiastic partisan of the Revolution. In the same way the Emperor Leopold II approved of much of the work of the Constituent Assembly. Even when the more violent and disruptive aspects of events in France had become clearly visible, it was often the methods as much as the objectives of the revolutionaries which aroused opposition. Increasingly in the later eighteenth century it was felt, at least in intellectual and opinion-forming circles, that monarchy was on trial, that kings must now provide not merely good government but progressive government. By the 1770s or 1780s there were few European rulers who could feel the same unquestioning self-assurance as Louis XIV a century earlier.

NOTES AND REFERENCES

1   Quoted in P. Dukes, *The Making of Russian Absolutism, 1613–1801* (London, 1982), pp. 144–5.

2   These involved, apart from palace revolutions and conspiracies, the murder of two rulers: Ivan VI (1740–41) and Peter III (1762), assassinated in 1764 and 1762 respectively; and of one heir to the throne (Alexis, son of Peter I, put to death on his father's orders in 1718).

208

3   Abbé le Blanc, *Letters on the English and French Nations* (London, 1747), vol. I, pp. 106–7.

4   A. von Arneth (ed.), *Maria Theresia und Joseph II. Ihr Correspondenz* (Vienna, 1867–68), vol. I, p. 133.

5   G. Sénac de Meilhan, *Du Gouvernement, des Moeurs, et des Conditions en France avant la Révolution* (Hamburg, 1795), p. 91.

6   G. P. Gooch, *Louis XV: the monarchy in decline* (London, 1956), p. 77.

7   *Les Fastes de Louis XV* (n.p., 1782), vol. I, preface, p. i.

8   A. L. von Schlözer, *Neuverändertes Russland, oder Leben Catherina der Zweyten, Kaiserinn von Russland* (Riga-Mittau-Leipzig, 1771–72), vol. I, Vorrede.

9   W. Hubatsch, *Frederick the Great* (London, 1975), p. 125.

10 R. Augstein, *Preussens Friedrich und die Deutschen* (Frankfurt, 1968), p. 264.

11 W. Richardson, *Anecdotes of the Russian Empire* (London, 1784), p. 26.

12 F. P. Masson, *Secret Memoirs of the Court of St Petersburg.* (2nd edn, London, 1801), p. 61.

13 A. von Arneth (ed.), *Joseph II und Leopold von Toscana, ihr Briefwechsel von 1781 bis 1790* (Vienna, 1872), p. 23.

14 Quoted in K. O. Freiherr von Aretin (ed.), *Der Aufgeklärte Absolutismus* (Cologne, 1974), p. 109.

15 A. Wandruszka, 'Joseph II und der Verfassungsprojekt Leopolds II', *Historische Zeitschrift*, vol. CXC (1960), p. 21.

7

ARMIES AND NAVIES

In 1764 James Boswell's friend Rose claimed, in a conversation which the two men had at Leyden, that 'wars were going out nowadays, from their mildness'.[1] Nearly three decades later a British publicist had no doubt that 'the refinement of modern ages has stripped war of half its horrors'.[2] They were expressing a point of view widespread among their contemporaries, at least in Western Europe, a feeling that for several generations warfare had been becoming steadily milder and its influence on the ordinary man more limited. Many historians have shared this view.

Are such judgements justified? Certainly as far as Western Europe is concerned there is a good deal of evidence to support them. For nearly a century and a half after the end of the Thirty Years War in 1648 there was a tendency for the ratio of casualties to total numbers engaged in West European wars to fall and for that of prisoners to dead and wounded to rise. These are clear signs that warfare was tending to become less bloody. By the end of the seventeenth century a pamphleteer commenting on this tendency could write that now, in contrast to the attitude of former times, '20,000 Men are accounted great Slaughter'.[3] Widespread looting of the kind which had disfigured almost every war of the sixteenth and early seventeenth centuries was very largely brought under control in this period (in the interests of discipline rather than humanity). It was replaced by contribution agreements by which the local authorities in an area occupied by a foreign army undertook, often with the consent of their own ruler, to pay the occupying force a fixed sum in return for a promise that it would not pillage. These became more and more normal in

Western and Central Europe. Adam Smith even argued in 1763 that 'war is so far from being a disadvantage in a well-cultivated country, that many get rich by it. When the Netherlands is the seat of war, all the peasants grow rich, for they pay no rent when the enemy is in the country, and provisions sell at a high rate.'[4] It is true also that warfare had little influence on the arts, the most obvious indicator of the 'climate of opinion', during the eighteenth century. The best example of this is the fact that none of the greatest music of the period was inspired by the idea of military conflict (as some of that written by Beethoven in the following generation clearly was). Its 'military' music is that of courts and *Te Deums*, or at most of parade grounds, not that of battlefields.

The element of ritual and formality bulked large in much eighteenth-century warfare in West Europe. This was particularly marked in attacks on fortresses and fortified towns. 'The art of conducting sieges', wrote Frederick II, 'has become a trade like that of carpenter or clock-maker. Certain infallible rules have been established, and we carry on an unvarying routine in which we apply the same theory to the same cases.'[5] The idea of a siege as a ritual conducted according to well-defined rules is clearly illustrated by the answer of the commander of the Spanish garrison at Gaeta in southern Italy when faced in the 1730s with an Austrian demand for surrender: 'It is not yet time, since no batteries have been formed and no cannon are yet in place which would be a cause for surrender. The general must be patient for a while.' Moreover the armies of all West European States tended to be slow-moving, tied to fixed magazines and supply depots and further restricted by the ever-present fear of desertion. These limitations did not make rapid movement impossible, as Marlborough showed in 1704 and Frederick II in 1757; but they ensured that it should be the exception rather than the rule. Also commanders were not usually eager to fight decisive battles; and victories were seldom followed up with real energy. (The obvious if partial exception here is again Frederick II; but he never had the material resources needed for a truly Napoleonic strategy and became steadily more cautious and conservative in his later years.) Indeed it was the accepted orthodoxy that battles should in general be avoided as too risky and that skill in manoeuvre was the real criterion of ability in a commander. 'A battle', said the Saxon *Dienstreglement* of 1752, 'is at once the most important and the most dangerous operation of war. A great general shows his mastery by attaining the object of his campaign by sagacious and sure manoeuvres, without incurring any risk.' A good many observers even doubted whether wars between States at approximately the same level of civilization could have any decisive result. The growth in Europe's population and the increased number of fortified towns to be found on every frontier, wrote a pamphleteer at the end of the seventeenth century, made it more difficult than ever before to conquer great areas of territory. The diffusion of military techniques, he went on, had the same effect, for 'now both Parties are Equally Disciplin'd and Arm'd; and the Successes of War are not so great; Victory is seldome gained without some Considerable Loss to the Conquerour'.[6] A hundred years later the same ideas were still widespread. 'Conquests are never very extensive or rapid,' wrote the historian Robertson, 'but among nations, whose progress in improvement is extremely unequal.'[7]

None of this meant that war was a rare or unimportant phenomenon in the eighteenth century or that the demands which it made on the peoples of Europe were negligible. The political and diplomatic history of the period was dominated by warfare. With the partial exception of the two decades which followed the Treaty of Utrecht (and even then there were probably never less than half a million men under arms in Europe) there was scarcely a year in the century during which a large-scale struggle was not either raging or threatened in some part of the continent. Europeans, almost as much as in preceding generations, took war for granted as a normal part of their lives. These struggles, moreover, could still inflict intense and widespread suffering. Wounded men and prisoners could still have much to fear if they found themselves at the mercy of their opponents. In 1706, after his victory at Turin, Prince Eugene had to interfere in person to prevent a general massacre of the French wounded by the imperial forces; and after the battle of Zorndorf in 1758 many of the wounded Russians left on the field were buried alive by Prussian soldiers and local peasants. Civilian non-combatants could also on occasion have much to fear, especially when a city was taken by storm with all the looting, killing and destruction which this involved. The French ravaging of Bergen-op-Zoom in 1747 or the Russian sack of Memel ten years later are good cases in point. On occasion whole provinces could be savagely treated in an effort to deny their resources to an enemy, as the French devastation of Westphalia in 1759 showed. It is true that among intellectuals, influenced by the cosmopolitanism of the Enlightenment, there was a fairly general feeling that war was unworthy of an age in which reason was taking control of human affairs. 'Nothing is so evident', wrote Sir James Steuart, one of the most important economists of the period, 'as that war is inconsistent with the prosperity of a modern State.'[8] By the last years of the period there were indications that anti-militarist ideas were beginning to influence even the policies of a few important statesmen – Turgot, Vergennes, possibly the younger Pitt. They had little importance, however, outside a small minority of the educated classes.

A tendency towards a general, though slow, increase in the size of most European armies is visible during this period. That of France, the greatest European State, did not again reach the level achieved in the War of the Spanish Succession, when in 1710 Louis XIV had some 360,000 soldiers at his disposal; but most others grew. There was, however, a widespread feeling that very large armies were undesirable because they were difficult to supply and manœuvre. The Maréchal de Saxe, one of the best-known military theorists of the century and himself a highly successful commander, thought the 'acting body' of an army should not exceed 46,000 men, 'for multitudes serve only to perplex and embarrass'.[9] It was also possible to argue that the size of armies must be limited by the capacity of society to maintain them: Montesquieu believed that a ruler could hardly afford to have more than one per cent of his subjects under arms simultaneously, and other writers put the proportion still lower. But such ideas were unduly cautious. Half a century before Saxe wrote, the forces engaged in the great battles of the War of the Spanish Succession had sometimes amounted on each side to 60,000–90,000 men and the French army had been equivalent to about two per cent of the country's population: he himself is said to have commanded 130,000 at Raucoux in 1746 and 98,000 at Lawfeldt in the following year. This numerical growth is seen strikingly in the extraordinary development of the Prussian army. At the most critical moment of the Seven Years War it amounted to 4.4 per cent of the total population of the country, the highest proportion of this kind reached in any State during the century. Even more remarkable in some ways was the emergence of the

Russian army. Still an inefficient and partly feudal force at the end of the seventeenth century, it had become by the last years of Peter I one of the most powerful in Europe. In 1731 its strength was fixed at over 132,000 men: by 1796 (i.e. before Russia had begun to play an active part in the struggle against the French Revolution) it numbered 458,000. The same tendency to growth is seen, less strikingly, in Spain and some of the smaller States, notably Savoy-Piedmont.

Also if the destructiveness of warfare was declining, militarism was increasing, and was indeed largely a creation of this period. Louis XIV, during much of his reign an aggressive ruler, was not a soldier by taste, outlook or training. He would have regarded it as a breach of etiquette for a French nobleman to present himself at court in uniform. All his war ministers were civilians; and the commanders of his armies tended to be aristocrats first and professional soldiers second. The Marquis de Chamlay, his most important military adviser in his later years, had the title of *Maréchal-Général des Logis*; but he had little experience of active service and was often employed on non-military tasks. The same attitudes held sway in Vienna. Prince Eugene of Savoy, until his death in 1736 the most famous commander in Europe, had to wear civilian dress when he appeared at the Habsburg court.

From the beginning of the eighteenth century this position changed rapidly. There was a striking increase in the attention paid by most European rulers to military details of all kinds. A number of monarchs – Charles XII of Sweden, Frederick William I of Prussia, Paul of Russia, to some extent Peter I and Frederick II – began to regard uniform as their normal dress. In England George I and George II devoted their energies to the organization and discipline of their army in a way that no Stuart king had ever done. Even in Spain, none of whose rulers had any pretension to military ability, royal interest of this kind can be seen in the frequency with which military uniforms were remodelled under Charles III and Charles IV. It is true that over much of Europe military administration at its highest level was still largely in the hands of civilians. This was so in Britain, where the post of Secretary at War was held by politicians and changed hands with the ebb and flow of party politics. It was also the case in the very unmilitary Dutch Republic; and in the Habsburg territories the *Kriegskommissariat* set up in 1657 and reformed by Haugwitz in the 1740s was made up largely of civilians. Even in this respect, however, some signs of change can be seen. In France the post of Secretary of State for War was given for the first time to a soldier (the Maréchal de Belle-Isle) in 1758; and in the second half of the century there was a slow but steady tendency for the most important officials concerned, the *intendants d'armées* and the *contrôleurs des guerres*, to be military men. In a number of ways also armies became more conscious of themselves than ever before as entities clearly distinguished from civilian society. There was a marked multiplication of military decorations and orders, distinctions of a kind hitherto very rare. To the first important one, the Order of St Louis created by Louis XIV, were now added the Prussian Pour le Mérite in 1740 (though until 1810 this was also awarded to civilians), the Habsburg Order of Maria Theresa (1757) and the Russian Order of St George (1769). In 1771, a significant innovation, the French army began to award to old soldiers of twenty-five years standing the first long-service medal. During the second half of the century, moreover, there was a tendency in several States to house soldiers in purpose-built barracks rather than, as hitherto, to quarter them mainly in the houses of civilians; by 1775, 200,000 French soldiers were living in barracks. This meant that the population in general was increasingly spared an irritating and resented burden; but it also meant yet another hardening of the distinction between the soldier and those he defended.

More important, as armies became more highly organized, more permanent and more self-conscious, the temptation to use them as moulds in which civilian societies might be recast became stronger, at least in the relatively poor and backward States of Eastern and Northern Europe. In these a clear tendency developed to militarize society in general in the quest for greater political and economic efficiency. This bore fruit in Peter I's Table of Ranks of 1722 (see p. 50), itself based largely on Swedish precedents, and in the subjection in Prussia of the administration and much of the economic life of the country to the needs of the army.

Finally many of the checks on the ferocity of West European warfare did not exist, or were less effective, farther east. In the West most eighteenth-century campaigns were fought in densely populated and wealthy areas. In the East Russian, Turkish, Swedish and Polish armies struggled with one another in country which was usually poor and sometimes almost uninhabited. There sieges were less frequent and pitched battles more important. In

215

the West armies were cosmopolitan and religious animosities relatively insignificant. In the East the Russian and Swedish forces
were remarkable for their national character and resulting
homogeneity; and every Russo-Turkish war was a religious at
least as much as a political struggle to the ordinary soldier on both
sides. The result was that in the long Russo–Swedish conflict of
1700–21 both combatants endured sacrifices surpassing those of
any Western country in the War of the Spanish Succession, while
Russia's wars with the Ottoman Empire were fought almost in
the spirit of a crusade. In the West, again, warfare was largely,
though by no means completely, dominated by a defensive spirit.
There tactics were strongly influenced by reliance on line formation and fire-power, as against attack at close quarters. In Russia,
on the other hand, commanders such as Rumyantsev and Suvorov
had developed to a high pitch of effectiveness by the end of this
period the more aggressive method of attack in column with the
bayonet (though the contrast between Russian and West European
tactics has been greatly exaggerated by some Soviet historians).
Above all, in the West warfare was increasingly governed by rules
which gave some protection to prisoners and civilians. In the East
these restrictions were either almost unknown, as in the Ottoman
Empire, or were only slowly winning acceptance, as in Russia.
Thus the early years of the century, when war was taking on 'so
decorous an aspect' in Western Europe, saw the conquered provinces of Livonia ravaged by the armies of Peter I with a ferocity
which shocked Western observers. Later events, such as the
devastation of East Prussia by Russian troops in 1758 or the
terrible slaughter which followed the storming of the Turkish
fortress of Ismail in 1790 in which some 30,000 were killed,
underlined to contemporaries the freedom from conventional
restraints which characterized warfare in Eastern Europe.

The nature and value of every European army was determined
largely by its recruiting system. Most States developed during the
century some system of compulsory service; but all of these were
in varying degrees incomplete, haphazard and inequitable. In
many countries militias of widely differing efficiency existed. In
some they played a role of significance as sources of recruits for
the regular army in time of war – for example in France, where
a system of militia service was established by Louvois in 1688 and
revived in 1726, in Spain, in Piedmont and in England after the
passage of the Militia Act of 1757. In others forces of this kind

were unimportant or non-existent: in these the defence of the State rested as a rule upon armies raised largely by some modified and limited form of conscription. Such was Prussia, where a new system of recruiting, based on the allocation to each regiment of a defined area, a canton, upon which it could draw for its manpower, was introduced in the 1730s. The cantonists, as the conscripts were called, were however trained reserves rather than regular soldiers. After their first year of service they were normally on active duty for only two months in each year. In the hereditary provinces of the Habsburgs a somewhat similar system was introduced in 1771; but in Russia things were very different. There Peter I had developed at the beginning of the century a system by which a specified number of peasant households had to provide, in periodic levies, a recruit to serve for life. The Prussian army was unique among those of the major States in relying for its manpower neither on any militia system nor on voluntary recruiting.

Thus many though by no means all European States had at their disposal means of recruiting by compulsion considerable numbers of men for military service. With the exception of Russia, however, no major European power attempted to raise the bulk of its forces, at least in peacetime, by this means. In most States the army was still dependent largely on voluntary enlistment.

There were several motives which might bring a man to commit himself to a fairly long period (eight years in France from 1762 onwards) of military service. One, significant in a few parts of Europe, was the growth of a genuine popular military tradition and a willingness to regard the army as a respectable, even honourable, occupation. In the frontier areas of eastern and north-eastern France, especially those near main roads where the sight of columns of soldiers on the march was a familiar one, this factor clearly operated. These provinces produced, in proportion to their population, enormously more recruits than the centre, south and west of the country. Similar feelings were at work to some extent in the later decades of the century in the Scottish Highlands, both a cause and a result of the growing prominence of Scottish regiments in the British army. Men were also led to become soldiers by the desire to escape the monotony, drudgery and narrow horizons of rural life, or by a difficult domestic situation. Often a young man might be led to join up by the death of his mother, the remarriage of his father, and a resulting feeling that he was no longer wanted at home. But over most of Europe the most effective of all recruiting-sergeants was poverty. Army service offered poor living conditions, low pay and severe discipline; but at least it usually gave security against starvation. Moreover some governments, notably the British one, offered cash bounties to men willing to enlist. Everywhere, however, the burden of service fell most heavily on the poorer groups in society. The fact that a man liable to army or militia service could almost always provide a substitute if he had the money to pay for one accentuated still further this inequality. Over most of Europe any form of military service was generally unpopular. That in the militia was one of the most deeply resented burdens on the ordinary man in France; and in England the Militia Act of 1757 was widely resisted. Where a system of conscription operated all sorts of expedients were used to avoid service. Since married men were normally exempt, youths in some areas might for this reason marry as young as fourteen or fifteen and be given a small piece of land by their parents to maintain themselves: the proliferation of very small peasant holdings in Denmark has been attributed to this factor. Even self-mutilation to avoid service was not unknown. The size of the forces which might be raised by these primitive and inequitable means, especially at moments of real crisis, should not be under-estimated. In France during the most critical years of the Spanish Succession war in 1704–8 and 1712, one in six of the male population was serving in the army or the militia; and in the period 1700–63 about two million men were enrolled for military service there (though some 300,000 of these were foreigners).

The idea that the army should be a microcosm of the nation, or representative of it in any true sense, would have seemed to most contemporaries ridiculous or even shocking. It was generally agreed that it should be raised as far as possible from the social groups of least value. 'It would undoubtedly be desirable,' wrote the Comte de Saint-Germain, perhaps the greatest French war minister of the century, 'if we could create an army of dependable and specially-selected men of the best type. But in order to make up an army we must not destroy the nation; it would be destruction to a nation if it were deprived of its best elements. As things are, the army must inevitably consist of the scum of the people and of all those for whom society has no use.' Frederick II himself had argued a few years earlier that 'useful hard-working people should be guarded as the apple of one's eye, and in wartime recruits should be levied in one's own country only when the bitterest necessity compels'. This assumption that the productive and educated parts of society were too valuable to be squandered in battle, that their function was to pay for wars not to fight them, was almost universally accepted. A few military theorists – Saxe in his *Rêveries* (1757), Justus Möser in his *Patriotische Phantasien* (1775–1804), Guibert in his *Essai générale de tactique* (1772) – as well as political writers such as Montesquieu, Morellet and Mably, might advocate some form of extensive or even universal service; but there was no serious possibility of their ideas being adopted by any government. One result of this attitude was that the strain placed by warfare on the economies of most European States was less than the mere number of men engaged in fighting might seem to indicate, since these were drawn so largely from the least productive elements of society. Another was greatly to minimize the impact on the educated and property-owning classes (and hence often on the towns) of the rudimentary conscription systems of the period. It was calculated that in Prussia at the end of the century 1,700,000 men in a total population of 8,700,000 were completely exempt from military service (1,170,000 because of privileges possessed by most of the Prussian towns, 530,000 because of their social status or occupation). In 1745 the municipality of Seville, one of the largest cities in Spain, claimed that only 201 of its inhabitants were liable for military service, all the others being covered by exemptions of some kind. In France the more well-to-do cultivators (those who paid 50 livres or more in *taille*) were exempt from militia service, as were the servants of nobles or clerics, though exemptions of this kind were increasingly cut down as the century went on. It was only in 1742, moreover, that the militia there began to recruit from the urban as well as the rural population. Even in Russia the years after the death of Peter I saw the exemption from service of considerable social groups hitherto liable – the merchants of Astrakhan in return for a money payment, the arms-makers of Tula, Church servants, some groups of the better-off peasantry.

In these circumstances almost every eighteenth-century army was likely to contain a large element of ne'er-do-wells, social misfits and even criminals. In Britain, where suspicion of the army as a possible instrument of tyranny together with a generally rising level of prosperity made recruits unusually hard to obtain,

219

this element was prominent. In the War of American Independence three British regiments were composed entirely of reprieved criminals, while vagrants and other undesirables were often forced into the army as an alternative to prison. Such elements could be found in varying degrees in the fighting forces of most European States. The desire to shelter large sections of the population from military service also strengthened the willingness of most governments to employ foreign mercenaries, who retained throughout this period much of the importance they had possessed since the Renaissance. The French army included in the middle of the century over 50,000 foreigners, and still had over 40,000 serving in it on the eve of the Revolution. Of 133 battalions of infantry in the Spanish army in 1751 twenty-eight were composed of foreigners; and it was seriously proposed in that year to raise twenty more abroad. The United Provinces had a Scottish brigade in their service until the last years of the century. The most striking example of all of the employment of foreigners, however, was Prussia. There in 1751 in an army of 133,000 only 50,000 were natives of the various Prussian provinces; and even in 1786 the proportion had risen only slightly, to 80,000 in a total of 190,000. The Swiss cantons in particular continued, as in the previous century, to provide considerable numbers of recruits for foreign armies. In 1789 there were a dozen different States which made use of Swiss units; and probably one Swiss in every twelve of military age was serving in a foreign army in time of peace. In time of war the proportion was probably as high as one in eight. Switzerland was now challenged as an exporter of military manpower, however, by some of the smaller German States, above all by Hesse-Kassel. Nor were mercenaries supplied only by very small or weak States. Denmark and Saxony hired out considerable forces to the anti-French coalition during the War of the Spanish Succession, while Britain employed Russian auxiliaries in 1747–48 and confidently expected to obtain others for use against the American colonists in 1775.

Armies so non-national and drawn so largely from the lowest strata of the social pyramid were prone to lose men by desertion. This was so serious a threat to their efficiency, especially in wartime, that officers and NCOs had to spend much of their energies in checking and forestalling possible efforts by their men to desert. Thus in the army of Frederick II it was a rule that when passing through wooded country in which escape would be relatively easy infantry units must always be surrounded by cavalry patrols; and that when detached to fetch wood or water ordinary soldiers must always be accompanied by an officer. The need to guard against desertion had considerable influence even on the development of tactics; and governments naturally made efforts to repress a practice which so obviously threatened the strength and morale of their armies. In 1710 Prince Eugène ordered that all soldiers found more than a hundred paces from his army on the march and more than a thousand from it when it was in camp should be hanged. A year later Frederick I of Prussia ordered that in future deserters should have their nose and one of their ears cut off and be sent to hard labour for life, while after the Seven Years War a chain of military posts was set up on France's frontiers to prevent the escape abroad of soldiers fleeing from their units. That eighteenth-century generals and governments were justified in the attention they gave to this problem is clear. In 1713–40, a period during which it did hardly any fighting, the Prussian army lost over 30,000 men by desertion. During the Seven Years War the Austrian army is said to have lost over 62,000 men in this way, that of France about 70,000, and that of Prussia about 80,000. In the 1780s it was estimated that of the troops raised in Great Britain on the Irish establishment one-sixth deserted every year. Even in Russia, which was to some extent spared these difficulties by the relatively high morale and national feeling of her soldiers, 20,000 deserters were counted in 1732. It should be remembered, of course, that quite often a man who deserted would rejoin the same army a short time later in a different unit, perhaps under another name, to gain a new enlistment bounty. This means that the figures quoted in this paragraph have to be taken with a small pinch of salt. Nevertheless there is no doubt of the reality of the problem which desertion presented to every eighteenth-century army.

These armies of peasant conscripts, mercenaries and ne'er-do-wells were officered predominantly and in many cases over-whelmingly by nobles. In the seventeenth century army service had sometimes offered to ambitious men of low birth the prospect of raising themselves in the social scale, and perhaps of acquiring nobility for themselves and their descendants. Even then, however, the great majority of successful commanders were of noble origin; and by the early eighteenth century it was becoming increasingly difficult in many countries for a commoner to acquire commissioned rank in any but the more technical branches of the service, and almost impossible for him to rise to high rank. This tendency was not universal. In Spain for example, where the social importance of a commission was comparatively slight, would-be officers were required to prove noble descent only in a few calvary regiments. Nevertheless in some of the most important European States social status became increasingly the passport to military rank as the century progressed. For this growing noble monopoly of commissions there were a number of reasons. Rulers often felt that a hereditary privileged class alone possessed the sense of personal honour, which was seen as an essential ingredient in the make-up of a successful officer. The middle classes, it was argued, attached to their own comfort and influenced by rational calculations of private profit, could never make good officers. To allow them to attain commissioned rank, wrote Frederick II in 1775, would be 'the first step toward the decline and fall of the army'. Even a relatively liberal and progressive administrator like Saint-Germain was extremely unwilling to grant commissions to *parvenus* at the expense of poor but military-minded nobles. Sometimes the landowning class might be the only social group possessing the qualities of leadership and the minimum of education without which an officer was useless. This was the case in Russia, where Peter I, in the face of great hostility and obstruction, succeeded in forcing the privileged landowning class to become in effect a group of hereditary State servants (see p. 51). It also applied, to a lesser extent, in Prussia. There Frederick William I, again in spite of much opposition, achieved a similar success and became the real creator of the Junker officer.

In many countries, especially in the later decades of the century, the privileged classes came to regard a monopoly of commissions (except in the artillery and engineers) as a right to be jealously defended against bourgeois encroachments. This attitude can be seen in Prussia, and more strikingly in France. There the officer class, which consisted at the regimental level largely of provincial nobles with a well-developed military tradition, showed itself increasingly hostile to the purchase of commissions by rich bourgeois, even if recently ennobled, and to the invasion of the army by the power of money. Buying a commission for one of its members, it must be remembered, could impoverish a poor noble family for decades; and if the holder died in the performance of his duties the sum paid was lost to it. The dependence of many French nobles on army pay or pensions for their livelihood added bitterness to the social struggle involved. It also led to a marked inflation of the number of high-ranking officers. 'I have officers whom I do not need,' said Louis XV, 'but I am sure that they need me.'[10]

The eighteenth century was not an age of rapid development in military techniques. Nevertheless it was also not a period of stagnation in this respect. It saw the introduction of new arms, tactics and methods of organization, which made the armies of the 1780s appreciably different from those of the 1700s.

It was in the first place a great age in the growth of military education. Apart from recruitment the greatest problem most armies faced was that of giving adequate training to their officers. The *Accademia Reale* set up in Turin in 1677, the Noble Cadet Corps established in Saint Petersburg in 1731, the *Ecole Royale Militaire* which came into existence in Paris in 1751, the military academies established at Wiener-Neustadt in 1752 and Zamora in 1790, were all essentially intended to prepare young nobles for a military career. In 1776 twelve schools of this kind were set up in the French provinces, largely in an effort to cope with the military pretensions of the poorer nobility. One of these, at Brienne, was soon to have the young Napoleon Bonaparte as one of its pupils. On a different level the academy established at Woolwich in 1741, the great engineering school set up at Mézières in 1748, the combined artillery and engineer school created in Russia in 1756, and a number of similar establishments, provided the armies of Europe with a greater fund of technical knowledge than they had hitherto possessed. From such new creations, notably in France, came a high proportion of the most important writing on military problems produced during the century.

The technical improvements of this period centred around the problem of increasing the fire-power of armies; and towards this end a good deal of progress was made. At the beginning of the century the average well-trained soldier could fire about one round per minute. By its middle years the introduction of a number of relatively minor improvements, such as cartridges and iron ramrods, had allowed this rate of fire to be trebled in the most efficient European armies. The excellent French musket of 1777, for example, could maintain a rate of fire of three rounds per minute with an effective range of 200 metres and could fire

8,000 shots without needing modification or repairs. A general tendency towards making artillery lighter and more mobile can also be seen in the later decades of the century. It is visible especially in France, where the changes introduced by Gribeauval in the 1770s were of revolutionary importance. After his reforms a French 12-pounder gun could be drawn by only six horses and an 8-pounder by only four (in each case about one-third of the number needed two centuries earlier) while the interchangeable parts which he introduced made it possible to carry out repairs and replacements with hitherto unheard-of speed. From the 1760s onwards both the British and French armies made intermittent and rather unsuccessful experiments with explosive shells, while shrapnel was first demonstrated publicly at Gibraltar in 1787. The bayonet, perhaps the greatest contribution to warfare made by the seventeenth century, was well established almost everywhere in Europe by the beginning of this period.

Nevertheless the scope and importance of these technical changes should not be exaggerated. Compared to those of the century which followed they were slight. The smooth-bore muskets which British soldiers used against Napoleon did not differ very substantially from those which their ancestors carried against Louis XIV. Marlborough, if brought back to life, would have found on the field of Waterloo comparatively little with which he was not already familiar. On the battlefield armament was still much less important than discipline and fighting spirit. It is significant that the Prussian army, the most successful and admired of the age, used a heavy musket which was generally regarded as the worst in Europe.

In the field of tactics the main interest of the eighteenth century lies in the slow modification of the traditional line formation of troops on the field of battle by the new or rediscovered idea of attack in column. In Western Europe the idea of attack by columns in close formation seems to have been put forward for the first time by the Chevalier de Folard in his *Nouvelles Découvertes sur la Guerre* (1724). It was soon taken up by other French writers, many of whom were attracted by its reminiscences of the Greek phalanx of classical times, and a prolonged controversy between the advocates of the new system and those of the traditional line formation developed. The supporters of the new school of thought were not completely victorious. Columns of men in close order moved slowly and were very exposed to enemy fire. Moreover to change quickly from column to line and vice versa was a complicated business, though methods of doing this were evolved, notably by Guibert, the greatest military theorist of the century. Nevertheless the rigidity of the traditional line tactics which dominated most European battlefields in the eighteenth century had been shaken, with important results for the future. In Russia too, where ideas of linear formation had never taken such deep root as in the West, attack in column became, in the hands of generals such as Suvorov, a weapon capable of achieving great results. Moreover all tactical systems were, in the eighteenth century, becoming more effective simply because of improvements in discipline and the increasingly effective training to which the ordinary soldier was now subjected. More and more armies were becoming reliable though still very cumbersome machines, mechanisms which could be relied on to perform competently on the battlefield the evolutions in which they had been trained, and to stand enemy fire without flinching. This development is usually associated particularly with the Prussian and Russian forces. But the same trend is clearly visible in Western Europe also. From the Spanish Succession war onwards, for example, there was an increasing tendency for French soldiers to receive wounds in the left side – the part of the body which in line formation was exposed to the enemy's fire. This is one of the most convincing of all proofs of increasingly rigid discipline on the battlefield.

This period also saw the introduction into every major European army of various forms of mobile and lightly-armed troops to supplement the slow-moving line regiments. Units of this kind were first used on a considerable scale by the Austrian army in the 1740s; and the Croat sharpshooters who composed them were considered by Frederick II the most dangerous opponents he had to face. They were soon copied by the French, who developed formations of this kind on a large scale from the 1760s onwards, while light infantry were used for the first time in Europe by the Russians at the siege of Kolberg in 1761. The British army created a regiment of light infantry in 1757 for scouting duties in North America; and in the war of the American Revolution troops of this kind were the most effective part of Britain's forces in the colonies. To some military theorists such as Guibert, who was influenced by Rousseau and to whom the soldier of republican Rome was an ideal, formations of this kind seemed not merely useful in a military sense but possible signposts towards a different political system and society. The qualities of initiative, responsibility and loyalty which they demanded from the soldier were very different from the passive obedience and mechanical discipline typified by the army of Frederick II (which, significantly, found it difficult to create units of this kind). They could therefore be seen, with some stretch of the imagination, as forerunners of a new army and a new society, more austere, more national and patriotic, even more egalitarian, than any hitherto known.

Finally, important changes took place in the eighteenth century in the means by which armies were controlled and maintained by the governments for which they fought. Even before it opened they had become emanations of the State, a branch of the machinery of government. There was little scope left for the *condottiere*, no possibility of the rise of a new crop of Wallensteins or Mansfelds, the warlords and military entrepreneurs who had played so great a part in the struggles of the 1620s and 1630s. The last great assertion by the government of a major European State of its monopoly of military power in its own territory can be seen in the whittling away by Peter I of the autonomy of the Zaporozhian Cossacks on the Dnieper from 1709 onwards, and in its final destruction by Catherine II in 1775–83. Many aspects of military life, however, were still only indirectly controlled by the State, at least in Western Europe, at the beginning of the eighteenth century. Many armies still relied on civilians to drive their artillery train and baggage-wagons, and on draught animals commandeered from civilians to pull them. Civilian contractors were normally responsible for provisioning these armies, and often for supplying them with arms, ammunition and uniforms. Military hospitals also were often left in civilian hands, usually with unhappy results.

The period saw in most Western countries a series of intermittent and disjointed efforts to remedy this state of affairs. Thus the British government acquired a powder-mill of its own in 1759, though it seems to have made little use of it, and another in 1787. In 1793 two companies of horse artillery were formed, the first British artillery units to have their own drivers; and this reform was later extended to the whole of this branch of the army. The same increasing central control and rationalization can be seen also in the introduction in 1720 of a regular tariff for the purchase of commissions; in the 1750s of the custom of numbering regiments rather than referring to them by their colonel's name; and in 1792 of a common system of drill, based on that of Prussia, for the whole army. In France State-owned arms factories were set up at Maubeuge and Charleville in 1718; the government made itself responsible for the supply of uniforms in 1747; and the old system of military hospitals, which had left them largely in private hands, was abolished in 1788. More important, in 1762 recruitment was made for the first time a direct concern of the government, taking it out of the hands of the regimental officers who had hitherto controlled it. The most important assertion of central control over all aspects of military life made by any government during this period came, however, in the Habsburg Empire. There during the first half of the century, as in other armies, notably that of France, regiments were in effect the property of their colonels. These had not only control of promotions in them, with powers of life and death over their men, but even the right to impose their own systems of drill and tactics. The military crisis of the early 1740s (see pp. 290ff) made it impossible for this situation to continue. In 1749 for the first time a single system of tactics was laid down for the entire army, while in 1765 the *Hofkriegsrath* assumed the power to appoint to all ranks above that of captain and from 1776 an organized State military transport corps began to be built up.

The eighteenth century was thus a period of slow evolution rather than radical change in military affairs. It saw the continuation of a number of tendencies already visible in the reign of Louis XIV – a growth in the size of armies, a formalization of tactics, a rise in the importance of the technical branches of the service, an increase in the effectiveness of State control. It was by no means a period of stagnation. It was an age of militarism, though not yet of popular militarism; its wars and battles were a good deal more than the courtly and rather ineffective rituals which some historians have tended to imagine.

Eighteenth-century navies fluctuated in size and efficiency more, and more rapidly, than armies. For almost all European States with vulnerable land frontiers it was easier and safer to neglect the navy than the army. Also navies were, in proportion to the manpower they employed, far more expensive than armies. A ship of war with its armament and equipment was costly both to produce and to maintain: even a moderate-sized naval squadron involved a concentration of expensive artillery far larger than that of any field army. Great dockyards such as Chatham, Brest or Kronstadt were the biggest and most complex unified industrial enterprises of the age. Naval bases, with the fortifications and dock facilities they involved, were more expensive than any fortress on land: the new one built by the French government at Cherbourg in the 1780s was the most ambitious and costly public work undertaken anywhere in Western Europe during this period. By 1790 the European navies numbered in all about 470 ships of the line (the large vessels which formed the line of battle in important naval conflicts) together with about a thousand frigates and a thousand smaller ships. It is true that in peacetime a large proportion of these ships were normally laid up and had their crews paid off: only when war was imminent or had broken out were they brought back into service. This meant that a high proportion of the manpower of many European navies was available in time of peace for use in the civilian economy. The British navy which had 76,000 sailors at the end of the Seven Years War in 1763, for example, had only 17,500 in the following year. Nevertheless naval power on a large scale meant a very heavy commitment of resources: the temptation to economize on the navy in times of financial stringency was correspondingly strong.

Throughout this period Britain had the largest fleet in the world. She emerged from the War of the Grand Alliance in 1697 as the greatest of European naval powers; and this position she never lost. In 1721 she had 124 ships of the line and 105 smaller vessels, of which roughly a quarter had been built since 1714. These figures were virtually unchanged when war broke out with Spain in 1739; but lack of maintenance under the Walpole regime meant that she had only 35 of the line fit for immediate use. By 1762, however, she had 141 of the line and 224 smaller vessels; while by 1783 these figures had risen to 174 and 294, by far the most powerful fleet hitherto possessed by any State. The development of the French navy was a good deal more erratic. The War of the Spanish Succession and the financial strain it involved reduced France's strength at sea to a very low ebb, so that in 1719 she possessed only 49 ships of all rates. Yet twenty years later, largely as a result of the work of Maurepas, an energetic Secretary of State, she had nearly 50 ships of the line and was once more clearly the second-greatest European naval power. The war of 1744–48 with Great Britain meant fairly heavy losses; but by 1754 she possessed 57 ships of the line and 24 frigates. Even during the much more disastrous Seven Years War she made strenuous efforts under the Duc de Choiseul to recover her lost seapower, and these were continued in the 1760s and 1770s. In 1773 she had 66 ships of the line: by 1780, when she had 81, she was stronger at sea than ever before in her history. The development of Spanish naval strength was in step to some extent with that of France. Her fleet, which had almost ceased to exist by the end of the War of the Spanish Succession, was rapidly revived in the next two decades by able ministers such as Alberoni and Patino. By 1737 it included 33 ships of the line. Her losses in the great wars of the mid-century were smaller than those of France; and after 1748 the attention given to the navy by another Spanish statesman, Ensenada (which included the recruitment of a considerable body of shipbuilders and technicians in Britain) led to a fairly rapid increase in its strength. By 1774 she had 58 ships of the line: she is said to have possessed 72 in 1789.

More dramatic still was the growth of the Russian fleet. Its Baltic squadron, always the most important part of it, began to take shape only after Russia had acquired a foothold on that sea in 1703. Yet in the face of almost every conceivable difficulty – widespread and bitter popular hostility to the whole idea of naval development, the need to import from abroad officers and technicians of all kinds, the surrender of Azov and consequent loss of the Black Sea fleet in 1711 (see pp. 271–2) – Peter I had by his death in 1725 made Russia one of the great naval powers of Europe. His successors did not share his passion for maritime affairs; and in the 1730s and 1740s the fleet he had created was allowed to decline sharply in numbers and efficiency. Under Catherine II it was rapidly revived; and by 1788 the Baltic fleet numbered 37 ships of the line. Moreover the later 1770s and 1780s saw the re-creation of a powerful Russian squadron in the Black Sea which by 1791 possessed 22 ships of the line. Russia had thus become a naval power equal to Spain and little inferior to France.

The minor European naval powers can be briefly dismissed. Neither the Swedish nor the Danish navies were able to recover after the Great Northern War (1700–21) the importance they had enjoyed before its outbreak. Both were now overshadowed by the superior power of Russia, a fact which was driven home by the general lack of success of the Swedish fleet in the war of 1788–90 with her great eastern neighbour. The United Provinces, still a great naval power at the end of the seventeenth century, sank rapidly to a second-rate position in the early years of this period. In the War of the Spanish Succession they were seldom able to keep more than fifty warships of all sizes at sea simultaneously; and declining economic strength and the complications of their federal constitution made a recovery of their former status impossible. Neither the decaying seapower of Venice, which after the Treaty of Passarowitz in 1718 was used only in unsuccessful punitive expeditions against the Barbary States; nor the insignificant squadrons of Tuscany and Naples; nor the small and inefficient navy of Portugal, were factors of much significance in the balance of European naval power. The Ottoman Empire possessed a substantial fleet; but its ships were poorly designed (Turkey was the last important Mediterranean State to use galleys on a large scale), often inadequately armed and until fairly late in the century very poorly manned. Its efficiency was still further reduced by the fact that, almost alone among European navies of any size, it saw no active service between 1718 and 1769. Efforts to strengthen and improve it in the last decades of the century had only moderate success.

Most eighteenth-century navies, like the armies of the period, were recruited by a mixture of inducements and compulsion. In Russia the latter element was uppermost, and peasants were conscripted as sailors in very much the same way as for the army. In France a more elaborate and complex coercive apparatus existed than anywhere else in Western Europe – the system of *classement* set up by Colbert in 1668–73. It involved the registration of the seafaring inhabitants of the coastal areas of France (and later also of the population on the banks of navigable rivers) and the creation in this way of a pool of experienced sailors who could be used in manning the fleet. Like the system of militia service it pressed heavily upon the poorer sections of the groups it affected and fell comparatively lightly on the middle classes of the French seaports. This, coupled with the corruption and favouritism of many of the officials who administered it, made it widely unpopular and led to much evasion of the obligations it imposed. As a result the French navy was normally short of seamen throughout the century. In Spain, where a somewhat similar system was introduced in 1737, the same difficulties were encountered and the same disappointing results achieved.

The very moderate success of these methods did not prevent suggestions that they be copied in Britain. Throughout the century proposals for the creation of some kind of reserve of seamen were put forward, all of them without success. Fear of encroachments by the government or the armed forces on the liberty of the subject, coupled with a feeling that it was unjust that one particular group should be singled out for treatment in this way, combined to defeat all such suggestions. The British navy continued to depend on what men could be allured by bounties, snapped up by the press-gang, or recruited more or less forcibly from convicts and debtors. Though the official figures are not easy to interpret it seems that at the outbreak of the Seven Years War about half its manpower was drawn either from the jails of London and other cities or from the crews of foreign ships. The results were what might be expected. 'In a man-of-war', wrote an officer in 1756, 'you have the collected filths of jails. . . . There's not a vice committed on shore but is practised here. The scenes of horror and infamy on board of a man-of-war are so many and so great that I think they must rather disgust a mind than allure it.'[11] As in eighteenth-century armies, moreover, the defects of naval recruiting-systems were reflected in a crippling rate of desertion. In 1757 only 62 British sailors were killed in battle or died of wounds; but 4,624 deserted. A little later, in the four years 1776–80, over 42,000 men deserted from the British navy; and there is no reason to suppose that this was an unusual number by contemporary standards. Apart from desertion the other force which continually sapped and depleted the strength of every navy was disease. Overcrowded and insanitary warships were an ideal breeding-ground for every kind of contagion, while the lack of fresh food meant that until the 1790s scurvy continually threatened every ship's company. In 1774–80 for every British seaman who lost his life in battle, fifteen died of disease, while in 1779 Britain was preserved from invasion partly by the scurvy which swept the French and Spanish squadrons then for a time in control of the Channel.

Both Britain and France found difficulty in obtaining sufficient volunteers for their fleets, partly because the wages they offered their sailors compared very poorly with what could be obtained by service on a merchantman, and still more so with what might be made on a successful privateer. The pay of a sailor in the French navy in 1789 was practically the same as it had been a century before, though during that period prices had almost doubled. In Britain the wages of an ordinary seaman remained unchanged (at 19*s*. per month) during the whole of the period 1651–1797. Moreover these inadequate wages were often months in arrears, and were paid, at least in the earlier years of the century, not in cash but in tickets which could be cashed only at the Navy Office in London. The complaint of Admiral Vernon, in a parliamentary speech of 1749, that 'our fleets, which are defrauded by injustice, are first manned by violence and maintained by cruelty',[12] was substantially justified. In spite of efforts to give some semblance of fair treatment to the ordinary sailor (the most notable was the passage of Grenville's Navy Act in 1758) no radical improvement in the methods or rate of payment was made until after the mutinies of 1797.

Like eighteenth-century armies the navies of the period benefited from a certain amount of technical progress, but progress of a limited and evolutionary kind. One obvious aspect of this was the elimination from naval warfare of the galley. Its importance even in the Mediterranean, the sea which had given it birth, was rapidly declining by the later seventeenth century. Galleys took some small part in the indecisive battle of Cape Matapan between the Turkish and Venetian fleets in 1717; but apart from the large fleets of them maintained in the Baltic by Russia and Sweden they had become obsolete long before the end of this period. The French *Corps des Galères* was suppressed in 1748; and by the time of the French Revolution, except for the few maintained by the Spanish fleet and one or two in the navies of the small Italian States, galleys had disappeared from the sea which they had so long dominated. Much was done, again, by the work of mathematicians such as Euler, Bernouilli and Borda on fluid resistance and floating bodies, to make possible an improvement in the lines of sailing-ships. Books such as the *Architectura Navalis Mercatoria* of the Swede Chapman (1768) and the *Examen Maritimo Teorico Practico* of the Spaniard Jorge Juan (1771) show that this was beginning to have some influence on shipbuilders. In France, where a new class of naval engineers concerned with the building and repair of ships was created in 1765, shipbuilding was perhaps carried to a higher pitch of perfection than anywhere else in Europe. To French builders, admitted a British historian of the early nineteenth century, 'is primarily owing the energetical improvement made in modern times in the form, dimensions, and general contour of vessels'.[13] The *États de Bourgogne* of 118 guns, designed by J.-N. Sané and launched in 1782, was technically the most successful ship of the age. She was used as a model until far into the nineteenth century and was still carrying an admiral's flag in 1848. In Britain by contrast the gap between theory and practice, between the discoveries of mathematicians and the rule-of-thumb traditionalism of shipbuilders, remained very wide. Apart from the *Treatise on Shipbuilding and Navigation* of Mungo Murray (1754) no book of a scientific kind on shipbuilding or ship design was written in English during this period. The Society for the Improvement of Naval Architecture, formed in 1791, was essentially a body of theorists and amateurs with little or no practical influence. The result was a general and generally admitted inferiority of British men-of-war to those of France. 'I have never seen or heard since my knowledge of things,' wrote a British admiral in 1745, 'that one of our ships alone, singly opposed to one of the enemy's of equal force, has taken her, and I have been in almost every action and skirmish since the year 1718, and yet we are daily boasting of the prowess of our Fleet.'[14] Complaints that British ships by comparison with those of France were too small, sailed badly and were encumbered by too many guns, continued to be heard to the end of the century and afterwards; while French prizes were frequently used as models for the design of new British men-of-war.

Nevertheless it was the British navy which pioneered the two inventions which did most to increase the efficiency of eighteenth-century men-of-war. These were the copper sheathing which greatly reduced the fouling of their bottoms by weeds and the loss of speed this entailed; and the carronade which greatly increased their fighting power. The use of copper as a protection for the underwater parts of ships' hulls had been suggested in England as early as 1708 and by the 1770s it had been generally adopted throughout the navy. In France the new technique was first used, by copying from a captured British vessel, in 1778. In the decades which followed it was generally diffused throughout the navies of Europe. The carronade, a short-barrelled large-calibre gun with a low muzzle velocity, easily handled and very effective at close quarters, was first developed in 1774 and by the end of the American War was mounted on several hundred British men-of-war of all sizes. It too was copied, first of all by France and later by other continental naval powers.

Eighteenth-century observers often argued that naval battles between opponents of more or less equal strength were almost certain to be indecisive, that naval warfare was by its nature unlikely to produce victories of the kind which might be expected on land. 'Do you know what a naval battle is?' asked the French minister, Maurepas. 'I will tell you: the fleets manœuvre, come to grips, fire a few shots, and then each retreats . . . and the sea remains as salt as it was before.'[15] Experience seemed to justify this view, for the period saw many indecisive encounters of this kind; while the naval battles which produced some decisive result – Cape Passaro (1718); Hawke's victory over the French Admiral Du Bois de la Motte (1744); Lagos and Quiberon Bay (1759); Rodney's 'midnight chase' of the Spanish Admiral Langara in 1780 – were nearly all marked by a preponderance of strength on one side. Not until the battle of The Saints in 1782 (see p. 345) did a struggle between two fleets of approximately equal size produce a clear-cut victory for one of them.

The rigidity of eighteenth-century naval tactics, embodied in detailed and restrictive fighting instructions and imbued with the idea of the importance of the line of battle and its preservation, undoubtedly discouraged initiative on the part of commanders. It thus contributed to the ineffectiveness of much of the warfare of the period. The very primitive signalling systems available and the extreme difficulty of ensuring that any order was understood and obeyed were equally important obstacles in the way of an original or aggressive admiral. The improvement in signalling methods which Kempenfelt and others brought about in the British navy in the last decades of the century was a greater contribution than the idea of 'breaking the enemy's line' to the defeat of Napoleon.

Decisive naval battles were also made less likely by ideas which persisted throughout the century as to the way in which wars at sea should be fought. In France and Spain, and to a lesser extent in Britain, it was widely believed that the most important function of a fleet was not to seek out and destroy that of the enemy but to protect the colonies and seaborne trade of the State to which it belonged and capture or harass those of its opponents. The restrictions which ideas of this kind imposed on the French navy were particularly serious, and can be seen influencing France's strategy at sea throughout the century. They underlay the division in 1744–48 of the ships at her disposal into small squadrons for commerce protection, which made impossible their use in any true strategic way. They inspired the efforts of Admirals D'Estaing and De Grasse in the War of the American Revolution to seize British West Indian islands and evade rather than destroy the fleets to which they were opposed. They can also be seen in the popularity in France of the idea of attacks on British commerce as a means of forcing the traditional enemy to her knees, the belief that a *guerre de course* of this kind, avoiding large-scale engagements and making extensive use of privateers, would be more effective than a strategy which aimed at securing effective control of the seas. Alone among French sailors the Bailli de Suffren showed himself willing, in his campaigns of 1781–83 in the Indian Ocean, to challenge this fundamentally defensive attitude and the emphasis it laid on minor tactical and territorial advantages.

Nor was a similar outlook unknown on the other side of the Channel. In 1695 and 1708 Parliament, stung to action by the clamours of the London merchants, passed legislation which compelled the Admiralty to allocate specified numbers of ships to the task of protecting commerce; an unsuccessful Bill for the same purpose was introduced in 1742. Only with the emergence in 1747, in an embryonic form, of a Western Squadron dedicated to cruising off the main French Atlantic bases of Brest and Roche-fort, did strategic considerations overcome purely commercial and tactical ones in British thinking on the functions of the navy. With its establishment in the Seven Years War as an integral part of the war effort at sea their victory became decisive.

The increase of State control which has already been seen as a feature of military organization in this period is also visible where navies are concerned. It meant the disappearance from the line of battle of every European fleet of the converted merchantmen which had remained so important in wars at sea until the second half of the seventeenth century. It meant an increasing tendency for all men-of-war, at least of the larger types, to be built in government dockyards rather than by private contractors. It meant an increasingly rational and symmetrical organization of navies, the division of their ships into well-defined classes, each with relatively specialized functions and a fixed quota of men and guns. Most important of all, it meant a decline in the relative importance of privateers and even, at least in Britain, a tendency to regard them as a hindrance to the work of the navy proper. Throughout the century intensive encouragement of privateering by any State was usually a result of inferiority at sea, an implied admission that the enemy's fleet could not be defeated in open combat.

War was the greatest single factor in the international history of eighteenth-century Europe. It established Russia and Prussia as great powers. It greatly reduced the influence of Sweden and accelerated the decline of the Ottoman Empire. It substituted Spanish for Austrian influence in southern Italy. It made Lorraine a French province. Though it probably did not benefit her economically as much as has sometimes been thought, it endowed Britain with a great colonial empire and virtually unlimited opportunities of further expansion. On the economic and social history of the period its influence was also enormous. It meant growing State intervention in the economy, in the building of barracks, dockyards and fortifications and sometimes in the creation of entire new industries for war purposes. The need to create powerful fighting forces had repercussions on Russian society which were almost revolutionary, and underlay almost every aspect of the development of Prussia. It was war expenditure which brought the French monarchy by the 1780s to bankruptcy and collapse. The governments of old regime Europe were more than anything else war-making machines; the maintenance of large armed forces absorbed more of their energies and resources than anything else. The history of the generations which preceded the French Revolution almost as much as of that which followed it must be written in terms of warfare.

NOTES AND REFERENCES

1   *Boswell in Holland, 1763–1764*, ed. F. A. Pottle (London, 1952), p. 164.

2   D. Ramsay, *The History of the American Revolution* (London, 1793), vol. II, p. 281.

3   N. Barbon, *A Discourse of Trade* (London, 1690), p. 43.

4   *Lectures on Justice, Police, Revenue and Arms* (London, 1896), p. 273.

5   Quoted in C. Duffy, *The Army of Frederick the Great* (Newton Abbot, 1974), p. 127.

6   Barbon, *op. cit.*, pp. 41, 49.

7   *The History of the Reign of the Emperor Charles V* (London, 1769), vol. III, pp. 430–1.

8   *An Inquiry into the Principles of Political Economy* (London, 1767), vol. I, p. 448.

9   *Reveries, or Memoirs concerning the Art of War* (Edinburgh, 1759), p. 76.

10 M. Loir, *La Marine royale en 1789* (Paris, 1894), p. 98.

11 Sir W. L. Clowes, *The Royal Navy: a history from the earliest times to the present* (London, 1897–1903), vol. III, p. 21.

12 Sir H. W. Richmond, *The Navy in the War of 1739–48* (Cambridge, 1920), vol. I, p. 274.

13 J. Charnock, *A History of Marine Architecture* (London, 1800–02), vol. III, p. 172.

14 H. W. Hodges and E. A. Hughes (eds), *Select Naval Documents* (Cambridge, 1936), p. 121.

15 J. Tramond, *Manuel d'histoire maritime de la France* (2nd edn, Paris, 1927), p. 459.

8

DIPLOMACY AND INTERNATIONAL RELATIONS

By the beginning of the eighteenth century the framework of European diplomacy was well established. From the fifteenth century onwards, first in Italy and then in Western Europe generally, States had begun to maintain representatives more or less permanently in each other's capitals. These representatives corresponded regularly and sometimes very frequently with the governments for which they acted; from the early sixteenth century onwards their despatches and reports, preserved in the official archives which were now beginning to be formed, are one of the most important sources of information available to the historian. More slowly, ministers and departments of State charged more or less specifically with the conduct of foreign affairs emerged in most West European countries, though it was not until late in the eighteenth century that this process began to reach completion. The conception of a balance of power, again originating in Italy, spread rapidly to the other States of Western and Central Europe. From the time of the Emperor Charles V (1519–56) onwards the idea, if not the phrase itself, was part of the common currency of European political life.

In this network of institutions and ideas the eighteenth century saw no fundamental change. It was not qualitatively different on the eve of the French Revolution from what it had been during the reign of Louis XIV. From the beginning of the century, however, it was being extended to include large areas hitherto only on the fringes of the European system of international relations. The greatest of these was Russia. Until the end of the seventeenth century her diplomatic contacts with the States of

Western Europe had been intermittent and usually unimportant (see p. 256). In 1695, when Peter I first acquired effective control of the government, Russia had no permanent diplomatic representatives in foreign capitals. The officials chosen to represent her on intermittent and shortlived embassies were usually ignorant of the languages of the countries to which they were sent and often 'Moscow Germans' (descendants of foreigners who had settled in Russia) rather than Russians by ancestry. The *Posolskii Prikaz* (Department of Embassies) had for several generations been a part of the central administration, but Russia's relations with the outside world were still very limited. Under Peter this position changed completely. From 1699 onwards, when A. A. Matveev was sent as minister to the United Provinces, a network of diplomatic representatives abroad comparable in its extent and efficiency to that of any European State was rapidly created. By 1721 Russia had twenty-one permanent diplomatic missions in foreign countries (including one in Pekin and another in Bokhara) a number which was not to be exceeded during the remainder of the century. Simultaneously the number of foreign diplomats more or less permanently resident in Russia also increased. In 1702 there were only four of these (apart from unofficial agents of the Hospodar of Wallachia and of some dissident Serbian groups). By 1719 there were eleven, a figure which would have been higher but for the continuing war with Sweden and the very strained relations with Great Britain which then existed.

This expansion of diplomatic contacts between Russia and the other States of Europe did not end with Peter's reign. Though the number of Russian diplomatic missions abroad tended to fall somewhat in the decades which followed his death – there were nineteen in 1779 and (largely for reasons of economy) only fourteen in 1800 – the country did not relapse into the isolation of the seventeenth century. European diplomacy had thus extended its frontiers far to the East; a new, large, and in some ways awkwardly shaped piece had now to be fitted into the jigsaw of international relations. A new and heavy weight was now available to be thrown on one side or the other of the balance of power. In 1716 the French *Almanach Royal* for the first time listed the Romanovs as one of the reigning families of Europe, an important recognition of Russia's new status: during the next generation the completeness and irrevocability of her emergence as a great power was fully brought home to most observers.

At the beginning of this period the Ottoman Empire occupied a position akin to that of Russia. From the end of the fifteenth century she had been a factor in European diplomacy. She had played an important part in the long series of struggles between France and the Habsburgs which dominated the age of Charles V. By the early seventeenth century France, England, Venice and the United Provinces were all maintaining permanent representatives in Constantinople (though the English and Dutch ones were commercial rather than diplomatic agents). Yet she was clearly not a European State, and she never became during the eighteenth century completely incorporated into the European diplomatic system. Until far into this period there were many important States which were not represented at Constantinople (Sweden had no resident minister there until 1734, Prussia none till 1758). More significant, it was not until after it ended that she began to possess permanent representatives of her own in the major capitals of Europe. Nevertheless the political and diplomatic links which bound her to the rest of the continent were slowly multiplying and becoming stronger. The importance of the role she was now, willy-nilly, being forced to play in European affairs, in spite (or perhaps because) of her increasing weakness and inefficiency, is shown by the great though indirect and unsought significance of her part in the first partition of Poland (see pp. 273ff). In the Balkans and the Levant, as in Russia, the European diplomatic system was extending its scope.

The increasing importance of the diplomatic network which bound together the States of Europe was reflected in the eighteenth century in the development in most countries of central institutions for the direction of foreign policy. Foreign Offices of a modern kind, specialized in their functions, subdivided (usually on a largely geographical basis) into departments with still more specialized duties and employing considerable numbers of experts of all kinds, now appear for the first time in the major European capitals.

In this development France led the way. By the end of the seventeenth century she already possessed what seemed to many contemporaries the most efficient diplomatic organization in Europe, one which had at its disposal able negotiators, plentiful funds, expert knowledge and the prestige of past success. In the two generations which followed the death of Louis XIV it was further extended and elaborated. In the last years of his reign a tendency towards the creation of specialized departments within the ministry had become visible. A *dépot des archives* was set up in 1688; while the Marquis de Torcy (Louis's last Foreign Minister) had begun about the same time the creation of a rudimentary Press bureau. Departments for the handling of current diplomatic business also began to develop, each under a high official, the *premier commis*, of whom there were usually two or three. The number of departments in the ministry and their functions changed frequently during the century; but there was a general tendency for them to become more numerous. Thus a *bureau des fonds* with a wide range of responsibilities including control of the ministry's finances was set up in 1725, a *bureau du chiffre* for the cyphering and decyphering of despatches in 1749 and a *bureau des interprètes* in 1768.

This organization was not always as efficient in fact as it should have been in theory. The accumulation and arrangement of its archives, for example, was not always thorough or complete. Thus in 1779, when it was desired to refer to Choiseul's despatches relating to the Family Compact of 1761, they could not be found and copies had to be obtained from Madrid. Nevertheless the ministry was probably the best and most complete of its kind in Europe. In the second half of this period, under Secretaries of State such as the Duc de Choiseul (1758–70) and the Comte de Vergennes (1774–87) it was becoming steadily a more and more effective machine. By 1789 it had assumed in most respects its nineteenth-century form.

Even more striking was the growth in Russia of the *Posolskii Prikaz* and its successor the College of Foreign Affairs. The great expansion of diplomatic contact between Russia and the rest of Europe brought about by Peter I inevitably led to an increase in the size and activity of the *Posolskii Prikaz*. As early as 1705 it was one of the largest Foreign Offices in Europe, with over forty translators at its disposal. Moreover it was becoming for the first time, as a result of Peter's administrative reforms, an institution concerned solely with diplomacy. It no longer supervised, as in the seventeenth century, the administration of certain Russian provinces, or acted as a tax-collecting body. This stripping away of extraneous duties continued under its successor, the College of Foreign Affairs, which began to function in 1719, and well before the end of the century this process of specialization had been completed. The college had become a body concerned with the formulation and execution of foreign policy and nothing else.

Like the French Foreign Ministry the *Posolskii Prikaz* and College of Foreign Affairs showed during the eighteenth century an increasing tendency to divide into specialized departments. As early as 1705 there were five of these with well-defined functions, each handling relations with a specific group of countries, and new departments were added as time went on (for example a Ceremonial Department which evolved in the reign of Catherine II). The growth in the complexity of Russian diplomatic machinery can be seen in the rapidly increasing number of people employed in its control and direction, especially under Catherine II, and its still more rapidly increasing cost.

No other Foreign Office grew with the speed of those of France and Russia; but in almost every European State existing arrangements for the central control of foreign policy became more complex and efficient. In the Habsburg territories Joseph I set up in 1709 a new permanent committee of nine officials to control foreign affairs. This, reorganized by Charles VI in 1721, continued to be one of the most important organs of government until the rise of the dominating figure of Kaunitz in the 1750s. Almost equally important was the ending, by a series of agreements in 1745, 1773 and 1790, of a struggle for influence which had been going on for generations between the *Reichskanzlei* (Imperial Chancery) under its hereditary head, the Elector of Mainz, and the *Hofkanzlei* (the Chancery of the Habsburg hereditary lands). In Sweden arrangements for the control of foreign affairs were complex and unstable during the period 1720–72; but strenuous efforts were made to improve them and Gustavus III's *coup d'état* in the latter year increased their efficiency. Britain, sheltered by the sea and the strength of her navy from the necessity of having a good diplomatic organization, never attempted to compete with the great continental States in this respect. Even in the 1780s the Foreign Office had probably fewer than twenty employees in all; and throughout the century the efficiency of British diplomacy was hampered by the lack of effective arrangements for preserving correspondence and by a shortage of translators. Nevertheless an important step forward was taken in 1782 by the creation of the office of Secretary of State for Foreign Affairs. This concentrated in the hands of one individual the control of foreign policy which had hitherto been entrusted, together with a vast range of other business, to the Secretaries of State for the Northern and Southern Departments. Even in Poland some attempt to improve existing arrangements for the control of what foreign policy the country had becomes visible after 1775.

This period therefore saw the culmination of tendencies already visible in previous generations which made the diplomatic services of Europe more technically efficient than ever before. It also saw frequent proposals that diplomats should be given some systematic training to fit them for the posts they were to occupy. The best-known effort of this kind was that made by Torcy in 1712 to prepare a small number of young men for the French diplomatic service by the creation of a 'Political Academy'. This however lasted only until 1720. A generation later, in 1747, Frederick II set up a training school for the Prussian diplomatic service, again on a small scale. This came to an end during the Seven Years War; and although it was refounded in 1775 it seems to have been designed merely to produce men capable of filling such relatively minor posts as those at Warsaw and The Hague, where it was not necessary for the Prussian representative to be of high social rank. A similar effort can be seen in the *ukaz* of 1797 by which the Tsar Paul ordered the admission to the College of Foreign Affairs of thirty young men who were to be trained there for diplomatic careers. None of these schemes had much practical importance. In almost every European State the majority of the more important diplomatic posts were filled by aristocrats, sometimes great aristocrats, who were unwilling to submit to the drudgery of specialized training and often unable to acquire large amounts of specialized knowledge. Moreover it was widely and probably correctly felt that good diplomats were formed by experience rather than by study, by mixing in good society and watching negotiations in progress rather than by poring over documents in archives. Would-be ambassadors thus continued to be trained, in so far as they were trained at all, by the time-honoured method of acting as secretaries to older and more experienced diplomats, or by being attached in some subordinate capacity to one of their country's embassies abroad.

Secret diplomacy, though in itself perfectly legitimate and indeed essential to the functioning of the European diplomatic system, on various occasions during the century complicated and stultified the policies of a number of European States. This was particularly marked in France, where from 1745 onwards Louis XV created a complex mechanism, the *Secret du Roi*, designed to give effect to his personal policies. This functioned side by side with the official diplomacy controlled by the king's ministers. Though completely ineffective in obtaining the results at which Louis feebly aimed, in particular the strengthening of Poland, it did much, until his death, to confuse and weaken French policy, particularly in Eastern Europe. Moreover diplomats, as in the seventeenth century, were frequently corrupt; and the attitude of contemporaries to short-comings of this kind remained remarkably casual by modern standards. Perhaps the most striking case of this is J. A. Thugut, Austrian representative at Constantinople in 1769–75, who was throughout these years an agent in French pay regularly transmitting confidential information to his French colleague, the Comte de Saint-Priest (though it is true that French and Austria were at that time allies, at least in name). This fact, which was well known in his own lifetime, did not prevent his succeeding Kaunitz as Chancellor in 1792. Espionage continued to be an essential and sometimes very important ingredient in the conduct of international relations. The most obvious example of the significance it could have is Frederick II's invasion of Saxony in August 1756. This attack, which made inevitable the outbreak of a great European war (see p. 298) was in part provoked by the contents of documents which a Saxon government clerk had been bribed to betray to the Prussians. On a lower level of importance there are numerous examples of the prevalence and occasional success of political espionage. For five years (1770–75) the entire correspondence of John Murray, British Ambassador to the Porte, was copied by one of his servants and the copies sent to his French colleague and rival; simultaneously the Cardinal-Prince de Rohan, French Ambassador at Vienna in 1772–74, obtained through an anonymous intermediary a great amount of confidential correspondence relating to the policies of Austria and many other States.

The interception and copying of the despatches of foreign diplomats by official organizations created for the purpose (*cabinets noirs*) was also a regular practice in many States. The Habsburg government in particular had a great reputation for its skill in this respect and maintained offices for the purpose in Liège, Brussels, Frankfurt and Regensburg, as well as in Vienna. The Thurn und Taxis family, which had since the sixteenth century controlled the postal services of the smaller German States, maintained on behalf of the Emperor similar establishments in many cities of the Holy Roman Empire. France too possessed a very efficient *cabinet noir*, and down to the fall of the Duc de Choiseul in 1770 most of her Foreign Ministers also held the post of *Surintendant-Général des Postes*, thus maintaining effective control over so valuable an auxiliary. By the 1780s it had twelve employees; and complaints against its interference with the correspondence of private citizens figured in a number of the *cahiers* presented to the States-General in 1789. In Britain the position was somewhat similar. It had been established by the Post Office Act of 1711 that private letters could be opened on the warrant of a Secretary of State; and in 1730 the Duke of Newcastle ordered the Postmaster-General to make copies of all correspondence passing through his hands addressed to any of a list of 112 people, including the sovereigns and leading statesmen of Europe. After 1765 lists of this kind were replaced by general warrants ordering the copying of all diplomatic correspondence passing through London. By 1741 the British version of the *cabinet noir*, the 'Secret Office', was employing nine people; and its cost tended to increase in the second half of the century. It was at least as successful as its French equivalent in intercepting the correspondence of foreign diplomats, and far more so in keeping its activities secret.

Secret diplomacy, bribery, the interception of correspondence – none of these was in any way peculiar to the eighteenth century. They had existed long before it: they were to exist long after it. They were the result, not of some unique wickedness of the age, but of the natural exigencies of a system of competitive States. It could indeed be argued with some force that international morality was tending to improve slightly during this period. There was at least no example in Western Europe in the eighteenth century of the premeditated murder by secret agents of one country of a diplomat belonging to another, a thing which had been seen under the rule of Louis XIV.[1]

The traditions and attitudes of the seventeenth century were also continued in the importance attached, particularly in the first half of this period, to questions of diplomatic precedence. To ensure that his sovereign's dignity was not slighted by any infringement of the precedence claimed by his representatives continued to be one of the major tasks of the European diplomat;

and the continuing importance of questions of precedence is shown by the continuing production of books which claimed to elucidate them. 'Points of honour, rank, precedence, are the most delicate aspects of political life', wrote the author of one of these. 'Princes will cede towns, even provinces, but all the ability of the most adroit negotiators cannot persuade them to give up a rank to which they believe themselves entitled.'[2] The great peace congresses which punctuated the history of the period gave particular scope, by bringing together in one place the representatives of a large number of different States, for disputes of this kind. Seating arrangements at conferences, forms of address and other issues of this kind remained a continual source of potential difficulty. It is a sign of the slowly increasing political maturity of the age that serious negotiations were less frequently impeded by such quibbles than in the previous century. Even so, the attention devoted to questions of precedence, though declining, remained great until late in this period. In particular the assumption of the title of Emperor by Peter I of Russia in 1721 set off a series of complicated controversies (notably with the Holy Roman Emperors who claimed a monopoly of the imperial title) which dragged on intermittently for decades.

The relations of the European States continued to be influenced in the eighteenth century, almost as much as in the age of Louis XIV, by the idea of the balance of power. Theoretical justifications of such a balance were frequent; and by the middle decades of the century it was being discussed more widely than ever before. By then Europe was clearly becoming a single State-system. The localized 'inferior balances' – between Sweden and Denmark in the Baltic, between France and the Habsburgs in Germany and Italy – in terms of which many writers and politicians had hitherto thought, were becoming merged in a general balance which covered the whole continent.

In the first half of the century this continental balance was envisaged as essentially one of France, supported at times by Spain and some of the German States (above all Bavaria), against the Austrian Habsburgs, supported in general by Great Britain and the United Provinces. The apparent symmetry of this arrangement was rapidly shown to be superficial and delusive. A number of diplomatic episodes (notably the Anglo-French alliance of 1716 and the Austro-Spanish combination of 1725: see pp. 328, 315) made it clear that in this respect the presumptions of the previous century were no longer valid. Moreover the fact that after 1713 no State in Western Europe was in a position to dominate the area, as France had done during much of the reign of Louis XIV, introduced into the politics of the period an element of flexibility which had previously been lacking. Most important of all, traditional conceptions of the balance of power were now being undermined by the rapid emergence of great new political forces in East and East Central Europe, those of Russia and Prussia. However the full significance of this went unperceived until the 1740s; and even then habit kept the minds of most observers running in the old channels of Bourbon-Habsburg rivalry till the Diplomatic Revolution of 1756. Louis XIV had seen in the last days of his reign the growing pointlessness of the traditional Franco-Austrian antagonism, but his efforts to achieve some agreement with the Habsburgs were not followed up by his successors. It was the Seven Years War which broke up completely and decisively the old system of balance four decades later.

With France and the Habsburgs now allies (see p. 296) the pivot on which the old system turned had disappeared. The tradition of Anglo-Austrian co-operation against France, wearing thin in the time of Walpole and strained unbearably by the peace settlement of 1748, was also submerged by the events of the 1750s. Prussia had established, at least for the time being, her position as one of the great European powers; and the personal prestige of her ruler stood higher than that of any other European monarch. The Habsburgs had been stung by the loss of Silesia into a series of far-reaching administrative reforms, while Russia had once more displayed her military strength and had consolidated her dominant position in Poland. The result of these changes was to move the centre of gravity of European diplomacy sharply to the east after 1763. The growth in the importance of Prussia and Russia, the renaissance of Habsburg power, now contrasted sharply with the isolation and internal divisions of Britain and the financial weakness and diminished military prestige of France. The main problems of European politics after the Seven Years War were Eastern ones, those of Poland and European Turkey, not, as a generation earlier, those of the Netherlands, the Rhineland or Italy. The inability of the States of Western Europe to play a decisive role in the solution of these new questions was shown clearly by the impotent resentment with which the French government had to watch the first partition of Poland in 1772 and the Russian annexation of the Crimea in 1783–84. The European balance of power was thus after the Seven Years War a more subtle problem in many ways than in the first half of the century. It now covered a greater geographical area and involved a greater number of powerful States than ever before.

Side by side with this European aspect of the balance of power went another and increasingly important one – that constituted by events on the oceans and in Europe's colonies overseas. Most contemporaries realized that the two aspects were intimately connected. In particular they believed that a State which could dominate the sea and Europe's trade with the outside world would have gone far towards making herself mistress of the continent. Defoe proclaimed that 'to be Masters of the Marine Power is to be Masters of all the Power and all the Commerce in Europe'.[3] Similarly a French pamphleteer in the middle of the century argued that 'the power which is strongest at sea must necessarily be the strongest commercially and thus the most formidable . . . dominance of the sea would give a nation universal monarchy'. From these assumptions there naturally followed the idea that a balance between the maritime strengths of the European States must be safeguarded in the same way as that between their territories in Europe. Such an idea was beginning to be put forward at least as early as the 1720s.

In this naval and colonial struggle the main protagonists were Great Britain and, in opposition to her, France normally supported by Spain. In most of the continental States this aspect of the balance of power aroused anti-British feelings. To them it was essentially an effort, on the whole an unsuccessful one, to restrict and if possible reverse the enormous growth of Britain's maritime strength and overseas possessions. The vigour, sometimes amounting to brutality, with which she utilized her seapower in time of war, by wholesale interference with neutral shipping carrying contraband or trading with her enemies, did much to increase the hostility with which she was now widely regarded. It meant that merchants and public opinion in the United Provinces, Sweden, Denmark or the Hanse towns were easy targets for French propaganda stressing the dangers of British seapower and the need for Europe to combine to restrain its use.

Propaganda of this kind was particularly marked during the Seven Years War, and spread the idea of a trade balance which must be defended against the excessive strength of Britain just as the territorial balance in Europe must be safeguarded from the over-grown influence of any continental State. The English, alleged the Duc de Choiseul, 'while pretending to protect the balance on land which no one threatens . . . are entirely destroying the balance at sea which no one defends'. Nor were these arguments without practical effect. The approaches made in 1759 by the Danish government to the United Provinces for the creation of a mari-time union to defend neutral rights were only one of a series of proposals for some anti-British combination of this kind which culminated in the Armed Neutrality of 1780.

Analyses of the working of the balance of power, whether continental or colonial, became increasingly numerous and elab-orate in the eighteenth century. It was now no longer sufficient to accept it as the more or less automatic result of the existence of a number of completely sovereign States bound together by geographical contiguity. More and more it tended to be regarded not merely as a useful political device but as something with a moral value and justification of its own. Arguments of this kind normally started from the assumption that the powers of Europe were still in a 'state of nature' with respect to each other and that each of them was engaged, consciously or not, in a ceaseless struggle to increase its influence at the expense of its neighbours. 'Each nation in its natural state,' wrote a widely read commen-tator in the 1740s, 'must be considered as the enemy of all others; or as disposed to be such.'[4] 'We cannot rely on virtue; it is weak and equivocal, or hidden and unknown; . . . we must thus take as our starting-point only the possible and even probable abuse of power,' wrote another two generations later.[5] If these pessi-mistic assumptions were justified, how could the smaller States protect their interests or even their existence? Only by a tacit but effective agreement to combine against any power which threat-ened them, in other words by the creation of a balance of power. A balance of this kind, it was contended, was an essential condition of the functioning of the European State-system. It was even argued that a State could justifiably be compelled, by the other members of that system, to sacrifice for the common good territory to which it had every legal right, just as it in its turn could compel one of its subjects if necessary to sacrifice some of

his wealth to its needs; for 'the most legitimate rulers must sometimes renounce their rights in order to maintain the balance'.[6]

Such theories were exposed to obvious practical objections. In
particular they assumed that it was possible, at any given
moment, to make reasonably precise comparisons of the real
strength of the States concerned, to estimate accurately the advantages of Britain's wealth as against Russia's population or Prussia's
efficient bureaucracy. The power of the various European States
was in practice estimated by commentators largely in the crude
terms of the extent of territory each possessed. This, however,
was seen by some of them to be an unreliable criterion. Spain
under her last Habsburg kings, it was pointed out, had controlled
far more territory than any other European country and had none
the less been a victim-State on the point of internal collapse. It
was also possible to classify the States of Europe according to
their ability to wage war, whether on their own or with the help
of subsidies and other encouragements from their more powerful
neighbours. This, though a more realistic standard of judgement,
was also not entirely satisfactory. Discussions of how the relative
strength of States should be evaluated were common, but none
of their authors succeeded in finding a clear or universally applicable solution to the problem.

It is easy to find in the political writing of the eighteenth
century, and especially in its vast pamphlet literature, frequent
rejection of the idea of the balance of power. On closer exam-
ination, however, most of this turns out to be the product, not
of reasoned consideration and reflection, but merely of some
political manœuvre or party attitude. Fundamental criticism of the
idea of safeguarding the rights and interests of individual States
by means of some form of balance came only from the authors
of the various peace projects produced during this period.

These writers, like the theorists whom they criticized, started
from the assumption that the governments of Europe were still
in a 'state of nature' and that some means must be found of
restraining their innate propensity to attack and injure one
another. They agreed in rejecting the balance of power as a hopelessly inefficient mechanism for this purpose. It was, wrote the
best-known and most influential of them, the Abbé de Saint-
Pierre, 'that vain Idol to which the Nations have Sacrificed so
blindly, so fruitlessly, and for so long a Time, so much Blood
and Treasure'.[7] Peace and security, they argued, could be achieved

only by the creation of some effective international authority able to override the selfish or aggressive impulses of any individual ruler and to persuade him, if necessary by force, to respect the rights of his neighbours. In other words what was wanted was something equivalent, on the international level, to the 'social contract' from which the States themselves were thought to have originated. Just as men had at some remote date in the past surrendered some of their individual rights to a sovereign and thus created civil society, so now each State must surrender some of its sovereignty to a supranational authority. The suggestion of a 'social contract' between States had already been made in the first half of the seventeenth century by Grotius. It had been repeated at the end of that century by Leibniz, who attempted in the collections of treaties and other documents which he published, the *Codex Juris Gentium Diplomaticus* (1693) and *Mantissa Codicis* (1700), to provide a basis for it. The form which this idea normally took, that of a federation of States ruled by some central body which included representatives of all of them, was probably encouraged by the great political and economic success achieved in the seventeenth century by the new federation of the United Provinces. Its practicability was also sometimes alleged to be proved by the existence of the Holy Roman Empire or the Swiss cantons, both of which could be considered as types of loose federation.

Various more or less precise suggestions as to the structure of such a federation were put forward by different writers in the earlier years of this period – by the Quaker William Penn in his *Essay towards the Present and Future Peace of Europe* (1693), by another Quaker, John Bellers, in his *Some Reasons for an European State* (London, 1710), by the author of the anonymous *Cardinal Alberoni's Scheme for reducing the Turkish Empire to the Obedience of Christian Princes* (London, 1736) and by Saint-Pierre himself. Similar proposals continued to be made in various forms in the second half of the century, though none was elaborated in as much detail as that of Saint-Pierre or attracted as much attention. Thus the English radical Richard Price suggested in very general terms in 1776 the creation of a senate in which all the States of Europe would be represented and which would have power to intervene in disputes between them. A decade later a greater radical, Jeremy Bentham, suggested that the armed forces of all the European States should be reduced to low fixed levels, that all colonies should be freed (one of the first recognitions in schemes of this kind of the importance which overseas possessions were now assuming in European politics) and that a 'common court of judicature' should be set up to settle international disputes. More original, though hardly more practical, was the proposal of Thomas Pownall, a former Governor of Massachusetts, for the creation of 'a Council of Commerce, for all Europe and North America (absolutely exclusive of all and every point of politics)'.[8] This he hoped would enforce freedom of the seas and promote freedom of international trade. It might also, he modestly suggested, tend to prevent wars, and would at least help to codify and enforce maritime law in time of war.

Pownall's suggestion exemplified an approach to the problem of international peace which, from the 1770s onwards, increasingly supplanted schemes of the essentially traditional sort typified by that of St Pierre. This involved most notably a stress on the power of economic forces to overcome existing divisions between States. Free trade, it was argued, would at last give effect to the natural harmony which should exist between peoples and end the artifical and destructive tradition of political and dynastic division which had hitherto kept them apart. Hopes of this kind owed much to the influence and example of the Physiocrats in France; but their power in the English-speaking world on both sides of the Atlantic was considerable. Associated with them was the potentially much more radical assumption that the foreign relations of States were indissolubly bound up with the structure of their internal politics. It followed from this that real international peace could be attained only through far-reaching political reform within the European States and the weakening or destruction of the monarchical, aristocratic and military influences which had hitherto dominated them. If this could be achieved, wrote the English radical Tom Paine in the early 1790s, 'the intrigue of courts, by which the system of war is kept up, may provoke a confederation of peoples to abolish it'. But ideas so uncompromising as this could hardly be voiced, at least on the eastern shores of the Atlantic, until after the French Revolution had broken out.

No eighteenth-century peace plan had the slightest chance of being put into practice. Not only the statesmen of the age but also public opinion, partly sheltered from the realities of war by the employment of mainly professional armies, were untouched by the enthusiasm for peace which usually prompted such schemes and indifferent to the dreams which they embodied. The only political figures of importance to be even slightly influenced by ideas of this kind were the Marquis d'Argenson, who controlled French foreign policy, with small practical success, in the years 1744–47, and perhaps the Comte de Vergennes, who occupied a similar position in 1774–87.

Eighteenth-century plans for universal peace were also weakened by the fact that, in an age in which the relative strengths of the European States were rapidly altering, they shared the conservative bias, the desire to maintain the *status quo*, which seems inherent in any scheme of this kind. All of them tended to assume that the territorial division of Europe as it stood at the moment of their publication was, or could be made, permanent and sacrosanct. In some cases their authors avowed openly their desire to perpetuate the distribution of territory which existed when they wrote. Thus Saint-Pierre specified that existing frontiers were not to be changed in any way, and that no exchanges of territory were to take place or treaties between States to be made except with the consent of the federation which he wished to create. Eighty years later Immanuel Kant, in his *Zum Ewigen Frieden, ein philosophisches Entwurf* (1795) proposed as one of the preliminary conditions of a lasting peace that no State should ever pass under the control of another by any means – inheritance, exchange, purchase or donation as well as conquest. To generations which had seen Russia's expansion in the Baltic, the Black Sea and the Caucasus, Frederick II's attacks on Silesia and Saxony, and the partitions of Poland, such ideas appeared utterly unrealistic.

NOTES AND REFERENCES

1   In 1739 the Swedish representative at Constantinople, while returning home, was murdered in Silesia by Russian agents; but such an outrage would hardly have been committed by those of Britain, France or the Netherlands.

2   J. Rousset de Missy, *Mémoires sur le Rang et la Préséance entre les Souverains de l'Europe* (Amsterdam, 1746), Introduction.

3   *A Plan of the English Commerce* (London, 1737), p. 147.

4 L. M. Kahle, *La Balance de l'Europe considérée comme la règle de la paix et de la guerre* (Berlin-Göttingen, 1744), p. 33.

5 J. P. F. Ancillon, *Tableau des révolutions du système politique de l'Europe* (Berlin, 1803–05), vol. I, Introduction, p. 32.

6 Kahle, *op. cit.*, pp. 143–4, 147.

7 C. I. Castel de Saint- Pierre, *A Project for Settling an Everlasting Peace in Europe* (London, 1739), p. 20. The first edition was published in French at Cologne in 1712.

8 *A Memorial most humbly addressed to the Sovereigns of Europe, on the present State of Affairs between the Old and New World* (London, 1780), pp. 120–2.

9

THE EXPANSION OF RUSSIA: POLAND, THE BALTIC AND THE NEAR EAST

We have seen in Chapter VI that the internal politics of most European States were powerfully influenced by the personalities of their rulers. This was even more true of their foreign policies. Dynastic considerations, though slowly becoming less important, still bulked very large in international relations. Except in States such as Great Britain, the United Provinces or Sweden, where the monarchy was in some way limited, it was still easy, at least in the first half of the century, for kings and ministers to assume that the interests of a people were identical with those of its ruling family. Sometimes this assumption was justified. Territorial or strategic advantages which increased the personal or family prestige of the ruler might also give his subjects greater security from invasion, or better access to the sea or to important routes of communication. The expansion of Russia to be described in this chapter, and the wars by which it was accomplished, were in the long run desirable from the point of view of the ordinary Russian. Moreover rulers knew well, as has been pointed out in Chapter V, that the prosperity of their peoples contributed to their own power. Nevertheless dynastic and national interests could conflict; and when they did the former usually prevailed. The purely dynastic policy pursued so tenaciously by Philip V of Spain and his wife in Italy (see Chapter 11), a policy of no benefit whatever to the country they ruled, is a good example of this.

The increasing efficiency of governments and diplomatic services and the growing size of armies meant that foreign policies could be carried out with increasing vigour and continuity. In a world in which monarchies were powerful and social problems largely ignored or assumed to be insoluble, foreign policy bulked larger in the calculations of most governments during this period than in the century which followed. In the great States of Europe the Foreign Minister was often the most important of all ministers. The greatest legacy of the eighteenth century to modern times is the changes in inter–State relationships which it saw. The emergence as major powers of Russia and Prussia, the expansion of the first British Empire, the achievement of American independence, are more directly relevant to the present day than much of the art, literature and intellectual life of the period.

In the later seventeenth century Russia was still, for most purposes, outside Europe. As yet she possessed no coastline except in the north, on the White Sea which was frozen for a large part of the year. In the west she was cut off from the Baltic by Sweden's possession of Livonia, Ingria and Finland. In the south the Ottoman Empire and its Tatar vassal-State in the Crimea barred her way to the Black Sea. To European economic life she contributed nothing except some raw materials and a limited market for manufactured goods. Russian embassies began to be sent to the States of Western Europe in increasing numbers in the later seventeenth century, above all in the 1680s; but the country still played a very modest part in European diplomacy. So little was known in Western capitals about even the most obvious aspects of her political life that in 1657 Louis XIV addressed an official letter to the Tsar Michael, who had then been dead for twelve years. The greatest of all obstacles to the westernization of the country, however, was the influence of the Orthodox Church, ruled by its Patriarch, which was extremely conservative and hostile to foreigners. The breaking of its political power by Peter I, which began at the end of the century (see p. 461), was thus an essential step towards the emergence of a modern State in Russia. To foreigners in the seventeenth century the Russians and most aspects of their life seemed Asiatic rather than European. Their drunkenness and cruelty, which surpassed even those common in the West, appeared proofs of their barbarism.

Peter I, who had become Tsar jointly with his imbecile half-brother Ivan V in 1682, was established in 1689 as more or less effective ruler of the country by a revolution which overthrew his half-sister, the Tsarevna Sophia, Regent for the last seven years. He dominated every aspect of its life with increasing completeness from about 1695 onwards. Even as a youth he gave evidence of a desire to break with the past – in his friendships with foreigners and interest in foreign techniques, in his first fumbling efforts to improve the mechanism of government and in his intense interest in the sea. Largely as a result of his attitude, contacts between Russia and Western Europe expanded very rapidly for a number of years from the 1690s onwards. He found that to raise his army to European standards of efficiency and to construct a navy (the most cherished of all his projects) he had to import large numbers of soldiers, sailors, engineers and shipbuilders from the West. His first military success, the capture from the Turks in 1696 of the port of Azov at the mouth of the Don, was made possible partly by Austrian engineers provided by the Emperor Leopold I. The construction of the first Russian fleet, the flotilla of light craft built on the Don in 1695–96 for the successful campaign against Azov, was carried out largely by foreign experts, mostly Italians and Dutchmen. Peter's great journey to the West in 1697–98, during which he visited Prussia, the Netherlands, England and the Habsburg territories, an event quite unprecedented in Russian history, was inspired in part by the desire to recruit foreign technicians of all kinds for his service. It led to the engagement of several hundred of them. Simultaneously numbers of young Russians began to be sent to Western Europe to study. The majority went to the Netherlands, Italy and England to learn shipbuilding and navigation, while others in Germany studied languages, fortification and even medicine.

Peter's attitude to the West and its culture was, at least until near the end of his reign, utilitarian and pragmatic. He was interested in its techniques rather than its ideas. He admired its power and wealth rather than its philosophy or political thought. Nevertheless Western influences of a non-material as well as a material kind were now steadily increasing in Russia, a tendency illustrated by the foundation in 1699 of the first Russian order of knighthood, that of St Andrew.

These developments had for some time little influence on Russia's political relationships with the rest of Europe. Since 1686 she had been the ally of Poland, and *de facto* also of the Emperor Leopold I and of Venice, in long struggle against the Ottoman Empire. The campaigns against Azov in 1695–96 had been the main Russian contribution to this conflict; and she had played very subordinate rôle in the anti-Turkish coalition. She had won no victories comparable to those gained by the Habsburg armies on the Danube from 1683 onwards and had never been able to influence the policies of her allies. When in 1699 the Emperor, Poland and Venice made peace with the Turks at Carlowitz, after a war which had lasted for nearly two decades, Russia played no part in the negotiation of the treaty and her interests were completely ignored in the drawing-up of its terms. Abandoned by his allies, Peter made peace with the Porte at Constantinople in 1700; and this agreement gave him Azov and the right to a minister in Constantinople on an equal footing with the representatives there of other Christian powers. But he failed to secure possession of Kerch, at the entrance to the Sea of Azov, and thus the secure outlet to the Black Sea for which he had hoped. He never forgot the way in which he had been left in the lurch by his allies, and drew from it the justified conclusion that Russia was still too weak and remote to be able to force the powers of Europe to pay attention to her wishes.

Only a few weeks after peace had been made with Turkey Peter joined in the attack which Denmark and Saxony had already launched, in the first months of 1700, against the Swedish Empire. (He had in fact been thinking seriously of action against Sweden since at least the summer of 1698.) The Great Northern War, thus begun, was to last for over two decades (1700–21). The Tsar's motives in entering it were mixed, but the main one was his desire to acquire an outlet to the Baltic, a recurring dream of Russian monarchs and statesmen for the last century and a half. By his action he brought his country into closer political contact that ever before with Western Europe. The war in the Baltic was, from the moment of its outbreak, closely linked with the simultaneous conflict over the Spanish Succession between Louis XIV and a hostile coalition which began in 1702 and lasted till 1713. In particular both France and her opponents hoped to end the Great Northern War by political action and then hire Swedish troops for use in their own quarrels. These hopes led to a series of efforts by Louis XIV and his English and Dutch adversaries to mediate in the Russo-Swedish struggle. None of these came to anything. This was partly because of the obstinacy of Charles XII, the young king of Sweden, and to a lesser extent because of the refusal of Peter to surrender the territory at the mouth of the river Neva which he overran in 1703 and on which he at once began to build his new capital of St Petersburg.

Both sides in the West also made efforts to use Russia more directly for their own purposes in the Spanish Succession struggle. In 1701 and 1707 there were proposals that she should intervene actively in the war on the French side, while in 1707–8 there were protracted discussions in London on her possible adherence to the anti-French coalition. These negotiations, however, were always very tentative and were not taken very seriously by the British and French statesmen concerned. Russia was still a remote and apparently weak country on the fringes of the European State-system. Moreover Charles XII seemed for some years to be invincible. He drove Denmark out of the war in 1700, after a landing on the island of Zeeland which seemed to threaten Copenhagen itself. In the same year he inflicted a humiliating defeat on Peter outside Narva, an important fortress in Esthonia to which the Tsar had laid siege. In 1707, after a series of brilliant successes in Poland (of which the Elector Augustus of Saxony was king), he forced the latter to make peace at Altranstädt. His victories made it appear very doubtful whether Russia could long withstand a Swedish onslaught. They thus greatly reduced her value as an ally in the eyes of contemporaries.

In July 1709 a Swedish army which had invaded Russia in the previous year, commanded by the king in person, was totally defeated by the Russians at the battle of Poltava in the Ukraine. This defeat led a few days later to its surrender and complete destruction as a fighting force: Charles himself took refuge in Turkey with a handful of followers. The battle revolutionized the whole position in Northern and Eastern Europe. It at once revived the coalition of Russia, Denmark and Saxony which had been destroyed by Sweden's earlier victories, and by so doing threatened the complete destruction of the Swedish Empire. Nor was the threat an empty one. Sweden's territories in Livonia and Esthonia were already in Russian hands before Poltava (though Peter temporarily withdrew his army of occupation from them after 1707, to meet the onslaught on Russia itself) and by 1716 she had lost her last German possessions. The first Russian raid on Sweden proper came in 1714. Even then she remained a formidable military power; but when Charles XII was killed in Norway in 1718, and Sweden thus plunged into a series of bitter dynastic and constitutional struggles, all hope of recovering the Baltic Empire built up in the seventeenth century vanished. Poltava also made Russia's influence dominant in Poland and opened up prospects of her control of much of the Baltic coastline and even of parts of North Germany. All this enormously raised her standing, and that of her ruler, in Western Europe. It endowed them with the prestige which military victory alone could give and made Russia appear clearly to the Western powers for the first time as an international force which could play an effective role in their own conflicts. In 1709–10 Louis XIV and his ministers, when France's military fortunes were at their lowest ebb, seriously hoped to use Russian mediation as a means of restoring her position in the War of the Spanish Succession: this was a striking illustration of how the situation had changed. After 1709 fear of Russia, an emotion hitherto suppressed though of considerable importance, became much more visible and active among her neighbours. Now far more than ever before she began to appear a source of danger to them. Almost as soon as news of the battle had been received in Vienna Baron Urbich, the Russian minister there, told Leibniz that 'people begin to fear the Tsar as formerly they feared Sweden', while the philosopher agreed that 'it is commonly said that the Tsar will be formidable to all Europe, that he will be a kind of northern Turk'.

Until 1713 the Western States had their hands full with the War of the Spanish Succession: they could not effectively resist the growth of Russian power even had they desired to do so. Moreover in 1714 George I, who as Elector of Hanover had territorial ambitions against Sweden, became king of England and gave that country's policy, for the time being, an anti-Swedish direction. The United Provinces, for their part, were too closely bound to Russia by the lucrative trade they carried on with her to be willing openly to oppose her. Not until 1716 did any of the West European States come into open conflict with her.

In the summer of that year it seemed that a Russo-Danish army, supported by British and Dutch squadrons under the command of Peter himself, was about to land in southern Sweden. At the last moment the Tsar, impressed by the strength of the Swedish defences and distrustful of the loyalty of his allies, very sensibly abandoned the enterprise. Many of the Russian troops assembled for the projected campaign were quatered in the Duchy of Mecklenburg, whose ruler had just married the Tsar's niece, during the winter of 1716–17; and this occupation of German territory aroused violent suspicions of Peter's intentions in Denmark and Hanover, and to some extent in England. The Russian forces were withdrawn in the summer of 1717; but the anti-Swedish coalition, already undermined by the rivalries and jealousies of its members, had now completely collapsed. Anglo-Russian relations, exacerbated by other factors – English fears of Russian help for the Jacobites and a Russian monopoly of the supply of naval stores from the Baltic – remained extremely strained for the next decade. In 1719 and 1720, when British squadrons were sent to the Baltic in an effort to bolster up Swedish resistance to Russia, the two countries came close to open war. In 1719, moreover, a treaty signed at Vienna bound together the Emperor Charles VI and the Electors of Saxony and Hanover in an alliance designed to drive Russian forces out of Poland. Uneasiness about her power was now becoming ingrained in her neighbours. Nevertheless the very violence of the emotions aroused by the events of 1716 and the following years showed how completely Russia was now becoming a part of the European political system. She might be feared but could no longer be ignored. The Treaty of Nystad, which ended the long struggle with Sweden in 1721 and gave her Esthonia, Livonia and part of Karelia, established her finally as a Baltic power: Peter's almost simultaneous assumption of the title of Emperor (*Imperator*) seemed to symbolize the astonishing rise in her international standing under his rule.

Side by side with this increase in the country's political importance after 1709 went a growth in her cultural and intellectual contacts with Europe. The great reforms of 1718–19, in particular the creation in these years of administrative colleges as important organs of central government (see p. 148), were powerfully influenced by German and Swedish models. Peter's financial policies and methods of taxation were also based to a considerable extent on foreign examples. Moreover the Tsar's attitude to Western culture and intellectual life changed in his later years. His outlook after about 1714, when the war with Sweden had clearly been won, became more liberal and less narrow and utilitarian. He now began, for the first time in his life, to show some interest in cultural matters in the wider sense of the term. In the last years of his reign he bought pictures and statues abroad and began to build palaces in the Western style, though as yet on a quite modest scale. Simultaneously young Russians were sent to study painting at the *Accademia di Disegno* in Florence, while artists and architects were imported from France, Germany, Switzerland and Italy. In particular St Petersburg, the new capital, owed much to foreign architects such as Härbel, Schlüter and Trezzini. The new width of Peter's outlook and interests is also visible in his efforts to develop education in Russia, and particularly in the foundation of the Academy of Sciences in 1725 (opened after his death but planned by him).

These foreign cultural influences came for the most part from Germany, Scandinavia and the United Provinces. In Russian life Britain and France, now the intellectual leaders of Europe, as yet counted for relatively little in this respect. British cultural and technical influences were never of great importance at any time during Peter's reign, except where the navy was concerned, and were further restricted by the decade of hostility which followed the crisis of 1716. French ones were also relatively slight, largely because of France's traditional friendship with Sweden and the Ottoman Empire, Russia's most dangerous opponents. Peter visited Paris in 1717 in an effort to conclude a Russo-French alliance, and aroused widespread curiosity and enthusiasm among its inhabitants (many of whom were even then still ignorant of his exact name and title). But his proposal of a French alliance had no practical result, though the idea was one to which he recurred several times in his last years. The French Government was now bound to Britain by the Triple Alliance of 1717 (see p. 328), and thus caught up to some extent in her hostility to Russia. Moreover it remained loyal, though with some misgivings, to Sweden, France's traditional ally. The Tsar had to content himself with the signature in Amsterdam of an innocuous and ineffective treaty of friendship with France and Prussia which was nevertheless a further recognition of his country's new status as a European power.

When he died in January 1725 Peter I had thus brought about a fundamental and irreversible change in Russia's relationship with Europe. Whether his internal reforms amounted to a true revolution is very doubtful. They aimed at making the mechanism of government work more efficiently and at providing it with greater material resources (see p. 104) rather than at changing its essential character. Precedents can be found in the reigns of his immediate predecessors for all his innovations, with the important exception of the abolition of the Patriarchate. Even the creation of a navy had been faintly anticipated in the 1660s. But his reign saw changes in Russia's international status which can fairly be called revolutionary. Neglected and despised at the end of the seventeenth century, when he died she was feared by her neighbours and courted as a political and military, if not yet a cultural and economic, equal by the greatest powers of Europe.

Her position as a leading European State was not, however, completely secure by 1725. The suffering and sacrifice which Peter's wars involved had provoked widespread discontent: his reforms were generally unpopular. Foreign cultural and intellectual influences had still only a limited hold, and conservative forces in Russia remained very powerful. In 1718 the heir to the throne, Peter's son Alexis, had been put to death because of his opposition to his father's policy of internal change and external expansion. The attitude which he typified was still widespread even among the landowning class and was almost universal among the peasantry. The position which the Tsar bequeathed to his successors was thus, though brilliant, unstable. Many contemporaries expected the country to relapse after his death into the weakness and unimportance of the seventeenth century.

These expectations were partially realized. Peter was followed by a series of weak and incompetent rulers – his wife Catherine I (1725–27), his grandson Peter II (1727–30) and his niece Anna (1730–40). Then after a period of great confusion in 1740–41, marked by factional struggles and palace revolutions, relative stability was restored during the reign of his daughter Elizabeth (1741–62). Her successor, Peter III, reigned only a few months before being deposed and murdered in a *coup d'état* led by his wife, who succeeded him as Catherine II. None of the rulers of Russia in 1725–62 possessed much strength of character or intellect; and the fact that most of them were women further weakened their position. Throughout this confused period of over a generation much real political power was therefore in the hands of the guards regiments in St Petersburg and of court favourites – Prince A. D. Menshikov under Catherine I, the Dolgoruky family under Peter II, Johann Bühren, Duke of Courland, under Anna, to a lesser extent Count K. G. Razumovskii under Elizabeth. In 1730 there was even an unsuccessful attempt by a group of nobles to impose on Anna what amounted to a written constitution drastically limiting her powers (see p. 149), an attempt whose failure has sometimes been regarded (quite wrongly) as a turning-point in Russian history. This internal instability naturally made an unfavourable impression on Western observers. 'The Crown of Russia,' wrote one English periodical in 1759, 'may now be deemed elective, and of the worst kind of elective monarchies.'[1]

Nevertheless the country continued to play a great part in European affairs. In 1726 an alliance was signed with Austria. It was renewed several times, notably in 1746, and remained the pivot of Russian foreign policy until the end of the Seven Years War. It was based partly on the mutual interest of the two States in maintaining their influence in Poland and the *status quo* there, and still more on their mutual hostility to the Ottoman Empire. It was replaced in 1764 by a Russo-Prussian alliance, which was also founded on a desire to co-operate in Poland as well as on the eagerness of Frederick II, after the lessons of the Seven Years War, to keep on good terms with his great Eastern neighbour. This was succeeded in its turn, in 1781, by an *entente* between Catherine II and the Emperor Joseph II again directed against the Turks. In other words Russian foreign policy during this period was dominated alternately by pro-Austrian and pro-Prussian influences. The former, typified by statesmen such as Count A. I. Ostermann and Count M. P. Bestuzhev-Ryumin, were in the ascendant in the generation from the 1720s to the 1750s; the latter, represented above all by Count N. I. Panin, were dominant in the 1760s and 1770s.

With France Russia's diplomatic relations were throughout this period generally bad: no real friendship between the two States was possible. This was above all because France was the traditional friend and protector of Sweden, Poland and the Ottoman Empire, the weak and in the last two cases decaying States at whose expanse Russia's expansion took place. This factor had nullified the efforts of Peter I to secure a French alliance; and for half a century after his death France clung to her traditional eastern policy and thus made really good relations with Russia impossible. Moreover the Russian agreements of 1726 with the Habsburgs also helped to strain relations between Paris and St. Petersburg. The *de facto* alliance which united Louis XV and Elizabeth against Prussia in 1757–62 (see pp. 298ff.) was never secure and involved no lasting change in the relationship between the two countries. 'Everything that may plunge Russia into chaos and make her return to obscurity', wrote Louis XV in September 1763, 'is favourable to our interests.'[2] The 1760s and 1770s saw, however, the beginning of an alteration in France's attitude. Her government in the last decades of the *ancien régime* became increasingly willing to abandon the Ottoman Empire to its enemies, and perhaps even share in the spoils if it were partitioned. This made possible a slow improvement in relations with Russia, so that a commercial agreement with her was signed in 1787 and active negotiations for a quadruple alliance of France, Spain, Russia and Austria were under way when the revolution broke out in Paris. At no time during the eighteenth century, however, were the two States able or willing to co-operate effectively on any major international issue.

With Britain on the other hand Russia's relations, at least from the 1730s onwards, were always relatively amicable. The antagonism which had emerged in 1716 evaporated rapidly after the death of Catherine I in 1727. For the next two generations they were on good though sometimes rather distant terms and tended to regard each other as traditional friends. For this there were obvious reasons. Britain had few territorial interests or commitments in Europe, and none in Eastern Europe: Russia had none overseas. Territorial rivalry between them was impossible. Britain with her wealth and naval power, Russia with her great armies, seemed to complement rather than compete with each other. The fact that Russia could be regarded as the enemy of France and that her victories tended to reduce French influence in Eastern Europe recommended her strongly to British opinion. Most important of all the two States were now bound together by a growing and lucrative trade on which the finances of many Russian nobles, whose estates produced timber, hemp and other raw materials for export, largely depended. It is noteworthy that even when Anglo-Russian relations were at their worst, in the last years of his reign, Peter I made no effort to interfere with British merchants in Russia; and in 1734 Anglo-Russian trade was put on a firm footing by one of the most important commercial treaties of the century. These factors aided the conclusion of somewhat ineffective Anglo-Russian treaties of alliance in 1742 and 1746, while serious though eventually unsuccessful negotiations for another alliance were carried on for many years in the 1760s and early 1770s.

The importance of the part Russia was able to play in international relations during the eighteenth century was increased by the very high reputation for courage and tenacity, if not for skill, enjoyed by her army. Its prestige had been raised to a high pitch by the defeat of Sweden in the Great Northern War. It was raised further by Russia's victories over the Turks in the wars of

1736–39 and 1768–74, and further still by her participation in the Seven Years War (see p. 300). The extraordinary courage and endurance shown by the ordinary Russian soldier when faced by the army of Frederick II at Zorndorf and Kunersdorf aroused widespread admiration. 'Experience has proved', wrote one observer a year or two later, 'that the Russian infantry is by far superior to any in Europe, in so much that I question whether it can be defeated by any other infantry whatever.'[3]

Russia's military strength had indirect as well as direct importance in international affairs. It not only increased her own influence but also allowed her if she wished to supply the other States of Europe with large contingents for use in their struggles with each other. In the spring of 1730 a force of 30,000 Russian soldiers was made ready to support the emperor Charles VI in the war he was then fighting with Spain, though in the event they were never used. Five years later 20,000 men were provided for the same ruler for use on the Rhine against the French army in the War of the Polish Succession, while in 1747–48 a large contingent of Russian troops was engaged by the British and Dutch governments for the defence of the Netherlands against France. In 1775 Lord North's Cabinet confidently though mistakenly expected to be able to hire 20,000 Russians for use against the American colonists; and in 1799 that of the younger Pitt discussed the possibility of garrisoning Ireland with Russian troops.

From the Russian point of view, however, the country's relations with her immediate neighbours – the Baltic States (above all Sweden), Poland and the Ottoman Empire – were more important than those with the greater but more remote powers of Western or Central Europe. This was reflected in the fact that during most of the century the Russian ministers in Stockholm, and still more those in Warsaw, were paid considerably higher salaries than those in London, Paris or Vienna. Events near the country's frontiers were normally of greater significance to Russia than those in the Netherlands, Italy or even Germany; and her relations with the greater European powers were often profoundly influenced by happenings in these border areas.

Russian policy in Sweden was dominated, after the peace of 1721, by the desire to preserve peace and the *status quo*. Any danger of a Swedish attempt to recover the lost Baltic provinces by a war of revenge must be warded off. This meant that Russia consistently supported the Swedish constitution of 1720 (which she had guaranteed by Article VII of the Treaty of Nystad). This constitution, drawn up during a violent reaction against the despotism of Charles XII and its disastrous results, severely limited the power of the monarchy and placed control of the country in the hands of the Council and the Estates. The latter were normally divided by party strife which was often bitter. They were thus very vulnerable to Russian influence, exerted usually by bribery and occasionally by threats. By these means it was hoped to maintain in power at Stockholm a moderate and hence by implication pro-Russian regime. This was achieved for two decades after the Treaty of Nystad; partly because in 1723–27 Russia and Sweden were acting together to support the claims of the Duke of Holstein-Gottorp to parts of Schleswig and Holstein; and partly because Count Arvid Horn, the most important Swedish politician of the 1730s, was anxious to avoid a war with Russia which he realized his country was unlikely to win.

Anti-Russian feeling nevertheless remained very powerful in Sweden, stimulated by the great influence which France continued to enjoy in Stockholm and by the judicious distribution of French money to the members of the noble oligarchy which ruled the country. In 1733, when Russia became involved in the War of the Polish Succession, and again three years later when she began hostilities against Turkey, there was a strong demand from the opposition in Sweden for intervention against her. In July 1741, after Horn had fallen from power, these feelings led to a Swedish declaration of war. This attempt at revenge ended disastrously two years later with the signature of the Treaty of Åbo, by which still more of Finland was surrendered to Russia. Though French influences remained very strong at Stockholm, it was now clear that a successful attack by Sweden on her great Eastern neighbour was at least for the time being out of the question.

From the early 1750s onwards a court party grouped around the Queen, Louisa Ulrica, began to emerge in the Swedish capital. Though for many years it had little influence over the country's policies it showed that there were now influential people in Sweden who were prepared to envisage a drastic revision of the constitution of 1720. From the 1760s onwards the French government, instead of trying to maintain a pro-French majority in the Council and the Estates, began to use its money and influence to overthrow the constitutional regime and restore the power of the monarchy. The feeble king, Adolphus Frederick, was hardly the man to carry through so revolutionary a change. After his death in February 1771, however, his abler son and successor, Gustavus III, was able in August 1772 to destroy the constitution and set up a strongly monarchical regime by a brilliantly successful and bloodless *coup d'état*. This revolution made impossible Russian influence in Stockholm of the kind so frequently seen in the previous half-century. It thus naturally aroused great anger and alarm in St Petersburg and was the most serious, indeed the only serious, diplomatic defeat suffered by Russia during the reign of Catherine II. Nevertheless it did not lead to the immediate Russo-Swedish conflict which was widely expected. Hopes of a recovery of Livonia and Esthonia were still far from dead in Swedish ruling circles and the young king in November 1772 thought seriously of trying to wrest Norway from Denmark (the scheme which had cost Charles XII his life in 1718). But it was not till 1788 that the ambitions of Gustavus III led him to try conclusions once more with Russia.

Relations with Poland were more important in Russian policy, and of greater significance for the country's future, than those with Sweden. Hardly anyone in Russia wished or expected to make territorial gains at the expense of Sweden proper. Even Finland, parts of which were acquired in 1721 and 1743, was desired, in so far as it was desired at all, for essentially defensive purposes – to protect St Petersburg and act as a buffer between the two States. By contrast Poland was the essential land link between Russia and the West. It was, as one historian has said, 'the threshold over which Russia stepped into Europe'. Any challenge to her leading position there, whether by the Poles themselves or by some third party, therefore raised issues of fundamental importance for Russia.

Her influence, as has been seen, had become predominant in Poland after the battle of Poltava. It tended to become even more complete as time went on. Its extent was shown by the action of the Russian minister in negotiating in 1717 the so-called Treaty of Warsaw, an agreement between Augustus II and the Polish nobility which, among other things, drastically limited the size of the army. Moreover the fact that the minister in question, Prince G. F. Dolgoruky himself signed the agreement gave it a kind of Russian guarantee and made it impossible to alter without Russia's consent. The extent of Russian influence was emphasized once more by the War of the Polish Succession (1733–35).

In these years Russia, supported by Austria, imposed on the Polish nobility a king (Augustus III, Elector of Saxony) whom most of them obviously did not want, at the expense of another claimant (Stanislas Leszczynski, father-in-law of Louis XV of France) whom most of them were prepared to accept. Russian power was shown most conclusively of all when in 1764 Catherine II, supported by her new ally Frederick II, established as the last king of an independent Poland one of her former lovers, Stanislas Poniatowski. This was one of the greatest political triumphs of her reign. Moreover the Duchy of Courland, still theoretically a fief of the Polish Crown, had been virtually annexed by Russia in 1718. Henceforth the appointment and maintenance in power of its rulers depended entirely on Russian goodwill, though it did not formally become Russian territory till 1795.

Under the last of her Saxon rulers, Augustus III (1733–63), Poland's internal weakness and political incoherence became, if anything, worse than before. Her kings were now merely the puppets of foreign powers and domestic factions. Her political life was little more than a series of struggles between a few great noble families; above all between the Potockis, who were pro-French, and the Czartoryskis, who looked for support, at least after 1756, to Russia. Her army, ridiculously small (perhaps 12,000 men) in proportion to the size of the country and the length of its exposed land frontiers, was poorly equipped and trained. Her public revenue, it has been estimated, amounted in the middle of the century to about one-thirteenth of that of Russia and one-seventy-fifth of that of France. In 1757–62 much of her territory was occupied and plundered by Russian troops *en route* to the battlefields of Brandenburg and Pomerania, and exposed to retaliatory raids by the forces of Frederick II. In the 1760s the helplessness of her government was underlined once more by the emergence of the powerful Confederation of Bar, which united a large part of the privileged classes in hostility to Russia. (Confederations – semi-legal associations of the nobility and gentry whose formation was usually the prelude to civil war – had for long been a feature of Polish political life and proliferated in the 1760s.) All things considered, it is surprising that the country survived for so long as an independent or pseudo-independent State.

Nevertheless until the end of the Seven Years War the idea of a partition played little part in Russian policy in Poland. It was by no means a new idea. It had first been put forward in the 1650s; and a number of plans for a division of the country had been proposed during and after the Great Northern War. There was some discussion of this possibility, for example, in a meeting between Peter I and Frederick William I of Prussia in 1711. Russian statesmen, however, had seldom shown much interest in such schemes. Poland seemed to them most useful if kept intact as a buffer-State under the control of her eastern neighbour, while a partition would bring Russia into direct contact with such dangerous potential rivals as Austria and Prussia. During and after the struggle with Frederick II, nevertheless, there were signs that a new attitude was beginning to develop in St Petersburg. In 1759 and 1761 revision of Poland's eastern frontier in favour of Russia was proposed by different Russian statesmen. In the autumn of 1763 Count Zakhar Chernyshev, one of the Empress's main advisers on military affairs, urged that large annexations in eastern Poland should be made when the now clearly imminent death of Augustus III took place. In November 1768 the State Council stressed once more the need for a revision of Poland's eastern boundaries in the interest of Russian security. Thus the idea of a seizure of Polish territory was beginning to attract attention in Russia well before 1772, while the intolerance with which the Roman Catholic Poles treated not only the Orthodox population of White Russia and Ruthenia but also the Uniates (Catholics of the Greek rite) who inhabited these areas provided obvious pretexts for Russian intervention.

There were still, however, many influential people in Russia who wished to avoid a partition of Poland. In particular Count N. I. Panin, the Chancellor who had great influence on Russian foreign policy for nearly two decades after the accession of Catherine II, hoped in the 1760s to make the country part of the 'Northern System' which he was trying to create in order to reduce French influence in Eastern and Northern Europe. The dream of an alliance of this kind, a combination of Russia, Prussia, Britain, Denmark-Norway, Sweden and Poland, dominated Russian policy for a number of years. Panin placed high hopes on it, believing that it would 'draw Russia away from her continual dependence on others and place her . . . in such a position that she will be able to play an important role in the affairs of Europe, and also to preserve quiet and stability in the North'.[4] But the Northern System, like so many alliance proposals of this period, was impossibly grandiose and unwieldy. The British government was unwilling to give Catherine II, as the price of an Anglo-Russian treaty, the support she demanded in Sweden and the Ottoman Empire. In particular it refused to promise her help in any future war with the Turks. Frederick II wished to remain the only important ally of Russia and threw his weight at St Petersburg against any treaty arrangement with Britain. The formal results of the whole Northern System idea were therefore confined to a Russo-Danish treaty of mutual aid and guarantee signed in March 1765. Nevertheless it had some influence on Russo-Polish relations. Panin, its main supporter, believed that if the political structure of Poland were modernized and overhauled she might become once again an effective State. She would then be able to act as Russia's main ally against the Ottoman Empire, assuming the place hitherto held by Austria in Russian policy. Not until early in 1771 did the idea of a partition of Poland become dominant in St Petersburg. To see why it did it is necessary to look at the course of events in the Near East.

Peter I was much less successful in his relations with the Turks than in his long struggle with the Swedes. The capture of Azov in 1696 failed, as has been seen, to secure for Russia an outlet to the Black Sea or permission for her ships to trade there. More serious, the Tsar suffered in 1711 at the hands of the Turks the greatest defeat of his reign, one which for the time being put a total stop to any hope of Russian expansion southwards. In November 1710 the Porte, under the influence of Charles XII and still more of Devlet-Girei, the very anti-Russian Khan of the Crimea, declared war on Russia. Peter was at first reluctant to accept the challenge while his hands were so full in Poland and the Baltic provinces: keeping the peace on his southern frontier had been a major preoccupation since the beginning of the struggle with Sweden. Nevertheless he carried on the struggle with his usual energy in the spring and summer of 1711. An appeal was issued to the Balkan Christians, urging them to rise against their Turkish overlords. For the first time since the tenth century a Russian army entered Moldavia and Russian cavalry watered their horses in the Danube. However numerical inferiority, shortage of supplies and failure of the Hospodar of Moldavia to provide the help which had been expected of him, led almost at once to a catastrophic defeat. In July, with his army surrounded on the river Pruth, Peter was forced to make peace

on humiliating terms. Azov, Taganrog and the naval squadron
based on them were to be given up: Russian interference in Poland
was to cease, as was Russian diplomatic representation at the
Porte.

The setback on the Pruth, though severe, was not final. In 1720
Peter forced the Turks to agree to the re-establishment of a
representative in Constantinople; and his efforts to conquer the
southern shores of the Caspian from 1723 onwards led to acute
Russo-Turkish rivalry for influence in Persia. Russia's relations
with the Ottoman Empire continued, in other words, after the
Pruth campaign as before, to be those of explicit or implicit
hostility. The points on which the two Powers differed were
numerous and important. Apart from their intermittent rivalries
in Persia they were divided by the plundering raids of the Crim
Tatars (still under Turkish suzerainty) in the Ukraine and South
Russia and the complaints they evoked from St Petersburg; by
Turkish dislike of Russian dominance in Poland; and by the
persisting and inevitable desire of Russia, for both strategic and
economic reasons, to secure an outlet to the Black Sea. Also there
was by now a long tradition of enmity between the two States,
one given emotional weight on both sides by religious prejudice.

For nearly two generations after the campaign of 1711 the
Turks held their own fairly successfully against pressure from the
north. Russia was hampered in any struggle with them by the
great difficulty of maintaining an army across the still largely
uninhabited steppe lands which bordered the Black Sea, by the
fact that maritime power on that sea was a Turkish monopoly and
by the constant possibility of a Swedish attack in the Baltic.
Supply difficulties had been the main reason for Peter's defeat in
1711; and they bulked very large in the Russo-Turkish war of
1735–39. (An observer estimated that a Russian army which
attempted to attack the Crimea needed 90,000 wagons to carry
its food and equipment.) This struggle, in which Russia was
rather ineffectively suppported by Austria from the beginning of
1737 onwards, seemed at one time to promise great results. The
Russian delegates to a peace conference which opened at Nemirov
in the Ukraine in August 1737 were ordered to press for the
cession by the Turks of all territory between the rivers Kuban and
Dniester, including the Crimea: in case of further Russian victories the independence of the Danubian principalities, which were
under Turkish suzerainty, might be demanded. Even Peter I had

seldom contemplated success on this scale. However the military weakness of the Austrians and the mutual distrust which divided Russia and her ally forced a drastic modification of this ambitious programme even before the conference broke up in October. When peace was made at Belgrade in September 1739 the Russians retained none of their conquests except Azov, which they had taken in 1737. They were forced, moreover, to promise to dismantle its fortifications and agree to maintain no warships on the Sea of Azov or the Black Sea. The effects of the disastrous campaign of 1711 had thus been only very partially nullified.

The generation which followed saw intermittent Russo-Turkish tension – over the activities of the Crim Tatars, over rivalries in the Caucasus, over the building by the Russians of fortifications in the Ukraine – but no serious conflict broke out until 1768. The war which began in October of that year was largely a result of the growth of Russian power in Poland. The resentment which this aroused in Constantinople was skilfully stimulated by the Comte de Vergennes, the able French ambassador, who had already almost persuaded the Turks to declare war on Russia in 1764. It was fanned to white heat when Ukrainian partisans in Russian service, in pursuit of members of the Confederation of Bar, crossed the Turkish frontier and burnt the little town of Balta in Moldavia. The ensuing explosion of rage at Constantinople led, in spite of the efforts of the Russian minister there to preserve peace by bribery, to an immediate declaration of war.

The struggle which followed was the most disastrous in Turkish history. Thirty years of peace had destroyed most of what little efficiency remained in the Ottoman army, while the fleet was in even worse condition. The result was that though Russia had neither desired nor expected the war she began almost at once to win spectacular victories. In 1769–70 most of Moldavia and Wallachia was occupied. In 1771 the Crimea was overrun. Most remarkable of all, in 1769–70 three squadrons of Russian men-of-war were sent from Kronstadt through the English Channel and the Bay of Biscay to the eastern Mediterranean. There they helped to stimulate a serious though unsuccessful revolt in the Morea; and in July 1770 they annihilated the Turkish fleet at Chesmé on the coast of Asia Minor. This remarkable naval campaign, though made possible only by British help, was a startling reminder of Russia's potentialities and the first really effective sign of Russian interest in the Mediterranean. Inevitably, such victories encouraged Catherine II and her ministers to think in terms of sweeping territorial and other gains. As early as November 1768 it had been agreed in St Petersburg that when peace was made Russia must obtain a port on the Black Sea and freedom of navigation for her ships there. By the end of 1770 there had been added a whole series of much more sweeping demands – for Russian control of the Straits of Kerch, leading from the Sea of Azov to the Black Sea proper; for the cession of one of the Greek inlands to be used as a Russian naval base; for the placing of Moldavia and Wallachia under Russian control for twenty-five years after the end of the war as an indemnity for Catherine's war expenses; most important of all, for the erecting of the Crimean Khanate into an independent State free from Turkish control (and therefore fully exposed to Russian influence).

These extraordinary successes, equally inevitably, aroused opposition. France was irritated by the spectacle of a Russian fleet circumnavigating Europe and, but for the attitude of the British government, might have attacked it on its way to the Levant. More serious, Austria, faced by the threat of Russian domination of the Lower Danube, was deeply alarmed. In July 1771 she signed a convention with the Porte by which, in return for Turkish subsidies and the promise of part of Wallachia, she agreed to aid the Turks against Catherine II. By the summer of that year a full-scale Austro-Russian war seemed imminent. Such a war was desired neither in Vienna nor St Petersburg, and the prospect of its outbreak greatly alarmed Frederick II. Already obliged by the treaty of 1764 to give Russia financial support in her struggle with the Turks, he now saw himself on the verge of being drawn into a new European conflict over issues in which he had no direct interest whatever. It had already become obvious some months earlier, however, that an alternative to the Austro-Russian war which no one wanted could be found in the partition of Poland which hardly anyone was willing to oppose.

Frederick II had realized on the outbreak of war in 1768 that he might be able to obtain part of Prussian Poland as the price of his support for Catherine II. In the following year he unsuccessfully put forward indirect proposals for a partition, using the Danish diplomat Count Lynar as a stalking-horse. The action of Austria was more important. By occupying in February 1769 the two Polish counties of Zips, an enclave within the Hungarian frontier to which she had a rather weak historical claim, she paved the way for further and more important seizures of territory. As early as May 1770 the Austrian government suggested to Frederick II the possibility of his acquiring West Prussia and Ermeland if there were a partition (though Kaunitz, the Austrian Chancellor, hoped to recover Silesia in compensation, and also perhaps to break up the Russo-Prussian alliance by encouraging Prussian aggression in Poland). Responsibility for the partition must therefore be shared among the participating powers, with Russia, it is arguable, shouldering less of the blame than the other two.

Events were precipitated by the visit to St Petersburg at the end of 1770 of Prince Henry of Prussia, brother of Frederick II. For over a year he, much more than the king, had been envisaging a possible annexation of West Prussia in the immediate future: in October he had drafted a plan for joint supervision of Polish affairs by Austria, Prussia and Russia. He made a good impression at the Russian court; and on 8 January 1771 Catherine II, seeking in Poland an escape from the threat of war with Austria, suddenly suggested to him a partition of the country. The Prince leapt at the idea. On his return to Berlin six weeks later he overcame his brother's fears that its application might unduly strengthen Russia and won his consent to the proposal. In May Count Panin, hitherto the leading Russian opponent of partition, proposed that Austria be allowed to retain the territory she had seized and that Prussia be given some Polish provinces. By October Catherine II had agreed to surrender her claims on the Danube in return for compensation in Poland. The country's fate was sealed. The moral scruples of Maria Theresa, which were genuine, were overcome by the urgings of Joseph II and Kaunitz: in August 1772, after much heart-searching, she reluctantly accepted the treaty of partition which had been drawn up in February–March. Its detailed application was settled in a series of conventions in 1775–76.

Poland thus lost nearly a third of her territory and over a third of her population, though in White Russia and Galicia, the areas annexed by Russia and Austria, a high proportion of that population was not Polish. Frederick II failed to secure Danzig, for which he and his brother had hoped, and obtained less territory than the other partitioning powers. But he was able, by the annexation of West Prussia, to achieve his great object of linking up East (or Ducal) Prussia with the core of his dominions in Bran-

denburg. The partition therefore undoubtedly strengthened
Prussia more than Russia or Austria. Russia in many ways gained
least, for in agreeing to a partition she sacrificed a very promising
prospect of maintaining Poland undivided as her satellite and
brought closer the day when she would have a common frontier
with such formidable neighbours as Prussia and Austria.

The partition of Poland, though it deprived the Turks of any
hope of effective help against Russia, did little to hasten the end
of the Russo-Turkish war. Indeed by freeing Catherine II from
the fear of a conflict with Austria it did something to stiffen her
attitude towards the Porte. Simultaneously, however, the *coup
d'état* of August 1772 in Stockholm caused acute though short-
lived alarm in St Petersburg, while in the following year the
outbreak in East and South-East Russia of the great peasant and
Cossack revolt led by Pugachev (see p. 45) added very heavily to
the empress's other preoccupations. There were nevertheless
certain demands, above all the insistence that the Crimea should
become an independent State, which she was not prepared to
abandon. Two prolonged peace congresses – at Foksiany, a small
town in Moldavia, in August 1772, and at Bucharest in
November 1772–March 1773 – broke down on this point. Finally
in July 1774, after two years of mediocre achievement, the
Russian army forced the issue. Advancing across the Danube,
Field-Marshal P. A. Rumyantsev compelled the Grand Vizier to
agree to peace terms at the Bulgarian village of Kutchuk-Kainardji. This treaty, one of the most important of the century, gave
Russia the Kuban and Terek areas, the Black Sea steppe between
the Bug and the Dnieper together with the mouth of the latter
(and therefore a small but direct southern outlet to the sea), a war
indemnity and freedom of navigation on the Black Sea. She also
obtained the right to make representations on behalf of 'the
church to be built in Constantinople and those who serve it'.
Upon this vague and therefore dangerous phrase was to be raised
in the following century a structure of far-reaching claims. The
Crimea became independent, except that the Sultan retained the
formal right of investing its Khans with their office.

The Russian victory was exploited to the full. The 'New
Russia' of the Black Sea steppe was energetically populated from
a variety of sources – Moldavian and Vlach immigrants, state
peasants, Kalmyk tribesmen, even convicts. The appointment of
consuls in the Principalities, in several of the Greek islands, even

in Egypt, provided Catherine with a fresh means of undermining the shaky structure of the Ottoman Empire. A new agreement, the Convention of Ainali-Kavak, reiterated in 1779 a number of the terms imposed on the Porte in 1774. Most important of all, a long series of conflicts in the Crimea between the Tatars, still loyal to Constantinople, and the puppet-Khans established by Catherine, culminated in the summer of 1783 in the annexation by Russia of the peninsula. She thus immensely extended her coastline on the Black Sea and secured new bases for the powerful naval squadron she was now constructing there.

The decade which followed the peace of 1774 therefore saw Russia make a new and very important territorial gain. It also saw the rise of her international importance and prestige to a level higher than any hitherto reached, one which was not to be attained again until after 1812. In 1779 the short and ineffective war which Austria and Prussia had been waging over the Bavarian Succession was ended, in the Treaty of Teschen, by Russo-French mediation (see p. 305). As a guarantor of the settlement Russia could claim to have achieved for the first time a formal *locus standi* in German affairs, and to have placed the influence she had exercised there since the reign of Peter I on a secure legal footing. In December 1778 the French representative to the Imperial Diet complained, with perfect truth, that Russia was now the leading foreign influence in the politics of Germany, not, as for the last century and a half, France.

Only a few months separated the Treaty of Teschen from the formation, under Russian leadership, of the Armed Neutrality of 1780. This heterogeneous combination of States (Sweden, Prussia, Denmark, Portugal and others), united only by their common hostility to the way in which Britain defined and enforced her 'maritime rights' in the war with France which had begun in 1778, had limited practical effect. Its main result was to weaken the good Anglo-Russian relations which had prevailed for the last-century. Nevertheless it helped to consolidate in Western Europe the impression of Russia's power which had been developing ever since Poltava. After brilliant military victories and impressive territorial gains she seemed to have become the arbiter of Europe, courted and sometimes feared by Prussia and Austria in their German rivalries, by Britain and France in their maritime struggles, 'dictating a new code of maritime laws to mankind'.[5]

The two generations which followed the death of Peter I saw, especially from the 1750s onwards, an accelerated growth of Western cultural influences in Russia. By the second quarter of the century the court and the higher nobility had become completely westernized, at least in externals. Foreign amusements such as dinner-parties, balls and card-playing, foreign drinks such as champagne and tokay, were rapidly adopted by the upper ranks of society. A whole series of guides to good (i.e. Western) manners and social accomplishments was published for the instruction of the landowning class and eagerly read by it. Foreign influences, as well as growing in scope, were also changing somewhat in character. Peter's visit to Paris in 1717 led to an increase in intellectual and cultural contacts with France; but until the 1740s Italian models were at least as eagerly imitated at the Russian court and among the higher nobility as French ones. From the 1750s onwards, however, French culture came to dominate almost every aspect of the lives of the Russian ruling class. The School of Fine Arts founded by Elizabeth in 1755 was staffed largely by French painters and sculptors. French books were translated in large numbers. French tutors were *de rigueur* for the children of the greater Russian nobles. French reigned undisputed as the language of St Petersburg society. Simultaneously Britain and Germany made less spectacular but still appreciable contributions to this westernizing process; the former through her literature and the role played by British officers in the development of the Russian navy; the latter through the activities of many German scholars in Russia and the training received by many young Russians at German universities.

The reign of Catherine II thus saw not merely the import into Russia of European techniques, as under Peter I, but also the establishment there, more securely than ever before, of European ideas – the ideas of Locke, of Voltaire, even of Rousseau. By the second half of the century an educated Russian shared with his British or French counterparts a culture which was cosmopolitan and a system of ideas which transcended national groups or State boundaries. It is true that in Russia more than anywhere else in Europe this brilliant culture was very superficial. There even more than elsewhere it percolated only a very short distance down the social hierarchy, widening the gap between the privileged and westernized few and the ignorant and conservative many. Nevertheless Russia's military and territorial advances westward into Europe were paralleled by a simultaneous intellectual conquest of the country by the West. Russia was now a European State. Her newly established relationship with Western Europe might sometimes be distorted by mutual hostility. It could never relapse into the indifference which had reigned on both sides during the seventeenth century.

NOTES AND REFERENCES

1   *Universal Magazine*, vol. XXV, p. 35.

2   Quoted in P. Rain, *La Diplomatie française d'Henri IV à Vergennes* (Paris, 1945), p. 265.

3   H. H. Lloyd, *The History of the late War in Germany* (London, 1766), vol. I, p. 145.

4   *Sbornik Imperatorskogo Russkogo Istoricheskogo Obshchestva*, vol. LXVII (St. Petersburg, 1889), p. 25.

5   *Annual Register*, 1780, p. 205.

10

THE GERMAN STATES AND THE RISE OF PRUSSIA

Germany in the eighteenth century was more divided politically than at any time before or since. The decline in the effective authority of the Holy Roman Emperor (still its nominal ruler) which had been going on since at least the thirteenth century, and his descent to the position of an elective monarch (he was now chosen by a group of nine princes – the king of Bohemia, the archbishops of Trier, Mainz and Cologne, and the rulers of Saxony, Brandenburg, the Palatinate, Bavaria and Hanover) had set this process in motion. The religious divisions introduced by the Reformation, the repercussions of the Thirty Years War, the influence of foreign States, had reduced Germany by the beginning of this period to a state of political atomization which, at least in the west and south-west, could hardly have been more complete.

Some institutions with jurisdiction over all the German States, at least on paper, continued to exist. The Emperor continued to command in theory the allegiance of the German rulers, who in 1648, at the end of the Thirty Years War, had been recognized as possessing not complete sovereignty but merely 'territorial supremacy' (*Landeshoheit*). An Imperial Diet consisting of representatives of the States continued to meet and deliberate at Regensburg. An Aulic Council continued to function at Vienna for the conduct of German affairs, and a *Reichskammergericht*, a supreme law court for the whole empire, to sit at Wetzlar. These institutions were not complete nullities; and the Empire continued, until its fall in 1806, to be widely regarded in Germany as guarantee of existing rights of all kinds and to enjoy genuine popular support. But their powers were essentially negative. They could, within fairly narrow limits, inhibit change. But their ability to do anything new or constructive was non-existent.

The Emperor, as Emperor, still possessed great prestige and considerable influence over the German princes; but he had no real authority. For close on four centuries (1439–1806), with one short but important gap in 1740–45, every holder of the imperial title was a member of the Habsburg family. Long before the eighteenth century it had become virtually hereditary. But the real powers of its holders were derived almost entirely from their own hereditary lands, from the fact that they were Habsburgs, not from the fact that they were Holy Roman Emperors. The German States provided them neither with an army nor with any significant amount of money. The Diet and the administrative Circles into which the Empire was divided could, if the rulers concerned agreed, raise a composite force to defend imperial territory against outside attack or to repel agression by any of the German States against its neighbours; but a force of this kind was never effective or lasting. The Emperor's revenues amounted to the derisory sum of less than 14,000 florins (derived from a tax on the Jews of Frankfurt and Worms and from small annual payments by the imperial free cities). Strictly speaking the rulers of the German States could impose tolls or strike coins only with his permission. Also he alone could give universities the right to confer degrees, or could grant titles of nobility (though his monopoly of this privilege was disputed). But these theoretical powers meant little in practice. The German princes were by now in fact independent, complete sovereigns in their own States. The Diet, which consisted of three *curiae*, those of the electors, the princes and the towns, met regularly throughout this period; indeed in theory it had been in permanent session since 1663, and the capitulations agreed to by various Emperors on their accession, in 1711, 1742 and 1745, provided that it must be summoned at least once in every ten years. Nevertheless it was in practice very ineffective. It was hampered by incessant disputes between and within the *curiae* (notably between the electors, anxious to maintain their privileges and superior status, and the other ruling princes). It was also weakened by religious differences. Article V of the Treaty of Osnabrück in 1648 had provided for its division into Catholic and Protestant groups whenever religious questions were to be discussed, and for the settlement of such questions, not by majority vote, but by amicable agreement between the two parties. It was normal, moreover, for a number of States to be represented in it by proxy and to share a single representative, a practice which had the advantage of making it a small and manageable body but which also showed how little importance many of its members attached to it. All these factors combined to make it almost impossible for the Diet to take decisions on matters of general importance to the Empire; and any decision it did reach could usually be safely ignored by the more powerful German princes.

Nor had the Aulic Council and the *Reichskammergericht* much real authority. The former occasionally issued decrees, even in the later eighteenth century, against rulers who abused their powers; but never against the more important ones. Its greatest achievement was perhaps to help in forcing the Duke of Württemberg, in 1770, to make an agreement with his Estates by which he confirmed their powers and restored the constitution: but Wüttemberg, though not completely negligible, was not a State of the importance of Prussia, Saxony or Bavaria. The *Reichskammergericht* was weakened by the hostility of the German princes, who regarded its existence as a threat to their authority and in many cases denied their subjects the right to appeal to it. The slowness with which it worked, which had been notorious for generations, was such that by 1772 there were over 61,000 cases awaiting trial. Moreover a ruler condemned at Vienna or Wetzlar would often appeal to the Diet and thus evade compliance with the decisions of the Aulic Council or the *Reichskammergericht*. In other words, eighteenth-century Germany was, as a contemporary put it, 'a Knot of independent States leagu'd together, with a Prince or Staadtholder at their Head, cloath'd with the Ornaments of Royalty, but without that Power which ought to be deem'd essential to it'.[1] It is not surprising that by the later 1770s Joseph II had decided that the imperial title was a liability rather than an asset to him and was thinking in terms of its abdication and the severing of all ties between the Empire and the Habsburg territories – the cleavage finally forced on his successors in 1866.

The States into which Germany was divided varied enormously in size, in wealth, in military strength and in their systems of government. They can be divided into four groups. The first two – nobles who held their land immediately from the emperor, and free cities – were politically unimportant. The territories of the former, nearly all in south-west Germany, had at the end of the century less than 500,000 inhabitants out of the empire's total population of 28–30 million. The free cities had in all 600,000–700,000 inhabitants: of them only Nuremberg and Ulm possessed much territory beyond their walls. Some of those in Swabia were mere villages with populations of a few hundreds. The towns which grew in size and importance in the German world in the later seventeenth and eighteenth centuries were, significantly, not the old imperial cities but the capitals of the more important territorial princes, *Residenzstädte* such as Munich, Berlin, Stuttgart and most of all Vienna. A third group, the ecclesiastical principalities, included a few States of some political significance – the Electorates of Cologne, Mainz and Trier, the Archbishopric of Salzburg, the Bishoprics of Bamberg and Münster – but the areas which it covered were inhabited by only three million people in all. Moreover the ecclesiastical States more than ever in the past were now anachronisms exposed to the greed and expansionism of their greater secular neighbours. Plans for their secularization were drawn up during the short reign of the Wittelsbach Emperor Charles VII (1742–45) and also during the Seven Years War; though these had no result they were clear anticipations of the events of the Revolutionary and Napoleonic epoch. Finally came a group of secular States – Brandenburg-Prussia, Saxony, Hanover, the Palatinate, Bavaria and a few others – which wielded varying degrees of real power and could play roles of varing importance not merely in German but in European politics. Out of the 360 or so 'States' into which the country was divided (the number rises to about 1,800 if all the imperial knights of the south-west are included) there were at most ten or twelve ecclesiastical principalities and twice as many secular ones which really deserved the title. To complete this picture of political atomization it should be pointed out that these States were very often divided into different provinces, constitutionally distinct and frequently geographically scattered, and that this division affected the smaller ones almost as much as the larger. Thus although Brandenburg-Prussia was split into twelve such units and Hanover into nine, little Saxe-Weimar was also divided into three, each of which was very conscious of its separate identity and very unwilling to be amalgamated with the others.

'It is scarcely possible', wrote an eighteenth-century expert, 'to conceive a greater difference in the internal constitutions of any countries whatever than there actually is between the various States of Germany.'[2] Certainly their political and administrative structures varied very widely. With the exception of the free cities, which were normally controlled by oligarchies (see pp. 67–8) nearly all the German States were under some form of absolute rule which was usually the result of the weakening or destruction of the estates of the principality concerned. Even this generalization did not hold good everywhere. In Mecklenburg-Schwerin the estates persuaded the Emperor to depose an unpopular duke in 1728 and extracted important concessions from another in 1755. In Württemberg also they were able to establish a strong position in a long struggle with Duke Karl-Eugen (1737–93). With few exceptions, however, the German States were absolutisms, and often absolutisms of a peculiarly oppressive kind. Brandenburg-Prussia, endowed with relatively large territories and favoured with a series of able rulers, was able to develop a fine army and a still more remarkable system of administration. The other principalities of Germany, lacking both such resources and such leadership, remained throughout the century, with few exceptions, sunk in tradition and narrow in political outlook. The greater States of Europe, in return for the sacrifices they demanded of their citizens, had something at least to offer – military glory, the real if often misguided satisfaction to be derived from membership of a powerful political unit, in some cases the economic opportunities which a large politically unified area alone could provide. Hardly any of the German ones could offer compensations of this kind to offset the burdens imposed by their very existence.

In almost all of them the demands of the ruler and his court were a heavy drain on the State's finances. Saxony in the first half of the century, under the Electors Augustus I and Augustus II, was particularly famous for the lavishness of its court and for the ostentatious luxury in which ministers such as Count Flemming and Count Brühl lived. Conspicuous consumption of this kind was normal, however, in most of the smaller German States. It explains the tendency of so many of their rulers to run heavily, sometimes hopelessly, into debt, and thus helps to account for the undignified greed which many of them displayed for foreign subsidies and pensions. In many States, again, the rulers tended to emphasize their importance, sometimes to a ludicrous degree, by the assumption of long and complicated titles. A French observer claimed that 'there is no small sovereign in the Empire with less than three times as many titles as the King of France'.[3] More serious, the German princes often gratified their *amour-propre* and provided appointments for their courtiers by maintaining oppressively large armies and grossly inflated bureaucracies. Thus the Elector Palatine at one time possessed thirty regiments (about a quarter of whose strength consisted of officers) and a Grand Admiral to command the few small craft he maintained on the Rhine; while in 1778 it was alleged that the Bavarian army of less than 4,000 was commanded by as many as forty generals. During the eighteenth century Germany had twice as many officials, in proportion to its population, as after the unification of 1866–71. The weakness of the imperial cities, the predominance in every sizeable state of military and bureaucratic influences, the fact that in the developing territorial capitals economic life revolved very largely around the court and its demands; all this meant a society in which an independent middle class of merchants, manufacturers or professional men was exceptionally weak by the standards of England, the Netherlands or even France.

Equally important was the constricting effect which the political division of Germany had on her intellectual life. The despotisms which ruled nearly the whole of the country were, with few exceptions, hostile to intellectual novelties or even modified freedom of thought. Newspapers and the publishing trade developed slowly. In the 1760s the total number of book titles published annually in Germany – about 1,500 – was no greater than it had been in 1610; and it was only at the end of the seventeenth century that Latin was replaced by German as the country's main literary language. In these circumstances it is not surprising that German intellectual life was in many ways at a low ebb in the first half of his period (although its recovery after about 1770 was rapid and impressive). Its growth was further retarded by the immense cultural prestige of France (see pp. 405–06), which made German art and literature appear backward and provincial (as indeed they were until the 1750s or 1760s). The contempt for their subjects' intellectual attainments which was widespread among the country's rulers until late in the century is epitomized by Frederick II's refusal to appoint the great classical scholar Winckelmann as his librarian at a salary of 2,000 thalers on the grounds that 'a thousand thalers is enough for a German'.

The political divisions of Germany and the military weakness of most of the German States made it inevitable that the political as well as the cultural life of the country should be greatly influenced by foreign pressures. These were already well-established at the beginning of the eighteenth century. France had been influencing the policies and playing upon the ambitions of the German rulers for centuries, and had thus made important territorial gains at the expense of the Holy Roman Empire. In 1648 most of Alsace had fallen under her control. In 1681, by one of the most naked of all Louis XIV's aggressions, she had seized the city of Strasbourg. It is true that these advances aroused a good deal of hostility. The French minister to the Diet reported in 1723 that 'the Germans in general see with bitterness the King in possession of Alsace', while the recovery of the province had been one of the Habsburg war aims in the Spanish Succession struggle. Nevertheless throughout the century her military power, her money and her cultural prestige made France an important factor in German politics. Moreover she was slowly and almost imperceptibly 'rectifying' her eastern frontier and establishing for the first time a clear-cut geographical boundary between French and German territory. Thus for example part of the *baillage* of Gemmersheim, which surrounded the French fortress of Landau and which Louis had tried to seize through his *Chambres de Réunion* in the 1680s, became French by agreement with the Duke of Zweibrücken and the Elector Palatine in 1766 and 1768. By 1786 Vergennes could claim that the enclaves of non-French territory left in Alsace by the Treaty of Ryswick ninety years earlier had been eliminated.

Sweden, which like France had gained important German territories in 1648, lost most of them in the first two decades of the eighteenth century. Simultaneously, however, new foreign influences were brought to play upon German politics by the choice of the Elector of Saxony as King of Poland in 1697 and by the accession of the Elector of Hanover to the British throne in 1714. Above all the power of Russia to influence events in Germany, first seen clearly in her occupation of Mecklenburg in 1716 (see p. 260), increased throughout the century. Inevitably, moreover, the German policy of the Habsburgs was continually influenced by their territories and interests outside the boundaries of the Holy Roman Empire. Thus in the eighteenth century, as in preceding generations, the German States, with few exceptions, were the impotent spectators and victims of the struggles of the greater powers of Europe.

It was against this depressing background that the political history of eighteenth-century Germany unfolded. That history was dominated by one overriding fact – the success of Brandenburg-Prussia in raising herself to the status of a great power and the profound and lasting enmity of the Habsburgs which resulted from that success.

She had already, in the later seventeenth century, shown signs of an ability to lift herself out of the ruck of the other German States. Larger than Saxony, Bavaria or the Palatinate, her considerable areas of uncultivated land gave her greater opportunities than they could hope for of increasing her population by immigration and internal colonization. The 'Great Elector' Frederick William (1640–88) had begun to create the army and administrative machine which were to decide her future evolution. The significance of these factors, however, took two generations or more to become obvious. In the War of the Spanish Succession Prussia, whose ruler acquired the title of king in 1701, played a respectable but unimpressive role on the anti-French side. Her gains at the end of the struggle – the principality of Neuchâtel and Spanish Gelderland – did little to increase her real power. Under Frederick William I the bureaucracy was remodelled and made the most efficient in Europe (see pp. 144–5). Simultaneously the army became in some ways the best in the world. The king was, in fact, providing the weapons with which his son was to transform Prussia's international position, a debt which Frederick II was explicitly to acknowledge more than once in later years. But he was too cautious, too little skilled in diplomacy, too loyal to the emperor and perhaps in his own way too moral, to use these weapons himself. During his reign Prussia's only territorial gain was part of West Pomerania, acquired with comparatively little effort in 1719 during the dismemberment of the Swedish Empire. The fact that for all his obsessive interest in military affairs Frederick William fought no war of any significance obscured, for most contemporaries, the real importance of his reign, in some ways the most crucial in the history of Prussia. The secondary role played by the country in the tortuous diplomacy of 1713–40 concealed from them his success in raising a very impressive structure of State power on narrow economic and demographic foundations.

The will to expand was active in Berlin throughout his reign. Indeed it could hardly be otherwise in such a State, spread discontinuously from East Prussia to the Lower Rhine, with her main territories separated by the lands of her neighbours (notably Poland and Hanover) and still partially cut off from the Baltic by Sweden's retention of West Pomerania. By the end of the seventeenth century Brandenburg-Prussia had reached a position in which it was impossible for her to remain indefinitely. She must expand or resign herself to stagnation and perhaps to eventual dismemberment. Frederick William I was allured by dreams of annexing Polish Prussia and the remainder of Swedish Pomerania; but in general he regarded such gains as lying in a more or less remote future. Throughout his reign, and especially in its second half, much of his foreign policy was decided by the desire to acquire for Prussia, on the death of their ruler the Elector Palatine, the small but strategically placed West German duchies of Jülich and Berg to which he had a dynastic claim. This claim he wished to have recognized by the powers of Europe, and above all by the Emperor, whose support in a matter of this kind was still extremely valuable. In 1723, by the Treaty of Charlottenburg, he secured British and Hanoverian support for his acquisition of the duchies. In December 1728 he made an agreement with Charles VI by which he was guaranteed the succession to Berg (Jülich was to go to the rival claimants, the Pfalz-Sulzbach family) in return for a Prussian guarantee of the Pragmatic Sanction.

The latter, one of the central facts of the European diplomacy of the period, was a formal act promulgated by the Emperor in April 1713. By it he attempted to ensure that his territories should pass undivided to his children in the male or female line or, on their failure, to the two daughters of his elder brother Joseph I. Dynastic provisions of this type had long been common in the German States; and the extent of the Habsburg territories, their geographical dispersion (which was accentuated by the acquisition of the Netherlands and the new Italian possessions in 1713), and the virtual autonomy of many of them in the regulation of their internal affairs, seemed to make such an arrangement almost indispensable. In 1720–23 Charles secured the acceptance of the Pragmatic Sanction by the Diets of all his Central European provinces. Henceforth, as his hopes of a son vanished and it became clear that he must be succeeded by his eldest daughter, the Arch-duchess Maria Theresa, Austrian diplomacy centred on a series of efforts to have it guaranteed by the major powers of Europe. Spain promised to uphold it by the Treaty of Vienna of 1725 and Russia by her alliance with the Emperor in the following year. Britain added her guarantee in 1731 and France hers in 1735. The worthlessness of many of these paper promises was soon to be shown by events.

Austro-Prussian relations remained good for some time after the treaty of 1728, but by the end of the War of the Polish Succession in 1735 they had become very strained. By 1738 it was clear that Charles, in spite of his undertakings, would oppose the inheritance of Berg by the Hohenzollerns. The result was a secret Franco-Prussian agreement of May 1739 by which Cardinal Fleury, who then controlled French policy, promised his support for the acquisition by Prussia of most of the duchy. Two years earlier Frederick William had begun to receive substantial French subsidies. Thus when he died in May 1740 he bequeathed to his son Frederick II both a grievance against the Habsburgs and a relatively close relationship with France. Within a few months of his death German politics suffered a revolutionary change.

Charles VI died on 19 October. Two months later Prussian troops invaded the Habsburg province of Silesia and thus began a struggle for mastery in Germany which was to last for a century and a quarter. The reasons for Frederick's dramatic and unscru-pulous action seem clear. He had always been conscious of Prussia's exposed position and of the way in which her political geography forced expansion upon her. As early as 1731, in one of his earliest surviving comments on international affairs, he had visualized increasing her geographical unity by the acquisition of Polish Prussia and Swedish Pomerania. It was true that the conquest of Silesia (to which he had legal claims, though very weak ones) would considerably lengthen the already very long frontiers which the Prussian army had to defend. At the same time, however, it would place at Frederick's disposal a province much wealthier than any he already possessed, and would weaken the Elector of Saxony by placing a solid wedge of Prussian territory between his German lands and his Polish kingdom. Nor had Frederick any illusions about the morality of international relations or any scruples about the use of force to uphold his claims. Already in 1737 and 1738 he had proposed the forcible seizure of Jülich and Berg as soon as the Elector Palatine died; while in a memorandum drawn up in November 1740 he stressed the need to attack at once in Silesia since delay might result in the invasion of the province by Saxony, which must be avoided at all costs. Young, ambitious, anxious to cut a figure in the eyes of Europe, he had at his disposal a full treasury and a fine army. His adversary was an inexperienced girl insecurely established on the throne of a disunited and badly governed collection of provinces whose army was weak, whose treasury was empty and whose ministers were mediocrities. When Frederick launched his attack on Silesia the province was defended by only 6,000 men with no field artillery to speak of. Great Britain and the Dutch, the traditional allies of the Habsburgs, would not, Frederick correctly believed, object seriously to a Prussian annexation of Silesia: if they did the hostility of France would hold them in check. Only the opposition of Russia seemed likely to disconcert his plans, and that might be nullified by bribing her ministers, or by internal confusion when the Empress Anna died. Even if the Russians did move against him they would probably find themselves opposed by the Swedes.

For all these reasons Frederick decided, very soon after the Emperor's death, to attack Silesia. He did not, now or at any other time in his life, desire war for its own sake; he was always far too conscious of the very limited resources of Prussia to indulge in such expensive follies as unnecessary battles. If possible he would have liked to acquire Silesia without a struggle. Thus when his representative in Vienna announced the invasion to the horrified Maria Theresa he was instructed to offer, in return for the cession of the province, a guarantee of all the other German possessions of the Habsburgs, the payment of a money indemnity, and his master's vote for her husband Francis, Grand Duke of Tuscany, in the forthcoming imperial election. A few days later Frederick even suggested that he might be content with only part of Silesia if he could obtain a 'reasonable and sincere agreement' with Austria. All these proposals were immediately and understandably rejected by Maria Theresa. War thus became inevitable.

Her action was all the more courageous in that she was now threatened by new enemies. The Elector of Bavaria, Charles Albert, had inherited claims to the whole Habsburg inheritance. They were not particularly strong claims, and by himself he had no chance of enforcing them; but behind him stood France, whose satellite Bavaria had been intermittently for two generations. Already in treaties of 1714, 1727 and 1733 French support for Bavarian territorial claims had been promised. Moreover it was obviously likely that Spain would attempt, in case of a serious war in Central Europe, to expand at the expense of the Habsburg possessions in Italy. The resources of Maria Theresa's dominions, at least her financial resources, were inadequate to maintain a war of any length against so powerful an array of foes and very hard to mobilize effectively. The result was that almost from the moment Prussian troops crossed the Silesian border she was heavily dependent on outside help, above all from Great Britain. A British subsidy was granted her at the end of April 1741 and continued to be paid, though with growing reluctance, until the end of the war. It was provided not because any British statesman cared much about the fate of Silesia but because support for the Habsburgs seemed the best way of checking the growth of French power in Europe.

The development of French policy was the key to events in the spring of 1741. Cardinal Fleury, who had controlled the country's diplomacy since 1726, was now an old man of almost ninety. He had no desire for a new struggle against the Habsburgs and saw that France was unlikely to gain much from one. Ranged against him, however, were the weight of a long anti-Habsburg tradition, and also powerful military and aristocratic groups which had forgotten the defeats of Louis XIV's last years and hoped to win glory in a new struggle on the old battlefields of the Rhineland and the Netherlands. This resistance to Fleury's cautious policy was led by the Maréchal de Belleisle, who as early as January 1741 had drawn up plans for French intervention on a large scale in the affairs of Germany. In March he was sent as the envoy of Louis XV to those German States which seemed likely to support Charles Albert of Bavaria, who had now put himself forward as a candidate for the vacant imperial title. In the next few months Belleisle constructed an extensive though flimsy anti-Habsburg coalition in Germany. In May Bavaria and Spain united against Maria Theresa by the Treaty of Nymphenburg; and in June France, by an agreement with Frederick II, committed herself to military intervention. Fleury had thus been overruled; but his struggle with Belleisle had virtually paralysed French policy for several months. It had thus given Maria Theresa at least a chance of survival. Nevertheless her position was extremely serious. Already in April the Prussian infantry had shown their quality by defeating the Austrians at Mollwitz in Silesia, the first battle of the war. In July George II, alarmed for the safety of his German Electorate of Hanover which seemed exposed to French or Prussian attack, signed without consulting his ministers in London a convention guaranteeing its neutrality. This made it almost impossible for Britain to give any direct help to her ally. In October French and Bavarian troops invaded Bohemia.

From this dangerous position Maria Theresa escaped mainly because of the disunity of her opponents. Frederick II was quite prepared to throw over the French whenever it suited him to do so, and early in October agreed to the Convention of Klein-Schnellendorf. By this he was allowed to occupy the whole of Silesia: in return he suspended operations against Maria Theresa. This allowed her to drive the French and Bavarians with heavy losses from Upper Austria and later Bohemia, to invade Bavaria and even to capture Munich. Charles Albert, with French backing, was elected Emperor in January 1742, but found himself almost at once driven from his own capital. In June of that year, by an agreement signed at Breslau, Frederick II obtained the cession of almost the whole of Silesia. Maria Theresa agreed to this only under heavy pressure from the British government, which demanded that her resources be concentrated on the struggle with France. Her need for British subsidies and her hope that a combined British, Dutch and Austrian force was about to launch a large-scale attack on France from the Austrian Nether-lands led her to accept the surrender of Silesia – a surrender which she hoped and expected would be only temporary.

By the summer of 1742 the real decisions of the War of the Austrian Succession, as far as Germany was concerned, had there-fore all been taken. Frederick's aggression had been successful: Silesia was now Prussian territory. It was clear, on the other hand, that the structure of Habsburg power in Central Europe was still too solid to be pulled down by the apparently overwhelming but in fact rather ineffective enemies who attacked it in the later months of 1741. Though the struggle dragged on for another six years the ebb and flow of war could not affect these essential facts.

Maria Theresa's position continued on the whole to improve in 1743. The 'Pragmatic Army' of British, Hanoverian and Austrian troops which had now been formed in the Austrian

Netherlands won an important victory over the French at Dettingen in June. A new invasion of Bavaria by the Austrians seemed for a time to threaten France herself with attack. These appearances, however, were misleading. In particular the wavering and lukewarm attitude of the Dutch made the British government unwilling to launch a direct attack on France (with whom Britain was not formally at war; she was still fighting merely as the ally of Maria Theresa). Moreover Anglo-Austrian relations were very seriously strained by the insistence of Lord Carteret, now the leading figure in British foreign policy, that the Austrians should make substantial concessions to Charles Emmanuel of Sardinia in order to secure his support in Italy. These concessions were made by the Treaty of Worms, signed in September, but were deeply resented in Vienna.

Austria's successes in 1742–43 were nevertheless striking enough to alarm Frederick II, who quite rightly suspected Maria Theresa of wishing to annex part of Bavaria. Already there can be seen in Berlin that determination to prevent any strengthening of Habsburg power in Germany which was to remain a permanent element in Frederick's foreign policy and which he bequeathed to his successors. His fears and suspicions drove him to sign a new alliance with France in June 1744 and to invade Bohemia immediately afterwards. Maria Theresa was, however, far better placed to meet this onslaught than she had been to face that of December 1740. In January 1745 Charles Albert of Bavaria died, and she was able to make peace with his successor in April. In September she secured the election of her husband as Emperor, and thus re-established Habsburg control of what was still, at least in theory, the highest position of secular authority in Europe. Moreover she now enjoyed the support of Saxony. The result was that in spite of defeats at Hohenfriedberg and Soor she stubbornly refused for many months to agree once more to recognize Silesia as Prussian territory. She was forced to, however, in December 1745, by the Treaty of Dresden; partly because of a threat that British subsidies would be cut off if she did not; partly by a brilliantly successful Prussian invasion of Saxony; and most of all perhaps by the failure of a series of efforts to make a separate peace with France.

With this treaty the war, so far as Germany was concerned, virtually ended. The next three years saw much fighting in Italy and the Netherlands (see pp. 318, 331), but the repercussions of this on German affairs were of secondary importance. French efforts to persuade Frederick II to launch yet a third attack on Austria were unsuccessful. Thus when peace was made at Aix-la-Chapelle by Britain, France, Austria and the United Provinces in October 1748, Prussia, who was no longer a belligerent, took no part in the negotiations. The treaty which the British and French representatives drew up was accepted by Maria Theresa only with the greatest reluctance. This was because one of its clauses guaranteed, though in rather vague terms, Frederick II's possession of Silesia, the one really important result for Germany and indeed for Europe of the complicated struggles of 1740–48. The Empress, however, was far from having abandoned hope of regaining the lost province. The administration of her great possessions in Central Europe, though still full of faults, was improving rapidly. Her army, though still inferior to that of Prussia, had performed during the war as well as that of France and probably better than that of Britain. Her resources, at least on paper, were still much greater than those of Frederick II. A reconquest of Silesia was by no means beyond her powers.

But it was clear that such a reconquest would not be achieved with the help of Austria's traditional allies, Great Britain and the Dutch. Throughout the war Britain had shown herself indifferent to the interests of the Habsburg monarchy. In 1742 and 1745 she had forced Maria Theresa to accept the Prussian seizure of Silesia. In 1743 Carteret had browbeaten her into promising large concessions to Sardinia. At Aix-la-Chapelle the British government seemed to have conspired with that of France against the Empress. Plainly Britain was interested in the Habsburg territories as an auxiliary against France and nothing more. Preoccupied with colonial and commercial problems, she had little in common with Austria, whose outlook was increasingly dominated by events in Central and Eastern Europe, above all by the question of Silesia. The Duke of Newcastle, who in the main controlled British foreign policy in the years after 1748, tried in the early 1750s to consolidate the Austrian alliance by securing the election of the Empress's eldest son, the Archduke Joseph, as King of the Romans (i.e. heir to the imperial title). These efforts, however, cut little ice in Vienna. As for the Dutch the events of 1745–48 had shown up clearly their military weakness, their internal divisions and the almost catastrophic fall in their international importance.

The result was that from 1749 onwards, under the influence of Count Wenzel von Kaunitz-Rietberg who became Chancellor in 1753, the Austrian government played intermittently with the idea of breaking the Franco-Prussian alliance, isolating Frederick II, and then crushing him with the help of Russia and perhaps France. The idea was slow to bear fruit. When in March 1749 Maria Theresa asked the members of her council to give her in writing their views on the future course of Habsburg foreign policy her husband, the Emperor Francis, was in favour of maintaining the traditional alliance with Britain and was strongly supported by the Vice-Chancellor, Count Colloredo. Kaunitz, in a very long memorandum, was the only council member to disagree clearly with this view. Moreover the three years which he spent in Paris as ambassador in 1750–53 failed to make much impression on the French court. However in the summer of 1755, when fighting between Britain and France had already broken out in America and at sea and when the divergence between British and Austrian interests had become unmistakable, a new approach to France was made, with very different results. The Abbé de Bernis, who had just returned to Paris after several years as French ambassador at Venice, was appointed by Louis XV to receive the proposals made by the Austrian ambassador, Starhemberg, and showed himself much more sympathetic than the ministers with whom Kaunitz had had to deal. Nevertheless it is very doubtful whether any important change in French policy would have been made, at least for the time being, but for the action of Frederick II.

By the end of 1755 the King of Prussia was seriously alarmed by the position in which he found himself. He knew that he must, in all probability, face the irreconcilable hostility of the Habsburgs for the rest of his life. He also realized that Russia, whose foreign policy was now strongly influenced by the bitterly anti-Prussian Chancellor, Count Bestuzhev-Ryumin, was likely to aid Maria Theresa against him when a favourable opportunity arose. Moreover the weakness and disunity of the French government and its feeble reaction to British aggression on the high seas indicated that it was unlikely to give him much effective support. His uneasiness was brought to a head when in September 1755 Britain signed a convention with Russia. By this the Empress Elizabeth, in return for a subsidy, promised to maintain a force of 55,000 men in her Baltic provinces and to support them if necessary with a galley-fleet. This army was intended by the British government (which had been negotiating in St Petersburg for some such agreement since March 1753) to protect Hanover against Prussian attack by threatening Frederick II from the rear, and the convention at once aroused in his mind fears of a concerted onslaught on him by Britain, Austria and Russia. From this dangerous position he decided to escape by an agreement with Britain for the neutralization of Germany and its exclusion from the Anglo-French war which was now raging. Such an agreement was achieved in January 1756 by the so-called Convention of Westminster.

This limited and *ad hoc* Anglo-Prussian co-operation had disproportionately severe repercussions in France and Russia. At Versailles Frederick's secret negotiations with France's enemy, his tacit assumption that he was the equal of Louis XV, his barely concealed contempt for the weakness of French policy, aroused a wave of bitter and somewhat irrational hostility. It was irrational because the neutralization of Germany, by forcing the French government to concentrate its energies on the colonial struggle with Britain, served France's real long-term interests. Moreover Frederick had been careful to exclude the Netherlands from the scope of the convention and thus leave the way open for French military action there. Nevertheless the Anglo-Prussian agreement made Louis XV and his advisers far more ready than ever before to listen to proposals from Vienna. They were still unwilling to contemplate offensive action against Prussia but, anxious to punish Frederick II for his independence, they concluded on 1 May 1756 with Starhemberg the defensive alliance usually known as the First Treaty of Versailles. This bound each of the contracting parties to supply the other, if it were attacked, with a force of 24,000 men or a money equivalent.

The treaty was not a complete victory for Kaunitz and Maria Theresa. The French government was almost as far as ever from being willing to join in the destruction of Prussia. Nevertheless it was regarded by contemporaries as marking a revolutionary change in the structure of international relations, and had widespread repercussions, above all in Russia. Frederick, with good reason, was even more worried about the position in St Petersburg than about that in Vienna; and the spring and summer of 1756 saw the desire for war with Prussia become constantly more active and menacing in Russian ruling circles. A conference of Russian ministers had agreed in October 1755 that Silesia should be returned to Maria Theresa, and at the end of March 1756 a scheme for an immediate attack on Frederick, which involved offering the Austrian government the backing of 80,000 Russian soldiers, was being actively discussed. Later this offer was increased to that of Russia acting 'with her full strength'. It was also agreed that efforts should be made to strengthen the Russian position in Poland to prepare for a military advance westwards; while the idea of giving the Poles East Prussia in exchange for Courland when Frederick's power had been destroyed began to attract a good deal of support in St Petersburg. Attention was also to be given to improving relations with France to pave the way for possible co-operation against the hated King of Prussia. It was even decided to suspend work on a Russian fortress in the Ukraine to avoid annoying the Turks and minimize any risk of their being used by Frederick to divert Russia's attention and resources to her southern frontier. By June Russian war preparations were far advanced: it was by then the Austrians who, more hesitant, were asking that any attack on Prussia should be postponed until the following year, when France might have agreed formally not to oppose it.

Frederick, though he was not fully informed about the position in St Petersburg, was well aware of the danger looming up from that quarter. To avert it he relied mainly on British influence at the Russian court; and in the first seven months of 1756 he stressed repeatedly to the British government the need for it to do everything possible to restrain the belligerence of the Russian military and political leaders. But Britain's ability to achieve this was rapidly declining. The Empress Elizabeth had agreed to the subsidy treaty of September 1755 only because it appeared to her a weapon for possible and probably imminent use against Prussia. The Convention of Westminster made it clear that it would not be used in this way. It therefore caused deep disappointment in St Petersburg and sharply reduced what influence the British government had hitherto possessed there. Frederick's hopes of avoiding a conflict with his great eastern neighbour were therefore very insecurely based. By the early summer of 1756, if not before, Russia had become the key to the entire situation, though it was not until the very last day of that year that she acceded to the Austro-French treaty of 1 May.

That treaty, the kernel of what is usually called the 'Diplomatic Revolution' of 1756, was very quickly followed by a new Austro-

Prussian struggle in Germany. This war was not the result of the treaty, which was defensive in form and, so far as France was concerned, in fact. It was, like those of 1740–42 and 1744–45, the result of Prussian aggression; in this case of the attack which Frederick II launched on Saxony at the end of August. He took this desperate step because he had now come to realize that there was no real chance of separating Russia from the rest of his enemies. If he did not act, he believed, he would be attacked in the following year by a great alliance of Austria, Russia and Saxony, supported by France; and this belief was almost certainly justified. Inaction would thus be fatal. His only chance of survival seemed to lie in a sudden onslaught on Austria through Saxony, before Maria Theresa and her ministers were fully ready for the fray. It was even possible for Frederick to persuade himself that such an attack was not as dangerous as it seemed. He had ready for immediate action a fine army of 154,000 men, not counting various second-line formations. He hoped, quite wrongly as events were to show, that the Russians would not commit more than 45,000 men to a war against him; and in that case he might be a match for both them and Austria. Moreover although the attack on Saxony was in essentials a defensive reaction to a very real threat it was also inspired by hopes of territorial gain if all went well. In the first days of the war Frederick played with ideas of annexing West Prussia from Poland or even retaining Saxony (whose ruler might be compensated with conquered Habsburg territory in Bohemia). Ambitions of this kind had figured prominently in the *Political Testament* which he had drawn up some years earlier, in 1752. Whatever the exact balance of motives behind it, however, the attack on Saxony unleashed one of the most desperate and dramatic struggles in European history.

The European phases of the Seven Years War saw extraordinary fluctuations of fortune. By the summer of 1757, after a year's fighting, Frederick's position was desperate. He had forced the Saxon army to capitulate at Pirna (October 1756); but a Prussian attack on Bohemia had failed with heavy loss (June 1757). More important, the French government signed with Austria on 1 May 1757 the Second Treaty of Versailles. By this France bound herself to maintain a force of 105,000 men in Germany, as well as 10,000 German mercenaries, and to pay Austria an annual subsidy of 12 million florins. She was to receive in return four cities in the Austrian Netherlands, the rest of which was to go to Don Philip,

Louis XV's favourite son-in-law; but these cessions of territory were conditional on the reconquest by Maria Theresa of the whole of Silesia. France thus sacrificed a very substantial bird in the hand (the army in Germany and the subsidy to the empress) in return for a small and problematic bird in the bush. This commitment was to cost her dear and many Frenchmen were later to regret it bitterly. An offensive alliance of Austria and Russia was concluded a few days later; while the Circles of the Empire had already agreed in January 1757 to supply contingents for use against Prussia, and Sweden had joined the anti-Prussian coalition in March. Moreover it was clear that Frederick could expect no active help from Hanover, which was overrun by the French during the summer. The Duke of Cumberland, commanding a considerable army of German troops there, signed at Klosterzeven in September 1757 an armistice which was virtually a capitulation. A Russian army invaded East Prussia in August (earlier Russian action had been prevented by the fact that the Empress Elizabeth seemed for some time in late 1756 to be on the point of death). In October an Austrian force occupied Berlin itself, though for only a few days. It is not surprising, therefore, to find Frederick making efforts during these disastrous summer and autumn months to come to terms with France and offering to renew his old alliance with her.

Nevertheless by the end of the year a brilliant victory over the Franco-Imperial army at Rossbach in November, and a more fiercely contested one over the Austrians at Leuthen a few weeks later, had done much to restore his position. They had also raised his personal reputation higher than ever before, at least in Prot-estant Germany, and made him appear quite undeservedly as a symbol and defender of German nationality. But the odds against Prussia were tremendous. The war had become what one German historian has called 'a struggle of five million against ninety million', and the country's long and exposed frontiers intensified her difficulties. Growing financial strain was reflected in a cabinet order of October 1757 which suspended payment of all salaries and pensions to Prussian civil servants and judges, with the one exception of diplomats serving abroad. Eventually partial payment was resumed so far as the lower ranks of the bureaucracy were concerned; but their superiors had to be content merely with promissory notes. The discontent and bribery which this produced, coupled with the disruption of communications, the long absences of the king on campaign and enemy occupations of Berlin, meant that the work of administering most of the Prussian provinces was carried on for several years with sharply reduced efficiency. It is true that Frederick received, after April 1758, a British subsidy of £670,000 a year. Moreover from then onwards his western flank was protected against French attack by an Anglo-German army in Westphalia paid by Britain and ably commanded by Prince Ferdinand of Brunswick. On the other hand the heavy losses suffered by the Prussian army in the first eighteen months of the war did much to reduce its quality: recruits could still be obtained, but the splendid fighting machine of 1756–57 could not be resurrected. Thus in the years 1758–61 Prussia's position became steadily worse.

In August 1758 Frederick defeated the Russians at Zorndorf in the most bloody battle of the century; but the same year saw a Swedish invasion of Prussian Pomerania and an Austrian victory in October at Hochkirch in Saxony. By 1759 it was clear that Prussia could not long continue the struggle on this scale. Frederick's army now numbered little more than 100,000 men (as against about 150,000 in the previous year) while his enemies could muster twice as many. His financial position was made tolerable only by the British subsidies, debasement of the coinage, and ruthless exploitation of the areas in Prussian occupation, above all Saxony. He was now willing to accept a peace settlement which gave East Prussia to Russia and left France in control of much of West Germany, provided he were compensated with Saxony; a change in the geographical structure of the Prussian monarchy which, if carried out, would have had large repercussions on its future. Finally in August the Russians inflicted on him at Kunersdorf the most disastrous defeat of his career, reducing him temporarily to despair. 'I have no resources left,' he wrote to his minister Finckenstein, 'and to tell the truth I believe all is lost. I will not survive the ruin of my country.'

In spite of appearances, all was not lost. The Russian commander, Saltykov, suspicious of the Austrians and perhaps influenced by expectations of the death of Elizabeth and her replacement by the pro-Prussian Grand Duke Peter, did not follow up his victory. Notwithstanding serious setbacks, therefore, Frederick managed, when the campaigning season ended, to retain control of most of Saxony. Moreover the French government had now decided, rather belatedly, to reduce its commitments in Germany. By the Third Treaty of Versailles, signed in March 1759, its subsidies to Maria Theresa were cut by half and its military support of the Empress was reduced to 100,000 soldiers for use in Germany.

In spite of all this Frederick's position was becoming more and more critical. In 1760 he put about 90,000 men in the field in face of the 232,000 maintained by his enemies, and admitted that it would probably be impossible to do as much in the following year. Debasement of the currency now meant that thirty talers were being struck from a single fine mark of silver, whereas before the war the accepted standard had been eighteen. Most serious of all, there were unmistakable signs that reluctance to shoulder the burdens of an unprecedented war effort was now rapidly growing in the Prussian provinces. In 1760 the landowners of the Electoral Mark of Brandenburg refused to contribute further; and in the following year the Estates of Pomerania protested that the province could give no more. It was the resources drawn from Silesia and Saxony, the richest and most efficiently administered of the areas under Frederick's control, which permitted the war to continue: according to one calculation Saxony yielded during the struggle 48 million talers to her Prussian masters, and Silesia 18 million, whereas all the other Prussian provinces combined provided only 25 million. Frederick was still able, none the less, to win victories at Leignitz and Torgau, while the strain was clearly beginning to tell on his opponents. Before the war Kaunitz had estimated that each year of fighting would cost Austria 10–12 million florins. In fact that in 1760 cost 44 million, and in December he had to warn Maria Theresa that would be possible to finance only one more campaign. In the spring of 1761 lack of money forced a reduction of 20,000 men in the strength of the Austrian army. That year, though no great battles were fought, saw the fortunes of Prussia reach their lowest ebb. By the end of the campaigning season Silesia and much of Saxony were held by the Austrians, Prussian Pomerania by the Russians. A little more initiative on the part of Frederick's enemies, particularly Russia, would have destroyed the Prussian monarchy. Efforts to persuade the Turks to attack Austria or Russia in the rear had no success. 'If fortune continues to treat me so pitilessly,' the king told his friend the Marquis d'Argens in January 1762, 'no doubt I shall succumb; she alone can deliver me from my present position.[4]

He had already been delivered, though he did not know it when he wrote these words. On 5 January Elizabeth of Russia, a more inveterate enemy even than Maria Theresa, died at last. Her successor, the unstable Peter III, was a fanatical admirer of Frederick, and German far more than Russian in outlook and temperament. He ordered an immediate armistice, and early in May made peace with Prussia and withdrew his troops from her territory. His murder in July and the accession of his German wife as Catherine II destroyed the Russo-Prussian alliance against Austria and Denmark which now seemed to be in the making, but did not upset the peace signed two months earlier. Maria Theresa, now virtually isolated (Sweden, which had never played a great part in the war, also made peace with Prussia in May 1762), could not hope to recover Silesia and was forced to abandon the struggle. At Hubertusburg on 15 February 1763 the German part of the Seven Years War ended on the basis of the *status quo ante bellum*. Saxony, part of which Frederick had hoped to retain, was restored in full to its ruler; though no compensation was paid for the immense losses it had suffered during the war. Silesia remained part of the Prussian monarchy which was now, at least during Frederick's lifetime, established as one of the great powers of Europe.

The *de facto* Anglo-Prussian alliance which had existed throughout the war collapsed in 1762 amid mutual recriminations. For its dissolution the British government, and above all the Earl of Bute, whose influence over the young George III was very great, have usually been blamed by German historians. The charge has some foundation. Bute was undoubtedly anxious to withdraw from the struggle in Germany, especially after the declaration of war by Britain on Spain in January 1762. Moreover both he and the Duke of Newcastle, who as First Lord of the Treasury still retained great influence on foreign policy, were conspicuously clumsy and tactless in their diplomacy. They alarmed Frederick by making advances to Maria Theresa for a renewal of the old Austro-British alliance. They angered him by giving the impression that they meant to force him to make territorial concessions to his enemies as the price of peace. Also opposition in Britain to the payment of subsidies to Prussia was steadily mounting now that the war with France was clearly won. On the other hand Frederick himself had never hesitated to sacrifice the interests of his ally to his own, or to make advances to his opponents for a separate peace when it seemed advisable to do so, notably in 1757. His relations with Peter III from March 1762 onwards, and in particular the way in which he encouraged the Tsar to assert against Denmark his dynastic claims in Schleswig-Holstein, were certainly contrary to the spirit of his connexion with Britain. What finally decided the British government in 1762 to refuse further subsidy payments was not mere stinginess, but much more fear that the money would be used by Frederick to finance a new war against Denmark or a continuation of the old one against Austria. Whatever the rights and wrongs of the quarrel the alliance, once broken, could not be reconstructed. In 1764 Frederick turned to Russia for support; Britain remained for the next two decades ingloriously and at length disastrously isolated.

The war of 1756–63 left its mark upon both Prussia and her ruler. During it 180,000 Prussian soldiers had died: of the 5,500 officers Frederick had at his disposal in October 1756 4,000 had been lost. The Prussian provinces felt the effects of the struggle very severely; some of them had been devastated in a way which recalled the Thirty Years War. Henceforth Frederick, though he never abandoned hope of new territorial gains, and in fact made very important ones in Poland in the first partition (see pp. 275–6), feared nothing so much as another great war. From the 1760s to the 1780s it was Austria which was the revolutionary and dynamic force in German affairs while Prussia, quiescent though by no means satiated, stood on the whole for conservatism and the existing balance of forces. The rivalry with the Habsburgs to which the aggression of 1740 had given rise thus continued to dominate all Frederick's calculations. It was intensified by the growing influence at Vienna of the ambitious young Archduke Joseph, who in 1765 succeeded his father as Emperor. A visit by him to Frederick at Neisse in Silesia in August 1769, and a return visit by the king at Neustadt in Moravia a year later, produced protestations of goodwill on both sides but did nothing to bridge the gulf which separated the two rulers. Their mutual dislike and suspicion was brought to a head by the question of the Bavarian Succession in 1778–79.

When the Elector Maximilian Joseph of Bavaria died at the end of 1777 he was succeeded by a distant relative, the Elector Palatine. The later, like his predecessor, had no legitimate children, but a number of illegitimate ones for whom it was his main ambition to provide suitably. To obtain the support of the Emperor in this he agreed in January 1778 to surrender more than a third of Bavaria to him, an arrangement which has been justifiably described as 'the *reductio ad absurdum* of the principle of personal rule in the eighteenth century.'[5] Behind this partition treaty lurked the idea, which had attracted statesmen in Vienna for almost a century, of acquiring the whole of the electorate in exchange for the Austrian Netherlands and thus creating a more powerful and compact block of Habsburg territories centred on the Danube valley. But even such a limited accession of strength to the Habsburgs as that provided for by the agreement with the new Elector, unbalanced by any compensation for Prussia, was certain to be opposed by Frederick II. He had already undertaken, in secret negotiations with France in the summer of 1777, to prevent Austrian expansion in Bavaria or the Balkans; and he was provided with a plausible pretext for opposing Joseph II by the fact that the Duke of Zweibrücken, the heir to the electorate, formally protested to the Diet against its dismemberment. Moreover the Elector of Saxony had claims of his own to part of the Bavarian inheritance.

The result was a struggle of Prussia and Saxony against what appeared to be the dangerous ambitions of the Emperor. In this Frederick and his ally had the sympathy of most of the German States; and understandably so. Joseph's appetite for territorial gain and the lack of scruple he showed in his efforts to satisfy it had already antagonized much German opinion. His handling of the Bavarian situation did nothing to still these fears. Maria Theresa herself, now near the end of her life and anxious for peace, admitted that the Austrian claims in Bavaria were 'outdated and poorly based' (the territory ceded in January 1778 was alleged in Vienna to consist of lapsed Austrian, Bohemian and imperial fiefs). Yet Joseph and Kaunitz were confident of success. They hoped for support from France, at least on paper the ally of the Habsburgs since 1756; and they expected that Catherine II would be too preoccupied by events in the Balkans and the Black Sea to be able to give Frederick any effective help. On both counts they were wrong. Vergennes, the French Foreign Minister, wished to concentrate France's energies on the struggle with Britain in America which was now clearly imminent. He had no intention of helping to strengthen the Habsburgs in Germany, where he aimed, on the contrary, at the maintenance of an

Austro-Prussian balance. In March 1778, therefore, he made it clear to the Austrian court that 'circumstances did not permit His Majesty to take any part but that of neutrality in the war which might break out in Germany'. Moreover the beginning of hostilities early in July was quickly followed by signs that Catherine was likely to support Frederick: by the end of the year negotiations were under way for the sending of a Russian auxiliary force for this purpose. Although Prussia failed completely to win any significant military success the Austrian government was therefore forced, in February 1779, to accept preliminary peace terms which gave it only a minor part of what had been hoped for in Bavaria. When peace was signed in May, at Teschen in Silesia under French and Russian mediation, Joseph had to abandon his Bavarian plans and to accept only the Innviertel (a relatively small area of eastern Bavaria) as a consolation prize. He also agreed not to oppose the eventual union with Prussia of the little South German principalities of Ansbach and Bayreuth, which were held by a junior branch of the Hohenzollern family now clearly on the verge of extinction. Frederick was thus justified in claiming that the war had ended in a victory for Prussia, and that 'in the Empire we shall in future be thought of as a useful counterweight to the despotism of Austria'.

Joseph was not slow in providing fresh evidence of his determination to dominate South and West Germany. His relations with the smaller States continued to show all the tactlessness and inflexibility which marked his entire life. When the Prince-Bishop of Passau died in February 1783, for example, those parts of his diocese which extended into Austrian territory were seized by the Emperor and used to form two new bishoprics of Linz and St Polten. This was the grossest breach of the imperial constitution which Joseph ever perpetrated, and one which aroused violent antagonism, particularly in catholic clerical circles by tradition favourable to the Habsburgs. Fear and dislike of the Emperor continued to haunt Frederick II until his death in August 1786. The breakdown in 1780 of the alliance with Russia which had been the main prop of his foreign policy for sixteen years intensified these feelings, especially as Catherine II replaced it in the following year by an *entente* with Austria. In May 1782 he solemnly warned his nephew and heir that Joseph now threatened to become more powerful than any ruler since Louis XIV and would sooner or later attempt to destroy the Prussian monarchy.

The last achievement of his life was the construction in July 1785 of the *Fürstenbund* (League of Princes). This united a number of important German rulers – the Elector of Saxony, the Archbishop of Mainz, George III as Elector of Hanover – with Prussia in opposition to the Emperor, and in particular to Joseph's scheme, now coming to a head, to acquire the whole of Bavaria in exchange for the Austrian Netherlands.

The growth of Austro-Prussian antagonism, of 'dualism' in Germany, was the most important development in the politics of eighteenth-century Europe apart from the emergence of Russia. Its significance for the future was great. By his victories Frederick laid the foundations of belief in the moral superiority of Prussia to the other German States, a belief whose wide acceptance is easy to understand but which was to have dangerous results. The achievements of his reign consolidated the military character of the State he had inherited from his father and established the Prussian army as one of the great factors in European politics. Most important of all, by challenging Habsburg leadership and weakening still further the Empire as an institution, Frederick made less likely the creation in the future of a unified 'Great Germany'. He thus helped (though many other factors entered into the process) to pave the way for the 'unity' achieved by Bismarck in 1866–71 – a 'unity' which deliberately excluded from the newly created Reich the many millions of Germans then under Habsburg rule. Not until the days of Hitler was this effect of the events of 1740–63 overcome, and then only momentarily.

NOTES AND REFERENCES

1 *The Present State of Germany* (London, 1738), vol. II, p.312.

2 J. S. Pütter, *An Historical Development of the present Political Constitution of the Germanic Empire* (London, 1790), vol. III, p. 270.

3 A. Fauchier-Magnan, *The Smaller German Courts in the Eighteenth Century* (London, 1958), p. 21.

4 *Oeuvres de Frédéric le Grand* (Berlin, 1846–56), vol. XIX, p. 283.

5 H. W. V. Temperley, *Frederick the Great and Kaiser Joseph* (London, 1915), p. 85.

11

SPAIN, ITALY AND THE MEDITERRANEAN

The Peace of Utrecht, which in 1713 ended the War of the Spanish Succession, made great changes in the balance of power in the western Mediterranean. It deprived Spain of much territory; established Britain as an important factor in the politics of the area; and set up the Habsburgs, at least for the time being, as the dominant power in Italy. It disappointed long-cherished French hopes of obtaining control of the kingdom of Naples. It marked an important stage in the slow rise of the north Italian State of Savoy-Piedmont. Changes so great and so rapid inevitably generated new ambitions and grievances in the States concerned; these emotions were to provide the driving force behind events in this area during the next generation.

Spain was the only real territorial sufferer by the war. Its close saw the loss of all her European possessions. The Spanish Netherlands, the Duchy of Milan, Sardinia and the Kingdom of Naples were surrendered to the Emperor. Sicily was lost to the Duke of Savoy. These losses were in many ways an advantage to the country. They relieved her of the obligation to protect distant and constantly threatened territories which her economic and demographic weakness had, in the later seventeenth century, made it impossible for her to defend effectively. They offered her an opportunity to reduce her financial and military commitments and to pursue a simpler and more realistic policy in international affairs. She could now concentrate her energies on the development of her own resources and those of her American possessions. However the Spanish government and the majority of Spaniards did not see the position in this light, and it was hardly to be expected that they should. The dismemberment of Spain's European empire, which in the later seventeenth century it had been the great object of Charles II (1665–1700) and his advisers to avoid, was accepted by most Spanish statesmen in 1713 as inevitable. It was nevertheless felt as a great blow to the country's international position and to the prestige of its ruler.

Worse still, Spain suffered the humiliation of being forced to surrender to her enemies, and to heretical enemies at that, parts of her metropolitan territory. Gibraltar had been seized in 1704 by an Anglo-Dutch fleet; and though it had never been regarded by the Spanish government as a fortress of great importance – its garrison when it fell consisted of only fifty-six regular soldiers and about a hundred militiamen – its retention by Britain at the peace was bitterly resented. The capture of Minorca in 1708 established Britain more securely as a leading force in the affairs of the western Mediterranean: for the next half-century English statesmen and merchants cherished delusive hopes that the island might become a great commercial entrepôt comparable to Leghorn or Marseilles. The British Mediterranean squadron based on its capital, Port Mahon, was never in peacetime very large, while no men-of-war were regularly stationed at Gibraltar (where till 1766 dockyard facilities were poor and the roadstead exposed). Nevertheless the strategic value to Britain of these bases was enormous. From them the ports of southern France and eastern and southern Spain could be observed, and in time of war blockaded. From them Britain could in wartime influence events in Italy far more effectively than ever before. By her possession of them she was brought into closer contact than hitherto with the Barbary States of North Africa, from which they imported a large proportion of their food. Most important of all, while she held them in force she could sever the Mediterranean squadrons of France and Spain, based on Toulon and Cartagena, from their Atlantic counterparts based on Brest, Rochefort, Corunna and Cadiz.

Spain's loss of her European possessions and Britain's acquisition of bases in the Mediterranean were probably inevitable. An imminent disruption of the Spanish Empire had been taken for granted throughout the tortuous negotiations over the Succession question from 1668 onwards; and as early as the 1650s the Commonwealth government had established a navy agent at Leghorn and made the port a base for the squadrons it then maintained in the Mediterranean. The growth of Austrian power in Italy, which was in some ways the most important result of the treaties of 1713, was less easy to foresee. The partition treaties of 1698 and 1699 (agreed to by Louis XIV, the English and Dutch governments, and in the case of the first one the Emperor) would, if carried out, have given France a dominant position there on condition that a Bourbon ruler was not established in Spain. In the peace negotiations of 1712–13 the British government had proposed an arrangement by which Philip V, if he renounced the Spanish throne, would receive as compensation Sicily and all the possessions of the Duke of Savoy. Austrian dominance in Italy was thus the price Louis XIV had to pay for his success in main-taining his grandson as king of Spain. The fate of Austrian rule was, however, very different in the two regions of Italy which saw its establishment in 1713. In Naples it was never popular, achieved little, and lasted a bare two decades. In the Duchy of Milan it endured till the wars of the French Revolution, did much to increase the prosperity and improve the administration of the area, and eventually gained considerable popularity.

The gains made in 1713 by the ruler of Savoy, Victor Amadeus II, were not the result of victories he had won, or of the intrinsic strength of his dominions. They were rather the outcome of the strategic position near the meeting-point of French and Austrian influences in North Italy enjoyed by this minor State, and of the skill with which Victor Amadeus manœuvred between the competing great powers during the war (notably in his well-timed desertion of Louis XIV in 1703). Savoy continued throughout this period to be one of the most conservative and backward of the Italian States; until well into the century which followed very few people dreamt of her as the eventual leader of an Italian *risorgi-mento*. Nevertheless she was already showing both an appetite and a capacity for territorial expansion which no other State in the peninsula could equal.

Apart from Savoy those parts of Italy which remained inde-pendent were now of little account in international affairs. Venice was clearly a declining State living on her past. Her political struc-ture continued to enjoy, at least in the early decades of the century, a certain reputation for efficiency and stability; it was none the less increasingly weakened by factions within the Vene-tian nobility and by the growing discontent of the city's possessions on the Italian mainland and the Dalmatian coast.

Moreover the stability of her constitution had now become a rigidity hostile to innovation of any kind: no government in Europe showed less sympathy with the ideas of the Enlightenment than that of Venice. Her industries suffered from the extreme tenacity with which guild privileges were maintained, and her commerce from the competition of Ancona, Trieste and Ragusa. As a result she found herself increasingly reduced to living on the profits of her position as a great tourist centre. The last real achievement of her armed forces was a successful defence of Corfu against the Turks in 1716 and that, significantly enough, was led by a German general. By the second half of the century her fleet was so little able to protect her commerce against the attacks of the Barbary corsairs that the British consul in Venice reported in 1766 that for many years past she had been able to send few ships to any port west of Malta (though the two decades which followed saw a short-lived revival of the Venetian merchant marine). It is not surprising therefore that she attracted, in the later decades of this period, covetous glances from her powerful and aggressive neighbour, the Emperor Joseph II. A generation or more before her surrender to Napoleon Bonaparte in 1797 Venice was clearly marked as a victim-State. The peace with Turkey which she signed in 1718 was her last action of any importance on the stage of European affairs.

The other independent States of Italy were able to exert still less influence on the policies of the great European powers. Genoa, like Savoy but with much less success, attempted to safeguard and even improve her position by balancing between France and Austria. Her smallness, her vulnerability to attack, her failure to maintain control of her island possession of Corsica where serious rebellions broke out in 1729, 1734 and 1745, all weakened her. Though she retained more of her former economic importance than Venice (see p. 111) she slowly declined into little more than a French protectorate. The Grand Duchy of Tuscany under its last Medici ruler, Gian-Gastone (1692–1737), remained a largely medieval State. In spite of its considerable wealth it played little part in European affairs under his Habsburg successors. The Duchies of Parma and Piacenza, the tiny Republic of Lucca, could never hope to have an active role of any significance.

The Barbary States in North Africa were even more on the periphery of European politics. Algiers, which had enjoyed a golden age as a centre of piracy and privateering (and also of legitimate trade) in the first half of the seventeenth century, was now quite unable to resist the pressure of great naval powers such as Britain and France. She was thus increasingly compelled to confine the attacks of her cruisers to the ships of weaker maritime States such as Sweden, the Netherlands, the Hanse towns and the Italian principalities. The city itself remained one of the greatest fortresses in the Mediterranean. It repulsed attacks by Spain in 1775 and by a combination of Spain, Portugal and the Knights of St John in 1784: the British squadron under Lord Exmouth which bombarded it in 1816 lost more men than Nelson's fleet at Trafalgar. Nevertheless the Algerines were never, in the eighteenth century, more than a minor nuisance as far as the major States of Western Europe were concerned. Tunis, which had never been so great a centre of piracy as Algiers, concentrated increasingly during this period on legitimate trade, became richer and militarily weaker, and was captured by the Dey of Algiers in 1756 though she soon recovered her independence. Tripoli, small, poor, devastated by plague and possessing only a few insignificant cruisers, was little able to fire the ambitions or arouse the fears of any European power. Morocco, stronger and far less vulnerable to naval pressure than any other of the Barbary States, was in 1713 ruled by the Emperor Mulay Ismail, one of the strongest and most bloodthirsty characters in her bloodstained history. His death in 1727 unleashed a series of complicated civil wars which paralysed the country for a generation, while her weakness at sea meant that she could never play more than a minor role in the affairs of the western Mediterranean.

Far from the Barbary States being able to disrupt European trade or terrorize the coasts of Spain and Italy as they had done in the sixteenth and seventeenth centuries, the boot was now increasingly on the other foot. Christian privateers and pirates (the distinction between the two meant little in practice) based on Malta, Leghorn or the Balearics captured and plundered Turkish and Barbary ships and their crews on a large scale. They thus provided the basis for a considerable trade in Muslim slaves; and their activities may have been one reason (though certainly not the only or the most important one) for the economic stagnation and even decline which is visible in most of the Arab and Turkish world in the eighteenth century.

The western Mediterranean after the Utrecht settlement thus presents the picture of a number of strong and ambitious powers

– France, Spain, Great Britain, Austria, on a smaller scale Savoy
– side by side with the smaller and weaker victim-States of Italy
and North Africa.

The international relations of the area in the two decades which
followed the peace of 1713 were dominated by the efforts of the
newly established Bourbon dynasty in Spain to recover its lost
influence and possessions in Italy. Strengthened by the final
subjection of Catalonia and the French-inspired administrative
reforms of the early years of the century (see pp. 182–3) it was
now able to contemplate a war of revenge against the Habsburgs.
In spite of the many personal defects of Philip V a new spirit, a
refusal to accept the losses of the war as permanent, a will to
power unknown for decades, were all beginning to be felt in
Madrid. These feelings were focused on Italian affairs by Philip's
marriage at the end of the war to his second wife, Elizabeth
Farnese, niece of the Duke of Parma. She was a woman of strong
character and narrow outlook who very soon acquired great
influence over her husband and Spanish policy. Her arrival led
almost immediately to a reduction in the hitherto dominant
French influences at Madrid and their partial replacement by
Italian ones. Orry, the very able Frenchman who had done more
than anyone to overhaul Spain's inadequate fiscal system, left the
country. So did the very influential French *Camarera Mayor*,
Madame des Ursins. Italians such as Cardinal del Guidice and
above all the Abbé Giulio Alberoni began to play a great part in
Spain's political life, notably in her foreign policy. Alberoni had
originally come to Spain as the agent of a French commander, the
Duc de Vendôme, during the Succession struggle. He remained
there after his patron's death, as diplomatic agent of the Duke of
Parma, and helped to arrange Philip's second marriage – his first
great success in international affairs. Though he was never to hold
any recognized Spanish administrative post or title his influence
over the queen made him for several years the leading personality
in the government of the country and a figure of European
importance.

Alberoni undoubtedly felt a personal hostility to the Habsburg
family and Germans in general, and may have dreamed of some
form of political unity in Italy after their influence had been
expelled from the peninsula. Moreover the Emperor Charles VI
had stubbornly refused, in the settlement of 1713–14, to abandon

his claim to be rightful King of Spain. This meant that relations between Madrid and Vienna were still those of an armed truce rather than of genuine peace. These factors, coupled with the imminent extinction of the Medici dynasty in Tuscany and the desire of Charles VI to acquire Sicily from the Duke of Savoy, to whom it had been given in 1713, made the position in Italy extremely unstable. The neutrality of the peninsula in the future struggles of the major European States which had been declared in vague terms by the Treaty of Utrecht was clearly unlikely to last very long. Overshadowing all these questions was the possibility that if the sickly Louis XV should die Philip V might assert, as grandson of Louis XIV, his claim to the throne of France, in spite of the renunciation of it he had been forced to make as part of the settlement of 1713. The effort of George I and the Regent d'Orléans to consolidate in the Anglo-French alliance of 1716 (see p. 328) the *status quo* from which both of them benefited was a failure as far as the Mediterranean was concerned.

The spark which ignited this combustible situation was struck at the end of May 1717. The Grand Inquisitor of Spain, a man of over eighty, was arrested by the Austrian governor of Milan while returning from a visit to Rome and died soon afterwards in prison. In spite of the doubts of Alberoni, who realized only too well the real limits of Spanish resources, Philip V declared war on the Emperor in July. The struggle which followed was short and dramatic. Sardinia, whose Austrian garrison was extremely weak, was quickly overrun by a Spanish expeditionary force. The efforts of Britain and France to appease Spain by promising that Don Carlos, the elder son of Philip V by Elizabeth Farnese, should inherit the Italian States of Tuscany, Parma and Piacenza, were a failure. Alberoni demanded some more tangible satisfaction than a promise; while even a suggestion that Gibraltar might be restored failed to appease the queen. The summer of 1718 saw a rapid conquest of Sicily which, though a possession of the ruler of Savoy and thus neutral territory, the Spanish government hoped to use as a base for the invasion of southern Italy. An imposing edifice of Spanish power in the Mediterranean had thus been erected in less than a year. But it was fundamentally unstable. It depended on seapower, and Spanish seapower was still much inferior to that of Great Britain. When, on 11 August, a British squadron under Admiral Byng destroyed off Cape Passaro near

Messina the fleet so painfully built up in the last four years, the whole structure collapsed.

Nevertheless Alberoni, who now hoped that Britain's difficulties in the Baltic (see p. 261) might weaken her position in the Mediterranean, at once declared war on her. The Jacobite Duke of Ormonde was provided with a Spanish squadron and some troops with which to attempt an invasion of England; and it became clear that only a direct attack on Spain herself would force the government in Madrid to submit. As a result in January 1719, after considerable hesitation on the part of the Regent, France declared war and invaded the Basque provinces and Catalonia. From this hopeless position Philip V had no escape but by surrender. In December he dismissed Alberoni. A month later he announced his adhesion to the Quadruple Alliance of Britain, France, Austria and the United Provinces which had been signed at the beginning of August 1718. The evacuation of Sicily and Sardinia and a new renunciation by him of his claims to the French throne followed in due course. In return it was promised that Don Carlos should inherit Tuscany, Parma and Piacenza, though he was to hold these territories as imperial fiefs. Thus the only immediate territorial result of the crisis of 1717–19 was the transfer of Sicily from Savoy to the Emperor in exchange for the far less valuable Sardinia. The events of these years had shown that the provisions of the Utrecht settlement, backed by the great conservative powers of Britain and France, could easily withstand the pressure of discontented and ambitious Spain.

The defeats of 1718–19 did not, however, force Philip V to abandon hope of improving his country's strategic and diplomatic position. He claimed, somewhat unrealistically, the fulfilment of the offer to return Gibraltar which had been made in 1718 before the outbreak of war with Britain. But for violent opposition in Parliament he might well have recovered the fortress, to which neither George I nor his ministers attached much importance. As it was, Philip had to content himself with a letter of June 1721 in which the king of England promised to consider the surrender of Gibraltar 'with consent of my Parliament . . . at the first favourable opportunity' – which in fact meant never. But in spite of this renewed check to her ambitions events were moving in Spain's favour in many ways in the early 1720s. Good relations with France had been restored by a convention of March 1721 which provided for the betrothal of Louis XV and the Infanta

Maria-Anna-Vittoria, the daughter of Philip V by his first wife. Simultaneously the efforts from 1722 onwards of Charles VI to establish a trade between his Netherlands dominions and the East Indies by the creation of a privileged Ostend Company caused acute friction with his British and Dutch allies. Nevertheless when in January 1724, after long delays, an international congress of diplomats met at Cambrai to work out in detail the settlement of Italian affairs reached four years earlier, France and Britain gave only half-hearted support to the demands of Spain. In particular she failed to secure her main objective, the occupation of the chief fortresses of Tuscany and Parma by Spanish troops, which she had demanded as a tangible guarantee of the eventual succession to these duchies of Don Carlos.

The result of this failure was perhaps the most remarkable diplomatic revolution of the century. Elizabeth Farnese, infuriated by the setback, resolved to attempt an alliance with the Habsburgs which would blot out the antagonisms of the past decade. Through a Dutch adventurer and Catholic convert, Ripperdà, she proposed in Vienna a marriage between her sons Don Carlos and Don Philip and two Austrian archduchesses, daughters of Charles VI. The marriage negotiations, which dragged on till 1729, came to nothing. However in February 1725 the Duc de Bourbon, who had been chief minister in Paris since the death of the Regent in August 1723, broke off without warning the betrothal of Louis XV to the Infanta Maria and sent the unfortunate princess back to Madrid. He did this because she was still so young that there was no hope of her producing a son for many years, and because if Louis died without a male heir the Crown would pass, by the terms of the Utrecht settlement, to the Orleans branch of the royal family who were Bourbon's personal enemies. His selfish and short-sighted action produced a natural outburst of resentment in Madrid. It threw Spain completely into the arms of the Habsburgs and led to the signature, on 30 April 1725, of an Austro-Spanish treaty of alliance. This was followed in November by a very secret offensive agreement which envisaged not merely the recovery of Gibraltar by Spain but even a dismemberment of France.

This new and unexpected combination of States proved less fragile than might have been expected. But it found itself faced almost immediately by the opposition of Britain, France and Prussia united in the so-called Alliance of Hanover, and collapsed after the outbreak of another Anglo-Spanish struggle early in 1727. This war, provoked partly by the Spanish desire to retake Gibraltar and partly by British resentment of commercial concessions which Philip V had granted to Austrian merchants, lasted only a few months. By June the pressure of France and Austria had forced the Spanish government to suspend the siege of Gibraltar which it had begun in February. Finally in November 1729, after another protracted and futile congress at Soissons, Britain and France agreed by the Treaty of Seville to the introduction of Spanish troops into the fortresses of Tuscany and Parma as a guarantee of the succession of Don Carlos; and in the following year they extorted the Emperor's consent to this. When at the end of 1731 an Anglo-French fleet disembarked 6,000 Spanish soldiers at Leghorn Elizabeth Farnese appeared to have triumphed.

However Italian politics had still problems in store for the statesmen of Europe. The confused struggle known as the War of the Polish Succession (1733–35) had, in its origins, nothing to do with the problems of the peninsula. The defeat of the French candidate for the Polish throne, Stanislas Leszczynski, by the nominee of Austria and Russia, the Elector Augustus of Saxony, nevertheless drove the French government to look for compensation in Italy at the expense of the Habsburgs. In this search it had the support of Spain and Savoy. In 1734 the Austrian army suffered a series of defeats at the hands of the French and Spaniards, at Parma, Guastalla and Bitonto, and when peace terms were agreed in October 1735 (the definitive treaty was signed at Vienna only in 1738) the Habsburgs surrendered Naples and Sicily to Don Carlos. They received in exchange, however, Parma and Piacenza. Tuscany (whose last Medici ruler died in 1737) was handed over to Francis, Duke of Lorraine, the husband-to-be of the Archduchess Maria Theresa. The Duchy of Lorraine was given as compensation for his lost Polish throne to Stanislas Leszczynski and was to revert to France on his death, a provision which promised her a very important acquisition. This complicated series of territorial exchanges, so typical in many ways of the diplomacy of the period, had a certain logic. It therefore proved more durable than most of the treaties of the first half of the eighteenth century. It established in the southern half of Italy the Bourbon dynasty which was to rule there for the next century and a quarter. It consolidated in Milan and set up in Tuscany that

Habsburg domination which was to last almost as long. It paved the way for the formal incorporation in 1766 of Lorraine in France, the last important success of that forward movement of the country's eastern frontier which had been in progress for centuries. Moreover it showed that the French and Spanish Bourbons were at last, after many vicissitudes, working in concert for their mutual advantage. The alliance between them which developed in the 1730s was to be a permanent factor in the politics of Europe for more than half a century.

After 1735 Italian questions, and particularly Spanish ambitions in Italy, no longer played the role in international relations of the previous two decades. The War of the Austrian Succession which was opened by Frederick II's attack on Silesia in December 1740 had indeed, more than that of the Polish Succession, a Mediterranean aspect. All the major belligerents except Prussia devoted a good deal of their energies to a struggle for territory and influence in Italy. Though Cardinal Fleury was strongly against another conflict with Austria he was, as has been seen (p. 291), overruled by the more bellicose elements in Paris and Versailles. Spain, still dreaming of a further extension of her influence in Italy, was anxious to take advantage of the apparent weakness of the Habsburgs and allied herself with the opponents of Maria Theresa in the spring of 1741. The King of Sardinia, who hoped to obtain the Duchy of Milan and an outlet to the sea by the seizure of Genoese territory, was willing to side with anyone who would promise him these acquisitions. Finally the 1740s saw the entry of Great Britain into the complexities of Italian politics on a scale hitherto unknown.

The danger of Spanish control of the peninsula seemed for a time very real. In 1742 only a British threat to bombard Naples forced Charles IV of the Two Sicilies (the former Don Carlos) to abandon his plans to attack the Austrians in north Italy in conjunction with the Spaniards. In January 1743 a Spanish army based in southern France occupied Chambéry, the capital of Savoy proper, which it held until the end of the war. In September of that year, however, Maria Theresa was at last prevailed on to purchase, with the promise of part of the Milanese, the help of Charles-Emmanuel III of Sardinia. Though he was never a reliable ally, even the lukewarm assistance he gave her was of vital importance at that moment. With the conclusion in the following month of an alliance of France and Spain directed against Austria and Great Britain the stage was set for a new outbreak of large-scale warfare in Italy.

The details of this struggle are unimportant. The British Mediterranean squadron maintained command of the sea, in spite of its failure to win any decisive victory and the continual shortage of small craft for scouting and blockade work from which it suffered. As a result Spain was unable, after 1741, to ship troops to Italy, and found it difficult to use effectively those she already had there. Moreover the Marquis d'Argenson, who became French Foreign Minister in November 1744, was no friend to the Spanish alliance. One of the most remarkable statesmen of the century, a visionary and an idealist, he dreamed of reorganizing Italy as a federation of independent States freed from both Austrian and Spanish influence. (The idea was not new: something similar had been proposed by Louis XIV's minister Pomponne in the 1690s, and schemes of this kind go back to the sixteenth century.) In spite of these difficulties the 'Gallispan' armies won considerable successes in 1745, though these were largely offset by defeats in the following year. Philip V, however, died in July 1746; and with his death the influence of Elizabeth Farnese on Spanish policy came to an end. His successor, Ferdinand VI, was almost as dominated by his wife as his father had been; but the wife in question was now Portuguese, favourable to Britain and little interested in Italy. The war there thus petered out in stalemate. The Treaty of Aix-la-Chapelle, which ended it in November 1748, made only minor changes in the political geography of the peninsula. Don Philip, the younger son of Philip V and Elizabeth Farnese, received the Duchies of Parma and Piacenza (mainly through the support of his father-in-law Louis XV) while Charles-Emmanuel of Sardinia was given the slice of the Milanese promised him in 1743.

The balance of forces established in Italy by 1748 was to endure almost unchanged until Bonaparte's campaigns of 1796–97. In 1752 Ferdinand VI, Charles-Emmanuel and Maria Theresa jointly guaranteed each other's possessions there; and the conflicts of the second half of the century left the peninsula untouched. After 1748 indeed the whole character of international relations in the western Mediterranean changed radically. Hitherto they had been dominated by a series of military struggles in Italy between France, Spain and Austria. Henceforth, with France and Austria at least formally allies after 1756 and the rulers of Spain little interested in Italian affairs, they were to centre on a series of naval conflicts between France, Spain and Great Britain.

These struggles had considerable repercussions on the balance of forces in the area. The Seven Years War saw British naval power in the Mediterranean carried to unprecedented heights, in spite of the capture of Minorca by a French expedition in 1756. The years which followed the Peace of Paris saw as a result a sustained effort by France to challenge that power. This can be seen in the reconstruction and strengthening of the French navy, in the consolidation of the alliance of 1761 with Spain (see p. 339), and, most notable in this context, in the purchase and annexation in 1768–69 of Corsica, hitherto an ungovernable and almost valueless dependency of Genoa. The island failed to provide the naval bases and easily accessible timber for shipbuilding which had been hoped for in Paris. Nevertheless its acquisition, the last significant territorial gain made in Europe by the France of the *ancien régime*, was accomplished without war in spite of the open hostility of the British government. It was thus widely and correctly interpreted as showing that domestic troubles and poor leadership were now making it difficult for Britain to maintain the international position which she had achieved during the Seven Years War. Moreover Spain, ruled from 1759 onwards by Charles III, a king of some ability and considerable energy, was now becoming a more serious threat than ever before to Britain in the Mediterranean. The war between them in 1761–63 had proved disastrous for Spain, but the losses she suffered by the Peace of Paris were relatively slight (see p. 338). After 1763 the improvement of her armed forces proceeded fairly rapidly, while in 1767 she helped to free her hands for action against Britain by a peace treaty with Morocco, with whom she had been intermittently at war throughout the century. An ambitious expedition against Algiers in 1775 was a humiliating failure, but none the less an index of the self-confident and even aggressive spirit which was once more, as in the days of Alberoni, gaining ground in Madrid.

The growing weakness of Britain's hold on the western Mediterranean was dramatically illustrated after 1778 during the War of the American Revolution. Faced by the most powerful hostile coalition she had yet had to meet, hampered by the Armed Neutrality of 1780 (see p. 277), suffering heavy losses at the hands of enemy privateers, her position contrasted strikingly with that she had enjoyed two decades earlier. On this occasion Minorca did not fall until the last stages of the struggle, in 1782. But long before then Britain's naval power in the Mediterranean had been destroyed, and her trade there had for the time being almost ceased to exist. Nevertheless she was able to maintain her most important foothold in the area. Gibraltar withstood the 'great siege' of 1779–82 by a powerful Franco-Spanish army; while feeling in Parliament and the country at large made it impossible for George III and his ministers to accept, as they otherwise would have done, Spanish proposals to exchange it for Puerto Rico. The end of the war meant, though this was not fully grasped at the time, the end of any hope of a Spanish recovery of the fortress. Britain while she retained it was always, even in defeat, potentially a Mediterranean power of the first rank.

The part played by the eastern Mediterranean in the politics of eighteenth-century Europe was as a rule little affected by what happened further west. In the Aegean and the Levant the course of events was underlain by the decline, at first slow and inter-mittent, eventually catastrophic, of the Ottoman Empire. This decline had become unmistakable in the struggles of the Turks with Austria, Poland and Venice which were ended by the Treaty of Carlowitz in 1699. It was already giving rise, at the beginning of the eighteenth century, to projects for a partition of the decaying bulk of the empire. The belief that Turkey was on the verge of collapse seemed justified by the clear and fundamental defects from which her government and society suffered.

In the first place the composition and policies of the Turkish government were extremely unstable, particularly in the early decades of the century. The Grand Vizier (the chief minister of State) was liable at any moment to lose his position and even his life as the result of some setback in war or diplomacy or some whim of the Sultan (there were thirteen occupants of the position in the years 1703–18 when instability of this kind was at its worst). Even the Sultan himself was not safe from deposition: Mustapha II was removed in this way in 1703 and Ahmad III in 1730. Moreover the empire lacked any real administrative unity or military efficiency. The emergence of powerful and virtually independent local warlords who were sometimes able to make their power hereditary (the most important example during this period was the rise of the Karaosmanoglu family in western

Anatolia from the end of the seventeenth century onwards) seemed both to illustrate and to intensify the incompetence of its rulers. The development of its economic life was impeded by a number of factors: misgovernment; religious conservatism; and not least the devastating epidemics from which the area continued to suffer as in the past (two-thirds of the population of Cyprus are said, probably with some exaggeration, to have died of plague in 1692, and a third or a half in 1759–60). Intellectual life was backward in the extreme. Constantinople had no printing press until 1726; and the activities of the one set up in that year (significantly by a Hungarian renegade, not a Turk) were short-lived. Above all the sharpness of the distinction between Muslim rulers and Christian ruled, a distinction which was often strengthened by differences of language, increasingly undermined the foundations of the European parts of the empire as time went on. 'Other nations,' wrote a British ambassador in Constantinople in 1736, 'may suit and adapt their maxims to their circumstances, but the Turkish Policy and Government is so interwoven with their religion that they cannot make any alterations, and without them they can neither annoy their neighbours nor defend themselves.'

The fate of the Balkan peoples under Ottoman rule varied very considerably. In a few areas, notably in Bosnia and much of Albania, the population had been converted *en masse* to Islam. In others, notably Bulgaria, almost all consciousness of belonging to a distinct national group had been lost. The Rumanian principalities of Moldavia and Wallachia remained Christian and retained a high degree of autonomy. They paid tribute to the Sultan and were ruled, or more usually misruled, by their hospodars (who from the early eighteenth century onwards were always Greeks appointed from Constantinople).

The relationship of the Greeks to their Turkish master was more complex and more important. The islands of the Aegean were perhaps less oppressively ruled than any other part of the Ottoman Empire; and in the barren and rocky Morea many Greek villages existed as virtually independent communities and had little contact with the Turkish administration. On the other hand the wealthy and educated 'Phanariot' Greeks of Constantinople (so called from the fact that they inhabited the Phanar or 'lighthouse' quarter of the city) played a leading role in that administration. In particular their knowledge of languages and their contacts with foreign countries made them valuable in the conduct of Turkish diplomacy; from 1661 onwards the position of Dragoman (i.e. chief interpreter) of the Porte, sometimes an office of real influence, was monopolized by them. From the ranks of the great Phanariot families, moreover – the Cantacuzènes, the Mavrocordatos, the Callimachis – were drawn the large majority of the hospodars of Moldavia and Wallachia during this period.

In general the Balkan peoples were becoming steadily more hostile to their Ottoman rulers during the eighteenth century. This was partly because the position of the peasantry was becoming worse in many areas as the *timar* system of land tenure (under which the peasant had enjoyed some security and fiefs had not been hereditary) gave way to the *chiflik* system (under which fiefs were hereditary and the peasants virtually serfs). At the same time the slow growth of trade tended to produce, especially in some seaports such as Salonika, a commercial middle class which was anti-Turkish in outlook; while by the end of this period contacts with Central and even Western Europe were beginning to stimulate national feeling in some parts of the peninsula. The first Greek and Serbian newspapers were published at Vienna in 1790 and 1791 respectively.

In spite of its internal difficulties the military weaknesses of the Ottoman Empire developed only slowly to their full extent. In 1711 the Turks were able to inflict a spectacular defeat on Peter I of Russia (see pp. 271–2) though it was the result of the Tsar's rashness as much as of their own military virtues. In a renewed struggle with the Habsburgs in 1716–18 they were heavily defeated by the great Austrian commander Prince Eugène, saw Wallachia invaded by an Austrian army and lost Belgrade, a Turkish fortress for over two centuries. These losses, though substantial, were not crippling. They were partly offset, moreover, by the fact that a simultaneous war with the Venetians, begun in 1714, resulted in the recovery of the Morea (which had been ceded to Venice by the Treaty of Carlowitz). Here, as to a lesser extent in Serbia, the dislike felt by an Orthodox population for rule by often intolerant Catholic masters was a source of strength to the Turks.

The war which Turkey waged with Russia and Austria in 1736–39 was by no means unsuccessful. The Habsburg armies showed themselves little more competent than the Ottoman ones; and the final loss of Azov to Russia, when peace was made at

Belgrade, was more than compensated for by the recovery from Austria of much of the territory ceded to her in 1718. The Austrian frontier, after a temporary advance to the south, had thus been pushed back once more to the line of the Danube and the Save, along which it still ran in 1914. Not until the disastrous struggle with Russia which began in 1768 did the extent to which Ottoman power had declined become fully visible to most observers.

Of the States of Western Europe, France was the only one with important political interests in the Levant during the first half of the eighteenth century. Britain's trade with the area continued to flourish until about 1730, after which it rapidly declined; but from the political point of view she was interested only indirectly in the eastern Mediterranean. The British Ambassador at Constantinople continued to be the representative of the Levant Company almost as much as of the government. Spain for her part regarded herself, in the tradition of the Counter-Reformation, as the natural enemy of Turkish and Muslim power in the Mediterranean. She had no diplomatic relations with Turkey during this period; the first treaty between the two States was signed only in 1783. Eighteenth-century France inherited, by contrast, a well-established tradition tracing from Francis I (1515–47) of political interest and activity in the Near East. This was inspired, now as in the past, mainly by her desire to use the Turks as a weapon against Austria and thus divert the attention and resources of the Habsburgs away from Western Europe to a struggle against the Ottomans in the Balkans. In Constantinople alone of the capitals of Europe, significantly enough, the representative of France took precedence over his Austrian colleague.

The memory of the defeats she had suffered on the Danube in the 1680s and 1690s prevented Turkey from playing any part in the War of the Spanish Succession. She did nothing to support the Hungarian nationalists who, under Francis Rákóczi, fought against the Emperors Leopold I and Joseph I in 1704–11. She gave little effective help to Charles XII against the Russians after the battle of Poltava and his flight to Turkey. Nor did she play any active part, as the French government had hoped, in opposing Austria and Russia in the War of the Polish Succession. Nevertheless her friendship with France was maintained, as can be seen in the sending to Paris in 1720 of a Turkish embassy, a mark of honour very rarely accorded any Christian State. Moreover a rapid expansion of France's commerce with the Levant from the 1720s onwards, which soon made her the dominant influence in the foreign trade of the area, bound the two States still more closely together. In the 1730s efforts to improve the Turkish army were made, with limited success, by one of the most remarkable figures of the century, the French renegade Comte de Bonneval (Bonneval Pasha) who also had considerable influence on the foreign policy of his adopted country. The peace of 1739, much more advantageous to Turkey than her achievements on the battlefield justified, was largely the work of the French Ambassador at Constantinople, the Marquis de Villeneuve, who was thus able to raise his country's influence at the Turkish capital to perhaps the highest pitch it ever attained. In the following year he succeeded in obtaining from the Porte a renewal of the Capitulations, the series of commercial and other concessions first granted to France by Suleiman the Magnificent in the sixteenth century and confirmed at intervals ever since.

The 'Diplomatic Revolution' of 1756, however, dealt Franco-Turkish relations the most severe blow they had suffered for generations. The Treaty of Versailles of May 1756 obliged each of the contracting powers to support the other in case of attack. It was from the French point of view essentially a weapon against Britain; but it meant nevertheless that if the Turks attacked the Habsburgs in the Balkans France would find herself, in spite of her traditional friendship with them, compelled to support Austria. The Porte could not fail to see this, and protested strongly to the Comte de Vergennes, the newly appointed French Ambassador at Constantinople, against his government's failure to exclude the Ottoman Empire from the scope of the treaty. The Franco-Russian *rapprochement* which followed the events of 1756, though it was very fragile, did even more to weaken Turkish faith in French goodwill and led some Turkish ministers to consider seeking safety in an approach to Prussia. A Prusso-Turkish treaty of friendship and commerce was indeed signed after long negotiations in 1761, but the hopes of Frederick II that the Porte might intervene actively in the war against Russia or Austria were never realized. In the following year the death of the Empress Elizabeth and the coldness which came over Russo-French relations with the accession of Catherine II paved the way for a resumption of the friendship with France which had been so marked at Constantinople before 1756. From 1762 onwards France and Turkey were bound together by their mutual fear of Russia, as they had been in the past by their mutual hostility to the Habsburgs.

The role of France in bringing about the Russo-Turkish war of 1768 and its disastrous results for the Ottoman Empire have already been mentioned (see p. 273). During the struggle France attempted more systematically than ever before to strengthen the Turkish army by supplying it with instructors and technicians; and this policy was continued, though never on a really large scale, down to the 1790s. In spite of this, her inability to give the Porte substantial aid against Russia or to help it avoid the humiliating peace of 1774 inevitably reduced her influence at Constantinople. In particular her powerlessness, in face of British hostility, to exclude the Russian fleet from the Mediterranean in 1770 did a good deal to shake Turkish faith in her value as an ally. Moreover in the decade which followed the Treaty of Kutchuk-Kainardji fear of Russia far more than friendship with France was the driving force behind the development of Turkish policy. As a result France, though represented at Constantinople by the very able Comte de Saint-Priest and still regarded by the Porte as its most reliable supporter, lost a good deal of the influence she had enjoyed in the 1760s. Vergennes, now Foreign Minister, had his attention fully occupied by events in America, by the war with Britain which broke out in 1778 and by the problem of the Bavarian Succession. He was thus neither willing nor able to involve his country in heavy Near Eastern commitments. He realized that the *entente* of 1781 between Austria and Russia exposed European Turkey to the risk of dismemberment by these rapacious neighbours, but could give the Porte little help except good advice. Even after France had made peace with Britain in 1783 his efforts to prevent the annexation of the Crimea by Russia, though they very nearly destroyed the thread-bare Austro-French alliance of 1756, did little to restrain Catherine II; while his insistence at Constantinople on the need to make further concessions to the Russians discouraged and antagonized the Turks.

The end of this period thus saw Russian influence in the Levant at the highest pitch it had hitherto reached. Intriguing in European Turkey through the consuls she had secured the right to maintain there in 1774 and through the contacts she kept up with local chieftains and religious dignitaries, expanding into the Crimea, laying the foundations of a powerful Black Sea fleet, exerting

increasing pressure on the Caucasian as well as the European frontiers of the Ottoman Empire, Catherine II seemed about to
dominate the whole area. Joseph II, though jealous of his new
ally's power and success, had no intention of breaking with her
and hoped increasingly to achieve in the Balkans the territorial
gains which had so far eluded him in Germany. France, still much
the greatest commercial power in the eastern Mediterranean,
nevertheless now saw her political influence there threatened as
never before during the century. Britain remained, as always,
uninterested in the Near East for its own sake and willing to
intervene actively in its affairs only when they seemed to affect
her position in Western Europe. Most significant of all the decline
of the Ottoman Empire, the source of most of the complexities
and peculiarities of Near Eastern politics, continued. By the end
of the eighteenth century some at least of the essentials of the
'Eastern Question' in the form in which Palmerston, Disraeli and
Bismarck knew it were already in existence.

12

THE ANGLO-FRENCH STRUGGLE FOR EMPIRE

The prolonged colonial struggle between Britain and France which began in 1689 and ended in 1815 was one of the greatest themes of eighteenth-century history. It was not, from a strictly European point of view, of greater importance than the rise of Russian and Prussian power which has already been described. In some respects indeed it was less significant. It involved no changes of European political boundaries or of the political allegiance of European populations comparable to those brought about by Peter I, Catherine II and Frederick II. None the less it deeply influenced the history of the continent. It had important repercussions, which were clearly visible to contemporaries (see pp. 248–9), on the balance of power. It allowed Great Britain, now becoming much more than a merely European State, to play in the politics of the continent a part far greater than her purely domestic resources justified. It was the most important political link between Europe and the non-European world.

The colonies of the European States were now becoming to some extent parts of the European political system and were influencing more and more the policies of some of its greatest members. The idea, so widespread in the previous century, that States might be in conflict in America or the East and still remain at peace in Europe was now clearly becoming outdated. Colonial events, at least transatlantic ones, now no longer took place in a different political world as well as a different continent. The Anglo-Spanish war of 1739 and the undeclared Anglo-French war of 1755, the first great struggles between European States to be provoked solely by commercial and colonial rivalries, showed unmistakably how things had changed in this respect.

In Europe the death of Louis XIV was followed by an unexpected and anomalous Anglo-French *rapprochement*. This was based, in both countries, on dynastic rather than national interests. In particular it was inspired by the wish of the Duc d'Orléans, Regent during the minority of Louis XV, to safeguard his position as heir to the French throne should the young king die and to exclude from the succession the rival claimant, Philip V of Spain, as had been agreed in the peace settlement of 1713. In other words, the government of France, for which the Treaty of Utrecht had been in many ways a defeat, as well as that of Britain for which it represented on the whole a victory, now desired to uphold the status quo. The result was an Anglo-French agreement in November 1716 which paved the way for the Triple Alliance of January 1717. By the latter Britain, France and the United Provinces combined to maintain the Utrecht settlement, the rule of the Hanoverian dynasty in Britain and the garrisoning by the Dutch of a number of 'barrier fortresses' in the Austrian Netherlands. The good, or at least officially good, Anglo-French relations thus created lasted, with some fluctuations, for well over a decade. In 1719–20 the two powers combined to oppose Spanish ambitions in Italy, and in 1725–27 to counterbalance the newly-formed Austro-Spanish alliance (see p. 315). Their co-operation, however, was always fragile and appeared to many contemporaries unnatural. With the death of Orléans in 1723 and the growth to manhood of Louis XV much of its original basis disappeared. By the 1730s, under Cardinal Fleury, French policy was once more acquiring much of its traditional anti-British colouring.

Nor could the tendency of the two States to combine in Europe during the years after 1716 conceal the fact that their interests and ambitions overseas now conflicted more violently than ever before. In 1713 the Treaty of Utrecht gave Britain a stronger position in America than she had hitherto possessed. Her acquisition of Acadia (Nova Scotia) did a good deal to protect New England against attack by the French in Canada. That of Newfoundland consolidated her position in the valuable cod fisheries of the Gulf of St Lawrence. That of Hudson's Bay, though less important, guaranteed her a share in the fur trade of Canada. Nevertheless Britain was still far from complete domination in North America and even farther in the Caribbean. Her mainland colonies, though their population and wealth were rapidly growing, were still widely separated; not merely by geography but by their differing histories and outlooks. The majority of them were ruled in a roughly similar way, through a governor appointed by the Crown and an elected assembly whose relations with him were often far from amicable. But in few other respects had they much in common. The New England colonies had for long periods of the seventeenth century been virtually independent republics. In some of them, notably Massachusetts, the assemblies even before the American Revolution were elected by something approaching manhood suffrage. They differed widely from the Carolinas, which had been founded under Charles II by a royal grant of lands and jurisdiction to a syndicate of noblemen and capitalists, and from Virginia. There, at least in the areas near the coast, aristocratic social traditions remained strong. Pennsylvania, still dominated by the Quaker tradition of its founders, differed almost as much from New York, the most cosmopolitan of the colonies and one which included, in families such as the Livingstons and the Van Rensselaers, many of the greatest landowners in British America. Geographical dispersal, social and economic differences, and the parochialism which still marked the outlook of many of the colonists, meant that the British settlements never combined effectively against the French or Spaniards. Their contribution to the struggles of this period against the French in Canada was provided mainly by one or two of them, above all by Massachusetts and Connecticut.

Politically and socially French Canada was far better adapted to a military struggle for survival. Her society, dominated by *seigneurs* and priests, and her administrative system, controlled by the military governor and the intendant, had been modelled on those of France herself. Her outlook was far more authoritarian than that of any important British colony. Her population, though small (about 19,000 in 1713, rising to about 56,000 in 1740) was incomparably better organized for military purposes than the far larger one of the British mainland colonies. France's position moreover was strengthened by her alliances with the Indian tribes on the frontiers of her territories, and by her possession in Louisbourg on Cape Breton Island (built from 1720 onwards) of the most powerful of all North American fortresses. Her struggling colony of Louisiana, which became administratively separate from Canada in 1717, had less military signifiance. Already, however, her exploration of the Mississippi basin was beginning to threaten an eventual junction of her possessions on the St Lawrence with those on the Gulf of Mexico, the hemming-in of the British colonies by a gigantic arc of French-held territory which would include the Great Lakes and the Ohio valley.

In the Caribbean also Anglo-French antagonism was constant and sometimes acute in the early decades of the century, notably over the possession of the four 'neutral islands' of St Vincent, St Lucia, Dominica and Tobago, which had been left in 1713 as a kind of no-man's-land. In this area, however, the position was complicated by the presence of other powers; the Dutch in Curaçao and St Eustatius, the Danes in St Croix (bought from France in 1733) and far more important the Spaniards in Cuba, San Domingo and their vast Central and South American Empire. It was with Spain, not with the more powerful and aggressive France, that Britain first came into serious conflict in the western hemisphere after the peace of 1713.

The *Asiento* agreement which she had extorted from an unwilling Spanish government in March 1714 provided for the sale each year by the English South Sea Company to Spanish America of a specified number of Negro slaves at a fixed price. It also permitted the company to send each year to trade in the Indies one ship, the *navio permiso*. It is now clear that this ship was not used as a cover for illegitimate trade on the scale which some historians used to believe; but the breach which it represented in Spain's traditional policy of confining trade with her American possessions strictly to the mother-country made it deeply suspect to the Spanish officials on whom the success of its voyages depended. Only eight such voyages were in fact made in the period 1717–33. By the 1730s persistent illicit trading with Spanish America by British ships and the often brutal efforts to prevent it of Spanish *guardacostas* were straining Anglo-Spanish relations very severely. A series of efforts to smooth over the situation had no success, largely because of the increasingly aggressive and anti-Spanish attitude of British public opinion. Attracted by dreams of the conquest of wealthy Spanish colonies, the opening-up of new opportunities for British trade and the capture of Spanish treasure-ships, an attitude summed up in the slogan 'Take and Hold', many Englishmen were not only ready but anxious for a war with Spain. This attitude was strengthened by disputes over the boundaries between the new British colony of Georgia and the Spanish possession of Florida, and over the right of British subjects to cut logwood (an important source of dyes for the textile industries) on the coast of Honduras. Its influence was increased by the growing weakness and division of the Walpole Cabinet. By October 1739 it had led to the outbreak of an Anglo-Spanish war.

But for Frederick II's attack on Silesia, which revolutionized the position in Europe, Britain would have found herself by 1741 engaged single-handed in a great naval and colonial struggle against France as well as Spain. Only the outbreak of the War of the Austrian Succession and the resulting French preoccupations in Germany postponed an open breach between Britain and France till 1744. With the formal outbreak of war between the two States in that year and the resulting involvement of the Netherlands, the Anglo-Spanish conflict which had been going on somewhat languidly since 1739 was transformed into the greatest colonial struggle hitherto known in European history. Its results in America were none the less indecisive. The capture of Porto-bello on the isthmus of Panama by Admiral Vernon in the first weeks of the war stimulated great hopes in Britain; but disease, rum and constant friction between military and naval commanders combined to stultify all other attempts to seize Spanish territory in the Caribbean. Two thousand miles to the north Louisbourg fell in June 1745 to a force consisting largely of New England militia. This was a striking reminder that the British colonies, in spite of their rivalries and the intractability of their assemblies, possessed material resources which French Canada, once cut off from the mother-country, could not hope to equal. Nevertheless their achievement had no permanent result. When peace was made Louisbourg was returned to France.

This was done, much to the annoyance of the New Englanders, partly because France found herself in a strong position in Europe when the war ended. In 1745–48 her armies, under the Maréchal de Saxe, had overrun the Austrian Netherlands and defeated a combined British, Austrian and Dutch force in a series of battles at Fontenoy (1745), Raucoux (1746) and Lawfeldt (1747). By the spring of 1748, with the great fortresses of Bergen-op-Zoom and Maastricht in his hands, Saxe was threatening a conquest of the United Provinces. Such gains were sufficient to offset much heavier losses overseas than France had suffered, and more than compensated her for two considerable naval defeats at the hands of Britain in 1747.

Britain was also compelled to return Louisbourg by her failures on the other side of the world, in India. Here the British and French East India Companies, the former established in the subcontinent for over a century, the latter since the time of Colbert, had shown until the 1740s few signs of increasing their military or territorial power. In spite of the breakdown of the Mughal Empire, which had begun to be visible even before the death of the Emperor Aurangzeb in 1707 and was greatly accelerated after that date, they remained for long mere trading companies. Their possessions in India were confined to a few forts and trading-stations – Bombay, Madras and Fort St George (Calcutta) in the case of the British Company; Pondicherry, Chandernagore and Mahé in that of the French one. Already Dumas, the French Company's *Commandant-Général*, had been forced in the later 1730s, in order to maintain France's position, to conclude political alliances with some of the independent rulers who were now emerging in South India. Mahé de la Bourdonnais, governor of the French islands in the Indian Ocean in 1735–40 and one of the greatest of French empire-builders, had dreamed of making Mauritius an important naval and privateering base. As yet, however, hardly anyone in London or Paris thought of a territorial empire in the East. Even in 1744, on the outbreak of war between Britain and France, Dumas's successor J.-F. Dupleix proposed that these countries' Indian possessions should take no part in the struggle. The only important event of the conflict which followed the British Company's rejection of this proposal was the fall of Madras to a French force in September 1746; it was largely to secure the return of this valuable commercial post that Louisbourg was given up when peace was made.

That peace, embodied in the Treaty of Aix-la-Chapelle of October 1748 was, in its colonial as in its European aspects, a mere truce. From it Britain and France 'gained nothing but the experience of each other's strength and power'.[1] France in particular received a very inadequate return for her victories in Europe. The comparatively trivial claims of the South Sea Company against Spain were settled two years later; but the increasingly acute and incomparably more important Anglo-French rivalry was obviously insoluble without further conflict. On both sides the events of the 1740s had roused resentments and whetted appetites. On both another naval and colonial conflict in the near future seemed clearly likely: thirty-eight new French ships of the line were built in 1749–54 in preparation for one. Within a very few years the two countries found themselves drifting into a state of undeclared war.

In North America the growing violence of the struggle can be seen in the capture by the British of Fort Beauséjour on the Chignecto isthmus in 1755 and the forcible deportation of 10,000 French-speaking and potentially disloyal Acadians from Nova Scotia. At the same time each power was seizing the other's merchant ships in the Gulf of St Lawrence and protracted negotiations were once more going on over the 'neutral islands' in the West Indies. More important were the conflicts now springing up around the forts which France was establishing in the Ohio valley. The danger that she might consolidate her grip on this area and thus prevent further expansion westwards by the British colonies seemed a very real one, with the building of Fort Presqu'île and Fort-le-Bœuf to the south of Lake Erie in 1749 and of Fort Duquesne on the Ohio in 1753. The British reply – the construction of Fort Necessity, also on the Ohio, and the unsuccessful efforts of expeditions under Washington in 1754 and Braddock in 1755 to shake French power in the area – meant that the two States were now in fact at war in America though still formally at peace in Europe.

Simultaneously a complex struggle between the British and French East India Companies was developing in the Carnatic in South India, each power acting ostensibly as the supporter of rival claimants to the position of Nawab, or ruler of the area. In this struggle the French were defeated. This was partly because of lack of money (though Dupleix spent during the conflict over £350,000 subscribed by himself and his friends). It was also because neither the French government, which was weak and preoccupied with events in America, nor the directors of the French Company, to whom Dupleix gave no detailed explanation of his plans till October 1753, provided adequate backing. His recall in 1754 was a symbol as well as a result of his defeat. In the powerful State of Hyderabad, however, a French force under the Marquis de Bussy, the ablest of French soldiers in India, had achieved by 1750 a strong position which it was to retain for the next eight years.

In 1755, therefore, the balance seemed still fairly even in the two great areas of Anglo-French rivalry. In June of that year the British Admiral Boscawen, on the orders of the government, attacked without any declaration of war a large French convoy taking reinforcements to North America. He did not succeed in destroying it, as had been hoped in London; but he captured two French men-of-war and in the following months the British fleet seized, still in time of peace, over 300 French merchantmen. A declaration of war by France was thus made inevitable: only the weakness of Louis XV and his ministers delayed it till May 1756.

The struggle which followed began badly for Britain. At the outset of the war Minorca, her largest overseas naval base, fell to French attack. The government led, in so far as it was led at all, by the fussy and uninspiring Duke of Newcastle, was discredited by the defeat and driven from power in November. It was succeeded at the end of June 1757, after a period of weakness and confusion, by the most successful British Cabinet of the century, that led by Newcastle and the elder William Pitt. Pitt, who was soon to prove himself the greatest war minister in British history, had first achieved prominence by the violence of his attacks on Walpole in the 1730s. Disliked by George II, his abilities as an orator and the strength of his personality made him a figure of importance in the politics of the 1740s and early 1750s. Now the climax of his career was at hand. His irritability, his lack of any capacity for friendship, his obsessive francophobia, make him an unsympathetic figure. Yet he gave British policy at a critical moment an energy and determination which were soon to produce a series of splendid victories. This could not be foreseen, however, by observers in 1757, and the new government was formed just in time to see the defeat and capitulation of the Duke of Cumberland in Hanover (see p. 299). 'We are no longer a nation,' wrote the very experienced Lord Chesterfield in the autumn of that year, 'I never yet saw so dreadful a prospect';[2] and other British statesmen echoed his gloom.

These misgivings were excessive. France, apart from the capture of Minorca, enjoyed almost as little success as Britain in the first months of the war. Her finances were strained and some of her leaders already demoralized. Most important of all she was now involved, as a result of her new commitments to Austria, in a series of large-scale campaigns in western Germany which inevitably diverted much of her energies away from the maritime and colonial struggle with Britain. 'The great object of the nation [i.e. Great Britain],' wrote a very well-informed contemporary, 'is the American war . . . the probability of our succeeding in our main point is . . . much increased by the part the French take in the affairs of Germany, which turns their attention, as well as their money, from their marine, and . . . making expeditions to our Colonies.'[3] These factors, coupled with the new impetus given by Pitt, soon brought a complete change in the situation.

In Europe a series of amphibious attacks were launched in 1758, though with only moderate success, on the north coast of France. In 1759 British supremacy at sea was consolidated by the victories of Boscawen at Lagos and Hawke at Quiberon Bay. In 1761 the capture of the island of Belleisle off the south coast of Brittany illustrated the potentialities of 'combined operations' and gave the British government a valuable bargaining counter when it came to negotiating peace terms.

In America, in spite of the brilliance of the French commander Montcalm (who captured the British base of Fort William Henry in August 1757 and won two considerable successes at Fort Carillon in 1758) Canada had been severed from Louisiana by the end of the latter year after the fall of Fort Frontenac and Fort Duquesne. Simultaneously Louisbourg fell into British hands once more, this time for good. British troops captured Fort Niagara in July 1759 and most important of all Quebec in September, the most successful amphibious operation in British history. A year later the surrender of Montreal completed the extinction of French power in Canada. The victory of Britain was one of numbers and material strength over equal or even superior military skill. Weakness at sea, an overwhelming numerical inferiority in North America and a constant threat of food shortage in Canada made the defeat of France inevitable. In the West Indies, where some of the same factors operated, the valuable sugar island of Guadeloupe fell to a British expedition in the spring of 1759. In the same year the French possessions of Gorée and Fort Louis in West Africa were captured.

In India the course of events was complicated by the existence of powerful native States with policies and problems of their own, States capable of raising armies many times larger than Britain or France could send to the East. But the fighting of the last decade had shown that European troops, if properly led, could more than hold their own against apparently overwhelming numbers of Indians; and this fact was soon to be driven home unmistakably. The capture of Calcutta in June 1756 by Siraj-ud-Daula, the ruler of Bengal (probably provoked by fear of the growing power of the East India Company) was merely a temporary setback. Six months later it was retaken by Robert Clive, who had already greatly distinguished himself in the Carnatic. This success was followed by the capture of the French station at Chandernagore and, in July 1757, by the complete defeat of Siraj-ud-Daula at Plassey. Though the French played little part in these events (their energies were diverted largely to the maintenance of Bussy's foothold in Hyderabad) Clive's victory fatally undermined their position in India. This was because it gave the British Company control through Mir Ja'far, their nominee as successor to Siraj-ud-Daula, of a large area of densely-populated and fertile country whose revenues could be used to maintain powerful native armies. By contrast the French forces farther south in the Carnatic, the main scene of direct conflict with the English, were now continuously and sometimes disastrously short of money. This contrast between the financial positions of the rivals does as much as anything to explain the defeat of France.

In India, as in America and in European waters, 1759 was a decisive year. The failure of the French, under the gallant but unfortunate Lally-Tollendal, to take Madras in February, and the British capture of Masulipatam in April, were the turning-point of the war there. Without control of the sea, weakened by the quarrels of their commanders, the French in India were now clearly fighting a losing battle. The defeat of Lally by Sir Eyre Coote at Wandewash in January 1760 and the fall a year later of Pondicherry, France's main stronghold in India, completed the British victory. An attempt by the Dutch to land troops in Bengal and supplant the British there had already been decisively defeated by Clive in November 1759: five years later the battle of Bakhsar led to the British conquest of Oudh and by 1765 the Nawab of Bengal had become the mere figurehead of a British-controlled administration. When Clive secured from the Mughal emperor at Delhi in that year control of the finances of Bengal, Bihar and Orissa, the East India Company had been launched by force of circumstances and the initiative of its servants on a career of territorial conquest which it had not wanted but from which it could not draw back.

Against these massive and world-wide British successes France could place nothing but the capture of Minorca. Moreover tentative peace negotiations at The Hague in 1760 and Paris in 1761 showed that Pitt, supported by British public opinion and the

Press, intended to drive a hard bargain when a treaty was signed. In particular it was clear that he was determined to exclude the French from any share in the Newfoundland fishery and thus, by depriving them of a great source of experienced seamen, to prevent the revival of their navy. Nevertheless the Duc de Choiseul, who had replaced the incompetent Bernis as French Foreign Minister in November 1758, still had a card to play. Charles III, who had in 1759 succeeded his half-brother Ferdinand VI as King of Spain, did not share his predecessor's freedom from anti-British feeling. In particular he was genuinely alarmed by the growth of Britain's power in North America, which he feared might be the prelude to attacks on Spain's possessions in South America and the West Indies. Already in 1759, soon after his accession, he had unsuccessfully offered to mediate between Britain and France. Choiseul hoped, by playing on his fears, to bring Spain into the war as the ally of France and thus limit the losses which the latter must inevitably suffer when peace was made. The involvement of Spain in this way proved remarkably easy: indeed in 1761 the advances for a Franco-Spanish alliance came from Charles III, who feared the conclusion of a peace which sacrificed Spanish interests in America, rather than from France. The Family Compact of August 1761 which united the two States against Britain was therefore, unlike previous agreements of this type made in 1733 and 1743, inspired by colonial rather than purely European rivalries. Its conclusion soon brought one advantage to the French; in October Pitt, who demanded an immediate attack on Spain, resigned when the Cabinet failed to support him. Nevertheless from the military and naval point of view France's new ally achieved little. Pitt's colleagues, belatedly adopting the policy he had advocated, declared war on Spain at the beginning of January 1762; and the year which followed saw a series of British victories comparable to those of 1759. In the West Indies Havana, the greatest Spanish base in the western hemisphere, was captured, as was the very valuable French sugar island of Martinique. In the Pacific an expedition from India took Manila, the capital of the Philippines. A Spanish attack on Portugal was repulsed with British help; and in West Germany Ferdinand of Brunswick drove the French from Kassel and Göttingen.

In the peace negotiations of 1761–63 Britain did not exploit these successes fully. The Earl of Bute, who had been the leading minister since Pitt's resignation, was anxious for peace and completely unskilled in diplomacy. The Duke of Bedford, who also played a leading part in these negotiations and who signed the Treaty of Paris (February 1763) as the British plenipotentiary, was even less willing to push France to extremes. Both he and Bute were worried by the cost of the war and the implications of the rapid and apparently threatening growth of the National Debt. To them it seemed that no further concessions which could be wrung from France by fighting on would be worth their cost. Moreover in one respect Choiseul occupied a favourable position, since he acted to some extent as an intermediary between Britain and Spain; this he was able to turn to advantage. The result was that the peace of 1763 was not for France the complete disaster of which Pitt had dreamed. Her losses were none the less severe. Canada was surrendered, and with it the vast undeveloped territory of which France had claimed possession to the east of the Mississippi. Grenada, St Vincent and Tobago were ceded; and perhaps only the unwillingness of British sugar-planters to expose themselves to the competition in the home market of the more fertile French islands prevented the loss of Guadeloupe or Martinique as well. In India, though she retained her trading stations, France was now clearly unable to compete with Britain. In West Africa her forts in Senegal were surrendered to her rival. These losses, moreover, had been incurred as a result of defeats in the colonies themselves. In Europe France was never directly threatened, in spite of the mediocre performance of her armies in Germany. Apart from British raids on her coasts her territory had never to fear invasion. In spite of Pitt's well-known phrase, America was not 'conquered in Germany'. It was conquered in America and on the high seas; and even the complete defeat of Frederick II could not have restored it to France. Spain for her part ceded to Britain in 1763 the comparatively valueless province of Florida and in exchange recovered Havana. She also regained Manila; while as compensation for her losses and to strengthen the alliance of 1761 she received from France the latter's territories and claims in that part of Louisiana which lay west of the Mississippi.

The colonial wars of the middle decades of the century had thus changed the political face of much of the world. On the empires of Spain and Portugal, which except in a few frontier areas had long reached the limits of their growth, their impact was slight.

That of France they reduced to a few islands – Guadeloupe, Martinique, the western half of San Domingo, Mauritius and the Seychelles. Many of these were valuable producers of tropical products, above all of sugar, but none of them offered any scope for territorial expansion. Britain these wars established conclusively as a world power. Nevertheless with all her victories she had not reduced France and Spain to the position of second-rate States: to do so was far beyond her ability. Moreover the collapse of her wartime relationship with Prussia (see pp. 302–13) left her isolated in Europe after 1763. Her enemies, by contrast, were united rather than divided by defeat; in the years which followed the war the alliance with Spain much more than that with Austria became the cornerstone of French policy. It is significant that although Choiseul ceased to be Foreign Minister in 1761 he was careful none the less to keep the correspondence with the embassy in Madrid in his own hands.

It was not to be expected that France would accept the decision of 1763 as final. The terms of peace seemed lenient to many Englishmen, particularly in allowing her to retain a share in the Newfoundland fishery and hence the possibility of resurrecting . her navy. In Paris, however, they stimulated a natural desire for revenge. Before his fall Choiseul did much to rebuild French military and still more naval power and strengthen the Franco-Spanish alliance. In 1770 he was willing to support Spain, even at the risk of war, in a dispute with Britain over the ownership of the Falkland Islands; and perhaps only the timidity of Louis XV, which led to the minister's dismissal in December of that year, prevented the outbreak of a new imperial struggle. Choiseul had also realized that the best chance of humbling Britain lay in encouraging and stimulating the growing unrest which was now showing itself in her American colonies.

That unrest had many causes. The best known is the effort of the British government from 1763 onwards to force the colonies to contribute more adequately to the costs of their own defence against French, Spanish or Indian attack. This it attempted to do partly by enforcing the legal restrictions (many of them disregarded for decades) which limited the commercial freedom of the colonists in the interests of the mother-country (see pp. 357–8). Led by the efficiency-minded George Greville, it tightened up in 1763–65 the hitherto very lax customs administration in the colonies and used vice-admiralty courts, which were independent of the colonial assemblies, to try smugglers. More serious, it attempted to tax the colonists, directly by the Stamp Act of 1765 and indirectly by the Townshend Acts of 1767. Almost simultaneously it tried, by a proclamation of October 1763, to restrict the westward movement of the frontier of settlement in North America and thus avoid friction with the native inhabitants. (A serious Indian rising, the 'revolt of Pontiac', which lasted till September 1764, was just then showing how dangerous the position on the frontier might become.) A few years later it reinforced hostility in Calvinist New England, by passing the remarkably liberal and enlightened Quebec Act of 1774 which recognized the position of the Catholic Church in Canada (at least by implication, in that its priests were given the right to collect tithes). All these measures, in varying degrees, were unpopular in America. Restrictions on trade, however well-grounded in law, aroused a great deal of understandable ill-will in the ports of the eastern seaboard. The levying of taxation by the British government for revenue purposes was an innovation which seemed to emphasize the inferior and dependent position of the colonies. Since the Parliament which authorized such taxation included no colonial representatives it was easy for idealists or trouble-makers to raise the seductive cry of 'no taxation without representation'. Efforts to suppress smuggling and protect the Indians again seemed, or could be made to seem, tyrannical interference with colonial liberties by a corrupt and overbearing government.

Moreover there was already in existence by the 1760s a tradition of friction between the British government and the colonial assemblies over a number of issues. One of these was the right claimed by the latter to issue paper currency and thus lighten the weight of the debts owed by many colonists to British merchants. Such issues were declared not to be legal tender by legislation of 1751 and 1764; and the debt of about £5 million owed in Britain by American traders and planters has been considered by some writers as an important factor in the final break with the mother-country. Other long-standing disputes were inspired by the claims of many colonial assemblies to control the governors appointed by the Crown, and by the right often though not very effectively exercised by rulers of Great Britain to veto legislation passed by such assemblies.

Underlying all these specific grievances and drawing strength from them was a growing feeling in America that the colonies were no longer mere offshoots of the mother-country; that they differed radically from her in their social and political structure; that they were now beginning to form a separate nation. This was based on the brute facts that the population of the colonies almost doubled in 1750–76, that their economies were rapidly growing and that after 1763 they had been freed from any real threat from France with a consequent weakening of their need for British protection. This profound though largely unconscious movement of separatist feeling in America is the real explanation of the American Revolution. It was this feeling (whose growth had been noticed by European travellers at least as early as the 1740s) which drove so many Americans to disregard legality, precedent and as it sometimes seemed common sense, in the pursuit of liberty. It was the emotions it generated, far more than any material grievance, which drove them to react against British rule; first by the Non-Importation Agreements of the 1760s (by which American merchants agreed not to purchase goods on which duties had been placed by Parliament); then by the stoning of British troops and the tarring and feathering of officials who attempted to enforce the law; and finally by armed rebellion.

It is true that even as late as 1775 only a minority, perhaps as little as a fifth, of the colonists wished for independence, and that perhaps a third or even half of them disapproved of outright resistance to British rule. These 'loyalists' provided many of the most bitter opponents of the movement towards independence and often suffered exile and loss when it had triumphed. The war in which the colonies threw off British rule was therefore in a very real sense an American civil war. Even in the closest family relationships these divisions can be seen. William Franklin, the son of Benjamin Franklin who more than anyone else came to typify for Europe the virtues of revolutionary America, was a leading and active loyalist, as was the brother of John Jay, one of the men who in 1783 negotiated American independence. Nevertheless by the 1760s the temper of many of the most politically conscious and politically active Americans, particularly in New England, was such that no concessions the British government could have made would have permanently satisfied them. As early as 1768 a Boston newspaper was talking of an appeal to France for aid in resisting British oppression.

The events of the later 1760s and early 1770s, as antagonism mounted between the colonists and the British government, need only be touched on here. The duties on stamped paper used for various legal documents in America, imposed by the Stamp Act of 1765, were repealed in the following year in response to colonial protests. Those placed by the Townshend Acts of 1767 on glass, paper, lead, tea and colours imported into the colonies were swept away, with the exception of that on tea, in 1770. As a result, tension relaxed somewhat in the following two or three years; but in 1773 the passage of the Tea Act (which gave the East India Company the right to export tea to America in its own ships and sell it there through its own agents) led to a new burst of colonial resentment. By allowing the company to dispose of a large stock of surplus tea at low prices it appeared to strike at the interests of both smugglers and legitimate traders in America. Events now moved swiftly to a crisis. The destruction by groups of colonists of supplies of tea, above all in Boston, was followed by British punitive measures directed against that city and the colony of Massachusetts. These in turn inspired the meeting, in April 1774, of the first Continental Congress, a gathering of representatives of most of the mainland colonies. This issued a Declaration of Rights, and by declaring its support of Massachusetts identified itself with rebellion. By 1775 fighting on a considerable scale between British troops and American militia had begun. In July 1776 another congress of colonial representatives meeting at Philadelphia declared the colonies independent.

When American discontent came to a head Britain was in a weaker position in Europe than at any other time during the century. She had made efforts in the middle 1760s to escape from political isolation by adopting the Russian idea of a Northern System which was to include Russia, Prussia, Sweden and Denmark, as well as Great Britain (see p. 270). These efforts were a failure. So were more prolonged and more promising negotiations, which dragged on till 1773, for a treaty with Russia alone. Moreover the unmistakable defeat of France in 1763 and her diplomatic setbacks in Poland and the Near East in the early 1770s made it difficult for Britain to gain support in Europe, as she had often tried to do in the past, by pointing to the alleged danger of French domination of the continent. The result was that she found herself in the 1770s, as in 1763, alone in face of a revengeful, envious or indifferent Europe. This isolation helps to explain her defeat in America.

She was also weakened by the unpopularity of the struggle in the colonies with important bodies of British opinion. It was opposed by merchants who saw their profitable colonial trade interrupted or destroyed. It was unpopular with Nonconformist groups who tended (with the notable exception of the Methodists) to sympathize with the largely Calvinist New England colonies and to suspect George III and his ministers as the representatives and tools of the aristocracy and the Established Church. These feelings moreover were used and played on by opposition politicians. Some of these (for example many of the Rockingham Whigs) were sincere believers in the rightness of the American cause, but others were animated merely by desire for office and in some cases personal hostility to the king. The good fortune which had provided the country with the leadership of Pitt during the Seven Years War was not repeated. The chief minister, Lord North (1770–82), had real administrative ability and considerable personal charm; but neither he nor any other statesman could embody the national cause and rally flagging energies in Britain as the colonial leader George Washington did in America. As the seriousness of the struggle became more apparent, notably after the surrender of a British army to the Americans at Saratoga in 1777, hostility to the government increased. In 1779–80, as has already been seen (see p. 172) the discontent brought to a head by the war for a short time reached almost revolutionary proportions. In 1782, in the last days of the struggle, the threat of revolt in Ireland allowed its Parliament in Dublin to recover the legislative independence it had lost almost three centuries earlier.

The decisive event of the war was the entry of France on the anti-British side early in 1778. This was undoubtedly stimulated by a desire for revenge after the defeats of the Seven Years War: the French government had from the beginning of the struggle been supplying the rebels with arms and equipment and sheltering American privateers. From the Stamp Act crisis of 1765 onwards British attitudes to America had been influenced by fears of intervention by France, very probably backed by Spain; and by 1778 the French naval budget was four times what it had been at the death of Louis XV. Moreover the victory at Saratoga made it clear that the colonists were not going to be easily defeated and were therefore worth backing: the almost simultaneous battle of Germantown, though an American defeat, had also a considerable encouraging effect in France. The ambitions of Vergennes, the French Foreign Minister, were however remarkably moderate. He

had no desire to recover Canada or Louisiana and aimed much
more at regaining the prestige which France had lost in the Seven
Years War, and at expanding French trade, than at the mere
acquisition of territory. French intervention, nevertheless, whatever its motive, made it extremely unlikely that Britain would be
able to subdue her rebellious colonies. Its importance was seen
when in 1778 the Americans rejected a series of very sweeping
concessions – abandonment of nearly all claims to tax the colonies, the right for them to maintain their own army, all offices
in the colonies to be reserved for Americans – offered them by
the British government through a commission headed by the Earl
of Carlisle. There seemed for a moment a chance that the British
proposals might be accepted by the rebels, and some of the more
extreme of the colonial leaders feared them as 'more dangerous
to our cause than ten thousand of their [the British government's]
best troops'. The availability of French support, however, was a
powerful incentive to continue the struggle; and with the rejection
of the British proposals the last real possibility of reconciliation
with the mother-country vanished.

Britain's difficulties were greatly increased when Spain joined
the ranks of her enemies in June 1779. Vergennes had proposed
as early as August 1776 that she and France should jointly attack
Britain; but it was only slowly and reluctantly that the Spanish
government took the plunge. Unlike that of France, it was
completely unwilling to recognize the independence of the thirteen British mainland colonies or to have any dealings with their
representatives. When John Jay reached Madrid as the envoy of
the rebels early in 1780 he found himself in an extremely difficult
and uncomfortable position. This was inevitable: signs, though
as yet relatively slight ones, of growing resentment of at least
some aspects of Spanish rule were now beginning to show themselves in South America. A general reassertion of control from
Madrid after a century of inertia, set in motion by the reforming
regime of Charles III from about 1765 onwards, partly explains
this. So does the very marked rise in emigration from Spain to
America in the later eighteenth century. This provoked bitter
complaints from small businessmen, artisans and minor office-
holders in the Spanish colonies, who resented the frequently
greater energy and success of the newcomers. In 1771, in an early
reflection of this attitude, the *cabildo* (town council) of Mexico
City demanded that all government offices in Mexico be reserved

for Mexicans and Spaniards treated as foreigners. In 1780 the British government seriously contemplated an attack on the Pacific coast of South America from bases to be seized in the Philippines: this, it was hoped, would set off a series of revolts over the whole area from Chile to Mexico. With great problems of this kind slowly beginning to emerge in her own possessions Spain was bound to see the revolt of the thirteen British colonies in a very different light from France. Also possible territorial gains bulked much larger at Madrid than in Paris. Spain entered the war above all to recover Gibraltar: the French government, by a treaty of alliance signed at Aranjuez in April 1779, bound itself not to make peace until she had done so. It was the refusal of the British government to contemplate the return of the fortress by negotiation which made a new Anglo-Spanish struggle inevitable. The declaration of war by Britain in December 1780 against the United Provinces, whose ships had for long been supplying the colonists with arms and supplies of all kinds, was an act of great boldness; but it made her position more difficult still. Moreover in June of the same year the ruler of Mysore, Hyder Ali, launched a serious attack on the British-held territories in the Carnatic: during the years which followed he was to prove the most determined enemy the East India Company ever had to face.

Britain therefore found herself fighting against odds unparalleled in her history, and fighting moreover in the most unfavourable circumstances – poorly led, divided by bitter party rivalries, and deprived by the revolt in America, according to a contemporary estimate, of a third of her merchant marine and 18,000 seamen. The Armed Neutrality of 1780 (see p. 277) did her little real harm but it weakened still further her influence in Europe.

From this desperate position she emerged less ingloriously than might have been expected. Hostility to France and Spain, the traditional enemies, did much to make the war popular and to ensure that it would be prolonged; in this sense French intervention harmed as well as helped the colonists. The numerical superiority which the French and Spanish fleets possessed in the early stages of the war was never fully utilized: by 1782 Rodney had restored British predominance at sea and averted any possibility of the loss of Jamaica by a decisive victory over the French at The Saints islands in the West Indies. During the war, in the exchanges of naval prisoners which were then normal while hostilities were in progress, Britain sent to France at least 31,000 men and probably far more: she received in return only a little over 16,000 British prisoners taken by the French. Not a single British ship of the line was captured by her enemies, while eleven French, seven Spanish and three Dutch ones were taken by the British navy. (Though against this it should be remembered that British losses of merchant ships to French, Spanish and American privateers were exceptionally heavy.) A very well-informed French observer spoke admiringly some years later of 'this so to speak miraculous struggle of the naval forces of England alone against those of the three greatest maritime powers in Europe'.[4] Moreover Gibraltar successfully withstood a siege of three years (1779–82) – by far the greatest military operation of the war. Canada and Newfoundland were retained, though this was partly because the French government had no desire to see the American colonists, by acquiring them, become strong enough to throw off its influence. Simultaneously the East India Company consolidated its position in South India at the cost of a difficult and expensive war with Hyder Ali. Most important of all in many ways, France was in no financial position to face a long war. By 1780, therefore, the desire for peace was strong in Paris; and during that year both Maurepas, the most influential of all the French ministers, and Necker, the Controller-General of Finance, made unofficial approaches to the British government. The negotiations of 1782–83, which ended the war, were conducted on the French side under the imminent threat of financial collapse.

But the thirteen mainland colonies in North America were irretrievably lost. Even without the intervention of France and her allies their enormous area, their remoteness and the great difficulties of moving a regular army within them, would have made them very hard to subdue. They were also greatly strengthened by the fact that there was no single centre whose loss could inflict really severe damage on the rebellion. At different times all the biggest American cities – Boston, New York, Philadelphia and Charleston – were in British hands; but this had little real influence on the outcome of the struggle. Moreover in spite of the hopes which were placed in loyalist support and 'helping the good Americans to overcome the bad', no British army ever controlled an area large enough to allow it to be fed from American resources. The British forces had therefore to be provisioned from home: every year a third of a ton of food had to be moved across the Atlantic for each soldier in the colonies with a consequent enormous drain on British shipping. In spite of all this, however, it was not until late in 1781 that it became clear that the rebellion would succeed. Until then it seemed quite possible that the colonies might be partitioned, with New England becoming independent and the more southerly ones remaining in British hands. It also seemed conceivable that their fragile unity might collapse and that Britain might negotiate separately with each of them, an idea briefly taken up by Vergennes in the spring of 1781, when the war was going badly for them and their morale and confidence were at a low ebb. However, with the surrender of Lord Cornwallis's army at Yorktown in October 1781 (a surrender compelled by France's temporary command of the sea in American waters) their independence was an accomplished fact, in spite of the determination with which George III continued to reject the idea. As late as the summer of 1782, in the peace negotiations at Paris, the British Prime Minister, Lord Shelburne, hoped that it might be possible to reunite them with the mother-country by conceding a high degree of self-government. It soon became clear that he had mistaken the temper of the colonists and that such ideas were totally impracticable. The Treaty of Versailles of September 1783, which recognized the independence of the thirteen colonies, also returned to France some of the West Indian islands she had lost in 1763 and her former trading-ports in Senegal. Spain recovered Minorca (which had been taken from Britain by a French expedition in 1782) and East Florida. The United Provinces, whose part in the war had been almost uniformly unsuccessful, signed a definitive treaty with Britain only in 1784, at the cost of a promise not to prevent British subjects from freely navigating the seas which the Dutch claimed to control around Indonesia.

Britain was able to emerge from an unprecedentedly difficult war without making great concessions to her European enemies largely because these enemies were so disunited. France and Spain never co-operated effectively during the struggle. Spain's ultimatum which paved the way for her entry into the war in 1779 was drawn up without any consultation with France and was almost as unacceptable to her as to Britain. In the following year Necker, by impeding the raising of a Spanish government loan, more or less deliberately deprived the ministers in Madrid of two million pesos which could have been used to support Spain's war effort. Divisions of this kind help to explain the failure of the Spaniards, in spite of bitter efforts which more than once brought the peace negotiation within sight of collapse, to recover Gibraltar, by far their most important objective. Vergennes, irritated by Spain's claims and the difficulties they created, spoke of her as 'a petty shopkeeper who thinks that the only way to get a fair price for his goods is to begin by asking ten times more than they are worth'.[5] Nor were relations between French and Americans anything like as good as later mythology on both sides of the Atlantic was to make them out to be. Formally allies, neither hesitated to sacrifice the interests of the other to its own. In its treaty of April 1779 with Spain the French government agreed to the exclusion of the colonists from the Newfoundland fisheries, a direct contravention of the Franco-American alliance of February 1778, while the French negotiating position at the end of the war was seriously weakened by the action of the colonists in agreeing to separate peace preliminaries with Britain at the end of November 1782. Yet in spite of all this Britain's influence and prestige in 1783 were perhaps lower than at any other moment in modern history. France had had her revenge, and had helped to create a new independent nation with unprecedented potentialities. She had done this, however, at a cost which ruined her finances and fatally undermined her system of government.

These colonial and naval struggles faced both Britain and France with strategic problems of a hitherto unknown magnitude. Both were, or were struggling to become, world powers. Both therefore had to work out a world strategy. Both had to face the difficulties created by the interaction of events in Europe with those in America or the East.

In each country hostility to the other remained a pervasive political emotion during this period. In France, however, its effects were tempered and diluted by a number of factors. Anti-British feeling there had to compete with an even more deeply ingrained hostility to the Habsburgs, at least in the first half of the century. It was further modified by the admiration which many educated Frenchmen increasingly felt for British intellectual life and the British constitution. Above all the fact that France had long land frontiers in Europe and a well-marked tradition of territorial expansion there, and that her people settled overseas only reluctantly and in small numbers, meant that colonial expansion never possessed for her the exclusive and dominant interest which it had for many Englishmen.

In Britain anti-French feeling was more profound than anti-British feeling on the other side of the Channel. France offered a more serious threat to Britain than Britain ever could to France. The latter's intrinsic strength was in most respects far superior to that of her rival. Her population was about three times as large as that of Britain and her taxable capacity was greater than the British one. She possessed a better and far larger army than Britain. As early as the 1670s Louis XIV had managed for a time to maintain under arms about 400,000 men, a force greater than any seen before in European history. By contrast the Duke of Marlborough himself argued in the early eighteenth century that Britain could not afford to keep the total strength of her armed forces for any length of time at a figure of more than 70,000. This was a gross underestimate: by the end of the War of the Grand Alliance, in 1697, the soldiers alone in British pay numbered about 90,000 men. Nevertheless the military inferiority of Britain to France continued to be marked. In 1760 the total number of soldiers voted by Parliament, including the very large foreign levies then in British pay, amounted to 170,000. This was the greatest exertion of British military strength at any time before the 1790s; but even so it represented little more than half the number of men then at the disposal of Louis XV's generals. During the Seven Years War an effort was made to provide more adequate forces for home defence by the passage of an important Militia Act in 1757. Two years later, however, at the height of one of the most serious invasion threats of the century, only a little over 17,000 men had been raised under this very unpopular Act; and of these only a little over 6,000 were ready for service.

France's material strength threatened Britain's position in two ways. It might allow her to establish her hegemony on the continent, destroying British influence there and perhaps even excluding much of British trade from Europe by the organization of a 'Continental System' on the lines later attempted by Napoleon. Suggestions for action of this kind were put forward by more than one French writer during the Seven Years War. Much more serious, France, once in control of the Channel for a few hours, might invade and overrun Britain without encountering effective resistance. The successes won by a few thousand untrained and poorly equipped Highlanders during the Jacobite rebellion of 1745–46 lent point to such fears. Moreover the existence until the middle of the century of Jacobitism as a force to be reckoned with, at least in Scotland, was an additional inducement to French statesmen to risk a bold stroke against Britain, even across seas which the French fleet controlled imperfectly or not at all. It is not surprising therefore to find that British governments during this period were frequently alarmed by the spectre of French invasion and that their policies were influenced by their alarm. In 1739 Walpole, at the outbreak of war with Spain, was unwilling to send a really powerful fleet to the West Indies because of fears of this kind. The capture of Minorca by the French in 1756 was made possible by the justified refusal of the government, for the same reason, to dispatch a large squadron to the Mediterranean.

None of the numerous plans and suggestions put forward in France during this period for an invasion of Britain had any success. Some were impeded by bad luck. Thus in March 1744 the Maréchal de Saxe had actually begun to embark troops in the Austrian Netherlands for an attack on England (with which France was still officially at peace) when bad weather brought his activities to a halt. Other invasion schemes failed because of lack of determination in their leaders – for example the small-scale landing made at Torbay in 1690, at a time when the French fleet was in control of the Channel. Others again were stultified by a combination of both factors. By far the most important instance was in 1779, when temporary control of the Channel by French and Spanish squadrons seemed to make practicable a French plan to seize the Isle of Wight and make a large-scale landing in the Portsmouth area. Poor leadership and disease in the Franco-Spanish fleet meant that the opportunity was lost; but the panic which reigned for a time along the south coast of England is understandable. In St Malo and Le Havre 31,000 French soldiers were poised to invade at a time when there were only 21,000 regulars available in the whole of England.

The chances of successful French invasion were enormously reduced by the strength of the British navy and its normal superiority to that of France. This more than anything else explains Britain's victory over her opponents in the colonial struggles of 1739–63. In no eighteenth century war was her navy effectively inferior for any length of time to those of France and Spain combined. Moreover its superiority to its rivals tended to increase as each of the struggles of this period progressed. This was partly because it lost many fewer ships in battle than those of France and Spain (though since it spent much more time at sea it lost many more by wreck, fire and other accidents). It was also because, by maintaining an effective blockade of French and to a lesser extent of Spanish ports, it could make it difficult for these countries to import naval stores from the Baltic. More important still, by reducing the activities of their merchant marines it restricted the supply of trained seamen on which their fleets could draw.

The responsibilities which fell on the British navy were extremely heavy. The country depended on it not merely for physical security from foreign attack but also for the maintenance of much of its economy and particularly of its financial system. Throughout this period much of Britain's economic strength depended on her ability to import and export freely and to act as an entrepôt from which colonial and Oriental goods could be distributed over much of Europe. Any sustained interuption of her trade might well bring down in ruins the complex and sophisticated structure of public finance which was normally one of her greatest assets. In general the navy rose to its responsibilities with remarkable success. The French fleet, normally unable to challenge Britain openly for control of the seas, tended increasingly as the century went on to fall back on defensive tactics, on commerce-raiding by individual ships or small squadrons (see p. 234). This policy, though it sometimes caused much loss to British merchants, depended for ultimate success on France's ability to send out her fleets and win a clear-cut victory at sea, an ability which she never possessed. The result was that the outbreak of an Anglo-French war was usually followed by a temporary drop in Britain's seaborne trade as French cruisers and privateers got to work, but that this in turn gave way to a steady rise in both imports and exports towards the end of each struggle, as British naval superiority was increasingly asserted. Simultaneously French seaborne trade would fall, sometimes as in 1747–48 and 1759–62 to a mere trickle. France, however, was far less vulnerable to pressure of this kind than Britain. She could lose much of her fleet and trade and still remain one of the greatest European States, as she showed in the second half of the Seven Years War. Similar losses would reduce Britain almost overnight to the position of a second-rate power.

British superiority at sea had also profound repercussions on events in the British and French colonies. It meant above all that France was prevented from translating her material superiority in Europe into a corresponding superiority overseas. She might possess great armies; but unless adequate parts of them could be transported to Canada, the West Indies or India, their existence could have little direct bearing on the outcome of the colonial struggle. British seapower made it impossible for them ever to be deployed effectively outside Europe. In the Seven Years War, the real crisis of the Anglo-French conflict, very few of the 300,000 men whom France had under arms in Europe were sent overseas. The only French colonial expeditions of any significance during the war, those of Montcalm to Canada and Lally-Tollendal to India, mustered between them only about 10,000 fighting men. By contrast Britain had as early as 1757 over 70,000 regular troops in her North American colonies alone. Moreover the French West Indian islands were very vulnerable to blockade – much more so than France herself. This fact was never adequately exploited, largely because British commanders in the area were chronically short of light vessels suitable for blockade purposes. Nevertheless many French West Indian islands were prepared for British conquest by this means, both in the War of the Austrian Succession and the Seven Years War. More than once (notably in 1747–48) more rigorous and effective use of blockade might have led to the surrender through starvation of all France's possessions in the area.

Naval power was thus by far the sharpest weapon at Britain's disposal in her colonial struggles with France. Was it by itself sufficient to ensure victory? Could Britain, in spite of her great inferiority in numbers and resources, defeat her rival in single combat without European allies?

The vast majority of Englishmen hoped and believed that the answer to this question was 'Yes'. It was widely felt throughout this period that Britain should as far as possible fight only at sea and for objectives of some commercial value, potential if not actual. In the terms used by contemporaries, public opinion was heavily biased against 'continental' and in favour of 'American' or 'colonial' warfare. 'Sea war, no Continent, no subsidy,' wrote the Duke of Newcastle in July 1755 at one of the most critical moments of the Anglo-French struggle, 'is almost the universal language. It would be betraying the king to say otherwise, or to conceal the truth.'[6] For this attitude, with its undertones of hostility to and suspicion of Europe, there were various explanations. In part it was merely the result of the contempt and dislike for foreigners which was now more deep-rooted in Britain, or at least in England, than in most other parts of the continent. To a large extent it was also the product of a desire to wage war as cheaply as possible. Experience showed that continental allies had usually to be encouraged or bribed by British subsidies before they were willing, or often able, to set their armies in motion against France. Sometimes it was necessary, to make sure of their support in wartime, to pay them subsidies in time of peace as a kind of retaining fee, a practice which was fiercely opposed by the majority of both politicians and public opinion in Britain. Moreover bitter experience showed that many of the rulers on whom subsidies were lavished, especially many of the smaller German princes, failed to justify the hopes placed in them or to make a military effort commensurate with the sums they received. Naval warfare on the other hand, it was widely believed, could be made to pay for itself, since it involved the capture of valuable enemy prizes and led to the seizure of lucrative colonies and trading-posts. Finally the idea of maintaining the balance of power in Europe, which underlay much of the policy of subsidizing continental States against France, made little appeal to the ordinary Englishman. Many politicians, especially if they were out of office, tended to challenge the validity of the whole concept and to allege that it was being used by the government as a pretext to squander British money on foreign princes.

Opposition to 'continental' warfare was always stronger in Parliament and among the general public than in the Cabinet. In the vital decades of the 1740s and 1750s ministers such as Henry Pelham (First Commissioner of the Treasury, 1743–54 and in many ways the most important influence in British politics during these years) tended to share the popular prejudice against continental entanglements; but others – Lord Carteret, the Duke of Newcastle and eventually Pitt himself – saw the advantages to be gained by pinning down a large part of France's energies and resources in Europe. 'A naval force,' wrote Newcastle in 1749, 'tho' carried never so high, unsupported with even the appearance of a force upon the Continent, will be of little use . . . France will outdo us at sea when they [*sic*] have nothing to fear by land . . . I have always maintained that our marine should protect our alliances upon the Continent; and they, by diverting the expense of France, enable us to maintain our superiority at sea.'[7] This was the formula which, backed by the energy and vision of Pitt, brought unprecedented and unrepeatable victory in 1759–62.

Moreover Britain could not in practice withdraw completely from Europe, however much she might wish to do so. She was linked to the continent, most unfortunately in the eyes of nearly all Englishmen, by the fact that her ruler was also, as Elector of Hanover, ruler of an important German State. Under George I and George II the connexion with Hanover was almost universally unpopular in Britain, and understandably so. The fact that both rulers were interested in the Electorate at least as much as in Britain meant that British policy was often influenced by their desire to safeguard or extend their German territories. Thus Anglo-Russian relations in the last years of Peter I were affected very much for the worse by George I's territorial ambitions in North Germany and by Hanoverian fears of the Tsar's influence there. A projected Anglo-Prussian alliance in 1740 was stultified by George II's jealously of Frederick II, while in the following year he seriously disorganized British policy by making an agreement for the neutrality of Hanover in the struggle which was then beginning (see p. 292).

More serious, the fact that Hanover was exposed to French attack could be used in wartime to put pressure on Britain and perhaps to extort concessions from her when peace was made. If the Electorate were overrun by France Britain might be compelled, in order to recover it, to return conquests made overseas at the cost of British blood and money. But to abandon Hanover to its fate, though most Englishmen in their hearts would have been happy to do so, was hardly practical politics. Such a step was certain to be violently opposed by the king. Moreover the loss of the Electorate would greatly damage British prestige, while control of it would greatly strengthen France's influence in the Holy Roman Empire and Northern Europe. Thus Hanover could neither be safely abandoned nor easily defended. So long as it was associated with Britain, even by the slender bond of a personal union, British governments were willy-nilly involved in the politics of Germany. It was therefore impossible during this period for Britain to fight a purely naval and colonial war against France unless France herself were willing to fight on these terms.

Both in 1740 and in 1755 it seemed that this might be the case. In the former year Cardinal Fleury was actively preparing to support Spain in a struggle of this kind against Britain. In the latter British aggression at sea, though it led to proposals for a French attack on the Electorate, produced no immediate threat to Hanover. In neither case, however, did France in the event confine her war effort to the oceans and the colonies. By 1741 she had become involved in a struggle to destroy Habsburg power in Central Europe; and from 1756 onwards she played a part, though an ineffective one, in efforts to partition Prussia. To many French statesmen action in Europe still seemed the most effective means of redressing the balance, otherwise favourable to Britain, at sea and in America.

The disastrous experience of the Seven Years War shook this view severely. The maintenance in western Germany of a powerful French army, the payment to German princes of very large French subsidies, did little or nothing to strengthen France's position in the negotiations of 1761–63 or to reduce the losses which she suffered by the Treaty of Paris. The idea that Britain's colonial supremacy might be weakened by French action in Europe was not, however, abandoned. The Duc de Choiseul, for example, argued at the end of 1765 that in any future war with her France should seize the United Provinces, which could be set off, when it came to peacemaking, against any further losses of French territory overseas. He asserted that he would have proposed this course of action in 1763 if peace had not been made in that year. To the Comte de Vergennes, on the other hand, such ideas made little appeal. More influenced than almost any other leading statesman of the century by the humanitarian and pacifist aspects of the Enlightenment, he regarded another conflict with Britain as inevitable, and as necessary to weaken her over-mighty position in the overseas trade and expansion of Europe. But he did not believe that France should gain territory in Europe. Throughout his years as Foreign Minister (1774–87) he worked for peace and stability on the continent. The result was that the Anglo-French war of 1778–83 was the only one of the century which did not involve large-scale land warfare in Europe (apart from the great siege of Gibraltar in 1779–82). For once French resources were not diverted to the Rhine, the Netherlands or Italy. This, combined with the help of Spain, the Dutch and the American rebels, allowed Vergennes to achieve his object. By the

end of the struggle he had reduced Britain's power and prestige
and established, as he hoped, the basis for a more stable relationship between her and France. The misgivings of Newcastle and
other British statesmen about their country's ability to win a
purely naval and colonial war against France had been justified,
though under conditions which would never recur.

NOTES AND REFERENCES

1   W. Coxe, *Memoirs of Horatio, Lord Walpole* (London, 1802),
    p. 359.

2   P. C. Yorke, *The Life of Lord Chancellor Hardwicke* (Cambridge,
    1913), vol. III, p. 123.

3   *Ibid.* p. 157.

4   A. M. Arnould, *Système maritime et politique des Européens pendant
    le dixhuitième siècle* (Paris, 1797), p. 322.

5   Quoted in R. B. Morris, *The Peacemakers: The Great Powers and
    American Independence* (New York, 1965), p. 392.

6   C. W. Eldon, *England's Subsidy Policy towards the Continent during
    the Seven Years War* (Philadelphia, 1938), p. 17.

7   Yorke, *op. cit.*, vol. II, p. 23.

13

EUROPE AND THE OUTSIDE WORLD

To the average European during the eighteenth century overseas colonies were chiefly areas in which the commerce of the mother-country could develop. They were an outlet for trade, a source of raw materials, particularly those which the mother-country could not produce for herself, and a market for manufactured goods. They were not primarily receptacles for surplus population or even a gratification of national pride, far less the embryos of new independent States.

All the imperial powers had now embodied these ideas in laws and regulations aimed at making their colonies complement and support the economy of the mother-country and thus contribute to the creation of an economically unified empire. The best-known of these bodies of legislation is the Navigation System in England. Originating with the Navigation Ordinance passed by the Commonwealth government in 1651, it was rapidly extended and consolidated, notably in 1663 and 1673. Though eighteenth-century statesmen altered and added to it in various ways they made little fundamental change in it. This legislation aimed at giving the staple products of the colonies, such as sugar or tobacco, as far as possible a monopoly of the British market. In return the colonists were to supply goods (mainly raw materials and foodstuffs) which Britain could not herself produce. Certain valuable colonial products, the so-called 'enumerated commodities', were to be exported only to the mother-country (this provision tended to be modified as time went on, notably by the removal of sugar from the list in 1739). Trade between Britain and her colonies was to be carried on only in British or colonial

357

ships and foreigners excluded as far as possible from commercial contacts with British possessions overseas. The system, at least at the time of its creation, had a certain symmetry and logicality and was never designed merely as an instrument of colonial exploitation. Throughout this period, in spite of conflicting pressures and propaganda from many different interest groups, British governments and public opinion adhered fairly steadily to its basic principles, though until the 1760s laws embodying them were often very poorly enforced in the colonies.

Comparable legislation in other European colonial powers was, at least on paper, more restrictive than in Britain. France did her best, notably in royal decrees of 1717 and 1727, to ensure that only French subjects traded with and benefited from the valuable French sugar islands of the West Indies. Spain's colonial trade was, in theory, channelled entirely through a government agency, the *Casa de Contratación*, which from 1717 was established in Cadiz; and trade with the great Spanish American market was, again in theory, in the hands of a small group of Cadiz merchants. Portuguese trade with the huge colony of Brazil was officially confined entirely to Portuguese subjects; and in the 1750s Pombal struggled to make this restriction a reality. All these systems of trade control were difficult to enforce at all thoroughly in practice; and smuggling and illegitimate trade of different kinds made the Spanish and Portuguese ones in particular little more than official shams. It was officially admitted in 1704 that only a sixth of the goods carried by the convoys going to Spanish America were in fact Spanish; and this proportion probably did not improve much during the eighteenth century. Nevertheless such policies reflected a set of assumptions about the position and value of colonies which was almost universal among the ruling groups of Europe. By the later years of the century these restrictions were becoming somewhat less rigid: the example and warning given by the independence of Britain's North American colonies, the slow growth of more liberal economic ideas, the sheer difficulties of enforcement, all played a part in this. In Spain the monopoly of colonial trade enjoyed by Cadiz was ended in 1765 and the restrictions on it progressively eased, while in 1784 the French West Indian islands were substantially opened to commerce with the newly independent American republic. But this freeing of colonial trade was slow, reluctant and very incomplete.

The value of a colony was therefore determined throughout this period mainly by its commercial potentialities. There was a strong tendency to regard the islands of the Caribbean, or slave-trading stations in West Africa, or commercial bases in India or South-East Asia, as more important than great overseas territorial possessions, most of which made a less striking and immediate contribution to the wealth of the mother-country. Tropical or subtropical colonies might even be regarded as more valuable than her territory in Europe. Thus in 1738 a pamphleteer argued that every British settler in the West Indies, by the British goods he consumed and the employment he gave to British shipping, contributed twenty times as much to the national wealth as he would at home. Four decades later in September 1779, at one of the most critical moments in Britain's history, George III argued that 'our [West Indian] Islands must be defended even at the risk of an invasion of this Island. If we lose our Sugar Islands it will be impossible to raise money to continue the war.'[1]

These very high contemporary estimates of the degree to which Britain (as distinct from individual Englishmen or Scots) profited from her West Indian possessions were often exaggerated. The tariff preference given in the British market to sugar from the British islands meant that the consumer paid higher prices than he need have done; and the capital attracted by these preferences into sugar production in the Caribbean could probably often have earned higher returns in some other field, especially if the cost of defending these colonies is set off against the profits made. Nevertheless there is no doubt of the extent of the British economic stake in these islands: in the years immediately before the American Revolution there were about £37 million of British money invested in the West Indies. Moreover in both Britain and France the tendency to overvalue the sugar islands was strengthened by the loss of their main colonies of settlement, actual or potential – French Canada and Louisiana in the Seven Years War, the British mainland colonies in America two decades later. These losses made small overseas possessions of purely commercial value appear not only the most lucrative but also the most manageable type of colony; so that the idea of an empire as a mechanism for the development and protection of trade was perhaps more firmly established at the end of the century than ever before. 'It would be making a great mistake', wrote the French Minister of Marine to the Governor of Martinique in 1765, 'to think of our colonies as French provinces separated only by the sea from the mother-country. They are absolutely nothing but commercial establish-ments.' Two decades later another French official made the same point more tersely – 'nothing need be considered but trade; that is the real mine of wealth'.

Such ideas were encouraged by the fact that the trade of all the great maritime powers with their colonies was increasing rapidly during the century, more rapidly than their trade in general. Thus commerce with America made up 19 per cent by value of all British overseas trade in 1715, but 34 per cent in 1785. For France the corresponding figures are 13 per cent and 28 per cent (though in this case most of the increase was concentrated in the two decades after 1763). In the same way Britain's trade with Africa and Asia, which represented 7 per cent of her total commerce in 1715, rose even more spectacularly to 19 per cent in 1785. For France, defeated in the struggle for power in India, the increase was merely from 5 per cent to 6 per cent. In other words by the end of this period over half of all Britain's foreign trade and over a third of that of France was being done with areas outside Europe. The same position can be seen in Portugal, which by the end of the century carried on almost half of all her trade with America, Africa and Asia. It was the revenues the Portuguese monarchy drew from the gold mines of Brazil which allowed it, after 1697, to rule without calling any further meetings of the *cortes* and running any risk, however small, of quasi-parliamentary control.

Europe was thus becoming less self-contained economically than ever before. An increasing proportion of her resources in manpower and capital was now employed in long-distance colo-nial trade. The distinction in wealth between the States of Western Europe which had important colonial possessions, and those of Germany, Italy, Scandinavia and Central Europe which had not, was becoming more apparent. The former benefited from colonial trade directly, in the markets it opened to their exports and the employment it provided for their ships and sailors, and also indirectly, in the ability it gave them to develop valuable re-export trades in tropical products – tea, coffee, tobacco, most of all sugar – to the parts of Europe which had no colonies, or no significant ones, of their own. Some French ports such as Bordeaux and Marseilles profited enormously in this way; while Portugal's entire commercial life depended very heavily, especially in the second half of the century, on her re-exports of Brazilian gold (mainly to Britain) and of Brazilian sugar. Several of the States without significant colonial empires made intermittent efforts to escape from what they saw, quite rightly, as a position of inferiority, for example by the creation of the Ostend Company by the Habsburgs in 1722 or of the Swedish and Danish East India Companies. But though bodies of this kind sometimes made considerable profits, at least for a number of years, they did not fundamentally alter the position. One or two countries, essentially Britain and Portugal, now looked outwards towards America, Africa or the East, at least as much as inwards towards Europe. They were thus ceasing to be European States in the fullest sense of the term. The parts of Europe which had virtually no direct trading links with the trans-oceanic world were still important. Even in the 1790s of all the goods exported across State boundaries three-quarters went merely from one European State to another. But that the favoured areas of Europe gained, and in more than a merely material sense, from their growing contacts with the world outside their own continent, there is no doubt. Here we see very clearly the contrast between the maritime western fringe, with the advantages given by access to the sea, and the landlocked bulk of the continent (see pp. 121–2).

From the western hemisphere Europe received during the eighteenth century a wide range of commodities, most of them in steadily increasing quantities, in exchange for her textiles, hardware, tools, paper, glass and other manufactured goods. From Canada came furs which were valuable in themselves and also formed the basis of an important hat-making industry. From Newfoundland came inexhaustible supplies of salt fish. This formed a staple export to the Catholic countries of the Mediterranean, where there was a demand which neither local supplies nor Norwegian stock-fish could satisfy. The New England colonies, however – Massachusetts, Connecticut, Rhode Island and others – though in many ways the most highly developed overseas possessions of any European State, produced little that was of use to Britain or to Europe in general. They were therefore criticized and suspected by many publicists. Undoubtedly they provided Britain with a very important market for manufactured goods; and the significance of this increased sharply during the first half of the century, a period during which British trade with many parts of Europe, notably the Mediterranean and the Levant, suffered considerably from French competition. But the New

England colonies supplied little that the mother-country could profitably import. As a result, it was calculated by one contemporary, Britain had in 1700–73 exported to them nearly £14 million more than she received from them. They sent much timber to the West Indies; but a long series of efforts to make them a source of naval stores had disappointing results. They exported considerable quantities of provisions and horses, but again only to the West Indies; and their important shipbuilding industry gave them the means of carrying on a large-scale illegitimate trade with the colonies of France or Spain, even when Britain was at war with these countries. Moreover the tentative industrial development of these colonies in the second half of the eighteenth century suggested that they might in the future compete with as well as supplement the economy of the mother-country. American industry was heavily handicapped, except in shipbuilding, by the high wages which prevailed in the colonies; but it offered at least an implicit threat to the British monopoly of the valuable colonial market for manufactured goods. Right down to the American Revolution, therefore, New England continued to fit awkwardly into the British colonial system.

Farther south, Virginia and Maryland produced large quantities of tobacco which was the basis of a great re-export trade. On the eve of the American Revolution of the 100 million pounds of tobacco which Britain was importing in a normal year 86 million found their way to other parts of Europe. Yet in the eighteenth century these colonies failed to maintain the prosperity and rapid development which had marked the first generations of their existence. Their planters thus became increasingly dependent on the British factors who marketed their crops and supplied them with manufactured goods and capital. Farther south again, however, in South Carolina and Georgia, the production of rice and indigo was increasing rapidly. The former was exported on a considerable scale to the Mediterranean and the latter used in the textile industries of Europe.

Almost all the islands of the West Indies based their economies on the production of sugar, varied in some cases by the cultivation of coffee, ginger, indigo, cochineal or cotton. These crops were produced by slave labour used on a very large scale; and a steady supply of slaves at reasonable prices was essential to the economic life of the area, particularly since the slave population did not maintain itself by natural increase. By the end of this period there were over half a million black slaves in the French Caribbean islands, about 400,000 in the British ones and perhaps 100,000 in the Spanish ones (sugar cultivation in Cuba, the largest Spanish island, did not become important until the last decades of the century). This meant that the economic connexion between the Caribbean and the slave-producing (or rather slave-exporting) parts of West Africa was very close. With the great slaving ports of Europe – Liverpool, Bristol and Nantes – these two areas formed the corners of the so-called 'triangular trade' which bulked large in much West European activity overseas in the eighteenth century. This trade could take a variety of shapes. In its simplest form it involved the export from Europe to West Africa of 'trade goods' such as textiles, firearms, beads and mirrors; the purchase with them of slaves; and the sale of these in the West Indies for sugar or sugar products such as rum or molasses. The slave trade was thus one in which the interval between investment and return was long. It was also a risky trade – slaves were not always easy to come by in West Africa and losses by disease on the transatlantic passage could be heavy. As a result it fell more and more in every country in the later eighteenth century into the hands of a relatively small number of large merchant houses. It remained throughout this period, however, an important branch of European commerce, and one which bulked large in the calculations of governments. It achieved this position not merely because it gave employment to ships and seamen and provided a rather minor outlet for manufactured goods; but far more because it was the basis of the whole economic life of the Caribbean and the southern colonies of North America, and to a lesser extent of that of Brazil and some parts of Spanish America as well.

Europe's trade with Latin America was quantitatively smaller than that with North America or the West Indies. It was none the less important. It brought to Europe dyestuffs and fine woods for cabinet-making from Central America and growing quantities of hides from the La Plata area. More important, it supplied her with gold and silver, as it had done for over two centuries. In Brazil the gold discoveries in Minas Gerais province in 1694 and on the Cuiaba river in 1719 paved the way for a great growth in Europe's gold imports between the 1750s and the 1770s, while throughout the century the silver production of Guanajuato in southern Mexico made it the largest mining town in the world. From Cadiz and Lisbon the precious metals of South America were diffused over Europe, largely by British, French, Genevan or German merchants or bankers, partly by smuggling. Broadly speaking France relied for her supplies of bullion during this period mainly upon silver from the Spanish colonies, Britain mainly though by no means entirely upon gold from Brazil. The importance of precious metals from America indeed far transcended the political boundaries of Europe. They played a great part in European trade with China and until fairly late in the century with India; while the Austrian *thalers* or *pataques* which became the most important form of currency in the Near East in the second half of this period were coined from silver imported from the western hemisphere.

The position was sharply different where Europe's trade with Africa and Asia was concerned. In America by the last decades of the century the number of European settlers (or settlers of European or part-European extraction) could be numbered in millions. In the British North American colonies the 250,000 inhabitants of 1700 had grown to ten times as many by the 1770s. It has been suggested that in Brazil some 500,000–600,000 people arrived in 1700–60 as immigrants from Portugal; and though this figure is almost certainly too high there is no doubt that the export of population was enormous for such a small country. In Asia by contrast resident Europeans were counted only in thousands, in some areas only in hundreds or even dozens. In British India there were in the 1780s about 5,000 of them protected by some 20,000 European soldiers; while in the princely States and the small settlements of the other European powers there were perhaps 2,000 more. At Canton, to which practically all European trade with China was confined, there were about 900–1,000 in 1720 and about 4,500 in 1785; but this was a constantly shifting merchant community without roots in the country. In 1745 there were only ninety resident European Portuguese (in a total population of 13,000) at Maçao, which had been a Portuguese possession for two centuries. Russia's vast Siberian colony, the only part of Asia in which large-scale white settlement was a practical possibility, remained throughout this period thinly peopled and neglected. Tentative efforts by Catherine II to increase its Russian population had little result, partly because of her unwillingness to see the existing social structure of European Russia weakened by a large exodus of peasants to the east. At the end of the century there were probably still fewer than 600,000 people in all living in Siberia. In the whole of Asia excluding Siberia there may have been about 50,000 Europeans in all in the 1740s and perhaps 75,000 by 1800. In Africa there were European trading establishments in the seaports of the Barbary States and Egypt, a few Spanish strongholds such as Ceuta and Oran on the coasts of Morocco and Algeria, slave-trading bases in the Gulf of Guinea, and decaying Portuguese fortresses on the coasts of Angola and East Africa (the most important of these, Mombasa, was finally lost to the Arabs of Oman in 1730). Apart from the Dutch colony at the Cape of Good Hope which was beginning to show important expansive tendencies (it had a white population of about 12,000 by the 1750s) there was no permanent European settlement. The majority of Africans still ended their lives without having seen a white man or been influenced by European ideas or techniques.

Again America provided a great and rapidly growing market for European goods while Asia and Africa consumed only small quantities of them: the Asian countries, above all China, because they were self-sufficient and unattracted by what Europe had to offer. The result was that the growing trade with China was made possible only by the expenditure at Canton of very large sums in silver. It was only from the 1780s that Indian opium began to emerge as a commodity which Europeans could supply and for which there was a growing Chinese demand. Africa for her part was simply too poor and inaccessible to be a large market for most European products. Finally and most important of all, in Asia alone of the non-European parts of the world were there indigenous States capable of withstanding serious European pressure with any hope of success.

The influence of these facts on Europe's trade with Africa and the East was immense. They meant in the first place that it was much smaller in volume than that with America. The British East India Company sent an average of only eleven ships a year to India in the early part of the century and only twenty a year in its middle decades. In spite of the legal monopoly which it enjoyed of Anglo-Chinese as of Anglo-Indian trade it sent only seven ships to Canton in 1751, only eight in 1776, and only twenty-one in 1789 when this aspect of its activities was increasing very rapidly. These figures contrast sharply with the hundreds of British ships which sailed westwards each year across the Atlantic. (In the 1730s it was claimed that trade with Jamaica employed 300 British merchant ships and that that with the little island of Barbados alone gave employment to a thousand seamen.) In the same way the Dutch East India Company sent on the average only about twenty-nine ships each year to all its eastern possessions in the first half of the century, a number which if anything fell slightly from the 1750s onwards; by contrast trade with the small Dutch South American colony of Surinam alone employed by the 1760s an annual average of sixty to seventy ships. These figures taken in isolation may give a somewhat unbalanced impression of the situation. It was possible for a trade to be very profitable even if the number of ships itemployed was relatively small. The trade with China which brought silk, tea and porcelain to Europe was the most rapidly growing branch of all European commerce by the end of this period and one in which large gains were made. As early as the 1750s more than half of the annual investment of the Dutch East India Company was often being sunk in this branch of its activities. Nevertheless the contrast in scale between trade with Asia and that with the western hemisphere was striking and important.

European trade with the East also differed from that with the Americas in that it was for the most part in the hands of a number of privileged trading companies. These were semi-official bodies which enjoyed great political influence, and their activities are fundamental to the history of Europe's relations with Asia in the seventeenth and eighteenth centuries. Companies of this kind were by no means unknown in trade with America. The Spanish government created a series of them during this period, of which the Caracas Company of 1728 was the most important and successful. Pombal made similar experiments in the regulation of Portuguese trade with Brazil. Nevertheless they had never in transatlantic commerce anything approaching the importance which they possessed in that with Asia. Moreover all the East India Companies traded not merely between Europe and Asia but between different parts of Asia – between India and the Red Sea and Persian Gulf, India and South-East Asia, the East Indies and Japan. This 'country trade' meant that the Dutch East India Company, for example, was involved in a complex web of exchanges spread from Mocha to Nagasaki: all these companies were therefore significant, to varying extents, not merely in Asia's trade with Europe but also in seaborne trade within Asia.

The British East India Company experienced during this period perhaps the strangest and most romantic turn of fortune which has ever overtaken any trading organization. From the 1750s onwards it was drawn, without any conscious plan and often against the will of its directors in London, into military conquest and territorial expansion on an immense scale. Within a few years the enterprise of its servants made it the dominant power in a large area of South India and, more important, in the province of Bengal (see p. 336).

These developments, it must be stressed, were unforeseen and undesired so far as both the Company and the British government were concerned. It was not until the last years of the century that both ceased to think of the British role in India as a primarily commercial one to be sustained by the use only of a minimum of military and naval force. Sometimes, therefore, opportunities of territorial gain were deliberately rejected: in both 1760 and 1784 areas in South India which had been occupied during struggles with native rulers were returned when these ended. Nevertheless by the 1760s the East India Company was ceasing, at least so far as its activities in India itself were concerned, to be primarily a trading organization. British pressure on the Indian States, partly to counter the French threat in the middle years of the century and partly in a simple quest for greater commercial privileges, was now undermining and destroying some of them – first Bengal in the decade after the battle of Plassey, then Oudh and the Carnatic. The economic basis of the Company's activities was ceasing to be trade and becoming the collection of taxes in the areas it controlled; while by lending money to local rulers and sometimes also supplying them with troops it was being drawn step by step into deeper territorial and political involvement in India. The personal interests of its representatives, war-like soldiers, ambitious governors, avaricious creditors of Indian potentates, pulled it constantly in the same direction – a fact of real import-ance since the very slow communications with England inevitably gave these representatives a great deal of independent initiative. The temptations to which they were exposed were certainly enor-mous. After the victory at Plassey even the most junior of the British officers involved received the then very large sum of £3,000 each, while Clive himself benefited to the tune of £234,000. During this formative period of British rule mere survival in Bengal for a decade or so was almost a guarantee that an officer or official could return home with a fortune. Yet the

Company was slow to transform itself into an effective political and administrative organism. For nearly a generation it remained an ineffective hybrid, unable to put its finances on a satisfactory basis, to make the large revenues it drew from taxation cover its administrative and commercial expenses, or to prevent many of its servants from making fortunes by dubious means. Not until the India Act of 1784 and the reforms undertaken by Lord Cornwallis in Bengal in the 1790s did the foundations of the great administrative structure of nineteenth-century British India begin to be laid.

To the French *Compagnie des Indes Orientales* the period brought a very different fate. Until the 1740s it sometimes sent more ships to the East than the British one. After that its decline was rapid; and in fact ever since its reorganization in 1719 its finances had been shaky. Defeated by its British rival and heavily in debt, it went into liquidation in 1769. Revived in 1785, it continued to maintain a narrow foothold in India until its remaining factories fell to the British during the revolutionary wars and, freed from the cares of administering large territories, probably made a small but genuine profit. As a serious factor in the history of India, however, it had ceased to count. It sent one or two ships to Canton each year, and in 1778 a French consulate was established there to protect its trade; but here too it was decisively inferior to the British company. The Danish Asiatic Company and the Swedish East India Company managed to prolong their existence throughout the century and to maintain small trading-stations on the Indian coast. Neither had great economic importance and neither attempted to become a political or military force in the East. Nor had the Royal Philippine Company, founded by Charles III of Spain in 1785 on the ruins of the old Caracas Company, any great significance.

On the other hand the Dutch East India Company, the most successful trading organization of the seventeenth century, in some ways increased its importance in this period. Until the 1730s it sent more ships to the East than any other trading company, although by then its 'country trade' was clearly in decline by comparison with that of the British. Like its British counterpart it found itself drawn almost insensibly into the assumption of political control over wide and wealthy territories. In Java, the centre of its power in the East, a long and complicated series of struggles in 1740–57 consolidated its position. One of the two main Javanese States, Mataram, became its vassal after 1743. A revolt against it in the other, Bantam, was suppressed in the 1750s. In 1765 a war with the native ruler of Ceylon ended in the fall of his capital and gave the company control of the main sugar-producing areas of the island. Efforts at expansion in the comparatively inhospitable islands of Borneo and Sumatra had less success.

Like the British company, however, the Dutch one tended to become less effective as a trading organization as its territorial power expanded. During the first half of the century it lost its hitherto leading position in the import of pepper into Europe; and during its second half it could never challenge the leading position of its British rival in the expanding tea trade of Canton. Its outlook was monopolistic and restrictive and its organization complex and cumbersome; it aimed consistently at selling small quantities of colonial products in Europe at the highest possible price. In the seventeenth century it had deliberately restricted the production of spices and sugar in order to keep up prices. From the 1730s onwards it extended this policy to the newly introduced crop of coffee, the production of which in Java was rapidly increasing. The rigidity of its structure, the conservatism of its ideas and the growing competition of the more enterprising British company, made its financial position steadily more difficult. In the last years of its life, before its final collapse in 1795, it was being maintained in existence only by the indirect aid of the Dutch taxpayer and was borrowing to pay dividends to its shareholders.

Europe's imports from Asia were important, but in a somewhat different way from those which she drew from America. From the East, as from the West, came raw materials for her industries and foodstuffs for her people – cotton from Bengal and the Near East, raw silk from Persia and China, sugar and spices from the East Indies, tea from China. In addition came manufactured goods, the only ones which Europe imported on an appreciable scale – fine textiles from India, silks and porcelain from China. These imports were small in quantity but had a psychological and artistic importance out of all proportion to their bulk. From them thousands of Europeans who had never set foot in Asia derived their ideas (often very misleading ones) of the East. Their beauty and the craftsmanship they displayed stimulated European manufacturers to imitate and finally in some respects to surpass them.

The rulers of Western Europe were well aware of the advantages given them by their overseas trade and colonial possessions. In particular they realized that the wealth thus placed at their disposal gave them an important superiority over the large but relatively undeveloped States of the east and central parts of the continent. 'The House of Austria,' wrote the Duc de Choiseul in 1760, 'Russia, the King of Prussia, are only second-rate States, since they can make war only when they are subsidised by the commercial powers.'[2] This was an exaggeration. The events of the next generation were to show that it was not necessary to possess maritime strength or colonial territories in order to have great, even dominant, influence in Europe. Nevertheless the profits of trade and empire gave the colonial powers, Britain in particular, the means of buying allies and hiring armies on the continent in a way that would otherwise have been impossible.

Nor were the peoples concerned indifferent to the significance of their overseas possessions. In Britain indeed public opinion if anything exaggerated their value and was too sensitive to any possible threat to them, while regarding almost with indifference great territorial changes in Europe. The excitement aroused in the 1730s by Spanish 'depredations' in the Caribbean, or in 1770 by a Spanish threat to the Falkland Islands, contrasts strikingly with the apathy which greeted the first partition of Poland. In the United Provinces also, increasingly dominated as the century wore on by the psychology of 'safety and three per cent', the preservation of the country's commercial and colonial position seemed more important than that of a largely mythical balance of power in Europe. Even in France attention and interest which in the reign of Louis XIV had been concentrated almost entirely on the affairs of Europe was now being increasingly diverted towards events in America and the East.

Both governments and peoples, when they turned their eyes outside Europe, looked first of all to the Americas, particularly in the first half of the century. There were a number of reasons why the western hemisphere should attract so much more attention than Asia or Africa. As has been seen, trade with it was far more extensive than with any other part of the non-European world. It had been for nearly two centuries a recognized field of international rivalry, a rivalry whose importance was increasing as Anglo-French conflicts became more acute. Moreover communications with America, however slow and imperfect, were far more rapid and reliable than those with the East. It was possible for a well-informed Englishman or Frenchman to have a knowledge of events in Canada or the Caribbean which was not hopelessly out of date. By contrast news from India, still more from China or Indonesia, seemed to come almost from another planet.

So close were the human and intellectual contacts between Western Europe and America in the later eighteenth century that a certain parallelism is visible, if not in their political development at least in their political aspirations. In each continent can be seen an increasing effort to modernize and rationalize administrative and financial methods. This was exemplified in British America by the legislation of the 1760s which attempted to enforce a more rigorous application of the Navigation System, and in the Spanish colonies by the remarkable efforts to improve the administration of Mexico by José de Galvez, *visitador* there in 1765–71. Strivings of this kind can be seen as the transatlantic equivalent of Enlightened Despotism in Europe. In each continent these changes were powerfully opposed by vested interests and local patriotism, forces which disrupted the British Empire in the 1770s and had almost disrupted that of the Habsburgs by 1790. In each the importance of the Press, and of public opinion organized and mobilized for political purposes, was increasing rapidly. In some respects at least an Atlantic civilization now existed, uniting Western Europe with North and to a lesser degree South America. The ocean, far from being a barrier to the movement of men and ideas, positively facilitated their transmission, for as has been seen (p. 93) until the coming of railways travel was normally swifter by sea than by land. It was usually far easier for a man or an idea to go from London to Boston or Philadelphia than to Constantinople or Moscow, or even Rome or Berlin.

Above all America was now the home of great numbers of emigrants from Western Europe; and conflicts there were decided in the main by forces recruited in the West European States. Campaigns on the Hudson or in the Antilles were fought by Englishmen and Frenchmen and might influence directly and immediately the lives of tens of thousands of English or French colonists. Campaigns in the Deccan or Bengal were fought largely by sepoys under European officers; they seemed to affect only the power and profits of two great trading companies.

The result of this concentration on the western hemisphere was that until quite late in this period no government in Europe devoted much attention to territorial expansion in Asia. Not until the 1760s did it become clear that a great Indian Empire had for some time been within the reach of both Britain and France, while until the end of the century the rapidly growing weakness of the Chinese Empire passed largely unnoticed in the West. By the last decades of this period, however, the indifference with which the British and French governments had hitherto contemplated the possibility of expansion in Asia was slowly beginning to be replaced by a more interested and acquisitive attitude. The victories of Clive and Coote in India showed their countrymen what could now be achieved, and stimulated France to seek elsewhere for compensations for what she had lost there. The result was what one historian has called a 'swing to the East' in the colonial and commercial activities of both States. This did not mean that Asia replaced America as the main focus of European overseas expansion; but from the 1760s onwards it received more attention than ever before from the governments and public opinion of these countries.

This rising interest in Eastern affairs showed itself in a number of ways. It contributed to a new burst of speculation about the possibility of discovering a north-west passage, a practicable sea route uniting the Atlantic and Pacific round the north coast of America. Of this the most important and enduring result was the discoveries made by Captain James Cook on his last voyage in 1776–79. It also stimulated a great deal of detailed survey and exploration work in the Pacific and Indian oceans: no less than ten hydrographic expeditions were sent from France to the East in 1784–89.

The new attitude also led to more serious attempts than ever before to extend European influence to the States of South-East Asia, hitherto almost untouched by it. In Burma the English East India Company held the port of Negrais for a few years in the 1750s; while a French shipyard was in operation at Rangoon for a decade after 1766. Warren Hastings, the greatest of all British proconsuls in India, made a short-lived effort to establish commercial relations with Cochin-China in 1778–79. In 1787 Louis XVI, by a treaty signed at Versailles, promised its ruler, who had been deposed two years earlier, help in recovering his throne. Much more important, however, was the active interest which was being taken in Paris from the 1770s onwards in the possibility of annexing Egypt. Wealthy, strategically placed and easily defended, the country seemed ideally suited to compensate France for what she had lost in India and the Caribbean. The growing weakness of the Ottoman Empire made it easy to argue that France should take Egypt as part of a general partition of Turkish territories among the States of Europe. The gross misgovernment of its rulers, the Mamluk Beys, who were in theory vassals of the Sultan, meant that the country would be easy to conquer. The result of all these factors was a series of proposals from 1770 onwards for a French seizure of Egypt, proposals which paved the way for the Napoleonic invasion of 1798.

None of these British or French attempts at expansion in the East had much immediate success outside India. The trading stations which were set up soon fell into decay. The treaties signed with native rulers were broken or never carried out. Nevertheless a change had taken place in the colonial policies of the two States during the last decades of the century, one with important implications for the future of large parts of the world. The preoccupation with America as the greatest, almost the only, area of European expansion overseas, which had marked their policies in the first half of this period, had now been tempered by a realization of the opportunities available in the East. For the first time in history it was becoming possible for one or two favoured nations to think of themselves not merely as European or even Atlantic powers but as potential world powers.

Europe's relations with the outside world in the eighteenth century affected not only her economy and politics but also her intellectual and artistic life. Exploration and colonization, the publication of increasingly full and detailed accounts of newly discovered lands, gave Europeans more clearly than ever before a sense of the immense variety of human habits and customs and of the difficulty of passing simple judgements on them. In particular contact with China, with its wealth, its apparently stable and enlightened government and its enormously long recorded history, challenged many received ideas and stimulated the growth of new attitudes. China was disturbing to Europeans in a number of ways. Efforts to reconcile Chinese and biblical chronology undermined hitherto unchallenged assumptions about the past. By the middle of the seventeenth century scholars were being forced to accept a date for the beginning of Chinese history much earlier than the traditional one for the Flood: in other words China had been inhabited before the days of Noah and the Flood had been a merely local event. More important, the Chinese had evolved a workable and indeed highly successful system of morality which was completely secular, even political, and which did not depend at all on religion in any normal European sense of the term. Such an achievement threw doubt on the hitherto virtually unchallenged assumption that revealed religion was the only source of true moral ideas and the only barrier between society and the anarchy which must follow a breakdown in morals. Moreover the separation of morality from religion opened the way to the dangerous idea that morals might be relative, not absolute, that each people might have a different moral system which suited its particular history and needs. Finally China appeared to Europeans as a striking proof that religious tolerance did not necessarily weaken or divide a State. The *Dictionnaire historique et critique* of Pierre Bayle (1697), a work which was to become one of the foundations of the eighteenth-century Enlightenment, illustrates well the way in which Chinese achievements could be used by critics of European religious obscurantism and intolerance to support their case.

Europe's interest in China had been developing throughout the seventeenth century, in its later decades with increasing speed. The first attempt at a translation of Confucius appeared in Paris in 1687. Ten years later the great German scholar Leibniz provided, in his *Novissima Sinica*, not merely a compendium of up-to-date information about the country (drawn largely from Jesuit sources) but also a powerful plea for further study of so fascinating and important a society. In the two or three generations which followed this interest grew in scope and intensity. The philosopher Christian Wolff, the most important figure in German intellectual life in the first half of the eighteenth century, was an admirer of the Chinese: his efforts to compare Chinese and Christian morality cost him his chair at the University of Halle in 1723. François Quesnay, the leading figure in the first generation of Physiocrats, was deeply influenced by what he thought to be Chinese practice in government and economic life: his followers referred to him admiringly as 'the European Confucius'. In the arts the same process is visible. The forty-nine volumes of Chinese paintings presented to Louis XIV by a Jesuit missionary in 1697 were only the most striking example of an influx which by the early and middle decades of the eighteenth century was beginning to influence seriously such artists as Watteau and Boucher. The German architect Fischer von Erlach, in his *Entwurff einer historischen Architektur* (1721) provided 'the first appreciative account of Chinese architecture to be published in Europe'; and by the middle of the century many rulers were building new palaces, or at least 'porcelain rooms' in existing ones, in what they or their architects imagined to be the Chinese style. This admiration for things Chinese reached its climax in Voltaire's *Essai sur les Mœurs* (1756), which presented Confucius as an anticipation of the *philsophes* of the eighteenth century and used China's alleged virtues, often unscrupulously, as a stick with which to beat the France of his own day. There were important figures in European intellectual life who did not share this uncritical admiration. In particular the more radical writers of the Enlightenment in France – Helvétius, d'Holbach, Diderot, most notably Rousseau – were all in varying degrees negative in their attitude to China. Nevertheless the dominant tone of European comment on the country and its government was favourable, sometimes very strongly so, especially during the first half of the eighteenth century. This comment was, however, still based on very limited and inadequate knowledge. In particular the widespread belief that China was dominated by rational and enlightened thought, that mysticism and superstition had no foothold there, was wildly untrue. The translation of Confucius nevertheless supported this misconception; while the works of the much more mystical and equally influential Lao Tzu, which would have done much to explode it, remained inaccessible to European readers.

The influence on European intellectual life of the rest of Asia was relatively unimportant. Mohammed had already been introduced to Europe through the interest of the seventeenth century in Turkish and Arabic studies. Zoroaster was made accessible by the translation of the *Zend-Avesta* which the French scholar Anquetil du Perron published in 1771. From the 1780s onwards Charles Wilkins and Sir William Jones made available English translations of the main Hindu classics – the *Bhagavad-Ghita*, the *Hitopadesa* and the *Sakuntala*. The growth of British power in India meant a greater need for men with a knowledge of Indian languages and of Persian, the main administrative and diplomatic language of much of the peninsula. But the Ottoman Empire,

Persia and India had no great intellectual or artistic impact on Europe. This was partly because they were all easier of access than China and thus less likely to be the object of flattering misconceptions; but also because, unlike China, they were all politically weak. Their civilizations lacked the prestige and attractive power which strength alone could give.

By the 1760s this situation was changing. By then there were clear signs that Europeans were beginning to think of themselves as members of a civilization inherently superior to any to be found in Asia. More and more the stability of Asiatic societies began to look like stagnation and the enlightened monarchy of China to seem merely another and not very impressive form of despotism. More and more, with the growth of Europe's political and military power in different parts of Asia, the great civilizations of the East began to seem poor, weak and vulnerable rather than as in the past rich, powerful and attractive. To a Europe in which religious tradition and patriarchal authority were increasingly questioned societies in which these forces were still completely unchallenged seemed obviously unable to produce the free and creative individual, intellectually daring and with an active sense of civic responsibility, who was the ideal of the Enlightenment. By the last years of this period we are clearly moving into a nineteenth-century situation in which Europe not merely led the world but felt proudly conscious of its right and responsibility to do so.

The intellectual influence of America on Europe in the eighteenth century was quite different from that of Asia. The American Indians, in either the northern or the southern half of the continent, could be presented to Europe by sympathetic missionaries as typifying the virtues inherent in man in a 'state of nature' or even as having many of the characteristics of primitive Christianity before it became corrupted by power and wealth. Alternatively they could be seen by more radical thinkers as showing that it was possible for good and virtuous societies to flourish without priests, kings or great social and economic inequalities, since they were supported by a natural morality founded on the good instincts and guiding reason which nature had implanted in all men. But until the achievement of independence by the British colonies America seemed in general a less attractive and less interesting model than China and a less effective stick with which to beat existing institutions in Europe.

The emergence in the early 1780s of an independent though as yet unstable confederation of the former British colonies completely changed this position. It was realized by some far-seeing contemporaries that the new State possessed material potentialities of a kind unknown and unattainable in Europe. It would become, wrote one, 'the Arbitress of the commercial, and perhaps . . . the Mediatrix of peace, and of the political business of the world, . . . the principal leading Power in Europe, in regulating the courses of the rest, and in settling the common centre of all'.[3] Of greater immediate importance was the stimulus which successful revolution in America gave to the forces making for change in Europe. Events across the Atlantic seemed a victory for liberty and natural rights, for the ideas which were increasingly challenging the *ancien régime*. Moreover this victory appeared to have been won by an egalitarian, predominantly agricultural and hence 'natural' society over the forces of tradition and social conservatism. It therefore appealed powerfully to emotions and prejudices increasingly widespread among the educated classes of Europe. In Spain, where 'enlightened' ideas were relatively weak, and in parts of Italy, this appeal aroused little response. But in Great Britain, the Netherlands, France and even Germany, the revolution in America aroused great interest. The immediacy of its impact, the extent to which it gave vicarious expression to resentments and tensions bottled up in the old world, are symbolized in the reaction of Count Vittorio Alfieri, perhaps the greatest poet then alive. When he dedicated his play *Bruto Primo* to Washington, or wrote in 1781–83 the five great odes grouped under the title of *America Libera*, he was not merely expressing approval of the rebellion of the thirteen colonies (of which he had no particular knowledge). He was rather throwing down the gauntlet to the government of his native State of Savoy-Piedmont, one of the most conservative in Europe.

For all these reasons the independence of British America was recognized clearly and immediately as something new, as a social and political experiment which was adding a new element to the collective experience of humanity. As such it aroused in the 1780s and 1790s a great volume of comment and discussion. Much of this was favourable, sometimes uncritically so. Some was pessimistic, jaundiced by the cultural backwardness of America and the persistence of Negro slavery there. Some was well-informed and the product of direct observation; much was based merely on theories and *a priori* judgements. All of it, however, was convinced of the immense importance of the subject. Not for well over a century was North America again to receive such attention, it might almost be said such reverence, in Europe. The 'spiritual flight from the Old Régime' which the achievement of American independence encouraged among radicals and reformers all over Western Europe was to be of great importance in the events of the next two decades there, though its exact significance is still very much a matter for debate.

The eighteenth century, which saw the bonds uniting Europe and her colonies drawn in many ways closer than ever before, also saw an unprecedented growth of hostility on moral grounds to overseas expansion. The argument that colonial empires as they developed were likely to involve injustice and oppression, an overriding of the rights of their aboriginal inhabitants by violent and unscrupulous conquerors, was not new. In the eighteenth century, however, it was more frequently advanced and more widely accepted than ever before. Montesquieu in his *Lettres Persanes* (1721), Swift in his *Gulliver's Travels* (1726), as well as many less well-known writers, satirized what they regarded as the immoral tendencies of overseas expansion. In Spain the statesman Macanaz in his *Testamento de España* (1740) showed clear signs of remorse for the methods by which the Spanish Empire in America had been acquired. In Britain the scandals of the East India Company's administration of its territories from the 1760s onwards produced a crop of protests which culminated in the protracted trial (1788–95) of Warren Hastings on charges of corruption and oppression. The attitude of many of his countrymen was summed up in Horace Walpole's remark, in a letter of 1783, that 'no man ever went to the East Indies with good intentions'. Such judgements, though often sharpened by envy of the wealth which lucky or unscrupulous 'nabobs' were able to bring home with them, were in part at least the result of a genuine repugnance for the methods by which this wealth had been gained. Simultaneously the anti-colonial feeling which had always been powerful in France, and which was now being fanned by the growing tendency to exalt the virtues of primitive non-Europeans at the expense of an over-civilized and over-sophisticated Europe, was expressed in an extreme form in one of the most popular and influential books of the century, G. T. F. Raynal's *Histoire . . . des Établissements et du Commerce des Européens dans les deux Indes* (1770). This book was also one of the first important expressions of what was to become the most influential and emotionally charged aspect of these anti-colonial attitudes – the attack on the slave trade. Almost every great figure of the Enlightenment (Hume is the only major exception) condemned this trade on moral grounds; and by the end of this period in Britain it was also being attacked, with considerably greater effect, by the evangelical and often emotional Christianity which was to be a major force in the nation's life for the next half-century or more. The formation of the London Abolition Committee in 1787 therefore marked the emergence of a significant new pressure group.

But anti-colonial ideas were never powerful enough to dominate the policies of States. The emotions which underlay them were sincere; and the achievement of American independence stimulated widespread cynicism about the permanence of great colonial empires. Nevertheless at no time during the eighteenth century did any government propose to relinquish voluntarily any important overseas possession. On the contrary, the development and increasing ramifications of Europe's economic life were making it less and less practicable for her to relax her growing control over the extra-European world. The significance of that world in European life was by the end of this period greater than ever before, greater in many ways than it was to be during the first three-quarters of the century which followed.

NOTES AND REFERENCES

1 *Correspondence of George III*, ed. Sir J. Fortescue (London, 1927), vol. IV. No. 2773.

2 A. Bourguet, *Le Duc de Choiseul et l'alliance espagnole* (Paris, 1906), p. 159.

3 T. Pownall, *A Memorial . . . to the Sovereigns of Europe* (London, 1780), pp. 77, 92.

14

EDUCATION AND CULTURAL LIFE

Schools and universities developed comparatively little during this period. In some countries the quality of formal education may even have declined. At the school level, especially at that of the primary school, shortage of trained teachers and money was often a serious obstacle to improvement. A still more serious one was the widespread feeling that it was unnecessary and might be dangerous to educate men who must gain their living by manual labour, in other words the great bulk of society. This idea was put forward by writers so different as the cynical Bernard Mandeville in his *The Fable of the Bees* (1714) and the fervent Jean-Jacques Rousseau in his *Nouvelle Héloise* (1762). It was universally agreed that education must be fitted to the social position of the recipients and designed to keep them in it: any idea of it as an engine of social mobility was rejected by almost everyone. 'Education should teach princes to reign,' wrote Holbach in his *Système social* (1773), 'the ruling classes to distinguish themselves by their merit and virtue, the rich to use their riches well, the poor to live by honest industry.' Even Diderot, the most radical of all the greater thinkers of the Enlightenment, though he insisted as hardly any other did on the right of the lower classes to literacy, wished to reserve secondary education for the nobility and 'comfortable citizens of the third estate'.

In Catholic countries the lack of teachers and other resources was partially alleviated, since there a high proportion of the teachers was normally provided by religious Orders. The Piarists in South Germany and the Habsburg provinces, the Oratorians in France, the Jesuits almost everywhere were particularly active in this respect. The control exercised by the clergy over the schools of Spain and Portugal was complete. In much of Italy also their influence, though resented and challenged by many intellectuals and statesmen, was very great. In France, where the majority of village schoolmasters were laymen, clerics had by the end of this period come to dominate education in the towns. The monks, nuns and priests who played so great a part in forming the youth of Catholic Europe very often made no charge for their work (this was usually the case in France for example): with all their faults they provided a body of teachers, conscientious if often conservative in their methods, which at this level most Protestant States could hardly match.

Several governments made efforts during this period to spread basic education to the majority at least of their male subjects. In France Louis XIV ordered in 1698 that each rural community should establish a school which all children were to attend up to the age of fourteen, and should pay the salary of a master to teach in it. This order was repeated in 1724, when the parents or guardians of children who did not go to school were threatened with prosecution. These edicts, though strongly supported by the Church, were not effectively enforced. In 1762 an anonymous author, possibly Diderot, estimated that there were two million boys of school age (6–16) in France, of whom less than a tenth received an effective education. This was certainly too gloomy a view of the situation. By 1789 every parish in Champagne was said to possess a school; and in what later became the *département* of the Aube 72 per cent of men and 22 per cent of women could read. These figures, however, were above the average for the country as a whole; and a very large part of the population, particularly of the female population, was still unable and often unwilling to acquire even the rudiments of education. La Chalotais, the procurator-general of the *Parlement* of Rennes, put forward in 1763, as the expulsion of the Jesuits from France was clearly approaching, the most elaborate proposal produced in any State during this period for a uniform and national system of education: but this remained only a dream. When a few years later Turgot urged Louis XV to set up a council which would control all educational institutions in France this advice bore equally little fruit. In Russia, where the shortage of trained men of all kinds was more acute than in any other major European State, the first effort to develop a system of primary education was made by

Peter I. In 1714 he ordered the establishment throughout the country of 'cyphering schools' to teach arithmetic and geometry, largely with the idea of producing the technicians needed to carry out his plans of military and economic development. The difficulties of realizing such a scheme were very great. Little more than forty such schools ever existed and in 1726, the year after the Tsar's death, only about 500 pupils were attending them. Under his immediate successors, though the idea of creating a system of primary education was not forgotten, very little was done to this end. Even Catherine II, whose last years saw some expansion of educational facilities in the towns, could do little to solve the intractable problem of extending some modicum of education to the peasants.

It was in Prussia, Scotland and the Habsburg hereditary lands that primary education was made genuinely available to the mass of the population. Frederick II made it compulsory for his subjects in 1763; and although this order was not completely enforced, by the end of the century the inhabitants of Prussia were better educated than those of any other country. In the Lowlands of Scotland an almost equally wide dissemination of basic education was achieved. This came about without legal compulsion or State action of any kind, through the influence of the Church and the pressure of public opinion. In Austria Joseph II, building on foundations laid by his mother, made strenuous and largely successful efforts to establish a system of universal primary education for his subjects. This was the first effort anywhere to use education as an aid to political unification; it therefore looked forward to very important and potentially dangerous nineteenth-century developments. In England by contrast education for the masses remained throughout this period comparatively backward. This was because the widespread distrust of strong central government made a State-controlled educational system impossible, because the position was complicated by the mutual antipathy of Established Church and Dissenters, and simply because popular demand for education was weak. The charity school and Sunday school movements made efforts, often devoted and not altogether unsuccessful, to spread a tincture of book-learning among the lower strata of society, above all in the towns. These attempts, however, were inspired by the desire to combat vice, drunkenness and irreligion, rather than by any belief in the desirability of knowledge for its own sake.

Primary education, like almost everything else in eighteenth-century Europe, thus varied enormously in scope and quality in different countries, from the relative efficiency of Prussia or Austria to the backwardness of Russia or Spain. Variations almost as marked can be seen in the continent's secondary schools and universities. The grammar and public schools of England, unadventurous in their teaching methods and still anchored to a curriculum dominated by the classical languages, contrasted strongly with the establishments for vocational training in such subjects as navigation, engineering and medicine established by Peter I in Russia and continued by his successors. These in turn were very different from the *collèges* to be found in every local capital in France, which were dominated by religious Orders, most of all the Jesuits until their expulsion in 1764 (see p. 454), and taught with greater efficiency a curriculum almost as narrow as that of the English grammar schools.

Secondary education developed and changed during this period more than its poor relation, the primary schools. From Locke and his followers it derived an emphasis (which increased as the century drew to a close) on education through the senses as well as through the printed word, on the importance of teaching practical accomplishments and developing useful abilities. Ideas and assumptions of this kind can be seen in such works as Saint-Pierre's *Projet de Perfectionnement de l'Éducation* (1728): they appear in their most extreme form in Rousseau's *Émile* (1762). Through pioneers such as Basedow, Pestalozzi and Froebel they were to influence the whole future development of educational techniques. From the scientific progress of the later seventeenth century secondary education also derived a high idea of the importance of mathematics and a perhaps exaggerated estimate of the subject's power to teach the art of logical reasoning. The development of economic life led to increasing demands for the teaching of such obviously useful subjects as book-keeping, navigation, geography and modern languages. At a higher social level it was sometimes argued that members of the various European nobilities spent far too much time in childhood on the study of Latin and merely decorative social accomplishments, and that to fit them to act as an effective ruling class they must devote more attention to studies which would give them some real understanding of political and economic problems. These new ideas and pressures were not easy to reconcile with a system of education which was still, over most of the continent, based upon the study of the classics and dominated by clerical influences. To some extent they were met by the foundation of new establishments designed to provide a purely professional and technical training. Such were the schools of mining set up at Brunswick in 1745, at Fribourg in 1755, at Clausthal in 1775 and in Paris in 1778; or the school of architecture created at Berlin in 1799; or the commercial schools and schools of agriculture which began to come into existence, notably in Germany, in the second half of the century.

More important, however, was the influence of these new demands in modifying the curricula of existing colleges and grammar schools and in stimulating the creation of new ones designed to provide a broader education. In Prussia the study of French was introduced into the secondary schools in 1763. Almost simultaneously French schoolboys began to receive for the first time some instruction in their own language and literature. In Scotland the foundation of Perth Academy in 1760 was one of the first recognitions of the need for schools with a more realistic curriculum. In England the 'dissenting academies', founded to educate the non-Anglican part of the population which was still by law debarred from public office, were at the height of their reputation in the third quarter of the century. The best of them, like the famous one at Warrington (1757–86) reached higher standards than the stagnant universities; and almost all the two hundred or so which existed by the end of this period provided a much wider education than the often moribund grammar schools. In Germany the first *Realschule*, designed to provide an education which would include such subjects as modern languages, geography and book-keeping for boys intended for a career in business or commerce, was founded by J. J. Hecker at Berlin in 1747. The fact that Germany played a leading role in adapting education to the needs of an age increasingly influenced by commerce and technology, and that France notably lagged behind, was of the highest importance for the future. In the second half of the century the schoolmasters of the German States were, for the most part quite unconsciously, helping to set their nation on the road to future greatness, indeed to leadership of Europe. In French schools by contrast can already be seen much of that intellectual rigidity and academic conservatism which was later to have profound repercussions on the country's political life and even her international position.

The universities of Europe differed at least as much as its schools – in their size, in the composition of their student bodies, in the ease with which they accepted new methods of teaching or recognized the importance of new subjects. On the one hand were a small group of institutions which were genuine centres of research and at which first-class teaching, at least in certain subjects, was to be had. These were among the most important factors in the intellectual life of the age. They included Leyden in the first half of the century and Göttingen, Edinburgh, and to a lesser extent Vienna, Halle and Glasgow in its later decades. Göttingen is of particular interest as the finest example of the new type of university which was now beginning to develop. In the emphasis it laid on the physical sciences, in the degree to which it was controlled by the Hanoverian State, and still more in its remarkably successful combination of teaching and research, it pointed the way, more than any of its contemporaries, towards the universities of the present day. The best index of its vitality and activity is the growth of its library. Though the university was founded only in 1737 the library, within less than a generation, included 60,000 books and 100,000 pamphlets, while the manuscript subject-index to it ran to eighty-six volumes. This was almost certainly the greatest university library of the century. At the other end of the scale were such places as Alcalá, where the chair of Greek was left vacant for over forty years (1693–1734); or Santiago, where in 1779 of the thirty-three chairs twenty-nine were unfilled or occupied by underpaid deputies appointed by the titular holders; or Graz, which in 1781 had only twenty-three matriculated students. (For that matter by the end of the century Leyden itself, now in decline, had only 150.)

Between these extremes were to be found a large number of institutions which continued to provide teaching of a tolerable standard without making much contribution to the age's stock of knowledge and ideas. Such were the twenty-two universities of France, the numerous though somewhat declining Italian colleges, and those of England and Scandinavia. Some of these, such as Paris and Oxford, remained important because of their size, their traditions and their political significance: few of them played a great part in Europe's intellectual life. The efflorescence of French political and scientific thought during this period owed as little to the French universities as Burke or Priestley did to the English ones. Giambattista Vico, the most original mind produced by

Italy during the century, held a poorly paid post at the University of Naples but was largely self-educated, and his work was very little known until the following century.

The universities of the eighteenth century can also be classified in terms of the social origins of their students. From this point of view the essential division was that between a group whose clientele was drawn exclusively or mainly from the aristocracy or wealthy bourgeoisie, and a larger group access to which was relatively free. The first included Oxford and Cambridge (whose exclusive character was probably intensified by the increasing cost, especially in the first half of the century, of maintaining a student there) as well as Strasbourg, Göttingen and a number of other German universities. The second was composed of the Scottish universities, most of the French and Italian ones and, surprisingly at first sight, the University of Moscow, the first to be established in Russia (1755). Whatever their social background, however, students were not a factor of the slightest political importance in this period. No eighteenth-century government paid or needed to pay any attention to student political activity or demands; for such activity and demands did not exist. Nevertheless there were beginning to be visible by the 1790s the first hopes and fears that the universities, or some of them, might become centres of political radicalism. It was not until well into the following century that this began to happen on any significant scale; but in the early 1790s a leading Austrian Jacobin was already envisaging a revolution which would begin with the seizure of Vienna by 3,000–4,000 student radicals who were then to kill army officers, aristocrats and eventually the emperor himself.[1] Totally unrealistic at the time of their formulation, these dreams were none the less a pointer to the future.

Most European universities, however they might differ in other respects, found themselves compelled during this period to pay increasing attention to the physical sciences and medicine, the departments of knowledge whose frontiers were advancing most rapidly. Opposition from theologians and classicists tended to hamper this change of emphasis, especially in Catholic Europe, and very few of the greatest scientific discoveries of the century were made by university teachers. (The most important exception is the fundamental work on the theory of heat done by Joseph Black, a teacher at both Edinburgh and Glasgow in the 1760s.) Nevertheless a good deal was achieved. In 1702 the first university textbook to be based on the principles of Newtonian physics and mathematics, David Gregory's *Astronomiae, Physicae et Geometriae Elementa*, was published at Oxford. The first continental scholar to base his teaching on Newton's discoveries was W. J. s'Gravesande, professor of astronomy and mathematics at Leyden from 1716 onwards. It was above all in physics and astronomy, and to a lesser degree in mathematics, that new ideas and new techniques filtered into the intellectual world of the universities. Leyden had an observatory of its own as early as 1706, and Uppsala acquired one in 1738. Even in Spain the government ordered in 1770 the drawing-up of new university curricula which emphasized the importance of mathematics and physics.

Medical teaching also developed with remarkable rapidity during this period. From Leyden, which by the beginning of the century had replaced Padua as the leading medical school of Europe, new methods and a new spirit, largely the work of the great professor Hermann Boerhaave, spread slowly to the rest of the continent. The important medical school which developed at Vienna after the middle of the century was created largely by a pupil of Boerhaave; while the Edinburgh medical school, whose fame was at its height in the last years of this period, also owed much to the example of Leyden. In medicine, however, as in the physical sciences, a high proportion of the most important discoveries were made by men who had no direct connexion with the universities – for example the work of Réaumur (1752) and Spallanzani (1780) on digestion, or the better-known studies of respiration by Priestley and Lavoisier. The gap between teaching and research, which had been opened by the Renaissance in almost every branch of intellectual activity, was still as wide as ever in the eighteenth century.

Nor did the scientific and learned societies of the age make much contribution to the progress of knowledge. New organizations of this kind were indeed founded in considerable numbers. Academies of Science came into existence in Russia (1725), Sweden (1737) and Denmark (1742); and societies of a less ambitious kind were founded in many large cities of Western Europe. There was a notable proliferation of learned academies in all the major French provincial towns during the first half of the eighteenth century; and by sponsoring literary competitions and subscribing to periodicals these made a considerable contribution to the spread of the ideas of the Enlightenment on political and social questions. Few of them however added much of importance to Europe's stock of scientific ideas, while the great institutions of the previous century in England, France and Italy were hardly more effective. The Royal Society in London during most of this period was little more than a gentleman's club, and the *Académie des Sciences* in Paris was almost as moribund. In some parts of Europe at least the spread of new ideas and knowledge owed more to the growth of learned periodicals, or at least of those designed for an educated public, which was rapid in the last years of the century, than to anything done in universities or academies. This was probably the case in Germany, whose growing intellectual vitality showed itself in a remarkable output of journals of this sort. Well over 4,000 periodicals of different kinds appeared in the German-speaking world during the eighteenth century. Many of these, of course, were trivial or short-lived; but some, such as the *Staats-Anzeigen* edited by A. L. von Schlözer, which appeared in 1783–95 and covered a wide field of politics, history and literature, were real educative forces in their own right.

The interest in the physical sciences which was slowly taking root in some of the universities was reflected in the attitude of the educated public. In particular the discoveries of Newton, which seemed to lay bare the inmost workings of the universe, appealed to the spirit of the age, and particularly to the love of intellectual and artistic symmetry which was so well developed in the early and middle decades of the century. They thus aroused the greatest interest and admiration. In France national pride and a resulting unwillingness to abandon the cosmology of Descartes, hitherto generally accepted there, delayed for decades the final acceptance of Newtonian physics. In 1742 the astronomer and mathematician Maupertuis published his *Discours sur la Figure des Astres*, the first scientific work in French to accept completely Newton's discoveries; but as late as 1759 the *Académie des Sciences* was still struggling to reconcile the Newtonian and Cartesian systems. Nevertheless the victory of Newton in France, though delayed, was absolute. A host of admirers headed by Voltaire used his name (often without having understood or perhaps even read his works) to symbolize the triumph of light over darkness, of knowledge over ignorance, and by implication of 'rational' and 'natural' religious belief (see pp. 437–40) over ecclesiastical tradition. The work of the mathematicians d'Alembert and

Lagrange completed the acceptance of Newtonian principles and gave them, by the use of more analytical mathematical techniques, more precise and systematic expression. In 1796 Laplace was able to provide, on the basis of their work, the most complete description hitherto produced of the universe as it appeared to the astronomer. His *Système du Monde* is in effect a hymn of praise to the physical sciences, or at least to physics, astronomy and mathematics, a kind of scientific poem. The almost arrogant self-confidence, the delight in the essential simplicity and logicality of the structure of the universe which it radiates, sum up one side of eighteenth-century science. They make the book a landmark in the history of philosophy, of religion and of ideas in general.

The refinements of Newtonian physics and mathematics remained beyond the reach of the ordinary man, even of the ordinary educated man. They none the less influenced, often without his knowledge, his attitude to the world around him and to the society in which he lived. A feeling of having at last acquired full understanding and hence potential control of his physical environment; a new consciousness of power; a belief in the ability of human reason to make even the most complex mysteries simple and comprehensible; a faith in deductive argument from general principles; a tendency to distrust tradition – all these were stimulated by the work of Newton and his followers.

The other sciences lagged far behind physics and astronomy in their development. The great biological discoveries of 1660–80 had no adequate sequel in the eighteenth century. This remains true in spite of the remarkable work of the Swedish botanist Linnaeus, who by the end of his life (he died in 1778) had come to see that new species might arise by crossings between existing ones, and of the French scholar Buffon, who realized that the earth was far older than was usually believed and that existing biological types were not fixed. Chemistry also was slow to develop. This was not merely because it was hampered by the mistaken 'phlogiston' theory (that of a substance with negative weight which was present in all other substances and was released by combustion). Advance was impeded far more by the fact that, until the work of Priestley and still more Lavoisier at the end of this period, the need for rigorous quantitative methods was hardly at all understood. Electricity moreover remained throughout the eighteenth century a completely mysterious subject, though one highly interesting to the ordinary man. Even the distinction between conductors and insulators was not clearly established until the 1730s. Nevertheless the general picture of eighteenth-century scientific life is one of progress, however uneven. One of the most important illustrations of this is the development of more elaborate and exact scientific vocabularies and systems of terminology (for example those created for botany by Linnaeus and later by Lavoisier for chemistry). Moreover mistaken theories and inadequate knowledge did nothing to shake the interest which the educated public increasingly took in the physical sciences and the faith which it increasingly felt in scientific progress.

This increasing interest is visible in a number of ways. The first and most obvious is the fact that works on scientific subjects make up an increasingly large proportion of total book publication as the century progresses. This has been most convincingly demonstrated for France; but there is no doubt that the same development took place at least in all the more developed parts of Europe. Another is the increasingly wide use in ordinary speech and writing of scientific and mathematical terms and even of metaphors drawn from the sciences. Another is the success of popular works on scientific subjects such as the Abbé Pluche's *Spectacle de la Nature* (1732) or Priestley's *History and Present State of Electricity* (1767) and the interest aroused by the courses of public lectures on elementary science which were now becoming increasingly common (the most famous is that given in Paris by the Abbé Nollet in 1734). Yet another is the unprecedented extent to which prominent figures of the political, intellectual and even religious worlds dabbled in the sciences. Thus George III took some interest in botany, Victor Amadeus III of Savoy performed the course of experiments prescribed by Nollet, Samuel Johnson dabbled in chemistry, Montesquieu wrote papers on drunkenness, fever, tides and echoes, and both Rousseau and Diderot took a semi-serious interest in mathematics.

Most of this public interest in science was very superficial. The lectures and writings of Nollet and his fellow-vulgarizers were designed to provide amusement as much as solid instruction; they had to be made palatable to an audience which was still in the main uneducated in scientific matters. The drawing-room experiments in physics or electricity which delighted so many people were a game or a social accomplishment rather than a serious exploration of nature. Even in the universities the primitive and undeveloped state of many of the physical sciences is clearly illustrated by the ease with which dilettanti could not merely obtain appointments but often hold them very successfully. Richard Watson, for example, knew nothing whatever of the subject when he became Professor of Chemistry at Cambridge in 1764; but within three years he was able to publish what at once became a standard academic work on metallurgy.

Nor was there, at least over most of Europe, any effective application of science to the development of new industrial processes or the improvement of existing ones. In the more developed parts of the continent, Britain, France, the United Provinces or Sweden, it is true, there was a growing understanding of the new possibilities of this kind. Thus in 1692 a committee of the *Académie des Sciences* produced, at the request of the French government, a detailed report on the proportions required in an optically satisfactory printing type. Two generations later the chemical laboratory in the Ashmolean Museum at Oxford was being used in the production of Worcester china. The work of John Dollond in the 1750s in improving the telescope shows a certain union of scientific knowledge with traditional techniques; Joseph Black did important work in industrial chemistry though he was a university professor; and in 1759 the great engineer John Smeaton made the first attempt to measure accurately the efficiency of different types of watermill and windmill. Lavoisier himself, the greatest chemist of the century, was employed in the 1780s as a government consultant in efforts to improve the manufacture of explosives in France. The Industrial Revolution in Britain developed against an intellectual background marked by the increasingly widespread dissemination among manufacturers and artisans of scientific knowledge and, equally important, scientific attitudes. Nevertheless the importance of all this should not be exaggerated. Technology, like so many other aspects of life, continued to be dominated by tradition, habit and rule-of-thumb. What counted in most industries was the knowledge which skilled workers, often only semi-educated or quite uneducated, had picked up through years of experience. A Platonic separation of science from the mundane processes of everyday life continued to prevail.

Nevertheless something had been gained. Scientific experiments, even of the most dilettante kind, were an advance on the cabinets of 'curiosities' (fossils, coins, shells, etc.) which had been popular in the previous century (and which continued to be so in this period). Public interest in science at least showed a more widespread realization than ever before that the physical world was governed by laws, that the phenomena of which it was composed could be logically classified and that these laws and classifications could be discovered by intelligent observation and careful measurement.

How far did this interest in the physical sciences promote the scepticism and the declining faith in religious dogmas which are visible in many parts of Europe during the eighteenth century? This is a complex question; but it seems clear that the importance of science in this respect, and indeed in the general development of radical thought during this period, has often been exaggerated. In Britain, which made through Newton the greatest single contribution to the century's stock of scientific ideas, scarcely anyone as yet thought of science as dangerous to faith. One historian has gone so far as to speak of 'that peculiarly English phenomenon, the holy alliance between science and religion'.[2] To all British scientists natural phenomena, however much they might be studied, however closely observed and subtly classified, had still their first cause in God. They were still manifestations of His being and nature. Many of the most popular writers and lecturers on science were themselves clergymen. The undermining of the intellectual foundations of revealed religion which was undoubtedly though very slowly taking place in Britain (see p. 439) was only indirectly the work of the mathematicians or astronomers. It owed more to moralists such as Mandeville, historians such as Gibbon, and above all philosophers such as Hume. It was Hume, not any of the scientists, who was first willing to argue openly against the credibility of miracles.

In France the position was similar. There the assault on traditional faith and the religious establishment was led, not by Maupertuis, Buffon or Lavoisier, but by philosophers, historians and publicists, by La Mettrie, Helvétius, Morellet, most of all Voltaire. The books and pamphlets produced by such authors were repeatedly condemned and criticized by the Assembly of the Clergy from 1765 onwards; but scientific writings as such were never attacked in this way. Not until the last years of the century did a scientist, Laplace, produce a description of the universe in which no place was allotted to God; whereas as early as 1770 the writer Holbach in his *Système de la Nature* had revived the Lucretian concept of the universe as the mere result of a fortuitous combination of atoms, and thus by implication ruled out the idea of a creator. Scepticism and materialism were certainly rife in the *salons* of Paris. As in England, however, they were the product of a philosophy hard to reconcile with traditional religious assumptions, of an increased knowledge of the peoples of the extra-European world which bred moral relativism, and of an intensified study of history which threw doubt on many clerical claims and traditions. The development of the physical sciences helped to create an atmosphere in which a widespread turning away from religion became possible; but it did little directly to stimulate such a movement.

The development of literature during the eighteenth century is usually described in terms of a transition from classicism to romanticism. The description is over-simplified and the terms it employs are vague; but some change of emphasis of this kind undoubtedly occurred. The classicism which still dominated aesthetic theory almost everywhere in Europe at the beginning of this period aimed at the imitation of Nature; but this was a Nature of a somewhat special kind, generalized, universal and unchanging. The writer was to concern himself with these aspects of his subject rather than with the more individual, intimate and fluctuating ones. Associated with these theories was the belief that literature, or at least the higher forms of literature, should be essentially if not overtly didactic, that art should be a mere intellectual statement of moral precepts, and that the various literary *genres* – tragedy, comedy, epic, lyric – were each governed by rules which could not be infringed without lowering the quality of the resulting work. The conventionality and rigidity, not to say dullness, of so much poetry of the first half of the century was produced by the influence of these ideas. This system of ideas moreover was suited to, and the product of, an aristocratic society. It presupposed on the part of the reading public some acquaintance with the literature of classical antiquity and a certain detachment from the processes and needs of contemporary life.

Theories so rigid and so abstract were never completely dominant in the literature of any European country, even in the early decades of the century. They were strongest of all in France, where classical traditions were deeply ingrained. There literature was still little influenced by the slowly growing current of romanticism and sensibility. Even in France, however, the *Réflexions critiques sur la Poésie et sur la Peinture* of the Abbé du Bos (1719) has been acclaimed as an important step in the development of a new attitude towards the literary expression of the emotions. Simultaneously in the hands of Lesage and Prévost the realistic novel reached a high pitch of development; while the plays of Marivaux show not merely wit but a psychological subtlety and realism uncommon in any period. In England acceptance of classical literary theories had always been limited to an educated upper class in which French influences were strong. Below this social level the old national writers uninfluenced by classical aesthetics, such as Shakespeare, remained widely read. Moreover the appeal of classicism was further limited by its association with pagan antiquity, and by a lingering popular preference for themes inspired by Christianity or at least drawn from the history of the Christian era. A moderate reaction against classical aesthetics can be seen as early as 1712 in Addison's series of essays 'On the Pleasures of the Imagination', which appeared in the *Spectator* of that year. As in France, the novel, a new form of writing with which classical aesthetics was hardly at all concerned, was sometimes highly realistic and popular – for example in Defoe's *Moll Flanders* and *Colonel Jack*. In Italy also the beginnings of a reaction against classical or neo-classical literary standards can be seen from the beginning of the century. It is clearly visible in L. A. Muratori's *Della Perfetta Poesia Italiana* (1706) and in the rediscovery of Dante (the greatest of all medieval poets, whose works had been virtually ignored for generations) by G. V. Gravina. In Germany classical ideals and standards were seen, as in England, largely as imports from abroad, in particular from France. Thus the new ideas on the importance of emotion and imagination which began to enter the country in the second quarter of the century, notably through the activities of the Swiss critics Bodmer and Breitinger, fell on comparatively fertile ground.

The middle decades of this period saw classicism in literature under increasingly heavy attack almost everywhere from a number of directions. Its adherents found themselves faced by a growing demand for greater naturalism, signs of which can be detected even in the writings of essentially conservative critics such as Diderot and Johnson. Novels or plays which dealt with recognizable individuals against a realistic and often middle-class background – Lessing's *Miss Sara Sampson* (1755) and Diderot's

Le Père de Famille (1758) are good examples – now won increasing popularity. Established critical ideas were also being undermined by the growing cult of 'sensibility', of intense emotion and high-minded suffering. In England this tendency can be seen gaining strength from the 1720s onwards in the works of such writers as Thompson, Shenstone and Young. Its full potentialities were first revealed in the prodigious success of Samuel Richardson's *Pamela* (1740) and later, in a somewhat different form, in the popularity of such books as Henry Mackenzie's *The Man of Feeling* (1771), Geothe's *Sorrows of Werther* (1774), and Bernardin de St Pierre's *Paul et Virginie* (1789). Already that archetypical romantic character, the lonely man deeply conscious of his isolation, of the failure of the world to understand him and of the intensity of his feelings, had taken shape. J. G. Zimmermann's *Ueber die Einsamkeit* (*On Loneliness*), whose mixture of melancholy and sentimentality was to make it one of the major texts of romanticism and ensure its translation into almost every European language, appeared first in 1756 as an essay of less than a hundred pages; but so popular did it prove that in its final form in the 1784–85 edition it had become a sturdy two-volume book. Most important of all was the growth of a more historical and relativist and less absolute attitude towards literature. Literary history of a modern kind, stressing the elements of growth and development inherent in every great literature, can be found in Italy as early as 1698, in G. M. Crescimbeni's *Istoria della volgar Poesia*. As this period drew to a close an increasing element of historicism, an effort to escape from absolute judgements divorced from any historical context, is visible in many critical works, notably in Thomas Warton's *History of English Poetry* (1774–81).

This trend bore fruit in the tendency to revalue (and often overvalue) the literature of primitive peoples or of the non-classical past which is usually referred to as 'primitivism'. This is seen most clearly in the amazing success all over Europe of James Macpherson's *Works of Ossian*, a collection of allegedly ancient Celtic poems (mostly the work of Macpherson himself though including genuine elements) published in 1765. It is also visible in the interest taken by such people as Bishop Percy in England, and above all J. G. Herder (see pp. 432–4) in Germany, in the collection and publication of folk-songs. The new attitude was clearly expressed in works such as Richard Hurd's *Letters on Chivalry and Romance* (1762) which claimed that the feudal period was more favourable to the production of great poetry than the Homeric one because of 'the improved gallantry of the feudal times' and the 'superior solemnity of their super-stitions', and argued that by the victory of the classicists 'we have lost . . . a world of fine fabling'. These anti-classical influences, typified also by the growing taste for wild natural scenery and for natural 'English' gardens as opposed to the highly artificial arrangements of *parterres*, topiary and statuary which French influ-ence had done so much to popularize in the first decades of this period, continued to gain strength as the century drew to a close. Classical models still had great influence on literature and aesthetic theory in its second half, an influence strengthened by the admir-ation for the classical past which was an important element in the Enlightenment in France (see p. 415). But this influence was now declining and changing its character. Europe, led by England and Germany, was now escaping from the rigidities and limitations of the French-dominated taste of the age of Louis XIV. The changing meaning for Europeans of classical models in the later eighteenth century can be seen most clearly in Germany. There, by way of such books as J.J. Winckelmann's *Thoughts on the Imitation of Greek Works in Painting and Sculpture* (1755) and above all Lessing's *Laocöon, or the Boundaries between Painting and Poetry* (1766) they came to be seen as illustrating the triumph of art, and the inner serenity which art can bestow, over the tragedy of human life, rather than as examples of style to be assiduously imitated.

The literature which has been described in the preceding para-graphs was that of the educated, of the reasonably affluent, of the town-dweller with at least partly developed tastes and fairly easy access to books. It was therefore quite untypical of the reading of the ordinary peasant or artisan, who enjoyed none of these advantages. We know little about the reading habits of the 95 per cent or more of Europeans in this period who were not well educated or well-to-do and who did not possess libraries of which there is some surviving record in wills or inventories. What frag-mentary information there is, however, suggests strongly that the reading of this vast majority (or of those members of it who read at all) remained highly traditional. In France, the one area in which popular reading habits have been seriously studied, there had since the early seventeenth century been a large output of small, cheap and often badly printed booklets for an unsophisticated mass market. During the eighteenth century there were about 150 printers producing literature of this kind (mainly in northern France, where literacy was much more widespread than in the south). Almanacs; collections of prophecies and works on astrology; collections of traditional and often very ancient tales (notably of Charlemagne and his paladins); manuals of practical advice on aspects of everyday life, health care, etc. – such appear to have been the staple reading of the ordinary man (in so far as that phrase has meaning) in France during this period. It was the reading of the uneducated: astrological predictions bulked large in it partly because they could be expressed in conventional signs rather than in words and thus 'read' by the illiterate or partly literate. It was the reading of those who wished to escape, however briefly, from a life often mercilessly hard; such feelings underlie the taste for the marvellous and the exotic which this type of literature so often expresses. It was the reading of men to whom change was something to be resisted and novelty an object of mistrust; hence the way in which works of this type could be reprinted for generations, even centuries, without alteration. (A poem giving general advice on health, *L'Escole de Salerne, en vers burlesques*, first published in 1474, had gone, without change, through almost three hundred editions by 1846.) It was, in the last analysis, a literature of submission, the reading of men in the grip of physical and social forces against which they felt it vain to struggle. If popular reading in other countries were studied in the same way it is hard to believe that this would not yield at least some similar conclusions. We must not forget that underlying the world of literature in the textbook sense of the term, the world of enlightenment, of scientific discovery and cosmopolitan high culture, was another intellectual universe, dark and barely penetrable by the historian but none the less inhabited by the overwhelming majority of Europeans.

In architecture and the visual arts changes of a kind very roughly similar to those in literature can be traced. The Baroque styles of the age of Louis XIV, with their highly developed plastic values, their efforts to impress and uplift rather than to amuse or attract, their occasional heaviness, were slowly transmuted by the new tendencies which developed during this period. The decorative style known as Rococo, which evolved in France towards the end of the seventeenth century and later enjoyed enormous popularity and influence in Germany, can be regarded as an offshoot of Baroque or even a degenerate form of it. Nevertheless it differed in a number of ways from its predecessor. The stress which it laid on curves and its general dislike of geometrical patterns; the fondness which it often showed, at least from the end of the 1720s, for asymmetry; its frequent use of newly discovered materials such as porcelain and later stucco; the way in which it was influenced in some of its forms by Chinese models – all these distinguish it from the art of the seventeenth century.

It was essentially a decorative style and little more. Its influence on the structure and plan of the buildings which it ornamented was inconsiderable. Italian architects, still in some ways the leaders of the profession, continued until the middle of the century to be strongly influenced by Baroque ideas and traditions, though the exuberance which that style had displayed in seventeenth-century Italy was now somewhat modified in the work of Juvara, Galilei and Vanvitelli. In France pseudo-classical Renaissance and 'Palladian' styles showed greater powers of resistance than in Italy and Baroque influence on architecture was limited, as can be seen in the work of Robert de Cotte or J.-A. Gabriel. In England Palladianism, and the ideas of regularity, symmetry, and restraint in external ornament associated with it, continued to be almost completely dominant in the early eighteenth century: Baroque models except in the design of furniture had little influence there.

The painting of the early eighteenth century is hard to describe briefly, but is perhaps best regarded as a continuation of the Baroque art of the later seventeenth century with its stress on movement and colour, on visual rhetoric and (except in England) on religious and mythological subjects. Even as late a painter as the Venetian G. B. Tiepolo (1692–1769) has been acclaimed as 'the epitome and the perfection of Baroque art'. Already, however, such unity as the Baroque style and tradition still possessed was breaking down in the paintings of Watteau, one of the most difficult of all great artists to classify satisfactorily, and in the different types of realism exemplified by Hogarth in England and Chardin in France.

The middle decades of the century saw the pace of change accelerate. Like poetry, though in a rather different way, the visual arts were now becoming more and more historically-minded. The art of Greece and Rome was suddenly being made more accessible than ever before, partly by the excavation of Pompeii and Herculaneum from the 1740s onwards and partly by the publication of the first accurate descriptions and drawings hitherto available of the great buildings of classical antiquity, particularly of Greece. In architecture this flood of new knowledge stimulated the growth of a conscious and often highly elegant neo-classical style. First developed in England by the Adam brothers from about 1759 onwards, this had spread to France by the 1770s; later it inspired the construction of the Brandenburger Tor in Berlin (1778–91) and had considerable influence even in Russia. In interior decoration and the design of furniture it not merely popularized classical or pseudo-classical motifs (well illustrated in the pottery produced in Staffordshire by Josiah Wedgwood from the 1760s onwards) but also gave rise to the often exaggerated and fanciful 'Etruscan' and 'Egyptian' styles of the later decades of the century.

In painting the influence of newfound classical models and neo-classical theories can be seen even more clearly during the last decades of this period. It is visible in the distrust felt by artists such as Sir Joshua Reynolds for mere manipulative skill, and in a tendency to exalt form at the expense of colour, draughtmanship at the expense of decorative effect, repose at the expense of movement. Moreover the typical neo-classical belief in the educative effect of great art, and in the artist's obligation to select from and generalize Nature in order to produce this effect, were now becoming almost as influential in discussions of painting as they had been in literary theory a generation or more earlier. This was an art strongly didactic in its ambitions, one which deliberately turned away from the frivolity and even occasional licentiousness of the Rococo and strove to return to the high standards of purity and morality which the best classical models were thought to embody.

The past to which the art and architecture of the later eighteenth century returned was, as in the case of literature, medieval as well as classical, Gothic as well as Greek. In England an interest in Gothic architecture had begun to develop even before the end of the seventeenth century, one which both stimulated and was stimulated by the formation of the Society of Antiquaries in 1718. The slow growth of a taste of this kind in the decades which followed is illustrated by the publication in 1742 of Batty Langley's *Ancient Architecture Restored . . . in the Gothic Mode*, and by the building and rebuilding by Horace Walpole of his house at Strawberry Hill (1750–76). The *dilettanti* of the eighteenth century were still far from a genuine understanding of or sympathy with medieval architecture. Strawberry Hill, as has often been pointed out, was really a ridiculous and anachronistic jumble of styles; and to the end of this period Gothic continued to have much less influence on the development of architecture in England than Palladianism and neo-classicism. 'The Saxon and Gothic antiquities', wrote a commentator in 1798, 'tho' justly objects of curiosity and even of admiration, are still the remains of society in its infancy and therefore barbarous and false'.[3] Even in continental Europe, however, where classical traditions were in general stronger than in England, Gothic art attracted some interest. As early as 1741 the great French architect Soufflot published a defence of it in his *Parallèle des églises Gothiques avec les églises modernes*, and in 1776 the Prince of Anhalt can be found building for himself at Wörlitz a palace in the 'Gothic' style. But in neither France nor Germany was it an important element in the artistic life of the age.

The painting of the later eighteenth century, like its literature, was powerfully influenced by the ideas of sensibility and Nature. The influence of the former is seen most clearly in the work of Greuze, who was praised by Diderot and is known to have been influenced by the writings of Rousseau. His scenes of family life, with their emotional and moralistic overtones, are one of the best visual reflections of the spirit of the decades before the French Revolution: a similar attitude can be found, in slightly different forms, in the work of many other painters of the period – Madame Vigée-Lebrun, Fragonard, perhaps Gainsborough.

The eighteenth century, or at least its middle and later decades, was thus a period of rapid aesthetic and stylistic change. In architecture and decoration Baroque and Palladian traditions struggled with the influences of Rococo and neo-classicism, while the position was further complicated by an appreciable admixture of Chinese or pseudo-Chinese influences (see pp. 374–5). The stylistic confusion which resulted, and which was at its height just after the middle of the century, is well reflected in the pattern-books of Thomas Chippendale and other cabinet-makers. In painting Baroque slowly gave way to neo-classicism and also to a style, or rather a group of styles, which were more realistic and above all more intimate and more sensitive. In literature the classical taste of the early part of the century (which had in any case been largely confined to poetry and tended to ignore prose as beneath serious criticism) was steadily eroded and transmuted by the growth of sensibility and by a more generous and realistic view of the literature of the past.

No art was in the eighteenth century more widely appreciated and practised than music. It attracted the interest, often a keen and well-informed one, of some of the most important writers and scholars of the period. Rousseau was the author of an opera (*Le Devin du Village*) and his *Lettre sur la Musique française* (1753) was one of the most influential critical works of the century. Voltaire in the 1730s played a leading role in the controversies between the French composer Rameau and his critics. An enormous quantity of music, most of it now totally neglected and forgotten, was written in the eighteenth century; in some parts of Europe at least it was more accessible than literature to the ordinary man. Twelve hundred operas were produced in Venice alone during the century and in the 1780s one observer claimed that the Papal States possessed forty opera-houses. Its sheer abundance, however, makes it difficult to describe or analyse briefly. Moreover music is by its very nature the most abstract, the most timeless of the arts, the one least influenced by the climate of ideas surrounding it.

Parallels between its development and that of literature and the visual arts are thus hard to draw with any certainty. Some nevertheless can be suggested. The Rococo art of the early decades of the century has, it can be argued, an analogy in much of the music (or at least the instrumental music) of the same period – music which was highly decorated, designed to please, melodically often somewhat impoverished and often rather lacking in both lyricism and architectural sense. From the 1740s onwards, as the true classical musical style begins to take shape, there is a much greater emphasis than before on melody; and by the later decades of the century a growing stress on making music simpler and more comprehensible to the ordinary man is visible. This led to a considerable infusion of folk elements even into some of the greatest achievements of the period: Mozart's *Magic Flute* (1791) is the supreme example of this. Such a development is in marked contrast to the early decades of the century, when folk music had attracted very little attention from professional composers. The same movement towards simplicity, comprehensibility, a wider and less aristocratic audience, it has been argued, underlies the tendency in the second half of the century towards the use only of a limited range of simple keys (D, F, G, and B flat) and its marked preference for major rather than minor ones. It is tempting to see such developments as a parallel in musical life to the movement towards naturalism and sensibility which has already been seen in novels, plays and painting. Some other analogies can be tentatively suggested. For example the rationalism, the taste for firmness and clarity, which made up another strand in the intellectual life of the early eighteenth century and were strongest in France, are perhaps reflected in the music of Jean Philippe Rameau, the greatest French composer of this period. His *Traité de l'harmonie reduite à ses principes naturels* (1722), the most important and systematic work of the century on musical theory, reflects the faith in rules and systems, the belief that success in any of the arts is above all a matter of correctness, of choosing a suitable model and taking it as a guide, which was so powerful in the Europe of Louis XIV. In the same way the neo-classicism which becomes so powerful in the visual arts in the last decades of this period is echoed in a sterner and more masculine tone in the remarkable operas of Gluck – particularly *Orfeo ed Euridice* (1762) and *Alceste* (1767) – which made their effect by placing on the stage 'monumentally simplified character types which led . . . back to the classical tragedy of antiquity'.

These analogies, however seductive, cannot be pressed too far: they break down when applied to the greatest composers of the age. To classify J. S. Bach, whose most important works were in a quite different tradition, that of the church music of Protestant Germany, in terms of the well-worn and somewhat shapeless concepts of Rococo, Baroque or Classicism is difficult and perhaps pointless. Like the other towering musical geniuses of the century – Mozart and perhaps Handel – he transcends all classifications and cannot be confined to any of these battered pigeonholes.

Eighteenth-century music was none the less a function of society where its forms if not its spirit were concerned. Like every other art it had to adapt itself to a given political and economic structure. This is seen most clearly in the domination of much of it by the needs and tastes of rulers and the greater nobility. Monarchies and aristocracies provided the most lucrative market for music as for so many of the arts. Virtually all the greatest composers of the period were directly employed by rulers or great nobles, from Rameau at the court of Louis XV and Handel at that of George II through Haydn in the service of Prince Esterhazy to Mozart the unwilling servant of the Archbishop of Salzburg. The great importance of opera as a musical form, especially in the first half of the century, was also largely a result of this position. In the seventeenth century operas, often mounted on the most lavish scale and combined with ballets, aquatic spectacles, firework displays and other extraneous elements, had been a means by which the rulers of the Italian States displayed their wealth and their patronage of the arts. By the early decades of the eighteenth century a taste for opera was spreading from Italy, by way of the Habsburg court at Vienna, to many parts of Germany. By the middle years of the century it had penetrated even as far as St Petersburg. The result was the creation at many of the courts of Europe of opera-houses served by professional musicians and singers and often, in the larger States, with composers and librettists permanently attached to them. Thus for example a line of Italian composers of real eminence – Galuppi, Traetta, Paisiello, Cimarosa – were associated with the development of opera in St Petersburg in the last generation of the century.

Opera-houses of this type, created by princes, were generally accessible to the ordinary man in Italy and South Germany. In the main, however, they were closed to him in North Germany and other parts of Europe. The type of work which they produced, the *opera seria* normally by Italian composers, drew heavily upon classical mythology for its subjects and was usually designed to give the utmost scope to the singers. (In no other period perhaps have supremely accomplished singers been so numerous or so lavishly rewarded.) It therefore tended to become somewhat stereotyped, and as the century progressed encountered increasing competition from new and more realistic operatic forms, especially in countries whose cultural life was less dominated by courts and princes than that of Germany. In England the ballad opera (the most famous example is John Gay's *Beggar's Opera*, produced in 1728), in France the *opéra comique* which developed from the 1750s onwards, in Spain the *tonadilla* (a kind of inter-mezzo often based on popular tunes), in Austria the *Singspiel* which culminates in Mozart's *Magic Flute*, even in Italy itself the realistic *opera buffa*, can all be considered as different forms of this reaction against the *opera seria* inherited from the previous century.

Thus in spite of the fact that so much music was written for courts and so many composers depended for employment on monarchs and nobles, music was not an art designed purely for the enjoyment of the privileged classes. This was especially the case where a large educated bourgeoisie existed. It was in such areas that the concert open to the public, which can be regarded as a declaration of middle-class cultural independence, had its origins. A series of public concerts was founded at Hamburg in 1722 and the first concert organizaton of a modern type, the *Concerts Spirituels*, was set up in Paris three years later. With the concert-hall and the anonymous audience came the first printed music criticism, originally in periodicals such as the *Mercure Galant* and the *Spectator*, later on a more professional scale in journals such as J. Matteson's *Critica Musica* (1722–25) and books such as J. A. Scheibe's *Der Critische Musicus* (1737). It is important, however, to remember that much eighteenth-century music, like much eighteenth-century poetry, was written for a small and relatively expert audience, not for the common man. Unless this is grasped neither its strengths nor its limitations can be completely understood.

Opera was not the only important musical form in Europe even in the first half of the century. On the contrary instrumental music of various types continued to be produced in great quantities, and the demand for chamber works for performance by groups of amateurs was very considerable. In the later decades of this period the balance began to tilt more and more towards instrumental music, a development clearly illustrated by the emergence of orchestras bigger and more highly disciplined than any hitherto seen. This was essentially a German development. It was at Mannheim under the Bohemian Stamitz and at Stuttgart under the Italian Jomelli that the first great European orchestras took shape; and by the end of the century the largest might include a hundred or more players. Combinations of this size, properly trained and controlled, opened to composers a whole new world of possible symphonic effects.

Germany's leadership in the development of the orchestra warns us not to overestimate, in spite of the enormous prestige of Italian composers and performers, the importance of Italy in eighteenth-century music. Even in the first decades of the century

Bach owed little, at least directly, to Italian influences; and in France an important and active school of native musicians struggled with some success against the threat of Italian dominance. With the advantages of hindsight, indeed, it is clear that the 1740s saw the beginning of a German leadership of the musical world (in large part the work of Bohemian composers of whom Gluck was the greatest) which has lasted until well into our own century. Even England was able to retain a distinct musical tradition of her own; though her relative backwardness is shown by the survival there until the end of this period of forms such as the concerto grosso, the organ concerto and the French-type orchestral overture long after they had been discarded elsewhere in Europe. Nevertheless the first half of the century saw an Italian, particularly Neapolitan, pre-eminence which lasted in some ways until the 1780s or even later. Lulli, who had founded the French school in the 1660s and 1670s, was a Florentine: Handel was profoundly influenced by a visit to Italy. Not until the end of this period did Haydn become the first German composer to achieve a truly international reputation (and incidentally the first great European musician to have his works performed in the new United States of America).

How far is it justifiable to speak, as many writers have done, of French cultural domination in eighteenth-century Europe? One of the period's main intellectual currents, that of romantic sensibility, owed little to French influence or example. In music France's influence, as has just been pointed out, was much less than that of Italy. In many respects, none the less, it is possible to consider the century as one of French cultural leadership. During its early decades in particular the example and enormous prestige of Louis XIV stimulated the creation of a whole galaxy of imitations of Versailles – by Philip V of Spain at La Granja, by John V of Portugal at Queluz, by the Dukes of Parma at Colorno, by the Dukes of Modena at Rivalta, by Charles IV of Naples at Caserta, by Frederick I of Prussia at Charlottenburg, and by many of the minor German rulers. Even in Russia one of the pavilions in the park at Peterhof, the palace begun by Peter I, was called *Marly* and others *Mon Plaisir* and *l'Hermitage*, while great Russian and Polish noble families built themselves vast country houses in whose construction the example of Versailles played some part. Many of these palaces were designed by French or French-trained architects. Almost all of them owed something to the work of French painters, sculptors and cabinet-makers. Throughout this period, moreover, the development not merely of the content but of the formal teaching of art was greatly influenced by French example. The rules of the Academies of Art founded at Berlin in 1697 and Vienna in 1705 were drawn almost word for word from those of the *Academie Royale de Peinture et Sculpture* in Paris.

The eighteenth century also saw the pre-eminence of French as the language of European scholarship, culture and polite society. As early as 1697 a writer could claim that 'the French language has succeeded the Latin and Greek languages . . . it has become so general that it is spoken today throughout almost the whole of Europe and those who frequent society feel a kind of shame if they do not know it'.[4] A natural result of this position was that educated Frenchmen developed a contempt for the languages of other peoples. 'We entertained so high an idea of ourselves and of our language', wrote one in 1792, 'that we looked upon foreign idioms as the jargon of barbarians: accordingly we neglected to learn them.'[5] France's linguistic dominance, like her influence on the arts, was particularly marked in countries such as Poland, Russia (see p. 278), Sweden and the German States, whose literary life was still developing and whose languages were sometimes only beginning to take shape as literary media. The uncritical acceptance of French by their ruling classes and the contemptuous rejection of the native language which it often involved are seen in their most extreme form in the attitude of Frederick II of Prussia. Born and growing to manhood in an age in which the attraction of French models was at its height, he remained till his death a wholehearted admirer of French literature and, as his own works show, of the strictest and most arid classicism. Despising German as a barbaric dialect, he used it only when he had to, and ordered in 1743 that the papers read to the Academy of Sciences at Berlin should be published in French.

Even in the first half of the century, however, French cultural influence was much weaker in countries such as England and Spain, which had well-established literatures of their own, than in the less developed States of Central and Eastern Europe. The generation which followed the Seven Years War saw moreover a tendency for this influence to decline in many areas. The decline was most marked in Germany, where the growth of a great national literature was now well under way. Thus the Academy of Sciences began after Frederick II's death in 1786 to transact business in German as well as French, while Herder and Lessing published attacks on the artificiality and lack of natural feeling which they considered the main characteristics of French literature. In Spain distrust of the sceptical and irreligious character of so much French writing raised a further barrier in the way of any widespread adoption of ideas or literary models from beyond the Pyrenees, while even in Russia there were faint signs in the last years of the century of a reaction against French cultural dominance.

Moreover France herself was now being influenced to a degree unknown for at least a century by foreign books, buildings, paintings and ideas. The English novel, particularly as represented by Richardson, enjoyed a considerable vogue there. It was largely from England that neo-classical architectural styles were popularized in France. By the 1760s there were even signs that German poetry was beginning to attract some attention in Paris. In the years before the Revolution French cultural influence in Europe was still much greater than that of any other State; but France was rapidly becoming a mere *primus inter pares* in this respect and was no longer the unchallenged leader of the whole continent.

NOTES AND REFERENCES

1 P. P. Bernard, *Jesuits and Jacobins* (Urbana-Chicago-London, 1973), p. 166

2 B. Willey, *The Eighteenth Century Background* (London, 1940), pp. 136–7.

3 W. Jackson, *The Four Ages* (London, 1798), p. 4.

4 Janssaeus, *La Véritable Clef de la Langue Française*, quoted in H. Kohn, *The Idea of Nationalism* (New York, 1945), p. 194.

5 J. P. Rabaut Saint-Étienne, *The History of the Revolution of France* (London, 1792), p. 15.

15

THE ENLIGHTENMENT AND
ITS COMPETITORS

The small minority of Europeans who were educated and respon-
sive to currents of intellectual change were conscious during much
of the eighteenth century of living in an age of 'Enlightenment'.
What did this term mean?

The Enlightenment meant very different things in different
parts of the continent and even as between different individuals
in the same country. In some areas and in the work of some
writers it took a form which was radical, aggressively critical,
contemptuous of the past and particularly of the religious assumptions which had done so much to shape the history of Christian
Europe. Elsewhere it was more moderate. Sometimes its influence, at least on the educated and opinion-forming sections of
society, was very great. In other circumstances, where such
groups were smaller and weaker, or where they were protected
against radical intellectual challenge by strong feelings of self-
interest or powerful religious influences, it had much less
purchase. The thinkers of the Enlightenment were never a unified
school, a disciplined intellectual phalanx, even in any single
European state. In so far as they were united at all it was merely
by a generic or family likeness; and many of the most original
thinkers of the age largely escaped from or even reacted against
what are usually considered typical 'enlightened' influences. There
were several different Enlightenments in eighteenth-century
Europe, reacting with and influencing one another in complex
ways; while outside this circle of intellectuals, prominent above
all in France, the great bulk of European society, traditional and
resistant to all new influences, remained largely unaffected.

Moreover the vitality and influence of the Enlightenment in its radical and mainly French version fluctuated sharply as between different parts of the century. Most of its basic ideas and assumptions had taken shape before the death of Louis XIV, even before 1700. But it was not until the 1740s that it emerged as a clearly identifiable movement of ideas with recognizable leaders and a certain degree of internal coherence. This was the decade of Diderot's *Pensées philosophiques* (1746) and *Lettre sur les aveugles* (1749), and above all of the most radical and iconoclastic philosophical work of the century, David Hume's *Enquiry concerning Human Understanding* (1748). The 1760s and early 1770s see the Enlightenment at its height: by the middle and later 1770s it was in decline. Of its greatest figures Voltaire, Rousseau (if he can justly be considered a man of the Enlightenment at all), Diderot, Condillac, d'Alembert and Mably all died in the years 1778–85. Well before the outbreak of the French Revolution, therefore, it had shot its bolt and was increasingly challenged and undermined by new intellectual and emotional currents – romanticism, sensibility, incipient nationalism and various forms of more or less unconcealed irrationalism.

None of this, however, means that this remarkable intellectual current, however confused and complicated by eddies and even counter-currents, was unimportant. Both its partisans and its enemies were conscious of its power. By the 1760s, when the Enlightenment was at the peak of its influence, the intellectual life of Europe was very different from what it had been half a century earlier at the death of Louis XIV. This change, however violently it was later to be denounced, even vilified, in the aftermath of the French Revolution, could never be undone.

What historians have generally agreed to regard as the central strand in the Enlightenment, its critical, rationalistic, intellectually liberating element, suspicious of tradition and received ideas, scornful of what were seen as the destructive follies of the past, was predominantly French. It was from Paris that ideas and attitudes of this kind spread, with widely varying effect in different parts of the continent, to the rest of Europe. Much of the intellectual style of the French Enlightenment – and it was, it must be emphasized, a style, a set of attitudes, much more than a systematic body of doctrine – is encapsulated in the writings of Voltaire. In a series of brilliant and piercingly amusing stories or short novels: *Zadig* (1747); *Micromégas* (1752); *Candide* (1759), as well as in his *Dictionnaire philosophique* (1764) he attacked conventional attitudes, most of all conventional religious beliefs and prejudices, with unparalleled effect. Savage irony, sarcasm raised to the level of devastating intellectual and political criticism, became in his hands weapons with which to attack churches, clerics and their allegedly stultifying effects on human liberty and happiness. This attack he launched with a cultivated ferocity, a venomous elegance, never seen before. No one did more than he to spread the ideas of 'natural religion' and deism, the opposition to religious intolerance, which are briefly discussed in the last chapter of this book (see pp. 437ff). He was not a man of great intellectual depth. His range of sympathies was in many ways narrow. But within his own limits he was the most brilliant and persuasive of all propagandists of ideas. His popularity and influence in the later decades of his life were immense. In 1779, the year after his death, the publisher Panckoucke was able to sell his rights in Voltaire's remaining unpublished works alone for the enormous sum of 300,000 livres.

The second great monument to many of the ideas of the French Enlightenment is the *Encyclopédie: ou dictionnaire méthodique des sciences, des arts et des métiers* which appeared in Paris in twenty-eight volumes in 1751–72, and for the production of which Denis Diderot was mainly responsible. This famous work, which had enormous success and influence in France and was the largest single publishing venture of the century, attempted to summarize the whole of human knowledge as it then existed. But besides its function merely as a vast assembly of information it had another, a more dynamic one – that of popularizing and disseminating attitudes which, in spite of variations between different contributors, in all essentials epitomized the radical and French form of the Enlightenment. As propaganda it was highly successful. In spite of its size and inevitably high cost (the first four editions were luxurious folios) at least 25,000 sets in different formats were in circulation throughout Europe by 1789. When the cheaper quarto edition was being produced in 1779–80 there were probably a hundred different printing-presses at work on it; and the first folio edition alone yielded for the publishers a net profit of four million livres.

The intellectual currents which Voltaire and the *Encyclopédie* represented had a largely non-French ancestry. In particular the English contribution to them was very great. Newton had shown more dramatically and on a larger scale than any other scientist the existence in nature of fundamental regularities, basic laws of the widest scope which gave coherence and meaning to otherwise shapeless masses of facts. His example strengthened and gave force to a fundamental Enlightenment belief, that in the possibility of transforming, by the use of human reason, a world of apparent chaos and contradiction into one of intellectual unity, one comprehensible to and therefore controllable by the intelligent man of good will. Even more important, from John Locke, in his *Essay concerning Human Understanding* (1690) and *Thoughts concerning Education* (1693), can be traced the Enlightenment belief that the human mind is formed by the sense impressions which it receives from the outside world, in other words by experience and environment. Man was thus seen as highly teachable. His mind, when this line of argument was pushed to its logical conclusion, became merely a *tabula rasa* upon which, through education, enlightened ideas and beliefs could be imprinted. In one sense such a view was, by implication at least, pessimistic. If all knowledge were limited by man's sense perceptions, then he could know only the external aspects of the universe; knowledge of essences and final causes, for which so many philosophers and mystics had striven in the past, was forever beyond his reach. The French writer Condillac, whose *Traité des sensations* (1754) is the most extreme statement of this view of man's psychology, frankly admitted as much. On the everyday level, however, the implications of this view of the human mind were highly optimistic. Man might, it seemed, be made virtuous merely by providing him with the right environment, the appropriate set of stimuli both positive and negative. This meant, in practical terms, subjecting him to simple, just and comprehensible laws and, most important of all, appropriate education. It is from the Enlightenment and its inheritance from Locke that there stems that faith in the power of education to reform man and society, a faith sometimes noble though often deluded and even pathetic, which has continued to inspire radicals of different types down to our own day.

But if the Enlightenment in its French, or French-centred, form depended heavily on English ingredients, it transformed them into something distinctively its own. What then did it, as seen at full maturity, involve?

The most famous answer to this question is that given by the

German philosopher Immanuel Kant, a strong partisan of the Enlightenment and later for a time of the French Revolution, in his article, 'Beantwortung der Frage: Was ist Aufklärung' (An Answer to the Question: What is Enlightenment), published in the *Berlinische Monatschrift* in December 1784. In this he identified the essential characteristics of the great intellectual change as 'man's leaving his self-caused immaturity'. Hitherto he had been in intellectual tutelage, unable to use his mind freely without outside control and guidance. Now he had grown up. His unrestricted search for knowledge, his achievement of intellectual autonomy, would lead him to discard his former prejudices and bring him to a new freedom and the full realization of his potentialities. '*Sapere aude!* Dare to use your own intelligence! That is the motto of the Enlightenment!' Kant summed up. This well expresses the most fundamental aspect of the Enlightenment; its search for freedom. Man, guided by reason, was now to make his own way in the world without relying as in the past on the supports offered him by revelation and religious tradition, supports which had crippled even while they appeared to aid him. His newfound freedom was to be very largely the product of criticism, criticism of the past, of custom, of received ideas of any kind which could not stand the test of reason. From this criticism was to come man's power to make sense of the world and hence to control his own destinies. Philosophy was to become 'disciplined aggression against concrete problems'.

The purpose of this aggression was human happiness. The greatest single emotional drive behind the Enlightenment was that towards making men happy in the here and now; and as it progressed it became more and more easy to believe that no other objective really counted for very much. The potentially explosive idea of happiness as a right, something to which all men were entitled and which only ignorance and external obstacles – bad government, archaic laws, worst of all cramping and irrational religious influences – denied them, was now for the first time in history gaining wide acceptance. Such an idea, impossible to reconcile with traditional Christian faith, was still challenged by one or two thinkers of real stature (the most important was the Marquis de Vauvenargues, the greatest moralist of the century). But these were increasingly regarded as perverse and unworthy of serious attention. Happiness was the overriding objective; and the general happiness so eagerly sought could be ensured by correct engineering of government and society.

The methods by which Newton had explained the physical universe and Locke and Condillac that of the mind and the emotions could be applied to political and social problems. Man was to be seen as a part of nature and studied by the methods which obviously worked when applied to other parts of it. Such an application of reason to human affairs would make possible for the first time a just and virtuous, and therefore happy, society. This society would be just, virtuous and happy because it was natural, no longer distorted by unfairness and irrationalities sanctioned merely by time and tradition. Its members would enjoy their natural rights, be ruled by natural law and practice the natural religion of which God had implanted an instinctive consciousness in their hearts. They might even enjoy, according to one or two of the more extreme advocates of such ideas, natural equality, though what this could or should mean in practice was seldom spelt out. The Enlightenment's faith in the potentialities of intellectual freedom, in the application of reason and intelligence to the problem of human life, was therefore profoundly optimistic. Few thinkers of the period had any naïve belief in the inherent or absolute goodness of human nature; but almost all were deeply hopeful about what could be achieved even with very imperfect human beings through the workings of science, education and good government, and through the rebuilding of society along lines dictated by reason. Social usefulness, the maximization of human happiness, must become the criterion of morality.

It must be emphasized once more that the Enlightenment was a complex and in many ways disorganized intellectual movement which extended over a considerable period of time. What has been given in the preceding paragraphs is merely a highly simplified account of its main attitudes and beliefs. The full reality was much more complex; for different writers inevitably stressed different aspects of the set of ideas and attitudes which was shaking French intellectual life by the middle of the century. Voltaire represents its fierce anticlericalism and its demand for religious toleration; but in political terms he was a moderate, a believer in efficient monarchical government. His view of society (perhaps this is not surprising in a man who was both extremely wealthy and also well into middle age by the 1740s) was markedly conservative. Diderot, both politically and socially, was a far more genuine radical; he was one of the few *philosophes* who consistently displayed an open dislike for any form of despotism, even for those which attempted to be enlightened. In the secondary figures of the period in France a wide range of different forms of extremism can be seen. La Mettrie, in his *L'Homme machine* (1748) represents the materialist currents which the Enlightenment inherited from the seventeenth century carried to dogmatic and almost ludicrous lengths; Holbach, in his *Le Christianisme dévoilé* (1767) and *Système de la Nature* (1770) shows anti-religious feeling expressed as explicit atheism; Morellet in his *Code de la Nature* (1755) and Mably in his *De la Législation* (1776) exemplify the visionary and utopian aspects implicit in the whole system of 'enlightened' ideas.

The attitudes and beliefs of the *philosophes*, though they were often held with great force and sincerity, were in many ways unrealistic. This was partly because, while so sweeping and grandiose in some respects, they were surprisingly limited, even narrow, in others. They were concerned with Man in the abstract rather than with specific societies or communities; underlying them was a general assumption that the problems of government and society were at bottom much the same everywhere, that policies did not need to be carefully adapted to varying conditions or to the differing feelings, traditions and potentialities of those affected by them. What was required for good government, it was assumed, was a firm grasp of correct principles, not detailed study of particular problems and conditions. This attitude underlies the contempt with which so many writers of the Enlightenment regarded mere erudition and their indifference or even hostility towards scholarship and minute knowledge. 'Details', wrote one of them, 'can take care of themselves; in fundamentals everything is to be seen in relation to general principles, simple but unchanging. It is of the highest importance to understand them, and this is the main study of the statesman.' Much important work was done during the eighteenth century in accumulating knowledge of non-European societies, in laying some of the foundations of modern anthropology and sociology. But the extent to which this overlapped with or influenced political and social speculation, though not negligible; was in many ways surprisingly small. (The only important exception to this generalization is the interest in China as an example of good government and a well-organized society referred to on p. 374). Moreover Enlight-

enment theorizing was weakened by the indifference or contempt
with which it tended to regard history, or at least most of what
had happened since the great days of the Roman Empire. Good
government and the just and happy society were to be achieved
by analysis, criticism of what already existed, the use of reason,
rather than by trying to deduce lessons from the past. What had
existed proved nothing about what might, far less what should,
exist in the future. 'The rights of men in society', wrote Turgot,
who more sincerely than anyone else during the century
attempted to give ideas of enlightened government practical effect
in France, 'are based not on their history but on their nature.' In
particular the Middle Ages, permeated by the Catholic Christianity which the *philosophes* regarded as their greatest enemy,
aroused widespread contempt and revulsion. Kant spoke of them
as 'an incomprehensible aberration of the human mind', a phrase
no more severe than many other thinkers of the period used. Such
an attitude grossly overestimated the extent to which men could
escape from their past and the speed and ease with which radical
change of any kind could be introduced. It therefore contributed
substantially to the optimism which many *philosophes* felt about
the possibility of rapid political and social progress.

In so far as the Enlightenment appealed to history, it was to
that of Greece and Rome. In so far as it looked for models in the
past they were models of classical grandeur and urbanity, those
to be found in Virgil and still more in Horace and Cicero, the
most popular Latin authors of the period. 'Nature and the
ancients' was a slogan frequently used by the *philosophes*; and it
is clear that many of them saw themselves as the heirs of classical
antiquity fighting once more the struggle which 'the ancients' had
lost against Christian bigotry and repression. The classical tradition offered an alternative to Christianity which most of them
were glad to embrace. 'All over Europe and America', as a recent
historian has put it, 'for all philosophes alike, the ancients were
signposts to secularism.'[1] Even the physical condition of the city
of Rome in the eighteenth century, brokendown, dirty, with
perhaps a third of the population of its greatest imperial days,
seemed visible testimony to the conflict between classical antiquity
and Christian belief. It was this contrast, symbolized by 'bare-
footed friars . . . chanting their litanies in the temple of Jupiter'
which in 1764 inspired Edward Gibbon (the only great English
scholar of the century who can be considered as fully in the main-

415

stream of the Enlightenment) to begin his *Decline and Fall of the Roman Empire* (1776–88).

There were other, and equally serious, ways in which the *philosophes* and the Enlightenment showed their limitations. So far as effective social change was concerned, as distinct from mere speculation or the construction of paper Utopias, their radicalism was often a sham. Violence in words, especially when religion and established churches were being attacked, coexisted easily with a marked readiness in practice to accept with little or no demur society as it existed. The possibility of sweeping change through the application of reason might be envisaged; but the most daring speculation was very often underlain by a comfortable conviction that society as it stood was in essentials unchangeable. The *philosophes* were well aware that they wrote only for a small educated élite. They took it for granted that the great majority of Europeans would continue to be outside this charmed circle, largely uneducated and perhaps ineducable. Some of them, notably Voltaire, attacked the continued existence of serfdom in parts of France; but in general they paid little attention to the great and growing problems of land hunger, low productivity and general backwardness which weighed so heavily on much of the population. It is possible to find works by *philosophes* which can in some general and theoretical sense be called socialist. But these (the best examples are Morellet's *Code de la Nature* and Mably's *De la Législation*) were utopian schemes, not a response to immediate and specific grievances. They enunciated vast and far-reaching theories of social and legal equality, of the collective ownership of property, of the restriction or abolition of rights of inheritance; but this was a very different thing from a practicable programme of social change. A truer pointer to the future in many respects was the *Théorie des Lois civiles* of S. N. H. Linguet, which appeared in 1767. This attacked the claim of Locke and his followers that property originated from man's 'mingling' his labour with material objects and was therefore a natural right. On the contrary, Linguet argued, property had its roots merely in force and was at bottom nothing but the right of the stronger. Law and government, which existed to protect property rights, were thus 'a conspiracy against the most numerous part of the human race'. It is not surprising to find these assertions quoted with approval by Marx a century later. But Linguet was one of the most individual and idiosyncratic writers of the century, difficult to classify, not very influential, and in many ways quite untypical of the Enlightenment.

Moreover the genuine liberalism, the real concern for freedom (or at least for the intellectual freedom of the educated minority) which inspired so much of the work of the *philosophes* did not exclude from the French Enlightenment significant elements of intolerance, even of fanaticism. On one level this found expression in relatively trivial acts of personal self-seeking and group exclusiveness. Thus Diderot, while employed as a government censor, can be found demanding the suppression of a play (the *Satirique* of Palissot de Montenoy) which poked fun at enlightened ideas; while the publication of the Abbé d'Expilly's great statistical dictionary in 1762–70 (see p. 117) seems to have been delayed by the influence of the Physiocrats, since it dared to contradict their dogmatic belief that the population of France was declining. More important was the fact that by the end of the 1760s or the early 1770s the *philosophes* had gained complete control of organized intellectual life in France. The Academy in Paris, the numerous provincial academies, the literary societies, all were dominated by them; and they used this position to impose the ideas of the Enlightenment (in a moderate and watered-down form) as a kind of official orthodoxy. This cliquishness aroused much resentment among those denied the official posts and the publication opportunities which the dominant group monopolized.

But far more significant than these rivalries was the absolutism and intolerance inherent in many of the assumptions of the Enlightenment when they were pressed to their logical conclusion. In their more extreme form these postulated an ideal type of society and government which could, indeed must, be attained by the free workings of human reason. All existing political and social systems, the products merely of history and of the selfishness and obscurantism of rulers, aristocracies and churches, were thus destined to be replaced by a natural and rational order. This would come into existence when all the irrational and unnatural features of existing societies had been swept away. In such a society men would at last be free; but this would not lead to the emergence of differing opinions and parties among them. On the contrary, unfettered reason would produce complete harmony and unanimity. Such a society would also be one of perfectly virtuous men; and the idea of virtue (conceived

417

virtu

of in narrow terms of asceticism and intolerance of 'luxury') was
one which was gaining ground in radical circles in France during
the 1770s and 1780s. Side by side, therefore, with the mocking,
critical, worldly, sometimes cynical spirit represented so brilliantly by Voltaire there lurked within the Enlightenment another
which was utopian, messianic and at least potentially totalitarian.
In the works of Mably, and even more through those of Rousseau, this was to have considerable influence during the French
revolution. Later it was to become one thread in the complex
intellectual fabric of European radicalism in the nineteenth and
twentieth centuries.

The most impressive characteristic of the Enlightenment,
however, it must once more be emphasized, was its complexity,
its many-sidedness. To every generalization about it qualifications, sometimes serious and important ones, must be made if
any fair picture is to emerge. Certainly many of the *philosophes*
were buoyed up by a belief in the rationality of man and in his
ultimate perfectibility if he were placed in the correct environment
and subjected to the correct form of education. Yet at the same
time there was in the thinking of others a distinct vein of scepticism, even pessimism, a consciousness that consistent and
cumulative human progress over a long period of time might in
fact be difficult to achieve. In the middle of the previous century
the great philosopher and scientist Pascal, in opposition to
Descartes, had claimed to set distinct boundaries to the potentialities of human reason; and Descartes's successors a century
later had not really disproved the claim. It is true that in the 1790s,
when the Enlightenment proper was over, Condorcet in his
Esquisse d'un Tableau historique des Progrès de l'Esprit humain (1795)
restated the doctrines of human perfectibility and inevitable social
and intellectual advance in their most extreme form. But by then
this was a mere survival of earlier attitudes, attitudes which in any
case had never been fully accepted by most *philosophes*. It has been
argued with a good deal of force that, apart from Condorcet,
Turgot alone of eighteenth-century thinkers possessed 'a fully
articulated theory of progress'.[2] Again, most writers of this period
thought of nature as helpful to man, as something to be understood and then used by him. Yet Buffon, the French scientist
whose *Histoire naturelle* (1749–88) was by far the most detailed and
influential description of the natural world produced during the
century, became, as its thirty-six volumes appeared, increasingly

w/ things did change

inclined to see the natural world as hostile to man, an obstacle which he must overcome or even a foe which he must conquer. Here again pessimism crept into the picture.

Nor were the *philosophes* always uninterested in other ages than their own and unwilling to realize that human societies were the distinctive products of specific times and places. Voltaire himself, in his *Essai sur les Mœurs* (1756) made a remarkable pioneering effort to see the social development of humanity in historical and comparative terms. Moreover the Enlightenment, hard though it might try, could never completely cut itself off from its Christian roots. What it did, in essentials, was to erect a new orthodoxy, humanist and pseudo-scientific, to challenge that which had preceded it. To Christian, and above all Catholic, universalism it opposed its own, more liberal and optimistic. But what it preached was none the less a form of universalism; and this necessarily limited the genuineness of any claim it might make to be truly empirical in its outlook and methods. The contributors to the *Encyclopédie*, its greatest monument, clearly owed much to a legacy of Catholic orthodoxy of which they were the beneficiaries.

Perhaps the greatest difficulty of all in the way of any simple account of the Enlightenment, however, is the fact that the two most original and important French thinkers of the period, Montesquieu and still more Rousseau, stand in varying degrees apart from it and are difficult (in Rousseau's case impossible) to fit into any conventional Enlightenment mould.

Rousseau may not be the greatest of eighteenth-century writers on political and social problems. But he has certainly been the most influential. For this there are two reasons. He created a new view of the State; indeed he was the only writer of the period to put forward any significant theory of the State. He also went far towards creating a new sort of political and social consciousness, a new psychology. To the intellectual style of the mid-century Enlightenment typified by Voltaire and Hume, sceptical, witty, at least within certain limits genuinely liberal, he opposed another which was earnest, often introspective, deeply distrustful of the cosmopolitan high culture of the period, of wealth, great cities, sophistication of any kind. In political terms his greatest and most lasting achievement was to elevate the State to a position higher and powers more all-embracing than any of his predecessors had contemplated. Its functions in his eyes went much further than the mere protection of the individual and his property which Locke had assigned to it. On the contrary it was the fact that men lived in societies, and societies which were also States, which really distinguished them from animals. In his emphasis on this fact Rousseau can be seen, in a very general sense, as a major precursor of modern sociology; his exaltation of the State and its creative functions also gives his political philosophy some very general affinity with that which Hegel was to popularize in Germany, with such far-reaching effect, half a century later. It was the State, according to Rousseau's theory in its mature form, which made men fully human. That theory was embodied in a famous work, the *Contrat social* (1762). This envisaged men deciding to create a society, but none the less retaining in their own hands ultimate sovereign power which they would exercise by meeting periodically to legislate for their needs. The ideal, in other words, was direct democracy of a sort practicable only in a small State; Rousseau remained always deeply suspicious of any sort of representative system, which in his eyes must mean that the ordinary citizen would lose interest in and control over public affairs. This attitude owed something to admiration of the city-states of antiquity and still more to Rousseau's upbringing in Geneva, an early experience which deeply influenced his ideas. The citizens of his ideal State, when as a body they took decisions, declared the General Will, which must, by definition, always work for the advantage of society as a whole. It was nothing so mechanical as the mere will of a numerical majority. On the contrary, it expressed the 'real will' of every individual citizen, what each would desire if he were fully informed on the issues at stake and acted in accordance with the dictates of his higher nature. To the General Will factions and parties must give way; indeed group and sectional interests of any kind were a grave danger to the State and must as far as possible be suppressed. There are very obvious totalitarian possibilities inherent in such a view of political life and Rousseau recognized and welcomed this. To the State he assigned enormously far-reaching functions. It must enforce a high degree of economic equality between individuals (since this was essential for the preservation of society as Rousseau envisaged it). Even more important, it must control the private morals of citizens, must determine the education they received and must if possible be supported by a State religion systematically preaching patriotism and civic virtue.

All this is separated by a great gulf from the main stream of Enlightenment thought. Where the latter had little theory of the State or of political obligation and in general little interest in political philosophy as such, Rousseau made the State one of the cornerstones of his thought. Where the radical Enlightenment was sceptical if not downright hostile to any kind of religious feeling, he firmly believed that conscience, 'an innate principle of justice and virtue', had been implanted in man by God and was in itself a convincing proof of the existence of a supreme being. He thus, against the dominant current of Enlightenment philosophy, reverted to the venerable concept of innate ideas which were not merely the product of sense-impressions or social conditioning. Where the Enlightenment in general moved, though slowly and unevenly, towards greater economic liberalism, Rousseau demanded strict and pervasive economic controls (sumptuary laws; restriction of the right of inheritance; measures to preserve agriculture, the foundation of liberty and virtue, against the potentially corrupting effects of industry and finance). Where the Enlightenment was cosmopolitan, Rousseau showed a deep feeling for exclusive patriotism. Yet it must be stressed that he retained always a profound belief in the value and rights of the individual. It was to safeguard these, in his eyes, that the State and its machinery existed; they had no other justification.

The State of the *Contrat social*, as Rousseau himself admitted, was an ideal. It was not intended to have any direct relationship to the facts of everyday experience. He agreed that it could be realized only in small, geographically coherent societies – Geneva, Berne, perhaps Corsica for which he attempted in 1764 to draw up a constitution. His only attempt at practical constitution-making for a large territory, his *Considérations sur le Gouvernement de Pologne* (written in 1771 though not published until 1790) was by contrast remarkably moderate, almost conservative. In it he stressed that it was desirable 'to change nothing, either for retrenchment or addition, unless it is necessary', and envisaged the freeing of the Polish serfs only by stages and the continued exclusion of the mass of the population from any political power.

The puzzles and inconsistencies of his political doctrines by no means exhaust the interest of Rousseau for the historian. He was very much more than a merely political thinker. He was also the writer who, more than anyone else, popularized and indeed to a large extent created a new kind of consciousness, almost a new kind of man. His whole deeply unhappy life can be seen as a continuous effort to be himself, to realize his own potentialities without compromising with the world as it was, without succumbing to the longing for wealth, for worldly success, for the approval of the great and powerful. 'He provided', writes one of his biographers, 'an exemplary instance of the power of absolute integrity in a man whose life and thought were in perfect harmony, and of the tremendous impact, far-ranging effect and truly revolutionary value of that integrity.'[3] His struggles, his hopes and fears, his successes and failures, he revealed to the world with unprecedented frankness in his *Confessions*, the autobiography of which the first six volumes were published in 1782, four years after his death. This book is the greatest single monument of the later eighteenth-century cult of sensibility. In its revelation of the most intimate details of his private life, its preoccupation with feeling and emotion, its passionate response to natural scenery and its deep distrust of urban and intellectual society, it offers a revealing contrast with the *Memoirs of my Life and Writing* by Edward Gibbon (1796). Restrained, reticent, elegant, often ironic, Gibbon's book is the quintessence of many aspects of the Enlightenment. Rousseau's is both more and less. In it the Enlightenment in its rational and Roman aspects does not appear at all; but the *Confessions* points the way, as Gibbon does not, towards a new state of mind and a new set of psychological values. These also suffuse totally the most popular of all Rousseau's writings during his lifetime, his novel, *La Nouvelle Héloise* (1761) which by 1800 had appeared in at least seventy editions.

Throughout his life Rousseau was tormented by the need to choose between values good in themselves but apparently irreconcilable with one another. Could liberty really be combined with the progress of the civilization which both attracted and repelled him? Would the native virtues of the good heart be corrupted by the growth of knowledge? How was the patriotism which meant so much to him to be reconciled with a love of humanity in general? The fact that he was well aware of these questions and struggled to find answers to them is one source of his continuing fascination for generations of historians and commentators.

Montesquieu was the most many-sided, the most productive of stimulating ideas, of all the major French writers of the eighteenth century on politics and society. In these respects he had had no superior, perhaps no equal, since Aristotle himself. Of all the thinkers of the age he is in many ways the one whose methods of thought seem most modern, most relevant to the present day and its problems. He is also one of the few important figures amongst them who can be reasonably described as a conservative. His greatest work, *De l'Esprit des Lois* (1748) restated with great effect traditional ideas of 'mixed' government. In a well-regulated State one power would be balanced by another and no authority able to override all competitors. To the formation of this attitude both the practical example of the British constitution, which Montesquieu greatly admired but did not completely understand, and his own position as a member of an important family of the *noblesse de la robe* and the holder of high office in the *Parlement* of Bordeaux certainly contributed. He took it for granted that in all large European States monarchy was the only practicable and constructive form of government. Yet the monarch (whom Montesquieu distinguished very clearly from an arbitrary despot of the Asiatic type) must be limited in his actions by a powerful and responsible nobility and by laws which he could not override. Institutions of this kind, able to interpose effectively between the ruler and the mass of his subjects, were essential. 'Intermediate, subordinate and dependent powers', he argued, 'constitute the nature of monarchical government.' In an age of increasing political absolutism Montesquieu therefore stood, though in a limited, traditional and classbound way, for freedom.

From the dogmatism and universalism, the tendency to generalize widely on the basis of *a priori* assumptions and scanty or even non-existent evidence which marked much eighteenth-century political writing, he did not escape. His discussion, in the *Esprit des Lois*, of the essential characteristics of monarchical, aristocratic and republican forms of government is an example of this. It is based on the description of 'ideal types' of each of these, to a large extent divorced from time and place, rather than on the discussion of specific historical examples, while this threefold division goes back as far as Aristotle. Nevertheless his work (his earlier *Considérations sur les Causes de la Grandeur des Romains et de leur Décadence* (1734) as well as the *Esprit des Lois*) is unique in the writing of his own age in its effort to base analysis and explanation on a great body of detailed information. From the facts of history, from information about non-European peoples and their organization and achievements, Montesquieu tried to evolve laws which ruled the evolution of human societies. 'It is not Fortune that governs the world', he wrote. 'There are general causes, either moral or physical, which operate. . . . In a word, the dominant trend carries with it all particular incidents.' This attitude, in effect an effort to write a pioneering work of sociology on the largest scale, is Montesquieu's supreme claim to importance.

It led him, against the dominant current of Enlightenment thinking, to think of morality and government as relative, the product of specific times and places, and thus to be judged fairly only in their own context. Laws, he wrote, 'should be so adapted to the people for which they are created, that it should be a great coincidence if the laws of one nation suit another'. In other words, good government not only will vary but ought to vary radically, since different societies have quite different needs. His relativism also strengthened his conservatism; for the result of his work was usually to justify whatever customs or habits existed at any given moment in any particular society. Moreover the laws of development which he attempted to formulate – notably his, in modern eyes, naïve theory of the effects of differing climates on human psychology and hence on institutions, a theory which was in any case not at all novel – had little permanent value. Yet there is no denying the greatness of the effort; and Montesquieu's work at its best has a combination of realism and intellectual scope which puts it in a different class from almost anything else produced by the French Enlightenment. It is significant that his relativism, an attitude which gained increasing support from many writers during the later decades of the century, seems to have appealed particularly to statesmen and diplomats, men with direct experience of government and its problems. Thus Tanucci (in many ways no friend to the Enlightenment) agreed that 'universal laws in moral and political matters do not exist; laws arise from the position of the country and its people'.[4] In the same vein the Neapolitan ambassador in Paris, the Abbé Galiani, himself a voluminous writer on economic and social problems, proclaimed that 'good legislation is always that which corresponds to the constitution, strength and nature of each country'.[5] Intellectuals divorced from political responsibility, on the other hand, were often disconcerted by Montesquieu's moderation and conservatism. Many of his more radical contemporaries disliked his emphasis on the complexity of political and social problems and his insistence that 'nature always acts slowly', while Diderot strongly criticized his defence of feudalism and feudal privileges. Montesquieu, then, had no simple panacea for all social and political ills. More clearly than any other major writer of the century he realized that good government was difficult to achieve and maintain; this alone gives him a claim on the sympathies of our own age.

When has been said in the preceding pages is concerned almost entirely with the Enlightenment in France. It is inevitable that she should bulk very large in any discussion of the subject. It was in Paris that this whole movement of ideas appeared, between the 1740s and the 1770s, in its most concentrated and intellectually convincing form. It was French books, far more than German, Italian or English ones, which were translated into other languages during this period. It was French writers and scholars who found themselves invited by rulers elsewhere in Europe to visit their courts and to accept posts as advisers or as members of academies of sciences. Voltaire's unsuccessful visit to Prussia in 1750–53, the mathematician Maupertuis's years as President of the Berlin Academy in 1745–53, the fruitless journey of Diderot to Russia in 1773–74, are obvious examples of this. In so far as Europe was a single intellectual world in the eighteenth century it was a world of which France was in many respects the leader (see pp. 405–06). Nevertheless it would be a great mistake to imagine that the movement of ideas elsewhere in Europe was merely a copy of that in France. On the contrary; everywhere it was deeply influenced by local traditions, values and preferences. Nowhere is this more clearly seen than in England. There increasing political stability, economic growth and remarkable success in the building up of a great overseas empire meant that criticism, discontent and hankering after change, so strong in intellectual circles in France by the middle of the century, was relatively muted. Neither the support for Wilkes in the 1760s nor the movement for parliamentary reform in the later 1770s and 1780s owed much to the type of radical political speculation so widespread in France. Gibbon, the one great figure whom England contributed to the Enlightenment, spent much of his life abroad and remained in his own country isolated and untypical. Later in the century England produced a group of writers – Jeremy Bentham, Richard Price, William Godwin and Thomas

Paine – who stood squarely in the main continental 'enlightened' tradition of rationalism and anticlericalism. But most of these did not become significant until the 1790s, in an environment quite different from that of Voltaire and the *Encyclopédie*.

The country which led Europe in economic and technological development during the second half of the century thus showed itself almost immune to the ideas of the Enlightenment. This is perhaps the strongest of all grounds for rejecting the frequently repeated Marxist view of the latter as essentially the ideology of a developing middle class. It is true that in many parts of Europe an important role in disseminating new and critical ideas was played by societies of like-minded men who were often in some sense of that vague term 'bourgeois'. Such were the Friday Clubs in the Netherlands, the New Patriotic Society set up in Hamburg in 1765 and perhaps the *sociétés de pensée* which were numerous in France. But in general it is not easy to see any clear correlation between areas of middle-class strength and those in which radical ideas were generated. The weakness of any serious 'enlightened' impulse in England is thrown into sharper relief by the development of a very interesting and important Scottish Enlightenment. Its leading figures, Adam Ferguson, in his *Essay on the History of Civil Society* (1767) and John Millar, in his *Observations concerning the Distinctions of Ranks in Society* (1771), clearly inhabit the same intellectual world as the leaders of French intellectual life during these years. Perhaps an Enlightenment of this type, critical and hostile to many aspects of the status quo, can develop only in societies where modernity and backwardness confront each other at close quarters. Such stark discontinuities stimulate questioning and discontent. The contrasts in France between the high intellectual life of Paris and the ignorance of so much of the population in general, or in Scotland between the world of Adam Smith and David Hume and the archaic poverty of the Highlands, very recently emerged from tribalism, had this effect. In England, by contrast (and for that matter in the Dutch Republic also) society, in spite of gross inequalities and many regional disparities, was too well integrated for such a situation to be possible.

This argument is supported by the experience of Italy during this period. There also there were great disparities between different parts of the peninsula in the development of radical and critical ideas. The stagnation in this respect of Savoy or Venice contrasts sharply with the growth in Naples, during the later decades of the century, of a remarkable group of thinkers on political and economic questions: Genovesi, Galiani, Filangieri. The government of the Papal State, one of the most backward-looking and hostile to change in Europe, confronted the régime of Leopold in Tuscany, the most enlightened of all (see pp. 199ff). The country where clerical conservatism was stronger than anywhere else in Europe outside the Iberian peninsula and possibly Bavaria produced, in the *Delle Delitti e delle Pene* of Cesare Beccaria (1764), the book which began the development of modern penology, one of the key works of the Enlightenment as a movement of practical reform. The Italian Enlightenment, though it was in part a response to Italian conditions and problems, can none the less be seen as essentially an aspect of the great European movement of intellectual development, of questioning and criticism, of striving for liberty and rationality, which had its centre in France.

The greatest single figure in the intellectual history of eighteenth-century Italy, however, Giambattista Vico, stands quite outside this tradition and had done all his work before it came to fruition. His whole cast of mind was profoundly historical: he has been described as 'one of the most historically minded men who ever lived'. In this alone he differs radically from almost all the great figures of the French Enlightenment. Moreover he is important chiefly because of a quality of creative imagination lacking in their thinking. The central idea of his greatest work, the *Scienza nuova* (first published in 1725; the final version appeared in 1744, the year of his death) is that the true history of humanity is the history of its mental states. But only by an immense effort of the imagination, a struggle by the historian to project himself into an intellectual environment quite foreign to that of his own day, can these be understood. The history of an age must therefore be approached not merely through documents and inscriptions but even more through the study of its poetry and its use of language, and through the interpretation of its mythology. This attitude clearly foreshadows nineteenth-century developments and entitles Vico, more than any other thinker, to be called the founder of the philosophy of history. But it sets him apart from (many historians would now say above) the main stream of the French Enlightenment.

It is in Germany that we see most clearly an Enlightenment

which owed little to France and to the intellectuals of Paris. Some debt there undoubtedly was; but it was one mainly to the great untypical figures of the French movement, Montesquieu and Rousseau, both of whom achieved widespread popularity and influence east of the Rhine. The *Aufkärung* in Germany was based on foundations different from those of the Enlightenment in France. Its tone and style were very different. It is very significant that far more copies of the *Encyclopédie* were to be found in Italy and the Netherlands than in Germany. Empiricism, materialism, the sensationalist psychology which stemmed from Locke, utilitarianism with its simple and direct emphasis on happiness in this world; none of these became a leading element in German intellectual life during the century in the way that they did in France. While the dominant strains in French thought became increasingly hostile to ambitious metaphysical systems, which seemed merely to confuse simple issues and bamboozle honest men, in Germany thinking of this kind remained supreme. The prestige of the great German scientist and philosopher Leibniz, still enormous for long after his death in 1716, was one of the bases of this attitude; his idealism, his belief in a personal God and transcendental moral values, made a powerful appeal to German intellectual tastes. The leading *Aufklärer*, such as Christian Thomasius and Christian Wolff, sternly rejected empiricism. Later even Kant, a radical liberal and deeply interested in the physical sciences, thought it inadequate as a method for the understanding of either science or morality. No significant German thinker of the century ever advocated that men should be guided by principles derived from the study of physics or astronomy rather than by those drawn from their own insights and intuitions.

In practice this contrast between France and Germany showed itself most clearly in the great and continuing intellectual importance of religion in the latter. 'While French *philosophes* leaped into unbelief', one historian has written, 'their German brethren were seduced into it, step by reluctant step.'[6] Even this overstates the case; most of the *Aufklärer* managed to resist seduction more or less completely. Wolff, the most powerful figure of the century in German intellectual life, never abandoned his belief in the possibility of reconciling reason with the revealed truths of Christianity. Nor did the significance of religion and religious controversy in Germany show much sign of declining as the century drew to a close. 'When all other nations have given up respect for religion', wrote the Frenchman Chateaubriand in 1797, 'it will find a haven among the Germans.'

The generally un-French and strikingly moderate character of the *Aufklärung in Germany* was to have enormous long-term importance for the country's history. It helps, in particular, to explain the weakness throughout the nineteenth century of German liberalism as a political force. In the shorter term, however, it also had significance in one important respect outside Germany. Whereas the Enlightenment in Italy and Spain drew sustenance from the fountain-head in France, that in Russia was very largely German in inspiration. Though French cultural influences were very powerful in Russia from the 1750s onwards and the prestige of French literature and the French language very great, German philosophical and scientific influences were more important there than those stemming from France. The roots of the Enlightenment in Russia (in so far as it ever took root there) lay, it now seems clear, in the German universities which had been deeply influenced by Pietism, such as Halle, Marburg and Leipzig, rather than in France. Well before the end of the eighteenth century, therefore, the higher reaches of Russian intellectual life were being cast in a German rather than a French mould. This development was to be continued and intensified in the century which followed. It was one of the first indications that the German intellectual world, or at least the northern and mainly Protestant half of it, was from at least the 1770s onwards beginning to show in many respects a clear superiority to that of France. In mathematics and the sciences France still led Europe; but Goethe and Schiller in literature, Kant in philosophy, Herder in political thought (see pp. 432–4) were now figures which could not be matched west of the Rhine. Well before the French Revolution Germany was beginning to achieve that leadership of some aspects of European intellectual life which she was to maintain for the next century and more.

The intellectual currents which have been discussed in this chapter were among the most important legacies bequeathed by the eighteenth century to the future. Nevertheless their effect in their own day was in many ways limited. When we talk about the Enlightenment we are, as almost always in discussion of intellectual history, talking about a small élite. In France, the centre of the movement, with a total population in the later decades of the century of 26 million or more, the entire 'enlightened' public probably did not number more than 30,000–50,000 people. This was the tip of a social pyramid still based almost everywhere on unthinking routine and the ignorance of the uninstructed masses. The vast numerical majority of Europeans, the peasant at the plough, the artisan at his loom or forge, the ordinary man everywhere still often anxiously preoccupied by the price of bread, were totally unconscious of living in an age of enlightenment. To them government and society as they existed were something given and unchangeable, something to be endured. Revolt against specific injustices or acts of oppression was conceivable; fundamental change in traditional power structures was not. But even within the minority with enough leisure to read books and enough education to absorb abstract ideas the Enlightenment was never without serious competitors. 'In this century of reason', it has been said, 'people never ceased to delight in superstition.'[7] The remark is justified. Sometimes feelings of this kind took the more or less respectable form of adherence to Freemasonry or to religious mysticism or ritualism (see pp. 440ff). But besides these there was an unmistakable willingness, indeed eagerness, throughout the century, even among the educated and in the highest ranks of society, to embrace what now seem intellectually less defensible beliefs. Henri, Comte de Boulainvilliers, was one of the most radical thinkers of its first decades. His *Vie de Mahomed*, published posthumously in 1730, was an important contribution to the growth of religious scepticism and rationalist criticism in France. Yet he also believed firmly in astrology, one of the most ancient of all forms of superstition. In 1711, in his *Astrologie mondiale*, he attempted to prove its validity by drawing up parallel tables of historical events and astrological conjunctions in order to demonstrate the influence of the latter upon the former. In rather the same way a few years later the plague which devastated Provence in 1720 (the last great outbreak of the disease in Western Europe) was attributed by some doctors to the malign influence of the stars.

To a considerable extent the progress of the physical sciences undermined belief of this kind. The spectacular advance of astronomy meant that by the second quarter of the century astrology was increasingly ridiculed by the educated. (Though the much slower development of chemistry made it difficult to oppose alchemy, belief in the possibility of transmuting metals, of finding an universal solvent or even the elixir of life, with the same certainty.) However scientific progress was a two-edged weapon. On balance it encouraged a rationalist, analytical and materialist view of the world. But it also made it more intellectually respectable than in the past to see the universe as pervaded by forces beyond man's comprehension. The discovery of gravitation, of the fact that air and water, hitherto regarded as elements, were not simple substances, most of all the attention attracted by the still incomprehensible power of electricity, added to the mystery and wonder of the world for many. Science, it could be argued, pointed in this direction as much as in a rationalist one. 'Above science is magic', claimed a writer in the 1780s, 'because magic follows it, not as an effect, but as its perfection.' Attitudes of this kind, combining a taste for the marvellous with scraps of half-understood science, may well have been becoming more common over much of Europe in the 1770s and 1780s, as the dynamism and self-confidence of the Enlightenment rapidly ebbed. Certainly striking instances of a crude belief in magic can be found in the very highest reaches of society. Gustavus III of Sweden for example, in many of his policies an important exponent of Enlightened Despotism, was deeply attracted by the occult. He had his horoscope cast and consulted a female seer who claimed to foretell the future. Round his neck, in a gold box, he carried a magical powder intended to ward off evil spirits.

In France, the source of the Enlightenment in its most radical and uncompromising form, the growth of mysticism and irrationalism was especially remarkable. The German pseudo-scientist F. A. Mesmer, who claimed to effect miraculous cures through the powers of the 'universal fluid' which permeated and bound together the entire natural world, enjoyed immense success and popularity in Paris for a time in the early 1780s. So did the wonder-working Count Cagliostro, an adventurer who claimed to be a thousand years old, to have access to the mystic lore of the ancient Egyptians and to be able to transmute base metals into gold. Simultaneously L. C. de Saint-Martin, 'the unknown philsopher', was preaching an almost unintelligible but emotionally satisfying mysticism which, in its explicit rejection of the specific and the measureable, its assertion that the material world was subordinate to a more real spiritual one, had great appeal in many parts of Europe. By the 1780s the Enlightenment was dying in the city which more than any other had given it life, its deathbed surrounded by a whole family of exotic mysticisms. 'Never, certainly,' wrote one Parisian mesmerist in 1788, 'were Rosicrucians, alchemists, prophets, and everything related to them so numerous and so influential. Conversation turns almost entirely upon these matters; they fill everyone's thoughts; they strike everyone's imagination. . . . Looking around us, we see only sorcerers, initiates, necromancers and prophets. Everyone has his own, on whom he counts.'

This turning away from rationalism and materialism, this search for a mental diet which nourished the emotions as well as the intellect, is clearly connected with the growth of the cults of sensibility and primitivism and with the whole complex movement of early romanticism, which has already been briefly alluded to (see pp. 395–6). It has been said that 'the romantic mentality is the mentality of miracles' and certainly the phrase expresses one important aspect of the early stages of the romantic movement. More than anywhere else it was in Germany that many aspects of romanticism came to their fullest fruition in the later eighteenth century. It was German writers above all who propagated the belief, deeply hostile to the assumptions of the Parisian *philosophes*, that the merely rational is weak and impoverished whereas the primitive is creative and strong. This attitude was first put forward in the 1760s by one of the strangest and most enigmatic writers of the century, J. G. Hamann, 'the Magus of the North', a figure who defies categorization. It finds its supreme expression in the work of J. G. Herder, whose most important book, *Ideen zur Philosophie der Geschichte der Menschheit*, appeared in 1784–91. Herder, more than any other writer of the century except Rousseau, was to shape the mind, indeed the whole history, of Europe in generations to come. His greatest contribution to the future was to make the happiness of the individual and the full realization of his capacities depend absolutely on his membership of an organic and historically based community, a nation. This community was to be defined above all in terms of its language, the language in which Herder believed 'the whole heart and soul' of a nation were to be found. This view of humanity, with its complete rejection of universalism, of cosmopolitan and supranational standards of judgement, was impossible to reconcile with the main stream of the Enlightenment as it had developed in France. Herder's whole cast of mind, his love of all that is natural and deep-rooted and his deep dislike of uniformity and distrust of abstract reasoning, were quite foreign to the intellectual style of the French Enlightenment. So were his view of history, his passionate belief that a man must be of his own age and his own nation, that every historical moment and situation is unique and different from all others. It followed from this that different civilizations and cultures could never be fairly compared with one another. But to rule out comparisons of this kind, to reject the widespread Enlightenment belief in the inferiority of the Middle Ages and the superiority of Augustan Rome or Periclean Athens, was to abandon the search for an ideal State and an ideal man. This in turn meant giving up any easily optimistic idea of the inevitability of progress once man's intellect had been freed from artificial restrictions. Herder believed in the possibility of progress; but to him it was to be measured in terms only of a specific society and a given historical epoch, not in those of some utopian ideal. Assertions of this kind amounted to a revolution against the whole drift of much of European thinking for most of the last hundred years. Moreover although Herder himself was in political terms far from conservative (he opposed hereditary rule, serfdom, despotism and censorship) it was a revolution whose implications were, in the long run at least, to be conservative much more than radical.

Its importance in the history of ideas was enormous. It is Herder more than any other thinker who links the often vague and utopian political idealism of the eighteenth century with the organized and powerful liberalism of the nineteenth, a set of aspirations with a great political movement. Most important of all, he is the first and most constructive prophet of nationalism. He did not create or in his own lifetime do much to intensify national and patriotic feeling. This had been slowly taking shape, at least in parts of Western Europe, for many generations. It was clearly becoming more powerful in the second half of the eighteenth century quite independent of anything intellectuals did to bring this about. The disasters of the Seven Years War, which faced the *philosophes* in France with a difficult choice between cosmopolitanism and national pride, had considerable effect in accelerating this development; while the palace revolution of 1762 which placed Catherine II on the Russian throne was in part an expression of national resentment of apparently predominant German influences in St Petersburg. But it was Herder, far more than anyone else, who provided nationalism with an organized and convincing ideology. He thus provided the intellectual foundations for the most dynamic political emotion, the most seductive political style, of the world which was taking shape by the time of his death in 1803. No writer illustrates better the fecundity and variety of the intellectual life of eighteenth-century Europe and the impossibility of forcing it into a purely French, a rationalist and universalist, mould.

NOTES AND REFERENCES

1 P. Gay, *The Rise of Modern Paganism* (London, 1967), p. 44: Book I, Chap. i of this book is the best account of the debt of the Enlightenment to classical antiquity.

2 P. Gay, 'The Enlightenment in the history of political theory', *Political Science Quarterly*, vol. LXIX (1954), p. 380.

3 J. Guéhenno, *Jean-Jacques Rousseau* (London-New York, 1966), vol. I, Preface, p. xvi.

4 Quoted in H. Holldack, 'Der Physiocratismus und die absolute Monarchie', *Historische Zeitschrift*, vol. CXLV (1932), p. 521.

5 *Dialogues sur le Commerce des Blés* (Berlin, 1795), pp. 121, 475.

6 Gay, *The Rise of Modern Paganism*, p. 331.

7 L. Trenard, *Lyon de l'Encyclopédie au préromantisme* (Paris, 1958), vol. I, p. 175.

16

RELIGION AND THE CHURCHES

The geographical distribution of the major Christian communions in Europe altered little during this period. Lutheranism, normally of a highly orthodox and conservative kind, held sway over Scandinavia and much of North Germany. Anglicanism, though subjected to increasingly serious competition from the various dissenting sects and from the Methodists, remained dominant in England. In Scotland, the United Provinces, a few German States and some of the Swiss cantons, Calvinism maintained the ascendancy so painfully won in previous generations, while an important Calvinist minority existed in Hungary and appreciable ones in France, Poland and Bohemia. Catholicism retained its hold on the Iberian peninsula, Italy, France, Poland and most of the Habsburg Empire and South Germany. In White Russia and the Ukraine the Uniates, who acknowledged papal authority while retaining many Orthodox rites and customs, were strong. In the East the Orthodox Church, dominant in Russia, continued to claim the allegiance of large groups in eastern Poland and parts of the Habsburg Empire. In the Balkans, where its hierarchy was almost entirely Greek, it was, except in a few areas such as Bosnia and Albania, the Church of the great majority of the population.

Throughout Europe it was accepted without question by almost everyone that some form of religious faith was the essential foundation of all organized society. Without the belief which religion alone could give in a future world in which virtue was rewarded and vice punished there would be no self-imposed restraint on man's passions and desires; the only effective barrier against a tidal wave of crime and disorder would have been removed. Without the acceptance of gross social inequalities, fostered by the belief that they were an integral part of the divine plan for humanity and thus to be patiently endured, society would lose all form and structure and collapse into anarchy. Unsupported by religion, deprived of the legitimacy which its support alone could give, no government would be safe or lasting. Everywhere the alliance between Church and State was taken for granted. No country was without a privileged State Church; and in many it was the only form of religious practice with any recognized right to exist.

In many parts of Western Europe, however, above all in Britain and France, established Churches and the systems of belief for which they stood were being subjected to a process of intellectual erosion. Increasingly their self-confidence and their hold over the minds of educated men were being eaten away by the growth of new assumptions and the development of new attitudes. The theological systems inherited from the past, well attuned to the conditions and intellectual ambience of the Reformation and Counter-Reformation, became from the later seventeenth century onwards increasingly out of harmony with the spirit of the age; they were, it has been said, 'a Gothic shrine in a Palladian basilica'.[1]

Traditional forms of religious belief were challenged during this period from a number of directions. 'Infidelity' and outright atheism probably became somewhat more common, and were certainly more openly expressed than ever before. They continued, however, almost as much as in the past, to be confined to tiny groups of untypical intellectuals and *esprits forts*, the great majority of them French. In spite of the alarm they aroused in the ranks of the faithful, they had little practical importance. With few exceptions (Holbach is the most important one) even the most radical thinkers of the period were not prepared to advocate atheism or a purely secular State. Nor were theological deviations such as Arianism and Socinianism[2] a real threat to established belief except in a few parts of the continent. (The most important of those was England, where Socinianism, which stressed heavily the primacy of reason in any form of religious belief, developed in the later eighteenth century into a Unitarian movement small in the number of its adherents but strong in their intellectual quality.) Pure scepticism, again, in the sense of a denial of the possibility of certainty in solving religious problems, was rare throughout this period. More important than any of these was the challenge to conventional belief now being offered by the development of techniques of criticism which stressed the improbabilities and inconsistencies of the Bible from a historical point of view. Against this challenge scholars such as Hardouin and Berruyer attempted to defend Catholic orthodoxy by stressing the importance of tradition, an unbroken tradition embodied in the teachings of the Church as it actually existed.

By far the most profound and widespread threat to existing systems of belief in Western Europe, however, was that provided by 'natural religion'. This was based on two assumptions. Firstly its adherents took it for granted, like all believers, that the universe was divinely constructed, the work of God. More particularly, they believed that its divine authorship was manifested by the symmetry and regularity of its workings, by the fact that it clearly obeyed certain simple and universal laws. So complex a machine working so efficiently must be the product of some superhuman creative force: it could not be the result of chance. Scientific discoveries, above all those of Newton, helped to strengthen and disseminate this assumption. They did much to spread the feeling that the study of the physical world, rather than of the works of orthodox divines or even the Fathers of the Church, was the passport to a knowledge of true religion. Secondly, and perhaps more important, belief in natural religion involved the assumption that there were certain religious ideas innate in every man, ideas which were intuitive and universal. Such were the knowledge that God existed; that man would be rewarded or punished in a future life for his behaviour in this one; and that he owed certain fundamental duties both to God and his neighbour. Underlying this type of thinking was the powerful and very widely accepted assumption that the simplicity and rationality of a belief were reliable guarantees of its truth, that truth could hardly co-exist with complexity and still less with obscurity. Two of the English works which laid the foundations of 'natural religion' make this point well in their titles – John Locke's *The Reasonableness of Christianity* (1695) and John Toland's *Christianity not Mysterious* (1696).

Beliefs of this kind, though often very vaguely formulated, had considerable influence within the established Churches of Western Europe during this period. In France in particular they were pressed to remarkable lengths by a number of Jesuit scholars. Nevertheless they cut at the roots of orthodoxy, both Catholic

437

and Protestant. God's continual manifestation of himself through a universe which science could describe and measure seemed to reduce, even to destroy, the significance of any special act of revelation. Natural religion was therefore by implication hostile not merely to mysticism and metaphysics but to all forms of revealed religion, and even to the idea of a personal God. Thus the Jesuit Abbé Camier could argue, in a textbook published in 1769, that 'Natural Law has binding force independently of the existence of God', and that 'moral principles impose obligation independently of the existence of God'. It was also inevitably hostile to the claims of the various Churches to the exclusive possession of truth. Toland argued in his *Nazarenus* (1718) that it was possible to speak of 'Jewish, Gentile and Mahometan Christianity', while nearly seventy years later the Provost of Berlin Cathedral could claim that the Jews were 'true Christians', since they believed in God, virtue and immortality. Many contemporaries would have accepted the assumptions behind these phrases, even if they shied at the clarity with which they were expressed.

Moreover, if man came into the world with all the beliefs essential for salvation already imprinted on his heart, of what real value were the theological systems and dogmatic complexities, the liturgical and ceremonial elaborations, with which nearly all existing Churches were in varying degrees encrusted? Natural religion thus tended to be indifferent to the externals of belief and worship. It was also hostile to traditional theology, which it could easily regard as a mere breeding-ground of meaningless and unnecessary disputes. The division which really mattered was that between the moral and the immoral, not between the orthodox and the heterodox. 'The greatest heresy', said an English archbishop who sympathized with these attitudes, 'is a wicked life.' A Christianity cleansed of the corruptions which it had accumulated in the course of centuries and restored to primitive purity, a Christianity whose dogmas should be few and simple, a Christianity freed from priestly power and arrogance and from the theology which that power had created – this was a vision very attractive to many thinkers of the eighteenth century.

Feeling of this kind was strengthened by the growing interest in, and frequent admiration of, non-European peoples which was so marked during this period. The innate religious emotions and aspirations postulated by natural religion were the same for all men. All of them stood in the same relationship to God. Why then should a virtuous Brahmin or Confucian be considered the spiritual inferior of a Christian? Did they not all worship the same God? Was it not possible that Christians might learn something from a study of the holy books of other religions which were now beginning to be translated into European languages? (see p. 375). Several of the greatest critical thinkers of the century – Diderot in his *Lettre sur les Aveugles* (1749), Hume in his posthumously published *Dialogues on Natural Religion* (1779), Kant in his *Critique of Pure Reason* (1781) – showed that the intellectual bases of natural religion were far from unassailable: in particular they seriously undermined the whole 'argument from design' which was one of its foundations. But the influence of this criticism on the ordinary man, even on the ordinary educated man, was very limited. Natural religion appealed strongly to one of the most prominent aspects of much eighteenth-century intellectual life – its liking for simple and common-sense ideas and distrust of metaphysics.

Natural religion and the Deism and Latitudinarianism which it generated had during this period more influence in England than anywhere else. In the early decades of the century a galaxy of able writers – Samuel Clarke, Thomas Woolston, Matthew Tindal and others – by expounding its ideas undermined dogmas and assumptions which had for generations been the common currency of Anglicanism. Later the Unitarian Joseph Priestley, himself a great scientist, proposed in his *History of the Corruptions of Christianity* (1782) to purify Christian belief by stripping it of what all orthodox believers thought of as its essential doctrines – the Trinity, Original Sin, the Atonement and Predestination among others. But similar attitudes were influential elsewhere in Europe. In Germany the ideas of Christian Wolff had considerable affinities with those of his Deist contemporaries in England: they led to his expulsion by Frederick William I from his chair at the University of Halle. Above all the writings of Voltaire were, from the religious point of view, a sustained plea, usually superficial but often brilliantly effective, for Deism and natural religion.

Underlying all these new and radical attitudes were the forces of social change and development. The religion practised by the masses everywhere was still traditional, unintellectual, emotional and life-pervading. The more intellectual, self-conscious, limited and even sceptical forms of belief which have been described in the previous paragraphs were the faith merely of an educated minority, though an increasingly active and vocal one. Men of this stamp lived in a world increasingly dominated by ideas of accurate measurement and exact calculation, a world slowly but surely moving towards our own day and succumbing to the rule of statistics and balance-sheets. For them it was increasingly difficult to accept miracles, mysteries and legends, in fact many of the beliefs with which traditional religion was encrusted. Physics and astronomy had discovered laws by which the universe was ruled and which God himself, it was claimed, could not infringe. His power thus lost some of its total and awe-inspiring character and became almost contractual. An increasing emphasis on practical virtue and good citizenship meant that the overwhelming theological distinction between the saved and the damned became in practice less important than that between the man who did his duty in this world and the man who did not. Even the religious view of labour as the penalty exacted from the descendants of Adam in retribution for his sin was probably undermined by the growth in the amount of interesting and rewarding work which accompanied and underlay the slow emergence of the modern professional classes. Social forces of this kind, in their blind and almost unconscious workings, may have done more than the writings of the *philosophes* to undermine traditional religious values. Natural religion, Deism, and hostility to religious tradition and dogma were the product of a few West European States – Great Britain, the United Provinces, France and parts of Germany. In Spain, Portugal, the Habsburg territories and most of Italy they developed much more slowly and had far less influence. In Orthodox Christendom they were weaker still. In other words they were characteristic of States experiencing the intellectually liberating effects of scientific and geographical discovery, of societies which possessed a substantial educated middle class or at least a certain element of liberal-minded aristocracy. Where these factors were weak or absent such radical ideas found it almost impossible to take root.

The desire for a form of belief which was simpler, more rational, more in tune with the leading currents of secular thought, also provided the foundations for the growth of Freemasonry, or at least the most widespread type of Freemasonry, during this period. From its foundation in England (the Grand Lodge there was set up in 1717) it spread rapidly to the continent. The first French and Italian lodges were opened in 1726. Frederick II founded a lodge at Charlottenburg in 1740 and became Grand

Master of one in Berlin in 1744. In spite of condemnations by the
Papacy in 1738 and 1751 its growth was rapid in many parts of
Catholic Europe. In Lyons, for example, sixteen different lodges
were founded in 1760–89. Moreover Freemasonry drew support
not merely from the merchants and professional men who made
up most of its membership but also from many intellectuals,
nobles, clerics and even rulers. At the coronation in 1745 of the
Holy Roman Emperor Francis I (who had become a mason in 1731)
a masonic ceremony even formed part of the proceedings. In the
second half of the century it began to be influential in Poland
and Russia, where the statesman Count Z. G. Chernyshev and the
great journalist N. I. Novikov were among its leading adherents.

Many factors contributed to the popularity of Freemasonry. Its
vague stress on reason and virtue as opposed to tradition and
dogmatic subtleties; its equally vague emphasizing of human
brotherhood and the need to transcend national divisions; the fact
that it could, at least to a limited extent, bring together in its
lodges people of differing social class; all these help to explain its
rapid growth. But these factors should not be exaggerated. Its
supporters made some very high claims. A masonic pamphlet of
1786 asserted that 'Masonry . . . unites people of all nations, of
all religions, of all social orders; the Mexican and the Siberian, the
German and the Japanese, the Christian and the Muslim, and the
Jew, the minister, the Capuchin and the field-marshal embrace
one another in the lodge. The opinions of all sects are mutually
tolerated.' This, however, was a gross exaggeration. Masonic
lodges differed enormously in their social composition even
within a single city: two of those in Lyons drew over 40 per cent
of their members from the nobility while two others did not
include a single noble. Moreover there were serious differences
and rivalries between different forms of Freemasonry and sometimes considerable factional struggles within individual lodges.
Nowhere, except in England and the Dutch Republic, were Jews
accepted as members except in very unusual circumstances. Often
the lodges were merely sociable gatherings of men interested in
nothing higher than banqueting, conversation and the drinking
of toasts. Very often they were quite as class-conscious as society
in general. Thus the constitution of the Peace lodge at Toulouse
declared that 'no one may be received as a Mason or an officiate
who is not of a profession nearly equal to that of most brothers
in the lodge'.[3]

The liberalizing currents in eighteenth-century religious life which have been described above also aided the growth of religious toleration. Thus in England the laws which discriminated against Protestant Dissenters were either repealed (as were the Occasional Conformity and Schism Acts passed by the Tories in 1711 and 1714) or if they remained on the statute-book were usually enforced laxly or not at all for much of this period. (Catholics, however, had to wait till 1778 for the first step towards any alleviation of their legal disabilities.) In France the persecution of the Huguenots (the French Protestants), which had produced a serious revolt in the Cevennes in 1702–04, continued far into the century. It became, however, steadily less severe and less whole-hearted. Many French bishops, though remaining attached in principle to the idea of religious intolerance, were by the second half of the century ready to restore normal civil rights to the Huguenots. The edict of 1787 which partially effected this restoration was issued by a Cardinal, Loménie de Brienne, while one of the greatest dignitaries of the French Church, the Archbishop of Narbonne, congratulated Louis XVI on such a display of enlightenment. In 1781 Joseph II brought a large measure of religious toleration to the Habsburg territories. In Italy and the Iberian peninsula, though there was still no thought of toleration, attitudes were softening a little: even in Portugal the public burning of Jews and relapsed heretics was prohibited in 1774.

It can scarcely be emphasized too strongly, however, that what has been described in the preceding pages was only one side of eighteenth-century religious life. Man does not live by reason alone; and natural religion, toleration and the faiths of the Enlightenment in general proved too meagre and unsatisfying a diet for many people, even many educated people, in this period. Everywhere religious literature of varying intellectual quality but of a quite traditional kind – printed sermons, collections of saints' lives, catechisms – continued to be sold in greater quantities than almost any type of secular writing. Everywhere there was a huge demand for cheaply produced religious works of a popular kind. In the last decade before the Revolution well over a million copies of these were produced in France by provincial printers alone; and there were many others printed without official authorization which therefore do not appear in this total. Even in England, the fountainhead of natural religion, the best-seller of the century was a devoutly conventional tract, Bishop Sherlock's *Letter from our Lord Bishop of London to the Clergy and People of London on the Occasion of the Late Earthquake* (London, 1750), of which over 100,000 copies were sold or given away by the author's admirers. One form of traditional writing in particular continued to flourish. This was the tract intended to prepare the sinner for the all-important moment of death, the tremendous moment when, it was claimed, the fate of the soul was decided by its last conscious acts. This type of devotional work still attracted a large and very varied readership, much of it made up of educated people.

There are clear signs that at least in France, where this subject has been more and better studied than anywhere else, some conventional pious forms were losing their former hold on the well-to-do, urban and educated part of society. There is a marked tendency for religious phraseology and formulae to disappear from the preambles to wills, where they had been frequent in the seventeenth century. When Louis XIV died 80 per cent or more of all French wills contained an invocation of the Virgin; by the time of the Revolution only 10 or 20 per cent did so. These wills also show a clearly declining readiness on the part of testators to leave money for masses to be said for the repose of their souls. Pomp and ostentatious expense at funerals become less common, and it has even been argued that the increasing number of satirical epitaphs to be found on tombstones is a sign of a new and less respectful attitude to death. But these were developments in one country only, and that one the centre of the radical and critical aspects of the Enlightenment. How far they were paralleled among the wealthier and more educated groups in society else- where in Europe is far from clear; and even in France they tell us nothing about the faith of the great majority – poor, unedu- cated, and much more often than not rural. At that level traditional forms of popular belief – in the efficacy of relics and pilgrimages; in fasting and other forms of mortification of the flesh; in the cult of the Virgin – flourished as they had done for centuries over the whole of Catholic and Orthodox Europe.

Everywhere there was a great structure of popular belief, much of it pre-Christian, in the magical powers of particular rocks, streams, springs or other natural features, in omens, spells, charms and a wide range of quasi-religious rituals. Occasionally beliefs of this kind could even become politically threatening. One of the most serious outbreaks of popular disorder of the century, the Plague Riots of September 1771 in Moscow, was set off by the gathering of great crowds begging protection against the disease then devastating the city from a wonder-working icon of the Virgin and the efforts of the authorities to disperse them. Everywhere the formal religion of the literate, the urban and the well-to-do was underlain by powerful popular undercurrents of what now seem a deeply superstitious kind. There was, for example, a wide range of superstitions associated with those who had died as criminals on the scaffold. In England it was believed that the touch of a hanged man could cure a wide range of illnesses, while the rope which had been used in an execution, and even wood chippings from the gallows, were thought to have curative properties. When in 1777 in Paris an alleged criminal who was widely believed to be innocent was broken on the wheel and his body burnt the ashes were immediately combed through for bones to be sold to the highest bidder, since these were believed to have magical powers. It is important to remember, moreover, that everywhere in Europe high levels of formal religious observance, in terms of frequent church attendance and genuine attachment to traditional rituals, co-existed with much behaviour which all Churches disliked but could not prevent or repress. It has been shown, for example, that in parts of south-central France punctilious performance of formal religious duties went hand in hand with a great deal of infanticide, rape and sexual assault on children, while marriages which contravened the Church's teaching on the prohibited degrees of affinity were also very frequent. The situation was certainly similar in many other parts of Europe.

The faith of the humble, of people who published no books, compiled no memoirs and did not normally even write letters, is inherently a difficult subject to discuss with precision or to measure in any clear-cut way. The extent to which belief in sorcery and witchcraft still flourished is particularly obscure, since the ending of the witch trials so common over much of Europe until the second half of the seventeenth century deprives us of the evidence which they provide for earlier generations. There is no doubt, however, of the persistence of widespread popular fear and hostility towards witches, at least in rural areas, even in some of the more developed parts of Europe. In 1751 two old women were drowned in a horsepond in Tring, within twenty miles of London, on suspicion of being witches. In western France in 1780 a woman suspected of having bewitched animals had her feet burned by frightened and infuriated peasants and was then drowned in a pond. Two years later another was burned as a witch in one of the Swiss cantons. Nor was it very difficult, at least in parts of the continent, to find educated men prepared to give some support to such beliefs. A book published in Milan in 1742, which denied the existence of the magic arts in general, aroused a good deal of suspicion because of its alleged religious unorthodoxy; while in Bavaria (the most intellectually undeveloped of all the major German States) an attack on belief in witchcraft published by a priest in 1761 provoked sharp controversy.

Travellers from the more intellectually developed parts of the continent were frequently shocked and even frightened by the intensity with which popular religious emotion was given expression in Spain, Portugal, most of Italy and much of Catholic Germany and Switzerland. John Wilkes, at least ostensibly a radical and a freethinker (see pp. 174–5), was impressed in this way by the behaviour of the Neapolitans in 1765, when the liquefaction of the blood of St Januarius (San Gennaro), the most famous ritual miracle in all Europe, was delayed. As the cardinal conducting the ceremony vainly agitated the phial containing the miraculous fluid 'the people grew quite outrageous. The women shriek'd hideously, beat their breasts and tore their hair. The men seemed equally frantic. They began the most frightful yelling, and several were cutting themselves with knives.'[4] Over much of Catholic Europe the Church tried to restrain and even suppress extravagantly emotional cults and types of devotion in the interests of decency and order: this was a continuation of the efforts it had been making for centuries to control and systematize religious life by imposing on it order and regularity. These efforts, however, had at best mixed success.

Nor were beliefs of this kind confined to the lower strata of society. In 1716, when his son had died a few weeks after birth, the Emperor Charles VI made a pilgrimage to Mariazell and laid before the statue of the Virgin there an image of the Christ-child in silver weighing exactly the same as his own dead son. He then prayed for another male heir. In Spain the Duchess of Alva, a member of one of the greatest grandee families, attempted to cure the illness of her son by making him swallow, in powdered form, what was alleged to be a mummified finger of St. Isidore. Even in Britain and France faith in the efficacy of the touch of a legit-

imate ruler as a cure for scrofula lingered on to the end of this
period. Queen Anne was the last English ruler to 'touch for the
King's Evil'; but the Jacobite pretender Prince Charles Edward
and his brother, Cardinal York, kept up the practice till the latter's
death in 1807. Over 2,000 sufferers came to be touched by Louis
XV on the day before his coronation at Rheims in 1722, while
over 2,400 came to beg the help of Louis XVI on the same
occasion half a century later.

The continuing power of religious emotion can also be seen in
a growth in some parts of Protestant Europe of new sects, often
of a mystical or semi-mystical kind. This growth was largely a
reaction against the rationalism and Deism which were now
increasingly influential in these areas, and became more rapid
from the 1760s onwards.

The most important example of this tendency was the development of the Methodist movement in England. Methodism,
which began to evolve a separate organization in the 1740s though
its final break with the Anglican Church did not come till 1784,
can hardly be described as mystical. Nevertheless it was explicitly
hostile to religious liberalism and distrustful of some aspects of
the physical sciences. Wesley himself doubted 'whether any man
on earth knows either the distance or the magnitude, I will not
say of a fixed star, but of Saturn or Jupiter, yea of the Sun or
Moon', and complained that 'the infidels [i.e. rationalists and
liberals] have hooted witchcraft out of the world'.[5] He is known
greatly to have admired a number of Catholic mystics, notably
St Francis de Sales. The sermons he preached, sometimes allegedly to audiences as large as 20,000 often produced outbursts of
very violent religious emotion: certainty based on faith, an
explicit relegation of reason to a very inferior position, were the
keynotes of his teaching. A similar distrust of many leading ideas
of the age, a similar insistence on religion as a mode of experience
rather than a system of thought, is to be found in the growth of
Pietism in Germany. Here too the religion of the heart and the
idea of a 'second birth' of the convert were central. The doctrines
of the great Pietist writers of the previous century, Boehme and
Spener, revived and adapted by Count N. L. von Zinzendorf,
provided the basis for the Moravian movement, one of the most
remarkable of this period. Many of the forms it took – for
example its sometimes macabre use of traditional Christian
symbols such as the lamb and the wounds of Christ – seem bizarre

and even repulsive to modern eyes. Nevertheless its vitality was shown by its ability, like Methodism though on a smaller scale, to gain adherents. From its original strongholds at Bethelsdorf and Herrnhut, on Zinzendorf's estate in Lusatia, it spread not merely over much of Germany but also in North America. Pietism differed from Methodism in a number of ways. In particular it received a good deal of encouragement from some German nobles and even some rulers of minor German States, while few members of the English ruling class showed much sympathy for Wesley and his followers. Nevertheless the two movements had to a very large extent a common psychological basis. Both laid great emphasis on the part to be played by music in arousing religious emotion. More significant, the adherents of both were often guided, in making difficult decisions, by drawing lots, or by opening the Bible at random and drawing inspiration from the first text to offer itself. Such methods were an implicit rejection of the idea of man as an autonomous individual, a reassertion of his position as a mere instrument of God.

Freemasonry also developed in the later eighteenth century, particularly in Germany and Russia, a markedly mystical and irrational side. Its most extreme form, the Strict Observance, which claimed to derive its origins from the medieval order of the Templars, showed marked tendencies of this kind and in political terms was, at least by implication, strongly conservative. I. G. Schwarz, a German from Transylvania who held a chair at the University of Moscow in 1779–83 and imported into Russian Freemasonry a large element of mysticism and irrationalism, is a good example of tendencies of this sort. Side by side with the masonic lodges, moreover, there grew up in the second half of the century secret societies which carried mysticism, secrecy and a taste for exotic rituals to extreme lengths. The best known is that of the Illuminati, founded in 1776 in Bavaria by Adam Weishaupt, whose organization and ceremonies had some affinities with Strict Observance Masonry. The Rosicrucians, founded in Regensburg in 1755, went even further in this direction, for the leaders of the order were believed by their followers to possess divine powers and within it astrology and sorcery seem to have been fairly widely practised. It would be a mistake to regard these bodies as possessing great political or social influence (though Frederick William II of Prussia and two of his closest advisers were Rosicrucians and their policies were affected by this). But their growth is yet another warning against any easy overestimate of the rationalism and 'enlightenment' of the eighteenth century.

Nor was the movement towards religious toleration universal or unchallenged. It is understandable that in Spain, where the identification of Catholicism with the country's history and aspirations was closer than anywhere else in Europe, one leading cleric could refer to the ideas of the Enlightenment as 'a vile prostitute misnamed philosophy' and another could refuse to learn French because of all the dangerous books written in the language. But even in the most advanced states of Western Europe popular intolerance was still very much alive.

The movement towards religious toleration was neither continuous nor very profound. In England the penal laws against Prostestant Dissenters might no longer be enforced; but a series of efforts to secure their repeal in 1787–90 ended in complete failure. The legal disabilities of English Catholics began very slowly to be whittled away in the last years of the century; but the Gordon Riots of 1780 (a great outburst of violence directed mainly against Catholics which for a few days placed London at the mercy of the mob) showed how intense and how near the surface was the hostility to them which still existed. In France the Assembly of the Clergy was urging Louis XVI as late as 1775 to enforce more rigorously the very severe legislation against Protestantism. More serious was the position in Germany, Hungary and Poland. In all of these, generations of religious strife had left a legacy of extreme sensitivity on religious matters and of readiness to persecute. Thus in 1719 the action of the town council of Torun in Poland in putting to death a number of Calvinists found guilty of riotous behaviour led to a minor European crisis and provoked protests from Britain and Prussia. In Hungary, where there was a tendency to regard Protestantism as a relic of the long years of Turkish domination in the sixteenth and seventeenth centuries, this period saw systematic persecution of the Calvinists, in spite of the guarantees given them by the Peace of Szatmár (1711). In 1728 the Archbishop of Salzburg expelled 20,000 Protestants from his dominions at three days' notice. In Switzerland the efforts of the Abbots of St Gall to foster Catholicism in the Toggenburg, an area under their jurisdiction, provoked friction between the Catholic and Protestant cantons which led to open warfare in 1712 and did not finally die down till 1759.

By the later 1770s and 1780s, moreover, traditional and more or less unthinking prejudices against religious minorities were being sharpened, in many parts of Europe, by a more explicit and vocal clerical hostility to the Enlightenment than ever before. In France the royal edict of 1787 which granted civil rights to Protestants was widely unpopular. Two *parlements*, those of Dôle and Douai, refused to register it, while efforts were made to exclude Protestants from the electoral assemblies which chose members of the States-General in 1789. In Prussia an Edict Concerning Religion of July 1788 ordered all Protestant preachers to adhere strictly in their sermons to the orthodox Lutheran or Reformed creeds; any who indulged in rationalistic speculations or practices were threatened with severe punishment. Even the myth of a great anti-monarchical and anti-Christian conspiracy, international in scope and the work of Freemasons and perhaps Protestants, a myth to which the French Revolution was to give vitality and longevity, was beginning to be put forward in the 1780s.[6] The last years of the old régime, in fact, saw a kind of clerical counter-revolution which antedated the Revolution itself.

In religion then, as in most other aspects of life, the eighteenth century bore within itself the seeds of an immense change. But this process of change still affected directly only a small minority of Europeans. The liberal and rationalist tendencies which bulk so large in the works of most of the better-known writers of the period had not yet had much effect on the ordinary man. They were to be weakened and even reversed by the reaction which accompanied and to some extent antedated the French Revolution.

Faced by the intellectual and other challenges it had to meet during this period the Catholic Church showed real vitality and creativity. A good many new religious orders were created, both teaching and nursing ones like the Ursulines and the Sœurs de la Charité in France and missionary ones like the Redemptorists in Italy (though this was counterbalanced by a tendency for some old and well-established ones such as the Benedictines, Cistercians and Carthusians to decline). There was a spread of new devotions such as the Sacred Heart and the Stations of the Cross: these were significant as a form of religious practice which had widespread popular appeal and at the same time was securely under clerical control. They thus provided an alternative to the sort of grass-roots popular religion which the church increasingly distrusted and tried to curb. In France at least the clergy was becoming better educated, largely because of the training given in the diocesan seminaries. A recent survey has shown a steady and impressive growth in the ownership of books by French clerics throughout the eighteenth century. On the eve of the Revolution nine-tenths of them owned more than fifty books and one in three had a library of over three hundred, figures which it might be difficult to equal anywhere else in Europe. In some areas there is also evidence of increasing interest by bishops in the administration and spiritual life of their dioceses and of more careful supervision by them of parish priests.

There were none the less serious and intractable weaknesses in the Church. Its resources were unevenly spread geographically; their distribution bore little relationship to that of population (though this was a defect to be found in every Church and by no means confined to Catholicism). Its resources were too much concentrated in towns at the expense of the countryside whose tithes and rents were the most important contributors to clerical wealth. By the end of the century of the 19,000 parishes in Spain, for example, 3,000 had no priest; and this was in a country where clerics of all kinds made up about 1.5 per cent of the total population – somewhat above the European average. In striking contrast eighty-four monasteries and convents were to be found in Seville alone: there was no lack of priests in Spain but the countryside was badly served by them. In Portugal also, where clergy were relatively even more numerous, priests were in short supply in the rural areas, particularly in the south, whilst in the large towns, Lisbon and Oporto, they were very thick on the ground. In the cities themselves population growth and geographical spread tended often to mean very small parishes in the old central areas and very large ones in the new suburbs: one parish in Cadiz had a population of 57,000. Bishoprics were also strikingly unevenly distributed between different parts of Catholic Europe. The Austrian and Bohemian provinces of the Habsburgs had only fifteen of them in 1780, while Italy as a whole had about 315 (the Kingdom of the Two Sicilies alone had 131).

The Church was also weakened, at least in some areas, by the fact that its higher ranks were recruited mainly or exclusively from the aristocracy, a fact which opened a profound social and even intellectual gulf between its bishops and archbishops and the parish priests under their control. The latter, drawn for the most part from the peasantry (though seldom from the very poorest peasant families) and often very badly paid, had in many cases little in common with their superiors. This position was seen at its worst in France, where the episcopate during this period was entirely aristocratic in origin and often scandalously worldly in outlook. Perhaps the most striking illustration of these social distinctions was the Benedictine convent of Remiremont in Lorraine, where the nuns did not have to wear a habit or take perpetual vows and were each given an income of 2,000 livres pending their marriage: it was claimed that even French princesses would be ineligible for entry to it because of their Medici descent, so strict were its requirements in terms of aristocratic lineage. Even in the Papal States themselves an increasing assimilation of the higher ranks of the Church to the secular aristocracy can be seen in the reconstitution of the Roman nobility as a closed caste of 187 families by Benedict XIV in 1746.

A more obvious weakness was the divisions provoked by the question of Jansenism. This was originally a theological dispute concerned with one of the most obscure yet important parts of Christian theology – doctrines of grace, free-will and predestination. Jansen, Bishop of Ypres, who gave his name to a movement which came into existence only a generation after his death in 1638, restated traditional Augustinian doctrines on these issues in a remarkably rigorous form. His assertion that every man was irreversibly predestined to heaven or hell nullified by implication the significance, as roads to salvation, of virtue, reason and good works. From the ideas which he formulated (in varying forms and expressed with varying degrees of rigidity they had long formed a part of Christian belief) developed an imposing structure of Puritan idealism, an intense preoccupation with the idea of sin and a denial of the assumptions of natural religion.

Jansenism gained the support first of a group of Paris theologians and from the mid seventeenth century onwards of the great French convent of Port-Royal. By the end of the century it was arousing interest among much wider circles in France, lay as well as clerical. In 1693 Pasquier Quesnel restated its central doctrines, in his *Nouveau Testament en français avec des Réflexions morales*, in terms which seemed to call in question the ultimate authority in matters of faith of the hierarchy of the Church. However the closer relations between Louis XIV and the Papacy which dated from this very year led to a sustained effort by the

French government to stamp out the movement. This was encouraged by the Jesuits, who from the beginning had been the most implacable doctrinal enemies of Jansenism. Port-Royal was destroyed in 1710; and in 1713 a number of errors alleged to be present in Quesnel's book were condemned by Clement XI in the bull *Unigenitus.*

With the promulgation of this bull the eighteenth-century phase of the controversy began. In the decades which followed Jansenism ceased to be what it had hitherto remained, an essentially theological question which interested in the main only a small intellectual class. Henceforth it became increasingly involved with many aspects of French life. Around it crystallized patriotic opposition to papal claims and the growing hostility of the *parlements* to some aspects of absolute monarchy (since Louis XV, breaking with the traditions of his ancestors, tended to support the Papalist and anti-Jansenist party in the French Church) as well as the frustration and resentment felt by many of the lower clergy in face of the power and wealth enjoyed by the higher ranks of the Church.

Though they were given a good deal of official support during the Regency period, the Jansenists were greatly weakened by the accession to power of Cardinal Fleury in 1726. Two years later, when Noailles, the Archbishop of Paris who had been their supporter for over a generation, was at last forced to abandon them, they lost their last influential adherent within the French hierarchy. Increasing persecution led to the growth of a mystical and even hysterical wing of the movement, which was associated with the alleged miracles performed in 1730–32 at the tomb of the deacon Pâris in the cemetery of St Médard and which helped to bring into disrepute the more disciplined majority of Jansenists. The latter, however, were protected by the *Parlement* of Paris during a series of struggles with Fleury (1730–33), published a successful clandestine periodical, the *Nouvelles Ecclésiastiques* (1728–1803), and even thought of founding in Indo-China a mission independent of the Papacy. So great was their popularity in the capital that the lawyer and diarist Barbier estimated in the 1730s that two-thirds of the people of Paris were Jansenist in sympathy. By the middle decades of the century the movement, though driven underground to some extent by official pressure, was exerting extensive influence on French society. It was now changing its form, tending increasingly to stress the rights of the parish priest against his ecclesiastical superiors, and even to some extent those of the layman against the priest. In many parts of France, moreover, liturgical and ceremonial changes (for example greater use of the vernacular in services and communion in both kinds) had now been introduced by Jansenist *curés*. From 1749 onwards a number of prelates, notably de Beaumont, Archbishop of Paris, attempted to force penitents on the point of death, as a condition of receiving absolution, to prove their orthodoxy by producing a certificate signed by an orthodox priest. This effort to stamp out Jansenism aroused widespread and bitter opposition: clearly the movement still retained much popular sympathy. By the 1760s, however, it had shot its bolt in France. The last Jansenist bishop died in 1754; and in the later decades of the century it ceased to be a real danger, or even a serious nuisance, to either Church or State.

The influence of Jansenism was in many ways as great outside as inside France. It appealed to the fear, envy and distrust of the Jesuits which was widespread all over Catholic Europe, and often also to dislike of papal claims to authority. In some of the Catholic States of Germany, as in Spain and Portugal, it helped to inspire resistance to these claims. In the Habsburg Empire it received a considerable amount of official encouragement. Maria Theresa's confessor, the Abbé de Tesme, was a Jansenist; and Jansenist books were allowed by the censorship to enter the Habsburg dominions freely. In the Netherlands Utrecht was a notable centre of Jansenist teaching. In Italy Jansenism was widespread and influential and sometimes assumed (notably in Lombardy) a radical and even democratic form. Its ideas were one element in the Neapolitan revolution of 1799, and the hostility to the Papacy of Mazzini, the greatest prophet of nationalism in nineteenth-century Europe, was probably in part the product of the Jansenist influences he absorbed as a child in Genoa. In Tuscany it was even possible, in 1786, to hold a Jansenist synod at Pistoia with the support of the Grand Duke Leopold; though its decisions were condemned by the Pope in 1794 and its leader, Scipione de Ricci, the greatest figure in the history of the movement in Italy, submitted to the Papacy in 1805.

More spectacular than the threat of Jansenism, though less dangerous to the unity of the Catholic Church, was the wave of hostility to the Jesuits which the Jansenists did so much to stimulate. This reached a climax in the 1760s and led to the dissolution of the Order in 1773. The exaggerated hatred and fear felt for the Jesuits everywhere in Protestant Europe had always been echoed, sometimes with equal intensity, in many parts of the Catholic world. Their wealth (often grossly exaggerated by rumour), the great influence they normally possessed at Rome and in many of the courts of Europe, above all the unity and discipline which made them appear a kind of secret society, aroused widespread envy and dislike. By the middle of the century it was becoming difficult for the governments of Catholic Europe, increasingly centralized and efficient, to tolerate the activities or even the existence of a body so ultramontane and, by implication at least, so hostile to the existence of genuinely sovereign States.

The first overt action against the Society came in Portugal. There Pombal in 1757 drove from the court the Jesuits who had hitherto acted as the confessors of the royal family. Two years later he accused the Society, almost certainly without justification, of complicity in an attempt to murder the king; and in September 1759 its members were expelled from Portugal. These drastic attacks on Jesuit influence, which were the result of Pombal's fear of intrigues and opposition at court and not at all of religious considerations, set off a chain reaction elsewhere in Catholic Europe. In France popular hostility to the Order, stimulated by the dissemination of Jansenist ideas, was particularly acute. There matters were brought to a head by the bankruptcy of a leading Jesuit, Père Lavalette, who had hitherto been a leading figure in the trade of Martinique, the wealthiest of France's West Indian islands. Sued by his creditors in the consular court of Marseilles, the French Jesuits unwisely appealed from its decision to the *Parlement* of Paris, which had a long tradition of hostility to ultramontane influences. The *Parlement* seized the opportunity to demand that the statutes of the Order be submitted to it for approval, condemned them on a number of grounds, and in spite of the feeble opposition of Louis XV demanded in August 1762 the dissolution of the Society of Jesus in France. In this demand it was followed by most of the provincial *parlements*. The king, though he was supported by the great majority of the French bishops in his desire to maintain the Order in existence, gave way to this popular and institutional pressure. In November 1764 he issued the decree which banished it from France (and thus produced a severe though temporary crisis in the country's educational system).

In Spain the Society was little more popular. There riots in Madrid, Barcelona and other cities in 1766 were officially attributed to its machinations and were followed in the next year, after careful preparation, by the arrest and deportation of its members. This drastic action was supported by the majority of the Spanish bishops. Finally, encouraged by the French and Spanish governments, Naples, Parma and even the Order of St John in Malta expelled the Jesuits from their territories in 1767.

Pope Clement XIII had not hesitated to declare his support for them (notably in the bull *Apostolicum Munus* of January 1765). He had also attempted unsuccessfully at the end of 1768 to put pressure on the Duke of Parma, the weakest of the secular rulers who had expelled them, by excommunicating his ministers. His successor Clement XIV, who became Pope in May 1769, was a weaker man; it has been conjectured that he may, before his election, have given the French and Spanish governments a promise to suppress the Society completely if he were chosen as head of the Church. After his accession he tried for several years to evade a decision on this point by asking for time to consider the question and by promising to call a general council. However in face of pressure from France, which occupied the papal enclave of Avignon; from Naples, which seized a similar enclave, Benevento; and most of all from Spain, whose ambassador in Rome secured by bribery the support of many members of the Curia, Clement had to give way. In July 1773 the brief *Dominus ac Redemptor* abolished the Society of Jesus throughout Catholic Europe. It was not applied everywhere with the same degree of severity, for both Louis XV and Maria Theresa wished to treat the Jesuits with moderation, while in Poland and some parts of Italy and Germany there was considerable opposition to their disappearance. Some of them, moreover, were able to find refuge in the dominions of Frederick II and Catherine II, non-Catholic rulers ostentatiously tolerant in matters of religion. By consenting to destroy the Society, however, Clement XIV had swept away the greatest institution of the Counter-Reformation. He had destroyed the one Catholic order which might have been able to reconcile traditional forms of authority in the Church with the new ideas, based on philosophical speculation and scientific discovery, which were now gaining so much ground in Europe. He had both illustrated and accelerated the decline in the real power of the Papacy which was one of the main facts of the religious life of this period in Western Europe.

This decline had become clearly visible long before 1773. As a factor in international affairs the Papacy had for several generations counted for little. It was represented in the negotiations of 1713–14 which led to the signature of the Treaties of Utrecht and Rastadt, but had not the slightest influence on the peace terms. The negotiations of 1748 which culminated in the Treaty of Aix-la-Chapelle were attended merely by its semi-official agent, the Vicar-General of the Bishop of Liège, who was kept in complete ignorance of what was going on. Already Clement XII had seen his Italian territories invaded, plundered, and used without his permission as recruiting grounds by the Spanish and Austrian armies in the wars of 1733–35 and 1741–48. His suzerainty over the Duchies of Parma and Piacenza, always shadowy, had in effect ceased to exist in 1731. With no real army, ruling one of the most backward and impoverished States in Europe, the Papacy had completely lost by the middle of the century any claim to be an effective force in warfare or diplomacy.

Its position, moreover, was now being threatened even more seriously by the growing hostility of governments to the powers which it continued to claim throughout Catholic Europe. This hostility was by no means new. Resentment of papal claims had been felt for centuries by both rulers and people in many parts of Italy: the Republic of Venice for example had been notoriously anti-ultramontane during much of the seventeenth century. When the Archbishop of Taranto in 1788 wrote of 'Papalism, the perpetual enemy of this kingdom', he was thus expressing an attitude deeply ingrained over much of the peninsula. Similarly in France Gallicanism (the belief that the French Church was autonomous and that its internal organization should be free from papal control) retained much of the great popular appeal it had possessed in previous generations. Jansenism with its anti-papal implications drew much of its strength from the still flourishing Gallican tradition. The *parlements* were solidly Gallican. Louis XV seriously damaged his own popularity and the position of the monarchy by the support he gave to the opponents of Gallicanism. In Spain also there was a strong tradition of independence of Rome where the government and organization of the Church were concerned; and royal control over it steadily increased during the century. Even in ultra-Catholic Portugal a royal decree of 1782 forbade the creation of any new religious order; and another six years later made royal permission necessary before a young man became a priest.

The growing demand that kings and princes must be masters in their own houses – a demand which underlay the attacks on the Jesuits – forced the Papacy in the second quarter of the century to make a series of important concessions. By a series of concordats – with Spain in 1737 and 1753, with Portugal in 1740, with Sardinia and Naples in 1741 – the Popes surrendered to the rulers concerned rights which Rome had hitherto possessed in theory if not always in fact, notably over Church appointments. These surrenders did little to appease the enemies of the Papacy. The spread of 'enlightened' ideas and the general movement towards more effectively centralized administrative systems were alike hostile to its traditional powers and position. Both brought clerical privileges under increasingly heavy fire and intensified suspicion of the Popes as the symbols and defenders of these survivals of the past. Moreover rulers increasingly conscious of their own powers and responsibilities were increasingly reluctant to accept interference with their actions by any international authority. Feelings of this kind were stimulated in the capitals of Catholic Europe by a series of able anti-papal writers – Giannone in Naples, Van Espen in the Netherlands, Febronius (i.e. J. N. von Hontheim, Vicar-General of the Archbishop of Trier) in the Habsburg dominions and South Germany. In many areas indeed the Catholic hierarchy itself played a leading part in opposing papal and ultramontane claims. Bishops who believed themselves to have received their powers directly from Christ and often enjoyed a high degree of administrative autonomy in their own dioceses (as in France for example) were usually willing to obey the instructions of the Papacy on spiritual matters but were otherwise frequently almost independent of it. This attitude was intensified by the aristocratic character of the episcopate in many countries. 'The Pope has his rights,' said the Bishop of Lombez towards the end of the century, 'and we have ours.' The remark summarized a point of view increasingly widespread during this period.

The last decades of the century produced a series of attacks on the position of the Papacy and even of the Church in general more open and more violent than any hitherto seen. In 1776 the Neapolitan government, still influenced by the anticlerical Tanucci, refused to continue the payment to Rome of the traditional tribute of the *Chinea* (a white horse richly caparisoned and 7,000 ducats in gold) in acknowledgement of the feudal subjection of the kingdom to the Pope. In many States of Catholic Europe – in Naples and Sicily during the 1760s and 1770s, in Lombardy during the last years of Maria Theresa, in France from 1765 onwards – decayed or superfluous religious houses were swept away. Almost everywhere efforts were made to reduce the number of appeals to Rome, to control the enforcement and even the publication of papal bulls, and to reduce the economic privileges of the Church in such matters as mortmain and exemption from taxation. In Spain, where Catholicism was stronger than in any other major State, the power of the Inquisition declined rapidly (the last man to be burnt alive for a religious offence was executed at Seville in 1781, though others were put to death in the Indies even later than this) and those of other Church tribunals were steadily reduced. By the end of the century proposals were being made for the partial expropriation of the Spanish Church and the devotion of some of its wealth to secular purposes.

Most striking of all was the great offensive against clerical power and papal claims which was now under way in the Habsburg dominions. Even in the first decades of the century there were signs that the atmosphere at the Habsburg court was becoming less intolerantly Catholic than in the past. Both Joseph I (1705–11) and Charles VI (1711–40) married princesses of Protestant origin; while a long series of disputes with the Papacy, the result of the territorial gains made by the Habsburgs in Italy during the Spanish Succession struggle, helped to strengthen liberalizing tendencies in Vienna. Under Maria Theresa, one of the most sincerely Catholic rulers of the century, efforts at Church reform, and hence interference with religious institutions, began on a considerable scale. Thus in Lombardy a new body, the *Giunta Economale*, was set up in 1767 to supervise clerical affairs: later the Inquisition was prevented from acting in the province, the number of monasteries was halved and their income reduced by two-thirds, and the judicial privileges of the Church were reduced in various ways. During her reign, however, its purely spiritual powers were left more or less unchallenged. In his religious policy as in all other respects Joseph II (though he remained to his death a practising and believing Catholic) was more wholehearted, more dogmatic and less patient than his mother. To him the Church as it existed was a parasite on society, a useless consumer of resources which might otherwise be applied to constructive secular purposes. Worse still, by its intolerance and by the superstitions which it fostered it was the positive opponent of social and intellectual progress; while as an international institution it was a check on the sovereignty of secular rulers. Soon after his accession these ideas began to find legislative expression. In October 1781 religious liberty was granted to his non-Catholic Christian subjects in the hereditary provinces, Galicia and Transylvania. In the following year a limited degree of toleration was extended to the Jews; and the Inquisition, which had long ceased to have any practical importance, was formally abolished in the territories under his rule. Simultaneously religious houses were suppressed and their property secularized unless they maintained schools, relieved the poor, or engaged in scholarly work of some kind. A life of religious contemplation was, to Joseph, a life wasted. The funds provided by the dissolution of hundreds of religious institutions were used to extend education, notably to create five new seminaries designed to produce priests in sympathy with the Emperor's policies.

Most striking of all to contemporaries was the conflict with the Pope which was now clearly developing. Visits to Vienna by Pius VI in 1782 and by Joseph to Rome in the following year, even the signature of a concordat in 1784, did little to bridge the gulf which was opening between them. From 1784 onwards a litany in German, and not the traditional Latin one, began to be used in many churches in the Habsburg dominions. Moreover the religious policies of the Emperor were now being imitated in Catholic Germany, in some parts of which they had considerable influence. The Elector Friedrich-Karl of Mainz, for example, when he abolished all legal discrimination in his territories against the Jews in 1783–84, was clearly following in the footsteps of Joseph II: Habsburg influence in the electorate was traditionally strong. As early as 1769 the Electors of Mainz, Trier and Cologne, meeting at Coblenz, had asserted forcibly the rights, as they saw them, of Catholic bishops against the Papacy. Only a General Council, they claimed, possessed supreme legislative and judicial power over the Church. Secular power was directly instituted by God and thus independent of spiritual power. A bishop's administration of his diocese could not be interfered with by the Papacy. In 1785 the same three clerical electors, with the Archbishop of Salzburg, jointly protested against the appointment of a Papal Nuncio to Bavaria. In the following year, in a meeting at Ems, they demanded that the publication of papal bulls in any part of Catholic Germany should depend on the consent of the bishops concerned, that appeals to Rome should be limited and that Papal Nuncios should no longer be appointed to any of the German States. By the later 1780s, therefore, 'Josephism', apart from its importance in the Habsburg territories themselves, was a significant factor in relations between the Papacy and the whole German world.

The movement was in the long run a failure. It was weakened by the stubborn resistance to Joseph's schemes of religious reorganization in the Austrian Netherlands and later, more fundamentally, by the conservative reaction against the French Revolution. For the next half-century or more, however, Josephist ideas continued to be important in the religious life of the Habsburg Empire and in its relations with the Papacy.

The Orthodox Church underwent during this period a series of organizational disputes and to a lesser extent intellectual challenges in some ways comparable to those faced by Catholicism and the Protestant sects. In the Balkans much controversy was provoked in the middle decades of the century by the assertion of Auxentios, Archdeacon of Galata, that converts to Orthodoxy from some other branch of the Christian faith must be rebaptized before being admitted to the Church. The suppression in the 1760s by the Ottoman government of the Patriarchates of Ipek and Ochrida, which deprived the Serbs and Bulgars of any remnant of ecclesiastical independence and subjected them to the control of the Greek Patriarchs of Constantinople, was to have considerable influence on the development of Balkan nationalism in the nineteenth century. In particular it did much to stimulate the resentment of Greek intellectual and commercial dominance which was already growing in the Slav areas of the peninsula. These developments, however, were all of essentially local importance and passed almost completely unheeded in Western Europe.

In Russia very important changes took place in the organization of the Church. The death in 1700 of the Patriarch Adrian brought to an end the high degree of independence of the State which it had hitherto enjoyed. No successor to him was appointed by Peter I; and during the first two decades of the eighteenth century Church property and Church–State relations in Russia were controlled by a government department, the *Monastyrskii Prikaz* (Monastery Department). This was used by the Tsar as a means of diverting Church revenues, first to the needs of the war with Sweden and later to some extent to charitable and educational purposes. Many of Peter's attitudes in religious matters – his dislike of the contemplative and inward-looking aspects of traditional Orthodox piety; his efforts to prevent monks and priests becoming too numerous in his dominions; most of all his hostility to clerical wealth used, as he saw it, unproductively – clearly anticipate those of later rulers in Western and Central Europe. They are well illustrated by the new oath which Russian bishops, from 1716 onwards, had to take before consecration. This bound them not to increase the number of clergy in their dioceses or to build superfluous churches; to make sure that monks under their jurisdiction did not travel without their written permission, which was to be given only in exceptional cases; and in general not to interfere in secular affairs and legal proceedings. In 1721 the *Monastyrskii Prikaz* was replaced by a body of churchmen, the Most Holy Directing Synod, which was intended to act in religious matters as the equivalent of the Senate established a few years earlier for the supervision of secular administration. The lines along which it was to work were prescribed by the Tsar in a very detailed *Dukhovnyi Reglament* (Spiritual Regulation) issued in the same year, which again provides plentiful evidence of his desire to make the church in Russia an agency of secular improvement. (Fully a fifth of the Regulation dealt with education; and a supplement to it ordered that each priest should keep a register of births, marriages and deaths in his parish, though this never worked in practice.) By the time of Peter's death in 1725 the administration of the Church was becoming almost a part of the centralized bureaucratic machine to which all Russians were now subject. A great secularization of Church lands by Catherine II in 1764 continued and consolidated this process, which encountered throughout remarkably little effective resistance from the Orthodox hierarchy.

In one fundamental way the position of the Church in Russia was weak. The social status of the parish priest was very low, far lower than that of his counterpart in Catholic or Protestant Europe. He was forbidden to own serfs and during the century was increasingly subjected to the jurisdiction of secular as opposed to Church courts. He was with few exceptions poorer and worse educated than his counterparts in Western and Central Europe. What intellectual vitality there was in the Russian Church was to be found in the monasteries and the 'black' monastic clergy from which all the higher ranks of the hierarchy were recruited. Most fundamental of all, the Orthodox clergy had now come to form a distinct clerical estate (*dukhovnoe soslovie*), a rigid caste-like order distinct from the rest of society. Parish priests, who had to be married before ordination, always took as their wives the daughters of other parish priests, and their sons normally became parish priests in their turn. This combination of separateness and low status was a crippling disadvantage. As in some parts of Catholic Europe, there were considerable efforts in Russia to improve Church administration in this period. Dioceses became smaller and more manageable. Bishops made more frequent and searching visitations. The procedures for the ordination of priests were made more stringent. Leading figures in the Church often tried, with very little success, to combat peasant superstition, belief in magic and wonder-working icons and the tough substratum of folk-beliefs which was probably stronger in Russia than anywhere else in Europe. But in spite of all this Orthodoxy in Russia clearly had less intellectual creativity and vitality and less independence of secular authority than the Churches elsewhere in Europe.

From the intellectual point of view the main interest of this period in the history of the Russian Church is that it sees a complicated triangular struggle between Protestant ideas imported from Western and Northern Europe, Catholic tendencies from Poland and the Ukraine, and a strain of native mysticism which was hostile to all foreign beliefs. The reign of Peter I saw the victory of the Protestant and 'enlightened' influences typified by Feofan Prokopovich, the Tsar's main agent in Church affairs, over the Catholicizing trends represented by Stefan Yavorskii, Metropolitan of Ryazan. During the half-century which followed, a number of Lutheran doctrines – for example on original sin and justification by faith – made considerable headway, at least among the higher ranks of the Church. The last decades of this period, however, saw a pietist, mystical and ascetic reaction, typified in different ways by St. Tikhon Zadonskii and the monk Paissy Velichkovskii. This marked a return to Orthodox tradition and an increasing rejection of foreign doctrinal innovations. Russian mysticism was seen in a more extreme and spectacular form in the growth during the same period of a number of very radical nonconformist sects – the *Dukhobortsy*, the *Khlysty* and the *Skopsty*.

For the Jews, of whom in 1750 there were perhaps three million in all, the eighteenth century, or at least its later decades, held important developments. They remained, particularly in Eastern and much of Central Europe, a despised, distrusted and often persecuted group. In 1738, for example, a Jew accused of having converted a naval officer to Judaism was burned alive in St. Petersburg; and four years later all Jews were formally expelled from the Russian Empire. The myth of their ritual murder of Christian children was still repeated and often credited, in spite of the efforts of Popes Benedict XIII and Clement XIV to combat it. The early years of the century saw the publication of perhaps the most influential piece of anti-Semitic propaganda ever produced, J. A. Eisenmenger's *Das entdeckte . . . Judenthum* (Amsterdam, 1711). In England an effort in 1753 to make it possible for Jews to become naturalized met with so much popular resistance that it had to be abandoned. On a deeper level, the hostility of many of the *philosophes* in France to Christianity led them to attack Judaism, from which so many of what they regarded as the worst features of Christianity, in its intolerant and puritanical Old Testament form, had been derived. Voltaire's antagonism on these grounds to the Jews and what they appeared to stand for is particularly marked: one of his legacies to later generations was 'the fundamentals of the rhetoric of secular anti-Semitism'.[7] Nevertheless in many areas their position was improving quite rapidly in the latter part of the century. In France they were exempted from the payment of a special poll-tax to which they had hitherto been liable. In the Habsburg territories Joseph II allowed them, under certain conditions, to settle in Vienna where, as in many other German towns, they had previously been forbidden to live or own houses. In Prussia they came to enjoy a high degree of equality with their Christian neighbours, though complete legal equality was achieved only in 1811–12. Moreover they too were now being influenced, at least in Western and parts of Central Europe, by the rationalism, optimism and universalism of the Enlightenment. Figures such as the philosopher Moses Mendelssohn and his disciples were beginning to tear down the intellectual barriers which had for so long cut Judaism off from the life and thought of Europe. In this they were helped by the foundation in the later decades of the century of the first Jewish periodicals, at Königsberg and Dessau, and by the setting-up of the first modern Jewish school at Berlin in 1778. The sceptical and assimilationist attitude which they represented was still that of a small minority of European Jewry, and was opposed by powerful and deeply-entrenched forces of conservatism and orthodoxy. It was becoming an increasingly widespread Jewish attitude, however, even before the cataclysm which began in 1789.

It is impossible to regard the eighteenth century as a great age of religion. Nevertheless it was not an age of religious stagnation or indifference. It saw a considerable development of Christian, above all Catholic, missionary activity in America and the East. Catholic missions continued to be active in China, and to a lesser extent in India, Indo-China and Persia. They remained the most important channel through which Oriental art and philosophy were introduced to Europe. Across the Atlantic the conversion of the native inhabitants of Central and South America continued; and in 1791 a Vicar-Apostolic was appointed to the United States. On the Protestant side the foundation in England of the Society for the Propagation of the Gospel in Foreign Parts in 1701, and the missionary activities of Methodists, Moravians and even Lutherans, showed similar forces and ideals at work.

More important, to the ordinary man everywhere in Europe religion continued to be of fundamental importance. He still found consolation and reassurance in the rituals to which habit had accustomed him. He continued, with few exceptions, sincerely to desire to know God, to wish for a religion which would satisfy his feelings and his moral sense. Sometimes these desires took the form of mysticism, emotionalism and superstition. The age of the Enlightenment was also the age of the Jansenist excesses at St Médard, of the Moravians, of the Methodists, of the obscurantist movement of Jewish pietism known as Hassidism. It was against this background of strong emotions and traditional beliefs that the structure of 'rational' or 'natural' religion, so impressive in the number and ability of its literary advocates, was erected. Nevertheless this structure was of great importance. The controversy which the new ideas aroused was generally conducted at a high intellectual level (higher than that at which contemporary political ideas were discussed). Many of the arguments of the advocates of natural religion were superficial;

but after they had done their work it was difficult for an educated layman, at least in Western Europe, to think of God or the universe quite as he would have done a century earlier. Science and rationalism had not destroyed religious belief. In some respects they had strengthened it. But they had wrought in it a qualitative change of fundamental importance, and had helped to produce a great wave of hostility among the educated to much traditional dogma and ecclesiastical organisation.

NOTES AND REFERENCES

1   B. Willey, *The Eighteenth Century Background* (London, 1940), p. 169.

2   The heresies propounded respectively by Arius, a presbyter of Alexandria in the fourth century who denied that Christ was consubstantial with God, and by Laelius and Faustus Socinus, two sixteenth-century Italian theologians who denied the divinity of Christ.

3   L. R. Berlanstein, *The Barristers of Toulouse in the Eighteenth Century.* (Baltimore – London, 1975), p. 126.

4   Quoted in C. Hibbert, *The Grand Tour* (London, 1974), p. 155.

5   Quoted in R. A. Knox, *Enthusiasm* (Oxford, 1950), pp. 518–19.

6   For example, in the Abbé Lenfant's *Discours . . . sur le Projet d'accorder l'État Civil aux Protestants* (1787). The first important French attack on Masonry as a dangerous movement for liberty and equality directed against all existing authority had been launched forty years earlier in an anonymous work, *Les Francs – Maçons écrasés* (1747); but hostility of this kind did not become widespread until the 1780s.

7   A. Hertzberg, *The French Enlightenment and the Jews* (New York, 1968), p. 286.

17

CONCLUSION

The period covered by this book saw in Europe a mixture of
change, sometimes violent and drastic, and stability which verged
on stagnation. The forces of progress and movement were
affecting the continent, but their influence was fluctuating and
uneven.

Politically, the European State-system and the balance of power
were altered fundamentally by the dramatic rise in the international significance of Russia after 1709 and of Prussia after 1740.
These developments involved a great eastward extension of the
geographical scope of European diplomacy and the domination
of international relations by East European problems to a quite
unprecedented extent in the generation after 1763. Simultaneously
the degree to which a European State could be strengthened
economically and hence politically by the possession of colonies,
the fact that the balance of power on the continent depended
increasingly on events thousands of miles away, began to be fully
grasped for the first time. In both these ways a political system
whose scope and components had remained on the whole remarkably stable since the Renaissance was rapidly remodelled; from
this point of view the changes seen during the eighteenth century
were more important than those in any comparable period of
European history.

' In intellectual life also the age was in many ways one of change
and development. The ideas of the Enlightenment grew from seed
sown well before the end of the seventeenth century. Nevertheless
they had produced in Western Europe by the middle decades of
this period an intellectual climate which Descartes, or for that

matter Newton himself, would have found almost unrecognizable and in many ways repugnant. Religious impulses, though they were not seriously weakened by the Enlightenment except among a small educated class, had in many areas to find new institutional forms; while systematic religious persecution became increasingly difficult to carry out or justify. In some ways more important, romanticism, whether in literature, in art, or in political ideas, was introducing by the 1750s not so much new ideas as new attitudes and a new scale of values. These were to modify profoundly though indirectly many sides of European life, as from the 1770s the more analytical and classical aspects of the Enlightenment lost some of their vigour and were increasingly challenged by other forces – those of sensibility and even of outright irrationalism.

Some aspects of European life, however, showed themselves until near the end of this period remarkably resistant to change. The economic structure of the continent, though it developed fairly rapidly in some respects, remained as far as the majority of Europeans were concerned essentially what it had been for generations or even centuries. The sophistication of some eighteenth-century systems of banking and public finance had been foreshadowed by the Italian bankers of the later Middle Ages. The great extension of seaborne trade during much of the century was a quantitative rather than a qualitative change. Technology, little influenced by scientific discovery, advanced on the whole slowly and erratically. As late as 1776 Adam Smith could base his *Wealth of Nations* on the tacit and still unchallenged assumption that the economies of all European States were more or less static; the problems of an economic structure based on rapid growth and revolutionary technological change did not and could not engage his attention. Only in the very last years of this period did radically new methods of production or economic organization begin to be of fundamental importance even in Great Britain, now establishing herself as the most economically advanced country in the world.

The stability of Europe's economic life during this period meant almost inevitably that European society (if this question-begging term is permissible) was also relatively stable. The erosion of traditional lines of division between classes and the erection of new ones, the decay of some social groups and the rise of others, none the less proceeded more rapidly than the growth of factories

467

and the modernization of agriculture. Even before the industrial revolution had got properly under way the growth of trade and towns had gone some distance, at least in the more advanced parts of Western Europe, towards replacing a society of communities, 'orders' and privileged institutions by a more modern social structure based mainly though by no means entirely on wealth. Since in Russia a society like that traditional in Western Europe had never really existed, it was chiefly in the central areas of the continent, particularly in the German States, that the social heritage of the Middle Ages was transmitted on any considerable scale to the nineteenth century.

The end of the period covered by this book is much more clearly and sharply defined than its beginning. By the 1780s a few favoured areas on or near Europe's western seaboard were beginning to develop a type of economic organization so different from anything hitherto known, so complex, rational and productive, that its growth constitutes the most revolutionary change in the human condition since Neolithic times. Simultaneously the American revolution, in combination with many other factors, was helping to generate dreams, ambitions and grievances more far-reaching than any since the days of the Anabaptists and the Fifth Monarchy Men. They were dreams and ambitions, moreover, whose popular appeal was potentially almost unlimited. This meant that they might become far more of a challenge to the existing state of things than the restricted sectarian radicalism of the past. What made them a threat to stability in some parts of Europe from the 1770s onwards, however, was not so much their own strength as the growing difficulties in which some governments now found themselves. The financial collapse which loomed in France by the end of the American war and the bitter opposition which Joseph II was encountering in Hungary and the Austrian Netherlands are the obvious examples of this: by the 1780s there were clear signs that the fabric of government over a good deal of Europe might simply not be tough enough to bear the burdens which, largely as the result of ambitious foreign policies and more expensive armed forces, were being placed upon it. It was the weaknesses of the old regime – the selfishness of privileged groups without whom governments could not function; the cumbersome administrative systems which so often failed to give these governments the effective control of their territories which they increasingly needed; the endless patchwork of institutional, regional and group privileges – which opened the way to revolution. The great majority of Europeans were still in the 1780s conservatives in the most profound because the most unthinking sense, that of being unable even to envisage the possibility of fundamental change. The age of large-scale factory production, of mass armies, of popular government, was not yet. Nevertheless it is possible, without an excessive use of the hindsight which is the historian's privilege and temptation, to see faint, and sometimes not-so-faint, portents of its approach. Modern history in the genuine as opposed to the textbook sense of the term was beginning.

APPENDIX

CHRONOLOGICAL LIST OF THE MAIN POLITICAL EVENTS MENTIONED IN THIS VOLUME

INTERNATIONAL EVENTS

1696   Peter I takes Azov from the Turks.

1699   Treaty of Carlowitz signed by Austria, Poland, the Ottoman Empire and Venice.

(1698, 1700)   First and Second Partition Treaties attempt to allocate the Spanish inheritance between the rival claimants.

1700   Outbreak of Great Northern War. Charles XII of Sweden forces Denmark to make peace (Treaty of Travendal) and defeats Peter I of Russia at Narva.

1702   Outbreak of War of the Spanish Succession.

1704   Britain takes Gibraltar.

1709   Battle of Poltava.

1711   Pruth campaign: Peter I restores Azov to the Turks.

1713   Peace made at Utrecht by France, Britain, Spain, the United Provinces, Savoy and Portugal.

1714   Peace made at Rastadt by France and the Emperor.

1717   Triple Alliance of Britain, France and the United Provinces (becomes the Quadruple Alliance when joined by the Emperor in the following year). Spanish conquest of Sardinia.

1718   Battle of Cape Passaro. Anglo-Spanish war. Treaty of Passarowitz (ends Austro-Turkish war in progress since 1716).

1719   France declares war on Spain.

1720   Savoy obtains Sardinia from the Emperor in exchange for Sicily.

1721   Treaty of Nystad signed by Sweden and Russia.

1725   Treaty of Vienna signed by Austria and Spain.

1731   Second Treaty of Vienna signed by Britain, the United Provinces, Spain and Austria.

1733   First Family Compact signed by France and Spain.

470

1733 –35	War of the Polish Succession (formally ended by Third Treaty of Vienna in 1738).

1733
–35   War of the Polish Succession (formally ended by Third Treaty of Vienna in 1738).

1735   Outbreak of Russo-Turkish war (Austrian participation on the Russian side from 1737).

1739   Russia, Austria and the Ottoman Empire sign Treaty of Belgrade.
Outbreak of Anglo-Spanish war.

1740   Prussian invasion of Silesia.

1742   Treaty of Berlin signed by Austria and Prussia.

1743   Treaty of Åbo ends Russo-Swedish war in progress since 1741. France and Spain sign Second Family Compact.

1744   France declares war on Great Britain.

1745   Treaty of Dresden ends new Austro-Prussian struggle which had broken out in the previous year.
British capture of Louisburg.

1746   French capture of Madras.

1748   Treaty of Aix-la-Chapelle signed by France, Britain, Spain, the Emperor and the United Provinces.

1755   Outbreak of undeclared war between Britain and France. (Fighting in America had begun in the previous year.)

1756   Convention of Westminster signed by Britain and Prussia, Treaty of Versailles by Austria and France. Outbreak of Seven Years War.

1757   Second Treaty of Versailles signed by Austria and France (modified by a third treaty signed in 1759).
Battle of Plassey.

1759   British capture of Quebec.

1761   Third Family Compact signed by France and Spain.

1762   Break-up of Anglo-Prussian alliance.

1763   Peace of Paris signed by Britain, France and Spain: Treaty of Hubertusburg by Austria and Prussia.

1764   Russo-Prussian alliance to control Poland.

1766   Duchy of Lorraine incorporated in France.

1768
–69   French purchase and conquest of Corsica.

1768   Outbreak of Russo-Turkish war.

1772   First Partition of Poland.

1774   Treaty of Kutchuk-Kainardji signed by Russia and Turkey.

1776   American Declaration of Independence.

1778   France enters the War of American Independence (followed by Spain in 1779).
War of the Bavarian Succession breaks out (ended in the following year by the Treaty of Teschen).

1780   Armed Neutrality formed. Britain declares war on the United Provinces.

1781   British surrender at Yorktown. Austro-Russian alliance against the Ottoman Empire.

1783   Treaty of Versailles signed by Britain, France, Spain and the United States.
Russian seizure of the Crimea.

GREAT BRITAIN

1689	Bill of Rights.
1694	Triennial Act.
1701	Act of Settlement.
1702	Death of William III, accession of Anne.
1707	Union of England and Scotland.
1714	Death of Anne, accession of George I.
1715 –16	Jacobite rising.
1716	Septennial Act.
1720	South Sea Bubble bursts.
1721	Robert Walpole First Lord of the Treasury (remains chief minister till 1742).
1727	Death of George I, accession of George II. First Indemnity Act in favour of Nonconformists.
1745 –46	Jacobite rising.
1757 –61	Coalition ministry led by William Pitt and the Duke of Newcastle.
1760	Death of George II, accession of George III.
1763	Wilkes case arises. Friction with American colonies begins to be serious.
1769	Wilkes expelled from Parliament, twice re-elected.
1770 –82	Lord North chief minister, personal influence of George III at its height.
1782	'Economical Reform' legislation.
1783	William Pitt the younger becomes chief minister.

FRANCE

1713	Bull *Unigenitus* condemns Jansenist doctrines.
1715	Death of Louis XIV, accession of Louis XV. (Philip Duc d'Orléans Regent till 1723.)
1720	Collapse of 'Mississippi Bubble' and financial schemes of Law.
1723 –26	Duc de Bourbon chief minister.
1726 –43	Cardinal Fleury chief minister.
1749	New tax, the *vingtième*, imposed by Controller-General Machault d'Arnouville.
1751	Failure of Machault's attempts to improve the government's financial position.

1758 Duc de Choiseul chief minister.
−70
1764 Expulsion of the Jesuits.
1771 *Parlement* of Paris exiled by Maupeou.
1774 Death of Louis XV, accession of Louis XVI.
　　 Fall of Maupeou and recall of the *parlements*.
　　 Vergennes Secretary for Foreign Affairs (till his death in 1787).
1774 Turgot Controller-General of Finances.
−76

RUSSIA

1689 Tsarevna Sophia (Regent since 1682) overthrown.
1695 Peter I begins the creation of a fleet for use against Azov and
−96　on the Black sea.
1697 Peter's journey to Western Europe.
−98
1703 Building of a Baltic fleet and of St Petersburg begun.
1711 Creation of the Senate.
1718 Murder of Tsarevich Alexis. Creation of administrative
　　 colleges begun.
1722 Table of Ranks issued.
1725 Death of Peter I, accession of Catherine I.
1727 Death of Catherine I, accession of Peter II.
1730 Death of Peter II, accession of Anna. Failure of attempt to
　　 impose restrictions on the power of the monarchy.
1740 Death of Anna. She is succeeded in 1741, after several palace
　　 revolutions, by Elizabeth.
1762 Death of Elizabeth; accession, deposition, and murder of Peter
　　 III; accession of Catherine III.
　　 Abolition of compulsory State service for the landowning
　　 class.
1767 Legislative Commission meets.
1773 Great peasant revolt led by Pugachev.
−75
1775 Far-reaching reform of provincial administration.
1785 Charters to the nobility and towns issued.

SPAIN

1714 Capture of Barcelona by Philip V.
1719 Fall of Alberoni.

1743   Ensenada chief minister.
−54
1746   Death of Philip V, accession of Ferdinand VI.
1759   Death of Ferdinand VI, accession of Charles III.
1767   Expulsion of the Jesuits.
1779   Unsuccessful siege of Gibraltar.
−82

THE HABSBURG MONARCHY

1711   Death of Joseph I, accession of Charles VI.
       Hungarian revolt ended by Peace of Szatmár.
1713   Pragmatic Sanction issued.
1740   Death of Charles VI, accession of Maria Theresa.
1749   *Directorium in Publicis et Cameralibus* set up.
1753   Kaunitz becomes Chancellor.
1760   Council of State set up.
1765   Joseph II becomes Holy Roman Emperor and co-ruler with his mother of the Habsburg territories.
1780   Death of Maria Theresa. Joseph II in sole control of the Habsburg territories.
1781   Numerous reforms introduced by Joseph II (most notable his
−85   efforts in 1781 to improve the position of the peasantry).

BRANDENBURG-PRUSSIA

1713   Death of Frederick I, accession of Frederick William I.
1722   General Directory established.
1728   Foreign Ministry (*Kabinetsministerium*) established.
1733   Modified form of conscription introduced.
1740   Death of Frederick William I, accession of Frederick II.
1766   New excise introduced.
1786   Death of Frederick II, accession of Frederick William II.
1794   New law code issued.

OTHER STATES

1702   Heinsius leading political figure in the United Provinces.
−20

474

1718 Death of Charles XII of Sweden.
1720 New constitution greatly reduces the power of the Swedish monarchy.
1747 Orangist revolution in the United Provinces.
1750 Pombal chief minister in Portugal.
–77
1759 Jesuits expelled from Portugal.
Tanucci in power in the Kingdom of the Two Sicilies (till 1776).
1764 Stanislas Poniatowski, last king of Poland, elected.
1765 Grand Duke Leopold ruler of Tuscany.
–90
1771 Gustavus III king of Sweden.
–92
1772 He re-establishes absolutism with French support.
1770 Struensee introduces reforms in Denmark.
–72

BIBLIOGRAPHY

Any short bibliography which attempts to cover, even in the most summary way, so enormous a subject, must be selective to the point of being arbitrary. In what follows works in languages other than English, and articles in learned periodicals, have been included when their importance seemed to justify it; but some effort has been made to give preference to what is available in English and to books rather than articles, since the former will often be more accessible to many readers. For ease of reference, the arrangement of the bibliography follows that of the chapters.

GENERAL WORKS

The most detailed general account of eighteenth-century Europe in English is that in the two relevant volumes of the *New Cambridge Modern History*: *The Old Regime, 1713–1763*, ed. J. Lindsay (Cambridge, 1957) and *The American and French Revolutions, 1763–1793*, ed. A. Goodwin (Cambridge, 1965), though both are inevitably beginning to be to some extent out of date. The three relevant volumes in the American *Rise of Modern Europe* series, edited by W. L. Langer: P. Roberts, *The Quest for Security, 1715–1740* (New York–London, 1947); W. L. Dorn, *Competition for Empire, 1740–1765* (London–New York, 1940); and L. Gershoy, *From Despotism to Revolution, 1763–1789* (New York–London, 1944) are even more dated but worth mentioning for the political and diplomatic detail they contain and their full bibliographies. A. Cobban (ed.), *The Eighteenth Century: Europe in the Age of Enlightenment* (London, 1969) is a collection of essays by experts on different aspects of the period and is magnificently illustrated. W. Doyle, *The Old European Order,*

1660–1800 (Oxford, 1978) is penetrating, up-to-date and very well written: its relatively heavy concentration on France is a reflection, probably unavoidable, of the quantity and originality of French research on this period. Olwen Hufton, *Europe: Privilege and Protest, 1730–1789* (London, 1980), a volume in the *Fontana History of Europe*, is shorter and in some ways more conventional, but a work of intelligence with the same strong French emphasis. G. Rudé, *Europe in the Eighteenth Century: Aristocracy and the Bourgeois Challenge* (London, 1972) is rather patchy; but I. Woloch, *Eighteenth-Century Europe: Tradition and Progress, 1715–1789* (New York, 1982), which is vol. 3 of the *Norton History of Modern Europe*, is a concise, intelligent and up-to-date American survey. Another American work, good on politics and political ideas, is L. Krieger, *Kings and Philosophers, 1689–1789* (New York, 1970). In French there is a useful though now a little dated single-volume discussion by R. Mousnier and E. Labrousse, *Le XVIIIᵉ siècle: Révolution intellectuelle, technique et politique, 1715–1815* (Paris, 1953) in the series *Histoire Générale des Civilisations*: the chapters relating to the eighteenth century were written by Professor Mousnier. French writing of the last generation has concentrated heavily on analysis of the social and economic forces which are argued to be the main impetus behind the movement of history: good examples of this are the surveys by P. Chaunu, *La Civilisation de l'Europe classique* (Paris, 1966), much of which deals with the seventeenth century, and *La Civilisation de l'Europe des lumières* (Paris, 1971). A recent collection of essays, some of which are of high quality, is J. Berenger and others, *L'Europe à la fin du XVIIIᵉ siècle (vers 1780–1802)* (Paris, 1985): in spite of its title many of them deal with the decades before 1780.

There are many national histories of the major states and peoples. For England the two relevant volumes of the *Oxford History of England* series: B. Willliams, *The Whig Supremacy, 1714–1760* (revised edn., Oxford, 1962) and J. Stephen Watson, *The Reign of George III, 1760–1820* (Oxford, 1960) remain the most comprehensive and balanced surveys, though they are becoming somewhat outdated. They contain large, though inevitably now incomplete, bibliographies. Two useful single-volume accounts are: Dorothy Marshall, *Eighteenth Century England* (London, 1962) and J. B. Owen, *The Eighteenth Century, 1714–1815* (London, 1975). The first half of I. R. Christie, *Wars and Revolutions: Britain 1760–1815* (London, 1982) is a useful though somewhat conventional account of the last decades of this period with a good bibliography. On Scotland T. C. Smout, *A History of the Scottish People, 1560–1830* (London, 1969) is very good; and B. Lenman, *Integration, Enlightenment, and Industrialization: Scotland, 1746–1832* (London, 1981), though short, is up-to-date and has a full bibliography. For France there is a good and clear summary in J. Lough, *An Introduction to Eighteenth Century France* (London, 1960): C. B. A. Behrens, *The Ancien Regime* (London, 1967) is an interpretative essay rather than a comprehensive treatment, but intelligent and stimulating. There is no completely satisfactory single volume in French in spite of the wealth of French research on the period. Older works with a predominantly political bias are H. Carré, *Le Règne de Louis XV* (Paris, 1911) and H. Carré, P. Sagnac and E. Lavisse, *Le*

Règne de Louis XVI (Paris, 1911) which are respectively volume viii, Part II and volume ix, Part I of E. Lavisse (ed.), *Histoire de France des Origines jusqu'à la Révolution*. Useful more recent works with a strong bias towards economic and social history are: R. Mandrou, *La France aux XVIIᵉ et XVIIIᵉ siècles* (Paris, 1967); P. Goubert, *L'Ancien Régime* (2 vols, Paris, 1969–73: the first volume is available in English translation (London, 1973)); and A. Soboul, *La Civilisation et la Révolution française*, vol. i, *La Crise de l'Ancien Régime* (Paris, 1970). On Germany W. H. Bruford, *Germany in the Eighteenth Century* (Cambridge, 1939) is still very useful on social and intellectual history, while H. Holborn, *A History of Modern Germany: 1648–1840* (Princeton, N.J., 1982) is the best up-to-date general account in English. On Prussia, for those who can read German, the most satisfactory general account is still perhaps O. Hintze, *Die Hohenzollern und ihr Werk* (9th edn; Berlin, 1926). The Habsburg territories are relatively well covered in a number of recent works. E. Wangermann, *The Austrian Achievement, 1700–1800* (London, 1973) is a good introduction; and there are two useful books by V.-L. Tapié, *Monarchies et peuples du Danube* (Paris, 1969) and *L'Europe de Marie-Thérèse* (Paris, 1973). On Hungary, H. Marczali, *Hungary in the Eighteenth Century* (Cambridge, 1910) has still not been superseded, though it focuses mainly on the later part of the century; and R. J. Kerner, *Bohemia in the Eighteenth Century* (New York, 1932) is important as almost the only treatment of this area in a western language, though it refers mainly to the later years of the century. H. Hantsch, *Die Geschichte Oesterreichs*, vol. ii (Vienna, 1950) is a useful general work written from an Austrian point of view. On Italy the best discussion in English, and probably at its length in any language, is Parts 1 and 2 of S. J. Woolf, *A History of Italy, 1700–1860: The Social Constraints of Political Change* (London, 1979): it contains a very large bibliography, but almost entirely of works in Italian. There is a brief summary in the last five chapters of J. Delumeau, *L'Italie de Botticelli à Bonaparte* (Paris, 1974): but this is very much a textbook. F. Valsecchi, *L'Italia nel Settecento* (Milan, 1959) is on a much larger scale and is lavishly illustrated. On Spain the best introduction is W. N. Hargreaves-Mawdsley, *Spain, 1700–1788: A Political, Diplomatic and Institutional History* (London, 1978), while the standard large-scale history is A. Ballesteros y Berretta, *Historia de Espana y su Influencia en la Historia universal* (Barcelona, 1918–41), of which volumes v and vi are relevant to the eighteenth century. The most important large-scale modern work in many ways is J. Vilar, *La Catalogne dans l'Espagne moderne* (3 vols; Paris, 1962), which is mainly concerned with the period 1714–1808 and is an outstanding example of the drive towards quantification which has inspired so much French historical writng in recent decades. On Russia there is a good general treatment in M. T. Florinsky, *Russia: A History and an Interpretation* (New York, 1955): P. Dukes, *The Making of Russian Absolutism, 1613–1801* (London, 1982) is short and rather conventional but of use as an introduction to the subject. The reign of Peter I is covered in two short books in English: B. H. Sumner, *Peter the Great and the Emergence of Russia* (London, 1951) and M. S. Anderson, *Peter the Great* (London, 1978). In other languages P. Milyukov, C. Seignobos and

L. Eisenmann, *Histoire de Russie* (Paris, 1932–33), vols ii–iii and V. Gitermann, *Geschichte Russlands* (Zurich, 1944–49), vol. ii are still useful in spite of their age, while there is an exhaustive treatment of Peter's work in R. Wittram, *Peter I, Czar und Kaiser* (2 vols, Göttingen, 1964). On Northern Europe there is a competent overview in P. Jeannin, *L'Europe du nord-ouest et du nord aux XVIIe et XVIIIe siècles* (Paris, 1969); while C. Nordmann, *Grandeur et liberté de la Suède* (Paris, 1971) is a good history of a country still of considerable significance throughout the eighteenth century, and M. Roberts, *Essays in Swedish History* (London, 1967) contains material of importance. It is less easy to suggest suitable general works on the Dutch Republic. P. J. Blok, *A History of the People of the Netherlands*, vol. v (New York, 1912) is now very old, and B. H. M. Vlekke, *The Evolution of the Dutch Nation* (New York, 1945) is also in many ways outdated. There is useful material in the first chapters of E. H. Kossmann, *The Low Countries, 1780–1840* (Oxford, 1978). On Poland *The Cambridge History of Poland*, vol. ii, ed. W. H. Reddaway and others (Cambridge, 1941) is still useful. On the difficult area of South-East Europe there are the older L. S. Stavrianos, *The Balkans since 1453* (New York, 1958), the first volume of Barbara Jelavich, *A History of the Balkans* (Cambridge, 1983) and P. F. Sugar, *Southeastern Europe under Ottoman Rule, 1354–1804* (Seattle–London, 1983), all of which give good general accounts of developments there. A sympathetic account of the Ottoman Empire's struggles with its problems can be found in S. J. Shaw, *History of the Ottoman Empire and Modern Turkey*, vol. i (Cambridge, 1976).

CHAPTER 2: THE SOURCES

The best general discussion of the historiography of modern Europe is E. Fueter, *Geschichte der neueren Historiographie* (Munich, 1936): in English there is the less penetrating J. W. Thompson, *A History of Historical Writing* (New York, 1942). The eighteenth century's ideas about history and the writing of it are discussed in R. N. Stromberg, 'History in the eighteenth century', *Journal of the History of Ideas*, xii (1951); H. Trevor-Roper, 'The historical philosophy of the Enlightenment,' *Studies on Voltaire and the Eighteenth Century*, xxvii (1963), and J. H. Brumfitt, *Voltaire Historian* (Oxford, 1958). K. Hammer and J. Voss (eds), *Historische Forschung im 18. Jahrhundert. Organisation: Zielsetzung: Ergebnisse* (Bonn, 1976) is an important collection of articles, several of them in French. Changing views on some of the most important questions of eighteenth-century history and the way in which they have been affected by the availability and use of different kinds of materials are illustrated in M. S. Anderson, *Historians and Eighteenth-Century Europe, 1715–1789* (Oxford, 1979). The remarkable contribution made to the subject by French historians during the last generaration or more is discussed in T. Stoianovich, *French Historical Method: The Annales Paradigm* (New

Brunswick, N.J., 1976); while the quantification which has bulked so large in that contribution is well illustrated by the articles collected in E. Le Roy Ladurie, *The Territory of the Historian* (Chicago, 1979). The growth of the newspaper press, which provides a major new source for historians, can be followed in C. Ledré, *Histoire de la presse* (Paris, 1958); C. Bellanger and others, *Histoire générale de la presse française*, vol. i (Paris, 1967); and L. Hanson *Government and the Press, 1695–1763* (Oxford, 1936).

Guides to the various national archives and to manuscript collections in great libraries are too numerous to mention here. D. H. Thomas and L. M. Case (eds), *Guide to the Diplomatic Archives of Western Europe* (Philadelphia, 1959) deserves attention, however, as a useful though sometimes rather summary introduction to one very important class of material.

CHAPTER 3: THE STRUCTURE OF SOCIETY

R. and Elborg Forster, eds, *European Society in the Eighteenth Century* (London, 1969) is a substantial and useful collection of extracts from contemporary, almost entirely printed, sources. There is no good discussion of European society as a whole; presumably the immensity of the subject has frightened off potential authors. For different states one or two titles may be mentioned. For France there is a challenging discussion in P. Goubert, *L'Ancien Régime*, vol. i, *La Société* (Paris, 1969). The last generation has also seen the production of very large, detailed and highly analytical studies of the social history of different regions of France. Parts of P. Goubert, *Beauvais et le Beauvaisis de 1600 à 1730* (Paris, 1960) and E. Le Roy Ladurie, *Les Pasysans de Languedoc* (2 vols, Paris, 1966) are relevant to the subject of this chapter; while A. Poitrineau, *La Vie rurale en Basse-Auvergne au XVIIIᵉ siècle (1726–1789)* (2 vols, Paris, 1965), M. Agulhon, *La Vie sociale en Provence intérieure au lendemain de la Révolution* (Paris, 1970), and G. Frêche, *Toulouse et la région Midi-Pyrénées au siècle des lumières (vers 1670–1789)* (n.p., ?1975) all contain a great deal of interesting information. For England there is R. Porter, *English Society in the Eighteenth Century* (London, 1982) which is also full of information, though on a smaller scale and with a strikingly different type of approach to the subject. Spain is covered by the solid work of A. Dominguez Ortiz, *La Sociedad espanola en el siglo XVIII* (Madrid, 1955), while for Venice there is the excellent study by M. Berengo, *La Società veneta alla fine del Settecento* (Florence, 1956). P. Villani, *Feudalità, riforme, capitalismo agrario: panorama di storia sociale italiano tra Sette e Ottecento* (Bari, 1968) provides a synoptic view of Italian writing up to the date of its publication. R. R. Palmer, *The Age of the Democratic Revolution*, vol. i *The Challenge* (Princeton, 1959) is a stimulating though controversial discussion of the relationship between social tensions and political events in the generation from 1760 onwards. Much of the best work on family structures and relationships is French. A. Armengaud, *La Famille et l'enfant en France et en Angleterre du XVIe au XVIIIe siècle* (Paris, 1975) is an analytical study by a demographer. J. L. Flandrin, *Les Amours paysannes: amour et sexualité dans les campagnes de l'ancienne France* (*XVIe–XIXe siècles*) is a collection of illustrative extracts with copious commentary by the editor; and the same author's *Families in Former Times: Kinship, Household and Sexuality* (Cambridge, 1979) contains much information but is again focused mainly on France. F. Lebrun, *La Vie conjugale sous l'ancien régime* (Paris, 1975), is an excellent short discussion much of which relates to the eighteenth century. A well-known older work, also focused on France, is P. Ariès, *Centuries of Childhood: A Social History of Family Life* (New York, 1962); while J. H. Plumb, 'The new world of children in eighteenth-century England,' *Past and Present*, No. 67 (1975) is an article of importance. On peasant life and agrarian problems in Eastern and East-Central Europe the best general work is J. Blum, *The End of the Old Order in Rural Europe* (Princeton, 1978); for Russia the same author's *Lord and Peasant in Russia from the Ninth to the Nineteenth Century* (Princeton, 1961) remains fundamental. W. E. Wright, *Serf, Seigneur and Sovereign: Agrarian Reform in Eighteenth-Century Bohemia* (Minneapolis, 1966) is slighter but useful. For France, apart from the great regional studies mentioned above, there are a large number of analyses of rural society in smaller areas, often single villages. Examples of what is available in English are: P. L.-R. Higonnet, *Pont-de-Montvert: Social Structure and Politics in a French Village, 1700–1914* (Cambridge, Mass., 1971); T. F. Sheppard, *Lourmarin in the Eighteenth Century: A Study of a French Village* (Baltimore–London, 1971); and D. Sutherland, *The Chouans: The Social Origins of Popular Counter-Revolution in Upper Brittany, 1770–1796* (Oxford, 1982). There is still much to be learned from the old works of A. Babeau, *La Vie rurale dans l'ancienne France* (2nd edn, Paris, 1885) and *Le Village sous l'ancien régime* (4th edn, Paris, 1891). The best comparative study of European nobilities is the excellent concise discussion in J. Meyer, *Noblesses et pouvoirs dans l'Europe d'ancien régime* (Paris, 1973); but the essays in A. Goodwin, ed., *The European Nobility in the Eighteenth Century* (London, 1953) are still useful. For England there are two very competent books by G. E. Mingay, *English Landed Society in the Eighteenth Century* (London, 1963) and *The Gentry: The Rise and Fall of a Ruling Class* (London, 1976). Three important articles by Sir John Habbakuk on 'The Rise and Fall of English Landed Families, 1600–1800', can be found in the *Transactions of the Royal Historical Society*, vols 29–31 (1979–81). For France the most challenging recent work is G. Chaussinand-Nogaret, *La Noblesse au XVIIIe siècle: De la féodalité aux lumières* (Paris, 1976), while J. Meyer, *La Noblesse bretonne au XVIIIe siècle* (2 vols, Paris, 1966) is a work of great learning and R. Forster, *The Nobility of Toulouse in the Eighteenth Century* (Baltimore, 1960) remains important. There is a considerable literature in western languages on the Russian landed ruling class. W. Leitsch, 'The Russian Nobility in the Eighteenth Century', *East European Quarterly*, vol. ix (1977) is a useful introduction. More specialised works are: M. Confino, *Domaines et seigneurs en Russie au XVIIIe siècle* (Paris, 1966); Brenda Meehan-Waters, *Autocracy and*

Aristocracy: *The Russian Service Elite of 1730* (New Brunswick, N.J.,
1982); and R. E. Jones, *The Emancipation of the Russian Nobility,
1762–1785* (Princeton, N.J., 1973). The nobilities of two of the Italian
states are covered in J. Nicolas, *La Savoie au 18e siècle: noblesse et bourgeoisie* (Paris, 1978) and J. C. Davis, *The Decline of the Venetian Nobility
as a Ruling Class* (Baltimore, 1962). Much has been written on urban
history, with France again very prominent. J.-P. Bardet, *Rouen aux XVIIe
et XVIIIe siècles. Les mutations d'un espace social* (2 vols, Paris, 1983) and
J.-C. Perrot, *Genèse d'une ville moderne: Caen au XVIIIe siècle* (2 vols,
Paris-The Hague, 1975) are both enormously detailed and far from easy
reading. Better proportioned are F. L. Ford, *Strasbourg in Transition,
1648–1789* (Cambridge, Mass., 1958); Olwen H. Hufton, *Bayeux in the
Late Eighteenth Century: A Social Study* (Oxford, 1969); F.-G. Pariset, ed.,
Bordeaux au XVIIIe siècle (Bordeaux, 1968); and in particular the excellent
book of M. Garden, *Lyon et les lyonnais au XVIIIe siècle* (Paris, 1975). G.
Lefèbvre, 'Urban society in the Orleannais in the late eighteenth century',
Past and Present, No. 18 (1961) is still useful, while C. Carrière, *Négociants
marseillais au XVIIIe siècle* (Marseilles, ?1975) is a more specialised study.
Two useful and readable books on London are M. Dorothy George,
London Life in the Eighteenth Century (London, 1925) and Dorothy
Marshall, *Dr. Johnson's London* (London, 1968). Some other great Euro-
pean cities are covered in F. G. Dreyfus, *Sociétés et mentalités à Mayence
dans la seconde moitié du XVIIIe siècle* (Paris, 1968); G. L. Soliday, *A
Community in Conflict: Frankfurt Society in the Seventeenth and Early Eight-
eenth Centuries* (Hanover, N.H., 1974); G. Aliberti, *Economia e società a
Napoli del Settecento al Novecento* (Naples, ?1975); and the enormously
detailed J. Georgelin, *Venise au siècle des lumières* (Paris-The Hague, 1978).
The weakness of urban life in Russia is brought out by J. M. Hittle, *The
Service City: State and Townsmen in Russia, 1600–1800* (Cambridge,
Mass., 1979). On poverty and the working class there are several excel-
lent contributions. Olwen H. Hufton, *The Poor of Eighteenth Century
France, 1750–1789* (Oxford, 1975) is outstanding, while J. Kaplow, *The
Names of Kings: The Parisian Labouring Poor in the Eighteenth Century* (New
York, 1972), though narrower in scope, is also good. Dorothy Marshall,
The English Poor in the Eighteenth Century (London, 1926) is still very
useful, while E. P. Thompson, 'The Moral Economy of the English
Crowd in the Eighteenth Century', *Past and Present*, No. 50 (1971) is a
brilliant short treatment of its subject. There is a useful short overview
of the problem of poverty in Europe generally in J. P. Gutton, *La Société
et les pauvres en Europe, XVIe–XVIIIe siècle* (Paris, 1974). Considerable
light is shed on English society, from a very different angle, by M.
Dorothy George, *Hogarth to Cruikshank: Social Change in Graphic Satire*
(London, 1967).

CHAPTER 4: ECONOMIC LIFE

The most satisfactory general account of the economic history of Europe in this period is perhaps that to be found in a collective work in French, P. Leon, ed., *Histoire économique et sociale du monde*, vol. 2, *Les Hésitations de la croissance, 1580–1740*, and vol. 3, *Inerties et révolutions, 1730–1840* (Paris, 1978). The first half of vol. 3 is particularly useful. In English there is much valuable material in *The Cambridge Economic History of Europe*, vols v and vi (Cambridge, 1977, 1966), though *The Fontana Economic History of Europe*, vol. 3 (London, 1973) will probably be found easier to use by most readers. The very long and somewhat mannered F. Braudel, *Civilization and Capitalism, 15th–18th Century* (3 vols, London, 1981–84) contains much of interest but is not always easy reading, while C. Wilson and G. Parker, eds, *An Introduction to the Sources of European Economic History, 1500–1800* (London, 1977), though short, provides a good deal of information in the form of tables and graphs. H. Kellenbenz, *The Rise of the European Economy: An Economic History of Continental Europe from the Fifteenth to the Eighteenth Century* (London, 1976), though rather poorly organised and focused too much on the German world, gives much interesting detail which cannot be easily found elsewhere. Some major developments in the later decades of this period are very well covered in D. S. Landes, *The Unbound Prometheus: Technological Change in Europe since 1750* (Cambridge, 1969), and S. Pollard, *Peaceful Conquest: The Industrialization of Europe, 1760–1970* (Oxford, 1981). So far as national economic histories are concerned, France and Britain are much better provided than most of the rest of Europe. For France there is F. Braudel and E. Labrousse, eds, *Histoire économique et sociale de la France*, vol. ii, *Des derniers temps de l'âge seigneurial aux préludes de l'âge industriel, 1660–1789* (Paris, 1970), which is written by an outstanding team of experts though not altogether well arranged. Two famous older works which have changed the whole course of thinking on the subject are C.-E. Labrousse, *Esquisse du mouvement des prix et des revenus en France au XVIIIᵉ siècle* (2 vols, Paris, 1933) and the same author's *La Crise de l'économie française à la fin de l'ancien régime et au début de la Révolution*, vol. i (Paris, 1944). Great Britain is well covered by T. S. Ashton, *An Economic History of England: The 18th Century* (London, 1966), which is short and challenging, by C. Wilson, *England's Apprenticeship, 1603–1763* (London, 1965) and by H. Hamilton, *An Economic History of Scotland in the Eighteenth Century* (Oxford, 1963). E. F. Heckscher, *An Economic History of Sweden* (Cambridge, Mass., 1954) is a very good book, while for Spain there is useful material in R. Herr, *The Eighteenth-Century Revolution in Spain* (Princeton, 1958) and R. J. Shafer, *The Economic Societies in the Spanish World (1763–1821)* (Syracuse, N.Y., 1958). In default of anything more recent in a western language B. Gille, *Histoire économique et sociale de la Russie* (Paris, 1949) is still useful; and there is an important account of Russia's greatest industrial achievement during this period in R. Portal, *L'Oural au XVIIIᵉ siècle* (Paris, 1951). The population growth which underlay much of Europe's economic life is a difficult and technical subject. An overall view is best found in M. W. Flinn, *The European Demographic System, 1500–1820* (Brighton, 1981), which gives a very clear summary, and in J. Dupâquier, M. Reinhard and others, *Histoire générale de la population mondiale* (3rd edn, Paris, 1968).

For France there is a good, fairly technical, but clear and concise account in J. Dupâquier, *La Population française aux XVIIᵉ et XVIIIᵉ siècles* (Paris, 1979), while for England there is an important recent article, E. A. Wrigley, 'The Growth of Population in Eighteenth-Century England: A Conundrum Resolved', *Past and Present*, No. 98 (1983). L. A. Clarkson, *Death, Disease and Famine in Pre-Industrial England* (London, 1975) is useful. This is an area in which scholarly work becomes outdated with frightening speed; but D. V. Glass and D. E. C. Eversley, eds, *Population in History* (London, 1965) contains articles which are still worth reading. On agriculture there is a good introduction, though one which covers a very long time-span, in B. H. Slicher van Bath, *The Agrarian History of Western Europe, A. D. 500–1850* (London, 1963): the same author's 'Eighteenth-Century Agriculture on the Continent of Europe: Evolution or Revolution?', *Agricultural History*, xliii (1969) is short but suggestive. For France a useful article is M. Morineau, 'Y a-t-il eu une révolution agricole en France au XVIIIᵉ siècle?', *Revue Historique*, ccxxxix (1968); this sums up some of the conclusions of the same author's *Les Faux-Semblants d'un démarrage économique: Agriculture et démographie en France au XVIIIᵉ siècle* (Paris, 1971). R. Forster, 'Obstacles to Agricultural Growth in Eighteenth Century France', *American Historical Review*, lxxv (1970) is also useful. For England two well-known and important books are J. D. Chambers and G. E. Mingay, *The Agricultural Revolution, 1750–1880* (London, 1966) and E. Kerridge, *The Agricultural Revolution* (1967). The overseas trade of England, the most dynamic element in European commerce, is briefly covered by R. Davis, *A Commercial Revolution: English Overseas Trade in the Seventeenth and Eighteenth Centuries* (London, 1967), in the same author's 'English Foreign Trade, 1700–1774', *Economic History Review*, Second Series, xv (1962–3), and in the older C. Wilson, *Anglo-Dutch Commerce and Finance in the Eighteenth Century* (Cambridge, 1941). On banking and finance there seems to be no suitable general survey: two outstanding works are H. Luthy, *La Banque Protestante en France de la révocation de l'Edit de Nantes à la Révolution* (2 vols, Paris, 1956–61) and P. G. M. Dickson, *The Financial Revolution in England* (London, 1967), but both are very detailed. J. G. Van Dillen, ed., *The History of the Principal Public Banks* (The Hague, 1934), a collection of essays in different languages, remains in many ways the best introduction in spite of its age. J. C. Riley, *International Government Finance and the Amsterdam Capital Market, 1740–1815* (Cambridge, 1980) assembles much information on borrowing by governments; while G. V. Taylor, 'Noncapitalist Wealth and the Origins of the French Revolution', *American Historical Review*, lxxii (1966–7), shows how little sophisticated financial institutions still meant in the greatest country in Europe. On industry J. Kulischer, 'La grande industrie aux XVIIᵉ et XVIIIᵉ siécles', *Annales d'Histoire Economique et Sociale*, ii (1931), is still well worth reading. On the origins and early stages of the Industrial Revolution in England R. M. Hartwell, ed., *The Causes of the Industrial Revolution in England* (London, 1967) is an important collection of articles: it includes in particular one by F. Crouzet, comparing British and French industrial growth in the eighteenth century, which has become a classic. T. S.

Ashton, *The Industrial Revolution, 1760–1830* (London, 1958), Phyllis Deane, *The First Industrial Revolution* (Cambridge, 1965), and P. Mathias, *The First Industrial Nation* (London, 1969) are all standard works, though inevitably most of what they have to says refers to the decades after the 1780s. The classical study of mercantilism is still E. F. Hecksher, *Mercantilism* (2 vols, London, 1935); but D. C. Coleman, ed., *Revisions in Mercantilism* (London, 1969) is a very useful collection of essays which provides an easier introduction to the subject. Much has been written on the Physiocrats. The most recent large-scale work is E. Fox-Genovese, *The Origins of Physiocracy: Economic Revolution and Social Order in Eighteenth-Century France* (Ithaca–London, 1976).

CHAPTER 5: GOVERNMENT AND ADMINISTRATION

There are very few studies of the administration of the European States during this period on anything more than a national scale. Sir Ernest Barker, *The Development of Public Services in Western Europe, 1660–1930* (Oxford, 1944) is intelligent but short and in many ways outdated. The estates and quasi-parliamentary bodies which still often played an important role in government and administration are discussed in A. R. Myers, *Parliaments and Estates in Europe to 1789* (London, 1973) and in an important article by D. Gerhard, 'Problems of Representation and Delegation in the Eighteenth Century', *Liber Memorialis Sir Maurice Powicke* (Louvain–Paris, 1965). On France there is the recent and very detailed R. Mousnier, *Les Institutions de la France sous la monarchie absolue, 1598–1715* (2 vols, Paris, 1974–80) and the very useful P. Goubert, *L'Ancien Régime*, vol. ii, *Les Pouvoirs* (Paris, 1973). One of the most important elements in the running of the country is covered by V. R. Gruder, *The Royal Provincial Intendants: A Governing Elite in Eighteenth-Century France* (Ithaca, 1968) and another in M. Antoine, *Le Conseil du Roi sous le règne de Louis XV* (Paris, 1970). On the *parlements* there is a very good treatment by J. Egret, *Louis XV et l'opposition parlementaire, 1715–1774* (Paris, 1970). For Britain M. A. Thomson, *The Secretaries of State, 1681–1782* (Oxford, 1932) is wide in scope and still very useful. On Brandenburg–Prussia, a State largely created by its administrative system, much has been written. R. A. Dorwart, *The Administrative Reforms of Frederick William I of Prussia* (Cambridge, Mass., 1953) is thorough and useful. H. Rosenberg, *Bureaucracy, Aristocracy and Autocracy: The Prussian Experience, 1660–1815* (Cambridge, Mass., 1958) is more schematic and less convincing. The long article of W. L. Dorn, 'The Prussian Bureaucracy in the Eighteenth Century', *Political Science Quarterly*, vols 46–47 (1931–32) is still important. More recent works are H. C. Johnson, *Frederick the Great and his Officials* (New York–London, 1975) and W. Hubatsch, *Frederick the Great: Absolutism and Administration*

(London, 1975): the latter is kinder to Frederick than many non-German historians would now be. There is an excellent discussion of the government of one of the smaller German states in T. C. W Blanning, *Reform and Revolution in Mainz, 1743–1803* (Cambridge, 1974). M. Raeff, *The Well Ordered Police State: Social and Institutional Change through the Law in the Germanies and Russia, 1600–1800* (New Haven–London, 1983) is very interesting on the paternalist elements in much German government during this period. On Russia more has been written in western languages on the reign of Catherine II than on the earlier part of the century. There is information in the biographies of Catherine and Peter I mentioned on pages 488 and 479; but the best specialised discussion of administrative reform from the 1760s onwards is to be found in the articles assembled in a special issue of *Canadian Slavic Studies*, iv, No. 3 (1970). An interesting and detailed recent work is J. P. Le Donne, *Ruling Russia: Politics and Administration in the Age of Absolutism, 1762–1796* (Princeton, 1984); but this is an opinionated book whose conclusions have been challenged. The political background to administrative reform is well discussed in D. Ransel, *The Politics of Catherinian Russia: The Panin Party* (New Haven–London, 1975). For the Habsburg Empire there is a short and relatively recent treatment in F. Walter, *Oesterreichische Verfassungs-und Verwaltungsgeschichte von 1500–1955* (Vienna–Köln–Graz, 1972), while many of the books on Joseph II mentioned on page 488 are also useful. An important specialised study is H. E. Strakosch, *State Absolutism and the Rule of Law: The Struggle for the Codification of Civil Law in Austria, 1753–1811* (Sydney, 1967). The weaknesses of the mechanisms for the maintenance of public order are brought out by I. A. Cameron, 'The Police of Eighteenth-Century France', *European Studies Review*, vol. 7 (1977) and A. J. Hayter, *The Army and the Crowd in Mid-Georgian England* (London, 1978). Disorder in England is illustrated in the essays on London in G. Rudé, *Paris and London in the Eighteenth Century: Studies in Popular Protest* (London, 1970) and on Spain in L. Rodriguez, 'The Spanish Riots of 1766', *Past and Present*, No. 59, (1973). A good deal has been written on the problems of taxation in the major European States. P. C. Hartmann, *Das Steuersystem der europäischen Staaten am Ende des Ancien Régime* (Munich, 1979), which is based on a French official enquiry of 1765, contains much detailed information about tax systems in North and Central Europe. For France Betty Behrens, 'Nobles, Privileges and Taxes in France at the End of the Ancien Regime', *Economic History Review*, Second Series, xv (1963) is a penetrating and influential article, while also in English there is the very solid J. R. Bosher, *French Finances, 1770–1795* (Cambridge, 1970). The very detailed Y. Durand, *Les Fermiers-Généraux au XVIIIe siècle* (Paris, 1971) is an able study of this group rather than of the system they operated. An important would-be financial reformer is covered in R. D. Harris, *Necker, Reform Statesman of the Ancien Régime* (Berkeley–Los Angeles–London, 1979). For England there are the very detailed J. E. D. Binney, *British Public Finance and Administration, 1774–1792* (Oxford, 1958) and W. R. Ward, *The English Land-Tax in the Eighteenth Century* (Oxford, 1953). A significant specialised study, though not well written, is D. M. Klang, *Tax Reform in Eighteenth-Century Lombardy* (Boulder, Col., 1977). On judicial systems there are several general books of interest: M. R. Weisser, *Crime and Punishment in Early Modern Europe* (Hassocks, 1979); J. Heath, *Eighteenth-Century Penal Theory* (Oxford, 1963); J. P. Dawson, *A History of Lay Judges* (Cambridge, Mass., 1960) which has interesting information on seigneurial courts; and the short but iconoclastic J. H. Langbein, *Torture and the Law of Proof: Europe and England in the Ancien Regime* (Chicago–London, 1977). Some aspects of this subject in France are covered in J. A. Carey, *Judicial Reform in France before the Revolution of 1789* (Cambridge, Mass., 1981) and in England in D. Hay and others, *Albion's Fatal Tree: Crime and Society in Eighteenth-Century England* (London, 1975).

CHAPTER 6: MONARCHS AND DESPOTS: TENSIONS WITHIN THE STATE

The fullest coverage of many aspects of monarchical government, and indeed of political life in general, is to be found in F. Venturi, *Settecento riformatore* (4 vols, Turin, 1969–84), which covers the period from 1730 to the French Revolution. It is a great work of learning but very long and detailed. A high proportion of what has been written about eighteenth-century monarchy centres around the difficult and rather unsatisfactory subject of Enlightened Despotism. F. Bluche, *Le Despotisme éclairé* (Paris, 1968) is solid and workmanlike. J. G. Gagliardo, *Enlightened Despotism* (London, 1968) and F. Hartung, *Enlightened Despotism* (Historical Association Pamphlet, London, 1968) are short introductions. There are two relevant collections of essays: P. Francastel, ed., *Utopie et institutions au XVIIIᵉ siècle: le pragmatisme des lumières* (Paris, 1963) and, perhaps more directly useful to most students, K. O. Freiherr von Aretin, ed., *Der Aufgeklärte Absolutismus* (Cologne, 1974). L. Krieger, *An Essay on the Theory of Enlightenend Despotism* (Chicago–London, 1975) is penetrating but far from easy reading. Three articles are worth mentioning in spite of their age: M. Lhéritier, 'Le Despotisme éclairé de Frédéric II à la Révolution française', *Bulletin of the International Commission of Historical Sciences*, ix (1937); C. Morazé, 'Finance et despotisme: essai sur les despotes éclairés,' *Annales*, iii (1948); and G. Lefèbvre, 'Le Despotisme éclairé', *Annales Historiques de la Révolution Française*, New Series, 21 (1949), which gives a Marxist view of the subject. On Frederick II of Prussia, who more than any other ruler seemed to contemporaries the paragon of enlightened monarchy, there is a useful but limited introduction in D. B. Horn, *Frederick the Great and the Rise of Prussia* (London, 1964). P. Paret, ed., *Frederick the Great: A Profile* (London, 1972) is a collection of articles and extracts of varying value; the most perceptive treatment in English is probably G. Ritter, *Frederick the Great: An Historical Profile* (London, 1968). W. O. Henderson, *Studies in the Economic Policy of Frederick the Great* (London,

1963) is informative on a more limited subject. R. Augstein, *Preussens Friedrich und die Deutschen* (Frankfurt-am-Main, 1968) is a hostile but well informed German view. On Joseph II there are good introductions in T. C. W. Blanning, *Joseph II and Enlightened Despotism* (London, 1970) and P. P. Bernard, *Joseph II* (New York, 1968). The standard large-scale work, which has held its place for many decades, is P. von Mitrofanov, *Joseph II. Seine politische und kulturelle Tätigkeit* (2 vols., Vienna-Leipzig, 1910) though the book is confusingly arraged. The intellectual aspects of Joseph's policies and his conflict with the Catholic church can be followed in P. P. Bernard, *Jesuits and Jacobins: Enlightenment and Enlightened Despotism in Austria* (Urbana–Chicago–London, 1971) and E. Winter, *Der Josefinismus. Die Geschichte des Österreichischen Reform-katholizismus, 1740–1848* (Berlin, 1962). The outstanding work in any language on the regime of Catherine II is Isabel de Madariaga, *Russia in the Age of Catherine the Great* (London, 1981), which is very thorough and complete. Two useful articles have appeared in the German journal *Jahrbücher für Geschichte Osteuropas*, Neue Folge: D. M. Griffiths, 'Catherine II: The Republican Empress', (21 (1973)) and D. Geyer, 'Der Aufgeklärte Absolutismus in Russland', (30 (1982)). The essays collected and reprinted in M. Raeff, ed., *Catherine the Great: A Profile* (London, 1972) illustrate the widely varying reactions of historians to the empress. On despotism elsewhere in Europe the available writing varies considerably in quality. The book by T. C. W. Blanning mentioned on page 486 is an illuminating discussion of the problems of enlightened government in a small German state. A. H. Hull, *Charles III and the Revival of Spain* (Washington, 1981) is biographical and narrative but useful so far as it goes. Chapter 4 of R. Herr, *An Historical Essay on Modern Spain* (Berkeley–Los Angeles–London, 1974) provides a brief summary. The remarkable reforming regime of the Grand Duke Leopold in Tuscany can be followed in the first volume of A. Wandruszka, *Leopold II. Erzherzog von Österreich, Grosshertzog von Toskana, König von Ungarn und Böhmen, Römischer Kaiser* (Vienna, 1963) and in H. Holldack, 'Die Reformpolitik Leopolds von Toskana', *Historische Zeitschrift*, clxv (1941–42). On Gustavus III of Sweden the best discussion is to be found in Book IV of the work by C. Nordmann mentioned on page 479. The peculiar position of the British monarchy is well brought out by R. Pares, *King George III and the Politicians* (Oxford, 1953) and more briefly in the same author's Historical Association pamphlet, *Limited Monarchy in Great Britain* (London, 1957). Betty Kemp, *King and Commons, 1660–1832* (London, 1957) is also useful, while J. Brooke *King George III* (London, 1972) is a perceptive and perhaps definitive study and Sir L. B. Namier, 'Monarchy and the Party System', an essay in his *Personalities and Powers* (London, 1955) is a brilliant analysis. The negative personalities of Louis XV and Louis XVI are reflected in the lack of any good biography of either. An Italian state whose government was certainly despotic and in some ways progressive, but hardly enlightened, is covered in G. Symcox, *Victor Amadeus II: Absolutism in the Savoyard State, 1675–1730* (London, 1983) and G. Quazza, *Le Riforme in Piemonte nella prima metà del Settecento* (2 vols, Modena, 1957) The paternalism which inspired much of the activities of monarchs is illustrated in S. L. Kaplan, *Bread, Politics and Political Economy in the Reign of Louis XV* (2 vols, The Hague, 1976), a very detailed work. Some aspects of conservative resistance to 'enlightened' policies can be followed in the first chapters of K. Epstein, *The Genesis of German Conservatism* (Princeton, 1966).

CHAPTER 7: ARMIES AND NAVIES

The best study of armies in their social background is A. Corvisier, *Armies and Societies in Europe, 1494–1789* (Bloomington, Indiana, 1979), which is a translation of the French original published in 1976. The relevant parts of J. U. Nef, *War and Human Progress* (London, 1950) are interesting but less convincing. E. Silberner, *La Guerre dans la pensée économique du XVIe au XVIIIe siècle* (Paris, 1939) is useful as giving many quotations from and references to the writers of the period. J. Childs, *Armies and Warfare in Europe, 1648–1789* (Manchester, 1982) is up-to-date and easy to read; it concentrates on armies rather than on their economic and social background. The relevant chapters of E. M. Earle, ed., *Makers of Modern Strategy* (Princeton, 1944) are useful on the evolution of strategic and tactical ideas, as is E. Carrias, *La Pensée militaire française* (Paris, 1960). The book edited by J. Berenger and others and mentioned on page 477 contains an excellent chapter by A. Corvisier on 'Les Armées et la Guerre'. Much has been written on the French army in this period. The outstanding work is A. Corvisier, *L'Armée Française de la fin du XVIIe siècle au ministère de Choiseul: Le Soldat* (Paris, 1964), which is one of the most detailed books on any aspect of eighteenth-century history. Two interesting articles with wide scope are: E.-G. Leonard, 'La question sociale dans l'armée française au XVIIIe siècle', *Annales*, iii (1948) and D. Bien, 'The Army in the French Enlightenment: Reform, Reaction and Revolution', *Past and Present*, No. 85 (Nov., 1979). The Prussian army is well covered in C. Duffy, *The Army of Frederick the Great* (Newton Abbot, 1974), while there is also a useful brief account, with emphasis on the army's relationship with society, in the first chapter of M. Kitchen, *A Military History of Germany from the Eighteenth Century to the Present Day* (Bloomington–London, 1975). For the Habsburg territories there is another good study by C. Duffy, *The Army of Maria Theresa: The Armed Forces of Imperial Austria, 1740–1780* (Vancouver, 1977). For Russia there is an outstanding book, J. H. L Keep, *Soldiers of the Tsar: Army and Society in Russia, 1462–1874* (Oxford, 1985). Great Britain is covered by the excellent D. Chandler, *The Art of Warfare in the Age of Marlborough* (London, 1976), which in fact covers the subject up to about 1740, and the shorter and more popular H. C. B. Rogers, *The British Army of the Eighteenth Century* (London, 1977). The old standard work by J. W. Fortescue, *History of the British Army* (2nd edn, London, 1910), of which volume ii is relevant here, is still of use. A biography of one of the greatest soldiers of the period which is well worth a

mention is D. McKay, *Prince Eugene of Savoy* (London, 1977). A subject
of great importance which has been grossly neglected by historians is
discussed briefly in M. Van Creveld, *Supplying War. Logistics from
Wallenstein to Patton* (Cambridge, 1977). There is a large literature on the
British navy. In spite of its age M. Lewis, *The Navy of Britain* (London,
1948) provides a good starting-point; and M. Duffy, ed., *The Military
Revolution and the State, 1500–1800* (Exeter, 1980) contains a good short
discussion by the editor of 'The Foundations of British Naval Power'.
For the French navy the old work of G. Lacour-Gayet, *La Marine militaire
de la France sous le règne de Louis XV* (2nd edn, Paris, 1910) is still of use,
while that of Spain is covered in a recent detailed study by J. P. Merino
Navarro, *La Armada espanola en el siglo XVIII* (Madrid, 1981). Other
books relevant to naval history are mentioned in the bibliography to
Chap. 12.

CHAPTER 8: DIPLOMACY AND INTERNATIONAL RELATIONS

The most useful general histories of international relations of a narrative
kind are G. Zeller, *De Louis XIV à 1789* (Paris, 1955), a volume in the
series *Histoire des Relations Internationales*, edited by P. Renouvin, and D.
McKay and H. M. Scott, *The Rise of the Great Powers, 1648–1815*
(London, 1983); these books are also very relevant to Chapters 9–12.
Chapters ii and iii of H. Duchhardt, *Gleichgewicht der Kräfte; Convenance,
Europäisches Konzert* (Darmstadt, 1976) provide a concise account of the
peace congresses of 1713–14 and 1763, while P. R. Rohden, *Die klassische
Diplomatie von Kaunitz bis Metternich* (Leipzig, 1939) is a general
discussion of the ideas and methods of eighteenth-century diplomacy.
Diplomatic organization is a somewhat dry subject which has none the
less produced some substantial studies. For France there are two well-
known older works, C. Picavet, *La Diplomatie française au temps de Louis
XIV* (Paris, 1930) and F. Masson, *Le Département des Affaires Étrangères
pendant la Révolution, 1787–1804* (Paris, 1897) which are still of value; and
J.-P. Samoyault, *Les Bureaux du secretariat d'état des Affaires Étrangères sous
Louis XV* (Paris, 1971) is a more recent specialized study. For Britain
D. B. Horn, *The British Diplomatic Service, 1689–1789* (Oxford, 1961) is
an excellent comprehensive study and for Sweden there is a detailed but
rather difficult official work, *Histoire de l'administration des Affaires
Étrangères de Suède* (Uppsala, 1940). On the balance of power there is the
rather sketchy G. Livet, *L'Équilibre européen de la fin du XVᵉ à la fin du
XVIIIᵉ siècle* (Paris, 1976) and the short discussion in M. S. Anderson,
'Eighteenth-century theories of the balance of power', in R. M. Hatton
and M. S. Anderson, eds, *Studies in Diplomatic History* (London, 1970).
M. Wright, ed., *Theory and Practice of the Balance of Power, 1486–1914*
(London, 1975) is a collection of extracts some of which relate to this

period. E. Kaeber, *Die Idee des europäischen Gleichgewichts in der publizistischen Literatur vom 16. bis zur Mitte des 18. Jahrhunderts* (Berlin, 1907) still contains much of interest. Perhaps the best discussion of the main eighteenth-century peace projects is that in K. von Raumer, *Ewiger Friede* (Freiburg–Munich, 1953), while T. Ruyssen, *Les Sources doctrinales de l'internationalisme* (3 vols, Grenoble, 1954–61) provides a wide-ranging survey of the subject. F. Gilbert, *To the Farewell Address: Ideas of Early American Foreign Policy* (Princeton, 1961) contains a good deal on European internationalist idealism. The best-known proposal for the systematic training of diplomats is discussed in H. M. A. Keens-Soper, 'The French Political Academy, 1712: a School for Ambassadors', *European Studies Review*, ii (1972). Finally there may be mentioned a well-known eighteenth-century work, F. de Callières, *The Art of Diplomacy*, edited by H. M. A. Keens-Soper and K. W. Schweizer (New York, 1983), which is a translation of a French original of 1716.

CHAPTER 9: THE EXPANSION OF RUSSIA: POLAND, THE BALTIC AND THE NEAR EAST

The relevant chapters of R. Wittram, *Peter I* (see p. 479) give a detailed account of the Tsar's foreign policy in general, while a large-scale biography of his great opponent, R. M. Hatton, *Charles XII of Sweden* (London, 1968), is the most informative book in English on the military events of the Great Northern War. Russia's relations with the German States down to 1756 can be followed in detail in W. Mediger, *Russlands Weg nach Europa* (Brunswick, 1952). On Russo-Swedish relations there is a good study by E. Amburger, *Russland und Schweden, 1762–1772*, which contains a long chapter on the period 1721–62; while M. Roberts, *British Diplomacy and Swedish Politics, 1758–1773* (Minneapolis, 1980) is an extremely detailed account. G. von Rauch, 'Zur Baltischen Frage im 18. Jahrhundert', *Jahrbücher für Geschichte Osteuropas*, Neue Folge, v (1957) is an important article. On the confused and confusing subject of the War of the Polish Succession there is a recent book in English, J. L. Sutton, *The King's Honor and the King's Cardinal: The War of the Polish Succession* (Lexington, 1980). The partition of 1772 can be followed in H. H. Kaplan, *The First Partition of Poland* (New York–London, 1962), which is good on the domestic politics of the country in 1762–73, while the old work of R. H. Lord, *The Second Partition of Poland* (Cambridge, Mass., 1915) includes a very useful introductory chapter dealing with events before the 1790s. On Russo-Turkish relations H. Übersberger, *Russlands Orientpolitik in den letzten zwei Jahrhunderten*, i (Stuttgart, 1913) is still the best overall study. B. H. Sumner, *Peter the Great and the Ottoman Empire* (Oxford, 1949) is concise and very good; while the first chapter of M. S. Anderson, *The Eastern Question, 1774–1923* (London, 1966) gives a short introductory account of the subject in the later eighteenth century. One of the great steps in Russian expansion is ably discussed in A. W. Fisher, *The Russian Annexation of the Crimea, 1772–1783* (Cambridge, 1970), and from a diplomatic point of view in M. S. Anderson, 'The Great Powers and the Russian Annexation of the Crimea, 1783–4', *Slavonic and East European Review*, xxxvii (1958–59). Some interesting general points about the situation in the Balkans and the Black Sea area are made in Chapters iv and v of W. H. McNeill, *Europe's Steppe Frontier, 1500–1800* (Chicago, 1964).

CHAPTER 10: THE GERMAN STATES AND THE RISE OF PRUSSIA

There are two useful short discussions in English of the Holy Roman Empire in its last years: the Prologue, 'The "German Problem" in the eighteenth century', of T. C. W. Blanning, *Reform and Revolution in Mainz, 1743–1803* (Cambridge, 1974) and Carol M. Rose, 'Empire and Territories at the End of the Old Reich', in *The Old Reich: Essays on German Political Institutions, 1495–1806*, eds J. A. Vann and S. W. Brown (Brussels, 1974). Discussion of the history of Germany in this period must centre largely on Frederick II. In additon to the books indicated in the bibliography to Chapter 6 there should be mentioned R. Köser, *Geschichte Friedrichs des Grossen* (7th edn, Berlin, 1921–25) which is still the standard large-scale biography, in three volumes with a considerable bias towards war and diplomacy, and A. Berney, *Friedrich der Grosse* (Tübingen, 1934), which takes the story only to 1756. Of the complex events of the War of the Austrian Succession the best short discussion in English is the chapter by M. A. Thomson in volume vii of the *New Cambridge Modern History*: the essays in R. Lodge, *Studies in Eighteenth-Century Diplomacy, 1740–1748* (London, 1930), though rather pedestrian and focused on Britain, still have value. The basic large-scale work on the Diplomatic Revolution of 1756 is still R. Waddington, *Louis XV et le renversement des alliances, 1754–1756* (Paris, 1896): there is an excellent short account by D. B. Horn in *New Cambridge Modern History*, vol. vii. Some of the origins of this famous change in diplomatic alignments can be followed in W. J. McGill, 'The Roots of Policy; Kaunitz in Vienna and Versailles', *Journal of Modern History*, xliii (1971), and in H. H. Kaplan, *Russia and the Outbreak of the Seven Years War* (Berkeley, 1968). The controversies among historians to which Frederick's attack on Saxony has given rise are summarized in H. Butterfield, *The Reconstruction of an Historical Episode* (Glasgow, 1951), while one aspect of the disunity of his enemies is discussed in L. Jay Oliva, *Misalliance: A Study of French Policy in Russia during the Seven Years War* (New York, 1964). There are useful accounts of the Austro-Prussian rivalries over Bavaria in H. W. V. Temperley, *Frederick the Great and Kaiser Joseph* (London, 1915) and the more recent P. P. Bernard, *Joseph II and Bavaria* (The Hague, 1965).

CHAPTER 11: SPAIN, ITALY AND THE MEDITERRANEAN

There is no single comprehensive work in English on the tangled diplomacy of the generation after 1713: much of the gound is covered in Italian in G. Quazza, *Il Problema italiano et l'equilibrio europeo, 1720–1738* (Turin, 1965), and the same author has produced a summary account in 'Italy's Role in the European Problems of the First Half of the Eighteenth Century', in *Studies in Diplomatic History*, R. M. Hatton and M. S. Anderson, eds (London, 1970). On British policy there is the recent and detailed J. Black, *British Foreign Policy in the Age of Walpole* (Edinburgh, 1985) and more generally P. Langford, *The Eighteenth Century, 1688–1815* (London, 1976): the latter is a sound introduction to all aspects of Britain's foreign relations during the eighteenth century. An important aspect of these relations is covered in S. Conn, *Gibraltar in British Diplomacy in the Eighteenth Century* (New Haven, 1942). On French policy there is the old but detailed A. Baudrillart, *Philippe V et la Cour de France* (Paris, 1890–1900), iii–v, and the very useful A. Mc.C. Wilson, *French Foreign Policy during the Administration of Cardinal Fleury* (Cambridge, Mass., 1936). All previous discussions of the internal structure of the Ottoman Empire are superseded by H. A. R. Gibb and R. Bowen, *Islamic Society and the West*, vol. i, *Islamic Society in the Eighteenth Century* (2 pts, Oxford, 1950–57), while the *Slavic Review*, xxi (1962) contains a number of useful articles on Ottoman rule in the Balkans; this is also discussed in Deena R. Sadat, 'Rumeli Ayanlari: The Eighteenth Century', *Journal of Modern History*, xliv (1974). Lavender Cassels, *The Struggle for the Ottoman Empire, 1717–1740* (London, 1968) is a readable though not very profound account of its subject and K. A. Roider, *Austria's Eastern Question, 1700–1790* (Princeton, 1982) is a short but useful narrative account.

CHAPTER 12: THE ANGLO-FRENCH STRUGGLE FOR EMPIRE

The best account of the Anglo-French colonial struggle is probably still that to be found in the first volume of the *Cambridge History of the British Empire* (Cambridge, 1929): there is a recent bird's-eye view in J. Meyer and J. Bromley, 'The Second Hundred Years' War', in D. Johnson and others, eds, *Britain and France* (Folkestone, 1980). From the French side H. I. Priestley, *France Overseas through the Old Regime* (New York, 1939); H. Blet, *Histoire de la colonisation française*, i (Grenoble, 1946); and J. Saintoyant, *La Colonisation française sous l'ancien régime*, ii (Paris, 1929) provide good starting-points. R. Pares, *War and Trade in the West Indies,*

1739–1763 (Oxford, 1936) is a very thorough study of a crucial area of conflict. Anglo-French naval warfare can be followed in Admiral H. W. Richmond, *The Navy in the War of 1739–1748* (Cambridge, 1920) and Sir J. Corbett, *England in the Seven Years War* (London, 1907); and from the French side in J. Tramond, *Manuel d'histoire maritime de la France* (2nd edn, Paris, 1927) and the more recent and very competent J. R. Dull, *The French Navy and American Independence* (Princeton, 1975). In spite of its age H. Dodwell, *Dupleix and Clive* (London, 1920) remains perhaps the best short account of the critical years of the struggle in India, while the *Cambridge History of the British Empire*, v (Cambridge, 1929) provides much detail. On the Seven Years War there is much material in the unfinished work of R. Waddington, *La Guerre de Sept Ans* (Paris, 1896–1914), though this deals mainly with the fighting in Europe; and from the British side valuable insights can be found in R. Whitworth, *Field-Marshal Lord Ligonier* (Oxford, 1958). R. Pares, 'American versus continental warfare, 1739–1763', *English Historical Review*, li (1936) is an outstanding discussion of the conflicting trends in British strategy during the middle decades of the century. The only substantial study of the Peace of Paris is Z. E. Rashed, *The Peace of Paris, 1763* (Liverpool, 1952); but this does not supersede the detailed accounts to be found in the books of Pares and Corbett mentioned above. British policy during the difficult two decades after the Peace of Paris is the subject of a masterly survey by M. Roberts, *Splendid Isolation, 1763–1780* (Reading, 1970). On the American Revolution there are the very useful J. C. Miller, *Origins of the American Revolution* (Stanford, 1959) and the thoughtful R. W. Tucker and D. C. Hendrickson, *The Fall of the First British Empire: Origins of the War of American Independence* (Baltimore, 1982). Its international aspects are well covered in R. B. Morris, *The Peacemakers: The Great Powers and American Independence* (New York, 1965) and R. W. Van Alstyne, *Empire and Independence: The International History of the American Revolution* (New York, 1965); and its military ones in P. Mackesy, *The War for America, 1775–1783* (Oxford, 1964). G. S. Graham, 'Considerations on the War of American Independence', *Bulletin of the Institute of Historical Research*, xxii (1949) provides a brief but stimulating commentary on the struggle as, at rather greater length, does R. B. Morris, *The American Revolution Reconsidered* (New York, 1967). The most recent discussion of French policy during the war can be found in the somewhat pedestrian O. T. Murphy, *Charles Gravier, Comte de Vergennes: French Diplomacy in the Age of Revolution, 1719–1787* (Albany, N.Y., 1982). There is no good book on the Anglo-Dutch war of 1780: the old work of P. Coquelle, *L'Alliance Franco-Hollandaise contre l'Angleterre, 1735–1788* (Paris, 1902) is still of use. Many aspects of the diplomacy of the war are best covered, however, in Isabel de Madariaga, *Britain, Russia, and the Armed Neutrality of 1780* (London, 1962). V. T. Harlow, *The Founding of the Second British Empire*, i (London, 1952) gives a somewhat discursive but penetrating account of the peace negotiations of 1782–83.

CHAPTER 13: EUROPE AND THE OUTSIDE WORLD

F. Mauro, *L'Expansion européenne, 1600–1870* (2nd edn, Paris, 1967); J. H. Parry, *Trade and Dominion: The European Overseas Empires in the Eighteenth Century* (London, 1971); and G. Williams, *The Expansion of Europe in the Eighteenth Century* (London, 1966) are all sound general accounts. A recent work covering North and South America is Peggy K. Liss, *Atlantic Empires: The Network of Trade and Revolution, 1713–1826* (Baltimore–London, 1983). Useful articles are D. A. Farnie, 'The Commercial Empire of the Atlantic, 1607–1783', *Economic History Review*, 2nd ser., xv (1962–63); J. Godechot and R. R. Palmer, 'Le Problème de l'Atlantique du XVIIIᵉ au XXᵉ siècle', in *X Congresso Internazionale di Scienze Storiche, Relazioni* (Florence, 1955), vol. v; and P. O'Brien, 'European Economic Development; The Contribution of the Periphery', *Economic History Review*, 2nd ser., xxxv (1982), which argues forcibly that the economic importance of colonial trade for Europe has often been overrated. The ideas about the value and justifiability of colonial expansion current in the two most rapidly expanding European States can be studied in K. E. Knorr, *British Colonial Theories, 1570–1850* (Toronto, 1944) and C. L. Lokke, *France and the Colonial Question, 1763–1801* (New York, 1932). The former in particular gives references to a great mass of eighteenth-century printed material. The early chapters of K. R. Maxwell, *Conflicts and Conspiracies: Brazil and Portugal, 1750–1808* (London, 1973) are relevant, though much of the book deals with Brazil rather than Portugal. On eastern trade H. Furber, *Rival Empires of Trade in the Orient, 1600–1800* (Minneapolis–Oxford, 1976) is outstanding; and the same author's *John Company at Work* (Cambridge, Mass., 1948) is a fine piece of scholarship. On India there are two very sound books by P. J. Marshall, *Problems of Empire: Britain and India, 1757–1813* (London, 1968) and *East India Fortunes: The British in Bengal in the Eighteenth Century* (Oxford, 1976), while the same author has produced a stimulating short analysis in 'British Expansion in India in the Eighteenth Century; a Historical Revision', *History*, lx (1975). The alleged 'swing to the East' in the imperial interests of Britain and France in the 1770s and 1780s is discussed in V. T. Harlow, *The Founding of the Second British Empire*, i (London, 1952). On trade with China the extremely detailed work of L. Dermigny, *La Chine et l'occident: le commerce à Canton au XVIIIᵉ siècle, 1719–1833* (4 vols, Paris, 1964) is fundamental. On slavery D. B. Davis, *The Problem of Slavery in the Age of Revolution, 1770–1823* (Ithaca, 1966) is thought-provoking, while P. D. Curtin, *The Atlantic Slave Trade: A Census* (Madison, 1969) is a thorough effort to establish the size of the trade: Chapters 5–7 are relevant to this period. The impression made on Europe by increasing knowledge of the rest of the world has been discussed very well in a number of books. P. J. Marshall and G. Williams, *The Great Map of Mankind: British Perceptions of the World in the Age of Enlightenment* (London, 1982) is learned and yet very readable. Conceptions of America are discussed in D. Echeverria, *Mirage in the West: A History of the French Image of American Society to 1815* (Princeton, 1957), of which the first three chapters cover the period 1767–83, and in the very handsomely illustrated H. Honour, *The New Golden Land; European Images of America from the Discoveries to the Present Time* (London, 1976). An earlier work, H. N. Fairchild, *The Noble Savage* (New York, 1928) is still useful. On Europe's discovery of China there are W. W. Appleton, *A Cycle of Cathay* (New York, 1951) and H. Honour, *Chinoiserie: The Vision of Cathay* (London, 1961). Finally M. Duchet, *Anthropologie et histoire au siècle des lumières* (Paris, 1971) is a detailed study of the intellectual impact of growing knowledge of the non-European world which concentrates on a group of major French thinkers.

CHAPTER 14: EDUCATION AND CULTURAL LIFE

The best book on education in any of the European States during this period is R. Chartier, Marie-Madeleine Compère and D. Julia, *L'Education en France du XVIe au XVIIIe siècle* (Paris, 1976), which is very thorough and covers education at all levels. More generally, N. Hans, *New Trends in Education in the Eighteenth Century* (London, 1951) is somewhat opinionated but contains much information. S. D'Irsay, *Histoire des universités françaises et étrangères*, ii (Paris, 1935) has some informative pages on this period with very full references; and J. de Vignerie, 'Quelques Remarques sur les universités françaises au dix-huitième siècle', *Revue Historique*, cclxii (1979) is a clear and pointed short account. B. Fay, 'Learned Societies in Europe and America in the Eighteenth Century', *American Historical Review*, xxxvii (1931–32) is also short and still useful in spite of its age. The growth of scientific knowledge can be followed in A. R. Hall, *The Scientific Revolution, 1500–1800* (London, 1954) and in rather bewildering detail in A. Wolf, *A History of Science, Philosophy and Technology in the Eighteenth Century* (2nd ed., London, 1952). Briefer and clearer is C. Singer, *A Short History of Scientific Ideas to 1900* (Oxford, 1959). There is a good specialized study in R. Hahn, *The Anatomy of a Scientific Institution: The Paris Academy of Sciences, 1666–1903* (Berkeley, 1971), of which Chapter 3 is especially relevant here. On literature and the arts a vast amount has been written. P. Lavedan, *Histoire de l'art*, ii (Paris, 1944) has much information and good bibliographies; and M. Levy, *Rococo to Revolution* (London, 1966) is a readable general account, as is H. Honour, *Neo-classicism* (Harmondsworth, 1968). R. Wellek, *A History of Modern Criticism, 1750–1950*, i (London, 1955) is still perhaps the best source of information about eighteenth-century literary standards and preconceptions. N. Pevsner, *Academies of Art* (Cambridge, 1940) gives a good account of its subject. On music P. H. Lang, *Music in Western Civilization* (New York, 1941) is a good general work; and the first half of F. Blume, *Classic and Romantic Music* (London, 1972) provides a close analysis in a brief compass of developments from the 1740s onwards. On literature useful works in English are: J. G. Robertson, *A History of German Literature* (Edinburgh–London, 1933); E. H. Wilkins, *A History of Italian Literature* (London, 1954); and on a larger scale the relevant volumes of the *Cambridge History of English Literature* (Cambridge, 1907–27). Much good writing is available on various aspects of French cultural life. D. Roche, *Le Siècle des lumières en province* (2 vols, Paris–The Hague, 1978) is a very detailed study of French provincial academies; and D. T. Pottinger, *The French Book Trade in the Ancien Regime, 1500–1791* (Cambridge, Mass., 1958) is interesting and wide-ranging. R. Darnton, 'Reading, Writing, and Publishing in Eighteenth-Century France: A Case Study in the Sociology of Literature', *Daedalus*, vol. 100, No. 1 (Winter, 1971) is by the acknowledged master of the subject. Geneviève Bollême, *La Bibliothèque Bleue: la littérature populaire en France du XVIᵉ au XIXᵉ siècle* (Paris, 1971); the same author's *Les Almanachs populaires aux XVIIᵉ et XVIIIᵉ siècles*; and still more some of the essays in Geneviève Bollême, J. Ehrard and others, eds, *Livre et société dans la France du XVIIIᵉ siècle* (2 vols, Paris–The Hague, 1965–70) are important correctives to any view based merely upon the reading of the educated and well-to-do. On French cultural influences L. Réau, *L'Europe Française au siècle des lumières* (Paris, 1933; new edn, 1971) is a standard work, though one which exaggerates the extent of French leadership in some respects. Finally, J. Queniart, *Culture et société urbaines dans la France de l'ouest au XVIIIᵉ siècle* (Paris, 1979) is an admirably thorough though very detailed study.

CHAPTER 15: THE ENLIGHTENMENT AND ITS COMPETITORS

The best single book in English on the Enlightenment is N. Hampson, *The Enlightenment* (*The Pelican History of European Thought*, iv; Harmondsworth, 1968) which is clear, concise and very informative. I. O. Wade, *The Intellectual Origins of the French Enlightenment* (Princeton, 1971) is learned though a little pedestrian; and R. Porter and M. Teich, eds, *The Enlightenment in National Context* (Cambridge, 1981) is a collection of thirteen essays of varying quality, some of them very useful. A. B. Cobban, *In Search of Humanity: The Role of the Enlightenment in Modern History* (London, 1960) is penetrating and suggestive; and Margaret C. Jacob, *The Radical Enlightenment: Pantheists, Freemasons and Republicans* (London, 1981) is a stimulating though idiosyncratic discussion of some of the radical materialist aspects of the early stages of the movement. Two works by P. Gay are also stimulating though a little idiosyncratic: *The Enlightenment: An Interpretation*, vol. i, *The Rise of Modern Paganism*

(London, 1967); vol. ii, *The Science of Freedom* (London, 1970), and *The Party of Humanity: Studies in the French Enlightenment* (London, 1964). E. Cassirer, *The Philosophy of the Enlightenment* (Princeton, 1951) is an older but still classic account. P. Hazard, *The European Mind, 1680–1715* (London, 1953) though the French edition appeared as long ago as 1935, remains the best general account of the 'pre-Enlightenment'; and the same author's *European Thought in the Eighteenth Century: from Montesquieu to Lessing* (London, 1954), though not so good, remains of importance. F. Venturi, *Utopia and Reform in the Enlightenment* (Cambridge, 1971) is an interesting attempt to relate the intellectual developments of the century to its political and social history, as is the essay 'The European Enlightenment', in his collection *Italy and the Enlightenment: Studies in a Cosmopolitan Century* (London, 1972). R. Pomeau, *L'Europe des lumières: cosmopolitisme et unité européenne au dix-huitième siècle* (Paris, 1966) provides much interesting background to the intellectual and cultural life of the period. H. Chisick, *The Limits of Reform in the Enlightenment: Attitudes towards the Education of the Lower Classes in Eighteenth-Century France* (Princeton, 1981) brings out well the narrowness of the social base of 'enlightened' attitudes. On individual figures a long list of books could be given. R. Shackleton, *Montesquieu: A Critical Biography* (Oxford, 1961) and A. McC. Wilson, *Diderot: The Testing Years* (New York, 1957) are both excellent. On Voltaire there are T. Besterman, *Voltaire* (London, 1969) and P. Gay, *Voltaire's Politics: The Poet as Realist* (Princeton, 1959), both somewhat uncritical in tone; and R. Pomeau, *La Réligion de Voltaire* (Paris, 1956). Rousseau is discussed in R. Derathé, *Le Rationalisme de J.-J. Rousseau* (Paris, 1948) and *Jean-Jacques Rousseau et la science politique de son temps* (Paris, 1950); and in R. Grimsley, *Jean-Jacques Rousseau: A Study in Self-Awareness* (Cardiff, 1961). On Vico there is the brief P. Burke, *Vico* (Oxford, 1985) and on Herder F. M. Barnard, *Herder's Social and Political Thought* (Oxford, 1965), while I. Berlin, *Vico and Herder* (London, 1976) covers both. Some aspects of the reaction against the Enlightenment are briefly and brilliantly discussed in R. Darnton, *Mesmerism and the End of the Enlightenment in France* (Cambridge, Mass., 1968), while the same author's *The Business of Enlightenment: A Publishing History of the Encyclopédie, 1775–1800* (Cambridge, Mass., 1979) is a book of great originality which throws light on many aspects of eighteenth-century life.

CHAPTER 16: RELIGION AND THE CHURCHES

The best general introduction to the subject is G. R. Cragg, *The Church and the Age of Reason, 1648–1789* (*The Penguin History of the Church*, vol. iv, Harmondsworth, 1960); and there is a large-scale treatment of the Catholic Church in E. Préclin and E. Jarry, *Les Luttes politiques et* *doctrinales au XVIIe et XVIIIe siècles*, Pt 2 (vol. xix of *Histoire de l'église depuis les origines jusqu'à nos jours*, Paris, 1956). W. J. Callahan and D. Higgs, eds, *Church and Society in Catholic Europe of the Eighteenth Century* (Cambridge, 1979) is a collection of essays of varying but sometimes high quality. O. Chadwick, *The Popes and European Revolution* (Oxford, 1981) deals in its first chapters with this period. On Jansenism A. Gazier, *Histoire générale du mouvement janseniste* (Paris, 1922) is still a standard work and L. Cognet, *Le Jansenisme* (3rd edn. Paris, 1968) is a short introduction. On the suppression of the Jesuits P. Dudon, 'De la suppression de la Compagnie de Jesus, 1758–73', *Revue des Questions Historiques*, cxxii (1938) is a useful short account. Several works on a national scale deserve mention. N. Sykes, *Church and State in England in the Eighteenth Century* (Cambridge, 1934) is thorough and sound; A. L. Drummond, *German Protestantism since Luther* (London, 1951) is a little pedestrian; and R. R. Palmer, *Catholics and Unbelievers in Eighteenth-Century France* (Princeton, 1939) is penetrating and very interesting. In this as in other aspects of history in this period France is better served than any other part of Europe. J. de Viguerie, 'Quelques aspects du catholicisme des Français au dix-huitième siècle', *Revue Historique*, cclxv (1981) is a convenient short discussion; and J. Queniart, *Les Hommes, l'Eglise et Dieu dans la France du XVIIIe siècle* (Paris, 1978) has much information on religious thought and psychology. One particular aspect of religious feeling which has recently attracted much attention is covered in R. Favre, *La Mort au siècle des lumières* (Lyon, 1978) and J. McManners, *Death and the Enlightenment* (Oxford, 1981); both deal exclusively with France. McManners has also produced an excellent regional study in *French Ecclesiastical Society under the Ancien Regime: A Study of Angers in the Eighteenth Century* (Manchester, 1960), as has T. Tackett, *Priest and Parish in Eighteenth-Century France: A Social and Political Study of the Curés in a Diocese of Dauphiné, 1750–1791* (Princeton, 1977). Two important specialised studies of the Orthodox Church in Russia are J. Cracraft, *The Church Reform of Peter the Great* (London, 1971) and G. L. Freeze, *The Russian Levites: Parish Clergy in the Eighteenth Century* (Cambridge, Mass., 1977). J. M. Roberts, *The Mythology of the Secret Societies* (London, 1972) covers well different aspects of irrationalism and superstition during this period, as do F. Venturi, 'Enlightenment versus the Powers of Darkness', in his collection *Italy and the Enlightenment* (London, 1972) and the early chapters of J. Rogalla von Bieberstein, *Die These von der Verschwörung, 1776–1945* (Frankfurt, 1978).

MAPS

Map 1. The westward expansion of Russia, 1696–1783

Map 2. The growth of Brandenburg – Prussia in the eighteenth century

Map 3. Italy on the eve of the French Revolution

Map 4. The Balkans in the eighteenth century

St. Johns

Ft. Beausejour
Louisbourg

Quebec

Montreal

Boston

New York

Ft. le
Boeuf
Ft. Duquesne Philadelphia

ATLANTIC OCEAN

Charleston

New
Orleans

FLORIDA

BAHAMA
ISLANDS (BR.)

Havana

CUBA

PORTO
RICO

Antigua (Br.)

St. Kitts (Br.)
Guadeloupe (Fr.)
Martinique (Fr.)

Vera Cruz

SAN DOMINGO

JAMAICA

St. Vincent (Fr.)

BELIZE

Curacao
(Dutch)

Barbados (Br.)

TRINIDAD

Mosquito
Coast

Cartagena

Porto Bello

LOUISIANA

CANADA

British possessions

French possessions

Spanish possessions

Map 5. European possessions in North America and the Caribbean at the outbreak of the Seven Years War

INDEX

Courland, 263
Bureau de Commerce, in France, 117
Bureau de Statistique, in France, 116
Burma, European activity in, 372
Bussy-Castelnau, Charles, Marquis de, French soldier, 333, 336
Bute, John Stewart, 3rd Earl of, British statesman, 302
and Peace of Paris, 337–8
Byng, George, Viscount Torrington, British admiral, 313

cabinet noir, in France, 245
Cagliostro, Alessandro, Count, adventurer, 432
Caisse d'Escompte, in France, 110, 120
Calas, Jean, case of, 142
Calcutta, 332, 335
Cambrai, Congress of (1724), 315
Camier, Abbé, French theologian, and Natural religion, 438
Campomanes, Pedro Rodriguez, Spanish statesman, 187, 198
Canada
French society in, 329
British conquest of, 335
furs from, 361
Canton
Europeans in, 364
trade with, 365
Cape Breton Island, 329
capitation, in France, 55, 125
Caracas Company, 366
Caribbean
Anglo-French rivalry in, 330
British trade with, 359
American trade with, 362
slavery in, 362–3
Carillon, Fort, 335
Carlisle, Earl of, envoy to American colonies, 344
Carlowitz, Treaty of (1699), 258
Carnatic, Anglo-French struggles in, 333, 336
Carolinas, British colonies, 329

Carron works, in Scotland, 99
carronade, 233
Carteret, John, Viscount, British statesman, 293, 353
Cartouche, French smuggler, 129
Casa de Contratación, in Spain, 358
Caserta, palace at, 405
Catalonia, incorporated in Spain, 182
Catherine I, Empress of Russia, 168, 263
Catherine II, Empress of Russia
and Russian nobility, 39, 51–2, 195
and Russian towns, 58–9
and Russian industry, 104
and immigration, 134
and religion, 143
administrative achievements of, 149–52
on monarchy in Russia, 165
and petitions, 166
as enlightened despot, 192–6
vanity of, 193
and serfdom, 193–4
continues policies of her predecessors, 194
intellectual life under, 195–6
and Poland, 275
and Ottoman Empire, 273–7, 325–6
and Bavarian Succession, 304–5
Catholic Church
vitality of, 450–1
weaknesses of, 450–1
and Jansenism, 451–3
and the Jesuits, 453–5
and the Papacy, 456–7
and Joseph II, 458–60
Caucasus, serfdom in, 44
censuses, attempts at, 116
Ceuta, 365
Chambéry, 317
Chamlay, Jules-Louis Bolé, Marquis de, French soldier, 214
Champagne, schools in, 381
Chandernagore, 332, 336

makes little impression in
Germany, 428
Enlightened Despotism, ideology
of, 184, 187
justifications of, 185–6
in Spain, 186–7
limitations of, 188–9, 206
in Prussia, 189–92
in Russia, 192–6
in Savoy-Piedmont, 196–7
in Portugal, 197–8
in the Two Sicilies, 198
in Tuscany, 199–201
in the Habsburg lands, 201–6
popular resistance to, 207–8
significance of, 208
Enlightenment
and society, 31
differing forms taken by, 408
fluctuations over time, 409
critical aspects of, 409–10
English ancestry of, 410–11
essential character of, 411–12
emphasis of on happiness,
412–13
optimism of, 413
lack of realism of, 414–15
admiration of for the ancients,
415
limitations of, 416
totalitarian aspects of, 417
pessimistic aspects of, 418
and middle classes, 426
in England and Scotland,
425–6
in Italy, 426–7
in Germany, 427–9
in Russia, 429
confined to an élite, 429–30
challenged by irrationalism,
430–2
clerical hostility to, 449
Ensenada, Cenon de Somodeville,
Marques de la, Spanish
statesman, 229
Entick, John, English writer, 15
Erie, Lake, 333
Esterhazy, Hungarian family of,
56

Esthonia, 194, 261
society in, 34–5
Eugene of Savoy, Prince,
Austrian soldier, 212, 214, 322
and desertion, 221
Euler, Leonhard, mathematician,
232
Expilly, Jean Joseph, Abbé,
French statistician, 64, 117, 417

Falkland Islands, dispute over
(1770), 339, 370
family
importance of in society, 26–7
weakening of traditional
attitudes to, 27–8
Family Compact (1761), 241, 337
famine
becoming rarer, 74
in Sicily (1763–64), 82
in Saxony and Bohemia
(1770), 83
Farnese, Elizabeth, 183
Italian ambitions of, 312–16
Febronius (J. N. von Hontheim),
Catholic theorist, 457
Felbiger, J. I., Austrian
administrator, 202
Ferdinand VI, King of Spain, 318,
337
Ferdinand, Prince of Brunswick,
300
Ferguson, Adam, Scottish writer,
426
Fielding, Henry, English novelist,
24
Filangieri, Gaetano, Neapolitan
economist, 427
Filmer, Sir Robert, English
political writer, 5
Fiscals, in Prussia, 145
Fischer von Erlach, Johann
Bernhard, German architect, 375
Fiume, 134
Flemming, Jacob-Heinrich,
Count, Saxon statesman, 284
Fleury, André Hercule de,
Cardinal, French statesman, 88,
180, 289, 355, 452

Graz, University of, 385
Great Britain
  trade statistics in, 8
  printed administrative
    documents in, 9
  newspapers and periodicals in,
    20–1
  nobility in, 53
  financiers in, 61
  population in, 73, 76
  agriculture in, 79–80
  secure food supply of, 83
  foreign trade of, 86–8
  roads and canals in, 93–4
  industrial revolution in, 96–9
  reasons for industrial growth,
    97–8
  banks in, 107
  South Sea Bubble in, 108
  financial strength of, 108–9
  Dutch investment in, 109
  attempts at census in, 116
  usury laws in, 121
  administration in, 125
  taxation in, 132
  relief of distress in, 135
  judicial system in, 136–7
  monarchy in, 155, 168–76
  administration in, 156
  justices of the peace in, 156–7
  parliament in, 169–71
  cabinet in, 172–3
  parties in, 173–5
  regarded as a factious country,
    175–6
  army in, 219–20, 226–7
  navy in, 228, 231
  Foreign Office in, 242–3
  interception of despatches in,
    245
  and Russia, 265
  and War of Austrian
    Succession, 291–4
  and Diplomatic Revolution,
    295–6
  and Frederick II, 300, 302–3
  and France in the
    Mediterranean, 308
  and Italy, 317

  power of in the
    Mediterranean, 318, 319–20
  importance of colonial conflict
    with France, 327
  colonies after 1713, 328–9
  colonial conflict with Spain,
    330–1
  colonial conflict with France,
    333, 335–6
  and unrest in American
    colonies, 339–42
  and War of American
    Revolution, 342–7
  difficulties in this war,
    346–7
  hostility of to France, 349
  fears of French invasion,
    349–50
  importance of naval strength
    to, 351–2
  prefers American to colonial
    warfare, 352–3
  and Hanover, 354
  colonial trade of, 361–2
  schools in, 382–3
  Enlightenment in, 425–6
  religious toleration in, 442,
    448
Greece, under Turkish rule,
  321–2
Gregory, David, Scottish
  mathematician, 387
Grenada, 338
Grenville, George, British
  statesman, 339
Greuze, Jean Baptiste, French
  painter, 400
Grey, Charles, 2nd Earl, British
  statesman, 53
Gribeauval, Jean Baptiste de,
  French soldier, 224
Guadalajara, woollen factory at,
  102
Guadeloupe, 335, 338
Guanajato, in Mexico, 363
Guastalla, battle of (1734), 316
guerre des farines, in France (1775),
  129
Guibert, Jacques Antoine, Comte

Mark, principality of, 192

Marlborough, John Churchill, 1st Duke of, 2, 211, 224, 349

Marseilles, Chamber of Commerce of, 89

Martini, Karl Anton von, Baron, Austrian cameralist, 200

Martinique, 337, 338

Maryland, 362

Massachusetts, 329, 342, 361

Massillon, Jean-Baptiste, Bishop of Clermont, 30

Masulipatam, 336

Matapan, Cape, battle of (1717), 232

Mataram, Javanese state of, 369

Matteson, Johann, German music critic, 404

Matveev, A. A., Russian diplomat, 239

Maubeuge, arms factory at, 227

Maupeou, René Nicholas, French statesman, 181
   and *Parlement* of Paris, 179

Maupertuis, Pierre Louis Moreau de, French mathematician, 388, 425

Maurepas, Jean Frederic Phelypeaux, Comte de, French statesman, 52, 234
   desires peace, 346

Mauritius, 332

Maximilian Joseph, Elector of Bavaria, 303

Mecklenburg-Schwerin, Duchy of, conflict in, 284
   occupied by Russia (1716), 260–1

Melon, Jean-François, French economist, 88

Memel, 212

memoirs and autobiographies, importance of to the historian, 13–14

Mendelssohn, Moses, Jewish liberal, 463

Menshikov, Prince A. D., Russian statesman, 263

mercantilism

ambiguities of, 113
ideas underlying, 113–14
limitations of, 114
rooted in contemporary realities, 114
challenges to, 114–15

Mesmer, Franz Anton, German mystic, 432

Mesnager, Nicholas, French merchant, 61

Messina, 94

Methodism, growth of, 446

Methuen Treaty (1703), 88

Mexico, grievances in, 344–5

Mézières, engineering school at, 223

Michael, Tsar of Russia, 256

Milan, Duchy of, Austrian rule in, 309

militarism, growth of, 214–15

Militia Act (1757), 218, 349

militias
   unpopularity of, 218
   in France, 219

Miller, John, Scottish writer, 426

millones, tax in Spain, 125

Minas Geraes, in Brazil, 363

Minorca
   strategic value of, 308
   capture of by France (1756), 334, 350
   recovered by Spain (1782), 347

Mir Ja'far, Indian ruler, 336

Mirabeau, Victor Riquetti, Marquis de, French economist, 115

Mississippi, 330

'Mississippi Bubble', in France, 110

Mohammed, prophet, 375

Moldavia, 273
   Russian defeat in (1711), 272
   under Turkish rule, 321

Mollwitz, battle of (1741), 292

Mombasa, 365

monarchy
   importance of, 160–1
   justifications of, 161–5

Speranskii, Count M. M., Russian statesman, 139
Squillace, Leopoldo de Gregario, Italian statesman, 129
Stamitz, Karl Philipp, German composer, 404
Stamp Act (1765), 340, 342
Starhemberg, Georg Adam, Count von, Austrian diplomat, 295
statistics
  limitations of, 8–9
  efforts to collect, 166
  inadequacy of, 118
steam-engines, 96, 99
Steuart, Sir James, Scottish economist, 115
  on war, 213
Strafpatent, in Habsburg lands (1781), 202
Strasbourg, 1, 286
  French rule in, 35
  municipal government in, 67
Strawberry Hill, house at, 400
Struensee, Johann Frederick, Danish statesman, 160
Suffren, Pierre André, French admiral, 235
Sumatra, 369
superstition, persistence of, 443–6
Surinam, 366
Suvorov, Prince A., Russian soldier, 216, 225
Sweden
  nobility in, 49, 57
  foreign trade of, 87, 91
  iron industry in, 104
  census in, 116
  monarchy in, 163–4
  foreign affairs in, 242
  and Great Northern War, 258–61
  constitution (1720), 266–7
  and Russia, 266–7
  revolution in (1772), 268
  and Germany, 286
  and Seven Years War, 299–300

Swift, Jonathan, Irish writer, 378
Szatmár, Peace of (1711), 153

Table of Ranks, in Russia (1722), 50
Taganrog, 272
taille, in France, 131
Tanucci, Bernardo, Neapolitan statesman, 424
  reforms of, 198
  and papacy, 457–8
Taranto, Archbishop of, 456
Tavora, Marquis of, in Portugal, 197
taxation
  defects in collection of, 130–1, 133
  forms of, 131–2
  in France, 131–2
  in Britain, 132
Tea Act (1773), 342
Terray, Joseph-Marie, Abbé de, controller-general in France, 181
Teschen, Treaty of (1779), 277, 305
Tesme, Abbé de, Jansenist, 453
Thomasius, Christian, German philosopher, 428
Thompson, William, English poet, 395
Thugut, J. A., Austrian statesman, 244
Thurn und Taxis, family of, 244
Tiepolo, Giovanni Batista, Venetian painter, 398
Tindal, Matthew, English Deist, 439
tithes, resentment of, 41
tobacco, trade in, 362
Tobago, 330, 338
Toggenburg, religious friction in, 448
Toland, John, English Deist, and Natural Religion, 437–8
Tolbooth, in Edinburgh, 127
Torbay, French landing at (1692), 350
Torcy, Jean-Baptiste Colbert,